ABOUT THE EDITOR

Robert S. Hirschfield is Professor and Chairman of the Department of Political Science at Hunter College/City University of New York. He received his Ph.D. from New York University and his A.B., LL.B., and M.A. from Harvard University. Author of THE CONSTITUTION AND THE COURT and editor of SELECTION/ELECTION: A FORUM ON THE AMERICAN PRESIDENCY, his articles, essays, and reviews have appeared in *Public Policy, Parliamentary Affairs, The American Political Science Review, The American Government Annual, The Nation, The New York Times,* and other journals. He has taught at Harvard, Fordham, and New York University. Dr. Hirschfield is Director of the New York Center for Education in Politics, and has been a political activist at both the national and local levels. He is also the producer and host of a public affairs television program in New York City.

THE POWER OF THE PRESIDENCY

Concepts and Controversy

Third Edition

EDITED BY

ROBERT S. HIRSCHFIELD

ALDINE PUBLISHING COMPANY
New York

Copyright © 1968, 1973, 1982 by Robert S. Hirschfield

Third Edition published 1982
Aldine Publishing Company
200 Saw Mill River Road
Hawthorne, New York 10532

ISBN 0-202-24159-9 cloth
ISBN 0-202-24160-2 paper
Library of Congress Catalog Number 81-67976

Printed in the United States of America
1 2 3 4 5 6 7 8 9 10

for
Muriel
and
Rebecca
and
David

PREFACE

Since the last edition of this book was published, the Presidency has gone through one of the most turbulent periods in its history. In the prior *Preface* I noted that the problem of presidential power had become a critical issue for the nation because of the war in Vietnam. Within a year that problem had been compounded by the Watergate affair.

The matter of defining the scope and limits of presidential power dominates American governmental affairs now as on only a few occasions in our history. This may be because the office has not yet adjusted to the twin blows of Vietnam/Watergate or because it is in a period of transition from the institution shaped by Franklin Roosevelt to one that must contend with difficult new political environments, both domestically and globally.

In any event the present result of all that has happened to and around the Presidency since this book last appeared is an extensively revised and enlarged volume:

The "Presidential Views" section now includes dramatic new material dealing with Richard Nixon's truncated second term, as well as items related to the presidencies of Gerald Ford, Jimmy Carter, and Ronald Reagan.

The Supreme Court's historic decision in *United States v. Nixon* has been added to the "Judicial Views" section.

The "Expert Views" section has undergone great change and expansion to reflect the different attitudes and approaches toward the Presidency that have emerged among students of the office since Vietnam and Watergate.

In all, about forty percent of the material in this third edition is new. My hope is that the volume has not only been made current, but that it also captures the searching mood that surrounds the contemporary Presidency.

My thanks to Julie Nadell, as always an indispensable aide, and to Rita Bates, Julian Baim, and Michele Stetz for their generous help.

PREFACE TO THE
SECOND EDITION

The four years since the original edition of this book appeared span the end of Lyndon Johnson's Presidency and the beginning of Richard Nixon's second term in the White House. But the problem with which the book is concerned—definition of the scope and limits of presidential power—remains the same despite changes of party or Presidents.

That problem became a critical issue for Americans during the late 1960s primarily because Mr. Johnson conducted a "presidential war" in Vietnam. And it was not resolved by the election of Mr. Nixon. On the contrary, Nixon's exercise of independent authority in attempting to end the war turned out to be even more assertive than Johnson's was in escalating it.

The problem of presidential power is persistent. It continues to trouble observers, students, and practitioners of American Government, as it has since the beginning of the Republic. Because of Vietnam, the contemporary generation has been forced to confront it directly, but we are no more likely to come up with solutions than our predecessors. Involving as it does the delicate balance between democracy and security, constitutionality and necessity, it is a problem with which Americans will have to deal recurrently so long as our political system endures.

In revising the book I have reviewed all of the readings and tried to strengthen each section by addition, substitution, or reediting of materials. The result, I hope, is that the volume has not only been brought up to date but that it has also been made more complete and therefore more useful.

I want to thank three associates who have helped me in preparing this revised edition: Julie Nadell, Martin Rosen and Anna Goldoff.

PREFACE TO THE
FIRST EDITION

The American Presidency is the most powerful political office in the world. But this impressive statement serves only to raise a whole series of fundamental questions: What is the scope of presidential power and what are its limits? Can the President use all the authority of his office or is that authority more formal than effective? Does the Presidency have sufficient power to meet today's needs or do the problems of the nuclear age demand a more powerful executive? Is there a danger of dictatorship in the growth of presidential authority or will the Presidency remain an office of constitutional democratic leadership?

This book explores such questions by presenting a wide range of views on presidential power from a variety of sources: original supporters and opponents of the office, Presidents themselves, Supreme Court decisions, and professional students of the Presidency. Throughout an effort has been made to select materials which emphasize the controversial nature of the subject, as well as its historical continuity and contemporary significance. While these readings inevitably discuss the roles and functions of the President, they have been chosen because they focus on his power, and because they stimulate serious thought about this essential aspect of the office. That the subject is important hardly needs stating. For the issue of presidential power—directly related as it is to the problems of war or peace, annihilation or survival, progress or stagnation—is among the most important political issues of our time.

I became interested in the subject of presidential power through contact with four teachers to whom I am much indebted: Carl J. Friedrich, Arthur E. Sutherland, and the late Zechariah Chafee, Jr., all of Harvard University; and Marshall E. Dimock, formerly of New York University. In preparing this volume, I had the valuable assistance of Denise Rathbun, Martin Rosen, Arthur Miltz, and Robert Laurenty, each of whom I want to thank. I am also grateful to the City University Doctoral Faculty Research Fund for a grant in support of this project. Finally, I want to express my appreciation to Mr. Charles D. Lieber and Miss Marlene Mandel of Atherton Press, colleagues and friends as well as publishers.

CONTENTS

The Emergence of the Modern Presidency

The Contemporary Presidency

III. JUDICIAL VIEWS 222

Presidential Power in Foreign Affairs

Presidential Power to Make War

If a war be made by invasion of a foreign nation, the President . . . is bound to accept the challenge without waiting for any special legislative authority. . . . He must determine what degree of force the crisis demands.

Presidential Power in Time of War

No doctrine involving more pernicious consequences was ever invented by the wit of man than that any of [the Constitution's] provisions can be suspended during any of the great exigencies of government.

. . . when under conditions of modern warfare our shores are threatened by hostile forces, the power to protect must be commensurate with the threatened danger.

In the framework of our Constitution, the President's power to see that the laws are faithfully executed refutes the idea that he is to be a lawmaker.

Presidential Power over Administrative Policy

We think it plain under the Constitution that illimitable power of removal is not possessed by the President.

Presidential Power to Protect the Peace

Is this duty [to "take care that the laws be faithfully executed"] limited to the enforcement of acts of Congress or of treaties of the United States according to their express terms; or does it include the rights, duties, and obligations growing out of the Constitution itself, our international relations, and all the protection implied by the nature of the government under the Constitution.

Presidential Power and Executive Privilege

IV. EXPERT VIEWS 276

The Scope of Presidential Power
[from Franklin Roosevelt to Vietnam/Watergate]

THE
POWER
OF THE
PRESIDENCY

INTRODUCTION
The Scope and Limits
of Presidential Power

The Presidency has been tested in our time as never before. During the past twenty years it has suffered a relentless series of shocks: in 1963 John Kennedy was assassinated; in 1968 Lyndon Johnson had to forego re-election because of the divisiveness generated by the Vietnam war; in 1974 Richard Nixon was forced to resign as a result of the Watergate affair; in 1976 Gerald Ford could not win election in his own right; and in 1980 Jimmy Carter became the first elected President in a half century to be rejected at the polls. From Kennedy to Ronald Reagan we have had five Presidents, and none has served two terms.

This discontinuity in the executive office is unprecedented in our history. And it is too early to tell whether Mr. Reagan's "politics of confidence" approach or his "new federalism" concept or his attempt to create a conservative coalition in Congress will result in stabilizing a political system that has become highly volatile. Although his stated goal is to lessen and limit governmental — including presidential — power, Reagan's first year in office was reminiscent in style of Franklin Roosevelt's strong Presidency. Notwithstanding the widespread disillusion that marked the 1980 presidential selection/election process, the Presidency may now be on the way to recovering its prestige and power. If the Reagan programs and policies are successful, its "time of troubles" could be at an end; if those efforts fail to meet the nation's problems, the office could face a crisis greater than any since it was created over two hundred years ago.

Meanwhile, regardless of misgivings about its current stability or future prospects the Presidency remains the keystone of our governmental structure and the grand prize in our political system. Despite repeated and serious blows, its essential nature and basic role have not changed. What contemporary events *have* done is to make us more aware of how important is the choice of a President, of how real is the potential for misuse or abuse of executive authority, and of how necessary it is that we concern ourselves constantly with the oldest and most difficult problem of American government: determining the scope and the limits of presidential power.

1

This problem has been the root of serious controversy since the inception of the office. From George Washington's time to our own, political leaders, students of public affairs, and ordinary citizens have argued that presidential authority is excessive or inadequate, effective or illusory, the basis for dictatorship or the best defense of democracy. Depending on the historial period or the political orientation from which the office is viewed, each of these seemingly contradictory assessments may be valid. But taken together they reflect two essential facts about presidential power—that it cannot be precisely defined and that there are many different conceptions of its scope and limits.

The power of the Presidency is a complex phenomenon. It cannot be determined simply by reference to the Constitution; nor does it become fully evident by reviewing the history of what Presidents have done or gotten away with. The reason for this elusiveness is that presidential power *varies*, with any President's capacity to influence or control the course of national or international affairs being dependent at any given time on five major factors: 1) the meaning currently attributed to the formal, constitutional sources of executive authority; 2) the state of the political system in which the specific Presidency is operating; 3) the personal attributes and attitudes of the incumbent President; 4) the particular set of circumstances, conditions, and events presently confronting the nation; 5) the popularity of the incumbent President and the degree to which he enjoys the public's trust and confidence. All of these factors change from time to time and from President to President. They are constantly in flux, and since the power of the Presidency is the product of interaction among all of them, the dimensions of that power are continually changing. As a result, no absolute definition of presidential power is possible, because that power is always in the process of being defined.

PRESIDENTIAL POWER AND THE CONSTITUTIONAL SYSTEM

When Professor Woodrow Wilson said "the President is at liberty, both in law and conscience, to be as big a man as he can," he indicated the range of possibilities open to a President in attempting to exercise power and emphasized that the essential attribute of the constitutional office is its flexibility. For the Presidency under the Constitution is only potentially, not necessarily, powerful. That document's executive provisions, even more than the others, are general, indefinite, and ambiguous. The basic characteristics of the office—its unitary form, independent functions, and national purview—are clear enough. But Article II provides at best only a hint of the Presidency's potential for power. In fact, those cryptic provisions raise more questions than they answer. The President is "commander-in-chief of the army and the navy of the United States."

But does this make him only the nation's "first general and admiral," as Hamilton insisted, or does it empower him to use the armed forces in such a way as to commit the nation to war? Does his authority to make treaties by and with the advice and consent of two thirds of the Senate require a sharing of power in the formulation and control of foreign policy, or does it mean, as the Supreme Court once stated, that the President is America's "sole organ of government" in the field of international relations? The President is to "take care that the laws be faithfully executed," but faithful according to what standard? Congressional intention? Judicial rulings? His own determination of constitutionality or political expediency? The very first words of Article II read: "The Executive power shall be vested in a President of the United States of America." But is this simply an introductory statement, or is it a grant of inherent power to act in any way the President deems necessary to protect the national interest?

Ostensibly, it is possible to get answers to such questions in the American governmental system. For interpretation of the Constitution's meaning is the function of the Supreme Court. But despite its vaunted reputation, judicial review has not been an effective method of defining presidential authority. Judicial pronouncements on such authority are rare, and in virtually every instance they have involved acquiescence in extraordinary actions taken during periods of grave national emergency. Although in the Court's latest major decision on presidential power it rejected Mr. Nixon's claim of absolute "executive privilege" and ordered him to make available information relevant to the Watergate affair, the lesson of history is that the Supreme Court usually restrains itself rather than the President. If, as in the Nixon case, the misuse of power is clear and the political climate compels, the Court may go further and attempt to impose limits on specific exercises of authority. But in checking strong Presidents the judiciary has generally functioned only as a symbol of restraint, a moral force, and a reminder of established principles.

The flexibility of the Constitution's language, combined with the diffidence of the Supreme Court and the intrinsic limitations of judicial review, have made it possible for the powerful Presidency to develop within a framework of governmental legitimacy. The constitutional system permits presidential passivity, indifference, ineptitude, or worse; but it also allows for presidential energy, resourcefulness, creativity, and leadership. Constitutional flexibility — the most distinctive and important feature of American government — has made the Presidency both the most dynamic and the most dangerous of our political institutions.

PRESIDENTIAL POWER AND THE POLITICAL SYSTEM

The American political system is also adaptable and amorphous. Operating simultaneously at two levels — national and local — it is exceedingly complex, allowing for the expansion of executive power when the President can mobilize broad support for himself and his policies, but providing formidable constraints on that power when he cannot. The growth of democracy has made the Presidency a tribunate office, so that today the President is politically as well as constitutionally, actually as well as symbolically, "the sole representative of all the people." This development, which had its beginnings in the Jacksonian era, has resulted in a Presidency potentially much more powerful than the monarchical office so feared by its early opponents. But presidential power is also subject to limitation because of its dependence on public attitudes, and because changes in those attitudes can be reflected through institutions—Congress, interest groups, the media, economic enterprises, state and local governments—that have countervailing power.

Leadership of a political system as complicated as ours is difficult to establish. And since the late 1960's it has become even more difficult, because of changes which were designed to democratize the system but which have also destabilized it. These changes or "reforms" have involved virtually every element of the political process and have affected the Presidency in many ways. The method of presidential selection has been revolutionized by the substitution of primary elections for party decisions as the principal mode of choosing state delegates to the national nominating conventions. This method has broadened the base of citizen participation in the selection process, and coupled with the reform of campaign financing it has opened the process to a larger field of candidates. But it has also dealt a severe blow to the two major national parties. They are no longer able to play their customary mediational role in accommodating the diverse groups and building the broad consensus on controversial issues that can help a President govern effectively. In addition, the state and local chieftains who once played a major part in selecting and electing their party's candidate have been largely displaced in the new system and are therefore unavailable or uninterested when it comes to helping "their" President mobilize support in his dealings with Congress or the country.

Concomitant with the decline of party has been an increase in voters who identify themselves as "independents," which adds to the undisciplined amorphousness of our politics; and a decrease in voter turnout, which encourages the growth of single-interest pressure groups with their uncompromising attitudes. Both of these phenomena further weaken the party system and exacerbate the problem of finding a firm center of popular or governmental support for measures that reflect the national interest. The greatly expanded influence of the mass media—particularly television—in our political process is also related to the decline of party, as the role of reporting, interpreting, and judging the significance of events and personalities has passed from party leaders to journalists. From the viewpoint of the Presidency the media factor is a two-edged sword. Candidates and Presidents gain popularity and support from media coverage, but they are also subject to intense and incessant scrutiny, which can have a withering effect; and the President is so constantly at center stage that he is often left alone to take the blame for anything that seems wrong.

Finally, the "new politics" has resulted in increasing the political vulnerability of an incumbent President, and in distracting him from his principal responsibilities for long periods of time. The proliferation of presidential primaries and the absence of party machinery to support a sitting President mean that the power of incumbency is no longer sufficient to assure renomination. This situation (plus federal campaign financing and the potential effectiveness of grass-roots media-oriented campaigning) encourages opponents from inside or outside the President's party to challenge him. Moreover, the need to organize for so many primaries over so long a period of time requires an incumbent to begin running for renomination at least a year before his term ends. The result of all this is that political considerations may supersede policy decisions, and that presidential power may be adversely affected by the very process of presidential selection and election.

Along with these fundamental changes in the political system as related to the parties and the selection/election process, there have also during the past decade been great changes and reforms in the operation of Congress, and these too have had serious effects on the power of the Presidency. On a day-to-day basis any President's biggest headache is not the Russians or NATO or the Middle East. It is Congress — and the problem of how to exercise leadership over the legislative process. While the modern President is charged with formulating major legislative policies, he does not have a congressional majority on which he can depend. Although he is ostensibly the head of his own party, this position does not give him control over the party's members in Congress. This situation existed long before the "new politics" made it worse. For the anomaly that there is no conformance between the President's role of national leader and the structure of American government is rooted in the fact that political power in America is locally rather than nationally based; that despite the quadrennial appearance of "national" parties, "national" candidates, and "national" elections related to the Presidency, essentially politics in America is local in organization, operation, and orientation.

Unlike parliamentary systems, ours deliberately separates the executive and legislative branches of government politically as well as functionally. The President and Congress are selected and elected independently of each other; they represent different constituencies and have different interests. To the extent that the new system still uses the form and framework of the old, our national parties remain only federations of state and local political organizations or factions which come together in tenuous alliance every four years to nominate or ratify the primary-determined nomination of a candidate for President. But candidates for local offices — Senators, Representatives, and other officials — are selected separately by local processes and local electorates, entirely without reference to the presidential nominee, and are in no way beholden to him.

The results of this process are as complicated as the system itself. Because our politics is neither national nor disciplined, party and government have little relationship to each other. Since the presidential and congressional elections are separate, a party's nominee may capture the White House while the party as a whole fails to win a majority of seats in one or both legislative houses. But even if a party gains control of both the executive and legislative branches the effect is not the same as in parliamentary systems. For whether the President's party does or does not control Congress, independently elected legislators are free to act independently of the President. Any President must bargain, cajole, or threaten to get what he wants in Congress. To achieve his legislative goals he must constantly try to form majority coalitions among members of both his own and the opposition party. As a result, every President finds that leadership of party and Congress is his most difficult and frustrating job, whether it be John Kennedy or Jimmy Carter, with a legislature dominated by their own party; Lyndon Johnson with 35 years' experience in fashioning working majorities on Capitol Hill; Richard Nixon or Gerald Ford, lacking party control in either house of Congress; or Ronald Reagan, dealing with a divided legislature. Moreover, because congressmen are extremely sensitive to the views of their own constituents, a President who has lost the confidence of the people finds that loss quickly reflected in Congress, as public criticism or hostility lead to legislative obduracy and opposition.

If the new system of politics has compounded the President's difficulties with Congress, so have the internal legislative reforms of the past decade. These changes have dispersed power in the legislature to such an extent that the President can no longer negotiate with a limited number of congressional leaders (the Speaker, majority and minority leaders, major committee chairmen and ranking members) to reach agreement on policy. Now on important and controversial matters, the White House must deal with virtually every member of Congress. The breakdown of the party system outside Congress has also affected the legislature by heightening the individual congressman's constituency-orientation and independence. Party discipline — never a major or continuing feature of congressional operations — is now almost nonexistent. And the growth of single-interest groups, coupled with a resurgence of ideological politics, has made the traditional principles of legislative compromise and accommodation increasingly difficult to apply.

Added to all this is the fact that in the wake of Vietnam and Watergate, Congress asserted its own power and prerogatives against presidential domination. This assertiveness has taken the form of attempts to constrain the President's power to make war, to impound funds, and to act contrary to the congressional will. It has also led Congress to prepare itself better for battle with the President by establishing a Budget Office and other information agencies of its own. The end result is a national legislature more independent, better informed, stronger and more aggressive. But one that is also less responsive to customary techniques of executive pressure and less amenable to presidential leadership.

Congress has again become—as the Framers intended—the President's principal antagonist and most effective restrainer. But it has not yet found a way to play a responsible role as the executive's governmental partner. The local orientation of Congress results in a structural fragmentation and dispersion of power that leaves the legislature without a cohesive majority or strong centralized leadership. In fact, if the President does not himself assume the role of legislative leader, Congress still cannot move on important or controversial issues. Moreover, the legislature's new information-gathering and problem-evaluating apparatus is not comparable to that of the Presidency. Nor is Congress properly equipped to oversee executive operations; on the contrary its supervisory function is to a large extent dependent on the executive's willingness to cooperate. The political longevity of congressional leaders and the absence of party discipline do allow for displays of independence which can embarrass or inhibit the executive, and legislative hearings and investigations can focus attention on alleged maladministration or misconduct in the Presidency. But by its nature Congress is not attuned to decisive action.

In the final analysis the key to control over the legislative process — whether by the legislators themselves or by the executive—lies outside the houses of Congress *and* the White House. It is to be found in the President's relationship with the American people. Congress can be mobilized against the President only when he has lost public approval and there is a general and sustained popular demand to impose restraints on him. Conversely, strong and broad public support of the President is the essential precondition for congressional acceptance of his leadership.

Because the American political system divides the nation into separate presidential and congressional constituencies representing different interests and divergent views, it raises the constant threat of governmental stalemate or dyarchy. And because that system is deeply rooted in the basic structural principles of the Constitution — federalism and the separation of powers — it is uncommonly resistant to change. Nonetheless it has been resilient enough to permit unity, leadership, and action when necessary. As the Depression and wartime experiences demonstrate, the executive and legislative powers *can* be fused, partisanship *has* been sublimated, and presidential primacy *is* accepted under the pressure of crisis. The wide distribution of political power in the United States generally provides constraints on executive authority, but it does not handcuff an activist President or preclude the use of extraordinary power when events demand leadership, when the President is prepared to act, and when the public is willing to support him. The political base of presidential power — like the constitutional base — is flexible. As the only national representative of the American people, the President's political position is potentially dominant, but it is dependent on his competence, character, and capacity for leadership; on his skill in gaining, holding and using power; and on the depth of public confidence and support he can command.

PRESIDENTIAL POWER AND PRESIDENTIAL PERSONALITY

The third element that must be considered in attempting to ascertain the scope and limits of executive authority is not systemic but human: the personal attributes and attitudes of the President himself. Because the Presidency is a personal office, the incumbent's personality — those inherent qualities that shape his relationship with the people — is an essential aspect of his leadership role. This personality factor is, in turn, largely a reflection of the individual's attitude toward his office, its authority, and the way in which he believes that authority should be used. In fact, a President's own view of his power plays an important part in shaping the dimensions of that power.

Presidents do not often indulge in theoretical exposition of their ideas, and only occasionally has one expressed himself clearly or systematically on the subject of his authority. But such formal statements are not necessary, since a President's views are revealed in the way he conducts his Presidency and confronts the problems of his time. Every President has some conception of the Presidency's power. In at least one instance (Woodrow Wilson) that conception was fully developed before the office was achieved. Among the other Presidents, some (like Lincoln) formulated their views of power under the pressure of events, some (like Kennedy) modified their views in accommodating to the realities of their situations, and a few (like Buchanan and Hoover) adhered to views which circumstances had made untenable. But however a President reaches his concept of presidential power, and whatever form that concept assumes, his own attitude and behavior are major determinants of the power he in fact possesses. Moreover, the President's conception of his functions and authority is a crucial factor in determining America's destiny, as John Kennedy pointed out in 1960 when he noted that "the history of this nation — its brightest and bleakest pages — has been written largely in terms of the different views our Presidents have had of the Presidency itself."

Here again there are no definite rules, for the office is open to a wide range of background, experience, and temperament. But professional observers and students of the Presidency have developed different kinds of classifications, typologies, and criteria in their attempts to categorize and assess Presidents and presidencies. Some, emphasizing a constitutional perspective, have seen Presidents as "strict-constructionists" or "broad constructionists"; others, looking at the Presidency in operational terms, have used "leader" or "clerk" to distinguish dissimilar types of incumbents; still others have analyzed Presidents from the point of view of their character or psychological makeup or personality, using "active" or "passive" —sometimes coupled with "positive" or "negative"—as the key elements in differentiating executive attitudes and behavior. But the most commonly used terms are those that reflect the ways in which the nation has traditionally tended to judge its Presidents and their presidencies: "strong" and "weak." These categories are of course too simple, the standards of judgment too varied, and the connotations of "weak" and "strong" too value-laden. But properly understood as incorporating aspects of the more sophisticated classifications, they may well be used to describe the different ways in which presidential power has been conceived and exercised.

The weak President regards the federal government as only one among many centers of power in American society and the Presidency as only a coequal branch of that government. He does not believe that government should play a role in solving all its citizens' problems, and he has no plan to change the nation or the world. By nature and philosophy he distrusts the notion of a popular will which must be obeyed, fears highly centralized leadership, and is unconvinced that decisive action is always a virtue. These views are translated into a literalist conception of the constitutional and political systems, and a limitationist interpretation of the President's power in those systems. The weak President believes that his office is bound by the principles of federalism and separation of powers. He is reluctant to advocate or enforce policies that expand national governmental control and impinge on state or local authority. He considers Congress an equal and coordinate (if not superior) organ of government, and often expects the legislature to reflect public opinion and formulate public policy. Viewing Pennsylvania Avenue as a moat rather than a bridge, he eschews legislative leadership. Having limited policy objectives, he does not attempt to organize or mobilize his party. He is not comfortable with and seeks to avoid "politics." The weak President is passive in the sense that he is a conservator and consolidator rather than an interventionist or innovator. The Presidency itself he sees as a moderative office, its influence as primarily moral and above partisanship. The weak President takes a narrow view of his independent constitutional authority, even in the field of foreign affairs, and he is comfortable in a political system of widely distributed power and responsibility. His hope is to pass on an efficient administration and a stable society to his successor.

The strong President regards the federal government as the appropriate instrument for meeting the needs of American society and the Presidency as the vital center of that government. Historically associated with the development of mass democracy and the growth of social consciousness, the strong Presidency is power oriented and attuned to assertive, charismatic, and visionary leadership. In terms of the governmental system, this Presidency reflects a latitudinarian attitude toward basic constitutional principles and an expansionist view of presidential power. National in his outlook, the strong President advocates the extension of national authority and is untroubled by the decline of localism. He attempts to bridge the separation of powers, to join the political branches of government, and to direct the legislative process. Needing widespread support to gain his policy objectives, he seeks to be both a popular and a party leader. To the strong President, the Presidency is a place of action, the only office representing the national interest, the focal position in American government and society. For him the Presidency's essential attribute is its power, and his purposes can be achieved only through the use of that power. Thus the strong President often resorts, particularly in foreign affairs, to independent action. Faced inevitably with resistance in Congress, he uses all the techniques at his command to overcome the constraints inherent in the political system, being constantly engaged in pressuring the legislature to enact his programs and going regularly to the people to generate support for those programs. His principal concern is not the administration of an inherited office but the use of that office to bring about change in American society.

Despite the oversimplification apparent in these descriptions, and notwithstanding the fact that there are significant gradations of strength or weakness among the Presidents in these classifications, each of the men who has held the presidential office could probably be fitted into one of the two general patterns. Those designated by history and by students of the office as "Great Presidents" — Washington, Jefferson, Lincoln, Wilson, and Franklin Roosevelt — were all charismatic personalities and forceful leaders who conceived their power broadly and used it boldly. Those Presidents who are universally regarded as "Failures" — Grant, Buchanan, and Harding — all suffered from an incapacity to lead, an inability to act, and confusion in dealing with presidential authority.

PRESIDENTIAL POWER AND THE TIMES

Caution is required in assessing Presidents, since even those who have been regarded as mediocre were not necessarily untalented or inept. Rather, Presidents and their administrations have almost invariably been reflective of the dominant mood of their times. More important than judging or rating Presidents, therefore, is the fact that the weak and strong presidencies have generally been associated with different historical conditions — the former with periods of "normalcy," of consolidation, of national reconciliation and "good feeling"; the latter with times of tension, movement, change and crisis. Nor is this surprising since no President operates in a vacuum, and since his own conception of the Presidency's power is not alone sufficient to determine the reality of that power. A President may conceive of his authority in the broadest terms and yet be unable to use it, or he may view his authority narrowly and still be compelled to act with vigorous independence.

Two factors in addition to the President's own proclivities determine whether or not power can or will be used: the existence of circumstances or conditions perceived by the nation as requiring action, and the nation's willingness to support the President if he chooses to act. While events — and particularly crises — can make vast authority available to the President, only a President who is prepared to act and whose popular support is firm can make the decision to use it. And conversely, no presidential decision can assure the availability of power without the existence of conditions that justify and legitimize its use. Harry Truman was able to act on his own initiative and according to his own broad view of inherent executive authority when the Cold War turned hot in Korea. But when the crisis atmosphere and aura of public approval passed he could not apply the same concept to seizure of the steel industry. John Kennedy could not move the country or Congress during a period of ostensible "normalcy" which he regarded as unperceived emergency, but he encountered no resistance when he alone decided the issue of national survival in the Cuban missile crisis. And while Lyndon Johnson found widespread support in 1964 for his attack on America's most critical domestic problems, by 1968 his ability to lead the nation had been dissipated by grave doubts regarding both the morality and the necessity of the war in Vietnam.

Only when it is apparent that the nation's fate is at stake does extraordinary power flow to the President. But in times of genuine crisis his authority reaches its zenith, as illustrated by Lincoln's "dictatorial" regime during the Civil War, by Wilson's highly centralized World War I administration, and by Franklin Roosevelt's executive-dominated government during the emergencies of domestic depression and global conflict. National peril creates conditions — psychological as well as constitutional and political — for the use of power by a power-oriented President. Partisanship and localism are sublimated, and Congress and the country alike turn to the President for leadership in time of evident emergency. It is not surprising, therefore, that all of the "Great Presidents" have held office during periods of great crisis.

THE BASIC SOURCES OF PRESIDENTIAL POWER

Although theoretically the twin fountainheads of executive authority are "the Constitution and the laws," in fact the sources of this prodigious power are democracy and necessity. The public need for clearly identified and deeply trusted leadership, and the governmental need for focus, initiative, and action form the dual base of the strong modern Presidency. Given this foundation, the edifice of presidential power is constructed through a combination of popular attraction to the President as a person and popular support for his policies as national leader.

The President's role as "tribune of the people" is essential to the acceptance of a need for action in defense of the national interest and to the exercise of whatever authority may be latent in the presidential office. Neither Lincoln nor Roosevelt could have acted with such spectacular independence in meeting the challenges confronting them had they lacked solid public support, but with that support they could push their powers to the limits of constitutionality and beyond. Conversely, two of our strongest Presidents received object lessons regarding the dependence of power on popular approval, namely Wilson during the fight over the League of Nations, and Roosevelt when he presented his plan to "pack" the Supreme Court. The power of a power-oriented President is virtually unlimited if he enjoys the trust of the people, but if a President loses the public's confidence his authority as Chief Executive is seriously impaired and his position as acknowledged leader of the nation may be jeopardized.

Depending on how intense, widespread, and sustained is the public reaction against a President, the consequences of popular disapproval can cover a broad range of constraints. Inevitably a President who cannot mobilize national support finds his leverage in Congress and his effectiveness in areas requiring congressional consent or cooperation curtailed. At a more serious level of confrontation, the legislature and other centers of countervailing power may assert their authority and rebuff the President, as the Supreme Court did in declaring Truman's seizure of the steel mills unconstitutional, and as Congress did by refusing to enact additional New Deal legislation in the wake of Roosevelt's abortive court-packing plan. Public pressure can become so great that a beleaguered President may be compelled to "campaign" for popular support or he may attempt, as Lyndon Johnson did, to calm the situation by announcing that he will not seek another term in office.

Ultimately, if public reaction to the President reaches a crescendo of outrage and opposition, Congress may turn to the only remedy for involuntary executive change provided by the Constitution — impeachment by a majority vote of the House of Representatives, followed by trial before the Senate with the Chief Justice presiding, in which a two-thirds vote for conviction results in the President's removal from office. This process, often threatened, has been carried to conclusion only once in the nation's history — against Lincoln's successor, Andrew Johnson — and in that single instance the Senate failed to convict by one vote. Thus no President has ever been removed from office, and only one — Richard Nixon — has ever been compelled to resign. But the power of any discredited President declines in direct proportion to his loss of popular approval. If public sentiment remains overwhelmingly negative, he cannot function effectively as the country's leader.

PRESIDENTIAL POWER AND THE FUTURE OF THE PRESIDENCY

In a governmental system noted for its pragmatism, the Presidency is our most pragmatic institution. The office is truly a mirror of our national life, reflecting accurately the events that have made our history, the men we have chosen, for better or worse, to deal with those events, and our own willingness to entrust them with enormous authority over the nation's destiny. It is a flexible and resilient office, whose form has remained undisturbed for more than 200 years, although its substance — that is, its power — has constantly varied. Because the dimensions of presidential power are dependent on changing combinations of individuals, events, and the nation's response to them, it cannot be defined abstractly and it is subject to varying interpretations and uses. This has been true since the creation of the office, and the contemporary acceptance of a strong Presidency does not make it less true in our time.

The institutionalization of presidential power in the modern period has, however, led to results which require a review of basic understandings and a reaffirmation of fundamental principles. If the need for a Presidency of leadership and action is still demanded by the uncertainties of our age, we should not forget that the ultimate purpose of our governmental system is not simply to provide national security but also to guarantee individual liberty; and that while the American system allows for the exercise of virtually unlimited executive authority in defense of the national interest, it is also designed to prevent that concentration of power in the executive which Madison characterized as "the very definition of tyranny."

Presidential power has been attacked in recent years as a result of the distrust and fear generated by Vietnam and Watergate. And this is not surprising, since a reaction against the "imperial" Presidency and attempts to devise means for restraining excessive presidential authority were inevitable in the wake of those disturbing events. But while a national rededication to the basic concept of constitutional government is long overdue, any attempt to change the fundamental nature of the executive office must be rejected. We know that its vast power creates real danger, but the answer to the problem of presidential power is not an emasculated Presidency. A strong executive has been our indispensable instrument in meeting crises at home and abroad since the Republic was born, and we still live in an era of protracted crisis. Moreover, while we should recognize that there are limits to what Presidents can do — that *our* expectations exceed *their* capabilities — it still remains true that there is no substitute for the President as the keystone of our governmental structure, the focus of our political system, and the chief protector of our national interest. Vietnam and Watergate have made us more aware than ever before of our own ultimate responsibility in choosing the person to whom we entrust these functions and powers, but nothing we have experienced changes the fact that for the foreseeable future there is no alternative to a strong Presidency.

The importance of the American President in today's world makes it certain that the subject of presidential power will continue to be controversial. In fact the perennial debate on that subject has been given new impetus by the election of Ronald Reagan, since he is perceived as favoring a less powerful and less pervasive executive office. But whether or not this turns out to be the case, it is reassuring to note that change has been characteristic of the Presidency since its inception and that both the office and the nation have survived intact. In the future as in the past some will fear the Presidency because it seems too strong and others will be concerned because it seems too weak, for dispute over the scope and limits of presidential power is part of our political heritage. It is also a sign of vitality in our society — welcome evidence that we continue to regard our most important institution of government as a great experiment in constitutional democratic leadership.

I

ORIGINAL
VIEWS

Controversy regarding the scope and limits of presidential power began even before the office was established. In fact, during the struggle over ratification of the Constitution, the proposed Presidency became the major target for those who were against the creation of a stronger central government. Committed to the idea of state sovereignty and to the principle of legislative supremacy within the framework of a strictly limited governmental system, they were wary of an independent and powerful national executive. And the constitutional office was potentially strong. Its chief architects, James Wilson and Gouverneur Morris, had persuaded the Convention that effective executive power was essential to the new system's success, and the assumption that General Washington would be the first President blunted most criticism even if it did not allay all fears. Indeed, if any single factor was responsible for the strong Presidency included in the Constitution, it was this anticipation that the country's most trusted, respected, and honored citizen would be its first Chief Executive.

In a document noted for its brevity, the executive provisions of the Constitution are notably brief. Like the document as a whole, but to a greater degree than in the provisions dealing with legislative authority, Article II is simply an outline of presidential functions and powers. General, vague, and ambiguous, the language leaves much room for interpretation. The basic attributes of the Presidency are, however, manifest: the personal nature of the office, its guaranteed tenure and independence from the legislature, its national character, and its potential for leadership.

It was this conception of the Presidency that the Constitution's protagonists, the federalists, ardently supported. Merchants and traders, creditors and speculators, nationalists and elitists, they wanted a central government powerful enough to maintain law and order, protect property interests, develop the nation's resources, and make America a factor in international affairs. Seeking stable, authoritative, and vigorous rule, they regarded a strong executive as essential to the achievement of their goals. Their antifederalist opponents—individualistic, parochial farmers and tradesmen, plus some landed interests—regarded all government, particularly a distant and impersonal one, with fear and suspicion. In their view, the Constitution granted more power to the new central government than had been exercised over the colonies by Britain; in the Presidency they saw the re-establishment of monarchical rule and the specter of tyranny.

The ratification campaign was bitter. Thousands of pamphlets, handbills, editorials, and essays were published by both sides, and all the leading political figures of the time were involved in the great debate. The two crucial battles were fought in Virginia and New York, for without the participation of these important states, the new government could not succeed.

In the Great Commonwealth, Patrick Henry, George Mason, James Monroe, and Richard Henry Lee led the fight against the Constitution, while James Madison, John Marshall, and ultimately Governor Edmund Randolph supported ratification. Virginia was the most doubtful state, and the discussion in its convention the most thorough, able, and spirited. Henry, the greatest orator of his day, made an impassioned plea for individual liberty under state sovereignty, and conjured up the nightmare of a "despot" President leading his national army in "one bold push for the American throne." Madison concentrated on the dangers and deficiencies of government under the Articles of Confederation. The debate reflected a full awareness of the authority Virginia was being asked to cede, but in the end General Washington's compatriots approved the new charter 89 to 79.

Most of the antifederalists in the other states also hammered at the theme of monarchy and tyranny, with its emotional appeal to such recent events, and the Pennsylvanian who adopted the pseudonym "An Old Whig" inveighed against the Presidency because it would establish the worst kind of despot—"an elective king." But it was in New York that the opposition to the Constitution and the Presidency came closest to success. For there most of the great landowners rejected the idea of a "consolidated government," and the antifederalists were led by the Governor, George Clinton. The pro-Constitution forces not only found support among the rising mercantile interests but also had the inestimable benefit of Alexander Hamilton's brilliant advocacy and political expertise.

Out of this confrontation came the most comprehensive and valuable commentary on the Constitution—*The Federalist Papers*—a series of essays written by Hamilton, Madison, and John Jay in support of the new governmental system and designed to convince New Yorkers that it would be neither unfamiliar nor excessively powerful. Hamilton defended the Constitution's presidential provisions, emphasizing the need for "decision, activity, secrecy, and despatch" in the executive, and taking full advantage of the fact that the governorship of New York under the state constitution of 1777 had been the principal model in creating the Presidency. The battle was long and the outcome uncertain, but by the narrow margin of 30 to 27 the federalists won. Ironically, the nine state ratifications required for the Constitution to become effective were achieved before the federalist cause prevailed in either Virginia or New York, but with their approval the "great experiment" was launched, and on April 30, 1789, George Washington was inaugurated as first President of the United States.

The selections included in this section present the two opposing views of presidential power at the nation's beginning. The section opens with the various constitutional provisions related to the Presidency, for they are the source from which all conceptions of presidential power flow and to which they all refer.

THE PRESIDENCY IN THE CONSTITUTION

☆

THE CONSTITUTION: *Provisions on the Presidency*

ARTICLE II

Section 1. The executive power shall be vested in a President of the United States of America. He shall hold his office during the term of four years, and, together with the Vice President, chosen for the same term, be elected as follows:

Each State shall appoint, in such manner as the legislature thereof may direct, a number of electors, equal to the whole number of senators and representatives to which the State may be entitled in the Congress: but no senator or representative, or person holding an office of trust or profit under the United States, shall be appointed an elector.

The electors shall meet in their respective States, and vote by ballot for two persons, of whom one at least shall not be an inhabitant of the same State with themselves. And they shall make a list of all the persons voted for, and of the number of votes for each; which list they shall sign and certify, and transmit sealed to the seat of the government of the United States, directed to the president of the Senate. The president of the Senate shall, in the presence of the Senate and House of Representatives, open all the certificates, and the votes shall then be counted. The person having the greatest number of votes shall be the President, if such number be a majority of the whole number of electors appointed; and if there be more than one who have such majority, and have an equal number of votes, then the House of Representatives shall immediately choose by ballot one of them for President; and if no person have a majority, then from the five highest on the list the said House shall in like manner choose the President. But in choosing the President, the votes shall be taken by

18

States, the representation from each State having one vote; a quorum for this purpose shall consist of a member or members from two thirds of the States, and a majority of all the States shall be necessary to a choice. In every case, after the choice of the President, the person having the greatest number of votes of the electors shall be the Vice President. But if there should remain two or more who have equal votes, the Senate shall choose from them by ballot the Vice President.[1]

The Congress may determine the time of choosing the electors, and the day on which they shall give their votes; which day shall be the same throughout the United States.

No person except a natural born citizen, or a citizen of the United States, at the time of the adoption of this Constitution, shall be eligible to the office of President; neither shall any person be eligible to that office who shall not have attained to the age of thirty-five years, and been fourteen years a resident within the United States.

In case of the removal of the President from office, or of his death, resignation, or inability to discharge the powers and duties of the said office, the same shall devolve on the Vice President, and the Congress may by law provide for the case of removal, death, resignation, or inability, both of the President and Vice President, declaring what officer shall then act as President, and such officer shall act accordingly, until the disability be removed or a President shall be elected.[2]

The President shall, at stated times, receive for his services a compensation, which shall neither be increased nor diminished during the period for which he shall have been elected, and he shall not receive within that period any other emolument from the United States, or any of them.

Before he enter on the execution of his office, he shall take the following oath or affirmation: "I do solemnly swear (or affirm) that I will faithfully execute the office of President of the United States, and will to the best of my ability, preserve, protect and defend the Constitution of the United States."

Section 2. The President shall be Commander in Chief of the army and navy of the United States, and of the militia of the several States, when called into the actual service of the United States; he may require the opinion, in writing, of the principal officer in each of the executive departments, upon any subject relating to the duties of their respective offices, and he shall have power to grant reprieves

[1] Superseded by the Twelfth Amendment.
[2] See the Twenty-fifth Amendment.

and pardons for offenses against the United States, except in cases of impeachment.

He shall have power, by and with the advice and consent of the Senate, to make treaties, provided two thirds of the senators present concur; and he shall nominate, and by and with the advice and consent of the Senate, shall appoint ambassadors, other public ministers and consuls, judges of the Supreme Court, and all other officers of the United States, whose appointments are not herein otherwise provided for, and which shall be established by law: but the Congress may by law vest the appointment of such inferior officers, as they think proper, in the President alone, in the courts of law, or in the heads of departments.

The President shall have power to fill up all vacancies that may happen during the recess of the Senate, by granting commissions which shall expire at the end of their next session.

Section 3.   He shall from time to time give to the Congress information of the state of the Union, and recommend to their consideration such measures as he shall judge necessary and expedient; he may, on extraordinary occasions, convene both Houses, or either of them, and in case of disagreement between them with respect to the time of adjournment, he may adjourn them to such time as he shall think proper; he shall receive ambassadors and other public ministers; he shall take care that the laws be faithfully executed, and shall commission all the officers of the United States.

Section 4.   The President, Vice President, and all civil officers of the United States, shall be removed from office on impeachment for, and conviction of, treason, bribery, or other high crimes and misdemeanors.

ARTICLE I

Section 3. . . .   The Vice President of the United States shall be President of the Senate, but shall have no vote, unless they be equally divided.

The Senate shall choose their other officers, and also a president *pro tempore*, in the absence of the Vice President, or when he shall exercise the office of the President of the United States.

The Senate shall have the sole power to try all impeachments. When sitting for that purpose, they shall be on oath or affirmation. When the President of the United States is tried, the chief justice shall preside: and no person shall be convicted without the concurrence of two thirds of the members present.

Judgment in cases of impeachment shall not extend further than to removal from office, and disqualifications to hold and enjoy any office of honor, trust or profit under the United States: but the party convicted shall nevertheless be liable and subject to indictment, trial, judgment and punishment, according to law.

Section 7. . . . Every bill which shall have passed the House of Representatives and the Senate, shall, before it becomes a law, be presented to the President of the United States; if he approves he shall sign it, but if not he shall return it, with his objections to that House in which it shall have originated, who shall enter the objections at large on their journal, and proceed to reconsider it. If after such reconsideration two thirds of that House shall agree to pass the bill, it shall be sent, together with the objections, to the other House, by which it shall likewise be reconsidered, and if approved by two thirds of that House, it shall become a law. But in all such cases the votes of both Houses shall be determined by yeas and nays, and the names of the persons voting for and against the bill shall be entered on the journal of each House respectively. If any bill shall not be returned by the President within ten days (Sundays excepted) after it shall have been presented to him, the same shall be a law, in like manner as if he had signed it, unless the Congress by their adjournment prevent its return, in which case it shall not be a law.

Every order, resolution, or vote to which the concurrence of the Senate and the House of Representatives may be necessary (except on a question of adjournment) shall be presented to the President of the United States; and before the same shall take effect, shall be approved by him, or being disapproved by him, shall be repassed by two thirds of the Senate and House of Representatives, according to the rules and limitations prescribed in the case of a bill.

Section 9. . . . The privilege of the writ of *habeas corpus* shall not be suspended, unless when in cases of rebellion or invasion the public safety may require it.

ARTICLE IV

Section 4. The United States shall guarantee to every State in this Union a republican form of government, and shall protect each of them against invasion; and on application of the legislature, or of the executive (when the legislature cannot be convened) against domestic violence.

AMENDMENT XII
Adopted September 25, 1804

The electors shall meet in their respective States, and vote by ballot for President and Vice President, one of whom, at least, shall not be an inhabitant of the same State with themselves; they shall name in their ballots the person voted for as President, and in distinct ballots the person voted for as Vice President and they shall make distinct lists of all persons voted for as President and of all persons voted for as Vice President, and of the number of votes for each, which lists they shall sign and certify, and transmit sealed to the seat of the government of the United States, directed to the President of the Senate; The President of the Senate shall, in the presence of the Senate and House of Representatives, open all the certificates and the votes shall then be counted; The person having the greatest number of votes for President, shall be the President, if such number be a majority of the whole number of electors appointed; and if no person have such majority, then from the persons having the highest numbers not exceeding three on the list of those voted for as President, the House of Representatives shall choose immediately, by ballot, the President. But in choosing the President, the votes shall be taken by States, the representation from each State having one vote; a quorum for this purpose shall consist of a member or members from two thirds of the States, and a majority of all the States shall be necessary to a choice. And if the House of Representatives shall not choose a President whenever the right of choice shall devolve upon them, before the fourth day of March next following, then the Vice President shall act as President, as in the case of the death or other constitutional disability of the President. The person having the greatest number of votes as Vice President shall be the Vice President, if such number be a majority of the whole number of electors appointed, and if no person have a majority, then from the two highest numbers on the list, the Senate shall choose the Vice President; a quorum for the purpose shall consist of two thirds of the whole number of Senators, and a majority of the whole number shall be necessary to a choice. But no person constitutionally ineligible to the office of President shall be eligible to that of Vice President of the United States.

AMENDMENT XX
Adopted January 23, 1933

Section 1.   The terms of the President and Vice President shall end at noon on the 20th day of January, and the terms of Senators and Representatives at noon on the 3rd day of January, of the years in which such terms would have ended if this article had not been ratified; and the terms of their successors shall then begin.

Section 2.   The Congress shall assemble at least once in every year, and such meeting shall begin at noon on the 3rd day of January, unless they shall by law appoint a different day.

Section 3. If, at the time fixed for the beginning of the term of the President, the President-elect shall have died, the Vice President-elect shall become President. If a President shall not have been chosen before the time fixed for the beginning of his term, or if the President-elect shall have failed to qualify, then the Vice President-elect shall act as President until a President shall have qualified; and the Congress may by law provide for the case wherein neither a President-elect nor a Vice President-elect shall have qualified, declaring who shall then act as President, or the manner in which one who is to act shall be selected, and such person shall act accordingly until a President or Vice President shall have qualified.

Section 4. The Congress may by law provide for the case of the death of any of the persons from whom the House of Representatives may choose a President whenever the right of choice shall have devolved upon them, and for the case of the death of any of the persons from whom the Senate may choose a Vice President whenever the right of choice shall have devolved upon them.

Section 5. Sections 1 and 2 shall take effect on the 15th day of October following the ratification of this article.

Section 6. This article shall be inoperative unless it shall have been ratified as an amendment to the Constitution by the legislatures of three fourths of the several States within seven years from the date of its submission.

AMENDMENT XXII
Adopted February 26, 1951

No person shall be elected to the office of the President more than twice, and no person who has held the office of the President, or acted as President, for more than two years of a term to which some other person was elected President shall be elected to the office of the President more than once.

But this article shall not apply to any person holding the office of President when this article was proposed by the Congress, and shall not prevent any person who may be holding the office of President, or acting as President, during the term within which this article becomes operative from holding the office of President or acting as President during the remainder of such term.

This article shall be inoperative unless it shall have been ratified as an amendment to the Constitution by the legislatures of three fourths of the several States within seven years from the date of its submission to the States by the Congress.

AMENDMENT XXIII
Adopted March 29, 1961

Section 1. The District constituting the seat of Government of the United States shall appoint in such manner as the Congress may direct:

A number of electors of President and Vice President equal to the whole number of Senators and Representatives in Congress to which the District would be entitled if it were a State, but in no event more than the least populous State; they shall be in addition to those appointed by the States, but they shall be considered, for the purposes of the election of President and Vice President, to be electors appointed by a State; and they shall meet in the District and perform such duties as provided by the twelfth article of amendment.

Section 2. The Congress shall have power to enforce this article by appropriate legislation.

AMENDMENT XXV
Adopted February 10, 1967

Section 1. In case of the removal of the President from office or of his death or resignation, the Vice President shall become President.

Section 2. Whenever there is a vacancy in the office of the Vice President, the President shall nominate a Vice President who shall take office upon confirmation by a majority vote of both Houses of Congress.

Section 3. Whenever the President transmits to the President *pro tempore* of the Senate and the Speaker of the House of Representatives his written declaration that he is unable to discharge the powers and duties of his office, and until he transmits to them a written declaration to the contrary, such powers and duties shall be discharged by the Vice President as Acting President.

Section 4. Whenever the Vice President and a majority of either the principal officers of the executive departments or of such other body as Congress may by law provide, transmit to the President *pro tempore* of the Senate and the Speaker of the House of Representatives their written declaration that the President is unable to discharge the powers and duties of his office, the Vice President shall immediately assume the powers and duties of the office as Acting President.

Thereafter, when the President transmits to the President *pro tempore* of the Senate and the Speaker of the House of Representatives his written declaration that no inability exists, he shall resume the powers and duties of his office unless the Vice President and a majority of either the principal officers of the executive department or of such other body as Congress may by law provide, transmit within four days to the President *pro tempore* of the Senate and the Speaker of the House of Representatives their written declaration that the President is unable to discharge the powers and duties of his office. Thereupon Congress shall decide the issue, assembling within forty-eight hours for that purpose if not in session. If the Congress, within twenty-one days after receipt of the latter written declaration, or, if Congress is not in session, within twenty-one days after Congress is required to assemble, determines by two thirds vote of both Houses that the President is unable to discharge the powers and duties of his office, the Vice President shall continue to discharge the same as Acting President; otherwise, the President shall resume the powers and duties of his office.

AMENDMENT XXVI
Adopted June 30, 1971

Section 1. The right of citizens of the United States, who are 18 years of age or older, to vote shall not be denied or abridged by the United States or by any state on account of age.

Section 2. The Congress shall have power to enforce this article by appropriate legislation.

ANTIFEDERALIST ATTACKS
ON THE PRESIDENCY

☆

PATRICK HENRY: *Speech Against Ratification*

This Constitution is said to have beautiful features; but when I come to examine these features, sir, they appear to me horribly frightful. Among other deformities, it has an awful squinting; it squints towards monarchy; and does not this raise indignation in the breast of every true American?

Your President may easily become king. Your Senate is so imperfectly constructed that your dearest rights may be sacrificed by what may be a small minority; and a very small minority may continue forever unchangeably this government, although horridly defective. Where are your checks in this government? Your strongholds will be in the hands of your enemies. It is on a supposition that your American governors shall be honest, that all the good qualities of this government are founded; but its defective and imperfect construction puts it in their power to perpetrate the worst of mischiefs, should they be bad men; and, sir, would not all the world, from the eastern to the western hemisphere, blame our distracted folly in resting our rights upon the contingency of our rulers being good or bad? Show me that age and country where the rights and liberties of the people were placed on the sole chance of their rulers being good men, without a consequent loss of liberty! I say that the loss of that dearest privilege has ever followed, with absolute certainty, every such mad attempt.

If your American chief be a man of ambition and abilities, how easy is it for him to render himself absolute! The army is in his hands,

Patrick Henry was a delegate to the Continental Congress (1774–1775) and Governor of Virginia (1776–1779, 1784–1786). The selection is from *Debates and Other Proceedings of the Convention of Virginia* (Richmond, 1805), p. 52. The speech was delivered on June 5, 1788.

and if he be a man of address, it will be attached to him, and it will be the subject of long meditation with him to seize the first auspicious moment to accomplish his design; and, sir, will the American spirit solely relieve you when this happens? I would rather infinitely—and I am sure most of this Convention are of the same opinion—have a king, lords, and commons, than a government so replete with such insupportable evils. If we make a king, we may prescribe the rules by which he shall rule his people, and interpose such checks as shall prevent him from infringing them; but the President, in the field, at the head of his army, can prescribe the terms on which he shall reign master, so far that it will puzzle any American ever to get his neck from under the galling yoke. I cannot with patience think of this idea. If ever he violates the laws, one of two things will happen: he will come at the head of his army, to carry every thing before him; or he will give bail, or do what Mr. Chief Justice will order him. If he be guilty, will not the recollection of his crimes teach him to make one bold push for the American throne? Will not the immense difference between being master of every thing, and being ignominiously tried and punished, powerfully excite him to make this bold push? But, sir, where is the existing force to punish him? Can he not, at the head of his army, beat down every opposition? Away with your President! we shall have a king: the army will salute him monarch: your militia will leave you, and assist in making him king, and fight against you: and what have you to oppose this force? What will then become of you and your rights? Will not absolute despotism ensue?

. . .

☆

AN "OLD WHIG": *The Dangers of an Elected Monarch*

[The] office of President of the United States appears to me to be clothed with such powers as are dangerous. To be the fountain of all honors in the United States—Commander in Chief of the army, navy, and militia; with the power of making treaties and of granting pardons; and to be vested with an authority to put a negative upon all laws, unless two thirds of both houses shall persist in enacting it, and put their names down upon calling the yeas and nays for that purpose—is in reality to be a king, as much a king as the king of Great Britain, and a king too of the worst kind: an elective king.

If such powers as these are to be trusted in the hands of any man, they ought, for the sake of preserving the peace of the community, at once to be made hereditary. Much as I abhor kingly government, yet I venture to pronounce, where kings are admitted to rule they should most certainly be vested with hereditary power. The election of a king whether it be in America or Poland, will be a scene of horror and confusion; and I am perfectly serious when I declare, that, as a friend to my country, I shall despair of any happiness in the United States until this office is either reduced to a lower pitch of power, or made perpetual and hereditary.

When I say that our future President will be as much a king as the king of Great Britain, I only ask of my readers to look into the constitution of that country, and then tell me what important prerogative the king of Great Britain is entitled to which does not also belong to the President during his continuance in office. The king of Great Britain, it is true, can create nobility which our President can-

This letter was originally published in the *Philadelphia Independent Gazeteer*, December 4, 1787.

28

not; but our President will have the power of making all the great men, which comes to the same thing. All the difference is, that we shall be embroiled in contention about the choice of the man, while they are at peace under the security of an hereditary succession. To be tumbled headlong from the pinnacle of greatness and be reduced to a shadow of departed royalty, is a shock almost too great for human nature to endure. It will cost a man many struggles to resign such eminent powers, and ere long, we shall find some one who will be very unwilling to part with them. Let us suppose this man to be a favorite with his army, and that they are unwilling to part with their beloved Commander in Chief—or to make the thing familiar, let us suppose a future President and Commander in Chief adored by his army and the militia to as great a degree as our late illustrious Commander in Chief; and we have only to suppose one thing more, that this man is without the virtue, the moderation and love of liberty which possessed the mind of our late general—and this country will be involved at once in war and tyranny.

So far is it from its being improbable that the man who shall hereafter be in a situation to make the attempt to perpetuate his own power, should want the virtues of General Washington, that it is perhaps a chance of one hundred millions to one that the next age will not furnish an example of so disinterested a use of great power. We may also suppose, without trespassing upon the bounds of probability, that this man may not have the means of supporting, in private life, the dignity of his former station; that like Caesar, he may be at once ambitious and poor, and deeply involved in debt. Such a man would die a thousand deaths rather than sink from the heights of splendor and power, into obscurity and wretchedness.

We are certainly about giving our President too much or too little; and in the course of less than twenty years we shall find that we have given him enough to enable him to take all. It would be infinitely more prudent to give him at once as much as would content him, so that we might be able to retain the rest in peace, for if once power is seized by violence, not the least fragment of liberty will survive the shock. I would therefore advise my countrymen seriously to ask themselves this question: Whether they are prepared to receive a king? If they are, to say so at once, and make the kingly office hereditary; to frame a constitution that should set bounds to his power, and, as far as possible, secure the liberty of the subject. If we are not prepared to receive a king, let us call another convention to revise the proposed constitution, and form it anew on the principles of a confederacy of free republics; but by no means, under pretense of a republic, to lay the foundation for a military government, which is the worst of all tyrannies.

☆

GEORGE CLINTON: *Fourth Essay of "Cato"*

I shall begin with observations on the executive branch of this new system; and though it is not the first in order, as arranged therein, yet being the *chief*, is perhaps entitled by the rules of rank to the first consideration. The executive power as described in the 2d article, consists of a President and Vice President, who are to hold their offices during the term of four years; the same article has marked the manner and time of their election, and established the qualifications of the President; it also provides against the removal, death, or inability of the President and Vice President—regulates the salary of the President, delineates his duties and powers; and, lastly, declares the causes for which the President and Vice President shall be removed from office.

Notwithstanding the great learning and abilities of the gentlemen who composed the convention, it may be here remarked with deference, that the construction of the first paragraph of the first section of the second article is vague and inexplicit, and leaves the mind in doubt as to the election of a President and Vice President, after the expiration of the election for the first term of four years; in every other case, the election of these great officers is expressly provided for; but there is no explicit provision for their election which is to set this political machine in motion; no certain and express terms as in your state constitution, that *statedly* once in every four years, and as often as these offices shall become vacant, by expiration or otherwise, as is therein expressed, an election shall

George Clinton served as Governor of New York (1777–1795) and as Vice President under Jefferson and Madison (1805–1812). This Fourth Essay of "Cato" was originally published in the *New York Journal*, November 8, 1787.

be held as follows, etc.; this inexplicitness perhaps may lead to an establishment for life.

It is remarked by Montesquieu, in treating of republics, that *in all magistracies, the greatness of the power must be compensated by the brevity of the duration, and that a longer time than a year would be dangerous.* It is, therefore, obvious to the least intelligent mind to account why great power in the hands of a magistrate, and that power connected with considerable duration, may be dangerous to the liberties of a republic. The deposit of vast trusts in the hands of a single magistrate enables him in their exercise to create a numerous train of dependents. This tempts his *ambition,* which in a republican magistrate is also remarked *to be pernicious,* and the duration of his office for any considerable time favors his views, gives him the means and time to perfect and execute his designs; he therefore fancies that he may be great and glorious by oppressing his fellow-citizens, and raising himself to permanent grandeur on the ruins of his country. And here it may be necessary to compare the vast and important powers of the President, together with his continuance in office, with the foregoing doctrine—his eminent magisterial situation will attach many adherents to him, and he will be surrounded by expectants and courtiers. His power of nomination and influence on all appointments; the strong posts in each state comprised within his superintendence, and garrisoned by troops under his direction; his control over the army, militia, and navy; the unrestrained power of granting pardons for treason, which may be used to screen from punishment those whom he had secretly instigated to commit the crime, and thereby prevent a discovery of his own guilt; his duration in office for four years—these, and various other principles evidently prove the truth of the position, that if the President is possessed of ambition, he has power and time sufficient to ruin his country.

Though the President, during the sitting of the legislature, is assisted by the Senate, yet he is without a constitutional council in their recess. He will therefore be unsupported by proper information and advice, and will generally be directed by minions and favorites, or a council of state will grow out of the principal officers of the great departments, the most dangerous council in a free country.

The ten miles square, which is to become the seat of government, will of course be the place of residence for the President and the great officers of state; the same observations of a great man will apply to the court of a President possessing the powers of a monarch, that is observed of that of a monarch—*ambition with idleness*

*—baseness with pride—the thirst of riches without labor—aversion
to truth—flattery—treason—perfidy—violation of engagements—contempt of civil duties—hope for the magistrate's weakness; but above
all, the perpetual ridicule of virtue*—these, he remarks, are the characteristics by which the courts in all ages have been distinguished.
The language and the manners of this court will be what dis-
tinguishes them from the rest of the community, not what assimi-
lates them to it; and in being remarked for a behavior that shows
they are not *meanly born,* and in adulation to people of fortune
and power.

The establishment of a Vice President is as unnecessary as it is
dangerous. This officer, for want of other employment, is made President of the Senate, thereby blending the executive and legislative
powers, besides always giving to some one state, from which he is
to come, an unjust pre-eminence.

It is a maxim in republics that the representative of the people
should be of their immediate choice; but by the manner in which
the President is chosen, he arrives to this office at the fourth or fifth
hand. Nor does the highest vote, in the way he is elected, determine
the choice—for it is only necessary that he should be taken from
the highest of five, who may have a plurality of votes. . . .

[A]nd wherein does this President, invested with his powers and
prerogatives, essentially differ from the king of Great Britain (save
as to name, the creation of nobility, and some immaterial incidents,
the offspring of absurdity and locality)? The direct prerogatives of the
President, as springing from his political character, are among
the following: It is necessary, in order to distinguish him from the
rest of the community, and enable him to keep, and maintain his
court, that the compensation for his services, or in other words, his
revenue, should be such as to enable him to appear with the splendor of a prince. He has the power of receiving ambassadors from,
and a great influence on their appointments to foreign courts; as
also to make treaties, leagues, and alliances with foreign states, assisted by the Senate, which when made becomes the supreme law
of land. He is a constituent part of the legislative power, for every
bill which shall pass the House of Representatives and Senate is to
be presented to him for approbation. If he approves of it he is to
sign it, if he disapproves he is to return it with objections, which in
many cases will amount to a complete negative; and in this view
he will have a great share in the power of making peace, coining
money, etc., and all the various objects of legislation, expressed or
implied in this Constitution. For though it may be asserted that
the king of Great Britain has the express power of making peace
or war, yet he never thinks it prudent to do so without the advice

of his Parliament, from whom he is to derive his support—and therefore these powers, in both President and king, are substantially the same. He is the generalissimo of the nation, and of course has the command and control of the army, navy and militia; he is the general conservator of the peace of the union—he may pardon all offences, except in cases of impeachment, and the principal fountain of all offices and employments. Will not the exercise of these powers therefore tend either to the establishment of a vile and arbitrary aristocracy or monarchy? The safety of the people in a republic depends on the share or proportion they have in the government; but experience ought to teach you, that when a man is at the head of an elective government invested with great powers, and interested in his re-election, in what circle appointments will be made; by which means an *imperfect aristocracy* bordering on monarchy may be established.

You must, however, my countrymen, beware that the advocates of this new system do not deceive you by a fallacious resemblance between it and your own state government [New York] which you so much prize; and, if you examine, you will perceive that the chief magistrate of this state is your immediate choice, controlled and checked by a just and full representation of the people, divested of the prerogative of influencing war and peace, making treaties, receiving and sending embassies, and commanding standing armies and navies, which belong to the power of the confederation, and will be convinced that this government is no more like a true picture of your own than an Angel of Darkness resembles an Angel of Light.

FEDERALIST DEFENSE OF
THE PRESIDENCY

☆

ALEXANDER HAMILTON: *The Federalist, No. 69*

To the People of the State of New York:
I proceed now to trace the real characters of the proposed Executive, as they are marked out in the plan of the convention. This
will serve to place in a strong light the unfairness of the representations which have been made in regard to it.

The first thing which strikes our attention is that the executive
authority, with few exceptions, is to be vested in a single magistrate.
This will scarcely, however, be considered as a point upon which
any comparison can be grounded; for if, in this particular, there
be a resemblance to the king of Great Britain, there is not less a
resemblance to the Grand Seignior, to the khan of Tartary, to the
Man of the Seven Mountains, or to the governor of New York.

That magistrate is to be elected for *four* years; and is to be re-
eligible as often as the people of the United States shall think him
worthy of their confidence. In these circumstances there is a total
dissimilitude between *him* and a king of Great Britain, who is an
hereditary monarch, possessing the crown as a patrimony descendi-
ble to his heirs forever; but there is a close analogy between *him*
and a governor of New York, who is elected for *three* years, and
is re-eligible without limitation or intermission. If we consider how
much less time would be requisite for establishing a dangerous influence in a single State, than for establishing a like influence
throughout the United States, we must conclude that a duration
of *four* years for the Chief Magistrate of the Union is a degree of

Alexander Hamilton was a delegate to the Constitutional Convention and the
leader of the Federalist Party in New York. This essay by "Publius" was originally
published in the *New York Packet*, March 14, 1788.

permanency far less to be dreaded in that office, than a duration of *three* years for a corresponding office in a single State.

The President of the United States would be liable to be impeached, tried, and, upon conviction of treason, bribery, or other high crimes or misdemeanors, removed from office; and would afterwards be liable to prosecution and punishment in the ordinary course of law. The person of the king of Great Britain is sacred and inviolable; there is no constitutional tribunal to which he is amenable; no punishment to which he can be subjected without involving the crisis of a national revolution. In this delicate and important circumstance of personal responsibility, the President of Confederated America would stand upon no better ground than a governor of New York, and upon worse ground than the governors of Maryland and Delaware.

The President of the United States is to have power to return a bill, which shall have passed the two branches of the legislature, for reconsideration; and the bill so returned is to become a law, if, upon that reconsideration, it be approved by two thirds of both houses. The king of Great Britain, on his part, has an absolute negative upon the acts of the two houses of Parliament. The disuse of that power for a considerable time past does not affect the reality of its existence; and is to be ascribed wholly to the crown's having found the means of substituting influence to authority, or the art of gaining a majority in one or the other of the two houses, to the necessity of exerting a prerogative which could seldom be exerted without hazarding some degree of national agitation. The qualified negative of the President differs widely from this absolute negative of the British sovereign; and tallies exactly with the revisionary authority of the council of revision of this State, of which the governor is a constituent part. In this respect the power of the President would exceed that of the governor of New York, because the former would possess, singly, what the latter shares with the chancellor and judges; but it would be precisely the same with that of the governor of Massachusetts, whose constitution, as to this article, seems to have been the original from which the convention have copied.

The President is to be the "Commander in Chief of the army and navy of the United States, and of the militia of the several States, when called into the actual service of the United States. He is to have power to grant reprieves and pardons for offences against the United States, *except in cases of impeachment*; to recommend to the consideration of Congress such measures as he shall judge necessary and expedient; to convene, on extraordinary occasions, both houses of the legislature, or either of them, and, in case of disagreement between them *with respect to the time of adjournment,* to adjourn them to such time as he shall think proper; to take care that the laws be faithfully executed; and to commission all officers of the United States." In most of these particulars, the power of the President will resemble equally that of the king of Great Britain and of the governor of New York. The most material points of difference are these: *First.* The President will have only the occasional command of such part of the militia of the nation as by legislative provision may be called into the actual service of the Union. The king of Great Britain and the governor of New York have at all times the entire command of all the militia within their several jurisdictions. In this article, therefore, the power of the President would be inferior to that of either the monarch or the governor. *Secondly.* The President is to be Commander in Chief of the army and navy of the United States. In this respect his authority would be nominally the same with that of the king of Great Britain, but in substance much inferior to it. It would amount to nothing more than the supreme command and direction of the military and naval forces, as first general and admiral of the Confederacy; while that of the British king extends to the *declaring* of war and to the *raising* and *regulating* of fleets and armies—all which, by the Constitution under consideration, would appertain to the legislature. The governor of New York, on the other hand, is by the constitution of the State vested only with the command of its militia and navy. But the constitutions of several of the States expressly declare their governors to be commanders in chief, as well of the army as navy; and it may well be a question, whether those of New Hampshire and Massachusetts, in particular, do not, in this instance, confer larger powers upon their respective governors, than could be claimed by a President of the United States. *Thirdly.* The power of the President, in respect to pardons, would extend to all cases, *except those of impeachment.* The governor of New York may pardon in all cases, even in those of impeachment, except for treason and murder. Is not the power of the governor, in this article, on a calculation of political consequences, greater than that of the President? All conspiracies and plots against the government, which have not been matured into actual treason, may be screened from punishment of every kind, by the interposition of the prerogative of pardoning. If a governor of New York, therefore, should be at the head of any such conspiracy, until the design had been ripened into actual hostility he could insure his accomplices and adherents an entire impunity. A President of the Union, on the other hand, though he may even pardon treason, when prosecuted in the ordinary course of law, could shelter no offender, in any degree, from the effects of impeachment and conviction. Would not the prospect of a total indemnity for all the preliminary steps be a greater temptation to undertake and persevere in an enterprise against the public liberty, than the mere prospect of an exemption from death and confiscation, if the final execution of the design, upon an actual appeal to arms, should miscarry? Would this last expectation have any influence at all, when the probability was computed, that the person who was to afford that exemption might himself be involved in the consequences of the measure, and might be incapacitated by his agency in it from affording the desired impunity? The better to judge of this matter, it will be necessary to recollect, that, by the proposed Constitution, the offence of treason is limited "to levying war upon the United States, and adhering to their enemies, giving them aid and comfort"; and that by the laws of New York it is confined within similar bounds. *Fourthly*. The President can only adjourn the national legislature in the single case of disagreement about the time of adjournment. The British monarch may prorogue or even dissolve the Parliament. The governor of New York may also prorogue the legislature of this State for a limited time; a power which, in certain situations, may be employed to very important purposes.

The President is to have power, with the advice and consent of the Senate, to make treaties, provided two thirds of the senators present concur. The king of Great Britain is the sole and absolute representative of the nation in all foreign transactions. He can of his own accord make treaties of peace, commerce, alliance, and of every other description. It has been insinuated that his authority in this respect is not conclusive, and that his conventions with foreign powers are subject to the revision, and stand in need of the ratification, of Parliament. But I believe this doctrine was never heard of, until it was broached upon the present occasion. Every jurist of that kingdom, and every other man acquainted with its Constitution, knows, as an established fact, that the prerogative of making treaties exists in the crown in its utmost plentitude; and that the compacts entered into by the royal authority have the most complete legal validity and perfection, independent of any other sanction. The Parliament, it is true, is sometimes seen employing itself in altering the existing laws to conform them to the stipulations in a new treaty; and this may have possibly given birth to the imagination that its cooperation was necessary to the obligatory efficacy of the treaty. But this parliamentary interposition proceeds from a different cause: from the necessity of adjusting a most artificial and intricate system of revenue and commercial laws, to the changes made in them by the operation of the treaty; and of adapting new provisions and precautions to the new state of things, to keep the ma-

chine from running into disorder. In this respect, therefore, there
is no comparison between the intended power of the President and
the actual power of the British sovereign. The one can perform
alone what the other can do only with the concurrence of a branch
of the legislature. It must be admitted, that, in this instance, the
power of the federal Executive would exceed that of any State Executive. But this arises naturally from the sovereign power which relates to treaties. If the Confederacy were to be dissolved, it would
become a question whether the Executives of the several States were
not solely invested with that delicate and important prerogative.

The President is also to be authorized to receive ambassadors
and other public ministers. This, though it has been a rich theme
of declamation, is more a matter of dignity than of authority. It is
a circumstance which will be without consequence in the administration of the government; and it was far more convenient that
it should be arranged in this manner, than that there should be a
necessity of convening the legislature, or one of its branches, upon
every arrival of a foreign minister, though it were merely to take
the place of a departed predecessor.

The President is to nominate, and, *with the advice and consent
of the Senate*, to appoint ambassadors and other public ministers,
judges of the Supreme Court, and in general all officers of the
United States established by law, and whose appointments are not
otherwise provided for by the Constitution. The king of Great Britain is emphatically and truly styled the fountain of honor. He not
only appoints to all offices, but can create offices. He can confer
titles of nobility at pleasure; and has the disposal of an immense
number of church preferments. There is evidently a great inferiority in the power of the President, in this particular, to that of the
British king; nor is it equal to that of the governor of New York,
if we are to interpret the meaning of the constitution of the State
by the practice which has obtained under it. The power of appointment is with us lodged in a council, composed of the governor and
four members of the Senate, chosen by the Assembly. The governor
claims, and has frequently *exercised*, the right of nomination, and
is *entitled* to a casting vote in the appointment. If he really has
the right of nominating, his authority is in this respect equal to
that of the President, and exceeds it in the article of the casting
vote. In the national government, if the Senate should be divided,
no appointment could be made; in the government of New York,
if the council should be divided, the governor can turn the scale,
and confirm his own nomination. If we compare the publicity which
must necessarily attend the mode of appointment by the President
and an entire branch of the national legislature, with the privacy
in the mode of appointment by the governor of New York, closeted

in a secret apartment with at most four, and frequently with only two persons; and if we at the same time consider how much more easy it must be to influence the small number of which a council of appointment consists, than the considerable number of which the national Senate would consist, we cannot hesitate to pronounce that the power of the chief magistrate of this State, in the disposition of offices, must, in practice, be greatly superior to that of the Chief Magistrate of the Union.

Hence it appears that, except as to the concurrent authority of the President in the article of treaties, it would be difficult to determine whether that magistrate would in the aggregate, possess more or less power than the governor of New York. And it appears yet more unequivocally, that there is no pretense for the parallel which has been attempted between him and the king of Great Britain. But to render the contrast in this respect still more striking, it may be of use to throw the principal circumstances of dissimilitude into a closer group.

The President of the United States would be an officer elected by the people for *four* years; the king of Great Britain is a perpetual and *hereditary* prince. The one would be amenable to personal punishment and disgrace; the person of the other is sacred and inviolable. The one would have a *qualified* negative upon the acts of the legislative body; the other has an *absolute* negative. The one would have a right to command the military and naval forces of the nation; the other, in addition to this right, possesses that of *declaring* war, and of *raising* and *regulating* fleets and armies by his own authority. The one would have a concurrent power with a branch of the legislature in the formation of treaties; the other is the *sole possessor* of the power of making treaties. The one would have a like concurrent authority in appointing to offices; the other is the sole author of all appointments. The one can confer no privileges whatever: the other can make denizens of aliens, noblemen of commoners: can erect corporations with all the rights incident to corporate bodies. The one can prescribe no rules concerning the commerce or currency of the nation; the other is in several respects the arbiter of commerce, and in this capacity can establish markets and fairs, can regulate weights and measures, can lay embargoes for a limited time, can coin money, can authorize or prohibit the circulation of foreign coin. The one has no particle of spiritual jurisdiction; the other is the supreme head and governor of the national church! What answer shall we give to those who would persuade us that things so unlike resemble each other? The same that ought to be given to those who tell us that a government, the whole power of which would be in the hands of the elective and periodical servants of the people, is an aristocracy, a monarchy, and a despotism.

☆

ALEXANDER HAMILTON: *The Federalist, No. 70*

To the People of the State of New York:
There is an idea, which is not without its advocates, that a vigorous Executive is inconsistent with the genius of republican government. The enlightened well-wishers to this species of government must at least hope that the supposition is destitute of foundation; since they can never admit its truth, without at the same time admitting the condemnation of their own principles. Energy in the Executive is a leading character in the definition of good government. It is essential to the protection of the community against foreign attacks; it is not less essential to the steady administration of the laws; to the protection of property against those irregular and high-handed combinations which sometimes interrupt the ordinary course of justice; to the security of liberty against the enterprises and assaults of ambition, of faction, and of anarchy. Every man the least conversant in Roman story, knows how often that republic was obliged to take refuge in the absolute power of a single man, under the formidable title of Dictator, as well against the intrigues of ambitious individuals who aspired to the tyranny, and the seditions of whole classes of the community whose conduct threatened the existence of all government, as against the invasions of external enemies who menaced the conquest and destruction of Rome.

There can be no need, however, to multiply arguments or examples on this head. A feeble Executive implies a feeble execution of the government. A feeble execution is but another phrase for a bad execution; and a government ill executed, whatever it may be in theory, must be, in practice, a bad government.

This essay by "Publius" was originally published in the *New York Packet*, March 18, 1788.

Taking it for granted, therefore, that all men of sense will agree in the necessity of an energetic Executive, it will only remain to inquire, what are the ingredients which constitute this energy? How far can they be combined with those other ingredients which constitute safety in the republican sense? And how far does this combination characterize the plan which has been reported by the convention?

The ingredients which constitute energy in the Executive are, first, unity; secondly, duration; thirdly, an adequate provision for its support; fourthly, competent powers.

The ingredients which constitute safety in the republican sense are, first, a due dependence on the people; secondly, a due responsibility.

Those politicians and statesmen who have been the most celebrated for the soundness of their principles and for the justice of their views, have declared in favor of a single Executive and a numerous legislature. They have, with great propriety, considered energy as the most necessary qualification of the former, and have regarded this as most applicable to power in a single hand; while they have, with equal propriety, considered the latter as best adapted to deliberation and wisdom, and best calculated to conciliate the confidence of the people and to secure their privileges and interests.

That unity is conducive to energy will not be disputed. Decision, activity, secrecy, and despatch will generally characterize the proceedings of one man in a much more eminent degree than the proceedings of any greater number; and in proportion as the number is increased, these qualities will be diminished.

This unity may be destroyed in two ways: either by vesting the power in two or more magistrates of equal dignity and authority; or by vesting it ostensibly in one man, subject, in whole or in part, to the control and cooperation of others, in the capacity of counsellors to him. . . .

Wherever two or more persons are engaged in any common enterprise or pursuit, there is always danger of difference of opinion. If it be a public trust or office, in which they are clothed with equal dignity and authority, there is peculiar danger of personal emulation and even animosity. From either, and especially from all these causes, the most bitter dissensions are apt to spring. Whenever these happen, they lessen the respectability, weaken the authority, and distract the plans and operations of those whom they divide. If they should unfortunately assail the supreme executive magistracy of a country, consisting of a plurality of persons, they might impede or frustrate the most important measures of the government, in the most critical emergencies of the state. And what is still worse, they might split the community into the most violent and irreconcilable factions, adhering differently to the different individuals who composed the magistracy.

Men often oppose a thing, merely because they have had no agency in planning it, or because it may have been planned by those whom they dislike. But if they have been consulted, and have happened to disapprove, opposition then becomes, in their estimation, an indispensable duty of self-love. They seem to think themselves bound in honor, and by all the motives of personal infallibility, to defeat the success of what has been resolved upon contrary to their sentiments. Men of upright, benevolent tempers have too many opportunities of remarking, with horror, to what desperate lengths this disposition is sometimes carried, and how often the great interests of society are sacrificed to the vanity, to the conceit, and to the obstinacy of individuals, who have credit enough to make their passions and their caprices interesting to mankind. Perhaps the question now before the public may, in its consequences, afford melancholy proofs of the effects of this despicable frailty, or rather detestable vice, in the human character.

Upon the principles of a free government, inconveniences from the source just mentioned must necessarily be submitted to in the formation of the legislature; but it is unnecessary, and therefore unwise, to introduce them into the constitution of the Executive. It is here too that they may be most pernicious. In the legislature, promptitude of decision is oftener an evil than a benefit. The differences of opinion, and the jarrings of parties in that department of the government, though they may sometimes obstruct salutary plans, yet often promote deliberation and circumspection, and serve to check excesses in the majority. When a resolution too is once taken, the opposition must be at an end. That resolution is a law, and resistance to it punishable. But no favorable circumstances palliate or atone for the disadvantages of dissension in the executive department. Here, they are pure and unmixed. There is no point at which they cease to operate. They serve to embarrass and weaken the execution of the plan or measure to which they relate, from the first step to the final conclusion of it. They constantly counteract those qualities in the Executive which are the most necessary ingredients in its composition—vigor and expedition, and this without any counterbalancing good. In the conduct of war, in which the energy of the Executive is the bulwark of the national security, every thing would be to be apprehended from its plurality.

It must be confessed that these observations apply with principal weight to the first case supposed—that is, to a plurality of magistrates of equal dignity and authority, a scheme, the advocates for which are not likely to form a numerous sect; but they apply, though not with equal, yet with considerable weight to the project of a council, whose concurrence is made constitutionally necessary to the operations of the ostensible Executive. An artful cabal in that council would be able to distract and to enervate the whole system of administration. If no such cabal should exist, the mere diversity of views and opinions would alone be sufficient to tincture the exercise of the executive authority with a spirit of habitual feebleness and dilatoriness.

But one of the weightiest objections to a plurality in the Executive, and which lies as much against the last as the first plan, is, that it tends to conceal faults and destroy responsibility. Responsibility is of two kinds—to censure and to punishment. The first is the more important of the two, especially in an elective office. Man, in public trust, will much oftener act in such a manner as to render him unworthy of being any longer trusted, than in such a manner as to make him obnoxious to legal punishment. But the multiplication of the Executive adds to the difficulty of detection in either case. It often becomes impossible, amidst mutual accusations, to determine on whom the blame or the punishment of a pernicious measure, or series of pernicious measures, ought really to fall. It is shifted from one to another with so much dexterity, and under such plausible appearances, that the public opinion is left in suspense about the real author. The circumstances which may have led to any national miscarriage of misfortune are sometimes so complicated that, where there are a number of actors who may have had different degrees and kinds of agency, though we may clearly see upon the whole that there has been mismanagement, yet it may be impracticable to pronounce to whose account the evil which may have been incurred is truly chargeable.

"I was overruled by my council. The council were so divided in their opinions that it was impossible to obtain any better resolution on the point." These and similar pretexts are constantly at hand, whether true or false. And who is there that will either take the trouble or incur the odium of a strict scrutiny into the secret springs of the transaction? Should there be found a citizen zealous enough to undertake the unpromising task, if there happen to be collusion between the parties concerned, how easy it is to clothe the circumstances with so much ambiguity, as to render it uncertain what was the precise conduct of any of those parties?

In the single instance in which the governor of this State is coupled with a council—that is, in the appointment to offices, we have seen the mischiefs of it in the view now under consideration. Scandalous appointments to important offices have been made. Some

cases, indeed, have been so flagrant that ALL PARTIES have agreed in
the impropriety of the thing. When inquiry has been made, the
blame has been laid by the governor on the members of the council, who, on their part, have charged it upon his nomination; while
the people remain altogether at a loss to determine, by whose influence their interests have been committed to hands so unqualified
and so manifestly improper. In tenderness to individuals, I forbear
to descend to particulars.

It is evident from these considerations, that the plurality of the
Executive tends to deprive the people of the two greatest securities
they can have for the faithful exercise of any delegated power, *first*,
the restraints of public opinion, which lose their efficacy, as well on
account of the division of the censure attendant on bad measures
among a number, as on account of the uncertainty on whom it
ought to fall; and, *secondly*, the opportunity of discovering with
facility and clearness the misconduct of the persons they trust, in
order either to their removal from office, or to their actual punishment in cases which admit of it.

In England, the king is a perpetual magistrate; and it is a maxim
which has obtained for the sake of the public peace, that he is un-
accountable for his administration, and his person sacred. Nothing,
therefore, can be wiser in that kingdom, than to annex to the king
a constitutional council, who may be responsible to the nation for
the advice they give. Without this, there would be no responsibility
whatever in the executive department—an idea inadmissible in a
free government. But even there the king is not bound by the resolutions of his council, though they are answerable for the advice
they give. He is the absolute master of his own conduct in the exercise of his office, and may observe or disregard the counsel given
to him at his sole discretion.

But in a republic, where every magistrate ought to be personally
responsible for his behavior in office, the reason which in the British
Constitution dictates the propriety of a council, not only ceases
to apply, but turns against the institution. In the monarchy of Great
Britain, it furnishes a substitute for the prohibited responsibility of
the chief magistrate, which serves in some degree as a hostage to
the national justice for his good behavior. In the American republic,
it would serve to destroy, or would greatly diminish, the intended
and necessary responsibility of the Chief Magistrate himself.

The idea of a council to the Executive, which has so generally
obtained in the State constitutions, has been derived from that
maxim of republican jealousy which considers power as safer in the
hands of a number of men than of a single man. If the maxim
should be admitted to be applicable to the case, I should contend

that the advantage on that side would not counterbalance the numerous disadvantages on the opposite side. But I do not think the rule at all applicable to the executive power. I clearly concur in opinion, in this particular, with a writer whom the celebrated Junius pronounces to be "deep, solid, and ingenious," that "the executive power is more easily confined when it is ONE"; that it is far more safe there should be a single object for the jealousy and watchfulness of the people; and, in a word, that all multiplication of the Executive is rather dangerous than friendly to liberty.

II

PRESIDENTIAL
VIEWS

BECAUSE THE POWER of the Presidency is to a
large extent what the President says it is, the most important views
of presidential power are those expressed by Presidents themselves.
Clear and systematic exposition of such views is rare, but the
speeches, messages, letters, memoirs, and other documentary materials of Presidents—before, during, and after their tenure of office—
reveal their perceptions of executive authority and constitute the
most meaningful definitions of its scope and limits.

Reflecting the different political orientations and personalities of
the Presidents, as well as the different problems with which they
had to deal, these presidential conceptions of presidential power
vary widely. Those that are historically as well as conceptually the
most significant are presented here, beginning with the first President's assertion of his independent authority to chart the nation's
course in foreign affairs, and ending with the strikingly similar position assumed by his latest successor.

The selections are grouped in four sets, each of which marks an
important turning point in the interpretation and development of
presidential power. The first group of readings deals with the establishment of the Presidency as an office of independent authority
and focuses on the controversy surrounding George Washington's
proclamation of neutrality in 1793. Based on a claim to executive
prerogative in determining American foreign policy, this action outraged not only democrats sympathetic to the French Revolution but
also unreconstructed antifederalists (now called republicans) who
had all along distrusted the central government and its "elected
monarch." Ultimately the argument involved interpretation of the
President's constitutional powers, and in a series of essays James

Madison—at the instigation of Secretary of State Thomas Jefferson and writing under the pseudonym Helvidius—attacked Washington's "usurpation" of congressional authority to decide the issue of war or peace. The Administration was defended by Alexander Hamilton who, using the pen-name Pacificus, contended that under his "executive power" the President could establish the nation's foreign policy, although the consequences of his actions might "affect" the legislature's exclusive power to declare war.

Thus the crucial issue of executive authority to determine America's position in world affairs—an issue of the most far-reaching importance for our own time—was raised at the inception of the Presidency. It was then resolved in favor of the Washington-Hamilton concept attributing broad and independent power to the President as the nation's "sole organ of foreign relations." But the controversy has continued and the arguments of Hamilton and Madison were heard again in 1967 when President Johnson's Undersecretary of State and Senator J. William Fulbright clashed at the Foreign Relations Committee's hearings on the Gulf of Tonkin Resolution and the President's authority to conduct the war in Vietnam.

The second set of selections deals with the greatest test of presidential power in American history—the crisis of secession and civil war—and includes the response to that crisis of three Presidents: Jackson, Buchanan, and Lincoln. The issue of presidential power as a means to prevent the Union's dissolution first arose in 1832, when South Carolina adopted an ordinance nullifying congressional tariff acts, denying the federal government's authority to enforce them, and threatening to secede if enforcement was attempted. Although incensed by the action of his native state, Andrew Jackson responded calmly and effectively. Strengthening the government's military position in South Carolina and preparing a political compromise, he also issued a proclamation firmly rejecting the doctrine of nullification and clearly asserting his intention to preserve the Union. The combination of forcefulness and conciliation worked, and the bloody showdown was postponed for a generation.

The decisive confrontation finally came in 1860. With Abraham Lincoln's election the movement toward Southern withdrawal began, and only a strong stand by the President might have averted civil war. But James Buchanan did not have a Jacksonian conception of the Presidency's power. Faced with the most agonizing decision any President before the nuclear age has had to make, Buchanan considered issuing a proclamation condemning secession but ended with a message to Congress adopting the equivocal position that while no state had a right to secede the President was powerless to prevent such action. Abdicating responsibility to a paralyzed legislature, he then withdrew from the political arena.

His successor had a radically different view of executive authority in time of crisis, and though initially he sought reconcilation, ultimately he was prepared to act. In his first address to the nation, Lincoln made it clear that he regarded secession as rebellion, and that as Chief Executive and Commander in Chief he had both the duty and the authority to use whatever means were necessary to preserve the Union. That he was resolute in his purpose became even clearer in the critical period that followed, and particularly during the eleven weeks after Fort Sumter's fall when he alone constituted the government of the United States. Lincoln's conception of executive power went beyond that of any President before or since. As expressed in his message to the special session of Congress in 1861 and in an 1864 campaign document, his view included the arrogation to himself of the "war power of the government," unlimited inherent authority to meet the crisis, and a popular mandate to transcend the bounds of constitutionality in defense of the nation. Responding to the emergency and prosecuting the war on his own initiative, without any reference to Congress at its inception and with as little as possible throughout its duration, Lincoln's Civil War regime was a "presidential dictatorship." Such a spectacular administration has not reappeared on the American scene, but the Lincolnian conception of presidential power became the model for all of his strong successors, and its basic principles have been adopted by all subsequent crisis Presidents.

The third set of readings reflects the long period of transition from the post-Civil War Presidency to the modern office. As with all institutional transformations, this development of the Presidency was directly related to fundamental economic, social, and political changes, and consequently was slow, uneven, and bitterly resisted. The selections reveal the basic conflict going on in American society at the time and take the form of a disputation involving three successive Presidents—Theodore Roosevelt, William Howard Taft, and Woodrow Wilson—each of whom contributed to the debate a classic conceptualization of the executive's position and power as the nation entered a new era.

Characterized by a laissez-faire economy, an isolationist foreign policy, and congressionally-dominated government, the period after the Civil War witnessed a sharp decline in executive authority. But as demands for economic reform and world involvement grew, there was a concomitant revival of interest in the strong Presidency. Indeed, by the turn of the century the issue of presidential power had again become controversial as a result of Theodore Roosevelt's accidental succession to the office. For TR's energetic tenure broke the pattern of executive subservience to Congress, and his "steward-ship theory" of the Presidency expressed the new, activist concep-tion of its authority. Roosevelt saw the President as the representative and protector of the "plain people" in a system controlled by spe-cial interests, and he acknowledged no restrictions on his power to further the "general welfare" except those specifically imposed by the Constitution or the laws.

This assertive view of the executive was anathema to Roose-velt's hand-picked successor, William Howard Taft, whose counter-argument reflected the basic philosophic differences as well as the personal antagonism between the two men. Taft's denial of inherent executive power to act in the public interest, as set forth in *Our Chief Magistrate and His Powers*, is the most explicit statement of the literalist-limitationist concept ever formulated by a President. But if this view was still dominant at the beginning of the century, Theodore Roosevelt's ideas pointed toward the future. Indeed it was in the next President, Woodrow Wilson, that TR found his intellectual successor and the powerful Presidency its most eloquent advocate. Wilson's conception of the office was drawn from many sources, both British and American, and it was infused with the democratic spirit of his two idols, Jefferson and Lincoln. Systemat-ically developed in a series of 1908 lectures and applied in practice during his administration, the Wilsonian view of the executive as "the representative of no constituency but of the whole people" and as the "vital place of action" in American government heralded the modern Presidency.

Wilson's World War I regime provided a full-dress preview of that office, but it was not until the current era of continuing crisis that the powerful Presidency concept became institutionalized. The final set of selections deals with this period and includes the views of all the modern Presidents, beginning with the dominant figure in the establishment of the contemporary office—Franklin Roose-velt — and ending with the current occupant of the White House, Ron-ald Reagan. A pragmatist of the first order, FDR never theorized about presidential power. But his performance in meeting the economic catastrophe of the 1930s and the war emergency of the 1940s gives ample evidence that no President since Lincoln has had a broader conception of that power. Encompassing the Lincolnian view of independent authority and the Wilsonian of legislative direction, Roosevelt's was the consummate crisis Presidency. Its keynotes were leadership and action. Sounded in every major public statement from his stirring Inaugural Address through the war years, these were the themes by which he captured the popular imagination and dominated the political scene more completely and for a longer time than any other President. Over the course of thirteen critical years, he created an office whose power was commensurate with its national and world responsibilities.

Harry Truman inherited those responsibilities as well as the Rooseveltian conception of power in meeting them. Domestic politics and the conditions of cold war made Truman's application of that concept difficult, but in formulating a policy which continues to govern American foreign affairs, and in acting independently to halt Communist aggression in Korea, he projected the crisis Presidency into the nuclear age. To Truman the Presidency was "the greatest office in the history of the world," and he guarded its prerogatives jealously. Despite the absence of charisma, he secured his place in the ranks of strong Presidents and passed the office undiminished in its authority to his successor.

Dwight Eisenhower had a more limited idea of the Presidency's power and functions, however, and a less assertive view of his own role as President. His emphasis on "organization" and "teamwork," his rejection of a "personality cult," and his fear of executive "autocracy" betrayed an emotional attachment to the Taftian school of thought, and his tenure made it clear that despite the institutionalization of its power the Presidency remains a highly personal position. But the Eisenhower years were more significant in demonstrating rather than disproving the contemporary need for and acceptance of a strong Presidency. For if his administration lacked the vigor of the Lincoln-Wilson-Roosevelt regimes, nonetheless Eisenhower's actual conduct of the office and his uses of its authority were more closely related to those power-oriented Presidencies than to the administrations of his limitationist predecessors. For all his failure to provide leadership and to act decisively, Eisenhower was neither a Buchanan nor a Hoover, and the powerful Presidency was maintained (or survived) during his incumbency.

More important, the end of the Eisenhower interlude saw an immediate return to the strong Presidency in both conception and practice. John Kennedy was the first presidential candidate since Woodrow Wilson to make his view of executive authority a major campaign issue, and like Wilson he sounded the call for "a Chief Executive who is the vital center of action in our whole scheme of government." Concept came into conflict with reality, as Kennedy himself admitted at mid-term, but his independent (indeed secret) handling of the Cuban Missile Crisis in 1962 gave Americans their first frightening glimpse of the Presidency's power—and limits—in the nuclear era.

Kennedy's view of that power, as expressed in a 1960 campaign statement and consistently during his brief tenure, was in the strong Presidency tradition. And so too was Lyndon Johnson's. Although Johnson came to office with greater governmental experience than any of his predecessors, he never conceptualized his thoughts about executive authority. But from the start of his public career he was committed by political inheritance and basic personality to the Presidency of leadership and action. This was reflected in his independent albeit misguided conduct of the Vietnam war, as well as in his earlier efforts to achieve the "Great Society" program. If Johnson was a strong President whose conception of the office was deeply rooted in Rooseveltian principles and practices, however, his war policy also generated concern about the strong Presidency — concern that did not die with his own political demise.

On the contrary, the issue of presidential power became the focus of a great national controversy and a major constitutional crisis under Richard Nixon. Stemming from continuation of the unpopular conflict in Southeast Asia and marked by a chain of unusual events — most notably Nixon's excessive response to the domestic unrest caused by that conflict, his overzealous campaign for reelection in 1972, and a bizarre aspect of that campaign, a break-in at the office of the Democratic National Committee in Washington's Watergate complex — the period culminated in the greatest scandal ever to engulf the White House and finally ended with the unprecedented resignation of the President.

During his 1968 campaign for the Presidency Mr. Nixon had projected an "activist" conception of the office. And while the tone of his first administration was more reminiscent of Eisenhower than of Roosevelt insofar as domestic affairs were concerned, in the area of foreign relations Nixon did act with unusual independence. Even as he attempted to "wind down" American involvement in Southeast Asia, he exercised exclusive control over all aspects of foreign and military policy, and in 1972 he moved on his own initiative to open relations with the People's Republic of China.

But the concept of power reflected in the actions and events that led Congress to consider impeaching Nixon and that ultimately forced his resignation went far beyond the assertive kind of conduct historically associated with the strong Presidency. Presidents had acted independently — even "dictatorially" — in the past, but none before Nixon had followed a course as replete with illegal activities pursued secretly on such questionable grounds with so little regard for their impact on our political and constitutional systems. Nixon later argued that he had acted in the tradition of Lincoln in attempting to meet a serious challenge to our national security. But in the absence of either a clearly discernible crisis such as Lincoln faced or candid public statements such as those in which Lincoln explained his extraordinary assertions of authority, Mr. Nixon's views on presidential emergency power are incompatible with the concept of "government under law."

Gerald Ford was the first person to succeed to the Presidency as a result of the 25th Amendment's provisions allowing an incumbent President (with congressional approval) to appoint a Vice President if a vacancy occurs in that office. As a result, and despite his long experience in the House of Representatives, Ford lacked a solid base of political support either in Congress or the country. Drawn to a passive concept of the Presidency by background and personality, Mr. Ford never brought his administration into clear focus, and much of the good will that a divided people looking for stable leadership were prepared to bestow on him was dissipated by his quick pardon of Richard Nixon. The first President without an electoral base, Ford became the first caretaker President as well.

By 1976 the "new politics" was operational, and its initial presidential product was Jimmy Carter—aided by the reforms which had taken place in his party's selection process, campaigning as an "outsider" untainted by national governmental experience, assuring the electorate that he could be "trusted," promoted as a fresh, attractive, appealing candidate by the media. Self-confident and self-righteous, Carter's approach to the Presidency was essentially in the tradition of his strong Democratic predecessors, but with a sense of the limitations imposed on his office by the immediate past. He presented an impressive agenda to the nation and proposed a long list of important measures to Congress. But his attempt to substitute moral exhortation for political skill was unsuccessful, and he was denied a second term by an electorate that found him lacking in those very qualities of strength, purpose, and forthrightness which he had tried to project.

Conversely, it was those qualities that helped elect Ronald Reagan in 1980. Long a spokesman for the conservative wing of the Republican Party, Reagan almost succeeded in displacing Gerald Ford as the party's centrist nominee in 1976. His campaign was the most ideologically oriented in recent political history, and its major socioeconomic themes challenged the last fifty years of governmental policy. Reagan's ideological commitments — as expressed during the election campaign and in his major policy statements after taking office — include such "weak" Presidency concepts as circumscribing the authority of the national government, respecting the principles of federalism and separation of powers, and returning resources to localities, enterprises, and individuals. But, paradoxically, the instrument he proposes to use in achieving these goals is a strong Presidency. He has clothed himself in the mantle of Franklin Roosevelt in order to undo the work that Roosevelt began a half century ago. Reagan has thereby added an original, though as yet untested, twist to the concept of presidential power.

THE INITIAL EXPANSION OF
PRESIDENTIAL POWER

☆

ON GEORGE WASHINGTON'S PROCLAMATION OF

NEUTRALITY: *The First Letter of "Pacificus"*

by Alexander Hamilton

As attempts are making, very dangerous to the peace, and, it is to be feared, not very friendly to the Constitution, of the United States, it becomes the duty of those who wish well to both, to endeavor to prevent their success. . . .

The objections which have been raised against the proclamation of neutrality, lately issued by the President, have been urged in a spirit of acrimony and invective, which demonstrates that more was in view than merely a free discussion of an important public measure. They exhibit evident indications of a design to weaken the confidence of the people in the author of the measure, in order to remove or lessen a powerful obstacle to the success of an opposition to the government, which, however it may change its form according to circumstances, seems still to be persisted in with unremitting industry. . . .

It will not be disputed, that the management of the affairs of this country with foreign nations, is confided to the government of the United States.

It can as little be disputed, that a proclamation of neutrality, when a nation is at liberty to decline or avoid a war in which other nations are engaged, and means to do so, is a *usual* and a *proper* measure. Its main object is to prevent the nation's being responsible

Alexander Hamilton served as Secretary of the Treasury under Washington (1789–1795). This essay was originally published in *The Gazette of the United States*, Philadelphia, June 29, 1793.

for acts done by its citizens, without the privity or connivance of the government, in contravention of the principles of neutrality; an object of the greatest moment to a country, whose true interest lies in the preservation of peace.

The inquiry then is, what department of our government is the proper one to make a declaration of neutrality, when the engagements of the nation permit, and its interests require that it should be done?

A correct mind will discern at once, that it can belong neither to the legislative nor judicial department; of course it must belong to the executive.

The legislative department is not the organ of intercourse between the United States and foreign nations. It is charged neither with making nor interpreting treaties. It is therefore not naturally that member of the government, which is to pronounce the existing condition of the nation, with regard to foreign powers, or to admonish the citizens of their obligations and duties in consequence; still less is it charged with enforcing the observance of those obligations and duties.

It is equally obvious, that the act in question is foreign to the judiciary department. The province of that department is to decide litigations in particular cases. It is indeed charged with the interpretation of treaties, but it exercises this function only where contending parties bring before it a specific controversy. It has no concern with pronouncing upon the external political relations of treaties between government and government. This position is too plain to need being insisted upon.

It must then of necessity belong to the executive department to exercise the function in question, when a proper case for it occurs.

It appears to be connected with that department in various capacities: As the *organ* of intercourse between the nation and foreign nations; as the *interpreter* of the national treaties, in those cases in which the judiciary is not competent, that is, between government and government; as the *power*, which is charged with the execution of the laws, of which treaties form a part: as that which is charged with the command and disposition of the public force.

This view of the subject is so natural and obvious, so analogous to general theory and practice, that no doubt can be entertained of its justness, unless to be deduced from particular provisions of the Constitution of the United States.

Let us see, then, if cause for such doubt is to be found there.

The second article of the Constitution of the United States, section first, establishes this general proposition, that "the EXECUTIVE

POWER shall be vested in a President of the United States of America."

The same article, in a succeeding section, proceeds to delineate particular cases of executive power. It declares, among other things, that the President shall be Commander in Chief of the army and navy of the United States, and of the militia of the several states, when called into the actual service of the United States; that he shall have power, by and with the advice and consent of the Senate, to make treaties; that it shall be his duty to receive ambassadors and other public ministers, and to take care that the laws be faithfully executed.

It would not consist with the rules of sound construction to consider this enumeration of particular authorities as derogating from the more comprehensive grant in the general clause, further than as it may be coupled with express restrictions of limitations; as in regard to the cooperation of the Senate in the appointment of officers, and the making of treaties; which are plainly qualifications of the general executive powers of appointing officers and making treaties. The difficulty of a complete enumeration of all the cases of executive authority, would naturally dictate the use of general terms, and would render it improbable, that a specification of certain particulars was designed as a substitute for those terms, when antecedently used. The different mode of expression employed in the Constitution, in regard to the two powers, the legislative and the executive, serves to confirm this inference. In the article which gives the legislative powers of the government, the expressions are, "All legislative powers herein granted shall be vested in a Congress of the United States." In that which grants the executive power, the expressions are, *"The executive power* shall be vested in a President of the United States."

The enumeration ought therefore to be considered, as intended merely to specify the principal articles implied in the definition of executive power; leaving the rest to flow from the general grant of that power, interpreted in conformity with other parts of the Constitution, and with the principles of free government.

The general doctrine of our Constitution then is, that the *executive power* of the nation is vested in the President; subject only to the *exceptions* and *qualifications*, which are expressed in the instrument.

Two of these have been already noticed; the participation of the Senate in the appointment of officers, and in the making of treaties. A third remains to be mentioned; the right of the legislature "to declare war, and grant letters of marque and reprisal."

With these exceptions, the executive power of the United States is completely lodged in the President. This mode of construing the Constitution has indeed been recognized by Congress in formal acts, upon full consideration and debate; of which the power of removal from office is an important instance. It will follow, that if a proclamation of neutrality is merely an executive act, as, it is believed, has been shown, the step which has been taken by the President is liable to no just exception on the score of authority.

It may be said, that this inference would be just, if the power of declaring war had not been vested in the legislature; but that this power naturally includes the right of judging, whether the nation is or is not under obligations to make war.

The answer is, that however true this position may be, it will not follow, that the executive is in any case excluded from a similar right of judgment, in the execution of its own functions.

If, on the one hand, the legislature have a right to declare war, it is, on the other, the duty of the executive to preserve peace, till the declaration is made; and in fulfilling this duty, it must necessarily possess a right of judging what is the nature of the obligations which the treaties of the country impose on the government: and when it has concluded that there is nothing in them inconsistent with neutrality, it becomes both its province and its duty to enforce the laws incident to that state of the nation. The executive is charged with the execution of all laws, the law of nations, as well as the municipal law, by which the former are recognized and adopted. It is consequently bound, by executing faithfully the laws of neutrality when the country is in a neutral position, to avoid giving cause of war to foreign powers.

This is the direct end of the proclamation of neutrality. It declares to the United States their situation with regard to the contending parties, and makes known to the community, that the laws incident to that state will be enforced. In doing this, it conforms to an established usage of nations, the operation of which, as before remarked, is to obviate a responsibility on the part of the whole society, for secret and unknown violations of the rights of any of the warring powers by its citizens.

Those who object to the proclamation will readily admit, that it is the right and duty of the executive to interpret those articles of our treaties which give to France particular privileges, in order to the enforcement of them: but the necessary consequence of this is, that the executive must judge what are their proper limits; what rights are given to other nations, by our contracts with them; what rights the law of nature and nations gives, and our treaties permit, in respect to those countries with which we have none; in fine, what are the reciprocal rights and obligations of the United States, and of all and each of the powers at war?

The right of the executive to receive ambassadors and other public ministers, may serve to illustrate the relative duties of the executive and legislative departments. This right includes that of judging, in the case of a revolution of government in a foreign country, whether the new rulers are competent organs of the national will, and ought to be recognized, or not; which, where a treaty antecedently exists between the United States and such nation, involves the power of continuing or suspending its operation. For until the new government is acknowledged, the treaties between the nations, so far at least as regards public rights, are of course suspended.

This power of determining virtually upon the operation of national treaties, as a consequence of the power to receive public ministers, is an important instance of the right of the executive, to decide upon the obligations of the country with regard to foreign nations. To apply it to the case of France, if there had been a treaty of alliance, *offensive* and defensive, between the United States and that country, the unqualified acknowledgment of the new government would have put the United States in a condition to become an associate in the war with France, and would have laid the legislature under an obligation, if required, and there was otherwise no valid excuse, of exercising its power of declaring war.

This serves as an example of the right of the executive, in certain cases, to determine the condition of the nation, though it may, in its consequences, affect the exercise of the power of the legislature to declare war. Nevertheless, the executive cannot thereby control the exercise of that power. The legislature is still free to perform its duties, according to its own sense of them; though the executive, in the exercise of its constitutional powers, may establish an antecedent state of things, which ought to weigh in the legislative decisions.

The division of the executive power in the Constitution, creates a *concurrent* authority in the cases to which it relates.

Hence, in the instance stated, treaties can only be made by the President and Senate jointly; but their activity may be continued or suspended by the President alone.

No objection has been made to the President's having acknowledged the republic of France, by the reception of its minister, without having consulted the Senate; though that body is connected with him in the making of treaties, and though the consequence of his act of reception is, to give operation to those heretofore made with that country. But he is censured for having declared the United States to be in a state of peace and neutrality, with regard to the powers at war; because the right of changing that state, and declaring war, belongs to the legislature.

It deserves to be remarked, that as the participation of the Senate in the making of treaties, and the power of the legislature to declare war, are exceptions out of the general "executive power" vested in the President; they are to be construed strictly, and ought to be extended no further than is essential to their execution.

While, therefore, the legislature can alone declare war, can alone actually transfer the nation from a state of peace to a state of hostility, it belongs to the "executive power" to do whatever else the law of nations, cooperating with the treaties of the country, enjoin in the intercourse of the United States with foreign powers.

In this distribution of authority, the wisdom of our Constitution is manifested. It is the province and duty of the executive to preserve to the nation the blessings of peace. The legislature alone can interrupt them by placing the nation in a state of war.

But though it has been thought advisable to vindicate the authority of the executive on this broad and comprehensive ground, it was not absolutely necessary to do so. That clause of the Constitution which makes it his duty to "take care that the laws be faithfully executed," might alone have been relied upon, and this simple process of argument pursued.

The President is the constitutional EXECUTOR of the laws. Our treaties, and the laws of nations, form a part of the law of the land. He, who is to execute the laws, must first judge for himself of their meaning. In order to the observance of that conduct which the laws of nations, combined with our treaties, prescribed to this country, in reference to the present war in Europe, it was necessary for the President to judge for himself, whether there was anything in our treaties, incompatible with an adherence to neutrality. Having decided that there was not, he had a right, and if in his opinion the interest of the nation required it, it was his duty, as executor of the laws, to proclaim the neutrality of the nation, to exhort all persons to observe it, and to warn them of the penalties which would attend its nonobservance.

The proclamation has been represented as enacting some new law. This is a view of it entirely erroneous. It only proclaims a fact, with regard to the existing state of the nation: informs the citizens of what the laws previously established require of them in that state, and notifies them that these laws will be put in execution against the infractors of them.

☆

ON WASHINGTON'S PROCLAMATION OF NEUTRALITY:

The First Letter of "Helvidius"
by James Madison

Several pieces with the signature of PACIFICUS were lately published, which have been read with singular pleasure and applause, by the foreigners and degenerate citizens among us, who hate our republican government, and the French revolution; whilst the publication seems to have been too little regarded, or too much despised by the steady friends to both. . . .

Had the doctrines inculcated by the writer, with the natural consequences from them, been nakedly presented to the public, this treatment might have been proper. Their true character would then have struck every eye, and been rejected by the feelings of every heart. But they offer themselves to the reader in the dress of an elaborate dissertation; they are mingled with a few truths that may serve them as a passport to credulity; and they are introduced with professions of anxiety for the preservation of peace, for the welfare of the government, and for the respect due to the present head of the executive, that may prove a snare to patriotism.

In these disguises they have appeared to claim the attention I propose to bestow on them; with a view to show, from the publication itself, that under color of vindicating an important public act, of a chief magistrate who enjoys the confidence and love of his country, principles are advanced which strike at the vitals of its Constitution, as well as to its honor and true interest.

As it is not improbable that attempts may be made to apply in-

James Madison, one of the Framers of the Constitution, was the 4th President of the United States (1809–1817). This essay was originally published in *The Gazette of the United States*, Philadelphia, August 24, 1793.

sinuations which are seldom spared when particular purposes are to be answered, to the author of the ensuing observations, it may not be improper to premise, that he is a friend to the Constitution, that he wishes for the preservation of peace, and that the present chief magistrate has not a fellow-citizen, who is penetrated with deeper respect for his merits, or feels a purer solicitude for his glory.

This declaration is made with no view of courting a more favorable ear to what may be said than it deserves. The sole purpose of it is, to obviate imputations which might weaken the impressions of truth; and which are the more likely to be resorted to, in proportion as solid and fair arguments may be wanting.

The substance of the first piece, sifted from its inconsistencies and its vague expressions, may be thrown into the following propositions:

That the powers of declaring war and making treaties are, in their nature, executive powers.

That being particularly vested by the Constitution in other departments, they are to be considered as exceptions out of the general grant to the executive department:

That being, as exceptions, to be construed strictly, the powers not strictly within them, remain with the executive:

That the executive consequently, as the organ of intercourse with foreign nations, and the interpreter and executor of treaties, and the law of nations, is authorized to expound all articles of treaties, those involving questions of war and peace, as well as others; to judge of the obligations of the United States to make war or not, under any *casus fœderis* or eventual operation of the contract, relating to war; and to pronounce the state of things resulting from the obligations of the United States, as understood by the executive:

That in particular the executive had authority to judge, whether in the case of the mutual guaranty between the United States and France, the former were bound by it to engage in the war:

That the executive has, in pursuance of that authority, decided that the United States are not bound: And

That its proclamation of the 22nd of April last, is to be taken as the effect and expression of that decision.

The basis of the reasoning is, we perceive, the extraordinary doctrine, that the powers of making war, and treaties, are in their nature executive; and therefore comprehended in the general grant of executive power, where not especially and strictly excepted out of the grant. . . .

If we consult for a moment, the nature and operation of the two powers to declare war and to make treaties, it will be impossible not to see, that they can never fall within a proper definition of executive powers. The natural province of the executive magistrate is to execute laws, as that of the legislature is to make laws. All his acts, therefore, properly executive, must presuppose the existence of the laws to be executed. A treaty is not an execution of laws: it does not presuppose the existence of laws. It is, on the contrary, to have itself the force of a law, and to be carried into execution, like all other laws by the executive magistrate. To say then that the power of making treaties, which are confessedly laws, belongs naturally to the department which is to execute laws, is to say, that the executive department naturally includes a legislative power. In theory this is an absurdity—in practice a tyranny.

The power to declare war is subject to similar reasoning. A declaration that there shall be war, is not an execution of laws: it does not suppose pre-existing laws to be executed: it is not, in any respect, an act merely executive. It is, on the contrary, one of the most deliberative acts that can be performed; and when performed, has the effect of repealing all the laws operating in a state of peace, so far as they are inconsistent with a state of war; and of enacting, as a rule for the executive, a new code adapted to the relation between the society and its foreign enemy. In like manner, a conclusion of peace annuls all the laws peculiar to a state of war, and revives the general laws incident to a state of peace.

These remarks will be strengthened by adding that treaties, particularly treaties of peace, sometimes have the effect of changing not only the external laws of the society but also the internal code, which is purely municipal, and to which the legislative authority of the country is of itself competent and complete.

From this view of the subject it must be evident, that although the executive may be a convenient organ of preliminary communications with foreign governments, on the subjects of treaty or war; and the proper agent for carrying into execution the final determinations of the competent authority; yet it can have no pretensions, from the nature of the powers in question compared with the nature of the executive trust, to that essential agency which gives validity to such determinations. It must be further evident, that if these powers be not in their nature purely legislative, they partake so much more of that, than of any other quality, that under a Constitution leaving them to result to their most natural department, the legislature would be without a rival in its claim.

Another important inference to be noted is, that the powers of making war and treaty being substantially of a legislative, not an executive nature, the rule of interpreting exceptions strictly must narrow, instead of enlarging, executive pretensions on those subjects.

It remains to be inquired, whether there be anything in the Constitution itself, which shows, that the powers of making war and peace are considered as of an executive nature, and as comprehended within a general grant of executive power.

It will not be pretended, that this appears from any *direct* position to be found in the instrument.

If it were *deducible* from any particular expressions, it may be presumed, that the publication would have saved us the trouble of the research.

Does the doctrine, then, result from the actual distribution of powers among the several branches of the government? or from any fair analogy between the powers of war and treaty, and the enumerated powers vested in the executive alone?

Let us examine:

In the general distribution of powers we find that of declaring war expressly vested in the Congress, where every other legislative power is declared to be vested; and without any other qualification than what is common to every other legislative act. The constitutional idea of this power would seem then clearly to be, that it is of a legislative, and not an executive nature.

This conclusion becomes irresistible, when it is recollected, that the Constitution cannot be supposed to have placed either any power legislative in its nature, entirely among executive powers, or any power executive in its nature, entirely among legislative powers, without charging the Constitution, with that kind of intermixture and consolidation of different powers, which would violate a fundamental principle in the organization of free governments. If it were not unnecessary to enlarge on this topic here, it could be shown, that the Constitution was originally vindicated, and has been constantly expounded, with a disavowal of any such intermixture.

The power of treaties is vested jointly in the President and in the Senate, which is a branch of the legislature. From this arrangement merely, there can be no inference that would necessarily exclude the power from the executive class: since the Senate is joined with the President in another power, that of appointing to offices, which, as far as relate to executive offices at least, is considered as of an executive nature. Yet on the other hand, there are sufficient indications that the power of treaties is regarded by the Constitution as materially different from mere executive power, and as having more affinity to the legislative than to the executive character.

One circumstance indicating this, is the constitutional regulation under which the Senate give their consent in the case of treaties. In all other cases, the consent of the body is expressed by a majority of voices. In this particular case, a concurrence of two thirds at least is made necessary, as a substitute or compensation for the other branch of the legislature, which, on certain occasions, could not be conveniently a party to the transaction.

But the conclusive circumstance is, that treaties, when formed according to the constitutional mode, are confessedly to have the force and operation of laws, and are to be a rule for the courts in controversies between man and man, as much as any other laws. They are even emphatically declared by the Constitution to be "the supreme law of the land."

So far the argument from the Constitution is precisely in opposition to the doctrine. As little will be gained in its favor from a comparison of the two powers, with those particularly vested in the President alone.

As there are but few, it will be most satisfactory to review them one by one.

"The President shall be Commander in Chief of the army and navy of the United States, and of the militia when called into the actual service of the United States."

There can be no relation worth examining between this power and the general power of making treaties. And instead of being analogous to the power of declaring war, it affords a striking illustration of the incompatibility of the two powers in the same hands. Those who are to conduct a war cannot in the nature of things, be proper or safe judges, whether a war ought to be commenced, continued, or concluded. They are barred from the latter functions by a great principle in free government, analogous to that which separates the sword from the purse, or the power of executing from the power of enacting laws.

"He may require the opinion in writing of the principal officers in each of the executive departments upon any subject relating to the duties of their respective offices; and he shall have power to grant reprieves and pardons for offences against the United States, except in case of impeachment." These powers can have nothing to do with the subject.

"The President shall have power to fill up vacancies that may happen during the recess of the Senate, by granting commissions which shall expire at the end of the next session." The same remark is applicable to this power, as also to that of "receiving ambassadors, other public ministers, and consuls." The particular use attempted to be made of this last power will be considered in another place.

"He shall take care that the laws shall be faithfully executed, and shall commission all officers of the United States." To see the laws faithfully executed constitutes the essence of the executive authority. But what relation has it to the power of making treaties and war, that is, of determining what the laws shall be with regard to other nations? No other certainly than what subsists between the powers of executing and enacting laws; no other, consequently, than what forbids a coalition of the powers in the same department.

I pass over the few other specified functions assigned to the President, such as that of convening the legislature, etc., etc., which cannot be drawn into the present question.

It may be proper however, to take notice of the power of removal from office, which appears to have been adjudged to the President by the laws establishing the executive departments; and which the writer has endeavored to press into his service. To justify any favorable inference from this case it must be shown that the powers of war and treaties are of a kindred nature to the power of removal, or at least are equally within a grant of executive power. Nothing of this sort has been attempted, nor probably will be attempted. Nothing can in truth be clearer, than that no analogy, or shade of analogy, can be traced between a power in the supreme officer responsible for the faithful execution of the laws, to displace a subaltern officer employed in the execution of the laws; and a power to make treaties, and to declare war, such as these have been found to be in their nature, their operation, and their consequences.

Thus it appears that by whatever standard we try this doctrine, it must be condemned as no less vicious in theory than it would be dangerous in practice. It is countenanced neither by the writers on law; nor by the nature of the powers themselves; nor by any general arrangements, or particular expressions, or plausible analogies, to be found in the Constitution.

Whence then can the writer have borrowed it?

There is but one answer to this question.

The power of making treaties and the power of declaring war, are *royal prerogatives* in the *British government*, and are accordingly treated as executive prerogatives by British commentators.

We shall be the more confirmed in the necessity of this solution to the problem, by looking back to the era of the Constitution, and satisfying ourselves that the writer could not have been misled by the doctrines maintained by our own commentators on our own government. That I may not ramble beyond prescribed limits, I shall content myself with an extract from a work which entered into a systematic explanation and defense of the Constitution; and to which there has frequently been ascribed some influence in conciliating the public assent to the government in the form proposed. Three circumstances conspire in giving weight to this contemporary exposition. It was made at a time when no application to persons or measures could bias: the opinion given was not transiently mentioned, but formally and critically elucidated: it related to a point in the Constitution which must consequently have been viewed as of importance in the public mind. The passage relates to the power of making treaties; that of declaring war, being arranged with such obvious propriety among the legislative powers, as to be passed over without particular discussion.

> Though several writers on the subject of government place that power [of making treaties] in the class of *executive authorities*, yet this is evidently an arbitrary disposition. For if we attend carefully to its operation, it will be found to partake more of the legislative than of the executive character, though it does not seem strictly to fall within the definition of either of them. The essence of the legislative authority, is to enact laws; or in other words, to prescribe rules for the regulation of the society: while the execution of the laws and the employment of the common strength, either for this purpose, or for the common defense, seem to comprise all the functions of the executive magistrate. The power of making treaties is plainly neither the one nor the other. It relates neither to the execution of the subsisting laws, nor to the enaction of new ones, and still less to an exertion of the common strength. Its objects are contracts with foreign nations, which have the force of law, but derive it from the obligations of good faith. They are not rules prescribed by the sovereign to the subject, but agreements between sovereign and sovereign. The power in question seems therefore to form a distinct department, and to belong properly neither to the legislative nor to the executive. The qualities elsewhere detailed as indispensable in the management of foreign negotiations, point out the executive as the most fit agent in those transactions: whilst the vast importance of the trust, and the operation of treaties as laws plead strongly for the participation of the whole or a part of the legislative body, in the office of making them [Federalist, 75, written by Hamilton].

It will not fail to be remarked on this commentary, that whatever doubts may be stated as to the correctness of its reasoning against the legislative nature of the power to make treaties; it is clear, consistent, and confident, in deciding that the power is plainly and evidently not an *executive power*.

PRESIDENTIAL POWER AND
THE GREAT CRISIS

☆

ANDREW JACKSON: *Proclamation on Nullification*

To preserve [the] bond of our political existence from destruction, to maintain inviolate [the] state of national honor and prosperity, and to justify the confidence my fellow-citizens have reposed in me, I, Andrew Jackson, President of the United States, have thought proper to issue this my proclamation, stating my views of the Constitution and laws applicable to the measures adopted by the convention of South Carolina and to the reasons they have put forth to sustain them, declaring the course which duty will require me to pursue, and, appealing to the understanding and patriotism of the people, warn them of the consequences that must inevitably result from an observance of the dictates of the convention.

Strict duty would require of me nothing more than the exercise of those powers with which I am now or may hereafter be invested for preserving the peace of the Union and for the execution of the laws; but the imposing aspect which opposition has assumed in this case, by clothing itself with State authority, and the deep interest which the people of the United States must all feel in preventing a resort to stronger measures while there is a hope that anything will be yielded to reasoning and remonstrance, perhaps demand, and will certainly justify, a full exposition to South Carolina and the nation of the views I entertain of this important question, as well as a distinct enunciation of the course which my sense of duty will require me to pursue. . . .

I consider . . . the power to annul a law of the United States, assumed by one State, *incompatible with the existence of the Union,*

Andrew Jackson was the 7th President of the United States (1829–1837). This selection is from his *Proclamation to the People of South Carolina,* December 10, 1832.

contradicted expressly by the letter of the Constitution, unauthorized by its spirit, inconsistent with every principle on which it was founded, and destructive of the great object for which it was formed. . . .

This, then, is the position in which we stand: A small majority of the citizens of one State in the Union have elected delegates to a State convention; that convention has ordained that all the revenue laws of the United States must be repealed, or that they are no longer a member of the Union. The governor of that State has recommended to the legislature the raising of an army to carry the secession into effect, and that he may be empowered to give clearances to vessels in the name of the State. No act of violent opposition to the laws has yet been committed, but such a state of things is hourly apprehended. And it is the intent of this instrument to *proclaim*, not only that the duty imposed on me by the Constitution "to take care that the laws be faithfully executed" shall be performed to the extent of the powers already vested in me by law, or of such others as the wisdom of Congress shall devise and intrust to me for that purpose, but to warn the citizens of South Carolina who have been deluded into an opposition to the laws of the danger they will incur by obedience to the illegal and disorganizing ordinance of the convention; to exhort those who have refused to support it to persevere in their determination to uphold the Constitution and laws of their country; and to point out to all the perilous situation into which the good people of that State have been led, and that the course they are urged to pursue is one of ruin and disgrace to the very State whose rights they affect to support.

Fellow-citizens of my native State, let me not only admonish you, as the First Magistrate of our common country, not to incur the penalty of its laws, but use the influence that a father would over his children whom he saw rushing to certain ruin.

[The] dictates of a high duty oblige me solemnly to announce that you can not succeed. The laws of the United States must be executed. I have no discretionary power on the subject; my duty is emphatically pronounced in the Constitution. Those who told you that you might peaceably prevent their execution deceived you; they could not have been deceived themselves. They know that a forcible opposition could alone prevent the execution of the laws, and they know that such opposition must be repelled. Their object is disunion. But be not deceived by names. Disunion by armed forces is *treason*. Are you really ready to incur its guilt? If you are, on the heads of the instigators of the act be the dreadful consequences; on their heads be the dishonor, but on yours may fall the punishment. On your unhappy State will inevitably fall all the evils of the conflict you force upon the Government of your country. It can not accede to the mad project of disunion, of which you would be the first victims. Its First

Magistrate can not, if he would, avoid the performance of his duty.
. . .

Fellow-citizens of the United States, the threat of unhallowed dis-union, the names of those once respected by whom it is uttered, the array of military force to support it, denote the approach of a crisis in our affairs on which the continuance of our unexampled prosperity, our political existence, and perhaps that of all free governments may depend. The conjuncture demanded a free, a full, and explicit enun-ciation, not only of my intentions, but of my principles of action; and as the claim was asserted of a right by a State to annul the laws of the Union, and even to secede from it at pleasure, a frank exposition of my opinions in relation to the origin and form of our Government and the construction I give to the instrument by which it was created seemed to be proper. Having the fullest confidence in the justness of the legal and constitutional opinion of my duties which has been ex-pressed, I rely with equal confidence on your undivided support in my determination to execute the laws, to preserve the Union by all constitutional means, to arrest, if possible, by moderate and firm measures the necessity of a recourse to force; and if it be the will of Heaven that the recurrence of its primeval curse on man for the shedding of a brother's blood should fall upon our land, that it be not called down by any offensive act on the part of the United States.

Fellow-citizens, the momentous case is before you. On your un-divided support of your Government depends the decision of the great question it involves—whether your sacred Union will be pre-served and the blessing it secures to us as one people shall be per-petuated. No one can doubt that the unanimity with which that decision will be expressed will be such as to inspire new confidence in republican institutions, and that the prudence, the wisdom, and the courage which it will bring to their defense will transmit them unim-paired and invigorated to our children.

May the Great Ruler of Nations grant that the signal blessings with which He has favored ours may not, by the madness of party or personal ambition, be disregarded and lost; and may His wise provi-dence bring those who have produced this crisis to see the folly before they feel the misery of civil strife, and inspire a returning veneration for that Union which, if we may dare to penetrate His designs, He has chosen as the only means of attaining the high destinies to which we may reasonably aspire.

☆

JAMES BUCHANAN: *Message to Congress*

Fellow-Citizens of the Senate and House of Representatives:
Throughout the year since our last meeting the country has been eminently prosperous in all its material interests. The general health has been excellent, our harvests have been abundant, and plenty smiles throughout the land. Our commerce and manufactures have been prosecuted with energy and industry, and have yielded fair and ample returns. In short, no nation in the tide of time has ever presented a spectacle of greater material prosperity than we have done until within a very recent period.

Why is it, then, that discontent now so extensively prevails, and the Union of the States, which is the source of all these blessings, is threatened with destruction?

The long-continued and intemperate interference of the Northern people with the question of slavery in the Southern States has at length produced its natural effects. The different sections of the Union are now arrayed against each other, and the time has arrived, so much dreaded by the Father of his Country, when hostile geographical parties have been formed.

I have long foreseen and often forewarned my countrymen of the now impending danger. This does not proceed solely from the claim on the part of Congress or the Territorial legislatures to exclude slavery from the Territories, nor from the efforts of different States to defeat the execution of the fugitive-slave law. All or any of these evils might have been endured by the South without danger to the Union (as others have been) in the hope that time and reflection

James Buchanan was the 15th President of the United States (1857–1861). The selection is from his *Fourth Annual Message to the Congress*, December 3, 1860.

might apply the remedy. The immediate peril arises not so much from these causes as from the fact that the incessant and violent agitation of the slavery question throughout the North for the last quarter of a century has at length produced its malign influence on the slaves and inspired them with vague notions of freedom. Hence a sense of security no longer exists around the family altar. This feeling of peace at home has given place to apprehensions of servile insurrections. Many a matron throughout the South retires at night in dread of what may befall herself and children before the morning. Should this apprehension of domestic danger, whether real or imaginary, extend and intensify itself until it shall pervade the masses of the Southern people, then disunion will become inevitable. Self-preservation is the first law of nature, and has been implanted in the heart of man by his Creator for the wisest purpose; and no political union, however fraught with blessings and benefits in all other respects, can long continue if the necessary consequence be to render the homes and the firesides of nearly half the parties to it habitually and hopelessly insecure. Sooner or later the bonds of such a union must be severed. It is my conviction that this fatal period has not yet arrived, and my prayer to God is that He would preserve the Constitution and the Union throughout all generations. . . .

How easy would it be for the American people to settle the slavery question forever and to restore peace and harmony to this distracted country! They, and they alone, can do it. All that is necessary to accomplish the object, and all for which the slave States have ever contended, is to be let alone and permitted to manage their domestic institutions in their own way. As sovereign States, they, and they alone, are responsible before God and the world for the slavery existing among them. For this the people of the North are not more responsible and have no more right to interfere than with similar institutions in Russia or in Brazil.

Upon their good sense and patriotic forbearance I confess I still greatly rely. Without their aid it is beyond the power of any President, no matter what may be his own political proclivities, to restore peace and harmony among the States. Wisely limited and restrained as is his power under our Constitution and laws, he alone can accomplish but little for good or for evil on such a momentous question. . . .

The most palpable violations of constitutional duty which have yet been committed consist in the acts of different State legislatures to defeat the execution of the fugitive-slave law. It ought to be remembered, however, that for these acts neither Congress nor any President can justly be held responsible. Having been passed in violation of the Federal Constitution, they are therefore null and void,

All the courts, both State and national, before whom the question has arisen have from the beginning declared the fugitive-slave law to be constitutional. The single exception is that of a State court in Wisconsin, and this has not only been reversed by the proper appellate tribunal, but has met with such universal reprobation that there can be no danger from it as a precedent. The validity of this law has been established over and over again by the Supreme Court of the United States with perfect unanimity. It is founded upon an express provision of the Constitution, requiring that fugitive slaves who escape from service in one State to another shall be "delivered up" to their masters. Without this provision it is a well-known historical fact that the Constitution itself could never have been adopted by the Convention. In one form or other, under the acts of 1793 and 1850, both being substantially the same, the fugitive-slave law has been the law of the land from the days of Washington until the present moment. Here, then, a clear case is presented in which it will be the duty of the next President, as it has been my own, to act with vigor in executing this supreme law against the conflicting enactments of State legislatures. Should he fail in the performance of this high duty, he will then have manifested a disregard of the Constitution and laws, to the great injury of the people of nearly one-half of the States of the Union. But are we to presume in advance that he will thus violate his duty? This would be at war with every principle of justice and of Christian charity. Let us wait for the overt act. The fugitive-slave law has been carried into execution in every contested case since the commencement of the present Administration, though often, it is to be regretted, with great loss and inconvenience to the master and with considerable expense to the government. Let us trust that the State legislatures will repeal their unconstitutional and obnoxious enactments. Unless this shall be done without unnecessary delay, it is impossible for any human power to save the Union. . . .

What, in the mean time, is the responsibility and true position of the Executive? He is bound by solemn oath, before God and the country, "to take care that the laws be faithfully executed," and from this obligation he can not be absolved by any human power. But what if the performance of this duty, in whole or in part, has been rendered impracticable by events over which he could have exercised no control? Such at the present moment is the case throughout the State of South Carolina so far as the laws of the United States to secure the administration of justice by means of the federal judiciary are concerned. All the federal officers within its limits through whose agency alone these laws can be carried into execution have already resigned. We no longer have a district judge, a district attorney, or a marshal in South Carolina. In fact, the whole machinery of the federal government necessary for the distribution of remedial justice among the people has been demolished, and it would be difficult, if not impossible, to replace it. . . .

Apart from the execution of the laws, so far as this may be practicable, the Executive has no authority to decide what shall be the relations between the federal government and South Carolina. He has been invested with no such discretion. He possesses no power to change the relations heretofore existing between them, much less to acknowledge the independence of that State. This would be to invest a mere executive officer with the power of recognizing the dissolution of the confederacy among our thirty-three sovereign States. It bears no resemblance to the recognition of a foreign *de facto* government, involving no such responsibility. Any attempt to do this would, on his part, be a naked act of usurpation. It is therefore my duty to submit to Congress the whole question in all its bearings. The course of events is so rapidly hastening forward that the emergency may soon arise when you may be called upon to decide the momentous question whether you possess the power by force of arms to compel a State to remain in the Union. I should feel myself recreant to my duty were I not to express an opinion on this important subject.

The question fairly stated is: Has the Constitution delegated to Congress the power to coerce a State into submission which is attempting to withdraw or has actually withdrawn from the Confederacy? If answered in the affirmative, it must be on the principle that the power has been conferred upon Congress to declare and to make war against a State. After much serious reflection I have arrived at the conclusion that no such power has been delegated to Congress or to any other department of the federal government. . . .

The fact is that our Union rests upon public opinion, and can never be cemented by the blood of its citizens shed in civil war. If it can not live in the affections of the people, it must one day perish. Congress possesses many means of preserving it by conciliation, but the sword was not placed in their hand to preserve it by force. . . .

The slavery question, like everything human, will have its day. I firmly believe that it has reached and passed the culminating point. But if in the midst of the existing excitement the Union shall perish, the evil may then become irreparable.

Congress can contribute much to avert it by proposing and recommending to the legislatures of the several States the remedy for existing evils which the Constitution has itself provided for its own preservation. . . .

This is the very course which I earnestly recommend in order to obtain an "explanatory amendment" of the Constitution on the subject of slavery. This might originate with Congress or the State legislatures, as may be deemed most advisable to attain the object. The explanatory amendment might be confined to the final settlement of the true construction of the Constitution on three special points:

1. An express recognition of the right of property in slaves in the States where it now exists or may hereafter exist.

2. The duty of protecting this right in all the common Territories throughout their Territorial existence, and until they shall be admitted as States into the Union, with or without slavery, as their constitutions may prescribe.

3. A like recognition of the right of the master to have his slave who has escaped from one State to another restored and "delivered up" to him, and of the validity of the fugitive-slave law enacted for this purpose, together with a declaration that all State laws impairing or defeating this right are violations of the Constitution, and are consequently null and void. It may be objected that this construction of the Constitution has already been settled by the Supreme Court of the United States, and what more ought to be required? The answer is that a very large proportion of the people of the United States still contest the correctness of this decision, and never will cease from agitation and admit its binding force until clearly established by the people of the several States in their sovereign character. Such an explanatory amendment would, it is believed, forever terminate the existing dissensions, and restore peace and harmony among the States. . . .

It ought not to be doubted that such an appeal to the arbitrament established by the Constitution itself would be received with favor by all the States of the Confederacy. In any event, it ought to be tried in a spirit of conciliation before any of these States shall separate themselves from the Union. . . .

☆

ABRAHAM LINCOLN: *First Inaugural Address*

Fellow-Citizens of the United States:
In compliance with a custom as old as the Government itself, I appear before you to address you briefly and to take in your presence the oath prescribed by the Constitution of the United States to be taken by the President "before he enters on the execution of his office."

I do not consider it necessary at present for me to discuss those matters of administration about which there is no special anxiety or excitement.

Apprehension seems to exist among the people of the Southern States that by the accession of a Republican Administration their property and their peace and personal security are to be endangered. There has never been any reasonable cause for such apprehension. Indeed, the most ample evidence to the contrary has all the while existed and been open to their inspection. It is found in nearly all the published speeches of him who now addresses you. I do but quote from one of those speeches when I declare that "I have no purpose, directly or indirectly, to interfere with the institution of slavery in the States where it exists. I believe I have no lawful right to do so, and I have no inclination to do so."

Those who nominated and elected me did so with full knowledge that I had made this and many similar declarations and had never recanted them; and more than this, they placed in the platform for my acceptance, and as a law to themselves and to me, the clear and emphatic resolution which I now read:

Abraham Lincoln, 16th President of the United States (1861–1865), delivered his *First Inaugural Address* on March 4th, 1861.

Resolved, That the maintenance inviolate of the rights of the States, and especially the right of each State to order and control its own domestic institutions according to its own judgment exclusively, is essential to that balance of power on which the perfection and endurance of our political fabric depend; and we denounce the lawless invasion by armed force of the soil of any State or Territory, no matter under what pretext, as among the gravest of crimes.

I now reiterate these sentiments, and in doing so I only press upon the public attention the most conclusive evidence of which the case is susceptible that the property, peace, and security of no section are to be in any wise endangered by the now incoming Administration. I add, too, that all the protection which, consistently with the Constitution and the laws, can be given will be cheerfully given to all the States when lawfully demanded, for whatever cause—as cheerfully to one section as to another. . . .

I take the official oath today with no mental reservations and with no purpose to construe the Constitution or laws by any hypercritical rules; and while I do not choose now to specify particular acts of Congress as proper to be enforced, I do suggest that it will be much safer for all, both in official and private stations, to conform to and abide by all those acts which stand unrepealed than to violate any of them trusting to find impunity in having them held to be unconstitutional.

It is seventy-two years since the first inauguration of a President under our National Constitution. During that period fifteen different and greatly distinguished citizens have in succession administered the executive branch of the Government. They have conducted it through many perils, and generally with great success. Yet, with all this scope of precedent, I now enter upon the same task for the brief constitutional term of four years under great and peculiar difficulty. A disruption of the Federal Union, heretofore only menaced, is now formidably attempted.

I hold that in contemplation of universal law and of the Constitution the Union of these States is perpetual. Perpetuity is implied, if not expressed, in the fundamental law of all national governments. It is safe to assert that no government proper ever had a provision in its organic law for its own termination. Continue to execute all the express provisions of our National Constitution, and the Union will endure forever it being impossible to destroy it except by some action not provided for in the instrument itself. . . .

It follows from these views that no State upon its own mere motion can lawfully get out of the Union; that *resolves* and *ordinances* to that effect are legally void, and that acts of violence within any State or States against the authority of the United States are insurrectionary or revolutionary, according to circumstances.

I therefore consider that in view of the Constitution and the laws the Union is unbroken, and to the extent of my ability I shall take care, as the Constitution itself expressly enjoins upon me, that the laws of the Union be faithfully executed in all the States. Doing this I deem to be only a simple duty on my part, and I shall perform it so far as practicable unless my rightful masters, the American people, shall withhold the requisite means or in some authoritative manner direct the contrary. I trust this will not be regarded as a menace, but only as the declared purpose of the Union that it *will* constitutionally defend and maintain itself.

In doing this there needs to be no bloodshed or violence, and there shall be none unless it be forced upon the national authority. The power confided to me will be used to hold, occupy, and possess the property and places belonging to the government and to collect the duties and imposts; but beyond what may be necessary for these objects, there will be no invasion, no using of force against or among the people anywhere. Where hostility to the United States in any interior locality shall be so great and universal as to prevent competent resident citizens from holding the federal offices, there will be no attempt to force obnoxious strangers among the people for that object. While the strict legal right may exist in the government to enforce the exercise of these offices, the attempt to do so would be so irritating and so nearly impracticable withal that I deem it better to forego for the time the uses of such offices. . . .

Plainly the central idea of secession is the essence of anarchy. A majority held in restraint by constitutional checks and limitations, and always changing easily with deliberate changes of popular opinions and sentiments, is the only true sovereign of a free people. Whoever rejects it does of necessity fly to anarchy or to despotism. Unanimity is impossible. The rule of a minority, as a permanent arrangement, is wholly inadmissible; so that, rejecting the majority principle, anarchy or despotism in some form is all that is left.

I do not forget the position assumed by some that constitutional questions are to be decided by the Supreme Court, nor do I deny that such decisions must be binding in any case upon the parties to a suit as to the object of that suit, while they are also entitled to very high respect and consideration in all parallel cases by all other departments of the government. And while it is obviously possible that such decision may be erroneous in any given case, still the evil effect following it, being limited to that particular case, with the chance that it may be overruled and never become a precedent for other cases, can better be borne than could the evils of a different practice. At the same time, the candid citizen must confess that if the policy of the government upon vital questions affecting the whole people is to be irrevocably fixed by decisions of the Supreme Court, the instant they are made in ordinary litigation between parties in personal actions the people will have ceased to be their own rulers, having to that extent practically resigned their government into the hands of that eminent tribunal. Nor is there in this view any assault upon the court or the judges. It is a duty from which they may not shrink to decide cases properly brought before them, and it is no fault of theirs if others seek to turn their decisions to political purposes.

One section of our country believes slavery is *right* and ought to be extended, while the other believes it is *wrong* and ought not to be extended. This is the only substantial dispute. The fugitive-slave clause of the Constitution and the law for the suppression of the foreign slave trade are each as well enforced, perhaps, as any law can ever be in a community where the moral sense of the people imperfectly supports the law itself. The great body of the people abide by the dry legal obligation in both cases, and a few break over in each. This, I think, can not be perfectly cured, and it would be worse in both cases *after* the separation of the sections than before. The foreign slave trade, now imperfectly suppressed, would be ultimately revived without restriction in one section, while fugitive slaves, now only partially surrendered, would not be surrendered at all by the other.

Physically speaking, we can not separate. We can not remove our respective sections from each other nor build an impassable wall between them. A husband and wife may be divorced and go out of the presence and beyond the reach of each other, but the different parts of our country can not do this. They can not but remain face to face, and intercourse, either amicable or hostile, must continue between them. Is it possible, then, to make that intercourse more advantageous or more satisfactory *after* separation than *before*? Can aliens make treaties easier than friends can make laws? Can treaties be more faithfully enforced between aliens than laws can among friends? Suppose you go to war, you can not fight always; and when, after much loss on both sides and no gain on either, you cease fighting, the identical old questions, as to terms of intercourse, are again upon you.

This country, with its institutions, belongs to the people who inhabit it. Whenever they shall grow weary of the existing government, they can exercise their *constitutional* right of amending it or their *revolutionary* right to dismember or overthrow it. I can not be ignorant of the fact that many worthy and patriotic citizens are desirous of having the National Constitution amended. While I make no recommendation of amendments, I fully recognize the rightful authority of the people over the whole subject, to be exercised in either of the modes prescribed in the instrument itself; and I should, under existing circumstances, favor rather than oppose a fair opportunity being afforded the people to act upon it. I will venture to add that to me the convention mode seems preferable, in that it allows amendments to originate with the people themselves, instead of only permitting them to take or reject propositions originated by others, not especially chosen for the purpose, and which might not be precisely such as they would wish to either accept or refuse. I understand a proposed amendment to the Constitution—which amendment, however, I have not seen—has passed Congress, to the effect that the federal government shall never interfere with the domestic institutions of the States, including that of persons held to service. To avoid misconstruction of what I have said, I depart from my purpose not to speak of particular amendments so far as to say that, holding such a provision to now be implied constitutional law, I have no objection to its being made express and irrevocable.

The Chief Magistrate derives all his authority from the people, and they have conferred none upon him to fix terms for the separation of the States. The people themselves can do this also if they choose, but the Executive as such has nothing to do with it. His duty is to administer the present government as it came to his hands and to transmit it unimpaired by him to his successor.

Why should there not be a patient confidence in the ultimate justice of the people? Is there any better or equal hope in the world? In our present differences, is either party without faith of being in the right? If the Almighty Ruler of Nations, with His eternal truth and justice, be on your side of the North, or on yours of the South, that truth and that justice will surely prevail by the judgment of this great tribunal of the American people.

By the frame of the government under which we live this same people have wisely given their public servants but little power for mischief, and have with equal wisdom provided for the return of that little to their own hands at very short intervals. While the people retain their virtue and vigilance no Administration by any extreme of wickedness or folly can very seriously injure the Government in the short space of four years.

My countrymen, one and all, think calmly and *well* upon this whole subject. Nothing valuable can be lost by taking time. If there be an object to *hurry* any of you in hot haste to a step which you would never take *deliberately*, that object will be frustrated by taking time; but no good object can be frustrated by it. Such of you as are now dissatisfied still have the old Constitution unimpaired, and, on the sensitive point, the laws of your own framing under it; while the new Administration will have no immediate power, if it would, to change either. If it were admitted that you who are dissatisfied hold the right side in the dispute, there still is no single good reason for precipitate action. Intelligence, patriotism, Christianity, and a firm reliance on Him who has never yet forsaken this favored land are still competent to adjust in the best way all our present difficulty.

In *your* hands, my dissatisfied fellow-countrymen, and not in *mine,* is the momentous issue of civil war. The government will not assail *you.* You can have no conflict without being yourselves the aggressors. *You* have no oath registered in heaven to destroy the government, while *I* shall have the most solemn one to "preserve, protect, and defend it."

I am loath to close. We are not enemies, but friends. We must not be enemies. Though passion may have strained it must not break our bonds of affection. The mystic chords of memory, stretching from every battlefield and patriot grave to every living heart and hearthstone all over this broad land, will yet swell the chorus of the Union, when again touched, as surely they will be, by the better angels of our nature.

☆

ABRAHAM LINCOLN: *Message to Congress in Special Session*

Fellow-Citizens of the Senate and House of Representatives:
Having been convened on an extraordinary occasion, as authorized by the Constitution, your attention is not called to any ordinary subject of legislation. . . .

[The] issue embraces more than the fate of these United States. It presents to the whole family of man the question whether a constitutional republic or democracy—a government of the people by the same people—can or cannot maintain its territorial integrity against its own domestic foes. It presents the question whether discontented individuals, too few in numbers to control administration according to organic law in any case, can always, upon the pretenses made in this case, or on any other pretenses, or arbitrarily without any pretense, break up their government, and thus practically put an end to free government upon the earth. It forces us to ask: "Is there, in all republics, this inherent and fatal weakness?" "Must a government, of necessity, be too strong for the liberties of its own people, or too weak to maintain its own existence?"

So viewing the issue, no choice was left but to call out the war power of the government; and so to resist force employed for its destruction, by force for its preservation. . . .

Our popular government has often been called an experiment. Two points in it our people have already settled—the successful establishing and the successful administering of it. One still remains —its successful maintenance against a formidable internal attempt

President Lincoln sent this Message to Congress on July 4, 1861.

80

to overthrow it. It is now for them to demonstrate to the world that those who can fairly carry an election can also suppress a rebellion; that ballots are the rightful and peaceful successors of bullets; and that when ballots have fairly and constitutionally decided, there can be no successful appeal back to bullets; that there can be no successful appeal, except to ballots themselves, at succeeding elections. Such will be a great lesson of peace: teaching men that what they cannot take by an election, neither can they take it by a war; teaching all the folly of being the beginners of a war.

Lest there be some uneasiness in the minds of candid men as to what is to be the course of the government toward the Southern States after the rebellion shall have been suppressed, the executive deems it proper to say it will be his purpose then, as ever, to be guided by the Constitution and the laws; and that he probably will have no different understanding of the powers and duties of the federal government relatively to the rights of the States and the people, under the Constitution, than that expressed in the inaugural address.

He desires to preserve the government, that it may be administered for all as it was administered by the men who made it. Loyal citizens everywhere have the right to claim this of their government, and the government has no right to withhold or neglect it. It is not perceived that in giving it there is any coercion, any conquest, or any subjugation, in any just sense of those terms.

The Constitution provides, and all the States have accepted the provision, that "the United States shall guarantee to every State in this Union a republican form of government." But if a State may lawfully go out of the Union, having done so, it may also discard the republican form of government; so that to prevent its going out is an indispensable means to the end of maintaining the guarantee mentioned; and when an end is lawful and obligatory, the indispensable means to it are also lawful and obligatory.

It was with the deepest regret that the executive found the duty of employing the war power in defense of the government forced upon him. He could but perform this duty or surrender the existence of the government. No compromise by public servants could, in this case, be a cure; not that compromises are not often proper, but that no popular government can long survive a marked precedent that those who carry an election can only save the government from immediate destruction by giving up the main point upon which the people gave the election. The people themselves, and not their servants, can safely reverse their own delibrate decisions.

As a private citizen the executive could not have consented that these institutions shall perish; much less could he, in betrayal of so vast and so sacred a trust as the free people have confided to him. He felt that he had no moral right to shrink, nor even to count the chances of his own life in what might follow. In full view of his great responsibility he has, so far, done what he has deemed his duty. You will now, according to your own judgment, perform yours.

He sincerely hopes that your views and your actions may so accord with his, as to assure all faithful citizens who have been disturbed in their rights of a certain and speedy restoration to them, under the Constitution and the laws.

And having thus chosen our course, without guile and with pure purpose, let us renew our trust in God, and go forward without fear and with manly hearts.

☆

ABRAHAM LINCOLN: *Letter to A. G. Hodges*

My dear Sir:

You ask me to put in writing the substance of what I verbally said
the other day, in your presence, to Governor Bramlette and Senator
Dixon. It was about as follows:

I am naturally anti-slavery. If slavery is not wrong, nothing is
wrong. I can not remember when I did not so think, and feel. And
yet I have never understood that the Presidency conferred upon me
an unrestricted right to act officially upon this judgment and feeling. It was in the oath I took that I would, to the best of my ability, preserve, protect, and defend the Constitution of the United
States. I could not take the office without taking the oath. Nor
was it my view that I might take an oath to get power, and break
the oath in using the power. I understood, too, that in ordinary
civil administration this oath even forbade me to practically indulge my primary abstract judgment on the moral question of slavery. I had publicly declared this many times, and in many ways.
And I aver that, to this day, I have done no official act in mere
deference to my abstract judgment and feeling on slavery.

I did understand, however, that my oath to preserve the Constitution to the best of my ability, imposed upon me the duty of
preserving, by every indispensable means, that government—that
nation—of which that Constitution was the organic law. Was it possible to lose the nation, and yet preserve the Constitution? By general law life *and* limb must be protected; yet often a limb must be
amputated to save a life; but a life is never wisely given to save a
limb. I felt that measures, otherwise unconstitutional, might become
lawful, by becoming indispensable to the preservation of the Constitution, through the preservation of the nation. Right or wrong,
I assumed this ground, and now avow it. I could not feel that, to

This letter to Albert G. Hodges, editor of the Frankfort, Kentucky, *Com-
monwealth*, was used as a campaign document in the election of 1864. From
The Complete Works of Abraham Lincoln, John Nicolay and John Hay, eds.
(New York: Francis D. Tandy Co., 1894), Vol. X, pp. 65–68.

the best of my ability, I had even tried to preserve the Constitution, if, to save slavery, or any minor matter, I should permit the wreck of government, country, and Constitution all together.

When, early in the war, Gen. Fremont attempted military emancipation, I forbade it, because I did not then think it an indispensable necessity. When a little later, Gen. Cameron, then Secretary of War, suggested the arming of the blacks, I objected, because I did not yet think it an indispensable necessity. When, still later, Gen. Hunter attempted military emancipation, I again forbade it, because I did not yet think the indispensable necessity had come. When, in March, and May, and July 1862 I made earnest, and successive appeals to the border states to favor compensated emancipation, I believed the indispensable necessity for military emancipation, and arming the blacks would come, unless averted by that measure. They declined the proposition; and I was, in my best judgment, driven to the alternative of either surrendering the Union, and with it, the Constitution, or of laying strong hand upon the colored element. I chose the latter. In choosing it, I hoped for greater gain than loss; but of this, I was not entirely confident. More than a year of trial now shows no loss by it in our foreign relations, none in our home popular sentiment, none in our white military force—no loss by it any how or any where. On the contrary, it shows a gain of quite a hundred and thirty thousand soldiers, seamen, and laborers. These are palpable facts, about which, as facts, there can be no cavilling. We have the men; and we could not have had them without the measure.

And now let any Union man who complains of the measure, test himself by writing down in one line that he is for subduing the rebellion by force of arms; and in the next, that he is for taking these hundred and thirty thousand men from the Union side, and placing them where they would be but for the measure he condemns. If he can not face his case so stated, it is only because he can not face the truth.

I add a word which was not in the verbal conversation. In telling this tale I attempt no compliment to my own sagacity. I claim not to have controlled events, but confess plainly that events have controlled me. Now, at the end of three years struggle the nation's condition is not what either party, or any man devised, or expected. God alone can claim it. Whither it is tending seems plain. If God now wills the removal of a great wrong, and wills also that we of the North as well as you of the South, shall pay fairly for our complicity in that wrong, impartial history will find therein new cause to attest and revere the justice and goodness of God.

THE EMERGENCE OF THE
MODERN PRESIDENCY

☆

THEODORE ROOSEVELT: *The "Stewardship Theory"*

The most important factor in getting the right spirit in my Administration, next to the insistence upon courage, honesty, and a genuine democracy of desire to serve the plain people, was my insistence
upon the theory that the executive power was limited only by specific restrictions and prohibitions appearing in the Constitution or
imposed by the Congress under its constitutional powers.

My view was that every executive officer, and above all every
executive officer in high position, was a steward of the people bound
actively and affirmatively to do all he could for the people, and not
to content himself with the negative merit of keeping his talents
undamaged in a napkin. I declined to adopt the view that what
was imperatively necessary for the nation could not be done by the
President unless he could find some specific authorization to do it.
My belief was that it was not only his right but his duty to do anything that the needs of the nation demanded, unless such action
was forbidden by the Constitution or by the laws. Under this interpretation of executive power I did and caused to be done many
things not previously done by the President and the heads of the
departments. I did not usurp power, but I did greatly broaden the
use of executive power. In other words, I acted for the public welfare, I acted for the common well-being of all our people, whenever and in whatever manner was necessary, unless prevented by
direct constitutional or legislative prohibition. . . .

Theodore Roosevelt was the 26th President of the United States (1901–
1909). This selection is from *The Autobiography of Theodore Roosevelt*, edited
by Wayne Andrews (New York: Scribner's, 1958), pp. 197–200. Copyright ©
1958 Charles Scribner's Sons. Reprinted by permission.

The course I followed, of regarding the Executive as subject only to the people, and, under the Constitution, bound to serve the people affirmatively in cases where the Constitution does not explicitly forbid him to render the service, was substantially the course followed by both Andrew Jackson and Abraham Lincoln. Other honorable and well-meaning Presidents, such as James Buchanan, took the opposite and, as it seems to me, narrowly legalistic view that the President is the servant of Congress rather than of the people, and can do nothing, no matter how necessary it be to act, unless the Constitution explicitly commands the action. Most able lawyers who are past middle age take this view, and so do large numbers of well-meaning, respectable citizens. My successor in office took this, the Buchanan, view of the President's powers and duties.

For example, under my administration we found that one of the favorite methods adopted by the men desirous of stealing the public domain was to carry the decision of the secretary of the interior into court. By vigorously opposing such action, and only by so doing, we were able to carry out the policy of properly protecting the public domain. My successor not only took the opposite view, but recommended to Congress the passage of a bill which would have given the courts direct appellate power over the secretary of the interior in these land matters. . . . Fortunately, Congress declined to pass the bill. Its passage would have been a veritable calamity.

I acted on the theory that the President could at any time in his discretion withdraw from entry any of the public lands of the United States and reserve the same for forestry, for water-power sites, for irrigation, and other public purposes. Without such action it would have been impossible to stop the activity of the land-thieves. No one ventured to test its legality by lawsuit. My successor, however, himself questioned it, and referred the matter to Congress. Again Congress showed its wisdom by passing a law which gave the President the power which he had long exercised, and of which my successor had shorn himself.

Perhaps the sharp difference between what may be called the Lincoln-Jackson and the Buchanan-Taft schools, in their views of the power and duties of the President, may be best illustrated by comparing the attitude of my successor toward his Secretary of the Interior, Mr. Ballinger, when the latter was accused of gross misconduct in office, with my attitude toward my chiefs of department and other subordinate officers. More than once while I was President my officials were attacked by Congress, generally because these officials did their duty well and fearlessly. In every such case I stood by the official and refused to recognize the right of Congress to interfere with me excepting by impeachment or in other constitutional manner. On the other hand, wherever I found the officer unfit for his position, I promptly removed him, even although the most influential men in Congress fought for his retention.

The Jackson-Lincoln view is that a President who is fit to do good work should be able to form his own judgment as to his own subordinates, and, above all, of the subordinates standing highest and in closest and most intimate touch with him. My secretaries and their subordinates were responsible to me, and I accepted the responsibility for all their deeds. As long as they were satisfactory to me I stood by them against every critic or assailant, within or without Congress; and as for getting Congress to make up my mind for me about them, the thought would have been inconceivable to me. My successor took the opposite, or Buchanan, view when he permitted and requested Congress to pass judgment on the charges made against Mr. Ballinger as an executive officer. These charges were made to the President; the President had the facts before him and could get at them at any time, and he alone had power to act if the charges were true. However, he permitted and requested Congress to investigate Mr. Ballinger. The party minority of the committee that investigated him, and one member of the majority, declared that the charges were well-founded and that Mr. Ballinger should be removed. The other members of the majority declared the charges ill-founded. The President abode by the view of the majority. Of course believers in the Jackson-Lincoln theory of the Presidency would not be content with this town-meeting majority and minority method of determining by another branch of the government what it seems the especial duty of the President himself to determine for himself in dealing with his own subordinate in his own department. . . .

☆

WILLIAM HOWARD TAFT: *Our Chief Magistrate and His Powers*

The true view of the Executive functions is, as I conceive it, that the President can exercise no power which cannot be fairly and reasonably traced to some specific grant of power or justly implied and included within such express grant as proper and necessary to its exercise. Such specific grant must be either in the federal Constitution or in an act of Congress passed in pursuance thereof. There is no undefined residuum of power which he can exercise because it seems to him to be in the public interest, and there is nothing in the Neagle case and its definition of a law of the United States, or in other precedents, warranting such an inference. The grants of Executive power are necessarily in general terms in order not to embarrass the Executive within the field of action plainly marked for him, but his jurisdiction must be justified and vindicated by affirmative constitutional or statutory provision, or it does not exist.

There have not been wanting, however, eminent men in high public office holding a different view and who have insisted upon the necessity for an undefined residuum of Executive power in the public interest. They have not been confined to the present generation. We may learn this from the complaint of a Virginia statesman, Abel P. Upshur, a strict constructionist of the old school,

William Howard Taft was 27th President of the United States (1909–1913) and 10th Chief Justice of the United States (1921–1930). This selection is from *Our Chief Magistrate and His Powers* (New York: Columbia University Press, 1916), pp. 139–145, 156–157. Copyright 1916 by Columbia University Press. Reprinted by permission.

who succeeded Daniel Webster as Secretary of State under President Tyler. He was aroused by Story's commentaries on the Constitution to write a monograph answering and criticizing them, and in the course of this he comments as follows on the Executive power under the Constitution:

> The most defective part of the Constitution beyond all question, is that which related to the Executive Department. It is impossible to read that instrument, without being struck with the loose and unguarded terms in which the powers and duties of the President are pointed out. So far as the legislature is concerned, the limitations of the Constitution, are, perhaps, as precise and strict as they could safely have been made; but in regard to the Executive, the Convention appears to have studiously selected such loose and general expressions, as would enable the President, by implication and construction either to neglect his duties or to enlarge his powers. *We have heard it gravely asserted in Congress that whatever power is neither legislative nor judiciary, is of course executive, and, as such, belongs to the President under the Constitution.* How far a majority of that body would have sustained a doctrine so monstrous, and so utterly at war with the whole genius of our government, it is impossible to say, but this, at least, we know, that it met with no rebuke from those who supported the particular act of Executive power, in defense of which it was urged. Be this as it may, it is a reproach to the Constitution that the Executive trust is so ill-defined, as to leave any plausible pretense even to the insane zeal of party devotion, for attributing to the President of the United States the powers of a despot; powers which are wholly unknown in any limited monarchy in the world.

The view that he takes as a result of the loose language defining the Executive powers seems exaggerated. But one must agree with him in his condemnation of the view of the Executive power which he says was advanced in Congress. In recent years there has been put forward a similar view by executive officials and to some extent acted on. Men who are not such strict constructionists of the Constitution as Mr. Upshur may well feel real concern if such views are to receive the general acquiescence. . . .

. . . Mr. Roosevelt, by way of illustrating his meaning as to the differing usefulness of Presidents, divides the Presidents into two classes, and designates them as "Lincoln Presidents" and "Buchanan Presidents." In order more fully to illustrate his division of Presidents on their merits, he places himself in the Lincoln class of

Presidents, and me in the Buchanan class. The identification of Mr. Roosevelt with Mr. Lincoln might otherwise have escaped notice, because there are many differences between the two, presumably superficial, which would give the impartial student of history a different impression. It suggests a story which a friend of mine told of his little daughter Mary. As he came walking home after a business day, she ran out from the house to greet him, all aglow with the importance of what she wished to tell him. She said, "Papa, I am the best scholar in the class." The father's heart throbbed with pleasure as he inquired, "Why, Mary, you surprise me. When did the teacher tell you? This afternoon?" "Oh, no," Mary's reply was, "the teacher didn't tell me—I just noticed it myself."

My judgment is that the view of . . . Mr. Roosevelt, ascribing an undefined residuum of power to the President is an unsafe doctrine and that it might lead under emergencies to results of an arbitrary character, doing irremediable injustice to private right. The mainspring of such a view is that the Executive is charged with responsibility for the welfare of all the people in a general way, that he is to play the part of a Universal Providence and set all things right, and that anything that in his judgment will help the people he ought to do, unless he is expressly forbidden not to do it. The wide field of action that this would give to the Executive one can hardly limit. . . .

I have now concluded a review of the Executive power, and hope that I have shown that it is limited, so far as it is possible to limit such a power consistent with that discretion and promptness of action that are essential to preserve the interests of the public in times of emergency, or legislative neglect or inaction.

There is little danger to the public weal from the tyranny or reckless character of a President who is not sustained by the people. The absence of popular support will certainly in the course of two years withdraw from him the sympathetic action of at least one House of Congress, and by the control that that House has over appropriations, the Executive arm can be paralyzed, unless he resorts to a coup d'état, which means impeachment, conviction and deposition. The only danger in the action of the Executive under the present limitations and lack of limitation of his powers is when his popularity is such that he can be sure of the support of the electorate and therefore of Congress, and when the majority in the legislative halls respond with alacrity and sycophancy to his will. This condition cannot probably be long continued. We have had Presidents who felt the public pulse with accuracy, who played their parts upon the political stage with histrionic genius and commanded the people almost as if they were an army and the President their Commander in Chief. Yet in all these cases, the good sense of the people has ultimately prevailed and no danger has been done to our political structure and the reign of law has continued. In such times when the Executive power seems to be all prevailing, there have always been men in this free and intelligent people of ours, who apparently courting political humiliation and disaster have registered protest against this undue Executive domination and this use of the Executive power and popular support to perpetuate itself.

The cry of Executive domination is often entirely unjustified, as when the President's commanding influence only grows out of a proper cohesion of a party and its recognition of the necessity for political leadership; but the fact that Executive domination is regarded as a useful ground for attack upon a successful administration, even when there is no ground for it, is itself proof of the dependence we may properly place upon the sanity and clear perceptions of the people in avoiding its baneful effects when there is real danger. Even if a vicious precedent is set by the Executive, and injustice done, it does not have the same bad effect that an improper precedent of a court may have, for one President does not consider himself bound by the policies or constitutional views of his predecessors.

The Constitution does give the President wide discretion and great power, and it ought to do so. It calls from him activity and energy to see that within his proper sphere he does what his great responsibilities and opportunities require. He is no figurehead, and it is entirely proper that an energetic and active clear-sighted people, who, when they have work to do, wish it done well, should be willing to rely upon their judgment in selecting their Chief Agent, and having selected him, should entrust to him all the power needed to carry out their governmental purpose, great as it may be.

☆

WOODROW WILSON: *The President's Role in American Government*

The makers of the Constitution seem to have thought of the President as what the stricter Whig theorists wished the king to be: only the legal executive, the presiding and guiding authority in the application of law and the execution of policy. His veto upon legislation was only his "check" on Congress—was a power of restraint, not of guidance. He was empowered to prevent bad laws, but he was not to be given an opportunity to make good ones. As a matter of fact he has become very much more. He has become the leader of his party and the guide of the nation in political purpose, and therefore in legal action. The constitutional structure of the government has hampered and limited his action in these significant roles, but it has not prevented it. The influence of the President has varied with the men who have been Presidents and with the circumstances of their times, but the tendency has been unmistakably disclosed, and springs out of the very nature of government itself. It is merely the proof that our government is a living, organic thing, and must, like every other government, work out the close synthesis of active parts which can exist only when leadership is lodged in some one man or group of men. You cannot compound a successful government out of antagonisms. Greatly as the practice and influence

Woodrow Wilson was Professor of Political Science at Princeton University (1890–1902), President of Princeton (1902–1910), and Governor of New Jersey (1911–1912) before becoming the 28th President of the United States (1913–1921). This selection is from his chapter on "The President of the United States" in *Constitutional Government in the United States* (New York: Columbia University Press, 1908), pp. 54–81. Copyright © 1908 by Columbia University Press. Reprinted by permission.

of Presidents has varied, there can be no mistaking the fact that we have grown more and more inclined from generation to generation to look to the President as the unifying force in our complex system, the leader both of his party and of the nation. To do so is not inconsistent with the actual provisions of the Constitution; it is only inconsistent with a very mechanical theory of its meaning and intention. The Constitution contains no theories. It is as practical a document as Magna Carta. . . .

[The] office of President, as we have used and developed it, really does not demand actual experience in affairs so much as particular qualities of mind and character which we are at least as likely to find outside the ranks of our public men as within them. What is it that a nominating convention wants in the man it is to present to the country for its suffrages? A man who will be and who will seem to the country in some sort an embodiment of the character and purpose it wishes its government to have—a man who understands his own day and the needs of the country, and who has the personality and the initiative to enforce his views both upon the people and upon Congress. It may seem an odd way to get such a man. It is even possible that nominating conventions and those who guide them do not realize entirely what it is that they do. But in simple fact the convention picks out a party leader from the body of the nation. Not that it expects its nominee to direct the interior government of the party and to supplant its already accredited and experienced spokesmen in Congress and in its state and national committees; but it does of necessity expect him to represent it before public opinion and to stand before the country as its representative man, as a true type of what the country may expect of the party itself in purpose and principle. It cannot but be led by him in the campaign; if he be elected, it cannot but acquiesce in his leadership of the government itself. What the country will demand of the candidate will be, not that he be an astute politician, skilled and practiced in affairs, but that he be a man such as it can trust, in character, in intention, in knowledge of its needs, in perception of the best means by which those needs may be met, in capacity to prevail by reason of his own weight and integrity. Sometimes the country believes in a party, but more often it believes in a man; and conventions have often shown the instinct to perceive which it is that the country needs in a particular presidential year, a mere representative partisan, a military hero, or some one who will genuinely speak for the country itself, whatever be his training and antecedents. It is in this sense that the President has the role of party leader thrust upon him by the very method by which he is chosen.

As legal executive, his constitutional aspect, the President cannot be thought of alone. He cannot execute laws. Their actual daily execution must be taken care of by the several executive departments and by the now innumerable body of federal officials throughout the country. In respect of the strictly executive duties of his office the President may be said to administer the Presidency in conjunction with the members of his Cabinet, like the chairman of a commission. He is even of necessity much less active in the actual carrying out of the law than are his colleagues and advisers. It is therefore becoming more and more true, as the business of the government becomes more and more complex and extended, that the President is becoming more and more a political and less and less an executive officer. His executive powers are in commission, while his political powers more and more center and accumulate upon him and are in their very nature personal and inalienable.

Only the larger sort of executive questions are brought to him. Departments which run with easy routine and whose transactions bring few questions of general policy to the surface may proceed with their business for months and even years together without demanding his attention; and no department is in any sense under his direct charge. Cabinet meetings do not discuss detail: they are concerned only with the larger matters of policy or expediency which important business is constantly disclosing. There are no more hours in the President's day than in another man's. If he is indeed the executive, he must act almost entirely by delegation, and is in the hands of his colleagues. He is likely to be praised if things go well, and blamed if they go wrong; but his only real control is of the persons to whom he deputes the performance of executive duties. It is through no fault or neglect of his that the duties apparently assigned to him by the Constitution have come to be his less conspicuous, less important duties, and that duties apparently not assigned to him at all chiefly occupy his time and energy. The one set of duties it has proved practically impossible for him to perform; the other it has proved impossible for him to escape.

He cannot escape being the leader of his party except by incapacity and lack of personal force, because he is at once the choice of the party and of the nation. He is the party nominee, and the only party nominee for whom the whole nation votes. Members of the House and Senate are representatives of localities, are voted for only by sections of voters, or by local bodies of electors like the members of the state legislatures. There is no national party choice except that of President. No one else represents the people as a whole, exercising a national choice; and inasmuch as his strictly executive duties are in fact subordinated, so far at any rate as all detail is concerned, the President represents not so much the party's governing efficiency as its controlling ideals and principles. He is not so much part of its organization as its vital link of connection with the thinking nation. He can dominate his party by being spokesman for the real sentiment and purpose of the country, by giving direction to opinion, by giving the country at once the information and the statements of policy which will enable it to form its judgments alike of parties and of men.

For he is also the political leader of the nation, or has it in his choice to be. The nation as a whole has chosen him, and is conscious that it has no other political spokesman. His is the only national voice in affairs. Let him once win the admiration and confidence of the country, and no other single force can withstand him, no combination of forces will easily overpower him. His position takes the imagination of the country. He is the representative of no constituency, but of the whole people. When he speaks in his true character, he speaks for no special interest. If he rightly interpret the national thought and boldly insist upon it, he is irresistible; and the country never feels the zest of action so much as when its President is of such insight and calibre. Its instinct is for unified action, and it craves a single leader. It is for this reason that it will often prefer to choose a man rather than a party. A President whom it trusts can not only lead it, but form it to his own views.

It is the extraordinary isolation imposed upon the President by our system that makes the character and opportunity of his office so extraordinary. In him are centered both opinion and party. He may stand, if he will, a little outside party and insist as if it were upon the general opinion. It is with the instinctive feeling that it is upon occasion such a man that the country wants that nominating conventions will often nominate men who are not their acknowledged leaders, but only such men as the country would like to see lead both its parties. The President may also, if he will, stand within the party counsels and use the advantage of his power and personal force to control its actual programs. He may be both the leader of his party and the leader of the nation, or he may be one or the other. If he lead the nation, his party can hardly resist him. His office is anything he has the sagacity and force to make it.

That is the reason why it has been one thing at one time, another at another. The Presidents who have not made themselves leaders have lived no more truly on that account in the spirit of the Constitution than those whose force has told in the determination of law and policy. No doubt Andrew Jackson overstepped the bounds meant to be set to the authority of his office. It was certainly in direct contravention of the spirit of the Constitution that he should have refused to respect and execute decisions of the Supreme Court of the United States, and no serious student of our history can righteously condone what he did in such matters on the ground that his intentions were upright and his principles pure. But the Constitution of the United States is not a mere lawyers' document: it is a vehicle of life, and its spirit is always the spirit of the age. Its prescriptions are clear and we know what they are; a written document makes lawyers of us all, and our duty as citizens should make us conscientious lawyers, reading the text of the Constitution without subtlety or sophistication; but life is always your last and most authoritative critic.

Some of our Presidents have deliberately held themselves off from using the full power they might legitimately have used, because of conscientious scruples, because they were more theorists than statesmen. They have held the strict literary theory of the Constitution, the Whig theory, the Newtonian theory, and have acted as if they thought that Pennsylvania Avenue should have been even longer than it is; that there should be no intimate communication of any kind between the Capitol and the White House; that the President as a man was no more at liberty to lead the houses of Congress by persuasion than he was at liberty as President to dominate them by authority—supposing that he had, what he has not, authority enough to dominate them. But the makers of the Constitution were not enacting Whig theory, they were not making laws with the expectation that, not the laws themselves, but their opinions, known by future historians to lie back of them, should govern the constitutional action of the country. They were statesmen, not pedants, and their laws are sufficient to keep us to the paths they set us upon. The President is at liberty, both in law and conscience, to be as big a man as he can. His capacity will set the limit; and if Congress be overborne by him, it will be no fault of the makers of the Constitution—it will be from no lack of constitutional powers on its part, but only because the President has the nation behind him, and Congress has not. He has no means of compelling Congress except through public opinion.

That I say he has no means of compelling Congress will show what I mean, and that my meaning has no touch of radicalism or iconoclasm in it. There are illegitimate means by which the President may influence the action of Congress. He may bargain with members, not only with regard to appointments, but also with regard to legislative measures. He may use his local patronage to assist members to get or retain their seats. He may interpose his powerful influence, in one covert way or another, in contests for places in the Senate. He may also overbear Congress by arbitrary acts which ignore the laws or virtually override them. He may even substitute his own orders for acts of Congress which he wants but cannot get. Such things are not only deeply immoral, they are destructive of the fundamental understandings of constitutional government and, therefore, of constitutional government itself. They are sure, moreover, in a country of free public opinion, to bring their own punishment, to destroy both the fame and the power of the man who dares to practice them. No honorable man includes such agencies in a sober exposition of the Constitution or allows himself to think of them when he speaks of the influences of "life" which govern each generation's use and interpretation of that great instrument, our sovereign guide and the object of our deepest reverence. Nothing in a system like ours can be constitutional which is immoral or which touches the good faith of those who have sworn to obey the fundamental law. The reprobation of all good men will aways overwhelm such influences with shame and failure. But the personal force of the President is perfectly constitutional to any extent to which he chooses to exercise it, and it is by the clear logic of our constitutional practice that he has become alike the leader of his party and the leader of the nation.

The political powers of the President are not quite so obvious in their scope and character when we consider his relations with Congress as when we consider his relations to his party and to the nation. They need, therefore, a somewhat more critical examination. Leadership in government naturally belongs to its executive officers, who are daily in contact with practical conditions and exigencies and whose reputations alike for good judgment and for fidelity are at stake much more than are those of the members of the legislative body at every turn of the law's application. The law-making part of the government ought certainly to be very hospitable to the suggestions of the planning and acting part of it. Those Presidents who have felt themselves bound to adhere to the strict literary theory of the Constitution have scrupulously refrained from attempting to determine either the subjects or the character of legislation, except so far as they were obliged to decide for themselves, after Congress had acted, whether they should acquiesce in it or not. And yet the Constitution explicitly authorizes the President to recommend to Congress "such measures as he shall deem necessary and expedient," and it is not necessary to the integrity of even the literary theory of the Constitution to insist that such recommendations should be merely perfunctory. Certainly General Washington did not so regard them, and he stood much nearer the Whig theory than we do. A President's messages to Congress have no more weight or authority than their intrinsic reasonableness and importance give them: but that is their only constitutional limitation. The Constitution certainly does not forbid the President to back them up, as General Washington did, with such personal force and influence as he may possess. Some of our Presidents have felt the need, which unquestionably exists in our system, for some spokesman of the nation as a whole, in matters of legislation no less than in other matters, and have tried to supply Congress with the leadership of suggestion, backed by argument and by iteration and by every legitimate appeal to public opinion. Cabinet officers are shut out from Congress; the President himself has, by custom, no access to its floor; many long-established barriers of precedent, though not of law, hinder him from exercising any direct influence upon its deliberations; and yet he is undoubtedly the only spokesman of the whole people. They have again and again, as often as they were afforded the opportunity, manifested their satisfaction when he has boldly accepted the role of leader, to which the peculiar origin and character of his authority entitle him. The Constitution bids him speak, and times of stress and change must more and more thrust upon him the attitude of originator of policies.

His is the vital place of action in the system, whether he accept it as such or not, and the office is the measure of the man—of his wisdom as well as of his force. His veto abundantly equips him to stay the hand of Congress when he will. It is seldom possible to pass a measure over his veto, and no President has hesitated to use the veto when his own judgment of the public good was seriously at issue with that of the houses. The veto has never been suffered to fall into even temporary disuse with us. In England it has ceased to exist, with the change in the character of the executive. There has been no veto since Anne's day, because ever since the reign of Anne the laws of England have been originated either by ministers who spoke the king's own will or by ministers whom the king did not dare gainsay; and in our own time the ministers who formulate the laws are themselves the executive of the nation; a veto would be a negative upon their own power. If bills pass of which they disapprove, they resign and give place to the leaders of those who approve them. The framers of the Constitution made in our President a more powerful, because a more isolated, king than the one they were imitating; and because the Constitution gave them their veto in such explicit terms, our Presidents have not hesitated to use it, even when it put their mere individual judgment against that of large majorities in both houses of Congress. And yet in the exercise of the power to suggest legislation, quite as explicitly conferred upon them by the Constitution, some of our Presidents have seemed to have a timid fear that they might offend some law of taste which had become a constitutional principle.

In one sense their messages to Congress have no more authority than the letters of any other citizen would have. Congress can heed or ignore them as it pleases; and there have been periods of our history when presidential messages were utterly without practical significance, perfunctory documents which few persons except the editors of newspapers took the trouble to read. But if the President has personal force and cares to exercise it, there is this tremendous difference between his messages and the views of any other citizen, either outside Congress or in it: that the whole country reads them and feels that the writer speaks with an authority and a responsibility which the people themselves have given him.

The history of our Cabinets affords a striking illustration of the progress of the idea that the President is not merely the legal head but also the political leader of the nation. In the earlier days of the government it was customary for the President to fill his Cabinet with the recognized leaders of his party. General Washington even tried the experiment which William of Orange tried at the very beginning of the era of cabinet government. He called to his aid the leaders of both political parties, associating Mr. Hamilton with Mr. Jefferson, on the theory that all views must be heard and considered in the conduct of the government. . . . But our later Presidents have apparently ceased to regard the Cabinet as a council of party leaders such as the party they represent would have chosen. They look upon it rather as a body of personal advisers whom the President chooses from the ranks of those whom he personally trusts and prefers to look to for advice. . . . Mr. Cleveland may be said to have been the first President to make this conception of the Cabinet prominent in his choices, and he did not do so until his second administration. Mr. Roosevelt has emphasized the idea.

Upon analysis it seems to mean this: the Cabinet is an executive, not a political body. The President cannot himself be the actual executive; he must therefore find, to act in his stead, men of the best legal and business gifts, and depend upon them for the actual administration of the government in all its daily activities. If he seeks political advice of his executive colleagues, he seeks it because he relies upon their natural good sense and experienced judgment, upon their knowledge of the country and its business and social conditions, upon their sagacity as representative citizens of more than usual observation and discretion; not because they are supposed to have had any very intimate contact with politics or to have made a profession of public affairs. He has chosen not representative politicians, but eminent representative citizens, selecting them rather for their special fitness for the great business posts to which he has assigned them than for their political experience, and looking to them for advice in the actual conduct of the government rather than in the shaping of political policy. They are, in his view, not necessarily political officers at all.

It may with a great deal of plausibility be argued that the Constitution looks upon the President himself in the same way. It does not seem to make him a prime minister or the leader of the nation's counsels. Some Presidents are, therefore, and some are not. It depends upon the man and his gifts. He may be like his Cabinet, or he may be more than his Cabinet. His office is a mere vantage ground from which he may be sure that effective words of advice and timely efforts at reform will gain telling momentum. He has the ear of the nation as of course, and a great person may use such an advantage greatly. If he use the opportunity, he may take his Cabinet into partnership or not, as he pleases; and so its character may vary with his. Self-reliant men will regard their Cabinets as executive councils; men less self-reliant or more prudent will regard them as also political councils, and will wish to call into them men who have earned the confidence of their party. The character of the Cabinet may be made a nice index of the theory of the presidential office, as well as of the President's theory of party government; but the one view is, so far as I can see, as constitutional as the other.

One of the greatest of the President's powers I have not yet spoken of at all: his control, which is very absolute, of the foreign relations of the nation. The initiative in foreign affairs, which the President possesses without any restriction whatever, is virtually the power to control them absolutely. The President cannot conclude a treaty with a foreign power without the consent of the Senate, but he may guide every step of diplomacy, and to guide diplomacy is to determine what treaties must be made, if the faith and prestige of the government are to be maintained. He need disclose no step of negotiation until it is complete, and when in any critical matter it is completed the government is virtually committed. Whatever its disinclination, the Senate may feel itself committed also.

I have not dwelt upon this power of the President, because it has been decisively influential in determining the character and influence of the office at only two periods in our history; at the very first, when the government was young and had so to use its incipient force as to win the respect of the nations into whose family it had thrust itself, and in our own day when the results of the Spanish War, the ownership of distant possessions, and many sharp struggles for foreign trade make it necessary that we should turn our best talents to the task of dealing firmly, wisely, and justly with political and commercial rivals. The President can never again be the mere domestic figure he has been throughout so large a part of our history. The nation has risen to the first rank in power and resources.

The other nations of the world look askance upon her, half in envy, half in fear, and wonder with a deep anxiety what she will do with her vast strength. They receive the frank professions of men like Mr. John Hay, whom we wholly trusted, with a grain of salt, and doubt what we were sure of, their truthfulness and sincerity, suspecting a hidden design under every utterance he makes. Our President must always, henceforth, be one of the great powers of the world, whether he act greatly and wisely or not, and the best statesmen we can produce will be needed to fill the office of Secretary of State. We have but begun to see the presidential office in this light; but it is the light which will more and more beat upon it, and more and more determine its character and its effect upon the politics of the nation. We can never hide our President again as a mere domestic officer. We can never again see him the mere executive he was in the thirties and forties. He must stand always at the front of our affairs, and the office will be as big and as influential as the man who occupies it.

How is it possible to sum up the duties and influence of such an office in such a system in comprehensive terms which will cover all its changeful aspects? In the view of the makers of the Constitution the President was to be legal executive; perhaps the leader of the nation; certainly not the leader of the party, at any rate while in office. But by the operation of forces inherent in the very nature of government he has become all three, and by inevitable consequence the most heavily burdened officer in the world. No other man's day is so full as his, so full of the responsibilities which tax mind and conscience alike and demand an inexhaustible vitality. The mere task of making appointments to office, which the Constitution imposes upon the President, has come near to breaking some of our Presidents down, because it is a never-ending task in a civil service not yet put upon a professional footing, confused with short terms of office, always forming and dissolving. And in proportion as the President ventures to use his opportunity to lead opinion and act as spokesman of the people in affairs the people stand ready to overwhelm him by running to him with every question, great and small. They are as eager to have him settle a literary question as a political; hear him as acquiescently with regard to matters of special expert knowledge as with regard to public affairs, and call upon him to quiet all troubles by his personal intervention. Men of ordinary physique and discretion cannot be Presidents and live, if the strain be not somehow relieved. We shall be obliged always to be picking our chief magistrates from among wise and prudent athletes—a small class.

The future development of the Presidency, therefore, must certainly, one would confidently predict, run along such lines as the

President's later relations with his Cabinet suggest. General Washington, partly out of unaffected modesty, no doubt, but also out of the sure practical instinct which he possessed in so unusual a degree, set an example which few of his successors seem to have followed in any systematic manner. He made constant and intimate use of his colleagues in every matter that he handled, seeking their assistance and advice by letter when they were at a distance and he could not obtain it in person. It is well known to all close students of our history that his greater state papers, even those which seem in some peculiar and intimate sense his personal utterances, are full of the ideas and the very phrases of the men about him whom he most trusted. His rough drafts came back to him from Mr. Hamilton and Mr. Madison in great part rephrased and rewritten, in many passages reconceived and given a new color. He thought and acted always by the light of counsel, with a will and definite choice of his own, but through the instrumentality of other minds as well as his own. The duties and responsibilities laid upon the President by the Constitution can be changed only by constitutional amendment—a thing too difficult to attempt except upon some greater necessity than the relief of an overburdened office, even though that office be the greatest in the land; and it is to be doubted whether the deliberate opinion of the country would consent to make of the President a less powerful officer than he is. He can secure his own relief without shirking any real responsibility. Appointments, for example, he can, if he will, make more and more upon the advice and choice of his executive colleagues; every matter of detail not only, but also every minor matter of counsel or of general policy, he can more and more depend upon his chosen advisers to determine; he need reserve for himself only the larger matters of counsel and that general oversight of the business of the government and of the persons who conduct it which is not possible without intimate daily consultations, indeed, but which is possible without attempting the intolerable burden of direct control. This is, no doubt, the idea of their functions which most Presidents have entertained and which most Presidents suppose themselves to have acted on; but we have reason to believe that most of our Presidents have taken their duties too literally and have attempted the impossible. But we can safely predict that as the multitude of the President's duties increases, as it must with the growth and widening activities of the nation itself, the incumbents of the great office will more and more come to feel that they are administering it in its truest purpose and with greatest effect by regarding themselves as less and less executive officers and more and more directors of affairs and leaders of the nation—men of counsel and of the sort of action that makes for enlightenment.

THE CONTEMPORARY
PRESIDENCY

☆

ON FRANKLIN ROOSEVELT: *from* Roosevelt's View
of the Big Job *by Anne O'Hare McCormick*

[Roosevelt] is a potent name, easily the most potent influence in the
destiny of Franklin Roosevelt. Yet, though the Governor's versatile
interests and unconventional methods are Rooseveltian, they do
represent, nevertheless, his own conception of the personal and
human relationship that should exist between the Executive and
his State and by extension, between the Chief Executive and the
nation. He thinks that the President should personify government
to the citizen, should express the ideas germinating, ready for realization, in the popular mind.

"The Presidency," he says, "is not merely an administrative
office. That's the least of it. It is more than an engineering job,
efficient or inefficient. It is preeminently a place of moral leadership.
All of our great Presidents were leaders of thought at times when
certain historic ideas in the life of the nation had to be clarified.
Washington personified the idea of federal union. Jefferson practically originated the party system as we know it by opposing the
democratic theory to the republicanism of Hamilton. This theory was
reaffirmed by Jackson. Two great principles of our government were
forever put beyond question by Lincoln. Cleveland, coming into
office following an era of great political corruption, typified rugged

Franklin D. Roosevelt, the 32nd President of the United States, was elected
to the office four times and served from 1933 to 1945. This selection is from
"Roosevelt's View of the Big Job" by Anne O'Hare McCormick, who inter-
viewed Governor Roosevelt during his first campaign for the Presidency. *The
New York Times Magazine*, September 11, 1932, © 1932 by The New York
Times Company. Reprinted by permission.

honesty. T.R. and Wilson were both moral leaders, each in his own way and for his own time, who used the Presidency as a pulpit.

"Isn't that what the office is—a superb opportunity for reapplying, applying in new conditions, the simple rules of human conduct we always go back to? I stress the modern application, because we are always moving on; the technical and economic environment changes, and never so quickly as now. Without leadership alert and sensitive to change, we are bogged up or lose our way, as we have lost it in the past decade."

"And you?" I asked. "Is that the reason you want to be President? What particular affirmation or reaffirmation is required of the national leader of today?"

The Governor laughed. "Months before the nomination I told you I didn't know why any man should want to be President. I repeat that I didn't grow up burning to go to the White House, like the American boy of legend rather than of fact. I have read history and known Presidents; it's a terrible job. But somebody has to do it. I suppose I was picked out because the majority of the party thought I was the best vote-getter. Now that I am picked out, naturally I want to be President. I want to win." He laughed again, then went on gravely:

"The objective now, as I see it, is to put at the head of the nation someone whose interests are not special but general, someone who can understand and treat with the country as a whole. For as much as anything it needs to be reaffirmed at this juncture that the United States is one organic entity, that no interest, no class, no section, is either separate or supreme above the interests of all or divorced from the interests of all. We hear a good deal about the interdependence of the nations of the world. In the pit of universal calamity, with every country smothered by its own narrow policies and the narrow policies of other countries—and that goes for us, too—every one sees that connection. But there is a nearer truth, often forgotten or ignored, and that is the interdependence of every part of our own country.

"No valid economic sectionalism exists in these States. There are opposed economic interests within every section, town against country, suburb against city, but as a nation we are all mixed up, fluid. All the States are in some degree like New York, a blend of agriculture and industry. The rural South is changing, the Western prairies are planted with factory towns. East and West, as we use the terms, are mostly states of mind, not localized but everywhere. What we need is a common mind, and, even more, common sense to realize that if we are not acting for the interest of the whole country we are acting against the interests of every section."

Perhaps this is Governor Roosevelt's answer to the charge that he is trying to be all things to all sections, conservative in the East, radical in the West; he simply denies that there are sections in that sense. He classifies himself as a liberal. I asked what he meant by that elastic term, how he defined the difference between the outlooks vaguely called conservative and progressive, or between his program and that of the opposing party.

"Let's put it this way," he explained. "Every few years, say every half generation, the general problems of civilization change in such a way that new difficulties of adjustment are presented to government. The forms have to catch up with the facts. The radical, in order to meet these difficulties, jumps, jumps in groups, because he doesn't count unless he's part of a group. One group usually differs from another in its program, but they are all equally definite and dogmatic about it. They lay down categorical terms—'my plan or none.' Their characteristic is hard-and-fast processes, cut-and-dried methods, uncompromising formulas. The conservative says: 'No, we're not ready for change. It's dangerous. Let's wait and see what happens.' Half way in between is the liberal, who recognizes the need of new machinery for new needs but who works to control the processes of change, to the end that the break with the old pattern may not be too violent.

"Or say that civilization is a tree which, as it grows, continually produces rot and dead wood. The radical says: 'Cut it down.' The conservative says: 'Don't touch it.' The liberal compromises: 'Let's prune, so that we lose neither the old trunk nor the new branches.' This campaign is waged to teach the country to move upon its appointed course, the way of change, in an orderly march, avoiding alike the revolution of radicalism and the revolution of conservatism."

☆

FRANKLIN ROOSEVELT: *First Inaugural Address*

President Hoover, Mr. Chief Justice, my friends:
I am certain that my fellow Americans expect that on my induction into the Presidency I will address them with a candor and a decision which the present situation of our nation impels.

This is pre-eminently the time to speak the truth, the whole truth, frankly and boldly. Nor need we shrink from honestly facing conditions in our country today. This great nation will endure as it has endured, will revive and will prosper.

So first of all let me assert my firm belief that the only thing we have to fear is fear itself—nameless, unreasoning, unjustified terror which paralyzes needed efforts to convert retreat into advance.

In every dark hour of our national life a leadership of frankness and vigor has met with that understanding and support of the people themselves which is essential to victory. I am convinced that you will again give that support to leadership in these critical days.

In such a spirit on my part and on yours we face our common difficulties. They concern, thank God, only material things. Values have shrunken to fantastic levels; taxes have risen; our ability to pay has fallen, government of all kinds is faced by serious curtailment of income; the means of exchange are frozen in the currents of trade; the withered leaves of industrial enterprise lie on every side; farmers find no markets for their products; the savings of many years in thousands of families are gone.

More important, a host of unemployed citizens face the grim problem of existence, and an equally great number toil with little

President Roosevelt's *First Inaugural Address* was delivered on March 4, 1933.

return. Only a foolish optimist can deny the dark realities of the moment.

Yet our distress comes from no failure of substance. We are stricken by no plague of locusts. Compared with the perils which our forefathers conquered because they believed and were not afraid, we have still much to be thankful for. Nature still offers her bounty and human efforts have multiplied it. Plenty is at our doorstep, but a generous use of it languishes in the very sight of the supply.

Primarily, this is because the rulers of the exchange of mankind's goods have failed through their own stubbornness and their own incompetence, have admitted their failure and abdicated. Practices of the unscrupulous money changers stand indicted in the court of public opinion, rejected by the hearts and minds of men.

True, they have tried, but their efforts have been cast in the pattern of an outworn tradition. Faced by failure of credit, they have proposed only the lending of more money.

Stripped of the lure of profit by which to induce our people to follow their false leadership, they have resorted to exhortations, pleading tearfully for restored confidence. They know only the rules of a generation of self-seekers.

They have no vision, and when there is no vision the people perish.

The money changers have fled from their high seats in the temple of our civilization. We may now restore that temple to the ancient truths.

The measure of the restoration lies in the extent to which we apply social values more noble than mere monetary profit.

Happiness lies not in the mere possession of money; it lies in the joy of achievement, in the thrill of creative effort. The joy and moral stimulation of work no longer must be forgotten in the mad chase of evanescent profits. These dark days will be worth all they cost us if they teach us that our true destiny is not to be ministered unto but to minister to ourselves and to our fellow men.

Recognition of the falsity of material wealth as the standard of success goes hand in hand with the abandonment of the false belief that public office and high political position are to be valued only by the standards of pride of place and personal profit; and there must be an end to a conduct in banking and in business which too often has given to a sacred trust the likeness of callous and selfish wrongdoing.

Small wonder that confidence languishes, for it thrives only on honesty, on honor, on the sacredness of obligations, on faithful protection, on unselfish performance; without them it cannot live.

Restoration calls, however, not for changes in ethics alone. This nation asks for action, and action now.

Our greatest primary task is to put people to work. This is no unsolvable problem if we face it wisely and courageously. It can be accomplished in part by direct recruiting by the government itself, treating the task as we would treat the emergency of a war, but at the same time, through this employment, accomplishing greatly needed projects to stimulate and reorganize the use of our natural resources.

Hand in hand with this we must frankly recognize the overbalance of population in our industrial centers and, by engaging on a national scale in a redistribution, endeavor to provide a better use of the land for those best fitted for the land.

The task can be helped by definite efforts to raise the values of agricultural products and with this the power to purchase the output of our cities.

It can be helped by preventing realistically the tragedy of the growing loss, through foreclosure, of our small homes and our farms.

It can be helped by insistence that the federal, state and local governments act forthwith on the demand that their cost be drastically reduced.

It can be helped by the unifying of relief activities which today are often scattered, uneconomical and unequal. It can be helped by national planning for and supervision of all forms of transportation and of communications and other utilities which have a definitely public character.

There are many ways in which it can be helped, but it can never be helped merely by talking about it. We must act, and act quickly.

Finally, in our progress toward a resumption of work we require two safeguards against a return of the evils of the old order; there must be a strict supervision of all banking and credits and investments; there must be an end to speculation with other people's money, and there must be provision for an adequate but sound currency.

These are the lines of attack. I shall presently urge upon a new Congress, in special session, detailed measure for their fulfillment, and I shall seek the immediate assistance of the several States.

Through this program of action we address ourselves to putting our own national house in order and making income balance outgo. Our international trade relations, though vastly important, are in point of time and necessity secondary to the establishment of a sound national economy. I favor as a practical policy the putting of first things first. I shall spare no effort to restore world trade by international economic readjustment, but the emergency at home cannot wait on that accomplishment.

The basic thought that guides these specific means of national recovery is not narrowly nationalistic.

It is the insistence, as a first consideration, upon the interdependence of the various elements in, and parts of, the United States—a recognition of the old and permanently important manifestation of the American spirit of the pioneer.

It is the way to recovery. It is the immediate way. It is the strongest assurance that the recovery will endure.

In the field of world policy I would dedicate this nation to the policy of the good neighbor—the neighbor who resolutely respects himself and, because he does so, respects the rights of others—the neighbor who respects his obligations and respects the sanctity of his agreements in and with a world of neighbors.

If I read the temper of our people correctly, we now realize as we have never realized before our interdependnce on each other; that we can not merely take but we must give as well; that if we are to go forward, we must move as a trained and loyal army willing to sacrifice for the good of a common discipline, because without such discipline no progress is made, no leadership becomes effective.

We are, I know, ready and willing to submit our lives and property to such discipline because it makes possible a leadership which aims at a larger good.

This I propose to offer, pledging that the larger purposes will bind upon us all as a sacred obligation with a unity of duty hitherto evoked only in time of armed strife.

With this pledge taken, I assume unhesitatingly the leadership of this great army of our people, dedicated to a disciplined attack upon our common problems.

Action in this image and to this end is feasible under the form of government which we have inherited from our ancestors.

Our Constitution is so simple and practical that it is possible always to meet extraordinary needs by changes in emphasis and arrangement without loss of essential form. That is why our constitutional system has proved itself the most superbly enduring political mechanism the modern world has produced. It has met every stress of vast expansion of territory, of foreign wars, of bitter internal strife, of world relations.

It is to be hoped that the normal balance of executive and legislative authority may be wholly adequate to meet the unprecedented task before us. But it may be that an unprecedented demand and need for undelayed action may call for temporary departure from that normal balance of public procedure.

I am prepared under my constitutional duty to recommend the measures that a stricken nation in the midst of a stricken world may require.

These measures, or such other measures as the Congress may build out of its experience and wisdom, I shall seek, within my constitutional authority, to bring to speedy adoption.

But in the event that the Congress shall fail to take one of these two courses, and in the event that the national emergency is still critical, I shall not evade the clear course of duty that will then confront me.

I shall ask the Congress for the one remaining instrument to meet the crisis—broad executive power to wage a war against the emergency as great as the power that would be given me if we were in fact invaded by a foreign foe.

For the trust reposed in me I will return the courage and the devotion that befit the time. I can do no less.

We face the arduous days that lie before us in the warm courage of national unity; with the clear consciousness of seeking old and precious moral values; with the clean satisfaction that comes from the stern performance of duty by old and young alike. We aim at the assurance of a rounded and permanent national life.

We do not distrust the future of essential democracy. The people of the United States have not failed. In their need they have registered a mandate that they want direct, vigorous action.

They have asked for discipline and direction under leadership. They have made me the present instrument of their wishes. In the spirit of the gift I take it.

In this dedication of a nation we humbly ask the blessing of God. May He protect each and every one of us! May He guide me in the days to come!

☆

FRANKLIN ROOSEVELT: *Message to Congress on Wartime Stabilization*

Four months ago, on April 27, 1942, I laid before the Congress a seven-point national economic policy designed to stabilize the domestic economy of the United States for the period of the war. The objective of that program was to prevent any substantial further rise in the cost of living.

It is not necessary for me to enumerate again the disastrous results of a runaway cost of living—disastrous to all of us, farmers, laborers, businessmen, the Nation itself. When the cost of living spirals upward, everybody becomes poorer, because the money he has and the money he earns buys so much less. At the same time the cost of the war, paid ultimately from taxes of the people, is needlessly increased by many billions of dollars. The national debt, at the end of the war, would become unnecessarily greater. Indeed, the prevention of a spiraling domestic economy is a vital part of the winning of the war itself.

I reiterate the 7-point program which I presented April 27, 1942:

1. To keep the cost of living from spiraling upward, we must tax heavily, and in that process keep personal and corporate profits at a reasonable rate, the word "reasonable" being defined at a low level.

2. To keep the cost of living from spiraling upward, we must fix ceilings on the prices which consumers, retailers, wholesalers, and manufacturers pay for the things they buy; and ceilings on rents for dwellings in all areas affected by war industries.

President Roosevelt sent this *Message to the Congress Asking for Quick Action to Stabilize the Economy* on September 7, 1942.

111

3. To keep the cost of living from spiraling upward, we must stabilize the remuneration received by individuals for their work.

4. To keep the cost of living from spiraling upward, we must stabilize the prices received by growers for the products of their lands.

5. To keep the cost of living from spiraling upward, we must encourage all citizens to contribute to the cost of winning this war by purchasing war bonds with their earnings instead of using those earnings to buy articles which are not essential.

6. To keep the cost of living from spiraling upward, we must ration all essential commodities of which there is a scarcity, so that they may be distributed fairly among consumers and not merely in accordance with financial ability to pay high prices for them.

7. To keep the cost of living from spiraling upward, we must discourage credit and installment buying, and encourage the paying off of debts, mortgages, and other obligations; for this promotes savings, retards excessive buying, and adds to the amount available to the creditors for the purchase of war bonds.

In my message of four months ago, I pointed out that in order to succeed in our objective of stabilization it was necessary to move on all seven fronts at the same time; but that two of them called for legislation by the Congress before action could be taken. It was obvious then, and it is obvious now, that unless those two are realized, the whole objective must fail. These are points numbered one and four: namely, an adequate tax program, and a law permitting the fixing of price ceilings on farm products at parity prices.

I regret to have to call to your attention the fact that neither of these two essential pieces of legislation has as yet been enacted into law. That delay has now reached the point of danger to our whole economy. . . .

Therefore, I ask the Congress to pass legislation under which the President would be specifically authorized to stabilize the cost of living, including the prices of all farm commodities. The purpose should be to hold farm prices at parity, or at levels of a recent date, whichever is higher.

I ask the Congress to take this action by the first of October. Inaction on your part by that date will leave me with an inescapable responsibility to the people of this country to see to it that the war effort is no longer imperiled by threat of economic chaos.

In the event that the Congress should fail to act, and act adequately, I shall accept the responsibility, and I will act.

At the same time that farm prices are stabilized, wages can and will be stabilized also. This I will do.

The President has the powers, under the Constitution and under

Congressional Acts, to take measures necessary to avert a disaster which would interfere with the winning of the war.

I have given the most thoughtful consideration to meeting this issue without further reference to the Congress. I have determined, however, on this vital matter to consult with the Congress.

There may be those who will say that, if the situation is as grave as I have stated it to be, I should use my powers and act now. I can only say that I have approached this problem from every angle, and that I have decided that the course of conduct which I am following in this case is consistent with my sense of responsibility as President in time of war, and with my deep and unalterable devotion to the processes of democracy.

The responsibilities of the President in wartime to protect the Nation are very grave. This total war, with our fighting fronts all over the world, makes the use of executive power far more essential than in any previous war.

If we were invaded, the people of this country would expect the President to use any and all means to repel the invader.

The Revolution and the War Between the States were fought on our own soil but today this war will be won or lost on other continents and remote seas.

I cannot tell what powers may have to be exercised in order to win this war.

The American people can be sure that I will use my powers with a full sense of my responsibility to the Constitution and to my country. The American people can also be sure that I shall not hesitate to use every power vested in me to accomplish the defeat of our enemies in any part of the world where our own safety demands such defeat.

When the war is won, the powers under which I act automatically revert to the people—to whom they belong. . . .

☆

HARRY TRUMAN: *Statement on the Situation*

in Korea

In Korea the government forces, which were armed to prevent border raids and to preserve internal security, were attacked by invading forces from North Korea. The Security Council of the United Nations called upon the invading troops to cease hostilities and to withdraw to the 38th parallel. This they have not done, but on the contrary have pressed the attack. The Security Council called upon all members of the United Nations to render every assistance to the United Nations in the execution of this resolution. In these circumstances I have ordered United States air and sea forces to give the Korean government troops cover and support.

The attack upon Korea makes it plain beyond all doubt that communism has passed beyond the use of subversion to conquer independent nations and will now use armed invasion and war. It has defied the orders of the Security Council of the United Nations issued to preserve international peace and security. In these circumstances the occupation of Formosa by Communist forces would be a direct threat to the security of the Pacific area and to United States forces performing their lawful and necessary functions in that area.

Accordingly I have ordered the 7th Fleet to prevent any attack on Formosa. As a corollary of this action I am calling upon the Chinese government on Formosa to cease all air and sea operations against the mainland. The 7th Fleet will see that this is done. The determination of the future status of Formosa must await the restoration of security in the Pacific, a peace settlement with Japan, or consideration by the United Nations.

Harry S. Truman was the 33rd President of the United States (1945–1953). This *Statement* was issued on June 27, 1950.

I have also directed that United States forces in the Philippines be strengthened and that military assistance to the Philippine government be accelerated.

I have similarly directed acceleration in the furnishing of military assistance to the forces of France and the Associated States in Indochina and the dispatch of a military mission to provide close working relations with those forces.

I know that all members of the United Nations will consider carefully the consequences of this latest aggression in Korea in defiance of the Charter of the United Nations. A return to the rule of force in international affairs would have far-reaching effects. The United States will continue to uphold the rule of law.

I have instructed Ambassador Austin, as the representative of the United States to the Security Council, to report these steps to the Council.

☆

HARRY TRUMAN: *Speech on Presidential Power*

. . . There's never been an office—an executive office—in all the history of the world with the responsibility and the power of the Presidency of the United States. That is the reason in this day and age that it must be run and respected as at no other time in the history of the world because it can mean the welfare of the world or its destruction.

When the founding fathers outlined the Presidency in Article II of the Constitution, they left a great many details out and vague. I think they relied on the experience of the nation to fill in the outlines. The office of chief executive has grown with the progress of this great republic. It has responded to the many demands that our complex society has made upon the Government. It has given our nation a means of meeting our greatest emergencies. Today, it is one of the most important factors in our leadership of the free world.

Many diverse elements entered into the creation of the office, springing, as it did, from the parent idea of the separation of powers.

There was the firm conviction of such powerful and shrewd minds as that of John Adams that the greatest protection against unlimited power lay in an executive secured against the encroachment of the national assembly. Then there were the fears of those who suspected a plot to establish a monarchy on these shores. Others believed that the experience under the Confederation showed above all the need of stability through a strong central administration. Finally, there was the need for compromise among these and many other views.

President Truman delivered this speech at a Birthday Dinner in his honor on May 8, 1954. © 1954 by The New York Times Company. Reprinted by permission.

The result was a compromise—a compromise which that shrewd observer, Alexis de Tocqueville, over 120 years ago, believed would not work. He thought that the presidential office was too weak. The President, he thought, was at the mercy of Congress. The President could recommend, to be sure, he thought, but the President had no power and the Congress had the power. The Congress could disregard his recommendations, overrule his vetoes, reject his nominations. De Tocqueville thought that no man of parts, worthy of leadership, would accept such a feeble role.

This was not a foolish view and there was much in our early history which tended to bear it out. But there is a power in the course of events which plays its own part. In this case again, Justice Holmes' epigram proved true. He said a page of history is worth a whole volume of logic. And as the pages of history were written they unfolded powers in the Presidency not explicitly found in Article II of the Constitution.

In the first place, the President became the leader of a political party. The party under his leadership had to be dominant enough to put him in office. This political party leadership was the last thing the Constitution contemplated. The President's election was not intended to be mixed up in the hurly-burly of partisan politics.

I wish some of those old gentlemen could come back and see how it worked. The people were to choose wise and respected men who would meet in calm seclusion and choose a President and the runner-up would be Vice President.

All of this went by the board—though most of the original language remains in the Constitution. Out of the struggle and tumult of the political arena a new and different President emerged—the man who led a political party to victory and retained in his hands the power of party leadership. That is, he retained it, like the sword Excalibur, if he could wrest it from the scabbard and wield it.

Another development was connected with the first. As the President came to be elected by the whole people, he became responsible to the whole people. I used to say the only lobbyist the whole people had in Washington was the President of the United States. Our whole people looked to him for leadership, and not confined within the limits of a written document. Every hope and every fear of his fellow citizens, almost every aspect of their welfare and activity, falls within the scope of his concern—indeed, it falls within the scope of his duty. Only one who has held that office can really appreciate that. It is the President's responsibility to look at all questions from the point of view of the whole people. His written and spoken word commands national and often international attention.

These powers which are not explicitly written into the Constitution are the powers which no President can pass on to his successor. They go only to him who can take and use them. However, it is these powers, quite as much as those enumerated in Article II of the Constitution, which make the presidential system unique and which give the papers of Presidents their peculiarly revealing importance.

For it is through the use of these great powers that leadership arises, events are molded, and administrations take on their character. Their use can make a Jefferson or a Lincoln Administration; their non-use can make a Buchanan or a Grant Administration.

Moreover, a study of these aspects of our governmental and political history will save us from self-righteousness—from taking a holier-than-thou attitude toward other nations. For, brilliant and enduring as were the minds of the architects of our Constitution, they did not devise a foolproof system to protect us against the disaster of a weak government—that is, a government unable to face and resolve—one way or another—pressing national problems. Indeed, in some respects, the separation of powers requires stronger executive leadership than does the parliamentary and cabinet system.

As Justice Brandeis used to say, the separation of powers was not devised to promote efficiency in government. In fact, it was devised to prevent one form of deficiency—absolutism or dictatorship. By making the Congress separate and independent in the exercise of its powers, a certain amount of political conflict was built into the Constitution. For the price of independence is eternal vigilance and a good deal of struggle. And this is not a bad thing—on the contrary, it is a good thing for the preservation of the liberty of the people— if it does not become conflict just for its own sake.

I've always said that the President who didn't have a fight with the Congress wasn't any good anyhow. And that's no reflection on the Congress. They are always looking after their rights. You needn't doubt that.

Having been in these two branches of government, legislative and executive, I think I am expressing a considered and impartial opinion in saying that the powers of the President are much more difficult to exercise and to preserve from encroachment than those of the Congress. In part, this comes from the difficulty of the problems of our time, and from the fact that upon the President falls the responsibility of obtaining action, timely and adequate, to meet the nation's needs. Whatever the Constitution says, he is held responsible for any disaster which may come.

And so a successful administration is one of strong presidential leadership. Weak leadership—or no leadership—produces failure and often disaster.

This does not come from the inherent incapacity of the people of the nation. It is inherent in the legislative government where there is no executive strong and stable enough to rally the people to a sustained effort of will and prepared to use its power of party control to the fullest extent.

Today, also, one of the great responsibilities and opportunities of the President is to lead and inspire public opinion. The words of a President carry great weight. His acts carry even more weight.

All of us remember the words of Franklin D. Roosevelt in his first inaugural address which did so much to rally the spirit of the nation struggling through the depths of a depression. He said "the only thing we have to fear is fear itself." Those words, however, would have had little effect if President Roosevelt had not backed them up by action. Following that speech, President Roosevelt plunged into a vigorous course, striking at the depression on all fronts. He backed his words by his action, and words and action restored the faith of the nation in its government and in its form of government, too.

. . . Today the tasks of leadership falling upon the President spring not only from our national problems but from those of the whole world. Today that leadership will determine whether our Government will function effectively, and upon its functioning depends the survival of each of us and also on that depends the survival of the free world. . . .

☆

DWIGHT D. EISENHOWER: *Some Thoughts on the Presidency*

In the late afternoon of January 22, 1953—my first full day at the President's desk—my old friend Gen. Omar Bradley, then chairman of the Joint Chiefs of Staff, phoned me. For years we had been "Ike" and "Brad" to each other. But now, in the course of our conversation, he addressed me as "Mr. President."

Somehow this little incident rocked me back on my heels. Naturally, I knew all about Presidential protocol, but I suppose I had never quite realized the isolation that the job forces upon a man.

I couple this with another seemingly small circumstance that also put me on notice at once that the Presidency is something apart. During my first few hours in the Oval Room, a White House aide showed me a large push button concealed in the kneehole of my desk. If I were to touch the button with my knee, Secret Service guards would appear instantly.

Doubtless every new President has experiences which quickly teach him that he has undertaken a lonely job. After these two episodes, I understood with deep impact that now, except for my immediate family, I would in a sense be alone—far more so than when I commanded the Allied forces in Europe. I have always liked people, and it was hard to surrender the easy camaraderie of the old days. Nor was it easy to accept the fact that I would always be under

Dwight D. Eisenhower, Supreme Commander of the Allied Forces in Europe in World War II, was the 34th President of the United States (1953–1961). This selection is from "Some Thoughts on the Presidency" in the *Reader's Digest*, November, 1968. © 1968 by Dwight D. Eisenhower. Reprinted by permission of the *Reader's Digest* and Doubleday and Company.

guard, that all movements must be planned, that I could never go anywhere unattended.

But these, after all, are minor frustrations, to which one grows accustomed. The American people respect the Presidency, and want the office to be conducted with dignity and with as much personal safety for the incumbent as can be devised—and it is right that they should.

Far more important than protocol or any other outward trappings of the office are certain inner qualities that any President must have to be effective. On several occasions I have said publicly that there are four prime requisites of the Presidency: Character, Ability, Responsibility, Experience. These need no explanation. But, on a more specific level, there are also many identifiable qualities, moods, characteristics and attitudes that contribute to the success or defeat of a President. It is some of these human characteristics that I wish to discuss.

To See Beyond Today. One of the most important necessities of the Presidency is vision—the ability to look far into the future and see. the needs of the nation. Coupled with this is the courage to implement this vision with the necessary hard decisions, despite almost sure criticism—often actual vilification—from the press, the opposition party, and even from within the incumbent's own party.

Thomas Jefferson certainly displayed the kind of vision I am talking about when he made the Louisiana Purchase from France in 1803. Jefferson's political enemies and some segments of the press scoffed at his determination to acquire this territory—a desert wilderness of a million square miles, inhabited chiefly by Indians and buffalo, largely unfit for human use. But he and his Cabinet ministers ignored the criticism and went ahead with the deal, at a cost of about four cents an acre. Today this area is occupied by all or parts of 13 states, and is perhaps the greatest food-producing region in the world.

Frequently throughout our history, a President has displayed magnificent vision in the enunciation of a great principle. Such, surely, was James Monroe's courageous promulgation of the Monroe Doctrine, which warned the acquisitive nations of Europe to keep their hands off the Western Hemisphere.

Such, also, was Andrew Jackson's tough refusal to permit the nullification of federal law by a state. The confrontation came in 1832, when South Carolina attempted to prevent the collection of import duties at the port of Charleston. It was an early historic test of the states' rights doctrine in defiance of federal supremacy. Old Hickory, himself a Southerner, issued a call for federal troops to put down the insurrection. South Carolina grumbled that it would secede, but backed down before there was a clash of arms.

History gives Lincoln the credit for saving the Union, but if Jackson had not acted wisely and firmly in 1832, the nation might well have fallen apart before Abe ever appeared on the scene.

It was left to Abraham Lincoln, of course, to preserve the Union in the supreme test, the agony of bloodshed. His vision, his rock-like determination, his compassion, his aloneness in the midst of the worst public abuse any President has ever suffered, are a familiar story. But consider for a moment the superb selflessness of the man. Some months before the national election of 1864, prestigious leaders of his own party came to Lincoln and begged him to end the war through any kind of compromise he could arrange with the Confederacy. Otherwise, they predicted, he would go down to defeat at the polls. Abe's answer was a firm, historic No. He added that his own political future was unimportant—that the preservation of the Union was all that mattered. Fortunately, the tide of battle turned in time, he was re-elected, and the Union forces went on to complete victory a few months later.

Incidentally, the rebellious spirit of nullification still crops up occasionally even today. It was in September of 1957 that Gov. Orval Faubus, of Arkansas, attempted to thwart federal court orders to integrate a Little Rock high school. He called up the Arkansas National Guard to enforce his outrageous defiance of the federal government. After a fruitless conference with the governor, I sent U.S. paratroopers into Little Rock—and then braced myself for the inevitable storm of criticism. For a time, the South was outraged at my "high-handed tactics." But order was peacefully restored and eventually integration was effected. Once more the principle of federal supremacy had been upheld.

Andrew Johnson, who succeeded to the Presidency upon Lincoln's assassination, is usually catalogued as a "weak" President. It is true that his personal habits and comportment were anything but exemplary, and in many ways he was ineffectual. Yet he did two farseeing things: he "squandered" $7,200,000 to buy Alaska from Russia; he saved the office of the Presidency from destruction by Congress. Both of these acts took courage—and he was castigated unmercifully for them.

Johnson had been quarreling with Secretary of War Edwin M. Stanton, and wanted to remove him. To thwart Johnson, Congress had passed an obviously unconstitutional measure called the Tenure of Office Act, which forbade the President to dismiss Cabinet members or other appointive officials without the consent of the Senate. Despite the Act, Johnson fired Stanton. The House angrily impeached him. But in the Senate the President won his fight against conviction by one vote. It was enough. The right of a President to run the executive department was upheld.

Humility, Humor, Optimism. There are certain deeply personal characteristics that any President needs to cope with the pressures and the buffeting of the job. One of these is a working balance between humility and vanity. I have been amused to read occasionally that I was a "humble President," while just as often I have been called an autocrat or a martinet. Every human being, and certainly a President, needs a certain amount of personal pride, but he shouldn't be so proud that he cannot change his mind or admit his mistakes. Nor can any President achieve his objectives if he permits others to walk roughshod over him.

Lincoln's humility was one of his storied qualities, but he also demonstrated over and over that he had iron in his soul. On the other hand, although Woodrow Wilson was surely a great President, I have always felt that his unbending pride kept him from being even greater. George Washington was, I think, the ideal in this respect. He possessed pride and dignity, but he was also considerate of others, consulted constantly with his subordinates, unfailingly weighed their advice.

As part of this working balance in a man's nature, a sense of humor can be a great help—particularly a sense of humor about himself. William Howard Taft joked about his own corpulence, and people loved it; it took nothing from his inherent dignity. Lincoln eased tense moments with bawdy stories, and often poked fun at himself—and history honors him for this human quality. A sense of humor is part of the art of leadership, of getting along with people, of getting things done.

On the other hand, I found that getting things done sometimes required other weapons from the Presidential arsenal—persuasion, cajolery, even a little head-thumping here and there—to say nothing of a personal streak of obstinacy which on occasion fires my boilers.

It is an essential quality of leadership to be able to inspire people. I have often thought how fortunate it was that the two great Allies of World War II were led by two men, Winston Churchill and Franklin D. Roosevelt, who had that ability and used it masterfully.

Although I have always disagreed with some of Roosevelt's domestic policies—notably the trend toward highly centralized government that he set in motion—I admired him greatly as a war leader. The man exuded an infectious optimism. Even during the dark days of our early reverses in the Pacific, he was somehow able to convey his own exuberant confidence to the American people. As a result, despite often justified political opposition on domestic measures,

F.D.R. had the nation almost solidly behind him in his conduct of the war.

The Power of Organization. Executive ability, whose cornerstone is a talent for good organization and skill in selecting and using subordinates, certainly is a vital attribute of the Presidency. Any Chief Executive who tries to do everything himself, as some Presidents have, is in trouble. He will work himself into a state of exhaustion and frustration, and drive everyone around him half crazy. Franklin Pierce, for example, was so preoccupied with patronage decisions and other petty matters that he never was able really to be President.

George Washington's skill in organizing was superb. When he became our first President, he had a Congress and a fragmentary judicial system, but only small bits and pieces of an executive establishment. There were no precedents, and his only instruction guide was our new Constitution, a great document which nevertheless told him only in the broadest terms what he could and could not do. Upon this he had to build the structure of government.

Washington did it. He had the good sense to surround himself with men of stature, and he got the most out of them. History offers few examples of organizational achievement to compare with the eight years of his administration.

To accomplish this gigantic task, Washington had to invest the office of President with powers that the Constitution only hinted at or said nothing at all about. Predictably, he incurred an avalanche of savage abuse from a populace still sensitive to the excesses of monarchy. When he assumed office, his popularity was almost boundless, but by the time he retired he was being jeeringly referred to as a "tyrant" and "King George." But he had made the Presidency meaningful, with the power that any effective executive must have. Had he not done so, the Presidency might easily have deteriorated into a largely ceremonial office.

The Final Decision. In my own administration, we developed a fine working team of highly competent people. We had efficient organization and good staff work. Some writers have said that I conducted the Presidency largely through staff decisions. This, of course, is nonsense. Naturally, I consulted constantly with my staff, and I valued their opinions. But staff work doesn't mean that you take a vote of your subordinates and then abide by the majority opinion. On important matters, in the end, you alone must decide. As a military leader I had learned this hard lesson. Many times, during my two terms, my decisions ran contrary to the majority opinion of my advisers.

As an example of how decisions are hammered out, I shall mention just one knotty domestic problem that confronted us early in my first term. Even before I assumed the Presidency, I had become convinced that for the economy to forge ahead, government controls of prices and wages must be banished. The political opposition predicted that this would throw the nation into a new spiral of inflation. Some of my own close advisers were opposed; others were divided on how it should be done and when—gradually over a considerable period, or immediately. The decision was mine, and I concluded that we should do it quickly, but step by step.

That's what we did, and in a matter of weeks most controls were dropped. Happily for the country, it worked, and it continued to work. There was very little inflation during my administration, which was an era of remarkable prosperity.

Of all the men in my Cabinet there was no one whom I respected more than Secretary of State John Foster Dulles. I depended greatly on his wisdom. Yet Foster made no important move without consulting the President. I reviewed in advance all his major pronouncements and speeches, and when he was abroad he was constantly in touch by cable and telephone. If we did not see eye to eye—and these instances were rare—it was, of course, my opinion that prevailed; this is the way it has to be. The persistent statement that I turned foreign policy over to Dulles is—to use a more civilized word than it deserves—incorrect.

There is a strange theory among some pundits that smooth organization in the White House indicates that nothing is happening, whereas ferment and disorder are proof of progress. I recall that we had plenty of crises during my administration, but we were able to handle them without turning double handsprings—and usually without unnecessary public flap. In my opinion, a table-pounding executive is ridiculous.

With good executive organization in the White House and the departments, I do not think the heavy burdens of the Presidency need become intolerable. Nor do I believe that a plural Presidency, which has sometimes been suggested, is necessary or would work. In our kind of government, divided authority surely would result only in confusion and frustration.

Finally, I believe deeply that every occupant of the White House, whether he be conservative, liberal or middle-of-the-road, has one profound duty to the nation: to exert moral leadership. The President of the United States should stand, visible and uncompromising, for what is right and decent—in government, in the business community, in the private lives of the citizens. For decency is one of the main pillars of a sound civilization. An immoral nation invites its own ruin.

☆

ON DWIGHT EISENHOWER: *from* The Ordeal of Power *by Emmet John Hughes*

The Eisenhower who rose to fame in the 1940s, under the wartime Presidency of Franklin Roosevelt, brought to the White House of the 1950s a view of the Presidency so definite and so durable as to seem almost a studied retort and rebuke to a Roosevelt. Where Roosevelt had sought and coveted power, Eisenhower distrusted and discounted it: one man's appetite was the other man's distaste. Where Roosevelt had avidly grasped and adroitly manipulated the abundant authorities of the office, Eisenhower fingered them almost hesitantly and always respectfully—or generously dispersed them. Where Roosevelt had challenged Congress, Eisenhower courted it. Where Roosevelt had been an extravagant partisan, Eisenhower was a tepid partisan. Where Roosevelt had trusted no one and nothing so confidently as his own judgment and his own instinct, Eisenhower trusted and required a consensus of Cabinet or staff to shape the supreme judgments and determinations. Where Roosevelt had sought to goad and taunt and prod the processes of government toward the new and the untried, Eisenhower sought to be both guardian of old values and healer of old wounds.

The contrast was quite as blunt in the case of an earlier—and a Republican—Roosevelt. For the Eisenhower who so deeply disliked all struttings of power, all histrionics of politics, would have found

Emmet John Hughes, a former Eisenhower adviser, is a columnist and editorial consultant for *Newsweek* magazine. The selection is from his *The Ordeal of Power* (New York: Atheneum, 1963), pp. 347–350. Copyright © 1962, 1963 by Emmet John Hughes. Reprinted by permission of Atheneum Publishers and the author.

the person and the Presidency of Theodore Roosevelt almost intolerable. He would have applied to this Roosevelt, too, the homely phrase of derision that he reserved for politicians of such verve and vehemence: they were "the desk-pounders." Echoing back across the decades would have come the lusty answer of T.R.—exulting in the Presidency as the "bully pulpit." And it is hard to imagine a concept of the Presidency more alien to Eisenhower: to preach and to yell.

A yet more exact and intimate insight into the Eisenhower Presidency was revealed by his particular tribute to the Abraham Lincoln of his admiration. He was asked, on one occasion, to describe this Lincoln. And he chose these adjectives: "dedicated, selfless, so modest and humble." He made no mention or suggestion of such possible attributes as: imagination, tenacity, single-mindedness, vision. Pressed gently by his interrogator as to whether Lincoln were not something of a "desk-pounder," Eisenhower denied such a notion and spontaneously related the one episode of Lincoln's life that surged to the surface of memory . . .

> Oh no. Lincoln was noted both for his modesty and his humility. For example, one night he wanted to see General McClellan. He walked over to General McClellan's house . . . but General McClellan was out. He . . . waited way late in the evening. But when the general came in, he told an aide . . . he was tired and he was going to bed, and he would see the President the next day. And when criticized later . . . someone told Mr. Lincoln he ought to have been more arbitrary about this. He said: "I would hold General McClellan's horse if he would just win the Union a victory."

The Eisenhower appreciation of Lincoln, in short, reflected one sovereign attitude: all esteemed qualities of the founder of Republicanism were personal and individual, and not one was political or historical. And if the logic of such an estimate were carried coldly to its extreme, it would end in the unspoken implication that the highest national office should be sought and occupied less as an exercise of political power than as a test of personal virtue. To excel in this test, the man would live not *with* the office but *within* it—intact and independent, proudly uncontaminated by power, essentially uninvolved with it. Rather than a political life, this would be a life in politics. Its supreme symbol would be not the sword of authority but the shield of rectitude.

While this self-conscious kind of idealism sprang from deep within the man who was Eisenhower, it found reinforcement—and rationalization—in his explicit theory of political leadership. This theory was profoundly felt and emphatically argued. It claimed even to bespeak a sense of responsibility more serious than the conventional shows of leadership. And no words of Eisenhower stated this theory more succinctly than these:

> I am not a . . . leader. I don't want you to follow me or anything else. If you are looking for a Moses to lead you out of the . . . wilderness, you will stay right where you are. I would not lead you into this promised land if I could, because if I could lead in, someone else could lead you out.

These words might have been spoken by Dwight David Eisenhower—at almost any moment in the years from 1952 to 1960—to the Republican party or, indeed, to the American people at large. They were actually spoken, however, by one of the great leaders of American labor, Eugene V. Debs, more than half a century earlier. And they are worthy of note here as simple evidence that, quite apart from all impulses of personal character, the political posture assumed by Eisenhower toward the challenge of national leadership could not, in fact, be curtly described as negligent, eccentric, or even entirely original.

This posture *was* Eisenhower—remarkably and unshakably—because it was prescribed for him by *both* the temper of the man and the tenets of his politics. In any President, or in any political leader, these two need not necessarily coincide: they may fiercely clash. A man of vigorous and aggressive spirit, restless with the urge for action and accomplishment, may fight frantically against the limits of a political role calling for calm, composure, and self-effacement. Or a man of easy and acquiescent temper, content to perform the minimal duties of his office, may strain pathetically and vainly to fill the vastness of a political role demanding force, boldness, and self-assurance. Eisenhower suffered neither kind of conflict. The definition of the office perfectly suited and matched the nature of the man. And neither critical argument nor anxious appeal could persuade him to question, much less to shed, an attire of leadership so appropriate, so form-fitting, so comfortable.

The want and the weakness in all this was not a mere matter of indecision. The man—and the President—was never more decisive than when he held to a steely resolve *not* to do something that he sincerely believed wrong in itself or alien to his office. The essential flaw, rather, was one that had been suggested a full half-century ago —when the outrageously assertive Theodore Roosevelt had occupied the White House—and Woodrow Wilson had then prophesied that "more and more" the Presidency would demand "*the sort of action that makes for enlightenment."* The requisite for such action, however, is not merely a stout sense of responsibility, but an acute sense of history—a discerning, even intuitive, appreciation of the elusive and cumulative force of every presidential word and act, shaped and aimed to reach final goals, unglimpsed by all but a few. And as no such vision ever deeply inspired the Eisenhower Presidency, there could be no true "enlightenment" to shine forth from its somber acts of prudence or of pride.

This is not to say that the record of the Administration wholly lacked zeal—of a kind. It is doubtful if the leadership of any great nation can endure for nearly a decade without at least the flickering of some such flame of commitment. The man who came closest to a display of such fervor in these years, however, was not the President but his Secretary of State. This man possessed at least his own understanding of what Theodore Roosevelt meant when he spoke of a "pulpit." And yet, this particular ardor of John Foster Dulles could not be enough. For this kind of zeal was neither creative nor impassioned. It was austere, constrained, and cerebral. And in lieu of fire, it offered ice.

Ultimately, all that Eisenhower did, and refused to do, as a democratic leader was rigorously faithful to his understanding of democracy itself. When the record of his Presidency was written and done, he could look back upon it and soberly reflect: "One definition of democracy that I like is merely the opportunity for self-discipline." He lived by this definition. And by all acts of eight years of his Presidency, he urged its acceptance by the people of his nation.

The implications of this simple political credo could not instantly be dismissed as shallow. Forbearance and constraint, patience and discipline—those are not virtues for a democracy to deride. They can be fatefully relevant to the ways of free men.

And yet, by the year 1960, they did not seem to serve or to suffice, as full statement of either the nation's purpose or a President's policy.

☆

JOHN KENNEDY: *Campaign Speech*
on the Presidency

The modern presidential campaign covers every issue in and out of
the platform from cranberries to creation. But the public is rarely
alerted to a candidate's views about the central issue on which all the
rest turn. That central issue—and the point of my comments this
noon—is not the farm problem or defense or India. It is the Presidency itself. Of course a candidate's views on specific policies are
important—but Theodore Roosevelt and William Howard Taft
shared policy views with entirely different results in the White
House. Of course it is important to elect a good man with good intentions—but Woodrow Wilson and Warren G. Harding were both
good men of good intentions—so were Lincoln and Buchanan—but
there is a Lincoln Room in the White House, and no Buchanan
Room.

The history of this nation—its brightest and its bleakest pages—
has been written largely in terms of the different views our Presidents
have had of the Presidency itself. This history ought to tell us that
the American people in 1960 have an imperative right to know what
any man bidding for the Presidency thinks about the place he is bidding for—whether he is aware of and willing to use the powerful
resources of that office—whether his model will be Taft or Roosevelt—Wilson or Harding.

Not since the days of Woodrow Wilson has any candidate spoken

John Fitzgerald Kennedy, a Pulitzer Prize winner for his *Profiles in Courage,*
was 35th President of the United States (1961–1963). This speech was delivered
to the National Press Club on January 14, 1960. © 1960 by The New York
Times Company. Reprinted by permission.

on the Presidency itself before the votes have been irrevocably cast. Let us hope that the 1960 campaign, in addition to discussing the familiar issues where our positions too often blur, will also talk about the Presidency itself—as an instrument for dealing with those issues —as an office with varying roles, powers, and limitations.

During the past eight years, we have seen one concept of the Presidency at work. Our needs and hopes have been eloquently stated—but the initiative and follow-through have too often been left to others. And too often his own objectives have been lost by the President's failure to override objections from within his own party, in the Congress or even in his Cabinet.

The American people in 1952 and 1956 may well have preferred this detached, limited concept of the Presidency after twenty years of fast-moving, creative presidential rule. Perhaps historians will regard this as necessarily one of those frequent periods of consolidation, a time to draw breath, to recoup our national energy. To quote the State of the Union Message: "No Congress . . . on surveying the state of the nation, has met with a more pleasing prospect than that which appears at the present time." Unfortunately this is not Mr. Eisenhower's last message to the Congress, but Calvin Coolidge's. He followed to the White House Mr. Harding, whose "sponsor" declared very frankly that the times did not demand a first-rate President. If true, the times and the man met.

But the question is what do the times—and the people—demand for the next four years in the White House?

They demand a vigorous proponent of the national interest— not a passive broker for conflicting private interests. They demand a man capable of acting as the commander in chief of the grand alliance, not merely a bookkeeper who feels that his work is done when the numbers on the balance sheet come out even. They demand that he be the head of a responsible party, not rise so far above politics as to be invisible—a man who will formulate and fight for legislative policies, not be a casual bystander to the legislative process.

Today a restricted concept of the Presidency is not enough. For beneath today's surface gloss of peace and prosperity are increasingly dangerous, unsolved, long-postponed problems—problems that will inevitably explode to the surface during the next four years of the next Administration—the growing missile gap, the rise of Communist China, the despair of the underdeveloped nations, the explosive situations in Berlin and in the Formosa Straits, the deterioration of NATO, the lack of an arms control agreement, and all the domestic problems of our farms, cities, and schools.

This Administration has not faced up to these and other problems. Much has been said—but I am reminded of the old Chinese proverb: "There is a great deal of noise on the stairs but nobody comes into the room." The President's State of the Union Message reminded me of the exhortation from "King Lear" that goes: "I will do such things—what they are I know not . . . but they shall be the wonders of the earth."

In the decade that lies ahead—in the challenging, revolutionary Sixties—the American Presidency will demand more than ringing manifestoes issued from the rear of the battle. It will demand that the President place himself in the very thick of the fight, that he care passionately about the fate of the people he leads, that he be willing to serve them at the risk of incurring their momentary displeasure.

Whatever the political affiliation of our next President, whatever his views may be on all the issues and problems that rush in upon us, he must above all be the Chief Executive in every sense of the word. He must be prepared to exercise the fullest powers of his office—all that are specified and some that are not. He must master complex problems as well as receive one-page memoranda. He must originate action as well as study groups. He must reopen the channels of communication between the world of thought and the seat of power.

Ulysses Grant considered the President "a purely administrative officer." If he administered the government departments efficiently, delegated his functions smoothly, and performed his ceremonies of state with decorum and grace, no more was to be expected of him. But that is not the place the Presidency was meant to have in American life. The President is alone, at the top—the loneliest job there is, as Harry Truman has said. If there is destructive dissension among the services, he alone can step in and straighten it out—instead of waiting for unanimity. If administrative agencies are not carrying out their mandate—if a brushfire threatens some part of the globe— he alone can act, without waiting for the Congress. If his farm program fails, he alone deserves the blame, not his Secretary of Agriculture.

"The President is at liberty, both in law and conscience, to be as big a man as he can." So wrote Professor Woodrow Wilson. But President Woodrow Wilson discovered that to be a big man in the White House inevitably brings cries of dictatorship. So did Lincoln and Jackson and the two Roosevelts. And so may the next occupant of that office, if he is the man the times demand. But how much better it would be, in the turbulent Sixties, to have a Roosevelt or a Wilson than to have another James Buchanan, cringing in the White House, afraid to move.

Nor can we afford a Chief Executive who is praised primarily for what he did not do, the disasters he prevented, the bills he vetoed—a President wishing his subordinates would produce more missiles or build more schools. We will need instead what the Constitution envisioned: a Chief Executive who is the vital center of action in our whole scheme of government.

This includes the legislative process as well. The President cannot afford—for the sake of the office as well as the nation—to be another Warren G. Harding, described by one backer as a man who "would, when elected, sign whatever bill the Senate sent him—and not send bills for the Senate to pass." Rather he must know when to lead the Congress, when to consult it and when he should act alone. Having served fourteen years in the Legislative Branch, I would not look with favor upon its domination by the Executive. Under our government of "power as the rival of power," to use Hamilton's phrase, Congress must not surrender its responsibilities. But neither should it dominate. However large its share in the formulation of domestic programs, it is the President alone who must make the major decisions of our foreign policy.

That is what the Constitution wisely commands. And even domestically, the President must initiate policies and devise laws to meet the needs of the nation. And he must be prepared to use all the resources of his office to insure the enactment of that legislation—even when conflict is the result. By the end of his term Theodore Roosevelt was not popular in the Congress—particularly when he criticized an amendment to the Treasury appropriation which forbade the use of Secret Service men to investigate congressmen! And the feeling was mutual, Roosevelt saying: "I do not much admire the Senate, because it is such a helpless body when efficient work is to be done." And Woodrow Wilson was even more bitter after his frustrating quarrels—asked if he might run for the Senate in 1920, he replied: "Outside of the United States, the Senate does not amount to a damn. And inside the United States, the Senate is mostly despised. They haven't had a thought down there in fifty years."

But, however bitter their farewells, the facts of the matter are that Roosevelt and Wilson did get things done—not only through their Executive powers but through the Congress as well. Calvin Coolidge, on the other hand, departed from Washington with cheers of Congress still ringing in his ears. But when his World

Court bill was under fire on Capitol Hill he sent no messages, gave no encouragement to the bill's leaders and paid little or no attention to the whole proceeding—and the cause of world justice was set back. To be sure, Coolidge had held the usual White House breakfasts with congressional leaders—but they were aimed, as he himself said, at "good fellowship," not a discussion of "public business." And at his press conferences, according to press historians, where he preferred to talk about the local flower show and its exhibits, reporters who finally extracted from him a single sentence —"I am against that bill"—would rush to file tongue-in-cheek dispatches, proclaiming that: "President Coolidge, in a fighting mood, today served notice on Congress that he intended to combat, with all the resources at his command, the pending bill. . . ."

But in the coming years, we will need a real fighting mood in the White House—a man who will not retreat in the face of pressure from his congressional leaders—who will not let down those supporting his views on the floor. Divided government over the past six years has only been further confused by this lack of legislative leadership. To restore it next year will help restore purpose to both the Presidency and the Congress.

The facts of the matter are that legislative leadership is not possible without party leadership, in the most political sense—and Mr. Eisenhower prefers to stay above politics (although a weekly news magazine last fall reported the startling news that "President Eisenhower is emerging as a major political figure"). When asked, early in his first term, how he liked the "game of politics," he replied with a frown that his questioner was using a derogatory phrase. "Being President," he said, "is a very great experience . . . but the word 'politics' . . . I have no great liking for that." But no President, it seems to me, can escape politics. He has not only been chosen by the nation—he has been chosen by his party. And if he insists that he is "President of all the people" and should, therefore, offend none of them—if he blurs the issues and differences between the parties—if he neglects the party machinery and avoids his party's leadership—then he has not only weakened the political party as an instrument of the democratic process—he has dealt a blow to the democratic process itself. I prefer the example of Abe Lincoln, who loved politics with the passion of a born practitioner. For example, he waited up all night in 1863 to get the crucial returns on the Ohio governorship. When the Unionist candidate was elected, Lincoln wired: "Glory to God in the highest! Ohio has saved the nation!"

But the White House is not only the center of political leadership. It must be the center of moral leadership—a "bully pulpit," as Theodore Roosevelt described it. For only the President represents the national interest. And upon him alone converge all the needs and aspirations of all parts of the country, all departments of the government, all nations of the world. It is not enough merely to represent prevailing sentiment—to follow McKinley's practice, as described by Joe Cannon, of "keeping his ear so close to the ground he got it full of grasshoppers." We will need in the Sixties a President who is willing and able to summon his national constituency to its finest hour—to alert the people to our dangers and our opportunities—to demand of them the sacrifices that will be necessary. Despite the increasing evidence of a lost national purpose and a soft national will, F.D.R.'s words in his first inaugural still ring true: "In every dark hour of our national life, a leadership of frankness and vigor has met with that understanding and support of the people themselves which is essential to victory."

Roosevelt fulfilled the role of moral leadership. So did Wilson and Lincoln, Truman and Jackson and Teddy Roosevelt. They led the people as well as the government—they fought for great ideals as well as bills. And the time has come to demand that kind of leadership again. And so, as this vital campaign begins, let us discuss the issues the next President will face—but let us also discuss the powers and tools with which he must face them. For he must endow that office with extraordinary strength and vision. He must act in the image of Abraham Lincoln summoning his wartime Cabinet to a meeting on the Emancipation Proclamation. That Cabinet had been carefully chosen to please and reflect many elements in the country. But "I have gathered you together," Lincoln said, "to hear what I have written down. I do not wish your advice about the main matter—that I have determined for myself." And later when he went to sign it after several hours of exhausting handshaking that had left his arm weak, he said to those present: "If my name goes down in history, it will be for this act. My whole soul is in it. If my hand trembles when I sign this proclamation, all who examine the document hereafter will say: 'He hesitated.' " But Lincoln's hand did not tremble. He did not hesitate. He did not equivocate. For he was the President of the United States. It is in this spirit that we must go forth in the coming months and years.

☆

JOHN KENNEDY: *Mid-Term Television Conversation on the Presidency*

WILLIAM H. LAWRENCE, American Broadcasting Company. As you look back upon your first two years in office, sir, has your experience in the office matched your expectations? You had studied a good deal the power of the Presidency, the methods of its operations. How has this worked out as you saw it in advance?

THE PRESIDENT. Well, I think in the first place the problems are more difficult than I had imagined they were. Secondly, there is a limitation upon the ability of the United States to solve these problems. We are involved now in the Congo in a very difficult situation. We have been unable to secure an implementation of the policy which we have supported. We are involved in a good many other areas. We are trying to see if a solution can be found to the struggle between Pakistan and India, with whom we want to maintain friendly relations. Yet they are unable to come to an agreement. There is a limitation, in other words, upon the power of the United States to bring about solutions.

I think our people get awfully impatient and maybe fatigued and tired, and saying "We have been carrying this burden for seventeen years; can we lay it down?" We can't lay it down, and I don't see how we are going to lay it down in this century.

So that I would say that the problems are more difficult than I had imagined them to be. The responsibilities placed on the United States are greater than I imagined them to be, and there are greater limitations upon our ability to bring about a favorable

This "Conversation with President Kennedy" was broadcast on December 17, 1962.

136

result than I had imagined them to be. And I think that is probably true of anyone who becomes President, because there is such a
difference between those who advise or speak or legislate, and between the man who must select from the various alternatives proposed and say that this shall be the policy of the United States. It
is much easier to make the speeches than it is to finally make the
judgments, because unfortunately your advisers are frequently divided. If you take the wrong course, and on occasion I have, the
President bears the burden of the responsibility quite rightly. The
advisers may move on to new advice.

MR. LAWRENCE: Well, Mr. President, that brings up a point that
has always interested me. How does a President go about making
a decision, like Cuba, for example?

THE PRESIDENT. The most recent one was hammered out really
on policy and decision over a period of five or six days. During that
period, the fifteen people more or less who were directly consulted
frequently changed their view, because whatever action we took had
so many disadvantages to it, and each action that we took raised
the prospect that it might escalate with the Soviet Union into a
nuclear war. Finally, however, I think a general consensus developed,
and certainly seemed after all alternatives were examined, that the
course of action that we finally adopted was the right one.

Now, when I talked to members of the Congress, several of
them suggested a different alternative, when we confronted them
on that Monday with the evidence. My feeling is that if they had
gone through the five-day period we had gone through in looking at
the various alternatives, the advantages and disadvantages of action,
they probably would have come out the same way that we did. I
think that we took the right one. If we had had to act on Wednes-
day in the first twenty-four hours, I don't think probably we would
have chosen as prudently as we finally did, a quarantine against the
use of offensive weapons.

In addition, that had much more power than we first thought it
did, because I think the Soviet Union was very reluctant to have
us stop ships which carried with them a good deal of their highly
secret and sensitive material. One of the reasons I think that the
Soviet Union withdrew the IL-28's was because we were carrying on
very intensive low-level photography. Now, no one would have
guessed, probably, that that would have been such a harassment.
Mr. Castro could not permit us to indefinitely continue widespread
flights over his island at 200 feet every day, and yet he knew if he
shot down one of our planes, that then it would bring back a much
more serious reprisal on him. So it is very difficult to always make
judgments here about what the effect will be of our decisions on

other countries. In this case, it seems to me that we did pick the right one; in Cuba of 1961 we picked the wrong one.

GEORGE E. HERMAN, Columbia Broadcasting System: I would like to go back to the question of the consensus and your relationship to the consensus. You have said and the Constitution says that the decision can be made only by the President.

THE PRESIDENT. Well, you know that old story about Abraham Lincoln and the Cabinet. He says, "All in favor, say 'aye,'" and the whole Cabinet voted "aye," and then, "All opposed, 'no,'" and Lincoln voted "no," and he said, "The vote is no." So that naturally the Constitution places the responsibility on the President. There was some disagreement with the course we finally adopted, but the course we finally adopted had the advantage of permitting other steps if this one was unsuccessful. In other words, we were starting in a sense at a minimum place. Then if that were unsuccessful, we could have gradually stepped it up until we had gone into a much more massive action, which might have become necessary if the first step had been unsuccessful. I would think that the majority finally came to accept that, though at the beginning there was a much sharper division. And after all, this was very valuable, because the people who were involved had particular responsibilities of their own; Mr. McNamara, Secretary of Defense, who therefore had to advise me on the military capacity of the United States in that area, the Secretary of State, who had to advise on the attitude of the OAS and NATO. So that in my opinion the majority came to accept the course we finally took. It made it much easier. In the Cuba of 1961 the advice of those who were brought in on the executive branch was also unanimous, and the advice was wrong. And I was responsible. So that finally it comes down that no matter how many advisers you have, frequently they are divided, and the President must finally choose.

The other point is something that President Eisenhower said to me on January 19th. He said "There are no easy matters that will ever come to you as President. If they are easy, they will be settled at a lower level." So that the matters that come to you as President are always the difficult matters, and matters that carry with them large implications. So this contributes to some of the burdens of the office of the Presidency, which other Presidents have commented on.

SANDER VANOCUR, National Broadcasting Company: Mr. President, during the Cuban crisis, there was some problem that you are apparently familiar with and bored with by now, about the possibility of a President talking in very private and secret conversations with his advisers, and that somehow leaking out. Do you think that this is going to inhibit the free, frank flow of advice that every President has to have?

THE PRESIDENT. No, I think it is unfortunate there are that sort of conversations, but there are what—1300 reporters accredited to the White House alone? There are I suppose 100 or 150 people who are familiar with what goes on in the Security Council meetings in one way or another. You have the people who are actually there. Then you have got the others who are given instructions as a result of the decisions there, and I suppose people do talk. And then as I said at the time of the Cuban disaster in April of 1961 that success has a hundred fathers and defeat is an orphan. I suppose when something goes well, there is more tendency to talk at all levels, and frequently the reports are inaccurate. I would say the security is pretty good at the National Security Council. It is unfortunate when it is breached.

MR. VANOCUR: Is it true that during your first year, sir, you would get on the phone personally to the State Department and try to get a response to some inquiry that had been made?

THE PRESIDENT. Yes, I still do that when I can, because I think there is a great tendency in government to have papers stay on desks too long, and it seems to me that is really one function. After all, the President can't administer a department, but at least he can be a stimulant.

MR. VANOCUR: Do you recall any response that you received from somebody who was not suspecting a phone call in the State Department, any specific response somebody made to you?

THE PRESIDENT. No, they always respond. They always say "yes." It takes a little while to get it. You know, after I met Mr. Khrushchev in Vienna and they gave us an aide memoire, it took me many weeks to get our answer out through the State Department coordinated with the British, the French, and the Germans. It took much too long. Now, it seems to me we have been able to speed it up, but this is a constant problem in various departments. There are so many interests that are involved in any decision. No matter whether the decision is about Africa or Asia, it involves the Europe desk, it involves the desk of the place, it involves the Defense Department, it might involve the CIA, it frequently involves the Treasury, it might involve the World Bank, it involves the United Nations delegation. So it seems to me that one of the functions of the President is to try to have it move with more speed. Otherwise you can wait while the world collapses.

MR. VANOCUR: You once said that you were reading more and

enjoying it less. Are you still as avid a newspaper reader, magazine—
I remember those of us who traveled with you on the campaign, a
magazine wasn't safe around you.

THE PRESIDENT. Oh, yes. No, no, I think it is invaluable, even
though it may cause you—it is never pleasant to be reading things
that are not agreeable news, but I would say that it is an invaluable
arm of the Presidency, as a check really on what is going on in the
administration, and more things come to my attention that cause
me concern or give me information. So I would think that Mr.
Khrushchev operating a totalitarian system which has many advantages as far as being able to move in secret, and all the rest—there
is a terrific disadvantage not having the abrasive quality of the press
applied to you daily, to an administration, even though we never
like it, and even though we wish they didn't write it, and even
though we disapprove, there isn't any doubt that we could not do
the job at all in a free society without a very very active press.

Now, on the other hand, the press has the responsibility not to
distort things for political purposes, not to just take some news in
order to prove a political point. It seems to me their obligation is
to be as tough as they can on the administration but do it in a way
which is directed towards getting as close to the truth as they can
get and not merely because of some political motivation.

MR. LAWRENCE: Mr. President, in the light of the election returns, which at the congressional level at least were certainly a defeat for the Republican hopes, how do you measure your chances
for significant success domestically in the Congress just ahead?

THE PRESIDENT. Well, I think we will be about in the same position as the last two years. As I say, what we have that is controversial will be very closely contested.

MR. LAWRENCE: Did the complexion of the House change a little
bit by these shifts?

THE PRESIDENT. I would say slightly against us more than it was.
We are not in quite as good shape as we were for the last two years,
but we are about where we were the last two years, which means
that every vote will be three or four votes either way, winning or
losing.

MR. LAWRENCE: Do you have a very crucial vote at the outset on
this Rules Committee fight again, do you think?

THE PRESIDENT. I hope that the Rules Committee is kept to its
present number, because we can't function if it isn't. We are through
if we lose—if they try to change the rules. Nothing controversial
in that case would come to the floor of the Congress. Our whole
program in my opinion would be emasculated.

MR. LAWRENCE: As a young Congressman, sir, you voted to impose a two-term limitation on Presidents. Now that you have held the office for a while, and also observed its effect on President Eisenhower's second term, would you repeat that vote, even if the amendment did not apply to yourself?

THE PRESIDENT. Yes, I would. I would. I know the conditions were special in '47, but I think eight years is enough, and I am not sure that a President, in my case if I were re-elected, that you are at such a disadvantage. There are not many jobs. That is not the power of the Presidency—patronage—at all. They are filled in the first months. Most of those jobs belong to the members of the Congress, anyway. So patronage is not a factor. I think there are many other powers of the Presidency that run in the second term as well as the first. . . . The fact is, President Eisenhower has great influence today in the Republican Party, and therefore in the country, and has great influence in foreign policy, and he does not even hold office. In some ways his influence is greater to some degree. So that the same is really also true of President Truman and President Hoover. I don't think that it depends—the influence of a President is still substantial in his second term, though I haven't had a second term—I think it is.

MR. VANOCUR: Mr. President, on that point, much of your program still remains to be passed by the Congress. There are some people who say that you either do it in the next two years, or it won't be done, should you be elected to a second term. Do you share that point of view?

THE PRESIDENT. No. In the first place, I think we have got a lot by. I was looking at what we set out to do in January of '61 the other day, and on taxes, and on social security, welfare changes, area redevelopment, minimum wage, Peace Corps, the Alliance for Progress, the Disarmament Agency, and strengthening the defenses and strengthening our space program—we did all those things, the trade bill, not perhaps to the extent in every case of our original proposal, but substantial progress. I think we can do some more the next two years. I would think there are going to be new problems if I were re-elected in 1965, and I don't think—I don't look at the second term as necessarily a decline. I don't think that at all. In fact, I think you know much more about the position.

It is a tremendous change to go from being a Senator to being President. In the first months, it is very difficult. But I have no reason to believe that a President with the powers of this office and the responsibilities placed on it, if he has a judgment that some things need to be done, I think he can do it just as well the second time as the first, depending of course on the makeup of the Congress. The fact is I think the Congress looks more powerful sitting

here than it did when I was there in the Congress. But that is because when you are in Congress you are one of a hundred in the
Senate or one of 435 in the House, so that the power is so divided.
But from here I look at a Congress, and I look at the collective
power of the Congress, particularly the bloc action, and it is a substantial power. . . .

MR. LAWRENCE: Mr. President, is your problem of getting an
education bill through this year made more difficult by the events
at Oxford, Mississippi, and the use of federal troops there?

THE PRESIDENT. Yes, I think so . . . this is a case of where we
have come very close, and President Eisenhower came close, and we
came close once, we got a bill through the House—through the
Senate, almost through the House—and we didn't get it. Then another try for higher education through the Senate and the House,
and then it failed—the conference failed. Now, Oxford, Mississippi,
which has made this whole question of the federal government and
education more sensitive, in some parts of the country I suppose
that is going to be a factor against us. I don't really know what
other role they would expect the President of the United States to
play. The court made up of Southern judges determined it was according to the Constitution that Mr. Meredith go to the University
of Mississippi. The Governor of Mississippi opposed it, and there
was rioting against Mr. Meredith, which endangered his life. We
sent in marshals, and after all, 150 or 160 marshals were wounded
in one way or another out of four or five hundred, and at least
three-fourths of the marshals were from the South themselves. Then
we sent in troops when it appeared that the marshals were going
to be overrun. I don't think that anybody who looks at the situation can think we could possibly do anything else. We couldn't
possibly do anything else. But on the other hand, I recognize that
it has caused a lot of bitterness against me and against the national
government in Mississippi and other parts, and though they expect
me to carry out my oath under the Constitution and that is what
we are going to do. But it does make it more difficult to pass an
education bill. . . .

MR. VANOCUR: Do you think we could turn for a moment to this
subject of the President's responsibility in foreign affairs? Now, when
some congressmen disagreed with your course of action over Cuba
on that Monday, the responsibility you have by the Constitution
in this is very clear, but in domestic matters the responsibility is
divided. How do you use the Presidency, in Theodore Roosevelt's
phrase "the bully pulpit," to move these men who really are kind
of barons and sovereigns in their own right up there on the Hill?

Have you any way to move them toward a course of action which you think is imperative?

THE PRESIDENT. Well, the Constitution and the development of the Congress all give advantage to delay. It is very easy to defeat a bill in the Congress. It is much more difficult to pass one. To go through a committee, say the Ways and Means Committee of the House subcommittee and get a majority vote, the full committee and get a majority vote, go to the Rules Committee and get a rule, go to the Floor of the House and get a majority, start over again in the Senate, subcommittee and full committee, and in the Senate there is unlimited debate, so you can never bring a matter to a vote if there is enough determination on the part of the opponents, even if they are a minority, to go through the Senate with the bill. And then unanimously get a conference between the House and Senate to adjust the bill, or if one member objects, to have it go back through the Rules Committee, back through the Congress, and have this done on a controversial piece of legislation where powerful groups are opposing it, that is an extremely difficult task. So that the struggle of a President who has a program to move it through the Congress, particularly when the seniority system may place particular individuals in key positions who may be wholly unsympathetic to your program, and may be, even though they are members of your own party, in political opposition to the President—this is a struggle which every President who has tried to get a program through has had to deal with. After all, Franklin Roosevelt was elected by the largest majority in history in 1936, and he got his worst defeat a few months afterwards in the Supreme Court bill.

So that they are two separate offices and two separate powers, the Congress and the Presidency. There is bound to be conflict, but they must cooperate to the degree that is possible. But that is why no President's program is ever put in. The only time a President's program is put in quickly and easily is when the program is insignificant. But if it is significant and affects important interest and is controversial, therefore, then there is a fight, and the President is never wholly successful.

MR. VANOCUR: Mr. President, which is the better part of wisdom, to take a bill which is completely emasculated, that you had great interest in and accept it, or accept its defeat in the hope of building up public support for it at a later time?

THE PRESIDENT. Well, I would say given the conditions you described, I think it would be better to accept the defeat, but usually what has happened, and what has happened to us in the last two years, a good many of our bills passed in reasonable position, not the way we sent them up, but after all, the Congress has its own will and its own feelings and its own judgment, and they are close to the people. The whole House of Representatives has just been elected. So that it is quite natural that they will have a different perspective than I may have. So I would say that what we ought to do is to do the best we can. But if it is completely emasculated, then there is no sense in having a shadow of success and not the substance.

MR. LAWRENCE: Mr. President, in the exercise of presidential power, and I think perhaps the best-known case and the most widely talked about was your rollback of steel prices after they had been announced by the steel companies, some people have suggested that in retrospect that perhaps you would not have acted so vigorously. Is there any truth in this suggestion?

THE PRESIDENT. I must say it would have been a very serious situation though I don't like to rake over old fires, I think it would have been a serious situation if I had not attempted with all my influence to try to get a rollback, because there was an issue of good faith involved. The steel union had accepted the most limited settlement that they had had since the end of the second war, they had accepted it three or four months ahead, they did it in part, I think, because I said that we could not afford another inflationary spiral, that it would affect our competitive position abroad, so they signed up. Then when their last contract was signed, which was the Friday or Saturday before, then steel put its prices up immediately. It seemed to me that the question of good faith was involved, and that if I had not attempted, after asking the unions to accept the noninflationary settlement, if I had not attempted to use my influence to have the companies hold their prices stable, I think the union could have rightfully felt that they had been misled. In my opinion it would have endangered the whole bargaining between labor and management, would have made it impossible for us to exert any influence from the public point of view in the future on these great labor-management disputes which do affect the public interest. So I have no regrets. The fact is, we were successful.

Now, supposing we had tried and made a speech about it, and then failed. I would have thought that would have been an awful setback to the office of the Presidency. Now, I just think, looking back on it, that I would not change it at all. There is no sense in raising hell, and then not being successful. There is no sense in putting the office of the Presidency on the line on an issue, and then being defeated. Now, an unfortunate repercussion of that was the strong feeling that the government might interfere in a good many labor-management matters, or that it might interfere in the whole question of the free enterprise system. It was regrettable that that general conclusion was drawn in this particular incident. Given the problem that I had on that Tuesday night, I must say I think we had to do everything we could to get it reversed. . . .

MR. VANOCUR: Mr. President, have you noted since you have been in office that this terrible responsibility for the fate of mankind has—notwithstanding the differences that divide you—drawn you and Mr. Khrushchev somewhat closer in this joint sense of responsibility? He seems to betray it, especially in his speech to the Supreme Soviet earlier.

THE PRESIDENT. I think in that speech this week he showed his awareness of the nuclear age. But of course, the Cuban effort has made it more difficult for us to carry out any successful negotiations, because this was an effort to materially change the balance of power, it was done in secret, steps were taken really to deceive us by every means they could, and they were planning in November to open to the world the fact that they had these missiles so close to the United States; not that they were intending to fire them, because if they were going to get into a nuclear struggle, they have their own missiles in the Soviet Union. But it would have politically changed the balance of power. It would have appeared to, and appearances contribute to reality. So it is going to be some time before it is possible for us to come to any real understandings with Mr. Khrushchev. But I do think his speech shows that he realizes how dangerous a world we live in.

The real problem is the Soviet desire to expand their power and influence. If Mr. Khrushchev would concern himself with the real interests of the people of the Soviet Union, that they have a higher standard of living, to protect his own security, there is no real reason why the United States and the Soviet Union, separated by so many thousands of miles of land and water, both rich countries, both with very energetic people, should not be able to live in peace. But it is this constant determination which the Chinese show in the most militant form, and which the Soviets also have shown, that they will not settle for that kind of a peaceful world, but must settle for a Communist world. That is what makes the real danger, the combination of these two systems in conflict around the world in a nuclear age is what makes the sixties so dangerous.

MR. VANOCUR: Ambassador Kennan, who has some knowledge of the Soviet Union, wrote in one of his recent books that what you are dealing with here is a conditioned state of mind, that there is no misunderstanding here, that the only thing the Soviets really understand is when you present them with a set of facts and say to them, "This is what we are going to do." This they understand. Have you found that there is any way to break through to Mr. Khrushchev, to make him really aware that you are quite sincere and determined about what you say, sir, or is this a total——

THE PRESIDENT. Well, it is difficult. I think, looking back on Cuba, what is of concern is the fact that both governments were so far out of contact, really. I don't think that we expected that he would put the missiles in Cuba, because it would have seemed such an imprudent action for him to take, as it was later proved. Now, he obviously must have thought that he could do it in secret and that the United States would accept it. So that he did not judge our intentions accurately.

Well, now, if you look at the history of this century, where World War I really came through a series of misjudgments of the intentions of others, certainly World War II, where Hitler thought that he could seize Poland, that the British might not fight, and if they fought, after the defeat of Poland they might not continue to fight, Korea, where obviously the North Koreans did not think we were going to come in, and Korea, when we did not think the Chinese were going to come in, when you look at all those misjudgments which brought on war, and then you see the Soviet Union and the United States so far separated in their beliefs, we believing in a world of independent sovereign and different diverse nations, they believing in a monolithic Communist world, and you put the nuclear equation into that struggle, that is what makes this, as I said before, such a dangerous time, and that we must proceed with firmness and also with the best information we can get, and also with care. There is nothing—one mistake can make this whole thing blow up. So that—one major mistake either by Mr. Khrushchev or by us here—so that is why it is much easier to make speeches about some of the things which we ought to be doing, but I think that anybody who looks at the fatality lists on atomic weapons, and realizes that the Communists have a completely twisted view of the United States, and that we don't comprehend them, that is what makes life in the sixties hazardous. . . .

MR. HERMAN: Would you explain, sir, why you said in your toast to Chancellor Adenauer that [Cuba] was a turning point, a new era in history?

THE PRESIDENT. I think it is a climactic period. We have had a number of them. It is not *the*, but it is—after all, Cuba was the first time that the Soviet Union and the United States directly faced each other with the prospect of the use of military forces being used by the United States and the Soviet Union, which could possibly have escalated into a nuclear struggle. That is an important fact. Secondly, the Chinese-Indian struggle, between these two enormous countries, the two largest countries in the world, when the Soviet has devoted so many years to building its policy of friendship with India, the fact that China then attacked them. And third, the relation between the Soviet Union and China, as a result of the Sino-Indian dispute, as a result of the United States dispute with the Soviet Union over Cuba, I would say that that makes this a very important period.

MR. VANOCUR: Sir, how do you as the leader of the Western alliance, of the strongest member nation, how do you get the European countries, which are becoming increasingly more independent, increasingly more prosperous, which is what you said you hoped they would become, how do you get them to follow your lead? Apparently Secretaries McNamara and Rusk have not come back with an altogether satisfactory report from the NATO meeting, the Europeans seem unwilling to build conventional forces. Do you have any great power to determine——

THE PRESIDENT. No, in the first place you can do your part. We are doing our part. We have—our troops in Western Europe are the best equipped, we have six divisions, which is about a fourth of all of the divisions on the Western front. They are the best equipped. They can fight tomorrow, which is not true of most of the other units. So we are doing our part there, and we are also providing the largest naval force in the world. We are also providing the nuclear force in the world, and we are also carrying out the major space program for the free world, as well as carrying the whole burden in South Vietnam. So the United States is more than doing its part. We hope Western Europe will make a greater effort on its own, both in developing conventional forces, and in assistance to the underdeveloped world.

Now, we can't force them to do it. We can't say, "Well, if you won't do it, we are going to withdraw our forces and leave Europe naked." But I think the United States has done pretty well in carrying its burdens, and we hope that Western Europe, now that it is prosperous, will do its part. . . .

MR. VANOCUR: Mr. President, back before you were elected, your father used to have a favorite story he told reporters. He asked you once why do you want the job, and he cited the reasons why you shouldn't want it, and you apparently gave him an answer—I don't know whether it satisfied him, but apparently you satisfied yourself. Would you give him the same answer today after serving in this office for two years?

THE PRESIDENT. Oh, you mean that somebody is going to do it?

MR. VANOCUR: Yes, sir.

THE PRESIDENT. Yes. I think that there are a lot of satisfactions to the Presidency, particularly, as I say, we are all concerned as citizens and as parents and all the rest, with all the problems we have been talking about tonight. They are all the problems which if I was not the President, I would be concerned about as a father or as a citizen. So at least you have an opportunity to do something about them. And if what you do is useful and successful, then of course that is a great satisfaction. When as a result of a decision of yours, failure comes or you are unsuccessful, then of course that is a great setback. But I must say after being here for two years, and having the experience of the Presidency, and there is no experience you can get that can possibly prepare you adequately for the Presidency, I must say that I have a good deal of hope for the United States. Just because I think that this country, which as I say criticizes itself and is criticized around the world, 180 million people, for seventeen years, really for more than that, for almost twenty years, have been the great means of defending first the world against the Nazi threat, and since then against the Communist threat, and if it were not for us, the Communists would be dominant in the world today, and because of us, we are in a strong position. Now, I think that is a pretty good record for a country with 6 per cent of the world's population, which is very reluctant to take on these burdens. I think we ought to be rather pleased with ourselves this Christmas.

☆

LYNDON JOHNSON: *Comments on the Presidency*

[The Presidency] is a much tougher job from the inside than I thought it was from the outside.

I have watched it since Mr. Hoover's days, and I realized the responsibilities it carried, and the obligations of leadership that were there, and the decisions that had to be made, and the awesome responsibilities of the office.

But I must say that, when I started having to make those decisions and started hearing from the Congress, the Presidency looked a little different when you are in the Presidency than it did when you are in the Congress, and vice versa. . . .

Thomas Jefferson said the second office of the land was an honorable and easy one. The Presidency was a splendid misery. But I found great interest in serving in both offices, and it carries terrific and tremendous and awesome responsibilities, but I am proud of this nation and I am so grateful that I could have an opportunity that I have had in America that I want to give my life seeing that the opportunity is perpetuated for others.

I am so proud of our system of government, of our free enterprise, where our incentive system and our men who head our big industries are willing to get up at daylight and get to bed at midnight to offer employment and create new jobs for people, where our men working there will try to get decent wages but will sit across the table and not act like cannibals, but will negotiate and reason things out together.

Lyndon B. Johnson, the 36th President of the United States (1963–1969), made these comments during a television interview on March 15, 1964; at a reception for members of the American Society of Newspaper Editors on April 17, 1964; at a campaign rally in Wilkes-Barre, Pennsylvania on October 14, 1964; and at a meeting of the National Association of Broadcasters on April 1, 1968.

I am so happy to be a part of a system where the average per capita income is in excess of $200 per month, when there are only six nations in the entire world that have as much as $80 per month, and while the Soviet Union has three times as many tillable acres of land as we have and a population that's in excess of ours and a great many resources that we don't have, that if properly developed would exceed our potential in water and oil and so forth, nevertheless we have one thing they don't have and that is our system of private enterprise, free enterprise, where the employer, hoping to make a little profit, the laborer, hoping to justify his wages, can get together and make a better mousetrap.

They have developed this into the most powerful and leading nation in the world, and I want to see it preserved. And I have an opportunity to do something about it as President.

And I may not be a great President, but as long as I am here, I am going to try to be a good President and do my dead-level best to see this system preserved, because when the final chips are down it is not going to be the number of people we have or the number of acres or the number of resources that win; the thing that is going to make us win is our system of government.

. . . One of the hardest tasks that a President faces is to keep the time scale of his decisions always in mind and to try to be the President of all the people.

He is not simply responsible to an immediate electorate, either. He knows over the long stretch of time how great can be the repercussions of all that he does or that he fails to do, and over that span of time the President always has to think of America as a continuing community.

He has to try to see how his decisions will affect not only today's citizens, but their children and their children's children unto the third and the fourth generation. He has to try to peer into the future, and he has to prepare for that future.

If the policies he advocates lack this dimension of depth and this dimension of staying power, he may gain this or that advantage in the short term, but he can set the country on a false course and profit today at the expense of all the world tomorrow. So it is this solemn and this most difficult responsibility, and it is always hard to interpret confidently the future patterns of the world.

There are always critics around imploring the President to stick to the facts and not to go crystal-gazing. Some of them tell me to try to keep my feet on the ground, if not my head in the sand.

But this is the point: The facts include today, the overwhelming, built-in, irresistible forces of change that have been unleashed by modern science and technology. And the very facts dissolve and re-group as we look into them.

To make no predictions is to be sure to be wrong. Whatever else is or is not that certain in our dynamic world, there is one thing that is very sure: Tomorrow will be drastically different from today. Yet it is in all of these tomorrows that we and our children and our children's children are going to be forced to live. We have to try to see that pattern and we have to try to prepare for it.

The President of this country, more than any other single man in the world, must grapple with the course of events and the directions of history. What he must try to do, try to do always, is to build for tomorrow in the immediacy of today.

For if we can, the President, and the Congress, and you leaders of the communities throughout the Nation, will have made their mark in history. Somehow we must ignite a fire in the breast of this land, a flaming spirit of adventure that soars beyond the ordinary and the contented, and really demands greatness from our society, and demands achievement from our government. . . .

The world is no longer the world that your fathers and mine once knew. Once it was dominated by the balance of power. Today, it is diffused and emergent. But though most of the world struggles fit-fully to assert its own initiative, the people of the world look to this land for inspiration. Two-thirds of the teeming masses of humanity, most of them in their tender years under forty, are decreeing that they are not going to take it without food to sustain their body and a roof over their head.

And from our science and our technology, from our compassion and from our tolerance, from our unity and from our heritage, we stand uniquely on the threshold of a high adventure of leadership by example and by precept. "Not by might, nor by power, but by my spirit, saith the Lord." From our Jewish and Christian heritage, we draw the image of the God of all mankind, who will judge his chil-dren not by their prayers and by their pretensions, but by their mercy to the poor and their understanding of the weak.

We cannot cancel that strain and then claim to speak as a Chris-tian society. To visit the widow and the fatherless in their affliction is still pure religion and undefiled. I tremble for this Nation. I trem-ble for our people if at the time of our greatest prosperity we turn our back on the moral obligations of our deepest faith. If the face we turn to this aspiring, laboring world is a face of indifference and contempt, it will rightly rise up and strike us down.

Believe me, God is not mocked. We reap as we sow. Our God is still a jealous God, jealous of his righteousness, jealous of his mercy, jealous for the last of the little ones who went unfed while the rich sat down to eat and rose up to play. And unless my administration profits the present and provides the foundation for a better life for all humanity, not just now but for generations to come, I shall have failed. . . .

. . . I think I know some of the things that Americans want. They want their President to be a source of leadership and responsibility. They know that a President who strides forward to do the people's business is a bulwark against the decline and chaos in this country. They know that a President who is willing to move ahead, whose means are just, whose ends are democratic, can be the difference between national stagnation and national progress.

And the people want progress. They want to keep moving.

Americans know that the Presidency belongs to all the people. And they want the President to act and be President of all the people.

Something else is very clear. The source of the President's authority is the people. A President who refuses to go out among the people, who refuses to be judged by the people, who is unwilling to lay his case before the people, can never be President of all the people.

The people want to see their President in person. They want to hear firsthand what he believes. They want to decide if he can act for them.

And unless the President goes to the people, unless he visits and talks with them, unless he senses how they respond as he discusses issues with them, he cannot do the President's job. The voice of the people will be lost among the clamor of divisions and diversities, and the Presidency will not become a clear beacon of national purpose.

As long as I hold it, I will keep the office of President always close to all the people. I think I know what it is the people want, and I make that as a solemn pledge. . . .

. . . The office of the Presidency is the only office in this land of all the people.

Whatever may be the personal wishes or the preferences of any man who holds it, a President of all the people can afford no thought of self. At no time and in no way and for no reason can a President allow the integrity or the responsibility or the freedom of the office ever to be compromised or diluted or destroyed, because when you destroy it, you destroy yourselves.

I hope and I pray that by not allowing the Presidency to be involved in division and deep partisanship I shall be able to pass on to my successor a stronger office, strong enough to guard and defend all the people against all the storms that the future may bring us.

☆

ON LYNDON JOHNSON: *Testimony of Undersecretary of State Katzenbach on the President's Power to Conduct the War in Vietnam*

J. W. FULBRIGHT, Chairman (Senate Foreign Relations Committee): Does the department support or oppose the enactment of Senate Resolution 151? [The resolution stated that it is the sense of the Senate "that a national commitment by the United States to a foreign power necessarily and exclusively results from affirmative action taken by the executive and legislative branches of the United States government through means of a treaty, convention, or other legislative instrumentality specifically intended to give effect to such a commitment."]

MR. KATZENBACH: I could not support the resolution, Mr. Chairman, because it seems to me that it tries to do precisely what the Founding Fathers of this country declined to do in writing the Constitution, and that it purports to take a position, through a Senate resolution, on matters that it seems to me have worked out successfully, have worked out well in terms of distribution of functions between the executive branch and the Congress, and it seems to me that it could be interpreted to seek to join with the President on those matters which I think the President, in his capacity of conducting foreign relations of the United States has the constitutional authority to do. So in short I see no need for it.

Q. Well, let us see if we can develop a few of the specific points.

Nicholas de B. Katzenbach, Undersecretary of State in the Johnson Administration, presented this testimony at Hearings of the Senate Foreign Relations Committee on August 17, 1967. From *The Congressional Record*, August 21, 1967, pp. 11882–11884.

. . . You say: "his"—that is the President—"his is a responsibility born of the need for speed and decisiveness in an emergency. His is the responsibility of controlling and directing all the external aspects of the nation's power."

How do you fit this in with the constitutional provision as to the declaration of war by the Congress?

Yesterday we had one of the nation's leading authorities, Professor [Ruhl] Bartlett. He interprets the Constitution as meaning that the Congress has the exclusive power to initiate war.

A. I believe that the Constitution makes it very clear that on a declaration of war that it is the function of Congress to declare. I believe our history has been that the wars that we have declared have been declared at the initiative and instance of the executive.

The function of the Congress is one to declare. It is not one to wage, not one to conduct, but one simply to declare. That is the function of Congress as expressed in the Constitution.

The use of the phrase "to declare war" as it was used in the Constitution of the United States had a particular meaning in terms of those events, in terms of the practices which existed at that time, and which existed really until the United Nations organization, but it existed for a long time after that, to build on the structure that war was recognized to be an instrument of that policy, not in the climate today, which rejects that, which rejects the idea of aggression, which rejects the idea of conquest. It came in that context.

Now, it came for a function. As you rightly say, it was recognized by the Founding Fathers that the President might have to take emergency action to protect the security of the United States, but that if there was going to be a use of the armed forces of the United States, that was a decision which Congress should check the executive on, which Congress should support. It was for that reason that the phrase was inserted in the Constitution.

It would not, I think, correctly reflect the very limited objectives of the United States with respect to Vietnam. It would not correctly reflect our efforts there, what we are trying to do, the reasons why we are there. To use an outmoded phraseology, to declare war.

Q. You think it is outmoded to declare war?

A. In this kind of a context I think the expression of declaring a war is one that has become outmoded in the international arena, that is not correctly reflected. But I think there is, Mr. Chairman, an obligation on the part of the executive to give Congress the opportunity, which that language was meant to reflect in the Constitution of the United States, to give the Congress of the United States an opportunity to express its views with respect to this. In this instance, in the instance if you will of Vietnam, Congress had an opportunity to participate in these decisions. Congress ratified the SEATO treaty by an overwhelming vote, which expressed the security concerns, the general obligation of the United States in accordance with its constitutional process to attempt to preserve order and peace and defense against aggression in Southeast Asia. That was debated, that was discussed, and it was affirmed by two thirds of the Senate, and in fact confirmed by an overwhelming vote.

Q. You are talking about the SEATO treaty?

A. I am talking about the SEATO treaty. That is not all that happened.

Q. You mentioned that as a basis for the Tonkin Gulf resolution?

[The Resolution—approved by Congress on August 7, 1964—read as follows:

Whereas naval units of the Communist regime in Vietnam, in violation of the principles of the charter of the United Nations and of international law, have deliberately and repeatedly attacked United States naval vessels lawfully present in international waters, and have thereby created a serious threat to international peace;

Whereas these attacks are part of a deliberate and systematic campaign of aggression that the Communist regime in North Vietnam has been waging against its neighbors and the nations joined with them in the collective defense of their freedom;

Whereas the United States is assisting the peoples of Southeast Asia to protect their freedom and has no territorial, military, or political ambitions in that area, but desires only that these peoples should be left in peace to work out their own destinies in their own way;

Now, therefore, be it resolved, by the Senate and House of Representatives of the United States of America in Congress assembled:

Sec. 1. The Congress approves and supports the determination of the President, as Commander in Chief, to take all necessary measures to repel any armed attack against the forces of the United States and to prevent further aggression.

Sec. 2. The United States regards as vital to its national interest and to world peace the maintenance of international peace and security in Southeast Asia. Consonant with the Constitution and the Charter of the United Nations and in accordance with its obligations under the Southeast Asia Collective Defense Treaty, the United States is, therefore, prepared, as the President determines, to take all necessary steps, including the use of armed force, to assist any member or protocol state of the Southeast

Asia Collective Defense Treaty requesting assistance in defense
of its freedom.
Sec. 3. This resolution shall expire when the President shall
determine that the peace and security of the area is reasonably
assured by international conditions created by action of the United
Nations or otherwise, except that it may be terminated earlier by
concurrent resolution of the Congress.]

A. Congress participated in that. As the situation there deteriorated, as American ships were attacked in the Tonkin Gulf, the President of the United States came back to Congress to seek the views
of Congress with respect to what should be done in that area and
with respect to the use of the military of the United States in that
area, and on those resolutions Congress had the opportunity to participate and did participate. The combination of the two, it seems to
me, fully fulfills the obligation of the executive in a situation of this
kind to participate with the Congress, to give the Congress a full and
effective voice, the functional equivalent, the constitutional obligation expressed in the provision of the Constitution with respect to
declaring war.

Q. Well, it is quite true, not only literally, but in the spirit of it.
You haven't requested and you don't intend to request a declaration
of war, as I understand it.

A. As I explained—that is correct, Mr. Chairman, but didn't that
resolution authorize the President to use the armed forces of the
United States in whatever way was necessary? Didn't it? What could
a declaration of war have done that would have given the President
more authority and a clearer voice of the Congress of the United
States than that did?

Q. The circumstances partook of an emergency, as an attack
upon the United States, which could fall within the procedures or
the principles developed in the last century of the temporary repelling
of attacks as opposed to a full-fledged war, which we are in, and he
[Professor Bartlett] was, I thought, quite critical of that, and the circumstances were such that we were asked to act upon this resolution
very quickly. As a matter of fact, he [the President] had already, before the resolution, had responded to the attack by I think an attack
upon the sources of the PT-boats.

It has been interpreted as equivalent to a declaration of war. I
think this is a very critical difference as to how we regard it.

A. It seems to me that if your complaint is the drafting of the
[Tonkin] Resolution of Congress, it ill becomes—

Q. That resolution was drafted by the executive and sent up here.

We didn't draft it, but we did, under the impeller of the emergency, accept it.

A. Mr. Chairman, it wasn't accepted without consideration.

Q. Yes, it was largely without any consideration.

A. Mr. Chairman, whether a resolution of that kind is or is not, does or does not perform the functions similar to a declaration of war must indeed depend upon what the language of that resolution is and what it says. Now the language of that resolution, Mr. Chairman, is a very broad language. . . . It was explained in the debate. You explained it, Mr. Chairman, as head of this committee.

Q. But I misinterpreted it.

A. You explained that bill and you made it clear as it could be what the Congress was committing itself to.

Q. I not only didn't make it clear, obviously, it wasn't clear to me, because I did make statements that I thought this did not entail nor contemplate any change in the then existing policy, and of course there has been great change in it.

It is the waging of war that really concerns us, together with commitments which are made which seem to entail and may eventually entail the waging of war. In this Tonkin Bay, the Tonkin Gulf Resolution, I think it illustrates this distinction that I think should be made clear between repelling of an attack and the waging of war as a matter of broad policy, and I think there was a certain confusion under the circumstances at that moment that at least helped in influencing the Congress in making the approval—

A. Mr. Chairman, the President didn't need such a broad authorization to repel an attack upon American ships in the Tonkin Bay.

Q. That is right.

A. And that isn't what the resolution says—you have authority to repel an attack against ships in the Tonkin Bay. The resolution goes on and that was the reason for the resolution and I do not think it is correct to characterize that resolution as something simply dealing with some PT-boats attacking. That was not the way you presented it, Mr. Chairman, it was not the way the Administration presented it. It was not the way the Congress understood it and it wasn't what it said.

Q. It seems to me that if the Administration had taken the position at the time that this was the equivalent of a declaration of war, in pursuance of the SEATO treaty, it might have made a difference. But it was a fact that at the time it was under consideration, the Administration position was it was not based upon the SEATO treaty. It was based upon repelling the attack, is that not so?

A. That is correct in the sense that at the time of that resolution the evidence with respect to the invasion of South Vietnam, the aggression of North Vietnam against South Vietnam was not so clear.

This is not the kind of thing that we are doing there. And I said that I thought that the reason for that was to give the Congress of the United States an opportunity to look at, to examine, to speak upon the use of armed forces of the United States, that that was the purpose of it.

It seems to me it is clear as anything can be to anyone who reads that resolution and reads the debate.

Q. Mr. Secretary, I don't wish to keep disagreeing with you, but I think it is anything but clear. I think the whole background of the situation then existing, the declarations not only by President Johnson but by President Kennedy before him that in Southeast Asia, in Vietnam, it was not the policy of this country to use American forces, that we were there only to help them. It wasn't our war. That the President shortly thereafter made many statements in which he didn't propose that American men would do the fighting of Asian youths, and so on. He emphasized this. It had been the same statement with President Kennedy, a very similar one.

In other words, the policy as expressed, the general policy, as to waging a war there was against it by the executive themselves. The resolution was in response to an emergency. It wasn't even based as you said upon SEATO, any considered treaty arrangement.

I think in all fairness the circumstances were we were responding to an attack. As you have said, the President didn't need this authority to respond to an attack. And I agree with that, under the previous decision. But we did resolve, we did act and I have said many times I think wrongly, precipitously, without due consideration, to giving authority far beyond that particular attack, that additional authority which the professor described yesterday. This was a mistake.

SENATOR GORE: Mr. Secretary, your presentation lends greater importance to this hearing than I had previously thought was involved. As I understand your statement, it is to the effect that the Tonkir Bay Resolution did in fact grant the broad authority which has beer predicated upon it, and that if Congress acted without understanding such import, then that was the fault of the Congress. This may be true.

MR. KATZENBACH: I do not wish to be misunderstood as saying that the Tonkin Resolution was tantamount to a direct declaration of war, because I have given you the reasons why I think the phraseology "declaration of war," the use of that, would make it misunderstood, our objectives there. What I attempted to say was that the

Tonkin Gulf Resolution gave Congress a voice in this, and that they expressed their will and their voice in that.

They expressed that will, Senator, in the language of that resolution in extremely broad terms. They made reference to the obligations under the SEATO treaty, and it said: "The United States is, therefore, prepared as the President determines to take all necessary action, including the use of armed forces, to assist any member or protocol state in the Southeast Asia Collective Defense Treaty requesting assistance in defense of its freedom."

Now, my point in saying this is that that is an expression of congressional will in this regard. It is an authorization to the President, and in my judgment it is as broad an authorization of war so-called as could be in terms of our internal constitutional process.

Q. I accept that clarification. Nevertheless, the fact stands that a resolution was passed which the President has regarded as a commitment on the part of the Congress that, I have heard speak, understood at the time that they were authorizing the commitment of ground troops, combat troops in Vietnam by the President. I regard this as one of the most tragic mistakes in American history. I did not intend to authorize it. Now, I think it is clear that Congress is in large part at fault in not being precise.

The President has now directed planes to bomb targets within seconds of the most populous nation on earth. Do you think that the President should seek authorization of the Congress to undertake such provocation to run such risk of war between the largest industrial nation and the most populous nation in the world?

A. No.

Q. Do you think the Tonkin Bay Resolution is sufficient?

A. I think our obligations under the SEATO treaty referred to in the Tonkin Bay Resolution, the broad language of that resolution, are adequate. But I would make an additional point if I could, Senator.

In any event, when the Congress has authorized, whether by resolution of this kind, whether by declaration of war, however, the use of the armed forces of the United States, I do not believe that the Congress can then proceed, and I think this was very clear in the constitutional base, can then proceed to tell the President what he shall bomb, what he shall not bomb, where he shall dispose his troops, where he shall not.

Q. Mr. Secretary, if I may respectfully suggest, it appears to me that you are saying on the one hand that Congress is at fault in not sufficiently debating, in not drafting its resolution with sufficient precision to exercise its function in the formulation of policy, and in the extension of authority, but on the other hand, when I raise the question of provocation of possible war between two of the world's greatest nations, you say no, Congress should not be that precise.

Now just how should we operate in this field?

A. I see no fault of the Congress in this respect. I do not think there is any lack of precision in that. I think it expresses the will of Congress. I think they did authorize the use of the armed forces.

Q. It seems to me, Mr. Secretary, that you are now in a way of saying that this resolution authorized a war with China.

A. No, I think the resolution is quite precise in what it authorized. . . . Now in the course of that authorization, there can be risks, there can be risks taken. Other people could be involved. You could have that situation arise. It seems to me that it is very clear in what it says, and I am quite convinced that Congress knew what it was doing when it said it.

Q. You hold that this resolution authorized the use of the United States forces to bomb targets in Laos?

A. I think as far as—that would depend very much, Senator, on what was necessary in terms of coming to the aid of South Vietnam, but it also would depend on many of the facts and circumstances because I do not think that the Congress sought to authorize any action unless that action was justified in repelling an aggression.

Q. Will you please respond to the same question, but I use the word "China" instead of "Laos"?

A. I think that the resolution authorized—

Q. You would give the same answer?

A. The necessary defensive measures in this respect. Now it is in defense of South Vietnam. I think that if China were to invade South Vietnam, that that would present a very different factual situation than exists today. I think the limitation on it, Senator, is a limitation on what is necessary and proper in carrying out the statement, the authorization as was made there.

Now, I think there are risks in the situation, and I think the President has been extremely careful in his conduct of this to avoid those risks.

Q. Now, in the event we discovered that Chinese military advisers were in South Vietnam serving as cadres, organizers, assistants in training and advice in combat against our troops, in those circumstances would you interpret the extent of the authority of the Tonkin Resolution with respect to an attack on China?

A. I do not think—it is difficult for me in a hypothetical situation to attempt to deal with a situation like that. My judgment is so clear on it that the President of the United States would not run the risk of further involvement on those facts that it just becomes to me a purely hypothetical question that it would be hard for me to see that anybody could have contemplated and could have discussed under this situation. . . .

Q. You say it would be difficult for you to interpret this resolution in the light of the hypothesis. It was equally difficult for the Congress. I doubt if any congressman could foresee the bombing of targets within ten miles of China. Taking into consideration the speed of supersonic missiles, the provocation which is involved. Therefore, I come back to the thing about which I started. It seems to me that the thrust of your testimony is that it is incumbent upon the Congress hereafter to consider in detail and precision the grant of authority involved in its action.

☆

RICHARD NIXON: *Campaign Speech on the Nature of the Presidency*

During the course of this campaign, I have discussed many issues with the American people. Tonight, I would like to talk with you about a subject often debated by scholars and the public, but seldom dealt with directly in a Presidential campaign: The nature of the Presidency itself.

What *kind* of leadership should a President give? Is the office too strong, or not strong enough? How can it be made more responsive? Should a President lead public opinion, or follow it? What are the priorities for Presidential attention, and the range of Presidential responsibilities?

Perhaps the best way to begin my own answer is with another question, one I am often asked as I travel around the country: "Why do you seek the office? With all the troubles that we have, why would *anyone* want to be President today?"

The answer is not one of glory, or fame; today the burdens of the office outweigh its privileges. It's not because the Presidency offers a chance to *be* somebody, but because it offers a chance to *do* something.

Today, it offers a greater opportunity to help shape the future than ever before in the nation's history—and if America is to meet its challenges, the next President must seize that opportunity.

We stand at a great turning point—when the nation is groping

Richard Milhous Nixon, the 37th President of the United States (1969-1974), delivered this speech on the CBS and NBC radio networks on September 19, 1968.

for a new direction, unsure of its role and its purposes, caught in a tumult of change. And for the first time, we face serious, simultaneous threats to the peace both at home and abroad.

In this watershed year of 1968, therefore, America needs Presidential leadership that can establish a firm focus, and offer a way out of a time of towering uncertainties. Only the President can hold out a vision of the future and rally the people behind it.

The next President must unite America. He must calm its angers, ease its terrible frictions, and bring its people together once again in peace and mutual respect. He has to take *hold* of America before he can move it forward.

This requires leadership that believes in law, and has the courage to enforce it; leadership that believes in justice, and is determined to promote it; leadership that believes in progress, and knows how to inspire it.

The days of a passive Presidency belong to a simpler past. Let me be very clear about this: The next President must take an activist view of his office. He must articulate the nation's values, define its goals and marshal its will. Under the Nixon Administration, the Presidency will be deeply involved in the entire sweep of America's public concerns.

The first responsibility of leadership is to gain mastery over events, and to shape the future in the image of our hopes.

The President today cannot stand aside from crisis; he cannot ignore division; he cannot simply paper over disunity. He must lead.

But he must bear in mind the distinction between forceful leadership and stubborn willfulness. And he should not delude himself into thinking that he can do everything himself. America today cannot afford vest-pocket government, no matter who wears the vest.

In considering the kind of leadership the next President should give, let us first consider the special relationship—the special trust— that has developed between President and people.

The President is trusted, not to follow the fluctuations of the public-opinion polls, but to bring his own best judgment to bear on the best *ideas* his administration can muster.

There are occasions on which a President must take unpopular measures.

But his responsibility does not stop there. The President has a duty to decide, but the people have a right to know why. The President has a responsibility to tell them—to lay out all the facts, and to explain not only why he chose as he did but also what it means for the future. Only through an open, candid dialogue with the people can a President maintain his trust and his leadership.

It's time we once again had an open administration—open to

ideas *from* the people, and open in its communication *with* the people—an administration of open doors, open eyes and open minds.

When we debate American commitments abroad, for example, if we expect a decent hearing from those who now take to the streets in protest, we must recognize that neither the Department of State nor of Defense has a monopoly on all wisdom. We should bring dissenters into policy discussions, not freeze them out; we should invite constructive criticism, not only because the critics have a right to be heard, but also because they often have something worth hearing.

And this brings me to another, related point: The President cannot isolate himself from the great intellectual ferments of his time. On the contrary, he must consciously and deliberately place himself at their center. The lamps of enlightenment are lit by the spark of controversy; their flame can be snuffed out by the blanket of consensus.

This is one reason why I don't want a government of yes-men. It's why I do want a government drawn from the broadest possible base—an administration made up of Republicans, Democrats and independents, and drawn from politics, from career government service, from universities, from business, from the professions—one including not only executives and administrators, but scholars and thinkers.

While the President is a leader of thought, he is also a user of thought, and he must be a catalyst of thought. The thinking that he draws upon—must be the best in America—and not only in government. What's happening today in America and the world is happening not only in politics and diplomacy, but in science, education, the arts—and in all areas a President needs a constant exposure to ideas that stretch the mind.

Only if we have an Administration broadly enough based philosophically to ensure a true ferment of ideas, and to invite an interplay of the best minds in America, can we be sure of getting the best and most penetrating ideas.

We cannot content ourselves with complacency, with an attiude that because something worked once before, it must be good enough for us now. The world is changing, America is changing, and so must our ideas and our policies change—and our pursuit of the new must be an unremitting pursuit of excellence.

When we think of leadership, we commonly think of persuasion. But the coin of leadership has another side.

In order to lead, a President today must listen. And in this time of searching and uncertainty, government must learn to listen in new ways.

A President has to hear not only the clamorous voices of the organized, but also the quiet voices, the *inner voices*—the voices that speak through the silences, and that speak from the heart and the conscience.

These are the voices that carry the real meaning and the real message of America.

He's got to articulate these voices so that they can be heard, rather than being lost in the wail and bellow of what too often passes today for public discourse. He must be, in the words of Woodrow Wilson, "the spokesman for the real sentiment and purpose of the country."

The President is the one official who represents every American —rich and poor, privileged and underprivileged. He represents those whose misfortunes stand in dramatic focus, and also the great, quiet forgotten majority—the non-shouters and the non-demonstrators, the millions who ask principally to go their own way in decency and dignity, and to have their own rights accorded the same respect they accord the rights of others. Only if he listens to the quiet voices can he be true to this trust.

This I pledge, that in a Nixon Administration, America's citizens will not have to break the law to be heard, they will not have to shout or resort to violence. We can restore peace only if we make government attentive to the quiet as well as the strident, and this I intend to do.

But what of the burdens of the Presidency? Have they, as some maintain, grown beyond the capacity of any one man?

The Presidency has been called an impossible office.

If I thought it were, I would not be seeking it. But its functions have become cluttered, the President's time drained away in trivia, the channels of authority confused.

When questions of human survival may turn on the judgments of one man, he must have time to concentrate on those great decisions that only he can make.

One means of achieving this is by expanding the role of the Vice President—which I will do.

I also plan a re-organized and strengthened Cabinet, and a stronger White House staff than any yet put together.

The people are served not only by a President, but by an Administration, and not only by an Administration, but by a government.

The President's chief function is to lead, not to administer; it is not to oversee every detail, but to put the right people in charge, to provide them with basic guidance and direction, and to let them do the job. As Theodore Roosevelt once put it, "the best executive is the one who has enough sense to pick good men to do what he wants done, and self-restraint enough to keep from meddling with them while they do it."

This requires surrounding the President with men of stature, including young men, and giving them responsibilities commensurate with that stature. It requires a Cabinet made up of the ablest men in America, leaders in their own right and not merely by virtue of appointment—men who will command the public's respect and the President's attention by the power of their intellect and the force of their ideas.

Such men are not attracted to an Administration in which all credit is gathered to the White House and blame parceled out to scapegoats, or in which high officials are asked to dance like puppets on a Presidential string. I believe in a system in which the appropriate Cabinet officer gets credit for what goes right, and the President takes the blame for what goes wrong.

Officials of a new Administration will not have to check their consciences at the door, or leave their powers of independent judgment at home.

Another change I believe necessary stems directly from my basic concept of government. For years now, the trend has been to sweep more and more authority toward Washington. Too many of the decisions that would better have been made in Seattle or St. Louis have wound up on the President's desk.

I plan a streamlined Federal system, with a return to the states, cities and communities of decision-making powers rightfully theirs.

The purpose of this is not only to make government more effective and more responsive, but also to concentrate Federal attention on those functions that can only be handled on the Federal level.

The Presidency is a place where priorities are set, and goals determined.

We need a new attention to priorities, and a new realism about goals.

We are living today in a time of great promise—but also of too many promises. We have had too much wishful imagining that all the ills of man could be set right overnight, merely by making a national "commitment."

A President must tell the people what cannot be done immediately, as well as what can. Hope is fragile, and too easily shattered by the disappointment that follows inevitably on promises unkept and unkeepable. America needs charts of the possible, not excursions into the impossible.

Our cause today is not a nation, but a planet—for never have the fates of all the peoples of the earth been so bound up together.

The tasks confronting the next President abroad are among the most complex and difficult ever faced. And, as Professor Clinton Rossiter has observed, "Leadership in foreign affairs flows today from the President—or it does not flow at all."

The whole structure of power in the world has been undergoing far-reaching changes. While these pose what may be our period of greatest danger, they open what also may be our greatest opportunity. This is a time when miscalculation could prove fatal; a time when the destructive power amassed by the world's great nations threatens the planet. But it is also a time when leaders both East and West are developing a new, sobering awareness of the terrible potential of that power and the need to restrain it.

The judgments of history can bestow no honor greater than the title of peacemaker. It is this honor—this destiny—that beckons America, the chance to lead the world at last out of turmoil and onto that plateau of peace man has dreamed of since the dawn of time. This is our summons to greatness. If we answer the call, generations yet unborn will say of this generation of Americans that we truly mastered our moment, that we at last made the world safe for mankind.

The President cannot stand alone. Today, more than ever in modern times, he must reach out and draw upon the strength of the people.

Theodore Roosevelt called the Presidency "a bully pulpit"; Franklin Roosevelt called it pre-eminently "a place of moral leadership." And surely one of a President's greatest resources is the moral authority of his office. It's time we restored that authority—and time we used it once again, to its fullest potential—to rally the people, to define those moral imperatives which are the cement of a civilized society, to point the ways in which the *energies* of the people can be enlisted to serve the *ideals* of the people.

What has to be done, has to be done by President and people together, or it won't be done at all.

In asking you to join this great effort, I am asking not that you give something *to* your country, but that you do something *with* your country; I am asking not for your gifts, but for your hands. Together, we can hardly fail, for there is no force on earth to match the will and the spirit of the people of America, if that will and that spirit are mobilized in the service of a common aim. . . .

Let me add a personal note. I made a point of conducting my campaign for the nomination in a way that would make it possible to unite the party after the convention. That was successful. I intend now to conduct my election campaign in a way that will make it possible to unite the nation after November. It is not my intention to preside over the disintegration of America or the dissolution of

America's force for good in the world. Rather, I want the Presidency to be a force for pulling our people back together once again, and for making our nation whole by making our people one. We have had enough of discord and division, and what we need now is a time of healing or renewal, and of realistic hope.

No one who has been close to the Presidency would approach its powers lightly, or indifferently, or without a profound sense of the awesome responsibility these powers carry.

Nor should the American people approach this time of challenge without a sense of the majesty of the moment.

Greatness comes from stepping up to events, not from sitting on the sidelines while history is made by others.

History will be made in these years just ahead—history that can change the world for generations to come. So let us seize the moment, and accept the challenge—not as a burden, and not in fear—but in the full confidence that no people has ever had such resources to meet its challenge. Ours is the chance to see the American dream fulfilled at last in the destiny of man. This is the role that history offers; this is the hope that summons us; this is our generation's call to greatness as a nation. This, today, is America's opportunity.

☆

RICHARD NIXON: *Veto Message* and *The War Powers Resolution*

To the House of Representatives:

I hereby return without my approval House Joint Resolution 542 —the War Powers Resolution. While I am in accord with the desire of the Congress to assert its proper role in the conduct of our foreign affairs, the restrictions which this resolution would impose upon the authority of the President are both unconstitutional and dangerous to the best interests of our Nation.

The proper roles of the Congress and the Executive in the conduct of foreign affairs have been debated since the founding of our country. Only recently, however, has there been a serious challenge to the wisdom of the Founding Fathers in choosing not to draw a precise and detailed line of demarcation between the foreign policy powers of the two branches.

The Founding Fathers understood the impossibility of foreseeing every contingency that might arise in this complex area. They acknowledged the need for flexibility in responding to the changing circumstances. They recognized that foreign policy decisions must be made through close cooperation between the two branches and not through rigidly codified procedures.

These principles remain as valid today as they were when our Constitution was written. Yet House Joint Resolution 542 would violate those principles by defining the President's powers in ways which would strictly limit his constitutional authority.

The President's message was sent to Congress on October 24, 1973. His veto was overridden by both Houses on November 7, 1973.

CLEARLY UNCONSTITUTIONAL

House Joint Resolution 542 would attempt to take away, by mere legislative act, authorities which the President has properly exercised under the Constitution for almost 200 years. One of its provisions would automatically cut off certain authorities after sixty days unless the Congress extended them. Another would allow the Congress to eliminate certain authorities merely by the passage of a concurrent resolution — an action which does not normally have the force of law, since it denies the President his constitutional role in approving legislation.

I believe that both these provisions are unconstitutional. The only way in which the constitutional powers of a branch of the Government can be altered is by amending the Constitution — and any attempt to make such alterations by legislation alone is clearly without force.

UNDERMINING OUR FOREIGN POLICY

While I firmly believe that a veto of House Joint Resolution 542 is warranted solely on constitutional grounds, I am also deeply disturbed by the practical consequences of this resolution. For it would seriously undermine this Nation's ability to act decisively and convincingly in times of international crisis. As a result, the confidence of our allies in our ability to assist them could be diminished and the respect of our adversaries for our deterrent posture could decline. A permanent and substantial element of unpredictability would be injected into the world's assessment of American behavior, further increasing the likelihood of miscalculation and war.

If this resolution had been in operation, America's effective response to a variety of challenges in recent years would have been vastly complicated or even made impossible. We may well have been unable to respond in the way we did during the Berlin crisis of 1961, the Cuban missile crisis of 1962, the Congo rescue operation in 1964, and the Jordanian crisis of 1970 — to mention just a few examples. In addition, our recent actions to bring about a peaceful settlement of the hostilities in the Middle East would have been seriously impaired if this resolution had been in force.

While all the specific consequences of House Joint Resolution 542 cannot yet be predicted, it is clear that it would undercut the ability of the United States to act as an effective influence for peace. For example, the provision automatically cutting off certain authorities after 60 days unless they are extended by the Congress could work to prolong or intensify a crisis. Until the Congress suspended the deadline, there would be at least a chance of United States withdrawal and an adversary would be tempted therefore to postpone serious negotiations until the 60 days were up. Only after the Congress acted would there be a strong incentive for an adversary to negotiate. In addition, the very existence of a deadline could lead to an escalation of hostilities in order to achieve certain objectives before the 60 days expired.

The measure would jeopardize our role as a force for peace in other ways as well. It would, for example, strike from the President's hand a wide range of important peacekeeping tools by eliminating his ability to exercise quiet diplomacy backed by subtle shifts in our military deployments. It would also cast into doubt authorities which Presidents have used to undertake certain humanitarian relief missions in conflict areas, to protect fishing boats from seizure, to deal with ship or aircraft hijackings, and to respond to threats of attack. Not the least of the adverse consequences of this resolution would be the prohibition contained in section 8 against fulfilling our obligations under the NATO treaty as ratified by the Senate. Finally, since the bill is somewhat vague as to when the 60 day rule would apply, it could lead to extreme confusion and dangerous disagreements concerning the prerogatives of the two branches, seriously damaging our ability to respond to international crises.

FAILURE TO REQUIRE POSITIVE CONGRESSIONAL ACTION

I am particularly disturbed by the fact that certain of the President's constitutional powers as Commander in Chief of the Armed Forces would terminate automatically under this resolution 60 days after they were invoked. No overt Congressional action would be required to cut off these powers — they would disappear automatically unless the Congress extended them. In effect, the Congress is here attempting to increase its policy-making role through a provision which requires it to take absolutely no action at all.

In my view, the proper way for the Congress to make known its will on such foreign policy questions is through a positive action, with full debate on the merits of the issue and with each member taking the responsibility of casting a yes or no vote after considering those merits. The authorization and appropriations process represents one of the ways in which such influence can be exercised. I do not, however, believe that the Congress can responsibly contribute its considered, collective judgment on such grave questions without full debate and without a yes or no note. Yet this is precisely what the joint resolution would allow. It would give every future Congress the ability to handcuff every future President merely by doing nothing and sitting still. In my view, one cannot become a responsible partner unless one is prepared to take responsible action.

STRENGTHENING COOPERATION BETWEEN
THE CONGRESS AND THE EXECUTIVE BRANCHES

The responsible and effective exercise of the war powers requires the fullest cooperation between the Congress and the Executive and the prudent fulfillment by each branch of its constitutional responsibilities. House Joint Resolution 542 includes certain constructive measures which would foster this process by enhancing the flow of information from the executive branch to the Congress. Section 3, for example, calls for consultations with the Congress before and during the involvement of the United States forces in hostilities abroad. This provision is consistent with the desire of the Administration for regularized consultations with the Congress in an even wider range of circumstances.

I believe that full and cooperative participation in foreign policy matters by both the executive and the legislative branches could be enhanced by a careful and dispassionate study of their constitutional roles. Helpful proposals for such a study have already been made in the Congress. I would welcome the establishment of a non-partisan commission on the constitutional roles of the Congress and the President in the conduct of foreign affairs. This commission could make a thorough review of the principal constitutional issues in Executive-Congressional relations, including the war powers, the international agreement powers, and the question of Executive privilege, and then submit its recommendations to the President and the Congress. The members of such a commission could be drawn from both parties — and could represent many perspectives including those of the Congress, the executive branch, the legal profession, and the academic community.

This Administration is dedicated to strengthening cooperation between the Congress and the President in the conduct of foreign affairs and to preserving the constitutional prerogatives of both branches of our Government. I know that the Congress shares that goal. A commission on the constitutional roles of the Congress and the President would provide a useful opportunity for both branches to work together toward that common objective.

☆

JOINT RESOLUTION
Concerning the war powers of Congress and the President.

Resolved by the Senate and House of Representatives of the United States of America in Congress assembled,

SHORT TITLE

SECTION 1. This joint resolution may be cited as the "War Powers Resolution."

SEC. 2. (a) It is the purpose of this joint resolution to fulfill the intent of the framers of the Constitution of the United States and insure that the collective judgment of both the Congress and the President will apply to the introduction of the United States Armed Forces into hostilities, or into situations where imminent involvement in hostilities is clearly indicated by the circumstances, and to the continued use of such forces in hostilities or in such situations.

(b) Under article I, section 8, of the Constitution, it is specifically provided that the Congress shall have the power to make all laws necessary and proper for carrying into execution, not only its own powers but also all other powers vested by the Constitution in the Government of the United States, or in any department or officer thereof.

(c) The constitutional powers of the President as Commander-in-Chief to introduce United States Armed Forces into hostilities, or into situations where imminent involvement in hostilities is clearly indicated by the circumstances, are exercised only pursuant to (1) a declaration of war, (2) specific statutory authorization, or (3) a national emergency created by attack upon the United States, its territories or possessions, or its armed forces.

CONSULTATION

SEC. 3. The President in every possible instance shall consult with Congress before introducing United States Armed Forces into hostilities or into situations where imminent involvement in hostilities is clearly indicated by the circumstances, and after every such introduction shall consult regularly with the Congress until United States Armed Forces are no longer engaged in hostilities or have been removed from such situations.

REPORTING

SEC. 4. (a) In the absence of a declaration of war, in any case in which United States Armed Forces are introduced—

(1) into hostilities or into situations where imminent involvement in hostilities is clearly indicated by the circumstances;

(2) into the territory, airspace or waters of a foreign nation, while equippped for combat, except for deployments which relate solely to supply, replacement, repair, or training of such forces; or

(3) in numbers which substantially enlarge United States Armed Forces equipped for combat already located in a foreign nation;

the President shall submit within 48 hours to the Speaker of the House of Representatives and to the President pro tempore of the Senate a report, in writing, setting forth —

(A) the circumstances necessitating the introduction of United States Armed Forces;

(B) the constitutional and legislative authority under which such introduction took place; and

(C) the estimated scope and duration of the hostilities or involvement.

(b) The President shall provide such other information as the Congress may request in the fulfillment of its constitutional responsibilities with respect to committing the Nation to war and to the use of United States Armed Forces abroad.

(c) Whenever United States Armed Forces are introduced into hostilities or into any situation described in subsection (a) of this section, the President shall, so long as such armed forces continue to be engaged in such hostilities or situation, report to the Congress periodically on the status of such hostilities or situation as well as on the scope and duration of such hostilities or situation, but in no event shall he report to the Congress less often than once every six months.

CONGRESSIONAL ACTION

SEC. 5. (a) Each report submitted pursuant to section 4(a) (1) shall be transmitted to the Speaker of the House of Representatives and to the President pro tempore of the Senate on the same calendar day. Each report so transmitted shall be referred to the Committee on Foreign Affairs of the House of Representatives and to the Committee on Foreign Relations of the Senate for appropriate action. If, when the report is transmitted, the Congress has adjourned sine die or has adjourned for any period in excess of three calendar days, the Speaker of the House of Representatives and the President pro tempore of the Senate, if they deem it advisable (or if petitioned by at least 30 percent of the membership of their respective Houses) shall jointly request the President to convene Congress in order that it may consider the report and take appropriate action pursuant to this section.

(b) Within sixty calendar days after a report is submitted or is required to be submitted pursuant to section 4(a) (1), whichever is earlier, the President shall terminate any use of United States Armed Forces with respect to which such report was submitted (or required to be submitted), unless the Congress (1) has declared war or has enacted a specific authorization for such use of United States Armed Forces, (2) has extended by law such sixty-day period, or (3) is physically unable to meet as a result of an armed attack upon the United States. Such sixty-day period shall be extended for not more than an additional thirty days if the President determines and certifies to the Congress in writing that unavoidable military necessity respecting the safety of United States Armed Forces requires the continued use of such armed forces in the course of bringing about a prompt removal of such forces.

(c) Notwithstanding subsection (b), at any time that United States Armed Forces are engaged in hostilities outside the territory of the United States, its possessions and territories without a declaration of war or specific statutory authorization, such forces shall be removed by the President if the Congress so directs by concurrent resolution.

CONGRESSIONAL PRIORITY PROCEDURES FOR JOINT RESOLUTION OR BILL

SEC. 6. (a) Any joint resolution or bill introduced pursuant to section 5(b) at least thirty calendar days before the expiration of the sixty-day period specified in such section shall be referred to the Committee on Foreign Affairs of the House of Representatives or the Committee on Foreign Relations of the Senate, as the case may be, and such committee shall report one such joint resolution or bill, together with its recommendations, not later than twenty-four calendar days before the expiration of the sixty-day period specified in such section, unless such House shall otherwise determine by the yeas and nays.

(b) Any joint resolution or bill so reported shall become the pending business of the House in question (in the case of the Senate the time for debate shall be equally divided between the proponents and the opponents), and shall be voted on within three calendar days thereafter, unless such House shall otherwise determine by yeas and nays.

(c) Such a joint resolution or bill passed by one House shall be referred to the committee of the other House named in subsection (a) and shall be reported out not later than fourteen calendar days before the expiration of the sixty-day period specified in section 5(b). The joint resolution or bill so reported shall become the pending business of the House in question and shall be voted on within three calendar days after it has been reported, unless such House shall otherwise determine by yeas or nays.

(d) In the case of any disagreement between the two Houses of Congress with respect to a joint resolution or bill passed by both Houses, conferees shall be promptly appointed and the committee of conference shall make and file a report with respect to such resolution or bill not later than four calendar days before the expiration of the sixty-day period specified in section 5(b). In the event the conferees are unable to agree within 48 hours, they shall report back to their respective Houses in disagreement. Notwithstanding any rule in either House concerning the printing of conference reports in the Record or concerning any delay in the consideration of such reports, such report shall be acted on by both Houses not later than the expiration of such sixty-day period.

CONGRESSIONAL PRIORITY PROCEDURES FOR CONCURRENT RESOLUTION

SEC. 7. (a) Any concurrent resolution introduced pursuant to section 5(c) shall be referred to the Committee on Foreign Affairs of the House of Representatives or the Committee on Foreign Relations of the Senate, as the case may be, and one such concurrent resolution shall be reported out by such committee together with its recommendations within fifteen calendar days, unless such House shall otherwise determine by the yeas and nays.

(b) Any concurrent resolutions so reported shall become the pending business of the House in question (in the case of the Senate the time for debate shall be equally divided between the proponents and the opponents) and shall be voted on within three calendar days thereafter, unless such House shall otherwise determine by yeas and nays.

(c) Such a concurrent resolution passed by one House shall be referred to the committee of the other House named in subsection (a) and shall be reported out by such committee together with its recommendations within fifteen calendar days and shall thereupon become the pending business of such House and shall be voted upon within three calendar days, unless such House shall otherwise determine by yeas and nays.

(d) In the case of any disagreement between the two Houses of Congress with respect to a concurrent resolution passed by both Houses, conferees shall be promptly appointed and the committee of conference shall make and file a report with respect to such concurrent resolution within six calendar days after the legislation is referred to the committee of conference. Nothwithstanding any rule in either House concerning the printing of conference reports in the Record or concerning any delay in the consideration of such reports, such report shall be acted on by both Houses not later than six calendar days after the conference report is filed. In the event the conferees are unable to agree within 48 hours, they shall report back to their respective Houses in disagreement.

INTERPRETATION OF JOINT RESOLUTION

SEC. 8. (a) Authority to introduce United States Armed Forces into hostilities or into situations wherein involvement in hostilities is clearly indicated by the circumstances shall not be inferred—

(1) from any provision of law (whether or not in effect before the date of the enactment of this joint resolution), including any provision contained in any appropriation Act, unless such provision specifically authorizes the introduction of United States Armed Forces into hostilities or into such situations and states that it is intended to constitute specific statutory authorization within the meaning of this joint resolution; or

(2) from any treaty heretofore or hereafter ratified unless such treaty is implemented by legislation specifically authorizing the introduction of United States Armed Forces into hostilities or into such situations and stating that it is intended to constitute specific statutory authorization within the meaning of this joint resolution.

(b) Nothing in this joint resolution shall be construed to require any further specific statutory authorization to permit members of United States Armed Forces to participate jointly with members of the armed forces of one or more foreign countries in the headquarters operations of high-level military commands which were established prior to the date of enactment of this joint resolution and pursuant to the United Nations Charter or any treaty ratified by the United States prior to such date.

(c) For purposes of this joint resolution, the term "introduction of United States Armed Forces" includes the assignment of members of such armed forces to command, coordinate, participate in the movement of, or accompany the regular or irregular military forces of any foreign country or government when such military forces are engaged, or there exists an imminent threat that such forces will become engaged, in hostilities.

(d) Nothing in this joint resolution —

(1) is intended to alter the constitutional authority of the Congress or of the President, or the provisions of existing treaties; or

(2) shall be construed as granting any authority to the President with respect to the introduction of United States Armed Forces into hostilities or into situations wherein involvement in hostilities is clearly indicated by the circumstances which authority he would not have had in the absence of this joint resolution.

SEPARABILITY CLAUSE

Sec. 9. If any provision of this joint resolution or the application thereof to any person or circumstance is held invalid, the remainder of the joint resolution and the application of such provision to any other person or circumstance shall not be affected thereby.

EFFECTIVE DATE

Sec. 10. This joint resolution shall take effect on the date of its enactment.

☆

RICHARD NIXON: *Interview on Watergate*

DAVID FROST (narration): The wave of dissent, occasionally violent, which followed in the wake of the Cambodian incursion prompted President Nixon to demand better intelligence about the people who were opposing him. To this end, the Deputy White House Counsel, Tom Huston, arranged a series of meetings with representatives of the CIA, the FBI and other police and intelligence agencies. These meetings produced a plan—The Huston Plan—which advocated the systematic use of wire-tappings, burglaries or so-called black-bag jobs, mail openings and infiltration against antiwar groups and others. Some of these activities, as Huston emphasized to Nixon, were clearly illegal. Nevertheless, the President approved the plan. Five days later, after opposition from J. Edgar Hoover, the plan was withdrawn, but the President's approval was later to be listed in the Articles of Impeachment as an alleged abuse of Presidential power.

DAVID FROST: Now, when you were concerned about street crime and so on, you went to Congress and got laws passed and so on. Wouldn't it have been better here . . .

RICHARD NIXON. Much too late.

DAVID FROST: . . . wouldn't it have been better here though, to have done what you were going to do legally, rather than doing something that was illegal? I mean, seizing evidence in this way and all of that. In retrospect, wouldn't it have been better to do . . . to combat that crime legally, rather than adding another crime to the list?

This interview with David Frost was televised on May 19, 1977. The transcript is reprinted by permission of Paradine Productions.

RICHARD NIXON. Ah, basically, the proposition you've just stated in theory is perfect; in practice, it just won't work. To get legislation, specific legislation, to have warrantless entries for the purpose of obtaining information and the rest, would not only have raised an outcry, but it would have made it terribly difficult to move in on these organizations, because basically they would be put on notice by the very fact that the legislation was on the books that they'd be potential targets. An action's either going to be covert or not.

DAVID FROST: So, what in a sense you're saying is that there are certain situations, and the Huston Plan or that part of it was one of them, where the President can decide that it's in the best interests of the nation or something, and do something illegal.

RICHARD NIXON. Well, when the President does it, that means that it is not illegal.

DAVID FROST: By definition.

RICHARD NIXON. Exactly. Exactly. If the President . . . if, for example, the President, approves something, approves an action, because of the national security, or in this case because of a threat to internal peace and order of significant magnitude, then the President's decision in that instance, is one that enables those who carry it out to carry it out without violating a law. Otherwise, they're in an impossible position.

DAVID FROST: But, . . . so that . . . just so we understand this. Equally, it would apply presumably. . . these burglaries that we were talking about, that the people would not be open to criminal prosecution at the end; equally, it would . . . in the theoretical case, where the action ordered by the President was a murder, it would also apply, presumably? . . .

RICHARD NIXON. I don't know any . . . I don't know anybody who has been President, or is now who would ever have ordered such an action.

DAVID FROST: No, no, no. I . . . I . . .

RICHARD NIXON. And, I haven't. And, the Huston Plan . . .

DAVID FROST: . . . nor do I . . . nor do I have evidence . . .

RICHARD NIXON. . . . and the Huston Plan . . . and the Huston Plan, as you know, is very carefully worded in terms of how limited it is to be.

DAVID FROST: Yeah. No. But all I was saying was: where do we draw the line? If you're saying that Presidential fiat can, in fact, mean that someone who does one of these black-bag jobs, these burglaries, is not liable to criminal prosecution, why shouldn't the same Presidential power apply to somebody who the President feels in the national interest should murder a dissenter? Now, I'm not saying it's happened. I'm saying: what's the dividing line between the burglar not being liable to criminal prosecution, and the murderer? Or, isn't there one?

RICHARD NIXON. Because, as you know, after many years of studying and covering the world of politics and political science, there are degrees, there are nuances, which are difficult to explain, but which are there. As far as this particular matter is concerned, each case has to be considered on its merits.

DAVID FROST: So that in other words, really, the only dividing line, really, you were saying in that answer, really, between the burglary and murder . . . again, there's no subtle way to say that there was murder of a dissenter in this country because I don't know any evidence to that effect at all. But, the point is: just the dividing line, is that in fact the dividing line is the President's judgment?

RICHARD NIXON. Yes, the dividing line . . . just so that one does not get the impression that a President can run amok in this country and get away with it, we have to have in mind that a President has to come up before the electorate. We also have to have in mind that a President has to get appropriations from the Congress. We have to have in mind, for example, that as far as the CIA's covert operations are concerned, as far as the FBI's covert operations are concerned, through the years, they have been disclosed on a very, very limited basis to trusted members of Congress. I don't know whether it can be done today or not.

DAVID FROST: But, on the other hand, I don't think that . . .

RICHARD NIXON. And that's a restraint.

DAVID FROST: Yes. I don't think, reading the documentation, that it was ever intended, was it, that the Huston Plan and the black-bag robbery should be revealed to the electorate or really . . .

RICHARD NIXON. No.

DAVID FROST: . . . discussed with Congress?

RICHARD NIXON. No, these were not. That's correct. That's correct. . . .

DAVID FROST: Pulling some of our discussions together, as it were . . . speaking of the Presidency and in an interrogatory filed with the Church Committee, you stated, quote, "It's quite obvious that there are certain inherently governmental activities, which if undertaken by the sovereign in protection of the interests of the nation's security are lawful, but which if undertaken by private persons, are not." What, at root, did you have in mind there?

RICHARD NIXON. Well, what I . . . at root what I had in mind I think was perhaps much better stated by Lincoln, during the War Between the States. Lincoln said, and I think I can remember the quote almost exactly, he said, "Actions which otherwise would be unconstitutional, could become lawful if undertaken for the purpose of preserving the Constitution and the nation." Now, that's the kind of action I'm referring to. Of course, in Lincoln's case, it was the survival of the Union. In war time, it's the defense of the nation, and who knows, perhaps the survival of the nation.

DAVID FROST: But, there was no comparison was there between the situation you faced and the situation Lincoln faced, for instance?

RICHARD NIXON. This nation was torn apart in an ideological way by the war in Vietnam, as much as the Civil War tore apart the nation when Lincoln was President. No, it's true that we didn't have the North and South . . .

DAVID FROST: Thirteen states . . .

RICHARD NIXON. . . . fighting each other . . .

DAVID FROST: . . . weren't seceding and there wasn't fighting in that sense.

RICHARD NIXON. I understand. I understand. We didn't have the North and South fighting each other . . . what I was saying, it was torn apart ideologically speaking. I mean, you were there at the time, I mean nobody can know what it means for a President to be sitting in that White House working late at night, as I often did, and to have hundreds of thousands of demonstrators around, charging through the streets. No one can know how a President feels when he realizes that his efforts to bring peace, to bring our men home, to bring our POWs home, to stop the killing, to build peace, not just for our time, but for time to come, is being jeopardized by individuals who have a different point of view as to how things are to be done. Now, that's how I felt about it . . .

DAVID FROST: But, to quote somebody in conflict . . . Chief Justice Charles Evans Hughes, for instance, wrote, "The greater the importance of safeguarding the community from incitements to the overthrow of our institutions by force and violence, the more imperative is the need to preserve inviolate the Constitutional rights of free speech, free press, and free assembly, in order to maintain the opportunity for free political discussion to the end that government may be . . . responsive . . . to the will of the people." Now, in other words, that from the beginning, the founding fathers had said that a little bit of the dangers, as he puts it there, of even incitement to overthrowing of institutions, has to be borne in the cause of freedom.

RICHARD NIXON. What he said has to be taken in the context of the times. When he was Chief Justice, let's remember what the times were. Oh, there was some concern, of course, a little, about domestic violence, and this and that, and some concern about perhaps the Communist threat, although not very great at that time, because Communist subversion hadn't reached a very significant level until long after Hughes left the bench. What we are talking about are two different periods here. The nation was at war when I was President. The nation was at war when Lincoln was President, and incidentally, since you've quoted Charles Evans Hughes, whom I respect incidentally as one of the great Chief Justices, I can go back to Jefferson. Jefferson, after he left the Presidency said, in essence, exactly what Lincoln said, that actions sometimes must be taken, which would otherwise be unlawful, if the purpose of those actions is to preserve the very system that will enable freedom to survive.

DAVID FROST: But, as you said when we were talking about the Huston Plan, you know, "if the President orders it, that makes it legal" as it were. Ah, is the President, in that sense ... is there anything in the Constitution or the Bill of Rights that suggests the President is that far of a sovereign, that far above the law?

RICHARD NIXON. No, there isn't. There's nothing specific that the Constitution contemplates in that respect. I haven't read every word, every jot and every tittle, but I do know this: that it has been, however, argued as far as a President is concerned, that in war time a President does have certain extraordinary powers, which would make acts that would otherwise be unlawful lawful if undertaken for the purpose of preserving the nation and the Constitution which is essential for the rights we're all talking about.

☆

GERALD FORD: *Pardon of Richard Nixon*

Ladies and gentlemen:

I have come to a decision which I felt I should tell you and all of my fellow American citizens, as soon as I was certain in my own mind and in my own conscience that it is the right thing to do.

I have learned already in this office that the difficult decisions always come to this desk. I must admit that many of them do not look at all the same as the hypothetical questions that I have answered freely and perhaps too fast on previous occasions.

My customary policy is to try and get all the facts and to consider the opinions of my countrymen and to take counsel with my most valued friends. But these seldom agree, and in the end, the decision is mine. To procrastinate, to agonize, and to wait for a more favorable turn of events that may never come or more compelling external pressures that may as well be wrong as right, is itself a decision of sorts and a weak and potentially dangerous course for a President to follow.

I have promised to uphold the Constitution, to do what is right as God gives me to see the right, and to do the very best that I can for America.

I have asked your help and your prayers, not only when I became President but many times since. The Constitution is the supreme law of our land and it governs our actions as citizens. Only the laws of God, which govern our consciences, are superior to it.

As we are a nation under God, so I am sworn to uphold our laws with the help of God. And I have sought such guidance and searched my own conscience with special diligence to determine the right thing for me to do with respect to my predecessor in this place, Richard Nixon, and his loyal wife and family.

President Ford (1974-77) assumed office on Richard Nixon's resignation. His *Remarks* were made and the pardon *Proclamation* was signed on September 8, 1974. *Public Papers of the Presidents of the United States: Gerald Ford Vol. I, pp. 101-104.* (Washington, D.C.: United States Government Printing Office, 1975.)

Theirs is an American tragedy in which we all have played a part. It could go on and on and on, or someone must write the end to it. I have concluded that only I can do that, and if I can, I must.

There are no historic or legal precedents to which I can turn in this matter, none that precisely fit the circumstances of a private citizen who has resigned the Presidency of the United States. But it is common knowledge that serious allegations and accusations hang like a sword over our former President's head, threatening his health as he tries to reshape his life, a great part of which was spent in the service of this country and by the mandate of its people.

After years of bitter controversy and divisive national debate, I have been advised, and I am compelled to conclude that many months and perhaps more years will have to pass before Richard Nixon could obtain a fair trial by jury in any jurisdiction of the United States under governing decisions of the Supreme Court.

I deeply believe in equal justice for all Americans, whatever their station or former station. The law, whether human or divine, is no respecter of persons; but the law is a respecter of reality.

The facts, as I see them, are that a former President of the United States, instead of enjoying equal treatment with any other citizen accused of violating the law, would be cruelly and excessively penalized either in preserving the presumption of his innocence or in obtaining a speedy determination of his guilt in order to repay a legal debt to society.

During this long period of delay and potential litigation, ugly passions would again be aroused. And our people would again be polarized in their opinions. And the credibility of our free institutions of government would again be challenged at home and abroad.

In the end, the courts might well hold that Richard Nixon had been denied due process, and the verdict of history would even be more inconclusive with respect to those charges arising out of the period of his Presidency, of which I am presently aware.

But it is not the ultimate fate of Richard Nixon that most concerns me, though surely it deeply troubles every decent and every compassionate person. My concern is the immediate future of this great country.

In this, I dare not depend upon my personal sympathy as a long-time friend of the former President, nor my professional judgment as a lawyer, and I do not.

As President, my primary concern must always be the greatest good of all the people of the United States whose servant I am. As a man, my first consideration is to be true to my own convictions and my own conscience.

My conscience tells me clearly and certainly that I cannot prolong the bad dreams that continue to reopen a chapter that is closed. My conscience tells me that only I, as President, have the constitutional power to firmly shut and seal this book. ~~My conscience tells me it is my duty, not merely to proclaim domestic tranquility but to use every means that I have to insure it.~~

I do believe that the buck stops here, that I cannot rely upon public opinion polls to tell me what is right.

I do believe that right makes might and that if I am wrong, 10 angels swearing I was right would make no difference.

I do believe, with all my heart and mind and spirit, that I, not as President but as a humble servant of God, will receive justice without mercy if I fail to show mercy.

Finally, I feel that Richard Nixon and his loved ones have suffered enough and will continue to suffer, no matter what I do, no matter what we, as a great and good nation, can do together to make his goal of peace come true. [*Mr. Ford then signed the following document.*]

PROCLAMATION GRANTING PARDON TO RICHARD NIXON

By the President of the United States of America a Proclamation

Richard Nixon became the thirty-seventh President of the United States on January 20, 1969 and was reelected in 1972 for a second term by the electors of forty-nine of the fifty states. His term in office continued until his resignation on August 9, 1974.

Pursuant to resolutions of the House of Representatives, its Committee on the Judiciary conducted an inquiry and investigation on the impeachment of the President extending over more than eight months. The hearings of the Committee and its deliberations, which received wide national publicity over television, radio, and in printed media, resulted in votes adverse to Richard Nixon on recommended Articles of Impeachment.

As a result of certain acts or omissions before his resignation from the Office of President, Richard Nixon has become liable to possible indictment and trial for offenses against the United States. Whether or not he shall be so prosecuted depends on findings of the appropriate grand jury and on the discretion of the authorized prosecutor. Should an indictment ensue, the accused shall then be entitled to a fair trial by an impartial jury, as guaranteed to every individual by the Constitution.

It is believed that a trial of Richard Nixon, if it became necessary, could not fairly begin until a year or more has elapsed. In the meantime, the tranquility to which this nation has been restored by the events of recent weeks could be irreparably lost by the prospects of bringing to trial a former President of the United States. The prospects of such trial will cause prolonged and divisive debate over the propriety of exposing to further punishment and degradation a man who has already paid the unprecedented penalty of relinquishing the highest elective office of the United States.

Now, THEREFORE, I, GERALD R. FORD, President of the United States, pursuant to the pardon power conferred upon me by Article II, Section 2, of the Constitution, have granted and by these presents do grant a full, free, and absolute pardon unto Richard Nixon for all offenses against the United States which he, Richard Nixon, has committed or may have committed or taken part in during the period from January 20, 1969 through August 9, 1974.

IN WITNESS WHEREOF, I have hereunto set my hand this eighth day of September, in the year of our Lord nineteen hundred and seventy-four, and of the Independence of the United States of America the one hundred and ninety-ninth.

☆

JIMMY CARTER: *Interview with the Candidate*

PRESIDENTIAL LEADERSHIP

QUESTION: Would you describe in your own words the style and character of leadership you would bring to the presidency?

MR. CARTER. The President ought to be a strong leader. . . . The nation is best served by a strong, independent and aggressive President, working with a strong and independent Congress, in harmony for a change, with mutual respect, in the open.

I have a great respect for the Congress, but I don't consider the Congress to be inherently capable of leadership. I think the Founding Fathers expected the President to be the leader of our country. The President is the only person who can speak with a clear voice to the American people and set a standard of ethics and morality, excellence, greatness. He can call on the American people to make a sacrifice and explain the purpose of the sacrifice, propose and carry out bold programs to protect, to expose and root out injustice and discrimination and divisions among our population. He can provide and describe a defense posture that will make our people feel secure, a foreign policy to make us proud once again.

The degree of strength of the White House is probably proportionate to the confidence and trust of the people in the office of President. There is not a time for timidity, but there is a time for careful, cautious consideration of complicated issues, searching for harmony among the disparate groups that comprise American society. I think the Democrats, and indeed the nation, are looking for an end to distrust. I think we've already seen strong evidence of this desire in the

This interview with Mr. Carter was published in *The National Journal*, July 17, 1976. © The National Journal. Reprinted by permission.

evolution of the Democratic platform, where very controversial issues were handled with sensitivity, and with an adequate degree of aggression, but still an inclination to arrive at a harmonious answer to complicated questions.

The consummation of the platform promises ought to begin in the fall elections when candidates seeking offices of Congress, Senate, possibly governorships, will comment in their own campaigns . . . on the Democratic Party commitments. This would be a good way to bridge the gap among the President and the other office seekers so that during and after that period detailed legislation might be evolved jointly by the President and congressional leaders to carry out the approaches of our party. I think that would be good politics and would also add some substance to the platform promises, which quite often in the past have not been adequately used.

Here is where the President should provide the leadership, and I intend to do that in my major statements during the fall campagin, to cover the items in the platform plus others I might add, to provide a general debate and a framework on which we Democrats can make commitments. So in relationship with Congress and the population of the country and other officials, the leadership, the role of the President is perhaps most important of all. I intend to provide that leadership as a candidate and hopefully as a President.

QUESTION: Would you say that the general tone and mode of leadership that you would exercise as President would be close to or substantially different from the tone and mode of leadership you exercised as governor of Georgia?

MR. CARTER. It would be similar. I can't change my basic character or basic approach. I learned a lot as governor that would stand me in good stead as President. I think I can do a better job now of being aggressive and innovative and dynamic as a leader and also have a closer relationship with the Congress.

Everything I did as governor was done jointly with the legislature. It had to be. But there was room for improvement in personal relationships between myself as governor and the leadership of the legislature that I would hope to realize as President with the leaders of Congress.

QUESTION: Some people have likened your approach to Theodore Roosevelt's — aggressiveness, activism, personal discipline, the theme of moral revitalization in American life. Do you see any parallel there in your own reading of American history?

MR. CARTER. That's a great compliment to me. It's too early to say that I would like to be able to measure up to that kind of standard. But I think it's too early just looking at the campaign to say what kind of President I would be. I've always admired Theodore Roosevelt. Truman had the same approach to the presidency in a much more quiet and less dramatic way. And I think to some degree, Franklin

Roosevelt did too. I've spent a lot of time in the last three to four years reading about various Presidents and their attitude toward the position. I think I would be strong and aggressive—maybe a good deal quieter about it than Theodore Roosevelt.

QUESTION: Is the description by James David Barber of the active-positive President along the lines you'd like to bring to the office?

MR. CARTER. Yes, I think so. Again, it's a very subjective expectation and analysis, I would guess. I would be active and, I think, positive in approach. I don't feel ill at ease. I don't feel afraid of the job. I think I would be able to admit a mistake publicly when one was made.

I would not be reticent to use the office of the White House. I think I would be sure enough about my performance to strip away a maximum amount of secrecy that surrounds the President's function.

DECISION-MAKING

QUESTION: How do you arrive at a decision on a major policy issue?

MR. CARTER. Exact procedure is derived to some degree from my scientific or engineering background—I like to study first all the efforts that have been made historically toward the same goal, to bring together advice or ideas from as wide or divergent points of view as possible, to assimilate them personally or with a small staff, to assess the quality of the points of view and identify the source of those proposals and, if I think the source is worthy, then to include that person or entity into a group I then call in to help me personally to discuss the matter in some depth. Then I make a general decision about what should be done involving time schedules, necessity for legislation, executive acts, publicity to be focused on the issue. Then I like to assign task forces to work on different aspects of the problem, and I like to be personally involved so that I can know the thought processes that go into the final decisions and also so that I can be a spokesman, without prompting, when I take my case to the people, the legislature or Congress.

I have always promised the people willing to help me that we would not yield to political expediency—only when absolutely necessary to save the whole project. I think this gives volunteer contributors a sense of purpose and feeling the governor or President will indeed pursue the ideas proposed aggressively and without reticence. Most of the studies that have been made in the past . . . (on welfare, tax reform, etc.) have wound up in a beautiful bound volume and the President has never put the force of his office behind it. But I don't intend to do that.

QUESTION: Many people suggest that after the many inputs have been made, you make the decision essentially alone. Is that a correct perception?

MR. CARTER. Yes, it is to some degree. In [the Georgia] reorganization, the members of the legislature, the civil service workers, the business, professional and educational communities were intimately involved in the process from the beginning. They also thought they had a role to play in it. Somebody has to make the final decision in areas of controversy. To some degree that circumstance can be minimized by the degree of harmony that you are able to weld among those who do the basic work, and to the extent that the executive leader is part of the whole process. Then the isolated decision-making role can be minimized.

QUESTION: Some persons say that though they admire your decision-making process, that either on policy or strategy, it takes heaven and earth to move you thereafter. Is that allegation of stubbornness on your part fair criticism?

MR. CARTER. I think so. But you have to be certain the position you propose is best, and it can't be a unilateral decision. You have to have a mutual agreement this is the best road to pursue.

Quite often there are alternative decisions that can be made on the same subject with very little to choose one above the other. In grey areas, the necessity to compromise is obvious.

I've always been inclined on a matter of principle or importance not to compromise until it's absolutely necessary. I don't see any reason to compromise away a position early in the stage of negotiations or early in the stage of passage through the Congress or the legislature.

There is a final forum that even transcends the inclination of the legislative body. That's the people themselves. When you do have a difference of opinion with the legislative body, then the people themselves ought to be acquainted with the discussion. I've never had the inclination nor the knowledge about the process to twist arms or force people to vote different from what they thought. But I've always seen the effectiveness of convincing the constituents back home about the question and then giving the legislative members maximum credit for the success achieved. If the legislative leaders can be involved in the initial stages of a project, if they can take credit for what is done, and not be placed in a combative attitude, then most of the disharmonies can be avoided.

QUESTION: Do you see any validity in people's suggestion that when you're convinced the principle is right, the brittleness could be so great you'd get into a Woodrow Wilson-League of Nations type of situation?

MR. CARTER. I can't recall an incident when that's happened yet in my public life.

I've been through profound changes in the Georgia government that involved prison reform, education reform, government reorganization, judicial reform, mental health programs. I can't remember any instance, minor or major, when an adamant position on my part doomed a desirable goal.

QUESTION: There were some comments that Jimmy Carter approached being governor like being skipper of a submarine. As President, would you like to avoid that type of feeling and have a more harmonious working relationship?

MR. CARTER. I don't accept that categorization as accurate. It was made by the present speaker of the Georgia House, Tom Murphy, who's always been a political critic of mine. I never tried to be autocratic as governor or to run other people's feelings.

If I had, I would have had an adamant resistance from the legislature instead of the cooperation we experienced. But I would be much more able now, with the experience of four years as governor, to assure harmony.

OPEN ADMINISTRATION

QUESTION: A constant theme of some observers of the presidency is the dangerous sense of invincibility and infallibility that pervades the White House, especially after there's been a successful campaign and the winning team and its leader are in office. Some talk of "groupthink" — a mutually reinforcing idea that we've conquered the opposition and therefore whatever problem lies ahead of us, even like a Bay of Pigs in the early 60s under Kennedy, we can conquer also. Have you thought about that type of occurrence in your presidency and do you see a way to prevent it happening?

MR. CARTER. Yes. I've thought about it. Obviously I've seen it in other administrations. It's a serious enough matter to make every effort to remember the possibility and also to prevent the eventuality. One obvious measure that can help to prevent that kind of circumstance is a maximum degree of openness in government—a constant relationship between the President and the people of this country and the President and Congress. I favor strong sunshine legislation, and I will pursue that aggressively through executive order. I'll open up as much as I can of the deliberations of the executive branch of government to public scrutiny.

Another measure that could prevent a recurrence of those tragedies is to have foreign and domestic policy shaped with a maximum interrelationship with the congressional leaders. I need their help.

I recognize my inexperience in Washington. Many congressional leaders have already pledged their support to me, if I should become President, in the most complete way. Another prevention that can be instituted is to maintain a staff with free access to me and encouragement of an almost unrestricted debate within the White House circles. I think we had this while I was governor. I guess there were 200 people in the Georgia government who had unimpeded access to me, through memoranda or personally. This was a problem that sometimes I had with department heads because the key members within their departments knew they could come to me directly whenever they chose. I won't go into detail about the sensitive relationship between them and their superiors, but it worked well.

I think this kind of mistake can be prevented. . . .

QUESTION: The type of open presidency you're describing—does that include "pressing the flesh"—or don't you think that's as essential as the kind of communication you're describing?

MR. CARTER. I really don't think that's as essential. It's enjoyable and it's great for the ego of the President. It's fairly nonsubstantial as far as communication is concerned. In transient moments of contact with individual persons, there's very little opportunity for exchange of ideas. I think that would probably be of less significance than earlier, but I would certainly do it on occasion.

QUESTION: People like George Reedy have talked about a republican officer as President—lower case "r"—less emphasis on "Hail to the Chief," great booming guns and so on. Have you given some thought to that?

MR. CARTER. Yes, I'd like to minimize the pomp and circumstance of the office. And I think the American people would appreciate that. I would not form a secret White House "palace guard." I would expect Cabinet members to play a much larger and more autonomous role, much like the role that was played by the cabinet heads when I was governor of Georgia.

I would try to appoint members of the Cabinet in whom I had complete confidence, who could speak clearly to the American people and had judgment enough to act on their own. I would monitor their performance and try to bring cohesion within the executive branch of government as different departments shared a common purpose. But I would not have anyone within the White House try to administer the affairs of the executive branch of government.

QUESTION: You have talked about your contact with everyday citizens, the help you felt that gave you to keep in touch with people when you were governor, and the help it could give in avoiding misadventures as President. Could you give me one or two examples of such contacts, when you were governor, that led you to new policy positions or new insights?

MR. CARTER. Every month I was governor, as I told you before, I had a visitors' day, when anyone who wanted to could come in and see me. On one of the first visitors' days, although my wife and I had already participated publicly in a program for hiring the handicapped, I had a young man with a withered hand who came in to talk to me. He said that it was impossible to take the merit system examination for employment in the state government because he was handicapped. "Well," I said, "I'm sure that your own relatively minor handicap of having one withered hand would not be an obstacle to employment." He said, "They won't even let me take the examination for employment." And I said, "That cannot possibly be the case." And he said, "Governor, I can tell you for a fact that it is." And so I went over and picked up the phone and called the head of our merit system, which is civil service in Georgia, and reported to the administrator of the system what the young man had reported to me. The head of the merit system said, "Yes, sir, that's right. Four or five governors ago a decision was made that we would not employ handicapped people in the state government." So the policy was changed. We later had an aggressive program for hiring the handicapped. But I could very well have gone through a large portion of my administration pushing hiring of the handicapped in private industry and other ways and then discovered that state government had a policy of not hiring handicapped people.

Another example was during my campaign for governor, when it became obvious toward the end of my campaign that I might very well be governor. People would quite quickly come up to me and say "Governor," or "Jimmy," or "Senator, I've got a handicapped child at home, and I hope you'll do something about it." And I would glibly say, "Yes, this is going to be one of the major thrusts of my administration if I'm elected" — just to get votes. I didn't really think seriously about what I was going to do. And after I got the nomination, one day in a grocery story a fellow came up and touched me on the shoulder, and I turned around and he said, "I'm going to vote for you for governor." I said, "Well, I really appreciate that." And he said, "Do you know why?" And I said, "No, why?" "It's because I've got a retarded child at home." And he turned around and walked away. And I stood there shocked in a way to realize that the kind of political statements that I'd been making in the campaign about retarded children was actually such a deep, personal thing for a lot of Georgians. So I marshalled then a major effort to revise completely the mental retardation system in Georgia. I did it successfully, I think. So that's the kind of contact to me that's very important. And under the zero-base budgeting technique, the instigation for change and for better delivery of services is deep within the department among people who actually deliver those services.

VICE PRESIDENCY

QUESTION: Is it possible to make the vice presidency a substantially important position? There's been certainly, with a strong White House staff, a constant tendency to downgrade the Vice President's role, to make sure that he gets neither the exciting nor credit-winning jobs, and he's left with very heavily partisan duties or going to funerals in other parts of the world. Do you think there's a way to prevent that from happening?

MR. CARTER. I think that's an inherent danger. I'm certainly determined to make the vice presidency a substantial position. I see no reason for the President to be worried about challenge in public acceptance or public stature from the Vice President or anyone else. The office of the presidency is so powerful and so much a center of attention that the idea of competition with a Vice President seems quite remote. I hope to have the kind of Vice President, if I am elected, who would share with me all the purposes of the Administration in an easy, unrestrained way. And I think both the President and Vice President are best served, no matter what their future aspirations might be, by working in harmony. I think the people would react adversely to any sort of disharmony or conflict. I think the country loses when a competent Vice President is deprived of an opportunity to serve in a forceful way. . . .

THE CABINET

QUESTION: Some of the experts on presidential leadership—Thomas E. Cronin in particular—say that there are really two Cabinets—the inner Cabinet of Secretary of State, Attorney General, the Secretaries of Treasury and Defense, and the outer Cabinet of Agriculture, Labor, HEW, Transportation, etc. The latter are said, after a few weeks of becoming Cabinet members, to become advocates of the special constituencies that they represent, and to become, as Vice President Charles G. Dawes once said, the natural enemies of the President because they're always trying to get more of the fiscal pie for their special concerns. Often Presidents do interpose staff members to fend off the outer Cabinet members. Do you think that's avoidable? Is there a way to treat your outer Cabinet as counselors rather than advocates?

MR. CARTER. I believe so. Of course the same situation, the same parallel exists in a state government. The best mechanism to minimize this problem is the establishment of long-range goals or purposes of the government and a mutual commitment to those goals by different Cabinet members, both so-called inner and outer Cabinet members. The preparation of the budget in accordance with the long-range goals of the nation would help to cement the different Cabinet functions to a common purpose. Another element is the relevant priorities of the President himself. HEW, for instance. President Johnson was probably more aggressive in trying to deal with human needs than even Secretaries of HEW were.

The same thing applied in other administrations, depending on the relative importance of different elements of government service to the President and his staff. In any instance when the President is laggard in meeting the needs of people, a given Cabinet member in that neglected area will probably be more of an advocate than a counselor. I think that's a good, built-in minor system of checks and balances. And I see nothing wrong with it.

QUESTION: You're saying that you will have no "oversecretaries of domestic affairs" in the White House to whom these Cabinet members speak. Are you making a pledge that if you're elected President these Cabinet members will have direct access to you?

MR. CARTER. That's right. But I would certainly reserve the option of using the Vice President in a major role to be determined later. I would expect the Vice President to help carry out, in a generic sense, the commitments of my Administration and to deal directly with the governors and other state officials, to work closely with the Congress and obviously work directly with the Cabinet members. I would not prevent, though, the governors, mayors, Congress and Cabinet members to have direct access to me.

QUESTION: What kind of people and qualities are you looking for in the Cabinet and other major policy-making roles? What kind of talent hunt method are you thinking of and what goals beyond just the brightest and best people in America—what types of directions are you looking in? How much would you be looking toward traditional establishment figures who've been in other administrations and have an understanding of federal policy making? How much fresh appeal?

MR. CARTER. I think my inclination would be to go toward a new generation of leaders. I would put a strong emphasis on executive management capacity and sensitivity to people's needs. Obviously compatibility would be an important factor—not only with me but with other members of the Cabinet. I would ensure that those who are most dependent on government to meet their human needs would be reassured by the record and reputation and attitudes of the appointments I would make in the field of human rights, civil rights, justice, health, welfare, education, housing, transportation.

I would choose those in whom I have complete confidence to orient government services where services are the most needed— among the poor, deprived, the illiterate, and minority groups—and at the same time have the competence to deliver those services in an efficient, economical way.

I will probably continue to form my opinions about potential Cabinet members in the period following the convention when we start detailed preparation of legislation for issue analysis for the fall election. I will observe personally as much as possible the relative competence of the people who might be in the Cabinet in the future. I would deliberately seek advisers during the pre-election period with that as a major factor. If someone recommended to me a future

Cabinet member, I'd be inclined deliberately to seek out that person as a working companion during the postconvention period so that I could become personally acquainted with him. I would seek the advice obviously of those who've served in previous administrations. I can't say I would never use somebody who had served in a previous administration. Obviously I will use some. But my inclination would be to go to a new generation.

QUESTION: Do you desire a high degree of independence among your Cabinet members?

MR. CARTER. Yes.

QUESTION: Should a President tolerate Cabinet members who dissent from Administration policy as heavily as James R. Schlesinger did as Secretary of Defense?

MR. CARTER. I believe I could prevent that disharmony occurring by being more heavily involved in the evolution of basic commitments. I always managed the affairs of Georgia on long-range goals and I can't imagine a basic strategic difference developing between myself and one of my Cabinet members if the understanding were that we worked toward the long-range goals. There might be some difference on tactics. But I think I could tolerate the degree of independence shown by James Schlesinger—yes.

QUESTION: You recently stated that foreign and domestic issues are becoming more and more interrelated, and "We must develop a policy-making machinery that transcends narrow perspectives." How would you propose to do that?

MR. CARTER. Within the Cabinet structure, and within the process of evolving well understood, publicly described, long-range policies in, for instance, economics and foreign political affairs, there's got to be some coordination. I would not make the Secretary of State the boss over his domestic counterparts. I think that the Secretary of Treasury, the Secretary of Agriculture, the Secretary of Defense, Secretary of Commerce and others all inherently play a major role in the carrying out of matters that relate to foreign policy. Rather than make one of those leaders dominant over all the rest, the coordination has got to come from the President, I would say within the structure of the National Security Council, or perhaps some other Cabinet structure. But I think there ought to be a realization on the part of the Secretary of State that these are the long-range commitments that I've made in the fields of agriculture, commerce, Treasury, and so forth, and that the other Cabinet members have a similar awareness of the long-range commitments in foreign policy, and let me ensure, as President, through proper administrative mechanisms, that the disharmonies among these leaders be minimized. . . .

CONGRESSIONAL RELATIONS

QUESTION: Do you think the recent moves toward increased congressional independence — the War Powers Act and most particularly the new congressional budget process — will make it more difficult for a Democratic President to deal with a Democratic Congress?

MR. CARTER. No. Not necessarily. I think it makes it much more incumbent on the President and Congress to share the responsibilities at the early stage of the evolution of foreign policy. I think the stronger the congressional budgeting process might be, the more sure the nation can feel that the final budget will be both proper, substantive and responsible. So I don't fear that at all. I'll prepare the executive budget, using the zero-base budgeting technique. I'll submit it to the Congress for final disposition. I'll reserve the right to use my influence within the Congress to prevail on recommendations in which I have a deep sense of conviction they're proper. But I don't see anything wrong with the Congress having a very strong, very competent, very responsible budgeting procedure. That's good.

QUESTION: Would you consider negotiation to set common budget goals with the Senate and House Budget Committees?

MR. CARTER. I think consultation would be better than negotiation. I'll reserve the right to make the final decision on the executive budget recommendation. I'll reserve the right to determine how much consultation there ought to be. As the Congress considers the budget that I propose to them, then will come the time for negotiation and consultation in a much more in-depth manner.

QUESTION: When you were governor and consumer legislation was blocked in the legislature, you were openly critical of the special interest lobbies and the legislature's listening to them. Are there circumstances under which a major piece of legislation could be blocked in Congress, and you would feel compelled to make a similar statement as President?

MR. CARTER. Yes. And I would not hesitate to do it. Unfortunately for Georgia, I started working on consumer protection legislation too late. I was so wrapped up in complete reorganization of the government, mental health programs, prison reform, a new basic law on education, judicial reform, zero-based budgeting, that I didn't start early enough in my administration on consumer protection, and the special interest groups prevailed on about half of it. I prevailed — rather the Georgia people prevailed — on the other half.

I would use that influence of going directly to the people and identifying special interest groups that block good legislation. And I believe the President's voice would be much more authoritative and much more clear than any governor's voice could be, because of the close attention paid to the President's statements by the news media — much more so than any governor. . . .

THE BUREAUCRACY

QUESTION: Can a President really control the permanent bureaucratic government in Washington? A corollary is—can the President use inspirational leadership to motivate the civil service?

MR. CARTER. The President can't control the bureaucracy if there's a disharmonious or combative relationship between the President and those responsible for carrying out executive responsibilities. I don't intend to have that kind of relationship. I'll consider the employees of the federal government to be my allies, not my enemies, and try to work intimately with them in the consummation of any changes that relate to their own public service. There's no other source of leadership of a comprehensive nature than the President. In the absence of that leadership, there is no leadership. . . .

FOREIGN POLICY

QUESTION: Would the heaviest priority of your administration be on foreign or domestic affairs?

MR. CARTER. The number one responsibility of any President, above everything else, is to guarantee the security of his country—freedom from fear of attack or successful attack or blackmail, the ability to carry out legitimate foreign policy. I would certainly place that aspect of life and world peace in a pre-eminent position. As far as the amount of time devoted to domestic or foreign affairs, I would guess that most of the time would be devoted to domestic affairs.

QUESTION: Some recent Presidents seem to have had a sickly fascination with foreign affairs—crisis management, the daily secret briefings, dealings with heads of state—all the while avoiding some hard domestic problems and slogging budget questions. Would you seek to avoid that type of diversion of time into foreign affairs?

MR. CARTER. Yes, I would. I think a crucial prerequisite of an effective foreign policy is to restore the confidence and morale and commitment of our people in their own domestic affairs. So I would not use foreign affairs or foreign trips as an escape mechanism to avoid responsibilities on the domestic scene. . . .

QUESTION: In the foreign policy area, would your priorities be more East-West, dealing with traditional allies and the Soviet Union, or North-South, in planning for future relationships with the underdeveloped world?

MR. CARTER. I really see three relationships. One is in our relationship with our natural allies and friends—the democratic, developed nations of the world: Canada, Western Europe, Japan, and others such as Australia, New Zealand, Israel. That's one solid base of strength, mutual purpose, consultation, and it must be maintained. It's been damaged severely, in my opinion, recently.

The second relationship would be the relationship between the democracies of the world and the socialist or Communist nations — our relationship with the Soviet Union and the People's Republic of China. Not a unilateral relationship between the United States and those nations, but as much as possible involving the other democracies of the world.

And third, of course, would be the relationship between the developed nations and the developing nations. And I would like to get as much as possible the OPEC (Organization of Petroleum Exporting Countries) countries and the Soviet Union, for instance, to join with the developed democracies of the world to share the responsibility for the less developed nations. . . .

☆

JIMMY CARTER: *Address on America's*
"Crisis of Confidence"

This is a special night for me. Exactly three years ago, on July 15, 1976, I accepted the nomination of my party to run for President of the United States. I promised you a President who is not isolated from the people, who feels your pain, and who shares your dreams and who draws his strength and his wisdom from you.

During the past three years I've spoken to you on many occasions about national concerns — the energy crisis, reorganizing the Government, our Nation's economy, and issues of war and especially peace. But over those years the subjects of the speeches, the talks, and the press conferences have become increasingly narrow, focused more and more on what the isolated world of Washington thinks is important. Gradually, you've heard more and more about what the Government thinks or what the Government should be doing and less and less about our Nation's hopes, our dreams, and our vision of the future.

Ten days ago I had planned to speak to you again about a very important subject — energy. For the fifth time I would have described the urgency of the problem and laid out a series of legislative recommendations to the Congress. But as I was preparing to speak, I began to ask myself the same question that I now know has been troubling many of you. Why have we not been able to get together as a nation to resolve our serious energy problem?

President Carter delivered this speech to the nation on July 15, 1979.

It's clear that the true problems of our Nation are much deeper — deeper than gasoline lines or energy shortages, deeper even than inflation or recession. And I realize more than ever that as President I need your help. So, I decided to reach out and listen to the voices of America.

I invited to Camp David people from almost every segment of our society — business and labor, teachers and preachers, Governors, mayors, and private citizens. And then I left Camp David to listen to other Americans, men and women like you. It has been an extraordinary ten days, and I want to share with you what I've heard.

First of all, I got a lot of personal advice. Let me quote a few of the typical comments that I wrote down.

This from a southern Governor: "Mr. President, you are not leading this Nation — you're just managing the Government."

"You don't see the people enough any more."

"Some of your Cabinet members don't seem loyal. There is not enough discipline among your disciples."

"Don't talk to us about politics or the mechanics of government, but about an understanding of our common good."

"Mr. President, we're in trouble. Talk to us about blood, sweat and tears."

"If you lead, Mr. President, we will follow."

Many people talked about themselves and about the condition of our Nation. This from a young woman in Pennsylvania: "I feel so far from government. I feel like ordinary people are excluded from political power."

And this from a young Chicano: "Some of us have suffered from recession all our lives."

"Some people have wasted energy, but others haven't had anything to waste."

And this from a religious leader: "No material shortage can touch the important things like God's love for us or our love for one another."

And I like this one particularly from a black woman who happens to be the mayor of a small Mississippi town: "The big-shots are not the only ones who are important. Remember, you can't sell anything on Wall Street unless someone digs it up somewhere else first."

This kind of summarized a lot of other statements: "Mr. President, we are confronted with a moral and a spiritual crisis."

Several of our discussions were on energy, and I have a notebook full of comments and advice. I'll read just a few.

"We can't go on consuming 40 percent more energy than we produce. When we import oil we are also importing inflation plus unemployment."

"We've got to use what we have. The Middle East has only five percent of the world's energy, but the United States has 24 percent."

And this is one of the most vivid statements: "Our neck is stretched over the fence and OPEC has a knife."

"There will be other cartels and other shortages. American wisdom and courage right now can set a path to follow in the future."

This was a good one: "Be bold, Mr. President. We may make mistakes, but we are ready to experiment."

And this one from a labor leader got to the heart of it: "The real issue is freedom. We must deal with the energy problem on a war footing."

And the last that I'll read: "When we enter the moral equivalent of war, Mr. President, don't issue us BB guns."

These ten days confirmed my belief in the decency and the strength and the wisdom of the American people, but it also bore out some of my longstanding concerns about our Nation's underlying problems.

I know, of course, being President, that government actions and legislation can be very important. That's why I've worked hard to put my campaign promises into law—and I have to admit, with just mixed success. But after listening to the American people I have been reminded again that all the legislation in the world can't fix what's wrong with America. So, I want to speak to you first tonight about a subject even more serious than energy or inflation. I want to talk to you right now about a fundamental threat to American democracy.

I do not mean our political and civil liberties. They will endure. And I do not refer to the outward strength of America, a nation that is at peace tonight everywhere in the world, with unmatched economic power and military might.

The threat is nearly invisible in ordinary ways. It is a crisis of confidence. It is a crisis that strikes at the very heart and soul and spirit of our national will. We can see this crisis in the growing doubt about the meaning of our own lives and in the loss of a unity of purpose for our Nation.

The erosion of our confidence in the future is threatening to destroy the social and the political fabric of America.

The confidence that we have always had as a people is not simply some romantic dream or a proverb in a dusty book that we read just on the Fourth of July. It is the idea which founded our Nation and has guided our development as a people. Confidence in the future has supported everything else—public institutions and private enterprise, our own families, and the very Constitution of the United States. Confidence has defined our course and has served as a link between generations. We've always believed in something called progress. We've always had a faith that the days of our children would be better than our own.

Our people are losing that faith, not only in government itself but in the ability as citizens to serve as the ultimate rulers and shapers of our democracy. As a people we know our past and we are proud of it. Our progress has been part of the living history of America, even the world. We always believed that we were part of a great movement of humanity itself called democracy, involved in the search for freedom and that belief has always strengthened us in our purpose. But just as we are losing our confidence in the future, we are also beginning to close the door to our past.

In a nation that was proud of hard work, strong families, close-knit communities, and our faith in God, too many of us now tend to worship self-indulgence and consumption. Human identity is no longer defined by what one does, but by what one owns. But we've discovered that owning things and consuming things does not satisfy our longing for meaning. We've learned that piling up material goods cannot fill the emptiness of lives which have no confidence or purpose.

The symptoms of this crisis of the American spirit are all around us. For the first time in the history of our country a majority of our people believe that the next five years will be worse than the past five years. Two-thirds of our people do not even vote. The productivity of American workers is actually dropping, and the willingness of Americans to save for the future has fallen below that of all other people in the Western world.

As you know, there is a growing disrespect for government and for churches and for schools, the news media, and other institutions. This is not a message of happiness or reassurance, but it is the truth and it is a warning.

These changes did not happen overnight. They've come upon us gradually over the last generation, years that were filled with shocks and tragedy.

We were sure that ours was a nation of the ballot, not the bullet, until the murders of John Kennedy and Robert Kennedy and Martin Luther King, Jr.

We were taught that our armies were always invincible and our causes were always just, only to suffer the agony of Vietnam. We respected the Presidency as a place of honor until the shock of Watergate.

We remember when the phrase "sound as a dollar" was an expression of absolute dependability, until ten years of inflation began to shrink our dollar and our savings. We believed that our Nation's resources were limitless until 1973 when we had to face a growing dependence on foreign oil.

These wounds are still very deep. They have never been healed.

Looking for a way out of this crisis, our people have turned to the Federal Government and found it isolated from the mainstream of our Nation's life. Washington, D.C., has become an island. The gap between our citizens and our Government has never been so wide. The people are looking for honest answers, not easy answers; clear leadership, not false claims and evasiveness and politics as usual.

What you see too often in Washington and elsewhere around the country is a system of government that seems incapable of action. You see a Congress twisted and pulled in every direction by hundreds of well financed and powerful special interests.

You see every extreme position defended to the last vote, almost to the last breath by one unyielding group or another. You often see a balanced and a fair approach that demands sacrifice, a little sacrifice from everyone, abandoned like an orphan without support and without friends.

Often you see paralysis and stagnation and drift. You don't like it, and neither do I. What can we do?

First of all, we must face the truth, and then we can change our course. We simply must have faith in each other, faith in our ability to govern ourselves, and faith in the future of this Nation. Restoring that faith and that confidence to America is now the most important task we face. It is a true challenge of this generation of Americans.

One of the visitors to Camp David last week put it this way: "We've got to stop crying and start sweating, stop talking and start walking, stop cursing and start praying. The strength we need will not come from the White House, but from every house in America."

We know the strength of America. We are strong. We can regain our unity. We can regain our confidence. We are the heirs of generations who survived threats much more powerful and awesome than those that challenge us now. Our fathers and mothers were strong men and women who shaped a new society during the Great Depression, who fought world wars, and who carved out a new charter of peace for the world.

We ourselves are the same Americans who just ten years ago put a man on the Moon. We are the generation that dedicated our society to the pursuit of human rights and equality. And we are the generation that will win the war on the energy problem and in that process rebuild the unity and confidence of America.

We are at a turning point in our history. There are two paths to choose. One is a path I've warned about tonight, the path that leads to fragmentation and self-interest. Down that road lies a mistaken idea of freedom, the right to grasp for ourselves some advantage over others. That path would be one of constant conflict between narrow interests ending in chaos and immobility. It is a certain route to failure.

All the traditions of our past, all the lessons of our heritage, all the promises of our future point to another path, the path of common purpose and the restoration of American values. That path leads to true freedom for our Nation and ourselves. . . .

I will continue to travel this country, to hear the people of America. You can help me to develop a national agenda for the 1980's. I will listen and I will act. We will act together. These were the promises I made three years ago, and I intend to keep them.

Little by little we can and we must rebuild our confidence. We can spend until we empty our treasuries, and we may summon all the wonders of science. But we can succeed only if we tap our greatest resources — America's people, America's values, and America's confidence.

I have seen the strength of America in the inexhaustible resources of our people. In the days to come, let us renew that strength in the struggle for an energy-secure nation.

In closing, let me say this: I will do my best, but I will not do it alone. Let your voice be heard. Whenever you have a chance, say something good about our country. With God's help and for the sake of our Nation, it is time for us to join hands in America. Let us commit ourselves together to a rebirth of the American spirit. Working together with our common faith we cannot fail.

Thank you and good night.

☆

RONALD REAGAN: *Inaugural Address*

Thank you. Senator Hatfield, Mr. Chief Justice, Mr. President, Vice President Bush, Vice President Mondale, Senator Baker, Speaker O'Neill, Reverend Moomaw, and my fellow citizens:

To a few of us here today this is a solemn and most momentous occasion. And, yet, in the history of our nation it is a commonplace occurrence.

The orderly transfer of authority as called for in the Constitution routinely takes places as it has for almost two centuries and few of us stop to think how unique we really are.

In the eyes of many in the world, this every-four-year ceremony we accept as normal is nothing less than a miracle.

Mr. President, I want our fellow citizens to know how much you did to carry on this tradition.

By your gracious cooperation in the transition process you have shown a watching world that we are a united people pledged to maintaining a political system which guarantees individual liberty to a greater degree than any other. And I thank you and your people for all your help in maintaining the continuity which is the bulwark of our republic.

SEVERE ECONOMIC PROBLEM

The business of our nation goes forward.

These United States are confronted with an economic affliction of great proportions.

The Inauguration of Ronald Reagan as 40th President of the United States took place on January 20, 1981.

206

We suffer from the longest and one of the worst sustained inflations in our national history. It distorts our economic decisions, penalizes thrift and crushes the struggling young and the fixed-income elderly alike. It threatens to shatter the lives of millions of our people.

Idle industries have cast workers into unemployment, human misery and personal indignity.

Those who do work are denied a fair return for their labor by a tax system which penalizes successful achievement and keeps us from maintaining full productivity.

But great as our tax burden is, it has not kept pace with public spending. For decades we have piled deficit upon deficit, mortgaging our future and our children's future for the temporary convenience of the present.

To continue this long trend is to guarantee tremendous social, cultural, political and economic upheavals.

You and I, as individuals, can, by borrowing, live beyond our means, but for only a limited period of time. Why then should we think that collectively, as a nation, we are not bound by that same limitation?

ACTION 'BEGINNING TODAY'

We must act today in order to preserve tomorrow. And let there be no misunderstanding—we're going to begin to act beginning today.

The economic ills we suffer have come upon us over several decades.

They will not go away in days, weeks or months, but they will go away. They will go away because we as Americans have the capacity now, as we have had in the past, to do whatever needs to be done to preserve this last and greatest bastion of freedom.

In this present crisis, government is not the solution to our problem; government *is* the problem.

From time to time we've been tempted to believe that society has become too complex to be managed by self-rule, that government by an elite group is superior to government for, by and of the people.

But if no one among us is capable of governing himself, then who among us has the capacity to govern someone else?

All of us together—in and out of government—must bear the burden. The solutions we seek must be equitable with no one group singled out to pay a higher price.

We hear much of special interest groups. Well our concern must be for a special interest group that has been too long neglected.

It knows no sectional boundaries, or ethnic and racial divisions and it crosses political party lines. It is made up of men and women who raise our food, patrol our streets, man our mines and factories, teach our children, keep our homes and heal us when we're sick.

Professionals, industrialists, shopkeepers, clerks, cabbies and truck drivers. They are, in short, "We the people." This breed called Americans.

Well, this Administration's objective will be a healthy, vigorous, growing economy that provides equal opportunities for all Americans with no barriers born of bigotry or discrimination.

Putting America back to work means putting all Americans back to work. Ending inflation means freeing all Americans from the terror of runaway living costs.

All must share in the productive work of this "new beginning," and all must share in the bounty of a revived economy.

With the idealism and fair play which are the core of our system and our strength, we can have a strong, prosperous America at peace with itself and the world.

INVENTORY AS A BEGINNING

So as we begin, let us take inventory.

We are a nation that has a government — not the other way around. And this makes us special among the nations of the earth.

Our Government has no power except that granted it by the people. It is time to check and reverse the growth of government which shows signs of having grown beyond the consent of the governed.

It is my intention to curb the size and influence of the Federal establishment and to demand recognition of the distinction between the powers granted to the Federal Government and those reserved to the states or to the people.

All of us — all of us need to be reminded that the Federal Government did not create the states; the states created the Federal Government.

Now, so there will be no misunderstanding, it's not my intention to do away with government.

It is rather to make it work — work with us, not over us; to stand by our side, not ride on our back. Government can and must provide opportunity, not smother it; foster productivity, not stifle it.

UNLEASHING ENERGY AND GENIUS

If we look to the answer as to why for so many years we achieved so much, prospered as no other people on earth, it was because here in this land we unleashed the energy and individual genius of man to a greater extent than has ever been done before.

Freedom and the dignity of the individual have been more available and assured here than in any other place on earth. The price for this freedom at times has been high, but we have never been unwilling to pay that price.

It is no coincidence that our present troubles parallel and are proportionate to the intervention and intrusion in our lives that result from unnecessary and excessive growth of Government.

It is time for us to realize that we are too great a nation to limit ourselves to small dreams. We're not, as some would have us believe, doomed to an inevitable decline. I do not believe in a fate that will fall on us no matter what we do. I do believe in a fate that will fall on us if we do nothing.

So, with all the creative energy at our command let us begin an era of national renewal. Let us renew our determination, our courage and our strength. And let us renew our faith and our hope. We have every right to dream heroic dreams.

HEROES AT FACTORY GATES

Those who say that we're in a time when there are no heroes — they just don't know where to look. You can see heroes every day going in and out of factory gates. Others, a handful in number, produce enough food to feed all of us and then the world beyond.

You meet heroes across a counter — and they're on both sides of that counter. There are entrepreneurs with faith in themselves and faith in an idea who create new jobs, new wealth and opportunity.

There are individuals and families whose taxes support the Government and whose voluntary gifts support church, charity, culture, art and education. Their patriotism is quiet but deep. Their values sustain our national life.

Now, I have used the words "they" and "their" in speaking of these heroes. I could say "you" and "your" because I'm addressing the heroes of whom I speak — you, the citizens of this blessed land.

Your dreams, your hopes, your goals are going to be the dreams, the hopes and the goals of this Administration, so help me God.

We shall reflect the compassion that is so much a part of your makeup.

LOVING OUR COUNTRYMEN

How can we love our country and not love our countrymen? And loving them reach out a hand when they fall, heal them when they're sick and provide opportunity to make them self-sufficient so they will be equal in fact and not just in theory?

Can we solve the problems confronting us? Well the answer is an unequivocal and emphatic yes.

To paraphrase Winston Churchill, I did not take the oath I've just taken with the intention of presiding over the dissolution of the world's strongest economy.

In the days ahead I will propose removing the roadblocks that have slowed our economy and reduced productivity.

Steps will be taken aimed at restoring the balance between the various levels of government. Progress may be slow—measured in inches and feet, not miles—but we will progress.

It is time to reawaken this industrial giant, to get government back within its means and to lighten our punitive tax burden.

And these will be our first priorities, and on these principles there will be no compromise.

THE FIGHT FOR INDEPENDENCE

On the eve of our struggle for independence a man who might've been one of the greatest among the Founding Fathers, Dr. Joseph Warren, president of the Massachusetts Congress, said to his fellow Americans, "Our country is in danger, but not to be despaired of. On you depend the fortunes of America. You are to decide the important question upon which rest the happiness and the liberty of millions yet unborn. Act worthy of yourselves."

Well I believe we the Americans of today are ready to act worthy of ourselves, ready to do what must be done to ensure happiness and liberty for ourselves, our children and our children's children.

And as we renew ourselves here in our own land we will be seen as having greater strength throughout the world. We will again be the exemplar of freedom and a beacon of hope for those who do not now have freedom.

To those neighbors and allies who share our freedom, we will strengthen our historic ties and assure them of our support and firm commitment.

We will match loyalty with loyalty. We will strive for mutually beneficial relations. We will not use our friendship to impose on their sovereignty, for our own sovereignty is not for sale.

PEACE THE HIGHEST GOAL

As for the enemies of freedom, those who are potential adversaries, they will be reminded that peace is the highest aspiration of the American people. We will negotiate for it, sacrifice for it; we will not surrender for it—now or ever.

Our forbearance should never be misunderstood. Our reluctance for conflict should not be misjudged as a failure of will.

When action is required to preserve our national security, we will act. We will maintain sufficient strength to prevail if need be, knowing that if we do so we have the best chance of never having to use that strength.

Above all we must realize that no arsenal or no weapon in the arsenals of the world is so formidable as the will and moral courage of free men and women.

It is a weapon our adversaries in today's world do not have.

It is a weapon that we as Americans do have.

Let that be understood by those who practice terrorism and prey upon their neighbors.

PRAYER ON INAUGURAL DAY

I am told that tens of thousands of prayer meetings are being held on this day; for that I am deeply grateful. We are a nation under God, and I believe God intended for us to be free. It would be fitting and good, I think, if on each inaugural day in future years it should be declared a day of prayer.

This is the first time in our history that this ceremony has been held, as you've been told, on this West Front of the Capitol.

Standing here, one faces a magnificent vista, opening up on this city's special beauty and history.

At the end of this open mall are those shrines to the giants on whose shoulders we stand.

Directly in front of me, the monument to a monumental man, George Washington, father of our country. A man of humility who came to greatness reluctantly. He led America out of revolutionary victory into infant nationhood.

Off to one side, the stately memorial to Thomas Jefferson. The Declaration of Independence flames with his eloquence.

And then beyond the Reflecting Pool, the dignified columns of the Lincoln Memorial. Whoever would understand in his heart the meaning of America will find it in the life of Abraham Lincoln.

MONUMENTS TO HEROES

Beyond those monuments, monuments to heroism, is the Potomac River, and on the far shore the sloping hills of Arlington National Cemetery with its row upon row of simple white markers bearing crosses or Stars of David. They add up to only a tiny fraction of the price that has been paid for our freedom.

Each one of those markers is a monument to the kind of hero I spoke of earlier.

Their lives ended in places called Belleau Wood, the Argonne, Omaha Beach, Salerno and halfway around the world on Guadalcanal, Tarawa, Pork Chop Hill, the Chosin Reservoir, and in a hundred rice paddies and jungles of a place called Vietnam.

Under such a marker lies a young man, Martin Treptow, who left his job in a small town barber shop in 1917 to go to France with the famed Rainbow Division.

There, on the Western front, he was killed trying to carry a message between battalions under heavy artillery fire.

We are told that on his body was found a diary.

On the flyleaf under the heading, "My Pledge," he had written these words:

"America must win this war. Therefore I will work, I will save, I will sacrifice, I will endure, I will fight cheerfully and do my utmost, as if the issue of the whole struggle depended on me alone."

The crisis we are facing today does not require of us the kind of sacrifice that Martin Treptow and so many thousands of others were called upon to make.

It does require, however, our best effort, and our willingness to believe in ourselves and to believe in our capacity to perform great deeds; to believe that together with God's help we can and will resolve the problems which now confront us.

And after all, why shouldn't we believe that? We are Americans.

God bless you and thank you. Thank you very much.

☆

RONALD REAGAN: *Message on the State of the Union* and *Speech on the Economic Recovery Program*

Thank you all very much. Mr. Speaker, Mr. President, distinguished members of Congress, honored guests and fellow citizens.

Only a month ago, I was your guest in this historic building and I pledged to you my cooperation in doing what is right for this nation that we all love so much.

I'm here tonight to reaffirm that pledge and to ask that we share in restoring the promise that is offered to every citizen by this, the last, best hope of man on earth.

All of us are aware of the punishing inflation which has, for the first time in 60 years, held to double-digit figures for two years in a row. Interest rates have reached absurd levels of more than 20 percent and over 15 percent for those who would borrow to buy a home. All across this land one can see newly built homes standing vacant, unsold because of mortgage interest rates.

Almost eight million Americans are out of work. These are people who want to be productive. But as the months go by, despair dominates their lives. The threats of layoff and unemployment hang over other millions, and all who work are frustrated by their inability to keep up with inflation.

One worker in a Midwest city put it to me this way — He said: "I'm bringing home more dollars than I ever believed I could possibly earn but I seem to be getting worse off." And he is. Not only have hourly earnings of the American worker, after adjusting for inflation, declined 5 percent over the past five years, but in these five years, Federal personal taxes for the average family have increased 67 percent.

President Reagan's first State of the Union Message was delivered to a joint session of Congress on February 19, 1981; his speech on economic recovery was delivered on April 28, 1981.

We can no longer procrastinate and hope that things will get better. They will not. Unless we act forcefully, and now, the economy will get worse.

Can we who man the ship of state deny it is somewhat out of control? Our national debt is approaching $1 trillion. A few weeks ago I called such a figure — a trillion dollars — incomprehensible. And I've been trying ever since to think of a way to illustrate how big a trillion really is. And the best I could come up with is that if you had a stack of $1,000 bills in your hand only four inches high you'd be a millionaire. A trillion dollars would be a stack of $1,000 bills 67 miles high.

The interest on the public debt this year we know will be over $90 billion. And unless we change the proposed spending for the fiscal year beginning Oct. 1, we'll add another almost $80 billion to the debt.

Adding to our troubles is a mass of regulations imposed on the shopkeeper, the farmer, the craftsman, professionals and major industry that is estimated to add $100 billion to the price of the things we buy, and it reduces our ability to produce. The rate of increase in American productivity, once one of the highest in the world, is among the lowest of all major industrial nations. Indeed, it has actually declined in the last three years.

Now I've painted a pretty grim picture, but I think I've painted it accurately. It is within our power to change this picture and we can act with hope. There's nothing wrong with our internal strengths. There has been no breakdown in the human, technological and natural resources upon which the economy is built.

Based on this confidence in a system which has never failed us — but which we have failed through a lack of confidence, and sometimes through a belief that we could fine-tune the economy and get a tune to our liking — I am proposing a comprehensive four-point program. Now let me outline and detail some of the principal parts of this program. You will each be provided with a completely detailed copy of the entire program.

This plan is aimed at reducing the growth in Government spending and taxing, reforming and eliminating regulations which are unnecessary and unproductive or counterproductive, and encouraging a consistent monetary policy aimed at maintaining the value of the currency.

If enacted in full, this program can help America create 13 million new jobs, nearly three million more than we would without these measures. It will also help us to gain control of inflation.

It's important to note that we're only reducing the rate of increase in taxing and spending. We are not attempting to cut either spending or taxing levels below that which we presently have. This plan will get our economy moving again, [achieve] productivity growth and thus create the jobs that our people must have.

And I'm asking that you join me in reducing direct Federal spending by $41.4 billion in fiscal year 1982, along with another — and it goes along with another $7.7 billion in user fees and off-budget savings for a total of $49.1 billion. And this will still allow an increase of $40.8 billion over 1981 spending.

Now I know that exaggerated and inaccurate stories about these cuts have disturbed many people, particularly those dependent on grant and benefit programs for their basic needs. Some of you have heard from constituents, I know, afraid that Social Security checks, for example, were going to be taken away from them. Well I regret the fear that these unfounded stories have caused and I welcome this opportunity to set things straight.

We will continue to fulfill the obligations that spring from our national conscience. Those who through no fault of their own must depend on the rest of us, the poverty-stricken, the disabled, the elderly, all those with true need, can rest assured that the social safety net of programs they depend on are exempt from any cuts.

[*The President proceeded to discuss the specific aspects of his program.*]

This, then, is our proposal. "America's New Beginning: A Program for Economic Recovery." I don't want it to be simply the plan of my Administration—I'm here tonight to ask you to join me in making it our plan. Together we can embark on this road not to make things easy, but to make things better.

Our social, political and cultural, as well as our economical institutions, can no longer absorb the repeated shocks that have been dealt them over the past decade.

Can we do the job? The answer is yes. But we must begin now.

We are in control here. There's nothing wrong with America that together we can't fix.

I'm sure there will be some who will raise the familiar old cry, "Don't touch my program—cut somewhere else."

I hope I've made it plain that our approach has been even-handed; that only the programs for the truly deserving needy remain untouched.

The question is, are we simply going to go down the same path we've gone down before—carving out one special program here, another special program there. I don't think that's what the American people expect of us. More important, I don't think that's what they want. They are ready to return to the source of our strength.

The substance and prosperity of our nation is built by wages brought home from the factories and the mills, the farms and the shops.

They are the services provided in 10,000 corners of America; the interest on the thrift of our people and the returns for their risk-taking. The production of America is the possession of those who build, serve, create and produce.

For too long now, we've removed from our people the decisions on how to dispose of what they created. We've strayed from first principles. We must alter our course.

The taxing power of Government must be used to provide revenues for legitimate Government purposes. It must not be used to regulate the economy or bring about social change. We've tried that and surely we must be able to see it doesn't work.

Spending by Government must be limited to those functions which are the proper province of Government. We can no longer afford things simply because we think of them.

Next year we can reduce the budget by $41.4 billion, without harm to Government's legitimate purposes or to our responsibility to all who need our benevolence. This, plus the reduction in tax rates, will help bring an end to inflation.

In the health and social services area alone, the plan we're proposing will substantially reduce the need for 465 pages of law, 1,400 pages of regulations, 5,000 Federal employees who presently administer 7,600 separate grants in about 25,000 separate locations. Over seven million man and woman hours of work by state and local officials are required to fill out Federal forms.

I would direct a question to those who have indicated already an unwillingness to accept such a plan: Have they an alternative which offers a greater chance of balancing the budget, reducing and eliminating inflation, stimulating the creation of jobs and reducing the tax burden? And, if they haven't, are they suggesting we can continue on the present course without coming to a day of reckoning?

If we don't do this, inflation and the growing tax burden will put an end to everything we believe in and our dreams for the future. We don't have an option of living with inflation and its attendant tragedy, millions of productive people willing and able to work but unable to find a buyer for their work in the job market.

We have an alternative and that is a program for economic recovery.

True, it will take time for the favorable effects of our proposal to be felt. So we must begin now.

The people are watching and waiting. They don't demand miracles. They do expect us to act. Let us act together.

Thank you.

☆

SPEECH ON THE ECONOMIC RECOVERY PROGRAM

Mr. Speaker, Mr. President, distinguished members of the Congress, honored guests and fellow citizens:

I have come to speak to you tonight about our economic recovery program and why I believe it's essential that the Congress approve this package which I believe will lift the crushing burden of inflation off of our citizens and restore the vitality to our economy and our industrial machine. . . .

Mr. Speaker and Senator Baker, I want to thank you for your cooperation in helping to arrange this Joint Session of the Congress. I won't be speaking to you very long tonight, but I asked for this meeting because the urgency of our joint mission has not changed.

Thanks to some very fine people, my health is much improved. [*The President had been wounded in an assassination attempt on March 30, 1981.*] I'd like to be able to say that with regard to the health of the economy.

It has been half a year since the election that charged all of us in this Government with the task of restoring our economy. Where have we come in these six months?

Inflation, as measured by the Consumer Price Index, has continued at a double-digit rate.

Mortgage interest rates have averaged almost 15 percent for these six months, preventing families across America from buying homes.

There are still almost eight million unemployed.

The average worker's hourly earnings, after adjusting for inflation, are lower today than they were six months ago and there have been over 6,000 business failures.

Six months is long enough. The American people now want us to act, and not in half-measures. They demand—and they've earned —a full and comprehensive effort to clean up our economic mess.

Because of the extent of our economy's sickness, we know that the cure will not come quickly, and that, even with our package, progress will come in inches and feet, not in miles. But to fail to act will delay even longer—and more painfully—the cure which must come.

And that cure begins with the Federal budget. And the budgetary actions taken by the Congress over the next few days will determine how we respond to the message of last Nov. 4.

That message was very simple. Our Government is too big, and it spends too much.

For the last few months, you and I have enjoyed a relationship based on extraordinary cooperation. Because of this cooperation we've come a long distance in less than three months. I want to thank the leadership of the Congress for helping in setting a fair timetable for consideration of our recommendations. And committee chairmen on both sides of the aisle have called prompt and thorough hearings.

We have also communicated in a spirit of candor, openness and mutual respect. Tonight, as our decision day nears, and as the House of Representatives weighs its alternatives, I wish to address you in that same spirit.

The Senate Budget Committee, under the leadership of Pete Domenici has just today voted out a budget resolution supported by Democrats and Republicans alike that is in all major respects consistent with the program we have proposed. And now we look forward to favorable action on the Senate floor. But an equally crucial test involves the House of Representatives.

The House will soon be choosing between two different versions, or measures, to deal with the economy. One is the measure offered by the House Budget Committee. The other is a bipartisan measure — a substitute introduced by Congressmen Phil Gramm of Texas and Del Latta of Ohio.

On behalf of the Administration, let me say that we embrace and fully support that bipartisan substitute. It will achieve all the essential aims of controlling Government spending, reducing the tax burden, building a national defense second to none, and stimulating economic growth and creating millions of new jobs.

At the same time, however, I must state our opposition to the measure offered by the House Budget Committee.

It may appear that we have two alternatives. In reality, however, there are no more alternatives left. The committee measure quite simply falls far too short of the essential actions that we must take. For example, in the next three years:

The committee measure projects spending $141 billion more than does the bipartisan substitute.

It regrettably cuts over $14 billion in essential defense spending — funding required to restore America's national security.

It adheres to the failed policy of trying to balance the budget on the taxpayer's back. It would increase tax payments by over a third — adding up to a staggering quarter-of-a-trillion dollars. Federal taxes would increase 12 percent each year. Taxpayers would be paying a larger share of their income to Government in 1984 than they do at present.

In short, that measure reflects an echo of the past rather than a benchmark for the future. High taxes and excess spending growth created our present economic mess; more of the same will not cure the hardship, anxiety and discouragement it has imposed on the American people.

Let us cut through the fog for a moment. The answer to a government that's too big is to stop feeding its growth. Government spending has been growing faster than the economy itself. The massive national debt which we accumulated is the result of the Government's high spending diet. Well, it's time to change the diet and to change it in the right way.

I know the tax portion of our package is of concern to some of you. Let me make a few points that I feel have been overlooked. First of all, it should be looked at as an integral part of the entire package, not something separate and apart from the budget reductions, the regulatory relief and the monetary restraints.

Probably the most common misconception is that we are proposing to reduce Government revenues to less than what the Government has been receiving. This is not true. Actually, the discussion has to do with how much of a tax increase should be imposed on the taxpayer in 1982.

Now I know that over the recess, in some informal polling, some of your constituents have been asked which they'd rather have: a balanced budget or a tax cut. And with the common sense that characterizes the people of this country, the answer, of course, has been: a balanced budget. But may I suggest, with no inference that there was wrong intent on the part of those who asked the question, the question was inappropriate for the situation. Our choice is not between a balanced budget and a tax cut. Properly asked, the question is: Do you want a great big raise in your taxes this coming year or, at the worst, a very little increase with the prospect of tax reduction and a balanced budget down the road a ways. With the common sense that the people have already shown, I'm sure that we all know what the answer to that question would be.

A gigantic tax increase has been built into the system. We propose nothing more than a reduction of that increase.

The people have a right to know that even with our plan they will be paying more in taxes, but not as much more as they will without it.

The option, I believe, offered by the House Budget Committee will leave spending too high and tax rates too high. At the same time, I think, it cuts the defense budget too much. And, by attempting to reduce the deficit through higher taxes, it will not create the kind of strong economic growth and the new jobs that we must have.

Let us not overlook the fact that the small, independent business man or woman creates more than 80 percent of all the new jobs and employs more than half of our total work force. Our across-the-board cut in tax rates for a three year period will give them much of the incentive and promise of stability they need to go forward with expansion plans calling for additional employees.

Tonight I renew my call for us to work as a team—to join in cooperation so that we find answers which will begin to solve all our economic problems and not just some of them.

The economic recovery package that I've outlined to you over the past few weeks is, I deeply believe, the only answer that we have left.

Reducing the growth of spending, cutting marginal tax rates, providing relief from over-regulation, and following a noninflationary and predictable monetary policy are interwoven measures which will ensure that we have addressed each of the severe dislocations which threaten our economic future.

These policies will make our economy stronger, and the stronger economy will balance the budget—which we're committed to do by 1984.

When I took the oath of office, I pledged loyalty to only one special interest group—"We the people." Those people—neighbors and friends, shopkeepers and laborers, farmers and craftsmen—do not have infinite patience. As a matter of fact, some eighty years ago, Teddy Roosevelt wrote these instructive words in his first message to the Congress: "The American people are slow to wrath, but when their wrath is once kindled, it burns like a consuming flame."

Well, perhaps that kind of wrath will be deserved if our answer to these serious problems is to repeat the mistakes of the past. The old and comfortable way is to shave a little here and add a little there. Well, that's not acceptable any more. I think this great and historic Congress knows that way is no longer acceptable.

I think you've shown that you know the one sure way to continue the inflationary spiral is to fall back into the predictable patterns of old economic practices.

Isn't it time that we tried something new?

When you allowed me to speak to you here in these chambers a little earlier, I told you that I wanted this program for economic recovery to be ours—yours and mine. I think the bipartisan substitute bill has achieved that purpose. It moves us toward economic vitality.

Just two weeks ago, you and I joined millions of our fellow Americans in marveling at the magic historical moment that John Young and Bob Crippen created in their space shuttle Columbia.

The last manned effort was almost six years ago, and I remembered, on this more recent day, over the years, how we'd all come to expect technological precision of our men and machines. And each amazing achievement became commonplace, until the next new challenge was raised.

With the space shuttle, we tested our ingenuity once again—moving beyond the accomplishments of the past into the promise and uncertainty of the future. Thus, we not only planned to send up a 122 foot aircraft, 170 miles into space, but we also intended to make it maneuverable and return it to earth—landing 98 tons of exotic metals delicately on a remote dry lake bed.

The space shuttle did more than prove our technological abilities, it raised our expectations once more; it started us dreaming again.

The poet Carl Sandburg wrote: "The republic is a dream. Nothing happens unless first a dream."

And that's what makes us as Americans different. We've always reached for a new spirit and aimed at a higher goal. We've been courageous and determined, unafraid and bold. Who among us wants to be first to say we no longer have those qualities? That we must limp along doing the same things that have brought us our present misery. I believe that the people you and I represent are ready to chart a new course. They look to us to meet the great challenge — to reach beyond the commonplace and not fall short for lack of creativity or courage. Someone, you know, has said that he who would have nothing to do with thorns must never attempt to gather flowers.

Well, we have much greatness before us. We can restore our economic strength and build opportunities like none we've ever had before.

As Carl Sandburg said, all we need to begin with is a dream that we can do better than before.

All we need to have is faith, and that dream will come true.

All we need to do is act, and the time for action is now.

Thank you and good night.

III

JUDICIAL
VIEWS

IN THE AMERICAN governmental system, the last word on the scope of presidential power ostensibly belongs to the Supreme Court as the ultimate interpreter of the Constitution. But in fact the judiciary's role in defining executive authority has been quite limited. Under normal conditions, the Court seldom comes into direct conflict with the executive, since most legal challenges to governmental action are tests of legislative rather than executive power. And under crisis conditions, when presidential resort to inherent authority is most likely to cause constitutional concern, the sort of action usually involved—the making of executive agreements, threats of war, commitments of armed forces—is of such a nature that no justiciable issue can be raised.

On occasion important questions of presidential power do come before the Court. But the Justices have almost always evinced great reluctance to engage in battle with the executive. There have been periods—the New Deal is the best example—when the judicial branch has attempted to overrule the policies of a presidentially-dominated government, and there have even been direct confrontations—like the Steel Seizure Case of 1952—in which it has rebuked a President for exceeding his authority. But when vital issues of presidential power are involved, the judiciary's usual approach has been to delay or avoid decision and, when this has not been possible, to uphold the executive's exercise of power. Indeed even in those rare instances when it has ruled against the President, the Court has generally blunted the effect of its adverse decisions by using cautious, qualified, and ambiguous language. In short, the Supreme Court has consistently given Presidents a wide berth in judging the validity of their claims to power.

Despite the fact that most assertions of presidential authority are never subjected to judicial review, however, and notwithstanding the judicial restraint displayed in this highly-charged political field, Supreme Court decisions provide the only formal exposition of the Presidency's constitutional power. If they are less authoritative than American governmental mythology insists, still those decisions set the standards for presidential actions and provide American society with norms by which to judge their legitimacy. Recognizing all of the qualifications that reality imposes on the Supreme Court's reviewing authority, its opinions nonetheless represent the "constitutional concept" of presidential power.

The case excerpts presented here deal with judicial interpretation of the President's authority in a number of important problem areas: foreign relations, warmaking, crisis government, control over administrative policy, and the preservation of domestic peace. The first selection constitutes a major pronouncement on presidential power to conduct the nation's external affairs. In this case, *United States v. Curtiss-Wright Export Corporation*, the Court not only upheld a broad delegation of legislative authority to the President, it also expounded on his independent power in the field of greatest contemporary concern. Much of the decision was *obiter dicta*, but in adverting to "the very delicate, plenary and exclusive power of the President as the sole organ of the federal government in the field of international relations," the Court in effect constitutionalized this Hamiltonian conception of executive authority.

In the second selection, from the Civil War *Prize Cases*, the Court provided constitutional answers to two vital questions regarding the President's power under crisis conditions, as it accepted the view that he may both determine the existence of an emergency and take whatever measures he deems necessary to meet it. The President cannot "declare" war in the legal or constitutional sense, but as Commander in Chief he may nonetheless commit the nation to military action without congressional approval when the nation's survival is at stake. He has independent authority, in other words, to make "defensive war"—a concept which has been projected into the era of international crisis by several of Abraham Lincoln's more recent successors.

The next series of three readings deals with presidential power over individual liberty and private property in time. of war. The excerpt from *Ex parte Milligan*, in which the Court declared unconstitutional Lincoln's establishment of martial rule during the Civil War, is a forceful rejection of the crisis doctrine of unlimited executive-military authority and an eloquent defense of constitutional principles. But the decision was handed down over a year after the war's end and the President's death; and its ringing insistence that "none of [the Constitution's] provisions can be suspended during any of the great exigencies of government" seems rhetorical in view of the extraconstitutional regime which Lincoln had instituted in his effort to preserve the nation. Indeed the next selection, from the World War II *Korematsu* decision, emphasizes the point. For in that case the Court put its constitutional imprimatur on just the sort of executive-military resort to power that the *Milligan* ruling had implicitly rejected. And though it tried to lessen the blow to constitutional standards by talking about the "war power of Congress and the Executive," in fact the World War II exclusion of Japanese-Americans from the West Coast was initiated under the authority of the President alone. Thus *Korematsu* is the leading example of the judiciary's reluctance to substitute its judgment of constitutionality for the executive's determination of necessity under wartime conditions. The third excerpt in this series is from the 1952 Steel Seizure Case and is the Supreme Court's most recent major decision regarding presidential power. Here the issue of executive authority to determine the existence of an emergency and to take steps in defense of the national security—seemingly established by *The Prize Cases*—was reopened. For despite a declaration of national emergency by President Truman, and although he insisted that seizure of the steel industry was necessary to assure continued production in support of the Korean War effort, the Court declared that the President had acted beyond his legitimate powers. There were many non-constitutional factors involved in this case—the absence of declared war, the President's lack of popular support, the Court's concern about projecting presidential emergency power into an era of recurrent emergencies—and it is significant that not even his concurring colleagues agreed with Justice Black's simplistic interpretation of the separation-of-powers principle as a check on presidential authority. But however qualified the ruling may have been, and whatever its merit or effectiveness as constitutional doctrine, *Youngstown Sheet & Tube Company* v. *Sawyer* remains a landmark decision as the only time the Supreme Court has struck down a resort to inherent executive power under wartime conditions.

The next selection is from a less spectacular but still important decision limiting presidential power. Here the issue was the scope of executive authority over the administrative agencies of government, and specifically in *Humphrey's Executor* v. *United States,* over those agencies established by Congress to operate as independent regulatory commissions. The Court handed down this opinion in the midst of its great struggle with President Roosevelt over the constitutional validity of the New Deal, and there is more than a little animosity in its statement that "one who holds his office only during the pleasure of another cannot be depended upon to maintain an attitude of independence against the latter's will." But the doctrine of *Humphrey's Executor* has been reiterated by later Courts, and its limitation on the President's power to implement policy through the removal of recalcitrant administrative officials remains in effect.

Another infrequently activated but potentially important area of presidential power is involved in *In re Neagle*, which dealt with the scope of executive authority under the President's constitutional duty "to take care that the laws be faithfully executed." Ostensibly this clause refers to laws passed by Congress, but in the *Neagle* decision, the Court broadened the concept to include "any obligation fairly and properly inferable" from the Constitution. The result was to provide a constitutional base for the President's power to protect "the peace of the United States." Arising out of a bizarre incident before the century's turn, this ruling gave the executive branch authority of undefined (and still largely unexplored) magnitude in domestic affairs. Resuscitated by Presidents Eisenhower and Kennedy in support of their efforts to enforce the law of the Constitution at Little Rock and Oxford, the idea of the President as protector of internal peace has important implications for contemporary American society.

The final selection in this section is also the most recent major Supreme Court decision concerned with presidential power: *United States v. Nixon*. This case arose out of the Watergate affair and involved the issue of "executive privilege." Mr. Nixon claimed an absolute right to withhold from a federal court tapes of conversations which had been subpoenaed for use in the trial of presidential aides indicted for criminal conspiracy. The President himself was charged with being an unindicted co-conspirator, and the decision coincided with congressional activity aimed at impeaching him. In this unprecedented and dramatic situation, the Court rejected Nixon's assertion of absolute executive privilege and held that the President must respond to a judicial demand for materials involved in a criminal prosecution. The decision made it abundantly clear that courts should act with great restraint in matters related to the confidentiality of presidential communications. But the case is nonetheless an historic expression of the concept that in the American constitutional system no one — including the President — is above the law.

Like the Presidents themselves, the Justices of the Supreme Court have adopted varying conceptions of presidential power. And like the presidential views, those of the judges have reflected the changing needs, demands, and moods of the nation and the world. But over the long course of American history, and particularly since the Roosevelt era, the Court has supported the development of a strong Presidency.

In any event, it has never been an insurmountable obstacle to the exercise of presidential power. Indeed, one of the great issues that has confronted the judicial branch during crisis periods is whether it should acquiesce in extraordinary exercises of presidential authority and thereby legitimize actions whose constitutionality is doubtful.

Justice Jackson raised this problem in his dissent in *Korematsu*, when he declared that "a civil court cannot be made to enforce an order which violates constitutional limitations even if it is a reasonable exercise of military authority." But the weight of judicial opinion rejects the notion of distinguishing between necessity and constitutionality, and a consistent majority of the Court has accepted the view that any necessary exercise of presidential authority can be encompassed within the Constitution. While the result of this attitude has been to allow for the growth of executive power without precipitating a constitutional crisis, it has also raised the question of whether the constitutional provisions dealing with that power are infinitely interpretable and illimitably expansible. The Supreme Court's answer would be "no"; the answer of experience is "yes." But in any event, Justice Jackson's conclusion was correct: that for restraints on our national leaders we must ultimately look not to the Supreme Court but "to the political judgments of their contemporaries and to the moral judgments of history."

PRESIDENTIAL POWER IN
FOREIGN AFFAIRS

☆

UNITED STATES V. CURTISS-WRIGHT EXPORT

CORPORATION

Mr. Justice Sutherland delivered the opinion of the Court:

On January 27, 1936, an indictment was returned in the court
below, the first count of which charges that appellees, beginning
with the 29th day of May, 1934, conspired to sell in the United
States certain arms of war; namely, fifteen machine guns, to Bolivia,
a country then engaged in armed conflict in the Chaco, in violation
of the Joint Resolution of Congress approved May 28, 1934, and
the provisions of a proclamation issued on the same day by the
President of the United States pursuant to authority conferred by
¶ 1 of the resolution. In pursuance of the conspiracy, the commission of certain overt acts was alleged, details of which need not be
stated. The Joint Resolution (chapter 365, 48 Stat. 811) follows:

"Resolved by the Senate and House of Representatives of the
United States of America in Congress assembled, That if the President finds that the prohibition of the sale of arms and munitions
of war in the United States to those countries now engaged in
armed conflict in the Chaco may contribute to the re-establishment
of peace between those countries, and if after consultation with the
governments of other American Republics and with their cooperation, as well as that of such other governments as he may deem
necessary, he makes proclamation to that effect, it shall be unlawful
to sell, except under such limitations and exceptions as the President prescribes, any arms or munitions of war in any place in the
United States to the countries now engaged in that armed conflict,
or to any person, company, or association acting in the interest of

299 U.S. 304 (1936).

either country, until otherwise ordered by the President or by Congress. . . ."

It is contended that by the Joint Resolution the going into effect and continued operation of the resolution was conditioned (a) upon the President's judgment as to its beneficial effect upon the re-establishment of peace between the countries engaged in armed conflict in the Chaco; (b) upon the making of a proclamation, which was left to his unfettered discretion, thus constituting an attempted substitution of the President's will for that of Congress; (c) upon the making of a proclamation putting an end to the operation of the resolution, which again was left to the President's unfettered discretion; and (d) further, that the extent of its operation in particular cases was subject to limitation and exception by the President, controlled by no standard. In each of these particulars, appellees urge that Congress abdicated its essential functions and delegated them to the Executive.

Whether, if the Joint Resolution had related solely to internal affairs, it would be open to the challenge that it constituted an unlawful delegation of legislative power to the Executive, we find it unnecessary to determine. The whole aim of the resolution is to affect a situation entirely external to the United States, and falling within the category of foreign affairs. The determination which we are called to make, therefore, is whether the Joint Resolution, as applied to that situation, is vulnerable to attack under the rule that forbids a delegation of the lawmaking power. In other words, assuming (but not deciding) that the challenged delegation, if it were confined to internal affairs, would be invalid, may it nevertheless be sustained on the ground that its exclusive aim is to afford a remedy for a hurtful condition within foreign territory?

It will contribute to the elucidation of the question if we first consider the differences between the powers of the federal government in respect of foreign or external affairs and those in respect of domestic or internal affairs. That there are differences between them, and that these differences are fundamental, may not be doubted.

The two classes of powers are different, both in respect of their origin and their nature. The broad statement that the federal government can exercise no powers except those specifically enumerated in the Constitution, and such implied powers as are necessary and proper to carry into effect the enumerated powers, is categorically true only in respect of our internal affairs. In that field, the primary purpose of the Constitution was to carve from the general mass of legislative powers *then possessed by the states* such portions as it was thought desirable to vest in the federal government, leaving those not included in the enumeration still in the states. That this doctrine applies only to powers which the states had is self-evident. And since the states severally never possessed international powers, such powers could not have been carved from the mass of state powers but obviously were transmitted to the United States from some other source. During the colonial period, those powers were possessed exclusively by and were entirely under the control of the Crown. By the Declaration of Independence, "the Representatives of the United States of America" declared the United [not the several] Colonies to be free and independent states, and as such to have "full Power to levy War, conclude Peace, contract Alliances, establish Commerce and to do all other Acts and Things which Independent States may of right do."

As a result of the separation from Great Britain by the colonies, acting as a unit, the powers of external sovereignty passed from the Crown not to the colonies severally, but to the colonies in their collective and corporate capacity as the United States of America. Even before the Declaration, the colonies were a unit in foreign affairs, acting through a common agency—namely, the Continental Congress, composed of delegates from the thirteen colonies. That agency exercised the powers of war and peace, raised an army, created a navy, and finally adopted the Declaration of Independence. Rulers come and go; governments end and forms of government change; but sovereignty survives. A political society cannot endure without a supreme will somewhere. Sovereignty is never held in suspense. When, therefore, the external sovereignty of Great Britain in respect of the colonies ceased, it immediately passed to the Union. . . .

The Union existed before the Constitution, which was ordained and established among other things to form "a more perfect Union." Prior to that event, it is clear that the Union, declared by the Articles of Confederation to be "perpetual," was the sole possessor of external sovereignty, and in the Union it remained without change save in so far as the Constitution in express terms qualified its exercise. . . .

It results that the investment of the federal government with the powers of external sovereignty did not depend upon the affirmative grants of the Constitution. The powers to declare and wage war, to conclude peace, to make treaties, to maintain diplomatic relations with other sovereignties, if they had never been mentioned in the Constitution, would have vested in the federal government as necessary concomitants of nationality. Neither the Constitution nor the laws passed in pursuance of it have any force in foreign territory unless in respect of our own citizens . . . ; and operations of the nation in such territory must be governed by treaties, international understandings and compacts, and the principles of international law. As a member of the family of nations, the right and power of the United States in that field are equal to the right and power of the other members of the international family. Otherwise, the United States is not completely sovereign. . . .

Not only, as we have shown, is the federal power over external affairs in origin and essential character different from that over internal affairs, but participation in the exercise of the power is significan ly limited. In this vast external realm, with its important, complicated, delicate and manifold problems, the President alone has the power to speak or listen as a representative of the nation. He *makes* treaties with the advice and consent of the Senate; but he alone negotiates. Into the field of negotiation the Senate cannot intrude; and Congress itself is powerless to invade it. . . .

It is important to bear in mind that we are here dealing not a'one with an authority vested in the President by an exertion of legislative power, but with such an authority plus the very delicate, plenary and exclusive power of the President as the sole organ of the federal government in the field of international relations—a power which does not require as a basis for its exercise an act of Congress, but which, of course, like every other governmental power, must be exercised in subordination to the applicable provisions of the Constitution. It is quite apparent that if, in the maintenance of our international relations, embarrassment—perhaps serious embarrassment—is to be avoided and success for our aims achieved, congressional legislation which is to be made effective through negotiation and inquiry within the international field must often accord to the President a degree of discretion and freedom from statutory restriction which would not be admissible were domestic affairs alone involved. Moreover, he, not Congress, has the better opportunity of knowing the conditions which prevail in foreign countries, and especially is this true in time of war. He has his confidential sources of information. He has his agents in the form of diplomatic, consular and other officials. Secrecy in respect of information gathered by them may be highly necessary, and the premature disclosure of it productive of harmful results. Indeed, so clearly is this true that the first President refused to accede to a request to lay before the House of Representatives the instructions, correspondence and documents relating to the negotiation of the Jay Treaty—a refusal the wisdom of which was recognized by the House itself and has never since been doubted. In his reply to the request, President Washington said:

"The natu.e of foreign negotiations requires caution, and their success must often depend on secrecy; and even when brought to a conclusion a full disclosure of all the measures, demands, or eventual concessions which may have been proposed or contemplated would be extremely impolitic; for this might have a pernicious influence on future negotiations, or produce immediate inconveniences, perhaps danger and mischief, in relation to other powers. The necessity of such caution and secrecy was one cogent reason for vesting the power of making treaties in the President, with the advice and consent of the Senate, the principle on which that body was formed confining it to a small number of members. To admit, then, a right in the House of Representatives to demand and to have as a matter of course all the papers respecting a negotiation with a foreign power would be to establish a dangerous precedent."

The marked difference between foreign affairs and domestic affairs in this respect is recognized by both houses of Congress in the very form of their requisitions for information from the executive departments. In the case of every department except the Department of State, the resolution *directs* the official to furnish the information. In the case of the State Department, dealing with foreign affairs, the President is requested to furnish the information "if not incompatible with the public interest." A statement that to furnish the information is not compatible with the public interest rarely, if ever, is questioned.

When the President is to be authorized by legislation to act in respect of a matter intended to affect a situation in foreign territory, the legislator properly bears in mind the important consideration that the form of the President's action—or, indeed, whether he shall act at all—may well depend, among other things, upon the nature of the confidential information which he has or may thereafter receive, or upon the effect which his action may have upon our foreign relations. This consideration, in connection with what we have already said on the subject, discloses the unwisdom of requiring Congress in this field of governmental power to lay down narrowly definite standards by which the President is to be governed. . . .

In the light of the foregoing observations, it is evident that this court should not be in haste to apply a general rule which will have the effect of condemning legislation like that under review as constituting an unlawful delegation of legislative power. The principles which justify such legislation find overwhelming support in the unbroken legislative practice which has prevailed almost from the inception of the national government to the present day. . . .

Practically every volume of the United States Statutes contains one or more acts or joint resolutions of Congress authorizing action by the President in respect of subjects affecting foreign relations, which either leave the exercise of the power to his unrestricted judgment, or provide a standard far more general than that which has always been considered requisite with regard to domestic affairs.

. . . A legislative practice such as we have here, evidenced not by only occasional instances, but marked by the movement of a steady stream for a century and a half of time, goes a long way in the direction of proving the presence of unassailable ground for the constitutionality of the practice, to be found in the origin and history of the power involved, or in its nature, or in both combined. . . .

We deem it unnecessary to consider, seriatim, the several clauses which are said to evidence the unconstitutionality of the Joint Resolution as involving an unlawful delegation of legislative power. It is enough to summarize by saying that, both upon principle and in accordance with precedent, we conclude there is sufficient warrant for the broad discretion vested in the President to determine whether the enforcement of the statute will have a beneficial effect upon the re-establishment of peace in the affected countries; whether he shall make proclamation to bring the resolution into operation; whether and when the resolution shall cease to operate and to make proclamation accordingly; and to prescribe limitations and exceptions to which the enforcement of the resolution shall be subject. . . .

PRESIDENTIAL POWER TO MAKE WAR

☆

THE PRIZE CASES

Mr. Justice Grier delivered the opinion of the Court:

There are certain propositions of law which must necessarily affect the ultimate decision of these cases, and many others, which it will be proper to discuss and decide before we notice the special facts peculiar to each.

They are, 1st. Had the President a right to institute a blockade of ports in possession of persons in armed rebellion against the government, on the principles of international law, as known and acknowledged among civilized States? . . .

1. Neutrals have a right . . . to enter the ports of a friendly nation for the purposes of trade and commerce, but are bound to recognize the rights of a belligerent engaged in actual war, to use this mode of coercion, for the purpose of subduing the enemy.

That a blockade *de facto* actually existed, and was formally declared and notified by the President on the 27th and 30th of April, 1861, is an admitted fact in these cases.

That the President, as the Executive Chief of the Government and Commander in Chief of the Army and Navy, was the proper person to make such notification, has not been, and cannot be disputed.

The right of prize and capture has its origin in the *jus belli*, and is governed and adjudged under the law of nations. To legitimate the capture of a neutral vessel or property on the high seas, a war must exist *de facto*, and the neutral must have a knowledge or notice of the intention of one of the parties belligerent to use this mode of coercion against a port, city, or territory, in possession of the other.

2 Black 635 (1863).

Let us enquire whether, at the time this blockade was instituted, a state of war existed which would justify a resort to these means of subduing the hostile force.

War has been well defined to be, "That state in which a nation prosecutes its right by force."

The parties belligerent in a public war are independent nations. But it is not necessary to constitute war, that both parties should be acknowledged as independent nations or sovereign States. A war may exist where one of the belligerents claims sovereign rights as against the other.

Insurrection against a government may or may not culminate in an organized rebellion, but a civil war always begins by insurrection against the lawful authority of the government. A civil war is never solemnly declared; it becomes such by its accidents—the number, power, and organization of the persons who originate and carry it on. When the party in rebellion occupy and hold in a hostile manner a certain portion of territory; have declared their independence; have cast off their allegiance; have organized armies; have commenced hostilities against their former sovereign, the world acknowledges them as belligerents, and the contest a *war*. *They* claim to be in arms to establish their liberty and independence, in order to become a sovereign State, while the sovereign party treats them as insurgents and rebels who owe allegiance, and who should be punished with death for their treason. . . .

As a civil war is never publicly proclaimed, *eo nomine* against insurgents, its actual existence is a fact in our domestic history which the Court is bound to notice and to know.

The true test of its existence, as found in the writing of the sages of the common law, may be thus summarily stated: "When the regular course of justice is interrupted by revolt, rebellion, or insurrection, so that the Courts of Justice cannot be kept open, *civil war exists* and hostilities may be prosecuted on the same footing as if those opposing the government were foreign enemies invading the land."

By the Constitution, Congress alone has the power to declare a national or foreign war. It cannot declare war against a State, or any number of States, by virtue of any clause in the Constitution. The Constitution confers on the President the whole Executive power. He is bound to take care that the laws be faithfully executed. He is Commander in Chief of the Army and Navy of the United States, and of the militia of the several States when called into the actual service of the United States. He has no power to initiate or declare a war either against a foreign nation or a domestic State. But by the Acts of Congress of February 28th, 1795, and 3d of March, 1807, he is authorized to call out the militia and use the military and naval forces of the United States in case of invasion by foreign nations, and to suppress insurrection against the government of a State or of the United States.

If a war be made by invasion of a foreign nation, the President is not only authorized but bound to resist force by force. He does not initiate the war, but is bound to accept the challenge without waiting for any special legislative authority. And whether the hostile party be a foreign invader, or States organized in rebellion, it is none the less a war, although the declaration of it be *unilateral*. . . .

The battles of Palo Alto and Resaca de la Palma had been fought before the passage of the Act of Congress of May 13th, 1846, which recognized *a state of war as existing by the act of the Republic of Mexico.* This act not only provided for the future prosecution of the war, but was itself a vindication and ratification of the Act of the President in accepting the challenge without a previous formal declaration of war by Congress.

This greatest of civil wars was not gradually developed by popular commotion, tumultuous assemblies, or local unorganized insurrections. However long may have been its previous conception, it nevertheless sprung forth suddenly from the parent brain, a Minerva in the full panoply of *war*. The President was bound to meet it in the shape it presented itself, without waiting for Congress to baptize it with a name; and no name given to it by him or them could change the fact. . . .

Whether the President in fulfilling his duties, as Commander in Chief, in suppressing an insurrection, has met with such armed hostile resistance, and a civil war of such alarming proportions as will compel him to accord to them the character of belligerents, is a question to be decided *by him,* and this Court must be governed by the decisions and acts of the political department of the government to which this power was entrusted. "He must determine what degree of force the crisis demands." The proclamation of blockade is itself official and conclusive evidence to the Court that a state of war existed which demanded and authorized a recourse to such a measure, under the circumstances peculiar to the case. . . .

If it were necessary to the technical existence of a war, that it should have a legislative sanction, we find it in almost every act passed at the extraordinary session of the Legislature of 1861, which was wholly employed in enacting laws to enable the government to prosecute the war with vigor and efficiency. And finally, in 1861, we find Congress *ex majore cautela* and in anticipation of such astute objections, passing an act "approving, legalizing, and making valid all the acts, proclamations, and orders of the President, etc., as if they had been *issued and done under the previous express authority* and direction of the Congress of the United States."

Without admitting that such an act was necessary under the circumstances, it is plain that if the President had in any manner assumed powers which it was necessary should have the authority or sanction of Congress, that on the well-known principle of law, *omnis ratihabitio retrotrahitur et mandato equiparatu.*, this ratification has operated to perfectly cure the defect. . . .

On this first question therefore we are of the opinion that the President had a right, *jure belli*, to institute a blockade of ports in possession of the States in rebellion, which neutrals are bound to regard. . . .

Mr. Justice Nelson, dissenting:

. . . In the case of a rebellion or resistance of a portion of the people of a country against the established government, there is no doubt, if in its progress and enlargement the government thus sought to be overthrown sees fit, it may by the competent power recognize or declare the existence of a state of civil war, which will draw after it all the consequences and rights of war between the contending parties. . . . But before this insurrection against the established government can be dealt with on the footing of a civil war, within the meaning of the law of nations and the Constitution of the United States, and which will draw after it belligerent rights, it must be recognized or declared by the war-making power of the government.

. . . Instead, therefore, of inquiring after armies and navies, and victories lost and won, or organized rebellion against the general government, the inquiry should be into the law of nations and into the municipal fundamental laws of the government. For we find there that to constitute a civil war in the sense in which we are speaking, before it can exist, in contemplation of law, it must be recognized or declared by the sovereign power of the State, and which sovereign power by our Constitution is lodged in the Congress of the United States—civil war, therefore, under our system of government, can exist only by an act of Congress, which requires the assent of two of the great departments of the government, the executive and legislative.

We have thus far been speaking of the war power under the Constitution of the United States, and as known and recognized by the law of nations. But we are asked, what would become of the peace and integrity of the Union in case of an insurrection at home or invasion from abroad if this power could not be exercised by the President in the recess of Congress, and until that body could be assembled?

[*The opinion proceeds to note the power of the President, under various Acts of Congress to call forth the militia in times of emergency.*]

It will be seen, therefore, that ample provision has been made under the Constitution and laws against any sudden and unexpected disturbance of the public peace from insurrection at home or invasion from abroad. . . .

[But the Acts referred to] did not, and could not under the Constitution, confer on the President the power of declaring war against a State of this Union, or of deciding that war existed, and upon that ground authorize the capture and confiscation of the property of every citizen of the State whenever it was found on the waters. The laws of war, whether the war be civil or *inter gentes,* as we have seen, convert every citizen of the hostile State into a public enemy, and treat him accordingly, whatever may have been his previous conduct. This great power over the business and property of the citizen is reserved to the legislative department by the express words of the Constitution. It cannot be delegated or surrendered to the Executive. Congress alone can determine whether war exists or should be declared; and until they have acted, no citizen of the State can be punished in his person or property, unless he has committed some offense against a law of Congress passed before the act was committed, which made it a crime, and defined the punishment. The penalty of confiscation for the acts of others with which he had no concern cannot lawfully be inflicted. . . .

Upon the whole, after the most careful consideration of this case which the pressure of other duties has admitted, I am compelled to the conclusion that no civil war existed between this government and the States in insurrection till recognized by the Act of Congress 13th of July, 1861; that the President does not possess the power under the Constitution to declare war or recognize its existence within the meaning of the law of nations, which carries with it belligerent rights, and thus change the country and all its citizens from a state of peace to a state of war; that this power belongs exclusively to the Congress of the United States, and, consequently, that the President had no power to set on foot a blockade under the law of nations, and that the capture of the vessel and cargo in this case, and in all cases before us in which the capture occurred before the 13th of July, 1861, for breach of blockade, or as enemies' property, are illegal and void, and that the decrees of condemnation should be reversed and the vessel and cargo restored.

PRESIDENTIAL POWER IN TIME OF WAR

☆

EX PARTE MILLIGAN

Mr. Justice Davis delivered the opinion of the Court:

. . . The importance of the main question presented by this record cannot be overstated; for it involves the very framework of the government and the fundamental principles of American liberty.

During the late wicked rebellion, the temper of the times did not allow that calmness in deliberation and discussion so necessary to a correct conclusion of a purely judicial question. Then, considerations of safety were mingled with the exercise of power; and feelings and interests prevailed which are happily terminated. Now that the public safety is assured, this question, as well as all others, can be discussed and decided without passion or the admixture of any element not required to form a legal judgment. We approach the investigation of this case, fully sensible of the magnitude of the inquiry and the necessity of full and cautious deliberation. . . .

The controlling question in the case is this: Upon the facts stated in Milligan's petition, and the exhibits filed, had the military commission [established under presidential authority] mentioned in it jurisdiction, legally, to try and sentence him? Milligan, not a resident of one of the rebellious States, or a prisoner of war, but a citizen of Indiana for twenty years past, and never in the military or naval service, is, while at his home, arrested by the military power of the United States, imprisoned, and, on certain criminal charges preferred against him, tried, convicted, and sentenced to be hanged by a military commission, organized under the direction of the military commander of the military district of Indiana. Had this tribunal the legal power and authority to try and punish this man?

No graver question was ever considered by this court, nor one

4 Wallace 2 (1866).

which more nearly concerns the rights of the whole people; for it is the birthright of every American citizen when charged with crime, to be tried and punished according to law. . . . The Constitution of the United States is a law for rulers and people, equally in war and in peace, and covers with the shield of its protection all classes of men, at all times, and under all circumstances. No doctrine involving more pernicious consequences was ever invented by the wit of man than that any of its provisions can be suspended during any of the great exigencies of government. Such a doctrine leads directly to anarchy or despotism, but the theory of necessity on which it is based is false; for the government, within the Constitution, has all the powers granted to it which are necessary to preserve its existence; as has been happily proved by the result of the great effort to throw off its just authority.

Have any of the rights guaranteed by the Constitution been violated in the case of Milligan? and if so, what are they?

Every trial involves the exercise of judicial power; and from what source did the military commission that tried him derive their authority? Certainly no part of the judicial power of the country was conferred on them; because the Constitution expressly vests it "in one Supreme Court and such inferior courts as the Congress may from time to time ordain and establish," and it is not pretended that the commission was a court ordained and established by Congress. They cannot justify on the mandate of the President, because he is controlled by law, and has his appropriate sphere of duty, which is to execute, not to make, the laws; and there is "no unwritten criminal code to which resort can be had as a source of jurisdiction." . . .

It is claimed that martial law covers with its broad mantle the proceedings of this military commission. The proposition is this: that in a time of war the commander of an armed force (if, in his opinion, the exigencies of the country demand it, and of which he is to judge) has the power, within the lines of his military district, to suspend all civil rights and their remedies, and subject citizens as well as soldiers to the rule of his will; and in the exercise of his lawful authority cannot be restrained, except by his superior officer or the President of the United States.

If this position is sound to the extent claimed, then when war exists, foreign or domestic, and the country is subdivided into military departments for mere convenience, the commander of one of them can, if he chooses, within his limits, on the plea of necessity, with the approval of the Executive, substitute military force for, and to the exclusion of, the laws, and punish all persons, as he thinks right and proper, without fixed or certain rules.

The statement of this proposition shows its importance; for, if true, republican government is a failure, and there is an end of liberty regulated by law. Martial law, established on such a basis, destroys every guarantee of the Constitution, and effectually renders the "military independent of, and superior to, the civil power"—the attempt to do which by the King of Great Britain was deemed by our fathers such an offense, that they assigned it to the world as one of the causes which impelled them to declare their independence. Civil liberty and this kind of martial law cannot endure together; the antagonism is irreconcilable; and, in the conflict, one or the other must perish.

This nation, as experience has proved, cannot always remain at peace, and has no right to expect that it will always have wise and humane rulers, sincerely attached to the principles of the Constitution. Wicked men, ambitious of power, with hatred of liberty and contempt of law, may fill the place once occupied by Washington and Lincoln; and if this right is conceded, and the calamities of war again befall us, the dangers to human liberty are frightful to contemplate. If our fathers had failed to provide for just such a contingency, they would have been false to the trust reposed in them. They knew —the history of the world told them—the nation they were founding, be its existence short or long, would be involved in war; how often or how long continued, human foresight could not tell; and that unlimited power, wherever lodged at such a time, was especially hazardous to freemen. For this, and other equally weighty reasons, they secured the inheritance they had fought to maintain, by incorporating in a written Constitution the safeguards which time had proved were essential to its preservation. Not one of these safeguards can the President, or Congress, or the judiciary disturb, except the one concerning the writ of habeas corpus.

It is essential to the safety of every government that, in a great crisis like the one we have just passed through, there should be a power somewhere of suspending the writ of habeas corpus. In every war, there are men of previously good character, wicked enough to counsel their fellow-citizens to resist the measures deemed necessary by a good government to sustain its just authority and overthrow its enemies; and their influence may lead to dangerous combinations. In the emergency of the times, an immediate public investigation according to law may not be possible; and yet the peril to the country may be too imminent to suffer such persons to go at large. Unquestionably, there is then an exigency which demands that the government, if it should see fit, in the exercise of a proper discretion, to make arrests, should not be required to produce the persons arrested in answer to a writ of habeas corpus. The Constitution goes no further. It does not say after a writ of habeas corpus is denied a citizen, that he shall be tried otherwise than by the course of the common law; if it had intended this result, it was easy by the use of direct words to have accomplished it. The illustrious men who framed that instrument were guarding the foundations of civil liberty against the abuses of unlimited power; they were full of wisdom, and the lessons of history informed them that a trial by an established court, assisted by an impartial jury, was the only sure way of protecting the citizen against oppression and wrong. Knowing this, they limited the suspension to one great right, and left the rest to remain forever inviolable. But, it is insisted that the safety of the country in time of war demands that this broad claim for martial law shall be sustained. If this were true, it could be well said that a country, preserved at the sacrifice of all the cardinal principles of liberty, is not worth the cost of preservation. Happily, it is not so.

It will be borne in mind that this is not a question of the power to proclaim martial law, when war exists in a community and the courts and civil authorities are overthrown. Nor is it a question what rule a military commander, at the head of his army, can impose on States in rebellion to cripple their resources and quell the insurrection. The jurisdiction claimed is much more extensive. The necessities of the service, during the late Rebellion, required that the loyal States should be placed within the limits of certain military districts and commanders appointed in them; and, it is urged, that this, in a military sense, constituted them the theater of military operations; and, as in this case, Indiana had been and was again threatened with invasion by the enemy, the occasion was furnished to establish martial law. The conclusion does not follow from the premises. If armies were collected in Indiana, they were to be employed in another locality, where the laws were obstructed and the national authority disputed. On her soil there was no hostile foot; if once invaded, that invasion was at an end, and with it all pretext for martial law. Martial law cannot arise from a threatened invasion. The necessity must be actual and present; the invasion real, such as effectually closes the courts and deposes the civil administration.

It is difficult to see how the safety of the country required martial law in Indiana. If any of her citizens were plotting treason, the power of arrest could secure them, until the government was prepared for their trial, when the courts were open and ready to try them. It was as easy to protect witnesses before a civil as a military tribunal; and as there could be no wish to convict, except on sufficient legal evidence, surely an ordained and established court was better able to judge of this than a military tribunal composed of gentlemen not trained to the profession of the law.

It follows, from what has been said on this subject, that there are occasions when martial rule can be properly applied. If, in foreign invasion or civil war, the courts are actually closed, and it is impossible to administer criminal justice according to law, then, in the theater of active military operations, where war really prevails, there is a necessity to furnish a substitute for the civil authority, thus overthrown, to preserve the safety of the army and society; and as no power is left but the military, it is allowed to govern by martial rule until the laws can have their free course. As necessity creates the rule, so it limits its duration; for, if this government is continued after the courts are reinstated, it is a gross usurpation of power. Martial rule can never exist where the courts are open, and in the proper and unobstructed exercise of their jurisdiction. It is also confined to the locality of actual war. . . .

If the military trial of Milligan was contrary to law, then he was entitled, on the facts stated in his petition, to be discharged from custody by the terms of the Act of Congress of March 3, 1863. The provisions of this law having been considered in a previous part of this opinion, we will not restate the views there presented. Milligan avers he was a citizen of Indiana, not in the military or naval service, and was detained in close confinement, by order of the President, from the 5th day of October, 1864, until the 2d day of January, 1865, when the circuit court for the district of Indiana, with a grand jury, convened in session at Indianapolis; and afterwards, on the 27th day of the same month, adjourned without finding an indictment or presentment against him. If these averments were true (and their truth is conceded for the purposes of this case), the court was required to liberate him on taking certain oaths prescribed by the law, and entering into recognizance for his good behavior. . . .

KOREMATSU V. UNITED STATES

Mr. Justice Black delivered the opinion of the Court:

. . . In the light of the principles we announced in the Hirabayashi Case, we are unable to conclude that it was beyond the war power of Congress and the Executive to exclude those of Japanese ancestry from the West Coast war area at the time they did. True, exclusion from the area in which one's home is located is a far greater deprivation than constant confinement to the home from 8 P.M. to 6 A.M. Nothing short of apprehension by the proper military authorities of the gravest imminent danger to the public safety can constitutionally justify either. But exclusion from a threatened area, no less than curfew, has a definite and close relationship to the prevention of espionage and sabotage. The military authorities, charged with the primary responsibility of defending our shores, concluded that curfew provided inadequate protection and ordered exclusion. [The military actions were based on Executive Order 9066 issued by the President.] They did so, as pointed out in our Hirabayashi opinion, in accordance with congressional authority to the military to say who should, and who should not, remain in the threatened areas. . . .

Here, as in the Hirabayashi Case, "we cannot reject as unfounded the judgment of the military authorities and of Congress that there were disloyal members of that population, whose number and strength could not be precisely and quickly ascertained. We cannot say that the war-making branches of the government did not have ground for believing that in a critical hour such persons could not readily be isolated and separately dealt with, and constituted a menace to the national defense and safety, which demanded that prompt and adequate measures be taken to guard against it."

323 U.S. 214 (1944).

Like curfew, exclusion of those of Japanese origin was deemed necessary because of the presence of an unascertained number of disloyal members of the group, most of whom we have no doubt were loyal to this country. It was because we could not reject the finding of the military authorities that it was impossible to bring about an immediate segregation of the disloyal from the loyal that we sustained the validity of the curfew order as applying to the whole group. In the instant case, temporary exclusion of the entire group was rested by the military on the same ground. The judgment that exclusion of the whole group was for the same reason a military imperative answers the contention that the exclusion was in the nature of group punishment based on antagonism to those of Japanese origin. That there were members of the group who retained loyalties to Japan has been confirmed by investigations made subsequent to the exclusion. Approximately five thousand American citizens of Japanese ancestry refused to swear unqualified allegiance to the United States and to renounce allegiance to the Japanese Emperor, and several thousand evacuees requested repatriation to Japan.

We uphold the exclusion order as of the time it was made and when the petitioner violated it. In doing so, we are not unmindful of the hardships imposed by it upon a large group of American citizens. But hardships are part of war, and war is an aggregation of hardships. All citizens alike, both in and out of uniform, feel the impact of war in greater or lesser measure. Citizenship has its responsibilities as well as its privileges, and in time of war the burden is always heavier. Compulsory exclusion of large groups of citizens from their homes, except under circumstances of direst emergency and peril, is inconsistent with our basic governmental institutions. But when under conditions of modern warfare our shores are threatened by hostile forces, the power to protect must be commensurate with the threatened danger. . . .

It is said that we are dealing here with the case of imprisonment of a citizen in a concentration camp solely because of his ancestry, without evidence or inquiry concerning his loyalty and good disposition toward the United States. Our task would be simple, our duty clear, were this a case involving the imprisonment of a loyal citizen in a concentration camp because of racial prejudice. Regardless of the true nature of the assembly and relocation centers—and we deem it unjustifiable to call them concentration camps with all the ugly connotations that term implies—we are dealing specifically with nothing but an exclusion order. To cast this case into outlines of racial prejudice, without reference to the real military dangers which were presented, merely confuses the issue. Korematsu was not excluded from the Military Area because of hostility to him or his race. He *was* excluded because we are at war with the Japanese Empire, because the properly constituted military authorities feared an invasion of our West Coast and felt constrained to take proper security measures, because they decided that the military urgency of the situation demanded that all citizens of Japanese ancestry be segregated from the West Coast temporarily, and finally, because Congress, reposing its confidence in this time of war in our military leaders—as inevitably it must—determined that they should have the power to do just this. There was evidence of disloyalty on the part of some, the military authorities considered that the need for action was great, and time was short. We cannot—by availing ourselves of the calm perspective of hindsight—now say that at that time these actions were unjustified.

Mr. Justice Frankfurter, concurring:

. . . The provisions of the Constitution which confer on the Congress and the President powers to enable this country to wage war are as much part of the Constitution as provisions looking to a nation at peace. And we have had recent occasion to quote approvingly the statement of former Chief Justice Hughes that the war power of the Government is "the power to wage war successfully." Therefore, the validity of action under the war power must be judged wholly in the context of war. That action is not to be stigmatized as lawless because like action in times of peace would be lawless. . . .

Mr. Justice Jackson, dissenting:

. . . [It] is said that if the military commander had reasonable military grounds for promulgating the orders, they are constitutional and become law, and the Court is required to enforce them. There are several reasons why I cannot subscribe to this doctrine.

It would be impracticable and dangerous idealism to expect or insist that each specific military command in an area of probable operations will conform to conventional tests of constitutionality. When an area is so beset that it must be put under military control at all, the paramount consideration is that its measures be successful, rather than legal. The armed services must protect a society, not merely its Constitution. The very essence of the military job is to marshal physical force, to remove every obstacle to its effectiveness, to give it every strategic advantage. Defense measures will not, and often should not, be held within the limits that bind civil authority in peace. No court can require such a commander in such circumstances to act as a reasonable man; he may be unreasonably cautious and exacting. Perhaps he should be. But a commander in temporarily focusing the life of a community on defense is carrying out a military program; he is not making law in the sense the courts know the term. He issues orders, and they may have a certain authority as military commands, although they may be very bad as constitutional law.

But if we cannot confine military expedients by the Constitution, neither would I distort the Constitution to approve all that the military may deem expedient. . . .

In the very nature of things military decisions are not susceptible of intelligent judicial appraisal. They do not pretend to rest on evidence, but are made on information that often would not be admissible and on assumptions that could not be proved. Information in support of an order could not be disclosed to courts without danger that it would reach the enemy. Neither can courts act on communications made in confidence. Hence courts can never have any real alternative to accepting the mere declaration of the authority that issued the order that it was reasonably necessary from a military viewpoint.

Much is said of the danger to liberty from the Army program for deporting and detaining these citizens of Japanese extraction. But a judicial construction of the due process clause that will sustain this order is a far more subtle blow to liberty than the promulgation of the order itself. A military order, however unconstitutional, is not apt to last longer than the military emergency. Even during that period a succeeding commander may revoke it all. But once a judicial opinion rationalizes such an order to show that it conforms to the Constitution, or rather rationalizes the Constitution to show that the Constitution sanctions such an order, the Court for all time has validated the principle of racial discrimination in criminal procedure and of transplanting American citizens. The principle then lies about like a loaded weapon ready for the hand of any authority that can bring forward a plausible claim of an urgent need. Every repetition imbeds that principle more deeply in our law and thinking and expands it to new purposes. . . . A military commander may overstep the bounds of constitutionality, and it is an incident. But if we review and approve, that passing incident becomes the doctrine of the Constitution. There it has a generative power of its own, and all that it creates will be in its own image. . . .

I should hold that a civil court cannot be made to enforce an order which violates constitutional limitations even if it is a reasonable exercise of military authority. The courts can exercise only the judicial power, can apply only law, and must abide by the Constitution, or they cease to be civil courts and become instruments of military policy.

Of course the existence of a military power resting on force, so vagrant, so centralized, so necessarily heedless of the individual, is an inherent threat to liberty. But I would not lead people to rely on this Court for a review that seems to me wholly delusive. The military reasonableness of these orders can only be determined by military superiors. If the people ever let command of the war power fall into irresponsible and unscrupulous hands, the courts wield no power equal to its restraint. The chief restraint upon those who command the physical forces of the country, in the future as in the past, must be their responsibility to the political judgments of their contemporaries and to the moral judgments of history. . . .

☆

YOUNGSTOWN SHEET & TUBE COMPANY V. SAWYER

Mr. Justice Black delivered the opinion of the Court:

We are asked to decide whether the President was acting within his constitutional power when he issued an order directing the Secretary of Commerce to take possession of and operate most of the Nation's steel mills. The mill owners argue that the President's order amounts to lawmaking, a legislative function which the Constitution has expressly confided to the Congress and not to the President. The Government's position is that the order was made on findings of the President that his action was necessary to avert a national catastrophe which would inevitably result from a stoppage of steel production, and that in meeting this grave emergency the President was acting within the aggregate of his constitutional powers as the Nation's Chief Executive and the Commander in Chief of the Armed Forces of the United States. . . .

The President's power, if any, to issue the order must stem either from an act of Congress or from the Constitution itself. There is no statute that expressly authorizes the President to take possession of property as he did here. Nor is there any act of Congress to which our attention has been directed from which such a power can fairly be implied. . . .

Moreover, the use of the seizure technique to solve labor disputes in order to prevent work stoppages was not only unauthorized by any congressional enactment; prior to this controversy, Congress had refused to adopt that method of settling labor disputes. When the Taft-Hartley Act was under consideration in 1947, Congress

343 U.S. 579 (1952).

rejected an amendment which would have authorized such governmental seizures in cases of emergency. . . .

It is clear that if the President had authority to issue the order he did, it must be found in some provision of the Constitution. And it is not claimed that express constitutional language grants this power to the President. The contention is that presidential power should be implied from the aggregate of his powers under the Constitution. Particular reliance is placed on provisions in Article II which say that "The executive Power shall be vested in a President . . ."; that "he shall take Care that the Laws be faithfully executed"; and that he "shall be Commander in Chief of the Army and Navy of the United States."

The order cannot properly be sustained as an exercise of the President's military power as Commander in Chief of the Armed Forces. The Government attempts to do so by citing a number of cases upholding broad powers in military commanders engaged in day-to-day fighting in a theater of war. Such cases need not concern us here. Even though "theater of war" be an expanding concept, we cannot with faithfulness to our constitutional system hold that the Commander in Chief of the Armed Forces has the ultimate power as such to take possession of private property in order to keep labor disputes from stopping production. This is a job for the Nation's lawmakers, not for its military authorities.

Nor can the seizure order be sustained because of the several constitutional provisions that grant executive power to the President. In the framework for our Constitution, the President's power to see that laws are faithfully executed refutes the idea that he is to be a lawmaker. The Constitution limits his functions in the lawmaking process to the recommending of laws he thinks wise and the vetoing of laws he thinks bad. And the Constitution is neither silent nor equivocal about who shall make laws which the President is to execute. The first section of the first article says that "All legislative Powers herein granted shall be vested in a Congress of the United States. . . ." After granting many powers to the Congress, Article I goes on to provide that Congress may "make all Laws which shall be necessary and proper for carrying into Execution the foregoing Powers, and all other Powers vested by this Constitution in the Government of the United States, or in any Department or Officer thereof."

The President's order does not direct that a congressional policy be executed in a manner prescribed by Congress—it directs that a presidential policy be executed in a manner prescribed by the President. The preamble of the order itself, like that of many statutes, sets out reasons why the President believes certain policies

should be adopted, proclaims these policies as rules of conduct to
be followed, and again, like a statute, authorizes a government official to promulgate additional rules and regulations consistent with
the policy proclaimed and needed to carry that policy into execution.
The power of Congress to adopt such public policies as those proclaimed by the order is beyond question. It can authorize the taking
of private property for public use. It can make laws regulating the
relationships between employers and employees, prescribing rules
designed to settle labor disputes, and fixing wages and working
conditions in certain fields of our economy. The Constitution does
not subject this lawmaking power of Congress to presidential or
military supervision or control.

It is said that other Presidents without congressional authority
have taken possession of private business enterprises in order to
settle labor disputes. But even if this be true, Congress has not
thereby lost its exclusive constitutional authority to make laws
necessary and proper to carry out the powers vested by the Constitution "in the Government of the United States, or any Department
or Officer thereof."

The Founders of this Nation entrusted the lawmaking power to
the Congress alone in both good and bad times. It would do no good
to recall the historical events, the fears of power and the hopes for
freedom that lay behind their choice. Such a review would but confirm our holding that this seizure order cannot stand.

Mr. Justice Frankfurter, concurring:
. . . The issue before us can be met, and therefore should be, without attempting to define the President's powers comprehensively.

. . . We must therefore put to one side consideration of what
powers the President would have had if there had been no legislation
whatever bearing on the authority asserted by the seizure, or if the
seizure had been only for a short, explicitly temporary period, to
be terminated automatically unless congressional approval were
given. These and other questions, like or unlike, are not now here.
I would exceed my authority were I to say anything about them.

The question before the Court comes in this setting. Congress
has frequently—at least sixteen times since 1916—specifically provided for executive seizure of production, transportation, communications, or storage facilities. In every case it has qualified this grant of
power with limitations and safeguards. This body of enactments
demonstrates that Congress deemed seizure so drastic a power as to
require that it be carefully circumscribed whenever the President
was vested with this extraordinary authority.

Congress in 1947 was again called upon to consider whether

governmental seizure should be used to avoid serious industrial shutdowns. Congress decided against conferring such power generally and in advance, without special congressional enactment to meet each particular need. . . . In any event, nothing can be plainer than that Congress made a conscious choice of policy in a field full of perplexity and peculiarly within legislative responsibility for choice.

. . . Previous seizure legislation had subjected the powers granted to the President to restrictions of varying degrees of stringency. Instead of giving him even limited powers, Congress in 1947 deemed it wise to require the President, upon failure of attempts to reach a voluntary settlement, to report to Congress if he deemed the power of seizure a needed shot for his locker. The President could not ignore the specific limitations of prior seizure statutes. No more could he act in disregard of the limitation put upon seizure by the 1947 Act.

It cannot be contended that the President would have had power to issue this order had Congress explicitly negated such authority in formal legislation. Congress has expressed its will to withhold this power from the President as though it had said so in so many words. . . .

. . . The powers of the President are not as particularized as are those of Congress. But unenumerated powers do not mean undefined powers. The separation of powers built into our Constitution gives essential content to undefined provisions in the frame of our government.

To be sure, the content of the three authorities of government is not to be derived from an abstract analysis. . . . In short, a systematic, unbroken, executive practice, long pursued to the knowledge of the Congress and never before questioned, engaged in by Presidents who have also sworn to uphold the Constitution, making as it were such exercise of power part of the structure of our government, may be treated as a gloss on "executive power" vested in the President by § 1 of Art. 2. . . . [But no such] practice can be vouched for executive seizure of property at a time when this country was not at war, in the only constitutional way in which it can be at war. . . .

A scheme of government like ours no doubt at times feels the lack of power to act with complete, all-embracing, swiftly moving authority. No doubt a government with distributed authority, subject to be challenged in the courts of law, at least long enough to consider and adjudicate the challenge, labors under restrictions from which other governments are free. It has not been our tradition to envy such governments. In any event our government was designed to have such restrictions. The price was deemed not too high in view of the safeguards which these restrictions afford. I know no more impressive words on this subject than those of Mr. Justice Brandeis:

"The doctrine of the separation of powers was adopted by the Convention of 1787, not to promote efficiency but to preclude the exercise of arbitrary power. The purpose was, not to avoid friction, but, by means of the inevitable friction incident to the distribution of the governmental powers among three departments, to save the people from autocracy." . . .

Mr. Chief Justice Vinson, joined by Mr. Justice Reed and Mr. Justice Minton, dissenting:
Because we cannot agree that affirmance is proper on any ground, and because of the transcending importance of the questions presented not only in this critical litigation but also to the powers of the President and of future Presidents to act in time of crisis, we are compelled to register this dissent.

In passing upon the question of presidential powers in this case, we must first consider the context in which those powers were exercised.

Those who suggest that this is a case involving extraordinary powers should be mindful that these are extraordinary times. . . .

One is not here called upon even to consider the possibility of executive seizure of a farm, a corner grocery store or even a single industrial plant. Such considerations arise only when one ignores the central fact of this case—that the Nation's entire basic steel production would have shut down completely if there had been no government seizure. Even ignoring for the moment whatever confidential information the President may possess as "the Nation's organ for foreign affairs," the uncontroverted affidavits in this record amply support the finding that "a work stoppage would immediately jeopardize and imperil our national defense." . . .

Accordingly, if the President has any power under the Constitution to meet a critical situation in the absence of express statutory authorization, there is no basis whatever for criticizing the exercise of such power in this case.

. . . Admitting that the government could seize the mills, plaintiffs claim that the implied power of eminent domain can be exercised only under an Act of Congress; under no circumstances, they say, can that power be exercised by the President unless he can point to an express provision in enabling legislation. . . .

Under this view, the President is left powerless at the very moment when the need for action may be most pressing and when no one, other than he, is immediately capable of action. Under this view, he is left powerless because a power not expressly given to Congress is nevertheless found to rest exclusively with Congress. . . .

A review of executive action demonstrates that our Presidents have on many occasions exhibited the leadership contemplated by the Framers when they made the President Commander in Chief, and imposed upon him the trust to "take Care that the Laws be faithfully executed." With or without explicit statutory authorization, Presidents have at such times dealt with national emergencies by acting promptly and resolutely to enforce legislative programs, at least to save those programs until Congress could act. Congress and the courts have responded to such executive initiative with consistent approval.

[*The Chief Justice proceeded to review the occasions on which Presidents—from Washington to Roosevelt—exercised emergency power without congressional authorization.*]

This is but a cursory summary of executive leadership. But it amply demonstrates that Presidents have taken prompt action to enforce the laws and protect the country whether or not Congress happened to provide in advance for the particular method of execution. At the minimum, the executive actions reviewed herein sustain the action of the President in this case. And many of the cited examples of Presidential practice go far beyond the extent of power necessary to sustain the President's order to seize the steel mills. The fact that temporary executive seizures of industrial plants to meet an emergency have not been directly tested in this Court furnishes not the slightest suggestion that such actions have been illegal. Rather, the fact that Congress and the courts have consistently recognized and given their support to such executive action indicates that such a power of seizure has been accepted throughout our history. . . .

. . . Much of the argument in this case has been directed at straw men. We do not now have before us the case of a President acting solely on the basis of his own notions of the public welfare. Nor is there any question of unlimited executive power in this case. The President himself closed the door to any such claim when he sent his Message to Congress stating his purpose to abide by any action of Congress, whether approving or disapproving his seizure action. Here, the President immediately made sure that Congress was fully informed of the temporary action he had taken only to preserve the legislative programs from destruction until Congress could act.

The absence of a specific statute authorizing seizure of the steel mills as a mode of executing the laws—both the military procurement program and the anti-inflation program—has not until today been thought to prevent the President from executing the laws. Unlike an administrative commission confined to the enforcement of the statute under which it was created, or the head of a department when administering a particular statute, the President is a constitutional officer charged with taking care that a "mass of legislation" be executed. Flexibility as to mode of execution to meet critical situations is a matter of practical necessity. . . .

Plaintiffs place their primary emphasis on the Labor Management Relations Act of 1947, hereinafter referred to as the Taft-Hartley Act, but do not contend that that Act contains any provision prohibiting seizure.

. . . Plaintiffs admit that the emergency procedures of Taft-Hartley are not mandatory. Nevertheless, plaintiffs apparently argue that, since Congress did provide the eighty-day injunction method for dealing with emergency strikes, the President cannot claim that an emergency exists until the procedures of Taft-Hartley have been exhausted. This argument was not the basis of the District Court's opinion and, whatever merit the argument might have had following the enactment of Taft-Hartley, it loses all force when viewed in light of the statutory pattern confronting the President in this case. . . .

When the President acted on April 8, he had exhausted the procedures for settlement available to him. . . . Faced with immediate national peril through stoppage in steel production on the one hand and faced with destruction of the wage and price legislative programs on the other, the President took temporary possession of the steel mills as the only course open to him consistent with his duty to take care that the laws be faithfully executed. . . .

The diversity of views expressed in the six opinions of the majority, the lack of reference to authoritative precedent, the repeated reliance upon prior dissenting opinions, the complete disregard of the uncontroverted facts showing the gravity of the emergency and the temporary nature of the taking all serve to demonstrate how far afield one must go to affirm the order of the District Court.

The broad executive power granted by Article II to an officer on duty 365 days a year cannot, it is said, be invoked to avert disaster. Instead, the President must confine himself to sending a message to Congress recommending action. Under this messenger-boy concept of the Office, the President cannot even act to preserve legislative programs from destruction so that Congress will have something left to act upon. There is no judicial finding that the executive action was unwarranted because there was in fact no basis for the President's finding of the existence of an emergency for, under this view, the gravity of the emergency and the immediacy of the threatened disaster are considered irrelevant as a matter of law.

. . . Presidents have been in the past, and any man worthy of the Office should be in the future, free to take at least interim action necessary to execute legislative programs essential to survival of the Nation. A sturdy judiciary should not be swayed by the unpleasantness or unpopularity of necessary executive action, but must independently determine for itself whether the President was acting, as required by the Constitution, "to take Care that the Laws be faithfully executed.". . .

As the District Judge stated, this is no time for "timorous" judicial action. But neither is this a time for timorous executive action. Faced with the duty of executing the defense programs which Congress had enacted and the disastrous effects that any stoppage in steel production would have on those programs, the President acted to preserve those programs by seizing the steel mills. There is no question that the possession was other than temporary in character and subject to congressional direction—either approving, disapproving or regulating the manner in which the mills were to be administered and returned to the owners. The President immediately informed Congress of his action and clearly stated his intention to abide by the legislative will. No basis for claims of arbitrary action, unlimited powers or dictatorial usurpation of congressional power appears from the facts of this case. On the contrary, judicial, legislative, and executive precedents throughout our history demonstrate that in this case the President acted in full conformity with his duties under the Constitution.

PRESIDENTIAL POWER OVER ADMINISTRATIVE POLICY

☆

HUMPHREY'S EXECUTOR V. UNITED STATES

Mr. Justice Sutherland delivered the opinion of the Court:

. . . William E. Humphrey, the decedent, on December 10, 1931, was nominated by President Hoover to succeed himself as a member of the Federal Trade Commission and was confirmed by the United States Senate. He was duly commissioned for a term of seven years expiring September 25, 1938; and, after taking the required oath of office, entered upon his duties. On July 25, 1933, President Roosevelt addressed a letter to the commissioner asking for his resignation, on the ground "that the aims and purposes of the Administration with respect to the work of the commission can be carried out most effectively with personnel of my own selection," but disclaiming any reflection upon the commissioner personally or upon his services. The commissioner replied, asking time to consult his friends. After some further correspondence upon the subject, the President, on August 31, 1933, wrote the commissioner expressing the hope that the resignation would be forthcoming and saying:

"You will, I know, realize that I do not feel that your mind and my mind go along together on either the policies or the administering of the Federal Trade Commission, and, frankly, I think it is best for the people of this country that I should have a full confidence."

The commissioner declined to resign, and on October 7, 1933, the President wrote him: "Effective as of this date, you are hereby removed from the office of Commissioner of the Federal Trade Commission."

Humphrey never acquiesced in this action, but continued thereafter to insist that he was still a member of the commission, entitled

295 U.S. 602 (1935).

to perform its duties and receive the compensation provided by law at the rate of $10,000 per annum. Upon these and other facts set forth in the certificate which we deem it unnecessary to recite, the following questions are certified:

"1. Do the provisions of § 1 of the Federal Trade Commission Act, stating that 'any commissioner may be removed by the President for inefficiency, neglect of duty or malfeasance in office,' restrict or limit the power of the President to remove a commissioner except upon one or more of the causes named?

"If the foregoing question is answered in the affirmative, then—

"2. If the power of the President to remove a commissioner is restricted or limited as shown by the foregoing interrogatory and the answer made thereto, is such a restriction or limitation valid under the Constitution of the United States?"

The Federal Trade Commission Act . . . creates a commission of five members to be appointed by the President by and with the advice and consent of the Senate, and § 1 provides:

"Not more than three of the commissioners shall be members of the same political party. The first commissioners appointed shall continue in office for terms of three, four, five, six, and seven years, respectively, from the date of the taking effect of this act, the term of each to be designated by the President, but their successors shall be appointed for terms of seven years, except that any person chosen to fill a vacancy shall be appointed only for the unexpired term of the commissioner whom he shall succeed. The commission shall choose a chairman from its own membership. No commissioner shall engage in any other business, vocation, or employment. Any commissioner may be removed by the President for inefficiency, neglect of duty, or malfeasance in office.". . .

First. The question first to be considered is whether, by the provisions of § 1 of the Federal Trade Commission Act already quoted, the President's power is limited to removal for the specific causes enumerated therein. . . .

. . . The statute fixes a term of office in accordance with many precedents. The first commissioners appointed are to continue in office for terms of three, four, five, six, and seven years, respectively; and their successors are to be appointed for terms of seven years— any commissioner being subject to removal by the President for inefficiency, neglect of duty or malfeasance in office. The words of the act are definite and unambiguous.

The government says the phrase "continue in office" is of no legal significance, and moreover, applies only to the first commissioners. We think it has significance. It may be that, literally, its application is restricted as suggested; but it, nevertheless, lends support to a view contrary to that of the government as to the meaning of the entire requirement in respect of tenure; for it is not easy to suppose that Congress intended to secure the first commissioners against removal except for the causes specified and deny like security to their successors. Putting this phrase aside, however, the fixing of a definite term subject to removal for cause, unless there be some countervailing provision or circumstance indicating the contrary, which here we are unable to find, is enough to establish the legislative intent that the term is not to be curtailed in the absence of such cause. But if the intention of Congress that no removal should be made during the specified term except for one or more of the enumerated causes were not clear upon the face of the statute, as we think it is, it would be made clear by a consideration of the character of the commission and the legislative history which accompanied and preceded the passage of the act.

The commission is to be nonpartisan; and it must, from the very nature of its duties, act with entire impartiality. It is charged with the enforcement of no policy except the policy of the law. Its duties are neither political nor executive, but predominantly quasi-judicial and quasi-legislative. Like the Interstate Commerce Commission, its members are called upon to exercise the trained judgment of a body of experts "appointed by law and informed by experience.". . .

The legislative reports in both houses of Congress clearly reflect the view that a fixed term was necessary to the effective and fair administration of the law. . . .

The debates in both houses demonstrate that the prevailing view was that the commission was not to be "subject to anybody in the government but . . . only to the people of the United States," free from "political domination or control," or the "probability or possibility of such a thing"; to be "separate and apart from any existing department of the government—not subject to the orders of the President.". . .

Thus, the language of the act, the legislative reports and the general purposes of the legislation as reflected by the debates, all combine to demonstrate the congressional intent to create a body of experts who shall gain experience by length of service—a body which shall be independent of Executive authority, *except in its selection*, and free to exercise its judgment without the leave or hindrance of any other official or any department of the government. To the accomplishment of these purposes it is clear that Congress was of the opinion that length and certainty of tenure would vitally contribute. And to hold that, nevertheless, the members of the commission continue in office at the mere will of the President, might be to thwart, in large measure, the very ends which Congress sought to realize by definitely fixing the term of office.

We conclude that the intent of the act is to limit the executive power of removal to the causes enumerated, the existence of none of which is claimed here; and we pass to the second question.

Second. To support its contention that the removal provision of § 1, as we have just construed it, is an unconstitutional interference with the executive power of the President, the government's chief reliance is *Myers* v. *United States*, 272 U.S. 52. . . . Nevertheless, the narrow point actually decided was only that the President had power to remove a postmaster of the first class, without the advice and consent of the Senate, as required by act of Congress. In the course of the opinion of the court, expressions occur which tend to sustain the government's contention, but these are beyond the point involved, and therefore, do not come within the rule of stare decisis. In so far as they are out of harmony with the views here set forth, these expressions are disapproved. . . .

The office of a postmaster is so essentially unlike the office now involved that the decision in the Myers case cannot be accepted as controlling our decision here. A postmaster is an executive officer restricted to the performance of executive functions. He is charged with no duty at all related to either the legislative or judicial power. The actual decision in the Myers case finds support in the theory that such an officer is merely one of the units in the executive department and hence inherently subject to the exclusive and illimitable power of removal by the Chief Executive, whose subordinate and aid he is. Putting aside dicta, which may be followed if sufficiently persuasive but which are not controlling, the necessary reach of the decision goes far enough to include all purely executive officers. It goes no farther; much less does it include an officer who occupies no place in the executive department and who exercises no part of the executive power vested by the Constitution in the President.

The Federal Trade Commission is an administrative body created by Congress to carry into effect legislative policies embodied in the statute, in accordance with the legislative standard therein prescribed, and to perform other specified duties as a legislative or as a judicial aid. Such a body cannot in any proper sense be characterized as an arm or an eye of the executive. Its duties are performed without executive leave and, in the contemplation of the statute, must be free from executive control. In administrating the provisions of the statute in respect of "unfair methods of competition"—that is to say in filling in and administering the details embodied by the general standard —the commission acts in part quasi-legislatively and in part quasi-judicially. In making investigations and reports thereon for the information of Congress under § 6, in aid of the legislative power it acts as a legislative agency. Under § 7, which authorizes the commission to act as a master in chancery under rules prescribed by the court, it acts as an agency of the judiciary. To the extent that it exercises any executive function—as distinguished from executive power in the constitutional sense—it does so in the discharge and effectuation of its quasi-legislative or quasi-judicial powers, or as an agency of the legislative or judicial departments of the government.

If Congress is without authority to prescribe causes for removal of members of the Trade Commission and limit executive power of removal accordingly, that power at once becomes practically all inclusive in respect of civil officers, with the exception of the judiciary provided for by the Constitution. The Solicitor General, at the bar, apparently recognizing this to be true, with commendable candor agreed that his view in respect of the removability of members of the Federal Trade Commission necessitated a like view in respect of the Interstate Commerce Commission and the Court of Claims. We are thus confronted with the serious question whether not only the members of these quasi-legislative and quasi-judicial bodies, but the judges of the legislative Court of Claims, exercising judicial power . . . continue in office only at the pleasure of the President.

We think it plain under the Constitution that illimitable power of removal is not possessed by the President in respect of officers of the character of those just named. The authority of Congress, in creating quasi-legislative or quasi-judicial agencies, to require them to act in discharge of their duties independently of executive control, cannot well be doubted; and that authority includes, as an appropriate incident, power to fix the period during which they shall continue, and to forbid their removal except for cause in the meantime. For it is quite evident that one who holds his office only during the pleasure of another cannot be depended upon to maintain an attitude of independence against the latter's will.

The fundamental necessity of maintaining each of the three general departments of government entirely free from the control or coercive influence, direct or indirect, of either of the others, has often been stressed and is hardly open to serious question. So much is implied in the very fact of the separation of the powers of these departments by the Constitution, and in the rule which recognizes their essential co-equality. The sound application of a principle that makes one master in his own house precludes him from imposing his control in the house of another who is master there. . . .

The power of removal here claimed for the President falls within this principle, since its coercive influence threatens the independence of a commission, which is not only wholly disconnected from the executive department, but which, as already fully appears, was created by Congress as a means of carrying into operation legislative and judicial powers, and as an agency of the legislative and judicial departments.

In the light of the question now under consideration, we have reexamined the precedents referred to in the Myers case, and find nothing in them to justify a conclusion contrary to that which we have reached. . . .

The result of what we now have said is this: Whether the power of the President to remove an officer shall prevail over the authority of Congress to condition the power by fixing a definite term and precluding a removal except for cause will depend upon the character of the office. The Myers decision, affirming the power of the President alone to make the removal, is confined to purely executive officers. And as to officers of the kind here under consideration, we hold that no removal can be made during the prescribed term for which the officer is appointed, except for one or more of the causes named in the applicable statute. . . .

To the extent that, between the decision in the Myers case, which sustains the unrestrictable power of the President to remove purely executive officers, and our present decision that such power does not extend to an office such as that here involved there shall remain a field of doubt, we leave such cases as may fall within it for future consideration and determination as they arise.

PRESIDENTIAL POWER TO PROTECT THE PEACE

☆

IN RE NEAGLE

Mr. Justice Miller delivered the opinion of the Court:

. . . Without a more minute discussion of this testimony, it produces upon us the conviction of a settled purpose on the part of Terry and his wife, amounting to a conspiracy, to murder Justice Field. And we are quite sure that if Neagle had been merely a brother or a friend of Judge Field, traveling with him, and aware of all the previous relations of Terry to the judge—as he was—of his bitter animosity, his declared purpose to have revenge even to the point of killing him, he would have been justified in what he did in defense of Mr. Justice Field's life, and possibly of his own.

But such a justification would be a proper subject for consideration on a trial of the case for murder in the courts of the State of California, and there exists no authority in the courts of the United States to discharge the prisoner while held in custody by the State authorities for this offense, unless there be found in aid of the defense of the prisoner some element of power and authority asserted under the government of the United States.

This element is said to be found in the facts that Mr. Justice Field, when attacked, was in the immediate discharge of his duty as judge of the Circuit Courts of the United States within California; that the assault upon him grew out of the animosity of Terry and wife, arising out of the previous discharge of his duty as Circuit Justice in the case for which they were committed for contempt of court; and that the deputy marshal of the United States, who killed Terry in defense of Field's life, was charged with a duty under the law of the United States to protect Field from the violence which Terry was inflicting, and which was intended to lead to Field's death.

135 U.S. 1 (1890).

To the inquiry whether this proposition is sustained by law and the facts which we have recited, we now address ourselves. . . .

We have no doubt that Mr. Justice Field when attacked by Terry was engaged in the discharge of his duties as Circuit Justice of the Ninth Circuit, and was entitled to all the protection under those circumstances which the law could give him.

It is urged, however, that there exists no statute authorizing any such protection as that which Neagle was instructed to give Judge Field in the present case, and indeed no protection whatever against a vindictive or malicious assault growing out of the faithful discharge of his official duties; and that the language of section 753 of the Revised Statutes, that the party seeking the benefit of the writ of habeas corpus must in this connection show that he is "in custody for an act done or omitted in pursuance of a law of the United States," makes it necessary that upon this occasion it should be shown that the act for which Neagle is imprisoned was done by virtue of an Act of Congress. It is not supposed that any special Act of Congress exists which authorizes the marshals or deputy marshals of the United States in express terms to accompany the judges of the Supreme Court through their circuits, and act as a bodyguard to them, to defend them against malicious assaults against their persons. But we are of opinion that this view of the statute is an unwarranted restriction of the meaning of a law designed to extend in a liberal manner the benefit of the writ of habeas corpus to persons imprisoned for the performance of their duty. And we are satisfied that if it was the duty of Neagle, under the circumstances, a duty which could only arise under the laws of the United States, to defend Mr. Justice Field from a murderous attack upon him, he brings himself within the meaning of the section we have recited. This view of the subject is confirmed by the alternative provision, that he must be in custody "for an act done or omitted in pursuance of a law of the United States or of an order, process, or decree of a court or judge thereof, or is in custody in violation of the Constitution or of a law or treaty of the United States."

In the view we take of the Constitution of the United States, any obligation fairly and properly inferable from that instrument, or any duty of the marshal to be derived from the general scope of his duties under the laws of the United States, is "a law" within the meaning of this phrase. It would be a great reproach to the system of government of the United States, declared to be within its sphere sovereign and supreme, if there is to be found within the domain of its powers no means of protecting the judges, in the conscientious and faithful discharge of their duties, from the malice and hatred of those upon whom their judgments may operate unfavorably. . . .

Where, then, are we to look for the protection which we have shown Judge Field was entitled to when engaged in the discharge of his official duties? Not to the courts of the United States; because, as has been more than once said in this court, in the division of the powers of government between the three great departments, executive, legislative and judicial, the judicial is the weakest for the purposes of self-protection and for the enforcement of the powers which it exercises. The ministerial officers through whom its commands must be executed are marshals of the United States, and belong emphatically to the executive department of the government. They are appointed by the President, with the advice and consent of the Senate. They are removable from office at his pleasure. They are subjected by Act of Congress to the supervision and control of the Department of Justice, in the hands of one of the Cabinet officers of the President, and their compensation is provided by Acts of Congress. The same may be said of the district attorneys of the United States, who prosecute and defend the claims of the government in the courts.

The legislative branch of the government can only protect the judicial officers by the enactment of laws for that purpose, and the argument we are now combating assumes that no such law has been passed by Congress.

If we turn to the executive department of the government, we find a very different condition of affairs. The Constitution, section 3, Article II, declares that the President "shall take care that the laws be faithfully executed," and he is provided with the means of fulfilling this obligation by his authority to commission all the officers of the United States, and, by and with the advice and consent of the Senate, to appoint the most important of them and to fill vacancies. He is declared to be Commander in Chief of the army and navy of the United States. The duties which are thus imposed upon him he is further enabled to perform by the recognition in the Constitution, and the creation by Acts of Congress, of executive departments, which have varied in number from four or five to seven or eight, the heads of which are familiarly called cabinet ministers. These aid him in the performance of the great duties of his office, and represent him in a thousand acts to which it can hardly be supposed his personal attention is called, and thus he is enabled to fulfill the duty of his great department, expressed in the phrase that "he shall take care that the laws be faithfully executed."

Is this duty limited to the enforcement of Acts of Congress or of treaties of the United States according to their express terms, or does it include the rights, duties, and obligations growing out of the Constitution itself, our international relations, and all the protection implied by the nature of the government under the Constitution? . . .

We cannot doubt the power of the President to take measures for the protection of a judge of one of the courts of the United States, who, while in the discharge of the duties of his office, is threatened with a personal attack which may probably result in his death, and we think it clear that where this protection is to be afforded through the civil power, the Department of Justice is the proper one to set in motion the necessary means of protection. . . .

But there is positive law investing the marshals and their deputies with powers which not only justify what Marshal Neagle did in this matter, but which imposed it upon him as a duty. In chapter fourteen of the Revised Statutes of the United States, which is devoted to the appointment and duties of the district attorneys, marshals, and clerks of the courts of the United States, section 788 declares:

"The marshals and their deputies shall have, in each State, the same powers, in executing the laws of the United States, as the sheriffs and their deputies in such State may have, by law, in executing the laws thereof."

If, therefore, a sheriff of the State of California was authorized to do in regard to the laws of California what Neagle did, that is, if he was authorized to keep the peace, to protect a judge from assault and murder, then Neagle was authorized to do the same thing in reference to the laws of the United States. . . .

That there is a peace of the United States; that a man assaulting a judge of the United States while in the discharge of his duties violates that peace; that in such case the marshal of the United States stands in the same relation to the peace of the United States which the sheriff of the county does to the peace of the State of California; are questions too clear to need argument to prove them. That it would be the duty of a sheriff, if one had been present at this assault by Terry upon Judge Field, to prevent this breach of the peace, to prevent this assault, to prevent the murder which was contemplated by it, cannot be doubted. And if, in performing this duty, it became necessary for the protection of Judge Field, or of himself, to kill Terry, in a case where, like this, it was evidently a question of the choice of who should be killed, the assailant and violator of the law and disturber of the peace, or the unoffending man who was in his power, there can be no question of the authority of the sheriff to have killed Terry. So the marshal of the United States, charged with the duty of protecting and guarding the judge of the United States court against this special assault upon his person and his life, being present at the critical moment, when prompt action was necessary, found it to be his duty, a duty which he had no liberty to refuse to perform, to take the steps which resulted in Terry's death. This duty was imposed on him by the section of the Revised Statutes which we have recited, in connection with the powers conferred by the State of California upon its peace officers, which become, by this statute, in proper cases, transferred as duties to the marshals of the United States. . . .

The result at which we have arrived upon this examination is, that in the protection of the person and the life of Mr. Justice Field while in the discharge of his official duties, Neagle was authorized to resist the attack of Terry upon him; that Neagle was correct in the belief that without prompt action on his part the assault of Terry upon the judge would have ended in the death of the latter; that such being his well-founded belief, he was justified in taking the life of Terry, as the only means of preventing the death of the man who was intended to be his victim; that in taking the life of Terry, under the circumstances, he was acting under the authority of the law of the United States, and was justified in so doing; and that he is not liable to answer in the courts of California on account of his part in that transaction. . . .

PRESIDENTIAL POWER
AND EXECUTIVE PRIVILEGE

☆

UNITED STATES V. NIXON

Mr. Chief Justice Burger delivered the opinion of the Court.

This litigation presents for review the denial of a motion, filed in the District Court on behalf of the President of the United States, in the case of United States v Mitchell to quash a third-party subpoena duces tecum issued by the United States District Court for the District of Columbia, pursuant to Fed Rul Crim Proc 17(c). The subpoena directed the President to produce certain tape recordings and documents relating to his conversations with aides and advisers. The court rejected the President's claim of absolute executive privilege, of lack of jurisdiction, and of failure to satisfy the requirements of Rule 17(c). The President appealed to the Court of Appeals. We granted both the United States' petition for certiorari before judgment and also the President's cross-petition for certiorari before judgment because of the public importance of the issues presented and the need for their prompt resolution.

On March 1, 1974, a grand jury of the United States District Court for the District of Columbia returned an indictment charging seven named individuals [John N. Mitchell, H. R. Haldeman, John D. Ehrlichman, Charles W. Colson, Robert C. Mardian, Kenneth W. Parkinson, and Gordon Strachan] with various offenses, including conspiracy to defraud the United States and to obstruct justice. Although he was not designated as such in the indictment, the grand jury named the President, among others, as an unindicted coconspirator. On April 18, 1974, upon motion of the Special Prosecutor a subpoena duces tecum was issued pursuant to Rule 17(c) to the President by the United States District Court and made returnable on

418 U.S. 683 (1974).

May 2, 1974. This subpoena required the production, in advance of the September 9 trial date, of certain tapes, memoranda, papers, transcripts, or other writings relating to certain precisely identified meetings between the President and others. The Special Prosecutor was able to fix the time, place, and persons present at these discussions because the White House daily logs and appointment records had been delivered to him. On April 30, the President publicly released edited transcripts of 43 conversations; portions of 20 conversations subject to subpoena in the present case were included. On May 1, 1974, the President's counsel filed a "special appearance" and a motion to quash the subpoena under Rule 17(c). This motion was accompanied by a formal claim of privilege. At a subsequent hearing, further motions to expunge the grand jury's action naming the President as an unindicted coconspirator and for protective orders against the disclosure of that information were filed or raised orally by counsel for the President.

On May 20, 1974, the District Court denied the motion to quash and the motions to expunge and for protective orders. It further ordered "the President or any subordinate officer, official, or employee with custody or control of the documents or objects subpoenaed," to deliver to the District Court, on or before May 31, 1974, the originals of all subpoenaed items, as well as an index and analysis of those items, together with tape copies of those portions of the subpoenaed recordings for which transcripts had been released to the public by the President on April 30. The District Court rejected jurisdictional challenges based on a contention that the dispute was nonjusticiable because it was between the Special Prosecutor and the Chief Executive and hence "intra-executive" in character; it also rejected the contention that the judiciary was without authority to review an assertion of executive privilege by the President. The court's rejection of the first challenge was based on the authority and powers vested in the Special Prosecutor by the regulation promulgated by the Attorney General; the court concluded that a justiciable controversy was presented. The second challenge was held to be foreclosed by the decision in Nixon v Sirica (1973).

The District Court held that the judiciary, not the President, was the final arbiter of a claim of executive privilege. The court concluded that, under the circumstances of this case, the presumptive privilege was overcome by the Special Prosecutor's prima facie "demonstration of need sufficiently compelling to warrant judicial examination in chambers. . . ." The court held, finally, that the Special Prosecutor had satisfied the requirements of Rule 17(c). The District Court stayed its order pending appellate review on condition that review was sought before 4 p.m., May 24. The court further provided that matters filed under seal remain under seal when transmitted as part of the record.

On May 24, 1974, the President filed a timely notice of appeal from the District Court order, and the certified record from the District Court was docketed in the United States Court of Appeals for the District of Columbia Circuit. On the same day, the President also filed a petition for writ of mandamus in the Court of Appeals seeking review of the District Court order.

Later on May 24, the Special Prosecutor also filed, in this Court, a petition for a writ of certiorari before judgment. On May 31, the petition was granted with an expedited briefing schedule. On June 6, the President filed, under seal, a cross-petition for writ of certiorari before judgment. This cross-petition was granted June 15, and the case was set for argument on July 8, 1974.

[*On the various procedural issues, the Court concluded: 1. that the case was properly before it, 2. that the matter presented was justiciable, and 3. that the issuance of a subpoena to the President was justified.*]

. . . [We] turn to the claim that the subpoena should be quashed because it demands "confidential conversations between a President and his close advisors that it would be inconsistent with the public interest to produce." The first contention is a broad claim that the separation of powers doctrine precludes judicial review of a President's claim of privilege. The second contention is that if he does not prevail on the claim of absolute privilege, the court should hold as a matter of constitutional law that the privilege prevails over the subpoena duces tecum.

In the performance of assigned constitutional duties each branch of the Government must initially interpret the Constitution, and the interpretation of its powers by any branch is due great respect from the others. The President's counsel, as we have noted, reads the Constitution as providing an absolute privilege of confidentiality for all Presidential communications. Many decisions of this Court, however, have unequivocally reaffirmed the holding of Marbury v Madison, that "it is emphatically the province and duty of the judicial department to say what the law is."

No holding of the Court has defined the scope of judicial power specifically relating to the enforcement of a subpoena for confidential Presidential communications for use in a criminal prosecution, but other exercises of power by the Executive Branch and the Legislative Branch have been found invalid as in conflict with the Constitution. In a series of cases, the Court interpreted the explicit immunity conferred by express provisions of the Constitution on Members of the House and Senate by the Speech or Debate Clause, US Const Art I, § 6. Since this Court has consistently exercised the power to construe and delineate claims arising under express powers, it must follow that the Court has authority to interpret claims with respect to powers alleged to derive from enumerated powers.

Our system of government "requires that federal courts on occasion interpret the Constitution in a manner at variance with the construction given the document by another branch." The Court [has] stated:

"Deciding whether a matter has in any measure been committed by the Constitution to another branch of government, or whether the action of that branch exceeds whatever authority has been committed, is itself a delicate exercise in constitutional interpretation, and is a responsibility of this Court as ultimate interpreter of the Constitution."

Notwithstanding the deference each branch must accord the others, the "judicial Power of the United States" vested in the federal courts by Art III, § 1, of the Constitution can no more be shared with the Executive Branch than the Chief Executive, for example, can share with the Judiciary the veto power, or the Congress share with the Judiciary the power to override a Presidential veto. Any other conclusion would be contrary to the basic concept of separation of powers and the checks and balances that flow from the scheme of a tripartite government. We therefore reaffirm that it is the province and duty of this Court "to say what the law is" with respect to the claim of privilege presented in this case.

In support of his claim of absolute privilege, the President's counsel urges two grounds, one of which is common to all governments and one of which is peculiar to our system of separation of powers. The first ground is the valid need for protection of communications between high Government officials and those who advise and assist them in the performance of their manifold duties; the importance of this confidentiality is too plain to require further discussion. Human experience teaches that those who expect public dissemination of their remarks may well temper candor with a concern for appearances and for their own interests to the detriment of the decision-making process. Whatever the nature of the privilege of confidentiality of Presidential communications in the exercise of Art II powers, the privilege can be said to derive from the supremacy of each branch within its own assigned area of constitutional duties. Certain powers and privileges flow from the nature of enumerated powers; the protection of the confidentiality of Presidential communications has similar constitutional underpinnings.

The second ground asserted by the President's counsel in support of the claim of absolute privilege rests on the doctrine of separation of powers. Here it is argued that the independence of the Executive Branch within its own sphere insulates a President from a judicial subpoena in an ongoing criminal prosecution, and thereby protects confidential Presidential communications.

, However, neither the doctrine of separation of powers, nor the need for confidentiality of high-level communications, without more, can sustain an absolute, unqualified Presidential privilege of immunity from judicial process under all circumstances. The President's need for complete candor and objectivity from advisers calls for great deference from the courts. However, when the privilege depends solely on the broad, undifferentiated claim of public interest in the confidentiality of such conversations, a confrontation with other values arises. Absent a claim of need to protect military, diplomatic, or sensitive national security secrets, we find it difficult to accept the argument that even the very important interest in confidentiality of Presidential communications is significantly diminished by production of such material for in camera inspection with all the protection that a district court will be obliged to provide.

The impediment that an absolute, unqualified privilege would place in the way of the primary constitutional duty of the Judicial Branch to do justice in criminal prosecutions would plainly conflict with the function of the courts under Art III. In designing the structure of our Government and dividing and allocating the sovereign power among three co-equal branches, the Framers of the Constitution sought to provide a comprehensive system, but the separate powers were not intended to operate with absolute independence.

"While the Constitution diffuses power the better to secure liberty, it also contemplates that practice will integrate the dispersed powers into a workable government. It enjoins upon its branches separateness but interdependence, autonomy but reciprocity."

To read the Art II powers of the President as providing an absolute privilege as against a subpoena essential to enforcement of criminal statutes on no more than a generalized claim of the public interest in confidentiality of nonmilitary and nondiplomatic discussions would upset the constitutional balance of "a workable government" and gravely impair the role of the courts under Art III.

Since we conclude that the legitimate needs of the judicial process may outweigh Presidential privilege, it is necessary to resolve those competing interests in a manner that preserves the essential functions of each branch. The right and indeed the duty to resolve that question does not free the judiciary from according high respect to the representations made on behalf of the President.

The expectation of a President to the confidentiality of his conversations and correspondence, like the claim of confidentiality of judicial deliberations, for example, has all the values to which we accord deference for the privacy of all citizens and added to those values the necessity for protection of the public interest in candid, objective, and even blunt or harsh opinions in Presidential decision-making. A President and those who assist him must be free to explore alternatives in the process of shaping policies and making decisions and to do so in a way many would be unwilling to express except privately. These are the considerations justifying a presumptive privilege for Presidential communications. The privilege is fundamental to the operation of government and inextricably rooted in the separation of powers under the Constitution. In Nixon v Sirica, the Court of Appeals held that such Presidential communications are "presumptively privileged," and this position is accepted by both parties in the present litigation. We agree with Mr. Chief Justice Marshall's observation, therefore, that "[i]n no case of this kind would a court be required to proceed against the President as against an ordinary individual."

But this presumptive privilege must be considered in light of our historic commitment to the rule of law. This is nowhere more profoundly manifest than in our view that "the twofold aim [of criminal justice] is that guilt shall not escape or innocence suffer." We have elected to employ an adversary system of criminal justice in which the parties contest all issues before a court of law. The need to develop all relevant facts in the adversary system is both fundamental and comprehensive. The ends of criminal justice would be defeated if judgments were to be founded on a partial or speculative presentation of the facts. The very integrity of the judicial system and public confidence in the system depend on full disclosure of all the facts, within the framework of the rules of evidence. To ensure that justice is done, it is imperative to the function of courts that compulsory process be available for the production of evidence needed either by the prosecution or by the defense.

Only recently the Court restated the ancient proposition of law, albeit in the context of a grand jury inquiry rather than a trial, "that 'the public . . . has a right to every man's evidence,' except for those persons protected by a constitutional, common-law, or statutory privilege."

The privileges referred to by the Court are designed to protect weighty and legitimate competing interests. Thus, the Fifth Amendment to the Constitution provides that no man "shall be compelled in any criminal case to be a witness against himself." And, generally, an attorney or a priest may not be required to disclose what has been revealed in professional confidence. These and other interests are recognized in law by privileges against forced disclosure, established in the Constitution, by statute, or at common law. Whatever their origins, these exceptions to the demand for every man's evidence are not lightly created nor expansively construed, for they are in derogation of the search for truth.

In this case the President challenges a subpoena served on him as a third party requiring the production of materials for use in a criminal prosecution; he does so on the claim that he has a privilege against disclosure of confidential communications. He does not place his claim of privilege on the ground they are military or diplomatic secrets. As to these areas of Art II duties the courts have traditionally shown the utmost deference to Presidential responsibilities. In C. & S. Air Lines v Waterman S. S. Corp. (1948), dealing with Presidential authority involving foreign policy considerations, the Court said:

"The President, both as Commander-in-Chief and as the Nation's organ for foreign affairs, has available intelligence services whose reports are not and ought not be published to the world. It would be intolerable that courts, without the relevant information, should review and perhaps nullify actions of the Executive taken on information properly held secret."

In United States v Reynolds (1953), dealing with a claimant's demand for evidence in a damage case against the Government the Court said:

"It may be possible to satisfy the court, from all the circumstances of the case, that there is a reasonable danger that compulsion of the evidence will expose military matters which, in the interest of national security, should not be divulged. When this is the case, the occasion for the privilege is appropriate, and the court should not jeopardize the security which the privilege is meant to protect by insisting upon an examination of the evidence, even by the judge alone, in chambers."

No case of the Court, however, has extended this high degree of deference to a President's generalized interest in confidentiality. Nowhere in the Constitution, as we have noted earlier, is there any explicit reference to a privilege of confidentiality, yet to the extent this interest relates to the effective discharge of a President's powers, it is constitutionally based.

The right to the production of all evidence at a criminal trial similarly has constitutional dimensions. The Sixth Amendment explicitly confers upon every defendant in a criminal trial the right "to be confronted with the witnesses against him" and "to have compulsory process for obtaining witnesses in his favor." Moreover, the Fifth Amendment also guarantees that no person shall be deprived of liberty without due process of law. It is the manifest duty of the courts to vindicate those guarantees, and to accomplish that it is essential that all relevant and admissible evidence be produced.

In this case we must weigh the importance of the general privilege of confidentiality of Presidential communications in performance of his responsibilities against the inroads of such a privilege on the fair administration of criminal justice. The interest in preserving confidentiality is weighty indeed and entitled to great respect. However, we cannot conclude that advisers will be moved to temper the candor of their remarks by the infrequent occasions of disclosure because of the possiblity that such conversations will be called for in the context of a criminal prosecution.

On the other hand, the allowance of the privilege to withhold evidence that is demonstrably relevant in a criminal trial would cut deeply into the guarantee of due process of law and gravely impair the basic function of the courts. A President's acknowledged need for confidentiality in the communications of his office is general in nature, whereas the constitutional need for production of relevant evidence in a criminal proceeding is specific and central to the fair adjudication of a particular criminal case in the administration of justice. Without access to specific facts a criminal prosecution may be totally frustrated. The President's broad interest in confidentiality of communications will not be vitiated by disclosure of a limited number of conversations preliminarily shown to have some bearing on the pending criminal cases.

We conclude that when the ground for asserting privilege as to subpoenaed materials sought for use in a criminal trial is based only on the generalized interest in confidentiality, it cannot prevail over the fundamental demands of due process of law in the fair administration of criminal justice. The generalized assertion of privilege must yield to the demonstrated, specific need for evidence in a pending criminal trial.

We have earlier determined that the District Court did not err in authorizing the issuance of the subpoena. If a President concludes that compliance with a subpoena would be injurious to the public interest he may properly, as was done here, invoke a claim of privilege on the return of the subpoena. Upon receiving a claim of privilege from the Chief Executive, it became the further duty of the District Court to treat the subpoenaed material as presumptively privileged and to require the Special Prosecutor to demonstrate that the Presidential material was "essential to the justice of the [pending criminal] case." Here the District Court treated the material as presumptively privileged, proceeded to find that the Special Prosecutor had made a sufficient showing to rebut the presumption, and ordered an in camera examination of the subpoenaed material. On the basis of our examination of the record we are unable to conclude that the District Court erred in ordering the inspection. Accordingly we affirm the order of the District Court that subpoenaed materials be transmitted to that court. We now turn to the important question of the District Court's responsibilities in conducting the in camera examination of Presidential materials or communications delivered under the compulsion of the subpoena duces tecum.

Enforcement of the subpoena duces tecum was stayed pending this Court's resolution of the issues raised by the petitions for certiorari.

Those issues now having been disposed of, the matter of implementation will rest with the District Court. "[T]he guard, furnished to [the President] to protect him from being harassed by vexatious and unnecessary subpoenas, is to be looked for in the conduct of a [district] court after those subpoenas have issued; not in any circumstance which is to precede their being issued." [U.S. v Burr] Statements that meet the test of admissibility and relevance must be isolated; all other material must be excised. At this stage the District Court is not limited to representations of the Special Prosecutor as to the evidence sought by the subpoena; the material will be available to the District Court. It is elementary that in camera inspection of evidence is always a procedure calling for scrupulous protection against any release or publication of material not found by the court, at that stage, probably admissible in evidence and relevant to the issues of the trial for which it is sought. That being true of an ordinary situation, it is obvious that the District Court has a very heavy responsibility to see to it that Presidential conversations, which are either not relevant or not admissible, are accorded that high degree of respect due the President of the United States. Mr. Chief Justice Marshall, sitting as a trial judge in the Burr case was extraordinarily careful to point out that "in no case of this kind would a court be required to proceed against the president as against an ordinary individual."

Marshall's statement cannot be read to mean in any sense that a President is above the law, but relates to the singularly unique role under Art II of a President's communications and activities, related to the performance of duties under that Article. Moreover, a President's communications and activities encompass a vastly wider range of sensitive material than would be true of any "ordinary individual." It is therefore necessary in the public interest to afford Presidential confidentiality the greatest protection consistent with the fair administration of justice. The need for confidentiality even as to idle conversations with associates in which casual reference might be made concerning political leaders within the country or foreign statesmen is too obvious to call for further treatment. We have no doubt that the District Judge will at all times accord to Presidential records that high degree of deference suggested in United States v Burr and will discharge his responsibility to see to it that until released to the Special Prosecutor no in camera material is revealed to anyone. This burden applies with even greater force to excised material; once the decision is made to excise, the material is restored to its privileged status and should be returned under seal to its lawful custodian.

Since this matter came before the Court during the pendency of a criminal prosecution, and on representations that time is of the essence, the mandate shall issue forthwith.

IV

EXPERT
VIEWS

PROFESSIONAL STUDENTS of government and politics have always been fascinated by the Presidency. Generations of both foreign and American scholars have regarded the office as a great experiment in constitutional-democratic leadership and have watched its development closely. Each of these observers has had his own ideas about the executive's proper role in American government and all have become engaged in the controversy over presidential power.

As with other commentators on the subject, the experts vary widely in their views. Among the foreign observers, Alexis de Tocqueville at the beginning of the Jacksonian era despaired of an effective executive because "All his important acts are directly or indirectly submitted to the legislature; and where he is independent of it he can do but little." In 1906, James Bryce voiced doubts about the office because the American system did not tend to bring "the highest gifts to the highest place." But Harold Laski, writing in the glow of Franklin Roosevelt's achievements, was hopeful that the social and economic changes of the 1930s would produce a new Presidency with power "commensurate to the functions he has to perform." And in 1960 Denis Brogan noted "the present predominance of the President." On the whole, foreign—and particularly British—students of the office, with their parliamentary proclivities, have argued for strong presidential leadership and have been troubled by those characteristics of American politics that tend to thwart the establishment of such leadership.

Despite the cogency of these views from abroad, the readings presented here are confined to the conceptions of Americans who have observed (and in some cases been associated with) the Presidency as professional students of the office and its power. Moreover, since the preceding selections have included much historical material, there is no attempt to include expert views from the inception of the office. The purpose in this final section is to concentrate on the modern Presidency and to focus in on the issue of whether the power of the contemporary office is adequate to meet the demands of our time. The readings are divided into two groups. The first represents the dominant pattern of professional thought about the Presidency in the period from Franklin Roosevelt to the Vietnam war and the Watergate affair; the second represents the thrust of expert thinking since those critical events.

Most commentators in the pre-Vietnam/Watergate period viewed the Presidency as an office of great and expanding power, and most regarded its development with enthusiasm and optimism. Among the first to recognize that the Presidency as it was emerging under Roosevelt would be a different and permanently strong office, Professor Edward Corwin warned against the "aggrandizement" of power by the President. He concluded that the Roosevelt Presidency was excessively and dangerously powerful, and he expressed concern lest it become a "matrix of dictatorship." Corwin proposed an institutional change — the inclusion of congressional leaders in the President's cabinet — to prevent such a result. His proposal was rejected and his admonition ignored, however, as the Presidency continued to grow in authority during World War II, and as its power became institutionalized during the era of protracted crisis that followed. Not for thirty years would any major scholar question the necessity or the efficacy of the strong Presidency.

On the contrary, the concept of the President as the paramount leader of both American society and the Free World community was universally and proudly proclaimed. Clinton Rossiter was in the forefront of those who praised and extolled this "new Presidency." He popularized the idea that the President plays a wide variety of roles which taken together make him "a leader without any equal in the history of democracy" and give him prodigious power to shape a better future. Rossiter cautioned against any major changes affecting the Presidency's focal position, since the office had served us so well. His advice to America was "Leave Your Presidency Alone!"

Similarly, James McGregor Burns, in his book *Presidential Government*, thought the Presidency had reached a pinnacle of prestige and power. Indeed, he feared that with what seemed to be the imminent achievement of its contemporary aims, the office might lose its dynamism and be unable to turn to new purposes. But Burns believed that "the stronger we make the Presidency, the more we . . . can hope to realize modern liberal democratic goals."

My own attempt to describe and analyze the power of the Presi-

dency at this high point in its development presented the view that it
had become an institutionalized version of the enormously powerful
crisis governments established by Lincoln and Wilson and Roosevelt,
and that in an age of recurrent emergencies it would probably grow
even more powerful. I regarded the Presidency as the nation's indispensable instrument in meeting the challenges of our time, and
believed that it would remain a model of constitutional democratic
leadership.

Virtually without exception this was the dominant theme of the
time. And when Richard Neustadt at "mid-century" cast a cool,
professional eye on the array of countervailing forces and systemic
restraints that limit a President's freedom to choose and to act, he too
was concerned with sustaining and strengthening the modern strong
Presidency. Describing the office in operational terms and confining
himself largely to domestic decision-making and problem-solving,
Neustadt concluded that on a day-to-day basis the Presidency's power
is primarily "the power to persuade," not to command. His realism
was cogent and refreshing, but Neustadt's purpose was to provide
instruction in the ways Presidents could operate within a system of
constraints to maximize their power and achieve their goals.

In approaching the Presidency as he did, Neustadt also made it
clear that despite the post-World War II institutionalization of the
office and its power, the Presidency remained a highly personal
place. And it is this personal element or "presidential character" that
James David Barber sought to analyze at a critical juncture in the
history of the presidential office. Barber's psycho-political typology
added a new dimension to the traditional "strong-weak" measures of
presidential efficacy, and his "activity-passivity" and "positive-
negative affect" baselines in defining presidential types were as much
a pioneering landmark as Neustadt's principles of operational reality.
But Barber's "scientific" approach to predicting presidential performance also was designed ultimately to indicate the sort of personality
best suited to lead the nation. Each of his character types has something to offer, but Barber's clear preference is for the "active-positive"
(the President who invests great energy in his job, and who gets great
satisfaction from it). As Neustadt sought to help Presidents enhance
their own chances of success, so Barber hoped to instruct all of us in
how to choose an effective national leader. His message—conveyed
just before Richard Nixon's re-election—was "look to character
first."

The idea that limitation of presidential power was either necessary
or desirable did not become a viable proposition among professionals
until Lyndon Johnson's "Great Society" Presidency sank into the
morass of Vietnam; it was not widely accepted until Richard Nixon
became entwined in the web of the Watergate affair. Then, in a wide

pendular swing impelled by these two events, many experts — along with a substantial part of Congress and the general public — agreed that presidential power had gotten out of control, that the strong Presidency had indeed developed into Professor Corwin's "matrix of dictatorship," and that its power had to be delimited, confined, and secularized.

Leading this post-Vietnam/Watergate reassessment Arthur Schlesinger, Jr., admittedly one of those who had previously glorified the strong Presidency, looked to enforcement of the "system of accountability" to counter the abuses of the "imperial Presidency." That he among others had been too "uncritical" in the past Schlesinger acknowledged, but he argued that the office had nonetheless served the nation well, and that what we needed was not structural reforms but a national "consciousness-raising" to restore the proper balance between power and accountability. Schlesinger still believes in a strong Presidency — but "a strong Presidency *within the Constitution.*"

Strengthening the political system as a whole in order to provide constraints against an unfettered Presidency is also the prescription of Aaron Wildavsky, who adds the admonition that all of us must simultaneously lower our expectations of what government and its leaders can or should do. The Presidency will remain a powerful office in the future, says Wildavksy, but it will be less able (and its incumbents will be less willing) to use presidential power as routinely as in the past. There will be an "offensive retreat" of the Presidency as Presidents become preoccupied with strategy rather than tactics, with systemic oversight rather than with solving society's problems.

Thomas Cronin elaborates the theme of unrealistic expectations by describing ten paradoxes or inherently contradictory demands related to presidential power and performance that no institution or person can satisfy, but which the American people nonetheless expect their President to fulfill. Thus Cronin points out that we want and expect our Presidents to lead but also to be responsive to public opinion, to be models of morality but always ready to compromise, to have a common touch but be uncommon people — in short, to possess all the talents, skills, and qualities necessary to assure effective and successful national and world leadership. Cronin suggests that Presidents must concentrate on those aspects of their jobs which are practicable for them personally and which require priority consideration in terms of the national interest. And he also notes that the rest of us must understand our own responsibility in insisting on the impossible. "Let us ask our Presidents to give us their best," writes Cronin, "but let us not ask them to deliver more than the Presidency — or any single institution — has to give."

The selection by Richard Pious is the most negative and pessimistic assessment of the state of the post-Vietnam/Watergate Presidency presented here. Pious forecasts great difficulty or ultimate failure for future Presidents in virtually every area of executive activity. Presidential attempts to control the national agenda, he believes, will be frustrated by interest groups, undisciplined legislators, and the media; Congress will be increasingly obstreperous and legislative-veto mechanisms more troublesome; coherent policies will be harder to initiate, develop, and effectuate; and finally "Presidents will not be able to manage foreign relations well." Except where emergency powers can be invoked, the Presidency in the 1980's will not be an effective office, and Pious sees no serious attempt by either presidential scholars or political practitioners to address the central problem of presidential power: "how to make collaborative government work." Pious admits that scholars make poor forecasters, but his analysis is both provocative and disturbing, as is his conclusion that the Presidency is the major destabilizing factor in our political system because it oscillates between "too little and too much power."

Louis Koenig agrees that since Vietnam and Watergate "the Presidency has been sustaining a downward turn in its efficacy and impact," even—perhaps especially—in the area of foreign affairs. He catalogues a number of changes which have "debilitated" the office, including: the decline of a vital two-party system; the disappearance of a congressional leadership available to support the President; the growth of legislative independence from him, indeed of competition with him; the increased number and influence of domestic pressure groups concerned about foreign policy; the ambivalent impact of the media, particularly television; and the end of America's "ready predominance" in the world. All of these changes have adversely affected presidential power in both foreign and domestic affairs. But Koenig places the current situation in historical perspective and points out that the Presidency has survived and adapted to major "swings and roundabouts in its usable power" before. Presidents may have to learn how to collaborate with Congress and our allies, but "history counsels continued reliance on the Framers' balancing mechanisms which ought soon to move the Presidency into an upswing."

The final selection by Fred Greenstein reviews and analyzes the development of the Presidency since Franklin Roosevelt's time. Starting with an account of how the modern institution evolved from FDR through Truman to Eisenhower, Greenstein focuses on three phases of change in the office since John Kennedy's election in 1960. The first phase, including Kennedy's own "New Frontier" and Lyndon Johnson's "Great Society" programs, was characterized by a "celebration of presidential strength"; the second, from Vietnam through Watergate, by "lamentation about the 'imperial' practices"

of Johnson and Richard Nixon. The third and present phase —
termed "postimperial" — is perceived as one in which the Presidency
has become "a highly restrained institution," where the tension
between the demands made on him and the limitations on his ability
to satisfy those demands puts the President in an untenable position.
The result of this has been a period of rapid alternations in the way the
Presidency has functioned since 1960, and these oscillations Greenstein attributes in large part to the fact that alone among our national
political institutions it is "so profoundly affected by the personal
characteristics and performance in office of the incumbent" and his
associates. In any event, he believes that a series of one-term presidencies may have helped to "demystify" the office, and that the
current search for a redefinition of the proper presidential role may
educate the American people and Presidents themselves "to view the
office in terms of a realistic assessment of what Presidents can in fact
accomplish in American politics."

The theme of this book — that the power of the Presidency is a
constantly changing phenomenon dependent on the interaction of
personal, systemic, and historical factors, and therefore not amenable to precise definition — is reflected clearly in this final section.
Since Franklin Roosevelt ushered in the modern Presidency there
has been a continuity of executive power based on the President's
roles of national and global leadership. But there have also been
dramatic shifts in presidential power occasioned by the myriad international, constitutional, political and personal changes that have
affected the office.

Professional commentators on the Presidency have not only
chronicled all of this, they have also played a part in shaping the
institution by helping to determine the way in which the public (and
perhaps even Presidents) perceive it. Because neither Presidents,
Congresses, nor Courts generally attempt to conceptualize their
views of executive authority, the task has been left primarily to
scholars, and in pursuing their vocation they have become deeply
involved in the continuing controversy over the scope and limits of
presidential power. This is the case now as it has been since the
earliest days of the Republic. Scholarly treatises have reflected the
country's moods and shifting political preferences, as well as "objective" institutional situations, from the modern Presidency's halcyon
days of purposeful optimism to its more recent time of troubles. As
have Supreme Court justices, congressional leaders, Presidents, and
the Framers of the Constitution, so too do experts differ in their
personal desires as well as in their professional assessments of what is
or should be the power of the Presidency. But taken as a whole the
readings presented here also reflect a serious attempt by students of
the office to find both the form and the substance of a Presidency
equal to the enormous challenges that now confront it.

THE SCOPE OF
PRESIDENTIAL POWER

From Franklin Roosevelt to Vietnam/Watergate

☆

EDWARD S. CORWIN: *The Aggrandizement of*
Presidential Power

It is a common allegation that the terms in which the President's powers are granted are the loosest and most unguarded of any part of the Constitution, and this is true when Article II is read by itself. But what warrant is there for reading it thus, rather than in its context, the Constitution as a whole? When it is read in this way the net impression left is quite different.

"The Executive power shall be vested in a President of the United States of America"; "the President shall be Commander in Chief of the Army and Navy"; with the advice and consent of the Senate he shall make treaties and appoint to office; he shall have power to "grant reprieves and pardons for offenses against the United States"; he shall recommend to Congress "such measures as he shall judge necessary and expedient"; and so on and so forth. Yet, in order to exercise any of these powers—in order, indeed, to subsist—he must have money, and can get it only when and if Congress appropriates it. Likewise, he is dependent on Congress for the very agencies through which he must ordinarily exercise his powers, and Congress is the judge as to the necessity and propriety of such agencies. Again, he is bound to "take care that the laws" which Congress enacts are "faithfully executed"—for this purpose all his powers are in servitude; and Congress has the power to investigate his every official act, and can, by a special procedure, if it

Edward S. Corwin was McCormick Professor of Jurisprudence at Princeton University. This selection on "Some Aspects of the Presidency" is from *The Annals*, November, 1941, pp. 122–131. Copyright 1941 by the American Academy of Political and Social Sciences. Reprinted by permission.

finds him guilty of "high crimes and misdemeanors," impeach him
and throw him out of office. Moreover, by the standard set by the
prerogative of the British monarch in 1787, his "Executive power"
and his power to protect that power were both seriously curtailed.
The power to "declare war" was vested in Congress; the Senate was
made a participant in his diplomatic powers; he was given a veto
upon all legislative acts, but one which the houses may override by
a two-thirds vote, whereas the supposed veto of the British monarch
was absolute.

TWO CONSTITUTIONAL CONCEPTIONS

In short, the Constitution itself reflects not *one* but *two* conceptions
of executive power: the conception that it exists for the most part to
serve the legislative power, wherein resides the will of society, and
the conception that it ought to be within generous limits autonomous
and self-directory. The source of this dualism was the eighteenth-
century notion of a *balanced constitution;* its consequence has been
a constantly renewed struggle for power between the political
branches. Nor has the struggle ceased to this day, although its total
result has been, especially within recent years, the vast aggrandizement of the Presidency.

The Constitution was hardly set going when an indicative and
decisive event occurred to head the Presidency toward its destiny.
"The Executive power shall be vested in a President of the United
States," was originally intended merely to settle the issue whether
the National Executive should be single or plural and to baptize the
office. Yet when the question arose in the first Congress as to how
nonjudicial officers appointed by the President and Senate should be
removed, Congress, under the leadership of Madison, took action
which, in reliance on the clause just recited, attributed this power
to the President alone; and 137 years later the Supreme Court,
speaking by a Chief Justice who had himself been President, ratified this "practical construction of the Constitution" as the theoretically correct one. Likewise Hamilton, in justifying Washington's
course in 1793 in issuing a Proclamation of Neutrality in view of
the outbreak of war between France and England, appealed to the
"Executive power" clause, which in effect he construed as endowing
the President with the complete prerogative of the British monarch
in the conduct of foreign affairs except only the "power to declare
war," that having been transferred by specific provision of the Constitution to Congress. This time Madison took a brief on the other
side; yet who can doubt that Hamilton's view has in the main won
out?

In the case of the "fifty destroyer" deal in 1940 the President violated statutes which had been enacted by Congress in the uncontroverted exercise of its specifically delegated powers, and was justified by his Attorney General in so doing, by an argument which empowers the President, as Commander in Chief—and as organ of foreign relations—to ride high, wide, and handsome over the legislative powers of the Nation whenever he deems it desirable to do so. Yet I have heard of no impeachment proceedings being initiated in Congress against either the President or the Attorney General. Quite to the contrary, the attainments of the latter as a constitutional lawyer have been recently proclaimed to the Nation by his elevation to the Supreme Court.

But this confrontation of Hamilton and Madison in 1793 is of importance for a second reason; it signalized the early differentiation of what may be termed the quasi-monarchical and the ultra-Whig conceptions of the Presidency. Under the first two Presidents the former conception prevailed as of course. The Presidency at once furnished what Walter Bagehot would have termed the "dignified element of government" and also directed the legislative process to a notable extent, although without diminishing in the least the spontaneous legislative initiative of the houses themselves—exactly as in contemporary Britain before the younger Pitt, the legislative initiative was divided. The famous Judiciary Act of 1789 was elaborated in the Senate; the acts creating the great executive departments came from the House; Hamilton's financial measures exemplified the legislative leadership of the executive.

JEFFERSON'S VIEW

Jefferson's conception of executive power, on the other hand, was more Whig than that of the British Whigs themselves in subordinating it to "the supreme legislative power." At the time when the presidential election of 1800 was pending in the House, John Marshall predicted that if Jefferson was chosen he would "embody himself in the House of Representatives, and by weakening the office of President" would "increase his personal power. He will . . . become the leader of that party which is about to constitute the majority of the legislature." Better political prophecy has rarely been recorded.

In Jefferson we encounter for the first time a President who is primarily a party leader, only secondarily Chief Executive. The tone of his messages is uniformly deferential to Congress. His first one closes with these words: "Nothing shall be wanting on my part to inform, as far as in my power, the legislative judgment, nor to carry that judgment into faithful execution." His actual guidance of Congress' judgment was none the less constant and unremitting even while often secret and sometimes furtive. The chief instruments of his leadership were the party caucus, which enabled the party membership to present on the floor a united front and over which he himself is alleged to have presided now and then, and his Secretary of the Treasury, Albert Gallatin, whose own influence with Congress was also enormous. At the same time, it should be noted that the principal issues with which Congress was asked to deal legislatively were issues of foreign policy. Nor was the flow of power all in one direction. Both in the enactment of the famous Embargo Act of 1807 and in its subsequent repeal at Congress' insistence, we have an outstanding example of departmental collaboration in the diplomatic field.

What, then, of Marshall's prophecy that Jefferson would weaken the office of President? This, too, was justified by events when the Ulysses' bow of party leadership passed to feebler hands. With the practical disappearance of the Federalist Party the Republican caucus became "the congressional caucus," by which Madison and Monroe were each in turn put in nomination for the Presidency, while the younger Adams was virtually elected by it, through the election being thrown into the House. Thus, for twenty years the plan rejected by the framers, of having the President chosen by Congress, was substantially in operation. During this period the practice grew up of each succeeding President's continuing a considerable part of his predecessor's Cabinet in office; and when he convened them in council the Chief Executive counted the votes of the heads of departments as of equal weight with his own. Hardly more than *primus inter pares* in his own sight, he was glad if Congress accorded him that degree of deference. In short, the Presidency was in commission.

JACKSON'S VIEW

With Jackson's accession this enfeebling tendency was checked as decisively as it was abruptly. Jackson's Presidency was, in truth, no mere revival of the office—it was a remaking of it. The credit, however, should not go to Jackson alone. He contributed an imperious temper, a military reputation, and a striking personality; and he had the good luck to have an admiring public in the shape of a new and ignorant electorate. But the lasting impact of the Jacksonian Presidency upon American constitutional practice also owed much to the constructive skill of his political lieutenants, and particularly to their invention of the National Nominating Convention. When

Jefferson retired in 1809 his party began at once to dissolve into local or personal followings. That the same thing did not happen on Jackson's retirement was due to the rise of the national convention and the political devices which cluster about it.

Backed by a party organization which reached far beyond the halls of Congress, indeed eventually penetrated the remotest corners of the Union, Jackson became the first President in our history to appeal to the people over the heads of their legislative representatives. At the same time, the office itself was thrust forward as one of three *equal* departments of government and to each and every one of its powers was imparted new scope, new vitality. The Presidency became tridimensional, and all of the dimensions underwent more or less enlargement. Jackson was a more dominant party leader than Jefferson; his claim to represent the American people as a whole went to the extent of claiming to embody them; his claim to be one of three *equal* departments inferred the further claim that *all* his powers were autonomous, even his purely executive powers.

The logical implications of Jackson's position, as stated in his famous Bank Veto Message of July 10, 1832, were not exaggerated by his Whig critics, although its practical effects were. "I look upon Jackson," Kent wrote Story early in 1834, "as a detestable, ignorant, reckless, vain, and malignant tyrant. . . . This American elective monarchy frightens me. The experiment, with its foundations laid on universal suffrage and our unfettered press, is of too violent a nature for our excitable people." "The President," thundered Webster in the Senate, "carries on the government; all the rest are subcontractors. . . . A Briareus sits in the center of our system, and with his hundred hands touches everything, controls everything." "We are in the midst of a revolution," lamented Clay, "hitherto bloodless, but tending rapidly towards a total change of the pure republican character of the Government, and to the concentration of all power in the hands of one man."

Actually, prior to the Civil War, the supposed menace was more apparent than real. For this there were several reasons. In the first place, while magnifying the powers of the Presidency, Jackson subscribed to the states' rights doctrine of strict construction of Congress' powers. His legislative role consequently was chiefly negative, being confined for the most part to a vigorous use of the veto power. In the second place, even though it had been otherwise, the further development in the houses since Jefferson's day of the committee system interposed obstacles in the way of presidential participation in legislation which had not existed at first. But a circumstance which contributed even more to the temporary declension of the Jacksonian Presidency was the emergence after 1846 of the issue of slavery in the territories. For the handling of this highly charged question by the devices of negotiation and compromise, Congress, and especially the Senate, offered a far better theater than the Presidency. So the forces making for compromise systematically depressed the Presidency by taking care that only secondary and manageable personalities should be elevated to it. Lastly, the recently enunciated Monroe Doctrine had asserted a restraining principle upon presidential adventuring in the foreign field which gradually became invested with all the moral authority of the Constitution itself—an eminence it was to retain till 1898.

LINCOLN'S VIEW

The last important contribution to the theory of the Presidency until recent decades was Lincoln's, whose ultimate conception of the office was as much an expression of temperament as was Jackson's. A solitary genius who valued the opportunity for reflection above that for counsel, Lincoln came to regard Congress as a more or less necessary nuisance and the Cabinet as a usually unnecessary one. Nor could it have escaped Lincoln's intuition—especially after Buchanan's Message of December 3, 1860—that, if the Union was to be saved, recourse must be had to some still untested source of national power, one which had not become entangled, as had Congress', in the strangulating sophistries of states' rights. So, for a double reason, Lincoln turned to the "Commander in Chief" clause, from which, read in conjunction with the "Executive power" clause, he drew the conclusion that "the war power" was his. Originally, it is true, he appears to have assumed that his power was a simple emergency power whose ad interim decisions Congress must ratify if they were to be permanently valid. But, as the problems of Emancipation and then of Reconstruction loomed, he shifted ground, and his final position was "that as President he had extraordinary legal resources which Congress lacked," and which it could not control.

The long-run effect of Lincoln's Presidency on conceptions of the office would be difficult to exaggerate. Here two points need to be specially noted. The first is that Lincoln's course, fortified by the Supreme Court's dictum in the Prize Cases, that insurrection is "war," affords a strong warrant for any President, called upon to deal with a widespread condition of violence in the country, to ignore all constitutional and statutory restraints in favor of personal liberty. The other is that presidential spokesmen have repeatedly turned to Lincoln's acts as if they supported the thesis of presidential autonomy—in other words, presidential autocracy—in all fields of presidential power, which of course they are far from doing.

Moreover, the immediate effect of Lincoln's incumbency was little short of calamitous for the office. A frontiersman, his conception of the requirements of sound administration were no less naive than Jackson's, whose record as a spoilsman he far surpassed; while except for an ineffectual endeavor to interest Congress in the subject of compensated emancipation, he left the task of procuring necessary legislation to his Cabinet secretaries, and especially to Chase and Stanton, theirs being the departments most concerned. The outcome in the latter case was the creation of a direct relationship between the War Department and the congressional Committee on the Conduct of the War which under Johnson brought the Presidency to the verge of disaster.

JOHNSON'S THEORY OF THE PRESIDENCY

Final appraisement of Johnson's incumbency for the theory of the Presidency is, nevertheless, not easy. Johnson escaped dismissal from office by the High Court of Impeachment by a single vote, but he *escaped!* What is more, it was during his Administration that the Supreme Court confessed its inability, in *Mississippi* v. *Johnson*, to enjoin a President from exceeding his constitutional powers or to order him to perform his constitutional duties. The principle which Marshall had stated in *Marbury* v. *Madison* as applicable to the President's "important political powers," that "in their exercise he is to use his own discretion, and is accountable only to his country in his political character, and to his own conscience," was thus extended *even to the President's duty to enforce the law.* Furthermore, whatever of popular glamour the office had lost under Johnson was promptly restored to it when "the man from Appomattox and its famous apple tree" became President.

Reflecting upon all this, Henry C. Lockwood, in his *The Abolition of the Presidency*, which appeared in 1884, advanced the thesis that only by replacing the President with an executive council after the Swiss model could American liberty be preserved. He wrote:

> The tendency of all people is to elevate a single person to the position of ruler. The idea is simple. It appeals to all orders of intellects. It can be understood by all. Around this center all nationality and patriotism are grouped. A nation comes to know the characteristics and nature of an individual. It learns to believe in the man. Certain contingencies are likely to take place.

It does not require a great amount of political knowledge to form an opinion as to the course of their favorite statesman, whose character they have studied. Under these circumstances, let a person be chosen to an office, with power conferred upon it equal to that of the Presidency of the United States, and it will make but little difference whether the law actually gives him the right to act in a particular direction or not. He determines a policy. He acts. No argument that the law has been violated will avail. He is the chief officer of the nation. He stands alone. He is a separate power in himself. The lines with which we attempt to mark the limits of his power are shadowy and ill-defined. A party, real or imaginary, stands back of him demanding action. In either event, the President acts. The sentiment of hero worship, which to a great extent prevails among the American people, will endorse him. Under our form of government, we do not think so much of what Congress may do. A great multitude declared: "Give us President Grant! We know him. He is strong! He will rule!"

It is interesting to lay alongside Mr. Lockwood's words the contention advanced by Mr. Kemler, in his recently published *Deflation of American Ideals,* that our only escape from totalitarianism is to make the President a perpetual hero!

ABANDONMENT OF LAISSEZ FAIRE

The great accessions to presidential power in recent years have been due in part to an enlarged foreign policy, and in part to the replacement of the laissez faire theory of government with the idea that government should make itself an *active, reforming* force in the field of economic enterprise, which has meant, necessarily, that the *National Government* should be active in this way, inasmuch as the field in question has long since come to transcend state lines.

The result for the Presidency of the latter development has been twofold. On the one hand, Presidents have made themselves spokesmen of the altered outlook, have converted their parties to it—a conversion not infrequently accompanied by backsliding—and, with the popular support thus obtained, have asserted a powerful legislative initiative. On the other hand, Congress, in responding to the President's leadership in its own peculiar field, has found it convenient to aggrandize his executive role enormously, by delegating to him the power to supplement its measures by a type of sublegislation called "administrative regulations." Not all this delegated power, it is true, has gone to the President, but a vast proportion of it has;

and it constitutes a realm of presidential power of which the framers had little prevision, although it began to appear in the field of foreign relations even as early as Washington's second Administration.

The first exponent of the new Presidency was Theodore Roosevelt, whose achievement was to some extent negated by faults of method. Woodrow Wilson was enabled by the advantage of having critically observed his predecessor, by his knowledge of political methods abroad, by a taste for institution building, which was later to divert him into an abortive effort at world organization, and finally by the opportunity afforded by our entrance into the First World War, to illustrate on an unprecedented scale both the new roles of the President—that of legislative leader and that of recipient of delegated legislative power. Our war with Germany was prosecuted for the most part under laws which were drafted under the appraising eye of the President and which conferred upon him far greater powers than those which Lincoln had exercised as Commander in Chief.

To be sure, the war being ended, some degree of reaction to earlier, conventional views of the relations of President and Congress ensued; but the really surprising thing is that the reaction was so slight. Candidate Harding announced that while as President he would recommend a program, as the Constitution required him to do, legislation would be the work of Congress; but there is good reason to believe that he later regretted the promise thus implied. His ultimate failure to lead was apparently due much less to lack of willingness than of will. Although to Mr. Coolidge's ingrained conservatism legislation was in itself thoroughly distasteful, he nevertheless asserted it to be "the business of the President as party leader to do the best he can to see that the declared party platform purposes are translated into legislative and administrative action." Mr. Hoover was rather less articulate regarding his views on the subject, but according to Mr. Luce, an excellent authority, "he sent drafts of several important proposals to the Capitol to be introduced by leaders." And thanks to his inaction at the time of framing the Hawley-Smoot tariff, he has had in retrospect the doubtful satisfaction of being responsible for the supreme legislative monument to the futility of the gospel of "hands off."

FRANKLIN D. ROOSEVELT'S PRESIDENCY

While President Franklin D. Roosevelt's accomplishment as legislator has surpassed all previous records, yet the story of it, so far as it is of interest to the student of constitutional practice, offers little of novelty. Old techniques have been sharpened and improved, sometimes with the aid of modern gadgets—radio, for instance. The President, said one columnist in 1933, "has only to look toward a radio to bring Congress to terms." And there are certain lessons for the future which the record underlines. Yet except for two features, the pleasure afforded by its study is—to employ Henry James's classification—that of recognition rather than of surprise.

The first of these features is Mr. Roosevelt's consistent championship of the demands of certain groups, especially Agriculture and Labor. Congressional legislation meant to promote the general welfare via the welfare of particular groups is, of course, as old as Congress itself. The element of novelty presented by the New Deal legislation in this respect is furnished by the *size and voting strength of the groups served by it*. The tendency of this development to aid the party in power to remain in power is obvious.

The second exceptional feature of Mr. Roosevelt's legislative achievement is its dissolving effect on the two great structural principles of the Constitution—the principle of the Separation of Powers and the principle of Dual Federalism. The Supreme Court's decisions sustaining the New Deal legislation all turn on the one essential idea, even when it is not distinctly stated, that the reserved powers of the states do not afford a valid constitutional test of national legislation. As to the Separation of Powers doctrine, I have already pointed out how the President today takes toll at both ends of the legislative process, by pressing a legislative program upon Congress and by rounding out Congress' completed work with administrative regulations.

Is the Presidency of today a potential matrix of dictatorship? The dictatorship theme is a familiar one in the history of the Presidency—Jefferson was a dictator, Jackson was a dictator, Lincoln was a dictator, Theodore Roosevelt was a dictator, and so was Wilson. Nevertheless, it seems we still have rights and free institutions to be menaced.

That a disturbing case can today be made out for regarding the President as a potential despot has to be conceded. By *Mississippi* v. *Johnson*, as I mentioned earlier, the President has no judicially enforceable responsibility either for nonperformance of his duties or for exceeding his powers. Impeachment is, as Jefferson discovered much earlier, a "scarecrow," and to galvanize this scarecrow into life would be to run the risk of reducing the Presidency to a nullity, as almost happened in 1868. Congress has, to be sure, the power of the purse, and could not be deprived of it except by a coup d'état; but the President dominates Congress by the hold which fat relief rolls give him over millions of votes, and so a vicious circle is created whereby Congress pays for its own slow enslavement. Moreover within recent times, propaganda, once the casual art of a gifted few, has been converted into a skilled technique, which is supplemented by the most ingenious gadgets of mechanical science. Today the President of the United States can at any time request that the Nation's broadcasting channels be cleared that he may chat with the people, and the request will be granted pronto, all the available frequencies being allocated to companies by a federal license which terminates every six months.

Then there is the role of the President as organ of foreign relations, the potential menace of which to American democracy has been pointed out by writers many times. By virtue of his powers in the diplomatic field, wrote Professor Pomeroy as far back as 1871, the President holds in his keeping "the safety, welfare, and even permanence of our internal and domestic institutions." And the Marquis de Chambrun, writing at the same period, voiced his concurrence in this judgment, for, said he, "An active and energetic foreign policy necessarily implies that the executive who directs it is permanent and clothed with powers in proportion to his vigor of action." And both these warnings, be it noted, were written at a time when the acknowledged field of American foreign policy was still limited in the main to the Western Hemisphere.

Finally, we must not forget what occurred in November 1940, when the most generally understood, most widely accepted usage of the Constitution was tossed casually into the discard. It is true that what occurred was by the approval of the American electorate, but that is precisely why the occurrence was so disturbing a portent, for the electorate in question contained millions of voters who were recipients of governmental bounty and other hundreds of thousands who were on the government's payroll, and the number of both classes seems likely to increase indefinitely. And surely it is not necessary to cite Aristotle to prove that the very processes of democracy, and the electoral process in particular, can be, and have been, used in times past to overthrow democracy.

The picture is somewhat overdrawn. Nevertheless, I doubt very much if it would be worth while to point out meticulously just wherein the exaggeration lies. Even after all the words of reassurance were spoken, important counts would remain unanswered. The real refutation of the above jeremiad is that it deals with *symptoms*, not with *causes*. The menace today of the Presidency to "liberty" and "democracy," as these have been conceived in the past, consists in the fact that the enlarged role of the President is the product for the most part of conditions which appear likely to continue operative for an indefinite future. The first of these conditions is the international crisis; the other is the persuasion of the American electorate that government does not exist primarily to supplement and reinforce private economic superiority, but ought on the contrary to correct and improve the operation of economic forces in the interest of the masses. And both these conditions spell one thing—increased and increasing governmental activity, which means, of course, increased activity and hence increased power for the National Government. The only question therefore which can be profitably raised from the point of view of those whose concern for "liberty" and "democracy" I have voiced is whether or not all this increased power is to go to the President; and if it is not, how such outcome is to be obviated.

NEED FOR CONSTITUTIONAL REFORM

My answer to this question, or rather to the latter part of it, is that *the present enlarged position of the President in the constitutional system requires of the American people a deliberate effort at constitutional reform,* though this need not mean resort to the formal process of constitutional amendment. The reform demanded, however, must have for its purpose not merely the preservation of "liberty" in the conventional sense of *liberty against government,* but also—and indeed primarily—the enhanced *responsiveness* of government to public opinion. Bearing this qualification in mind, I suggest that under the existing constitutional setup the solution must take the form of providing some method of equating easily and without constant jar to society the political forces which Congress at any time represents with those which the President represents at the same time, and of putting the relationship of the two branches on a *durable* and *understood* basis. And for this purpose I suggest a reconstruction of the Cabinet to include the principal leaders of Congress, men who do not owe their political salt to presidential bounty, and so can bring an independent judgment to bear upon presidential projects betimes.

The objection will no doubt be forthcoming that it is constitutionally impossible for an individual to be a member of Congress and to hold office at the same time. The answer is that membership in the Cabinet is not as such an office, though headship of a department is. The Cabinet as a body is as little known to the Constitution as is a "kitchen cabinet" or a "brain trust." All three comprise persons whom the President chooses to consult, the only difference being that the latter two are more apt to contain his real advisers, while the Cabinet goes neglected or is consulted only because Cabinet meetings have become an understood part of presidential routine.

More pauseworthy is the objection that such an arrangement could not long be adhered to, otherwise it must at times cut athwart the two-party system, and so weaken the political responsibility of the President. The objection has reference to the possibility that the President would belong to the party which was a minority in Congress. Actually, the supposed situation has obtained comparatively rarely—only twice, I believe, in the last seven Administrations, or four years out of twenty-eight. What is more to the point, the objection overvalues the importance of so-called "political responsibility," which operates in the main only *ex post facto*, that is, after the damage is done, *whereas the problem is to prevent the damage from being done in the first place*. Nor does cooperation between the President and Congress under present arrangements invariably stop at the party line, or even generally do so when conditions of crisis arise; and why should it require a crisis to bring forth the best methods? Suppose one takes the position that government is normally a species of *nation keeping*; then it is clear that much of the fuss and fury of politics is really factitious and a sheer waste to the community; that the chief objective to be sought in political discussion, whether carried on in Cabinet council, on the floors of Congress, or elsewhere, is *consensus* or compromise—in what light does the above proposal then appear?

Finally, it may be objected that the arrangement I propose would put the President as organ of foreign relations in leading strings to Congress. The answer is, that the Constitution itself already puts him there. Contrary to a common, but quite mistaken impression, no President has a mandate from the Constitution to conduct our foreign relations according to his own sweet will. If his power in that respect is indefinite, so is Congress' legislative power; and if he holds the "sword," so does Congress hold the "purse strings." Simply from constitutional necessity, therefore, the actual conduct of American foreign relations is a joint affair, and to my mind this is an altogether desirable arrangement which should be lived up to in spirit. Thanks especially to the bad tradition of secrecy which surrounds foreign policy and which ministers to the self-importance of State Departments and diplomats, there is no field where presidential whim has been more rampant or its solicitations for popular support more misleading and dangerous. But why not a foreign policy based on candor and a real attempt at securing popular understanding of its motivation, rather than on bamboozlement and hysteria? And would not frank recognition by the President that Congress is an equal in this field of power, and not a mere servitor, be apt to eventuate in just such a policy?

CONCLUSION

The Presidency of this present year of grace, in terms of power, is the product of the following factors: (1) social acceptance of the idea that government should be active and reformist, rather than simply protective of the established order of things; (2) the breakdown of the principle of dual federalism in the field of Congress' legislative powers; (3) the breakdown of the principle of the separation of powers as defining the relation of President and Congress in lawmaking; (4) the breakdown of the Monroe Doctrine and the enlarged role of the United States in the international field.

To repeat what I said before, it is my belief that the growth of presidential power within recent years confronts the American people with a problem of deliberate constitutional reform; otherwise what was the result of democracy may turn out to be democracy's undoing. And it is my further belief that the reform must consist in stabilizing by means of a reconstructed Cabinet the relationship between President and Congress, for there today lies the center of gravity of our constitutional system, therein lies enfolded the secret of our democracy's future.

The problem of the alleged undue influence of the President on public opinion, of course, remains. For that, I suspect, there is under our system no remedy except an unshackled public opinion itself. When the self-renewing stream of public opinion ceases to provide a cure for its own humors, free institutions fail of their main support and their main purpose, and the democratic process withers away for want of the juices of life. For while democracy implies leadership, it also implies criticism of that leadership, criticism outspoken and unremitting. Leadership immune from criticism is the very definition of totalitarianism. Mr. Kemler to the contrary notwithstanding, no President should be regarded as hero ex officio unless it is at the same time recognized that even heroes have their off days.

☆

CLINTON ROSSITER: *The Presidency as the*

Focus of Leadership

No American can contemplate the Presidency without a feeling of
solemnity and humility—solemnity in the face of a historically unique
concentration of power and prestige, humility in the thought that he
has had a part in the choice of a man to wield the power and enjoy
the prestige.

Perhaps the most rewarding way to grasp the significance of this
great office is to consider it as a focus of democratic leadership. Freemen, too, have need of leaders. Indeed, it may well be argued that
one of the decisive forces in the shaping of American democracy has
been the extraordinary capacity of the Presidency for strong, able,
popular leadership. If this has been true of our past, it will certainly
be true of our future, and we should therefore do our best to grasp
the quality of this leadership. Let us do this by answering the essential question: For what men and groups does the President provide
leadership?

First, the President is *leader of the executive branch.* To the extent that our federal civil servants have need of common guidance,
he alone is in a position to provide it. We cannot savor the fullness
of the President's duties unless we recall that he is held primarily
accountable for the ethics, loyalty, efficiency, frugality and respon-

Clinton Rossiter was John L. Senior Professor of American Institutions at
Cornell University. The first part of the selection is from "The Presidency: Focus of
Leadership," *New York Times Magazine,* November 11, 1956, p. 26. © 1956 by
The New York Times Company. Reprinted by permission. The second part is from
The American Presidency (New York: Harcourt, Brace, 1960), pp. 257-262.
Copyright © 1956, 1960 by Clinton Rossiter. Reprinted by permission of the
publisher and the author.

siveness to the public's wishes of the two and one-third million Americans in the national administration.

Both the Constitution and Congress have recognized his power to guide the day-to-day activities of the executive branch, strained and restrained though his leadership may often be in practice. From the Constitution, explicitly or implicitly, he receives the twin powers of appointment and removal, as well as the primary duty, which no law or plan or circumstances can ever take away from him, to "take care that the laws be faithfully executed."

From Congress, through such legislative mandates as the Budget and Accounting Act of 1921 and the succession of Reorganization Acts, the President has received further acknowledgment of his administrative leadership. Although independent agencies such as the Interstate Commerce Commission and the National Labor Relations Board operate by design outside his immediate area of responsibility, most of the government's administrative tasks are still carried on within the fuzzy-edged pyramid that has the President at its lonely peak; the laws that are executed daily in his name and under his general supervision are numbered in the hundreds.

Many observers, to be sure, have argued strenuously that we should not ask too much of the President as administrative leader, lest we burden him with impossible detail, or give too much to him, lest we inject political considerations too forcefully into the steady business of the civil service. Still, he cannot ignore the blunt mandate of the Constitution, and we should not forget the wisdom that lies behind it. The President has no more important tasks than to set a high personal example of integrity and industry for all who serve the nation, and to transmit a clear lead downward through his chief lieutenants to all who help shape the policies by which we live.

Next, the President is *leader of the forces of peace and war.* Although authority in the field of foreign relations is shared constitutionally among three organs—President, Congress, and, for two special purposes, the Senate—his position is paramount, if not indeed dominant. Constitution, laws, customs, the practice of other nations and the logic of history have combined to place the President in a dominant position. Secrecy, dispatch, unity, continuity and access to information—the ingredients of successful diplomacy—are properties of his office, and Congress, needless to add, possesses none of them. Leadership in foreign affairs flows today from the President—or it does not flow at all.

The Constitution designates him specifically as "Commander in Chief of the Army and Navy of the United States." In peace and war he is the supreme commander of the armed forces, the living guarantee of the American belief in "the supremacy of the civil over military authority."

In time of peace he raises, trains, supervises and deploys the forces that Congress is willing to maintain. With the aid of the Secretary of Defense, the Joint Chiefs of Staff and the National Security Council—all of whom are his personal choices—he looks constantly to the state of the nation's defenses. He is never for one day allowed to forget that he will be held accountable by the people, Congress and history for the nation's readiness to meet an enemy assault.

In time of war his power to command the forces swells out of all proportion to his other powers. All major decisions of strategy, and many of tactics as well, are his alone to make or to approve. Lincoln and Franklin Roosevelt, each in his own way and time, showed how far the power of military command can be driven by a President anxious to have his generals and admirals get on with the war.

But this, the power of command, is only a fraction of the vast responsibility the modern President draws from the Commander in Chief clause. We need only think back to three of Franklin D. Roosevelt's actions in World War II—the creation and staffing of a whole array of emergency boards and offices, the seizure and operation of more than sixty strike-bound or strike-threatened plants and industries, and the forced evacuation of 70,000 American citizens of Japanese descent from the West Coast—to understand how deeply the President's authority can cut into the lives and liberties of the American people in time of war. We may well tremble in contemplation of the kind of leadership he would be forced to exert in a total war with the absolute weapon.

The President's duties are not all purely executive in nature. He is also intimately associated, by Constitution and custom, with the legislative process, and we may therefore consider him as *leader of Congress*. Congress has its full share of strong men, but the complexity of the problems it is asked to solve by a people who still assume that all problems are solvable has made external leadership a requisite of effective operation.

The President alone is in a political, constitutional and practical position to provide such leadership, and he is therefore expected, within the limits of propriety, to guide Congress in much of its law-making activity. Indeed, since Congress is no longer minded or organized to guide itself, the refusal or inability of the President to serve as a kind of prime minister results in weak and disorganized government. His tasks as leader of Congress are difficult and delicate, yet he must bend to them steadily or be judged a failure. The

President who will not give his best thoughts to leading Congress, more so the President who is temperamentally or politically unfitted to "get along with Congress," is now rightly considered a national liability.

The lives of Jackson, Lincoln, Wilson, and the two Roosevelts should be enough to remind us that the President draws much of his real power from his position as *leader of his party*. By playing the grand politician with unashamed zest, the first of these men gave his epic administration a unique sense of cohesion, the second rallied doubting Republican leaders and their followings to the cause of the Union, and the other three achieved genuine triumphs as catalysts of congressional action. That gifted amateur, Dwight D. Eisenhower, has also played the role for every drop of drama and power in it. He has demonstrated repeatedly what close observers of the Presidency know well: that its incumbent must devote an hour or two of every working day to the profession of Chief Democrat or Chief Republican.

It troubles many good people, not entirely without reason, to watch the President dabbling in politics, distributing loaves and fishes, smiling on party hacks, and endorsing candidates he knows to be unfit for anything but immediate delivery to the county jail. Yet if he is to persuade Congress, if he is to achieve a loyal and cohesive administration, if he is to be elected in the first place (and re-elected in the second), he must put his hand firmly to the plow of politics. The President is inevitably the nation's No. 1 political boss.

Yet he is, at the same time if not in the same breath, *leader of public opinion.* While he acts as political chieftain of some, he serves as moral spokesman for all. It took the line of Presidents some time to sense the nation's need of a clear voice, but since the day when Andrew Jackson thundered against the Nullifiers of South Carolina, no effective President has doubted his prerogative to speak the people's mind on the great issues of his time, to serve, in Wilson's words, as "the spokesman for the real sentiment and purpose of the country."

Sometimes, of course, it is no easy thing, even for the most sensitive and large-minded of Presidents, to know the real sentiment of the people or to be bold enough to state it in defiance of loudly voiced contrary opinion. Yet the President who senses the popular mood and spots new tides even before they start to run, who practices shrewd economy in his appearances as spokesman for the nation, who is conscious of his unique power to compel discussion on his own terms and who talks the language of Christian morality and the American tradition, can shout down any other voice or chorus of voices in the land. The President is the American people's one authentic trumpet, and he has no higher duty than to give a clear and certain sound.

The President is easily the most influential leader of opinion in this country principally because he is, among all his other jobs, our Chief of State. He is, that is to say, the ceremonial head of the Government of the United States, the *leader of the rituals of American democracy*. The long catalogue of public duties that the Queen discharges in England and the Governor General in Canada is the President's responsibility in this country, and the catalogue is even longer because he is not a king, or even the agent of one, and is therefore expected to go through some rather undignified paces by a people who think of him as a combination of scoutmaster, Delphic oracle, hero of the silver screen and father of the multitudes.

The role of Chief of State may often seem trivial, yet it cannot be neglected by a President who proposes to stay in favor and, more to the point, in touch with the people, the ultimate support of all his claims to leadership. And whether or not he enjoys this role, no President can fail to realize that his many powers are invigorated, indeed are given a new dimension of authority, because he is the symbol of our sovereignty, continuity and grandeur as a people.

When he asks a Senator to lunch in order to enlist his support for a pet project, when he thumps his desk and reminds the antagonists in a labor dispute of the larger interests of the American people, when he orders a general to cease caviling or else be removed from his command, the Senator and the disputants and the general are well aware—especially if the scene is laid in the White House—that they are dealing with no ordinary head of government. The framers of the Constitution took a momentous step when they fused the dignity of a king and the power of a Prime Minister in one elective office—when they made the President a national leader in the mystical as well as the practical sense.

Finally, the President has been endowed—whether we or our friends abroad like it or not—with a global role as a *leader of the free nations*. His leadership in this area is not that of a dominant executive. The power he exercises is in a way comparable to that which he holds as a leader of Congress. Senators and Congressmen can, if they choose, ignore the President's leadership with relative impunity. So, too, can our friends abroad; the action of Britain and France in the Middle East is a case in point. But so long as the United States remains the richest and most powerful member of any coalition it may enter, then its President's words and deeds will have a direct bearing on the freedom and stability of a great many other countries.

Having engaged in this piecemeal analysis of the categories of presidential leadership, we must now fit the pieces back together into a seamless unity. For that, after all, is what the Presidency is, and I hope this exercise in political taxonomy has not obscured the paramount fact that this focus of democratic leadership is a single office filled by a single man.

The President is not one kind of leader one part of the day, another kind in another part—leader of the bureaucracy in the morning, of the armed forces at lunch, of Congress in the afternoon, of the people in the evening. He exerts every kind of leadership every moment of the day, and every kind feeds upon and into all the others. He is a more exalted leader of ritual because he can guide opinion, a more forceful leader in diplomacy because he commands the armed forces personally, a more effective leader of Congress because he sits at the top of his party. The conflicting demands of these categories of leadership give him trouble at times, but in the end all unite to make him a leader without any equal in the history of democracy.

I think it important to note the qualification: "the history of democracy." For what I have been talking about here is not the Fuehrerprinzip of Hitler or the "cult of personality," but the leadership of free men. The Presidency, like every other instrument of power we have created for our use, operates within a grand and durable pattern of private liberty and public morality, which means that the President can lead successfully only when he honors the pattern—by working toward ends to which a "persistent and undoubted" majority of the people has given support, and by selecting means that are fair, dignified, and familiar.

The President, that is to say, can lead us only in the direction we are accustomed to travel. He cannot lead the gentlemen of Congress to abdicate their functions; he cannot order our civil servants to be corrupt and slothful; he cannot even command our generals to bring off a coup d'état. And surely he cannot lead public opinion in a direction for which public opinion is not prepared—a truth to which our strongest Presidents would make the most convincing witnesses. The leadership of free men must honor their freedom. The power of the Presidency can move as a mighty host only with the grain of liberty and morality. . . .

. . . The strong Presidency is the product of events that cannot be undone and of forces that continue to roll. We have made our decisions for the New Economy and the New Internationalism, and in making them we have made this kind of Presidency a requisite for the effective conduct of our constitutional system. No government can exercise the supervision that ours does over the economy at home or honor the bargains that ours has made abroad unless it has a strong, unified, energetic executive to lead it.

I do not mean to say—I have not meant to say—that "strength" in the Presidency is to be equated with "goodness" and "greatness." A strong President is a bad President, a curse upon the land, unless his means are constitutional and his ends democratic. . . . We honor the great Presidents of the past, not for their strength, but for the fact that they used it wisely to build a better America. And in honoring them we recognize that their kind of Presidency is one of our chief bulwarks against decline and chaos.

In point of fact, the struggle over the powers of the Presidency, fierce though it may seem, is only a secondary campaign in a political war, now pretty well decided, over the future of America. Few men get heated up over the Presidency alone. Their arguments over its powers are really arguments over the American way of life and the direction in which it is moving. The strong Presidency is an instrument and symbol of the 1960s; the weak Presidency is an instrument and symbol of the 1920s. Those who truly yearn to "go home again," like John T. Flynn and Clarence Manion and the Daughters of the American Revolution, are right in thinking that a reduction in the power of the Presidency would be an excellent first step to the rear, although it would be only a first step. It should be clearly understood that an attack on the Presidency like the Bricker amendment is aimed beyond the Constitution at America's position in the world. The backers of this amendment may be greatly worried about the potential dangers of "presidential autocracy," but they are even more worried about the present consequences of the New Internationalism. Conversely, many voices that are raised for an even stronger Presidency are really raised for an even bigger government with even more control of society.

We should not look with equanimity on the Presidency and its huge arsenal of authority. We should be careful about giving the President additional powers, alert to abuses of those he already holds, cognizant that the present balance of the Constitution is not a cause for unlimited self-congratulation. But we can look on it with at least as much equanimity—each of us according to his own blend of blood, bile, phlegm, and melancholy—as we do upon the present state of the Union. For the strength of the Presidency is a measure of the strength of the America in which we now live. Those who reject this America and are alarmed by the course we are taking reject the strong Presidency angrily. Those who accept this America and do not fear the one that is coming accept the strong Presidency soberly.

As I look back, I detect a deep note of satisfaction, although hardly of complacency, with the American Presidency as it stands today. A steady theme seems to have run all through this final re view of its weaknesses and problems, a theme entitled (with apologies to the genius of Thurber) "Leave Your Presidency Alone!" This feeling of satisfaction springs, I am frank to admit, from a political outlook more concerned with the world as it is than as it is said to have been by reactionaries and is promised to be by radicals. Since this outlook is now shared by a staggering majority of Americans, I feel that I am expressing something more than a personal opinion. If we accept the facts of life in the 1960s, as we must, and if we shun the false counsels of perfection, as we do, then we are bound to conclude that we are richly blessed with a choice instrument of constitutional democracy. Judged in the light of memory and desire, the Presidency is in a state of sturdy health, and that is why we should not give way easily to despair over the defects men of too much zeal or too little courage claim to discover in it. Some of these are not defects at all; some are chronic in our system of government; some could be cured only by opening the way to others far more malign.

This does not mean that we should stand pat with the Presidency. Rather, we should confine ourselves to small readjustments— I have noted a dozen or more that might be worth a try—and leave the usual avenues open to prescriptive change. We should abolish the electoral college but leave the electoral system to pursue its illogical but hitherto effective way. We should plan carefully for mobilization in the event of war but take care that the inherent emergency power of the President—the power used by Lincoln to blockade the South, by Wilson to arm the merchantmen, and by Roosevelt to bring off the Destroyer Deal—be left intact and untrammeled. We should experiment with a joint executive-legislative council and the item veto but be on our guard against the urge to alter radically the pattern of competitive coexistence between Congress and President. We should give the President all the aides he can use but beware the deceptively simple solution of a second and even third Vice President for executive purposes. And we should tinker modestly with the President's machinery but wake from the false dream of perfect harmony in high places, especially in the highest place of all. For if the Presidency could speak, it would say with Whitman:

> Do I contradict myself?
> Very well then I contradict myself.
> (I am large, I contain multitudes.)

"Leave Your Presidency Alone": that is the message of this chapter, and I trust I have made clear why I transmit it so confidently. To put the final case for the American Presidency as forcefully as possible, let me point once again to its essential qualities:

It strikes a felicitous balance between power and limitations. In a world in which power is the price of freedom, the Presidency, as Professor Merriam and his colleagues wrote in 1937, "stands across the path of those who mistakenly assert that democracy must fail because it can neither decide promptly nor act vigorously." In a world in which power has been abused on a tragic scale, it presents a heartening lesson in the uses of constitutionalism. . . . The quest of constitutional government is for the right balance of authority and restraint, and Americans may take some pride in the balance they have built into the Presidency.

It provides a steady focus of leadership: of administration, Congress, and people. In a constitutional system compounded of diversity and antagonism, the Presidency looms up as the countervailing force of unity and harmony. In a society ridden by centrifugal forces, it is, as Sidney Hyman has written, the "common reference point for social effort." The relentless progress of this continental republic has made the Presidency our one truly national political institution. There are those who would reserve this role to Congress, but as the least aggressive of our Presidents, Calvin Coolidge, once testified, "It is because in their hours of timidity the Congress becomes subservient to the importunities of organized minorities that the President comes more and more to stand as the champion of the rights of the whole country." The more Congress becomes, in Burke's phrase, "a confused and scuffling bustle of local agency," the more the Presidency must become a clear beacon of national purpose.

It is a priceless symbol of our continuity and destiny as a people. Few nations have solved so simply and yet grandly the problem of finding and maintaining an office of state that embodies their majesty and reflects their character. Only the Constitution overshadows the Presidency as an object of popular reverence, and the Constitution does not walk about smiling and shaking hands. "The simple fact is," a distinguished, disgruntled Briton wrote at the end of the "Royal Soap Opera" of 1955, "that the United States Presidency today is a far more dignified institution than the British monarchy." In all honesty and tact we must quickly demur, but we can be well satisfied with our "republican king."

It has been tested sternly in the crucible of time. Our obsession with youth leads us to forget too easily how long our chief instruments of government have been operating in unbroken career. The

Presidency is now the most venerable executive among all the large nations of the earth, and if one looks back beyond 1787 to "times of ancient glory and renown," he will find that the formula has worked before. "The truth is," Henry Jones Ford wrote with grace and insight,

> that in the presidential office, as it has been constituted since Jackson's time, American democracy has revived the oldest political institution of the race, the elective kingship. It is all there: the precognition of the notables and the tumultuous choice of the freemen, only conformed to modern conditions. That the people have been able . . . to make good a principle which no other people have been able to reconcile with the safety of the state, indicates the highest degree of constitutional morality yet attained by any race.

It is, finally, an office of freedom. The Presidency is a standing reproach to those petty doctrinaires who insist that executive power is inherently undemocratic; for, to the exact contrary, it has been more responsive to the needs and dreams of giant democracy than any other office or institution in the whole mosaic of American life. It is no less a reproach to those easy generalizers who think that Lord Acton had the very last word on the corrupting effects of power; for, again to the contrary, his doctrine finds small confirmation in the history of the Presidency. The vast power of this office has not been "poison," as Henry Adams wrote in scorn; rather, it has elevated often and corrupted never, chiefly because those who held it recognized the true source of the power and were ennobled by the knowledge.

The American people, who are, after all, the best judges of the means by which their democracy is to be achieved, have made the Presidency their peculiar instrument. As they ready themselves for the pilgrimage ahead, they can take comfort and pride in the thought that it is also their peculiar treasure.

☆

JAMES M. BURNS: *Presidential Government*

. . . The Presidency today is at the peak of its prestige. Journalists
describe it as the toughest job on earth, the presiding office of the
free world, the linchpin of Western alliance, America's greatest contribution to the art of self-government. Foreigners are fascinated by
the Presidency, just as they are appalled by Congress and perplexed
by party and election shenanigans. Scholars describe it as the most
popular and democratic—and withal the most elevated and even
most elitist—part of American government. They lovingly dissect
the Presidency, slicing up its essentially indivisible power into that
of Chief Executive, Chief of State, Chief Legislator, and so on. And
they worry about its infirmities even as they marvel at its strength.

Even so, we may have underestimated the long-term impact of
presidential government on the whole structure of American government. Past trends and current tendencies may permit some guarded
speculations as to the future.

Conservatives have long held that the Presidency, as idealized
and operated by liberals and internationalists, was imperialistic and
exploitative and hence that it would eventually overpower the other
branches of government. They are substantially right. For almost a
century now, the Presidency has been warding off forays against its
own constitutional domain and drawing other governmental and
political institutions into the orbit of its influence. At least since the
days of President Grant the defense and expansion of the office have

James MacGregor Burns is Woodrow Wilson Professor of Government at Wil-
liams College. The selection is from *Presidential Government: The Crucible of
Leadership* (Boston: Houghton Mifflin, 1965), pp. 313-335. Copyright © 1965 by
James MacGregor Burns. Reprinted by permission of the publisher and the author.

been conducted not only by the strong Presidents but by "weak" ones; hence we can say that the growth of the Presidency has been in part an institutional tendency and not one turning merely on the accident of crisis and personality.

As we have noted earlier, Hayes successfully withstood a vigorous effort by the Senate to dominate his major appointments and thus to exercise direct influence over the executive establishment. Cleveland refused to give in to Senate demands that he submit to that body executive papers relating to the nomination of federal officials. The Tenure of Office Act, "designed to transfer control of the public service from the President to the Senate, and thus to strike a vital blow both to executive power and to the capacity of a President to maintain a coordinate position with the legislative branch," was hamstrung under Grant and Hayes and repealed under Cleveland. Hayes overcame an attack on the President's legislative power when he vetoed an appropriation bill to which House Democrats had attached a rider relating to reconstruction policy in the South.

All this was good defense; and it confirmed the President's formal control of the executive department. The President in recent decades has seemed to bring the Cabinet more certainly under his personal influence than was often the case in the nineteenth century. Lincoln's famous episode of "seven noes, one aye—the ayes have it" would be impossible today; Cabinet members would not dare risk such a posture of opposition to the chief. The Vice Presidency also has been tucked securely into the executive establishment. Some agencies, such as the Federal Bureau of Investigation, remain classic examples of the limitations of the President's control, but this independence is in part a product of unique personality and will probably diminish in time.

Presidential aggrandizement has been even more marked in the sphere of party politics. There was a time when conventions refused to renominate incumbent Presidents, when the national chairman was independent of presidential control, when the national party apparatus was dominated by competing leaders or factions. Things are very different now. The most important change affecting the nominating process since 1896 in the party in power, according to David, Goldman, and Bain, "has been the rising position of the Presidency and the increased recognition accorded the President as party leader. Other circles of influence continue to exist; but the group consisting of the President and his immediate associates has become the innermost inner circle; the others can now be regarded as a loose constellation of groups surrounding the White House as the center of power." Recently the national party chairman has been simply one more political lieutenant of the President's and one who often has less power than political aides in the White House. The President's party influence does not run much beyond the scope of the presidential party; but the scope of the presidential party may be expanding too, depending in part on the President's influence over other sectors of the whole government.

Perhaps the most extraordinary but least remarked expansion of presidential government lies in the extension of its influence to the Supreme Court. Prior to the modern presidential epoch, successive Presidents held sharply different doctrines and hence put men of varying viewpoints on the bench. Judicial appointees of a Theodore Roosevelt versus a Taft, of a Wilson versus a Harding, of a Hoover versus a Franklin Roosevelt, could hardly be expected to agree in their socioeconomic doctrine, and generally their decisions reflected their differences. This does not mean that Presidents always appointed men who slavishly expressed the presidential line. Indeed, they sometimes chose men who in time diverged widely from the President's basic doctrine, as in the case of Wilson's appointment of James C. McReynolds. But inescapably the type of appointment, and the appointee's social and economic doctrine on the bench, were affected by the general set of ideas, as well as by the political interrelationships, of a presidential administration. Thus it was not surprising that the Supreme Court of 1933–37, composed mainly of appointees of Republican Presidents, rejected major New Deal legislation. Since 1937, however, the Supreme Court has not invalidated a major piece of national social legislation'. The Court is composed of men who respond to the same general ideas of freedom and equality as have recent Presidents. Eisenhower's appointees are almost indistinguishable on social and economic legislation from Roosevelt's and Kennedy's; indeed, Eisenhower's major appointee, Earl Warren, has led the Court in some of its historic egalitarian decisions, notably the *Brown* school desegregation case. The election of Barry Goldwater, and the kind of judicial appointments he would have made, would of course have disrupted the harmony between the two branches, at least if Goldwater could have put enough of his own men on the bench, but Goldwater's rejection diminishes the likelihood of a sharp presidential-judicial break in the foreseeable future. As long as we elect liberal Presidents from either of the presidential parties we can anticipate a generally liberal Court.

Federalism has also felt the impact of presidential government. Modern Presidents have overturned old doctrines and practices of states' rights by extending their policy-making power into the urban areas of the nation. Historically the growth of cities has brought more need for public regulation and control and hence the growth of government. This tendency has been evident in public health, public transportation, social welfare services, traffic and crime control, and many other sectors. These developments in turn have produced financial crises in many cities; as the burden on city government has increased, its fiscal resources have proved inadequate. City officials have had to go cup in hand to state legislatures. But the states too have been struggling with financial limitations, and rurally dominated state legislatures have not been eager to hand out money to their city brethren. So the cities have turned to Washington. But here too they often have met frustration, for Congress too is heavily influenced by the rurally based congressional party coalition, especially in the appropriations committees. So the mayors head for the White House.

And the President is there to welcome them. Whatever his political party, the modern President must be sensitive to the needs of the cities. The alliance between the President and the cities is one of the oldest facts of American politics. As far back as 1800, a presidential candidate foresaw that his success might turn on the vote in New York City. In that year Jefferson wrote to Madison: "If the city election of New York is in favor of the Republican ticket, the issue will be Republican; if the federal ticket for the city of New York prevails, the probabilities will be in favor of a federal issue because it would then require a Republican vote both from New Jersey and Pennsylvania to preponderate against New York, on which we could not count with any confidence." The spread of urbanization and the electoral college "gerrymander" have made New York and the other big urban states "preponderate" in most recent presidential elections.

Thus the man in the White House has become the President of the Cities; he has become the Chief Executive of Metropolis. He has provided the main motive power for shaping legislation needed by the cities; he pushes through the federal money bills with their provision for matching grants; he commands the executive departments—Labor, Justice, Health, Education and Welfare—that work closely with metropolitan governments; he appoints the heads of promotional and regulatory agencies for housing, urban renewal, transportation, communication, that affect the city. The President of course extends aid to the cities with strings attached—strings in the form of presidentially approved standards, procedures, safeguards, and the like. But the community of doctrine and interest between presidential government and big-city government is so close that major conflicts of politics and policy do not arise. More often the President and the mayors are allied against hostile or indifferent officials in other parts of the "marble cake" of federalism—against state legislators, county officials, congressional appropriations committees and subcommittees, even Governors.

It is dangerous to generalize about such a complex set of governmental interrelationships as these. But the population explosion in metropolitan areas, the President's sensitivity to urban needs, the proliferation of urban and suburban areas cutting across county and state lines, the fiscal parsimony of municipalities, counties, and state legislatures, and the modern liberal assumption that government is an effective tool for realizing freedom and equality—all these forces are powerful ones that will operate for years to come. As a vital force behind the President's political and legislative leadership, the cities constitute a lasting foundation of presidential government. Inevitably, as presidential government cuts across and deranges the old formal division between local, state, and national authority, it will dominate policy making in and around metropolis.

Thus the Presidency has absorbed the Cabinet, the executive departments, the Vice Presidency. It has taken over the national party apparatus. Through consistently liberal appointments over the years it has a powerful influence on the doctrine of the Supreme Court. It has transformed the federal system. What about its impact on Congress, historically and constitutionally the great counterforce to the presidential office?

Here the change may be the most profound of all, at least in the long run. Our speculations need not be overly influenced by short-run developments, such as President Johnson's ·great success with Congress in his first two years in office. This success, coming on the heels of the congressional deadlock over many of Kennedy's major proposals, was largely due to some special circumstances: Johnson's standing on Capitol Hill, his particular legislative experience, the consolidation of presidential support after the rout of the Goldwater forces, and a congressional and popular urge to honor the late President's memory by supporting some of his major proposals. We must consider more basic and continuing forces that shape the relations of Congress and President as institutions.

One such force is reapportionment. The granting of greater representation in the House (and in state legislatures) to urban and suburban areas will bring the presidential and congressional constituencies into closer approximation and hence diminish some of the structural forces making for divergent policy. This shift may take longer than some expect, because it is the one-party district rather than the malapportioned district that lies at the heart of congressional party power on Capitol Hill. But in the long run reapportionment, along with the spread of heterogeneous urban and suburban population into presently rural districts, will diversify one-party areas and stimulate competitive two-party politics.

Another tendency that may bring Congress more into the presidential orbit is continuing congressional reform. Some of this might consist of formal change in organization and procedures, such as the strengthening of the Speaker early in 1965. Other changes will be less obvious, embracing the distribution of prestige and informal influence in the structure of both houses. The elected party leadership in Congress tends to support a President of the same party, as in the case of Senator Robert Taft lining up behind Eisenhower (just as the elected congressional leadership tends to diverge from the presidential party when the Presidency is in opposition hands). As the elected leadership continues to gain strength in Congress as compared to the committee chairmen—as in the long run I believe it will—the President will gain added influence over the legislature.

The most powerful force for unifying President and Congress will be the continuing and probably increasing consensus over freedom and equality. As long as the nation was deeply and closely divided over these goals, Congress with its bias toward conservatism was bound to be at odds with a President biased toward liberalism, except in times of crisis. Without a broad consensus it was impossible to mobilize steady congressional majorities behind presidential proposals for social welfare and other egalitarian measures. Congress has been slow to act when only a bare popular majority seemed to support Fair Deal or New Frontier programs, as suggested by the fate of major presidential proposals in Congress following the close popular majorities won by Truman in 1948 and Kennedy in 1960. Kennedy liked to quote Jefferson's remark that "great innovations should not be forced on slender majorities." They have not been, in Congress. Often a three-fifths or two-thirds majority of the electorate supporting liberal programs has been necessary to produce a dependable straight majority behind those programs in Congress, because of the distortions in congressional representation. But judging from polls, election data, and other indices, about three-fifths or two-thirds of the American voters have come to uphold in a general way federal welfare and regulatory measures at home and policies designed to support freedom and equality abroad. This consensus is bound to show in Congress.

This is not to predict joyous harmony between President and Congress. Relations will continue to be marked by misunderstanding, jealousies over status and protocol, and differences over policy. Oscillations between presidential and congressional power will continue, though probably with the balance of power continuing to shift toward the executive over the long run. Conflict will probably be especially acute in the fiscal sector, for the conservative grip on the spending and taxing committees and machinery of Congress will not soon be relaxed. But it is precisely in the fiscal sector of policy that the President will be under the greatest pressure to meet the claims of freedom and equality. The question will be whether the President has enough power to channel funds into federal programs for health, education, urban development, housing, and the like; whether he has the funds to staff effectively promotional, regulatory, and control agencies in civil rights and related fields. If congressional conservatives could not thwart passage of social legislation, they still might try to starve or cripple its implementation.

But even here the big guns seem to be on the President's side. The same consensus over freedom and equality that now pervades Congress as a whole should affect its fiscal policy making too in the long run. If in the short run fiscal conservatives in Congress are able to stymie presidential programs, the White House can retaliate by mobilizing interests that favor spending, dramatizing the social and economic ills that need to be attacked, returning to Congress for deficiency and emergency appropriations, using discretionary funds of the President, and other devices. The President has already been granted significant latitude in the use of funds to influence policy; the most notable example is the Civil Rights Act of 1964, which granted him power to withhold federal funds from any program or activity receiving direct or indirect federal assistance, in which racial discrimination was found to exist. President Kennedy asked Congress for presidential authority to change tax ratios within certain limits, in order to strengthen the arsenal of anti-recession weapons; Congress balked at granting this power, but may well change its mind in the future, especially in the face of a deepening economic recession. The actual coming of a recession would precipitate an even speedier and more drastic shift of fiscal authority to the White House, for no President today can afford to bear the political burden of a slump. In March 1933, Roosevelt warned that unless Congress acted in the economic emergency, "I shall ask the Congress for the one remaining instrument to meet the crisis—broad Executive power to wage a war against the emergency, as great as the power that would be given to me if we were in fact invaded by a foreign foe." No President could ask for less than this in a future crisis; he probably would ask for more. And no modern Congress could resist him, for part of the nation's consensus over freedom and equality is a commitment to federal action against depression and poverty. And because that commitment first and foremost binds the President and will do so indefinitely, it is part of the edifice of presidential government. . . .

The increasing dominance of the Presidency over the rest of the government, its embodiment of the national purpose, its symbolic expression of the nation's glory and solidarity, its tremendous impact on Americans during their most formative years—what does all this imply for the future of the nation and of the Presidency?

The old and accepted fears of presidential power, I have contended, do not seem justified on the basis of actual experience. Increased authority and scope have not made the Presidency a tyrannical institution; on the contrary, the office has become the main governmental bastion for the protection of individual liberty and the expansion of civil rights. The office "represents" the electorate at least as effectively and democratically as does Congress, though in a different way. The office has attracted neither power-mad politicians nor bland incompetents but the ablest political leaders in the land, and these leaders in turn have brought the highest talent to the White House. We must, under modern conditions, reassess the old idea that the *main* governmental protection of civil liberty, social and economic rights, and due process of law lies in the legislature or the courts or state and local government. The main protection lies today in the national executive branch. As a general proposition the Presidency has become the chief protector of our procedural and substantive liberties; as a general proposition, the stronger we make the Presidency, the more we strengthen democratic procedures and can hope to realize modern liberal democratic goals.

The danger of presidential dominance lies in a different and more subtle tendency. It lies not in presidential failure but in presidential success. It lies not in the failure to achieve our essential contemporary goals of freedom and equality but in their substantial realization and in the incapacity of presidential government to turn to new human purposes.

The prospects seem good that presidential government will continue to help broaden equality of opportunity at the same time that it protects our basic freedoms. All the Presidencies since that of Hoover have made some kind of commitment to this goal; they have aroused strong expectations; they have perfected the governmental machinery necessary to realize the goals; and we can expect that the contest between the presidential parties on domestic issues will turn mainly on the incumbent Administration's successes and failures in combating poverty, expanding opportunity, and enlarging civil rights, especially for Negroes. In foreign policy the election tests will be the efficient management of crisis plus the long-run effectiveness of military and economic programs abroad designed to strengthen the foundations of freedom and equality in other nations.

Given the harmony between ends and means—between the ends of freedom and equality and the means of presidential government— we can expect that well before the end of this century, and perhaps much sooner, we will have achieved substantial equality of opportunity in this nation. We need not expect equality of *condition*, nor full equality of opportunity, for gray areas of deprivation and discrimination will remain. Some of the old tension between equality and freedom will always be found in a diverse and changing society. But to the extent that public and private measures can realize freedom and equality, the goals will be substantially achieved.

And precisely here lies the problem. As freedom and equality are achieved presidential government will exhaust the purpose for which it has been such an eminently suited means. The great machinery of government that has been shaped to distribute welfare and overcome poverty and broaden opportunity and protect liberty will become devoted to increasingly automatic tasks. The passion will long since have disappeared, and increasingly the compulsion of purpose will be dissipated. Purpose will no longer be toughened in conflict; creativity will no longer rise from challenge and crisis. As the ends of government become increasingly agreed upon among the people, between the parties, between President and Congress, between national and state and local governments, issues will resolve mainly around questions of technique. And the more humdrum these matters become, the more the President will turn to his ceremonial and symbolic role to provide circuses to the people—the bread already being in abundance.

According to Morgenthau, we are already facing this problem, even with the goals of freedom and equality not yet achieved. In this nation there have been purposes, he reminds us, to which we could pledge our lives, our fortunes, and our sacred honor. "There is no such issue today. None of the contemporary issues of domestic politics of which the public at large is aware commands for its alternative solutions those loyalties out of which great political conflicts are made. There are divergent opinions and interests, to be sure; but there is no great issue that men deem worthy of sacrifice and risk. In consequence, the integrating principle of American society has lost both its dynamic and its substantive qualities. . . . The American consensus, which in the past was monistic in form and pluralistic in substance, has become monistic in both respects. In consequence, conformism now extends to the substance of policies and constitutional arrangements. Since no issue is any longer worth fighting over, a position must be 'moderate,' and what was once a compromise between seemingly irreconcilable positions now transforms itself into the adjustment of positions differing only in degree.

Since the purpose of America seems to have been achieved—the need
for improvement notwithstanding—the *status quo* tends to become
as sacred as the purpose itself, and an attack upon the *status quo*
almost as unpalatable as dissent from the purpose. Since there is
nothing left to fight for, there is nothing to fight against. . . ."
Morgenthau was writing during the Eisenhower Administration, and
he did not anticipate the force of Kennedy's challenge to Republicanism and of the Nergoes' revolt against the status quo in the
early 1960s. But he was right in a broader sense, for it was precisely Eisenhower's acceptance of the purposes of the New Deal
and the Fair Deal, and his blandness in his methods of realizing
them, that made his administration an ominous indication of the
likely nature of late twentieth-century politics in America.

Many would reject any call today for high purposes and fighting
issues. They prefer a polity that is not rent by great issues, scarred
by savage conflict, absorbed in passionate controversy, or even distracted by political problems. Considering the nature of the early
and middle epochs of the twentieth century, they would cherish a
period of calm in which people could indeed, in John Adams' words,
turn to painting, poetry, music, architecture, statuary, tapestry, and
porcelain. The very realization of the grand aims of freedom and
equality, they believe, would create a basis on which people could
turn to the enduring problems of the richness of quality of life,
and could forsake some of the old ideological quarrels.

Those who spurn ideology will contend, moreover, that progress
emerges not from the pursuit of central, synoptic visions or plans
or purposes, but from the pursuit of a wide range of alternative
policies, from flexible methods, from refusal to make an ultimate
commitment to any means or any end, from incremental and ad-
justive tactics that permit day-to-day reconciliation of differences.
Such an approach, they hold, produces innovation, creativity, and
excitement. It rejects the grand formulations of interrelated ends
and means in favor of special angles of vision, sharpened individual
or group motivation, the social dynamics of a loosely articulated,
highly accessible, and open-ended polity. The incrementalists would
proceed step by step, renouncing passion and commitment in favor
of prudence and calculation.

Yet many who have lived through the decades of traumatic and
even bloody political conflict, at home or abroad, will wonder about
a nation in which the great issues have dwindled to matters of
technique. They will worry first about a people so bored by the
relatively trivial political issues of the day that they have become
largely absorbed in the minutiae of their private lives. They will
doubt whether in the long run even architecture and poetry can

be kept out of politics. They will worry that people might fall into adjustment, conformity, undiscriminating tolerance, and aimless, time-filling activities, and that this will lead to the acceptance of mediocrity and a compulsive togetherness rather than the pursuit of excellence and individuality.

They will be concerned about the governors as well as the governed. For a government agreed on the larger issues and proceeding by calculation and adjustment is likely to attract to its service the little foxes who know many little things—the operators, the careerists, the opportunists, the technicians, the fixers, the managers. Some of these men may be resourceful, zealous, dedicated, flexible, and adjustable. But they will be so absorbed in technique that it will be difficult for them to separate issues of policy from questions of their own immediate self-enhancement. Certainly there would be little room for the Churchills who give up office in the pursuit of broader principles, or even for the administrative innovators who wish to create something more exalted than a better administrative mousetrap. Thus the governors too would lose their way, become lost in technique, would become absorbed in private motives, would substitute means for ends.

For this is the corruption of consensus—the attempt to find universal agreement on so many issues that great public purposes are eroded by a torrent of tiny problems solved by adjustment and adaptation. Ways and means are more and more rationally elaborated by increasing numbers of technicians for a society having less and less human purpose. In government this would mean Hamiltonianism gone wild; in the Presidency it would mean the submergence of the nation's supreme political decision-maker in an ever widening tide of incremental adjustments. The President might still be a hero to most of his people, but his policy and program would not be heroic, only his image. He would still seem a potent figure to children—and grownups—but his actual influence over events would be dwindling. He would still be visible as he mediated among the technicians and occasionally coped with crises; but it would be the visibility of the tightrope walker whom the great public watches with emotional involvement but without actual participation. The defeat of presidential government would be inherent in its very success. Having taken over the Cabinet and the rest of the government, presidential government would finally have taken over the President.

☆

ROBERT S. HIRSCHFIELD: *The Power of the*
Contemporary Presidency

In general terms the Presidency at the beginning of the 1960s is easily
described: It is the focus of both the American governmental system
and the free world coalition, an office of great authority and commensurate responsibility. Resting firmly on the twin supports of
democratic election and the necessities of a critical era, it is now a
permanently strong office, an institutionalized version of the "crisis
presidencies" of Lincoln, Wilson, Roosevelt, and Truman. And like
the regimes from which it stems, the outstanding feature of the
executive office today is its power.

The purpose of this article is to outline the power of today's
Presidency—to describe and analyze the kinds of authority which it
includes, the real sources from which it springs, and the system of
restraints to which it is subject. The result intended is a better understanding of the Presidency's full dimensions in a time of protracted
crisis, and of the opportunities for effective leadership open to the
new President.

THE KINDS OF PRESIDENTIAL AUTHORITY

Although the power of the Presidency is today so vast as to defy
precise definition, it may be divided into three major categories of
authority: statutory, constitutional, and extraconstitutional.

Much of the President's authority is delegated to him by Acts of

This selection is from "The Power of the Contemporary Presidency," *Parlia-*
mentary Affairs, Summer, 1961, pp. 353–377. Reprinted by permission of the
Hansard Society for Parliamentary Government.

Congress. In this manner he may be empowered to reorganize the Executive Branch of the government, raise or lower tariffs, exercise control over the nation's atomic resources, federalize the National Guard, or halt labor-management disputes. In fact, virtually all major domestic legislation includes grants of power to the executive so that he may effectuate national policies. In addition—and most significant under contemporary conditions—Congress, either on its own initiative or at the President's request, may delegate authority enabling the President to meet extraordinary situations abroad, as in the Formosa Resolution of 1954 or the Near East Resolution of 1956. In such cases, however, there is often a question regarding the necessity for congressional action, and the delegations may be viewed, at least by the President, as a way of indicating congressional support for a presidential policy already undertaken, rather than as a means for extending his authority. Wilson, Roosevelt, Truman, and Eisenhower all sought and received this kind of legislative approval in dealing with emergency situations abroad. All of them insisted, as Mr. Eisenhower did in the 1956 Near East crisis, that since the President already possessed all the power required to meet such situations there was no constitutional need for congressional action; but all nonetheless agreed that Congress should be consulted whenever possible so that there would be no doubt regarding the nation's unity.

Power delegated prospectively for discretionary use by the President in the event of a foreign emergency, though designed as an indication of legislative confidence in the executive and as a warning to potential aggressors, may in effect authorize or put a congressional seal of approval on presidential warmaking. The Lend-Lease Act of 1941 was of this nature, and so was the Near East Resolution. Conversely, the delegatory process may be used as a device for according retroactive legislative assent to actions already taken by the President on his own initiative. Thus the Congress which convened on July 4, 1861, sanctioned the crisis regime instituted by Lincoln, though in fact this amounted simply to its recognition of a *fait accompli*.

Whatever the reasons for congressional grants of authority, statutory delegations are an important part of a President's reservoir of power, and in the absence of overriding considerations which make resort to other forms of authority seem more desirable, he will utilize such grants. Indeed Presidents will occasionally try to justify their actions by citing delegatory statutes which are defunct or inapplicable in order to maintain a semblance of normal procedure (FDR, for example, resurrected the Trading with the Enemy Act of 1917 to support his closing of the banks in 1933). But usually it is not too difficult to find a relevant statute, since emergency measures have a way of remaining on the books after the crisis which impelled their

enactment has passed. Although an Attorney General must sometimes use ingenuity to find the proper reference, with the hundreds
of accumulated emergency provisions now on hand the task can
ordinarily be accomplished. In any event, Presidents have never had
great difficulty in persuading Congress to legitimize their independent actions or to make additional power available under crisis
conditions.

The second kind of presidential authority is constitutional: power
vested in the President by the basic law and exercisable by him on
his own initiative. And because problems of interpretation become
greater when the Constitution itself is involved, this is a trickier area
than that which deals with statutory law.

The extent of the President's constitutional authority has been
the subject for continuing national debate, and the dispute between
"broad" and "strict" construction of the powers barely outlined in
Article II is as old as the Republic. In this debate virtually every
President of note has joined. The crescendo passages have been
reached, of course, during the terms of those who acted most
"strongly"—Washington, Jefferson, Jackson, Polk, Lincoln, Theodore
Roosevelt, Wilson, Franklin Roosevelt, and Truman. However, only
the first Roosevelt (whose impetuous autonomy gave rise to much
controversy, though he never had a really serious crisis to test his
vigor) ever propounded a "theory" of broad presidential power, by
asserting that it was limited only by "specific restrictions and prohibitions appearing in the Constitution or imposed by the Congress
under its Constitutional powers." In TR's view the President is the
"steward of the people," having not only the right but the duty to
do whatever the needs of the nation demand, unless such action is
forbidden "by the Constitution or the laws."

Emphasizing the President's tribunate character, this "steward-
ship theory" places the executive in the center of the American
governmental system, but it does not help very much in defining
just what the obviously vast residue of power not constitutionally or
legally forbidden to the President includes. And indeed it is only by
reference to what Presidents have actually done (or gotten away
with) that Article II takes form. For the great builders of the powerful Presidency have been the powerful Presidents themselves. The
State of the Union message, for example, was not an element of
power until Woodrow Wilson made it the instrument for announcing his legislative program to the nation as well as Congress. It was
Lincoln who molded the Chief Executive and Commander in Chief
clauses into a combination strong enough to save the Union. And
every powerful President has helped to develop the Hamiltonian
conception of executive primacy in the conduct of foreign relations.

Much scholarship has been devoted to discovering the content of the President's constitutional power, with the result that many of its aspects have been spelled out. The President is, constitutionally, Head of State, Chief Executive, Head of Administration, Chief Foreign Policymaker, Commander in Chief, and Legislative Leader. Under these titles, he has independent power to perform, among many others, such varied and significant functions as recognizing new governments, enforcing legislative enactments and judicial decisions, subdelegating presidential authority, making executive agreements which have the force of treaties, deploying the armed forces, and recommending or vetoing legislation. These and all the other activities which flow from the Constitution either by direct sanction or reasonable implication comprise an impressive array of powers even if exercised by a President whose conception of the office is modest. When placed in the hands of a strong President they take on overwhelming proportions. And it is the strong view which is today the accepted one. Indeed this acceptance has resulted in a theory of the office that attributes to it "inherent" power which is virtually unlimited.

It is at this point, however, that the President's authority under the Constitution, no matter how broadly interpreted, must give way to yet another kind of power. For constitutionalism means limitation on governmental power, including that wielded by the President, and no matter how far his authority under the basic law may be pushed, it cannot transcend the concept of limitation and remain constitutional. He cannot, in short, have "constitutional" power to do *anything* which the needs of the nation require, and any theory of the Presidency which projects executive power into this limitless range of action, by definition goes beyond the bounds of constitutionality.

When Presidents in meeting emergencies have assumed extraordinary power on their own initiative, they have invariably sought to legitimize their actions by reference to the Constitution, relying on the "inherent power" concept and generally using the magic formula: "By virtue of authority as President of the United States and Commander in Chief of the armed forces under the Constitution and the laws." But while this formula undoubtedly covers a lot of ground, it cannot be made to include exercises of power which ignore or violate the basic law even though their use is necessary to defense of the nation and notwithstanding the fact that their ultimate purpose is to preserve that law.

There is a third kind of presidential power, therefore, and it is *extraconstitutional:* the American manifestation of that executive authority which John Locke defined as the power to act "according to discretion for the public good, without the prescription of the laws, and sometimes even against it." And it is this kind of power which forms the unique ingredient of presidential authority today— a kind of power which has been resorted to by every crisis leader, and which must be more clearly identified and understood in our time.

Extraconstitutional presidential prerogative is the most difficult to assay, however, because it is unacknowledged in our political theory and unrecognized in our jurisprudence. Unwilling to face the dilemma created by exercises of power which transcend the established bounds of legitimate authority, our public law has refused to distinguish between necessity and constitutionality in judging presidential actions. Jurists and political scientists have, instead, equated these two very different bases of action, with the result that while Presidents have in fact exceeded their legal and constitutional authority in every instance of major national emergency, it remains a dogma of our system that the Constitution is "equal to any of the great exigencies of government."

Among the Presidents who have resorted to extraconstitutional power, only Abraham Lincoln—whose dictatorial regime at the beginning of the Civil War remains the clearest example of reliance on such authority—ever admitted the true nature of his actions, expressing the hope that "measures otherwise unconstitutional might become lawful by becoming indispensable to the preservation of the Constitution through the preservation of the Nation." The Civil War President exceeded his constitutional authority in many instances, from the independent raising of an army to the unauthorized expenditure of public funds. Yet, when Woodrow Wilson used indirect sanctions to gain compliance with his war agencies' directives; when Franklin Roosevelt closed the banks, traded destroyers for bases, threatened to repeal existing legislation, and interned citizens solely because of their racial descent; and when Harry Truman committed the nation to war on his own initiative—all were acting in the Lincolnian tradition.

That tradition is at the core of the strong Presidency, and it flows from a conception of the office legitimized through public approval: that the President, as the "sole representative of all the people," possesses unlimited authority to preserve, protect, and defend the nation which gives the Constitution life and meaning. He may suspend the basic law in order to assure its ultimate survival, and the only standard by which the validity of his actions can be measured is necessity, not constitutionality. Regardless of what American political theory and jurisprudence may hold, history demonstrates clearly that the executive does possess extraconstitutional power, and its existence as an essential part of the office must be acknowledged if we are to understand the Presidency of our time.

THE SOURCES OF PRESIDENTIAL POWER

Although theoretically the twin fountainheads of executive power are the "Constitution and the laws," in fact the sources of this prodigious authority are now democracy and necessity.

The Presidency, like all offices of government, is only a paper institution until the political process supplies the personality which brings it to life. And Article II, though it outlines a potentially powerful executive office, has no effect until its words are translated into action. The real foundations of presidential power, therefore, are those forces which elevate the executive to a focal position in government, allowing him to interpret his authority broadly and to exercise it boldly.

The most important of these forces lies in the democratic nature of the modern Presidency. Not only constitutionally, but also politically and psychologically, the President is *the* leader of the nation. "His," as Woodrow Wilson said, "is the only national voice in affairs. Let him once win the admiration and confidence of the country, and no other single force can withstand him, no combination of forces will easily overpower him. His position takes the imagination of the country. He is the representative of no constituency, but of the whole people." Whether the explanation for the unique popular response to the Presidency be put in politico-constitutional terms (the election process and the singular form of the office) or in psycho-sociological terms (the desire for a father-image and the need for a symbol of national unity), the fact remains that its power flows from and is primarily dependent on its tribunate character.

The personality and political philosophy of the President are closely related to his democratic leadership. All of our strongest Presidents have had charismatic personalities, and all have been power-oriented in their philosophy of government, for it is the combination of popular attraction to the person and popular support for his political principles which makes the President's power effective. Thus his role as Popular Tribune is basic to the exercise of whatever authority may be latent in the Constitution and the laws. Neither Lincoln nor Roosevelt could have acted with such spectacular independence in meeting the challenges that confronted them had they lacked solid popular support, but with that support, they could push their powers to the limits of constitutionality and beyond. Indeed a number of strong Presidents have received object lessons regarding the dependence of power upon popular support: Truman in the 1952 steel dispute, Wilson during the League fight, Roosevelt when he presented the Court-packing plan, and Lincoln's successor after the Civil War's end. Extending one of Woodrow Wilson's observations, the President can dominate American government (Wilson said "his party") by being "spokesman for the real sentiment and purpose of the country, by giving direction to opinion, by giving the country at once the information and the statements of policy which will enable it to form its judgments alike of parties and of men."

All strong Presidents have recognized the importance of maintaining a close relationship with their major source of power. Jackson's election, heralding the era of mass democracy, established the popular Presidency, and Lincoln made clear its significance under crisis conditions. Wilson, following the lead of Theodore Roosevelt, gave the conception further impetus by his practice of "going to the people" on important issues. And Franklin Roosevelt, through masterful use of modern communications media, brought the tribunate Presidency to its contemporary form. Radio, television, and the press conference have made possible the development of a relationship between the President and the people which is exceedingly close. As a result of this intimate—almost familial—bond, the President's constitutional role as symbol of national unity has become an instrument of tremendous power, making him the center of our governmental system, and creating the basis for his leadership both at home and abroad.

The other, and no less important, source of presidential power is necessity. Not only the psychological need for clearly identifiable and deeply trusted authority, but also the governmental necessity for centralized leadership and decisive action in times of crisis.

Ours is a system constitutionally attuned to the requirements of the eighteenth century, and it is mainly through the development of the Presidency that the system has been adapted to the demands of the twentieth. The separation of powers, federalism, even the Bill of Rights and the rule of law, must sometimes be transcended under conditions of grave national emergency. Even under less pressing circumstances, the need for purposeful and efficient government is increasingly evident. But the legislative process—complex, deliberative, cumbersome, and designed to assure the compromise of manifold local interests—is ill-suited to meet these challenges. Only the President, possessing (as Alexander Hamilton noted) both unity and energy, can meet the demand for leadership under critical conditions.

Again, every strong President has recognized this fact and acted in accordance with it. Lincoln arrogated to himself all the powers of government during his eleven-week "dictatorship" in 1861 on the ground that "whether strictly legal or not" his actions were ventured upon "under what appeared to be a popular demand and a public necessity." In the atmosphere of world war, Congress accepted Wilson's leadership and delegated theretofore unprecedented power to the President. Similarly, it was the pressure of economic catastrophe which elevated FDR to the dominant position he occupied during the first hundred days of the New Deal administration, and the existence of an even greater emergency which made him supreme commander of the nation during the Second World War. Likewise, Truman's war-making power sprang from the need for decisive action to halt aggression. Necessity creates power, and presidential power has always been commensurate with the nation's needs.

Most significant for our time, however, is the fact—clearly demonstrated by the Korean conflict and other events since the end of World War II—that the Communist challenge has created a permanent demand for strong leadership and extraordinary power. Because crisis has become the normal condition of our times, the vast authority available to former Presidents only occasionally has today become a permanent part of the executive office.

Thus the needs of the nation and the support of its citizens are the real sources of presidential power, unlocking all the authority hidden in the Constitution and the laws, as well as availing the executive of powers which go beyond even the broadest interpretation of that prodigious combination. The modern President can draw upon extraordinary power because he is the democratic symbol of national unity and the necessary instrument of national action, because it is to him that the nation turns for crisis leadership and because he alone can supply that leadership. As a result, under critical conditions there are no effective constitutional or governmental limits on executive power, for democracy and necessity allow the President to transcend the limitational principle and assert his full authority as trustee of the nation's destiny.

THE RESTRAINTS ON PRESIDENTIAL POWER

In our society there are ostensibly many restraints on presidential power. The federal system, for example, establishes fifty centers of local authority to contend with the national executive. The nation's socio-economic "power elite" represents another potential element of countervailing force. Even within the executive branch itself there is the kind of restraint which flows from administrative inertia or obstruction. But whatever limitations appear to reside in these areas, basically there are three major forms of external restraint on presidential power: judicial supervision, legislative control, and public opinion.

Judicial restraint. Of these the least effective—despite its vaunted reputation—is judicial review of executive acts. And the basic reason is clear: in a showdown the President's power is greater than the Supreme Court's. The judicial branch has generally recognized this fact and either avoided conflict with the executive when possible or accepted his assertions of authority when forced to reach a decision. Indeed the Court has established a consistent pattern of acquiescence in judging presidential exercises of extraordinary power. This acquiescent attitude is not automatic, but in only one instance of direct conflict between the two branches during an emergency period has an important exercise of independent presidential authority been effectively overturned, and then the actual holding was so narrow as to have little permanent value. It is the lesson of history that where exercises of extraordinary power are involved, the Court restrains itself and not the President.

The occasion for the single effective declaration against presidential authority was Truman's seizure of the steel industry during the Korean War, and the Court's hesitancy in breaking even temporarily from its own tradition was apparent in the fact that each of the six majority justices wrote his own opinion. All six agreed that the President had acted *ultra vires* in the particular case, but a majority of this "majority" (four justices) seemed to accept the dissenting view that the President does have "inherent power" to take extraordinary actions in time of crisis—and this was the crucial point. For these four members of the Court, the decision turned on the fact that Congress had explicitly eliminated seizure and provided an alternative procedure (the emergency provisions of the Taft-Hartley Act) for dealing with the type of dispute involved, and that in these circumstances the President, at least initially, could not act in a manner contrary to the clearly expressed legislative will.

Thus the decision was abundantly qualified, and though the steel mills had to be returned, it is more significant that seven members of the Court were unprepared to deprive the President of ultimate authority to meet emergencies. Indeed had there not been such widespread disapproval of the President's action—from Congress, the press, and the general public—or had the Korean situation seemed more critical (truce talks were already underway) it is doubtful that the four majority justices would have written even the cautious opinions that they did. But in the circumstances they evidently seized the opportunity to admonish the President, Congress, and the nation against indiscriminate use of inherent presidential power.

In this sense the Steel Case is very much like the first great decision in the area of presidential emergency power, *Ex parte Milligan*. For in that often cited but no more meaningful Civil War case, the Court, by declaring Lincoln's establishment of martial rule unconstitutional, also attempted to restore the basic law to its normal operation after a crisis. But the issue had been avoided during the war, and the decision did not come until both the emergency and the President had passed from the scene. The Milligan Court spoke the strongest language of limitation—and its words have been quoted against independent exercises of presidential authority on a number of occasions since—but in view of the Court's actual crisis behavior that language was embarrassingly unsubstantial. As most of the judiciary's blasts against the executive, the decision is more quotable than applicable.

Probably the most effective exercise of judicial restraining power was its use to invalidate the early New Deal, though the issue involved was not simply presidential authority but rather the power of the combined political branches of government. In any event, even on that occasion the Court's "victory" was short-lived if not pyrrhic. For the final result of the struggle which reached its climax in the Court-packing plan of 1937 was judicial capitulation to President Roosevelt's demand that economic disaster be viewed as seriously as war and that the Court cease to obstruct governmental efforts to meet the crisis.

The judiciary is always placed in a difficult position by conditions which allow a strong President to assume extraordinary power. Compelled to acknowledge that the law of necessity is superior to the law of the Constitution, and lacking the kind of popular support which is accorded the political leader, it must accept many actions which under normal conditions would be outside the realm of legitimate power. The Court's infrequent *ex post facto* pronouncements regarding the limits of presidential authority have little direct effect in any case, and since no judicial decision is self-enforcing they are always essentially lectures rather than injunctions. The Court's primary function in checking a strong President is to act as a symbol of restraint, a moral force, and a constant reminder of established principles—a function which is by no means unimportant—but with regard to executive power, Article II of the Constitution is what the President, and not what the Court, says it is.

Legislative restraint. In our governmental system Congress is traditionally viewed as the President's principal antagonist and most effective restrainer. The constitutional separation of powers with its mechanism of checks and balances was designed to encourage an executive-legislative power struggle which would prevent either branch from gaining dominant authority. And the local orientation of congressional politics supposedly provides a counterweight to the national purview of the Presidency. But despite all this, Congress cannot easily control the exercise of presidential power. In fact, both the constitutional structure of the government, with its separation of the branches, and the nature of American politics, with its emphasis on local interest representation, often tend to make that task more rather than less difficult.

The separation of powers doctrine can become both a shield and a sword in the hands of a strong President. He can use it to ward off alleged congressional encroachments on executive authority, as Lincoln did in combating the Committee on the Conduct of the (Civil) War and as Wilson did in preventing the establishment of a similar body. Or he can use the doctrine to support his resort to independent authority, the approach adopted on so many occasions by the Civil War President (who achieved the greatest concentration of power in our history by insisting on the separation principle), as well as by every other strong executive who has relied on that principle in assuming extraordinary power on his own initiative.

As the separation of powers principle often creates a constitutional power-vacuum which the executive can fill, so too does the nature of congressional politics give rise to conditions which may enhance rather than limit presidential authority. The local orientation of Congress assures the representation of all the significant interests in our society, but at the same time it results in legislative fragmentation, leaving Congress without a cohesive majority or effective leadership. And this political power-vacuum the President may also enter. Indeed it is increasingly evident that if he does not assume the role of legislative leader, Congress cannot move on important and controversial issues. Attuned to the process of continuing compromise rather than to the achievement of definite goals, Congress must always give way to the executive when events demand unity of purpose and decisive action.

Congress itself knows this and looks increasingly to the President for leadership, not only with regard to matters of national defense and foreign affairs, but in other areas as well, like domestic economic policy and civil rights. It is in time of actual or impending emergency, however, that this need for presidential initiative is most clearly evident and most readily acknowledged by Congress, as it quickly accepts the President's direction in delegating to him whatever authority he requests. Despite the separation of powers principle, executive leadership of the legislature has become an established feature of our system, though the effect of Congress's reliance on presidential initiative and of its delegations of authority to the executive is to enhance his domination over the legislative process and to increase his freedom from legislative control.

Congress's difficulty in restraining presidential power is also a result of the tremendous range and complexity of contemporary governmental problems, and of its own inability to deal with them. Neither the individual legislator nor the Congress as a whole possesses the information-gathering and problem-evaluating apparatus of the Presidency, particularly in the foreign affairs and defense areas, but in others as well. Congress is increasingly dependent, therefore, upon members of the executive branch—department heads, military officers, economic and scientific advisers—for the technical information essential to its own activity. Thus, while information may be acquired through congressional inquiry or investigation (and despite the fact that the President's subordinates do not always accept his policy determinations), to a large extent the effectiveness of legislative supervision depends upon the executive's willingness to cooperate.

Further detracting from the legislature's ability to contend with the President is his control over formulation of the budget, since this function gives the executive a dominant position in determining the final plan for governmental expenditures. Indeed the congressional power over the executive traditionally assumed to be the greatest—the power of the purse—is often ineffectual. The President may present Congress with a situation which does not permit the withholding of funds, as Theodore Roosevelt did by sending the Great White Fleet on its famous global journey without enough coal to get it back home, and as other Presidents have done by more serious dispositions of the armed forces. Congress may even be forced to appropriate money without knowing the reason for the expenditure, as it did in supporting the secret, multi-billion dollar development of the atomic bomb. And Lincoln simply paid out $2,000,000 of public funds on his own initiative. Despite its celebrated reputation, therefore, even the restraining power of the purse is subject to suspension when the need for secrecy or speed is of the essence.

The most important limitation on Congress as a presidential restrainer, however, is public support for the executive. While the localism of congressional politics makes legislators peculiarly responsive to the desires of particular groups, it also leaves the advantage increasingly with the President in mobilizing the general public behind national policies. For with regard to such policies Congress can never present a single view or project a definite image to the country, while the President can do so forcefully. Emphasizing his roles as head of state and sole national representative, and utilizing all the media of mass communication, he is able to generate pressure which Congress cannot easily withstand.

Of course Congress is not impotent in exercising control over the President. The political longevity of congressional leaders and the absence of party discipline allow for displays of legislative independence which can and do check, embarrass, or inhibit the executive. Legislative debate and investigation—techniques which have been used to harass every strong President—can focus attention on alleged maladministration or misconduct in the executive branch. And widespread congressional hostility makes even the strongest President somewhat cautious in his exercises of power. But under emergency or semi-emergency conditions congressional antagonism is largely sublimated, and attempts to limit the President are generally more irritating than effective. Despite legislative fulmination, no crisis executive has ever been deterred by the legislature from accomplishing his major purposes.

Indeed, confronted with a strong President, Congress generally finds the task of imposing restraints both thankless and frustrating. For the public is likely to equate opposition to the President with obstruction of his efforts in the nation's behalf, and moreover there is the hard fact that a popular crisis President who encounters difficulties or delays in Congress—particularly in matters of foreign policy—may simply bypass the legislature and present it with a *fait accompli* by resort to his independent authority. Congress is certainly a more formidable check on presidential power than the courts, but in our time it does not and cannot fulfill the restraining function traditionally ascribed to it.

Popular restraint. As the President's principal source of power is public support, so too can popular opinion be the most important restraint on that power. So long as the nation's approval is firm and evident, his authority cannot be challenged effectively, but conversely, in order to use his full powers a President must continue to have such approval. His personal relationship with the public and his ability to guide popular opinion are the mainstays of his dominant position in government.

Some of our strongest Presidents discovered this truth the hard way. Franklin Roosevelt lost the Court-packing battle (though he ultimately won the war against judicial obstructionism) because the same public which had just given him the greatest electoral mandate in history refused to support his attempt to invade judicial independence. Woodrow Wilson failed to meet his own test of success in the League campaign, and the absence of popular support played a major role in Harry Truman's defeat on the steel seizure issue. Moreover, Congress quickly reflects public hostility to the President, and, though less immediately, so may the Court. Thus FDR could not assert his legislative leadership once his opponents in Congress sensed that Court-packing lacked popular support, and the Supreme Court was encouraged to act with dispatch to invalidate Truman's unpopular assertion of power in the steel dispute.

The major instrumentalities for mobilizing public support against the President are the opposition political party, organized pressure groups, and the press or other communications media. But under critical conditions particularly, the same factors that limit the efficacy of the formal (legislative and judicial) restraints also apply to these three informal restraining forces. The President's political opponents —often including members of his own party—must beware of boomerangs; pressure groups represent only single rather than national interests; and the media, perhaps the most important of the three, fear that by combining their reportorial and editorial functions in opposing the President, they may lose the public trust, limit their wide area of freedom, and cut off their best source of news. The press, radio, and television report and comment on opposition to the executive, but even when the diverse elements of the communications system agree with this opposition, they seldom attempt to incite public disapproval of his actions.

While popular support may, on rare occasions, be mobilized against the President, the opposite is the rule. For he is the principal molder of public opinion, and as a result, even this most important instrument of restraint is not often effective. The same psychology that creates a desire for presidential leadership in critical times assures the executive of popular support for the policies which he pursues. Moreover, it is important to recognize that this "crisis psychology" which elevates the President to a dominant position is itself partly created by the President. For, given the framework of objective facts surrounding a critical situation, it is largely the crisis leader's own reaction to those facts—the extent to which he emphasizes and dramatizes the situation's seriousness—that determines the form of public response. The fact of Southern secession was no less serious in 1860 than 1861, but where Buchanan's equivocation clouded the issue, Lincoln's action mobilized the nation to meet it. Similarly, the depression did not begin when Roosevelt took office, but it was FDR who marshalled opinion behind a program to overcome the economic disaster. Most significantly, it was Wilson, Roosevelt, and Truman who made the nation aware that foreign aggression constituted a threat to domestic security. And conversely, in the immediate past, the country did not face up to the dangers confronting it largely because President Eisenhower failed to impress upon the public the urgency of the international situation.

Whatever the objective facts may be, it is the President himself who plays a central role in defining the issues and creating the popular attitudes which make possible his own exercises of extraordinary power. Moreover, all of this is especially true in our own time, not only because the means by which the President may influence opinion have improved so greatly, nor because his ability to use those means is so far superior to that of any other person or group in the society, but because even that segment of the public which is not politically indifferent finds it increasingly difficult to make independent judgments regarding the significance or seriousness of particular events. That international Communist aggression poses a threat to American security and world peace is perhaps generally recognized, but is economic penetration of Afghanistan or the fomenting of revolution in Iraq or infiltration of the Cuban government aggression? Adequate military defense is an acknowledged necessity, but to achieve it do we require planes or missiles, and if missiles, are domestic launching facilities sufficient or must we also have overseas bases? Support for those who seek their independence from colonial rule is in keeping with American principles, but should we favor strong central governments or federal unions in the newly-established nations?

Confronted with fantastically complex problems and asked to determine the wisdom of policies involving all the areas of the world, even the responsible and informed citizen often ends up placing his trust in God and the President. In the sense of its direct influence on decision-making, therefore, public opinion is less a limitation on presidential power than the key to its full utilization—a fact which every strong President has recognized by placing the greatest emphasis on his position of popular leadership.

Effective restraints. But if public opinion is ultimately no more effective than legislative or judicial restraint, are there no real limitations on the Presidency? There does exist in our political system one factor which can generally be counted on to minimize the possibility of arbitrary executive rule, and that is the process by which the President is selected. Not merely the element of choice in voting, though that is important, but rather the complex procedure by which candidates are selected in party conventions, and even more, the personal attributes of those who are finally chosen to seek the highest office.

Because the Presidency (along with the Vice Presidency) is the only national elective office in an exceedingly diverse society, it is open only to those who are attuned to the virtues of political compromise and moderate in their political philosophy. The parties will nominate only such men, and though this tends to exclude from consideration many competent people whose views are too definite, it also acts as a "safety valve" against those who might disregard the welfare of significant segments of our population. A new President may reveal or find within himself the capacity for bold and decisive leadership, but the basic personality, shaped by the same forces that open the way to the office, remains, and even in his assertions of extraordinary power he will not depart essentially from the conservative, evolutionary, and pragmatic tradition of American government and politics.

The Presidency reflects this tradition with remarkable accuracy in its consistent rejection of dogmatism, of the Left and of the Right alike. It is not a position for radical or reactionary autocrats, or for demagogues, and none of our strong Presidents, despite their claims to power, has given any evidence of desiring to establish a permanent dictatorship. Nor has any of them ever attempted to use temporary powers to achieve fundamentally different forms of social or political organization. Some Presidents have assumed dictatorial authority to meet crises, but none has ever *been* a dictator. In power they may sometimes violate basic principles of the constitutional system temporarily, even unnecessarily—as Wilson did by allowing overzealous subordinates to engage in witchhunting during World War I, and as Roosevelt did in permitting the denial of basic rights to a racial minority during World War II—but in the final analysis all have displayed a deep attachment to, and a high regard for, those principles.

It is at least partly because of their personal commitment to constitutional democratic processes that crisis Presidents have always attempted to justify their extraordinary actions by reference to the basic law, and that whenever possible they have sought to include Congress as a partner in crisis government. For legitimacy is important to the President, as it is to the Presidency, and presidential self-restraint, reflecting both innate personal qualities and real concern for the opinion of the public and of history can be as meaningful a restraining force as countervailing power. Thus, while constitutional and political methods of restraining the executive may not always be effective, the Presidency has auto-limitational features which tend to mitigate those dangers to our system of government which are inherent in its vast power.

THE PRESIDENCY IN THE SIXTIES

The scope and effect of executive power are today so broad as to make valid Henry Jones Ford's observation that in the presidential office American democracy has revived "the oldest political institution of the race, the elective kingship." In fact, considering the absence of external restraints on this power, the question arises as to whether the contemporary Presidency is not, potentially, a "matrix for dictatorship."

The answer is certainly "no" if by dictatorship is meant absolute and arbitrary authority which denies the opportunity for political opposition and rejects the possibility of free, nonpolitical activity. But it is just as clear that the Presidency today is unquestionably the dominant organ of American government, an office permanently and inherently strong, reflecting the institutionalization of crisis concepts established by precedent, legitimized by public acceptance, and sustained by the abnormality of international affairs.

The Presidency has always mirrored the facts of our national life, and under present conditions there is no alternative to a strong executive. Because ours is an age of crisis, it is an age of executive government, and this political truth applies no less surely to the United States than it does to virtually every other country in the world. The powerful American Presidency is part of a global pattern —as evident in the West as in the East—characterized by the expansion and centralization of governmental authority; it is a modern form of a more primitive kind of rule, developed to meet extraordinary challenges and perpetuated while the search for peaceful normalcy continues.

Despite its present eminence, however, the Presidency during the decade ahead will most likely become an even more powerful institution. And not only in the event of war, nor only in the field of foreign affairs. For the '60s will be a critical period, both at home and abroad, even in the absence of armed conflict, and executive authority may have to be exercised in new ways to meet new challenges. Indeed, to a significant degree the outcome of the struggle between communism and democracy, as well as the resolution of important domestic issues, will depend on the actions of the President. "Without leadership alert and sensitive to change," as Franklin Roosevelt said, "we are bogged up or lose our way," and in our rapidly changing world there is a pressing need for such leadership on both the national and the international scenes.

There are many new ways in which the power of the Presidency may have to be exercised during the decade ahead. Should the ultimate crisis of thermonuclear war occur, the President would necessarily have to assume dictatorial authority over every aspect of whatever remained of our national existence. His power would be total, to meet the totality of the disaster, and the regimes of Lincoln, Wilson, and Roosevelt would seem pale in comparison. But aside from the dread possibility of an atomic emergency, there will probably be at least three major problems in the '60s requiring strong executive action: the occurrence or threat of limited war in various parts of the globe, increasing political and economic competition with the Soviet camp, and the perfection of democracy within the United States itself.

With regard to the problem of limited armed conflict, Mr. Truman broke new ground in the exercise of presidential power when he committed the nation—and its allies—to a major war in Korea entirely on his own initiative, and a future President might well have to act with similar boldness in defense of the national interest. In fact, the President's responsibility is no longer limited to the maintenance of American security; it now embraces the security of all the free nations. Nor is his new role limited to sporadic instances of military aggression; because of the more subtle threat of Communist political, social, and economic competition, it is a permanent position. In a very real sense, the American President has become the executive of the entire Western Coalition, and the major instrument for assuring peace and order throughout the world.

To play this expanded executive role will require that the President lead in the formulation of common Western policy and that he assume the task of articulating the basic principles on which the Western Coalition is established. In the struggle for the nations of Asia and Africa, his will be the crucial job of presenting the case for democracy and of capturing the imagination of the uncommitted peoples. This job really starts at home, for the President must first create a climate of public opinion which will support a bold program of international leadership. To meet the challenge of Communist competition will require an effort much greater than that which was made to save Western Europe from collapse after World War II, but it will require a similar sense of urgency and a similar kind of vision and vitality in the executive office.

The major domestic problem which the President will have to meet in the '60s is related to the achievement of our foreign policy goals, since he cannot be an effective spokesman for democracy abroad so long as equality in civil rights is denied to colored citizens within the United States. The law of the Constitution is now clear with regard to this matter, but only the President has the prestige and the power to help make that law meaningful. The civil rights issue is not regional but national, and its resolution will depend largely on presidential initiative in mobilizing national sentiment behind the responsible leaders of both races.

In these new and as yet largely unexplored areas of presidential activity lies much of the future development of executive power. The precise form which that development may take cannot be foretold, but its general direction during the years immediately ahead seems clear. For the new President has already expressed an intention to act in the tradition of his "strong" predecessors, viewing his authority broadly and exercising it boldly. Thus he has recognized that the power of the contemporary Presidency is the nation's principal weapon for meeting the extraordinary challenges which now confront it. And though a President's determination to provide effective leadership cannot alone decide the nation's destiny, it nonetheless constitutes our best hope that those challenges will be met successfully.

☆

RICHARD E. NEUSTADT: *The Reality of*

Presidential Power

There are many ways to look at the American Presidency. It can be done in terms juridical or biographical, political or managerial: the office viewed primarily as a compendium of precedents, a succession of personalities, a fulcrum for party politics, a focus for administrative management. This essay denies the relevance of none of these approaches and makes use, incidentally, of them all, but aims at observation from a rather different point of view. This is an effort to look at the Presidency *operationally*, in working terms, as an instrument of governance in the middle years of the twentieth century; as man-in-office, that is to say, in a time of continuing "cold war," spiralling atomic discovery (and vulnerability), stabilized "big government," and stalemated partisan alignment—the *policy* environment capsuled by Clinton Rossiter as "new economy" and "new internationalism"; the *political* environment billed by Samuel Lubell as "politics of twilight." . . .

[The] modern Presidency's powers and responsibilities—the "what," that is to say—are widely known, however we may differ on their import for our form of government, and anyone in doubt has only to review numerous recent writings in the field. But the "how" is relatively unexplored terrain for which there are no ready

Richard E. Neustadt is Littauer Professor of Public Administration at Harvard University. The selection is from "The Presidency at Mid-Century," from a symposium, *The Presidential Office*, appearing in *Law and Contemporary Problems*, Vol. 21, Autumn, 1956, pp. 609-645, published by the Duke University School of Law, Durham, North Carolina. Copyright, 1956, by Duke University. Reprinted by permission of the publisher and the author.

336

references outside the realm of selective particulars in press reports, case studies, memoirs, and the like. Granting the President his modern "roles," how does the work get done? What are his means? How may these be employed? Under what limitations? At what cost? With what effect? In what degree sufficient to the Presidency's purposes?

These are the central questions I should like to pose—to pose, note, not to "answer." . . .

There is, though, a prerequisite: If one would focus on the doing of the presidential job, one needs a characterization of the job, as such, that lends itself to operational appraisal; a characterization that defines what need be done in terms approaching those in which the doer does it. . . . For working purposes, the President is never "many men," but one; the Presidency, as an instrument of government, is indivisible; the White House has no separate rooms for the "Chief Legislator," "Chief of Party," "Chief Administrator," *et al.* Observations on the doing of the job must build upon a statement of what exists to be done in terms other than these.

Hence, having stressed an emphasis on means and advertised its claims, I must begin where everyone begins, with a review of presidential powers—a review of the Presidency's place, that is to say, in the contemporary governmental scene.

THE PRESIDENCY IN GOVERNMENT

"His is the vital place of action in the system," wrote Woodrow Wilson of the President toward the close of TR's term. And this, a new discovery for Wilson's generation, is now, at mid-century, a matter of course. Presidential leadership is now a matter of routine to a degree quite unknown before the Second World War. If the President remains at liberty, in Wilson's phrase, "to be as big a man as he can," the obverse holds no longer: he *cannot* be as small as he might choose.

Once, TR daringly assumed the "steward's" role in the emergency created by the great coal strike of 1902; the Railway Labor Act and the Taft-Hartley Act now make such interventions mandatory upon Presidents. Once, FDR dramatically asserted personal responsibility for gauging and guiding the American economy; now, the Employment Act binds his successors to that task. Wilson and FDR became chief spokesmen, leading actors on a world stage at the height of war; now UN membership, far-flung alliances, the facts of power, prescribe that role continuously in times termed "peace." Through both World Wars, our Presidents grappled experimentally with an emergency-created need to "integrate" foreign and military and domestic policies; the National Security Act now takes that need for granted as a constant of our times. FDR and Truman made themselves responsible for the development and first use of atomic weapons; the Atomic Energy Act now puts a com parable burden on the back of every President. In instance after instance, the one-time personal initiatives, innovations of this century's "strong" Presidents, have now been set by statutes as requirements of office. And what has escaped statutory recognition has mostly been absorbed into presidential "common law," confirmed by custom, no less binding: the unrehearsed press conference, for example, or the personally-presented legislative program.

The "vital place of action" has been rendered permanent; the *forms* of leadership fixed in the cumulative image of *ad hoc* assertions under Wilson and the two Roosevelts; past precedents of personality and crisis absorbed into the government's continuing routines. For the executive establishment and for the Congress, both, the Presidency has become the regular, accustomed source of all major initiatives: supplier of both general plans and detailed programs; articulator of the forward course in every sphere of policy encompassed by contemporary government. Bold or bland, aggressive or conciliatory, massive or minimal, as the case may be, the lead is his.

Thus, we have made a matter of routine the President's responsibility to take the policy lead. And at the same time, we have institutionalized, in marked degree, the exercise of that responsibility. President and Presidency are synonymous no longer; the office now comprises an officialdom twelve-hundred strong. For almost every phase of policy development, there is now institutional machinery engaged in preparations on the President's behalf: for the financial and administrative work plan of the government, the Budget Bureau; for the administration's legislative program, the White House counsel and the Budget's clearance organization; for programing in economic and social spheres, the Council of Economic Advisers (and to some degree the cabinet, Eisenhower-style); in foreign and military fields, the National Security Council; in spheres of domestic preparedness, the Office of Defense Mobilization; these pieces of machinery, among others, each built around a program-making task, all lumped together, formally, under the rubric, "The Executive Office of the President," an institutional conception and a statutory entity less than two decades old.

These are significant developments, this rendering routine, this institutionalizing of the initiative. They give the Presidency nowadays a different look than it has worn before, an aspect permanently "positive." But the reality behind that look was not just conjured up by statutes or by staffing. These, rather, are *responses* to the impacts of external circumstance upon our form of government; not causes but effects.

Actually or potentially, the Presidency has always been—at least since Jackson's time—a unique point of intersection for three lines of leadership responsibility: "executive" and partisan and national. The mandates of our Constitution, the structure of our political parties, the nature of the President's electorate, fused long ago to draw these lines together *at that point and there alone*: the Presidency at once the sole nationally elective office, independently responsible to a unique constituency; sole centralizing stake of power, source of control, in each party (as a glance at either party out of power shows); sole organ of foreign relations and military command; sole object of the "take care" clause and of the veto power; and with all this, sole crown-like symbol of the Union.

By Wilson's time, that combination, in the context of world power stakes and status, had brought a fourth line of leadership into play, a line of leadership abroad, its only point of intersection with the other three the White House, once again. Since then, there have been revolutionary changes in the world and in American society and in the character of government's commitments toward both; changes productive of fast-rising expectations and requirements for leadership transmitted toward the Presidency along each line—four streams of action impulses and obligations converging on the President, whoever he may be, their volume and their rate of flow varying with events, a source which never, nowadays, runs dry.

The contemporary President, in short, has *four constituencies*, each with distinctive expectations of him and demands upon him. One of these is his "government" constituency, comprising the great group of public officers—congressional as well as executive—who cannot do their own official jobs without some measure of performance on his part. A second is his "partisan" constituency, comprising at once his own party's congressional delegation, and its organization leaders, workers, even voters, all those whose political fortunes, interests, sentiments, are tied, in some degree, to his performance. A third is his "national" constituency, comprising all those individuals and groups among Americans who look to him, especially when crises come, for an embodiment and an expression of government's relationship to its citizenry, for a response to their needs, purposes, endeavors. And fourth, is his "overseas" constituency, comprising not alone the officers of foreign governments, but the political oppositions, the opinion molders, even the plain citizens to some degree, in every country where our power, policies, or postures have imposed themselves upon domestic politics.

In respect to the first three of these constituencies, membership is not a mutually exclusive matter. A number of American officials —among them cabinet officers and congressmen, are members of all three. And most Americans hold membership in two, as at once partisans and citizens. But whatever its effects on individual or group behavior, multiple membership does not preclude distinctly differentiated sets of Presidency-oriented expectations and demands, identifiable with each constituency, arising in the circumstances of mid-century from the pervasive needs of each for governmental action.

In these terms, it appears no accident that at a time when stakes of government are high for all the President's constituents, to him has passed, routinely, the continuing initiative in government. That role is both assured him and required of him by the very uniqueness of his place at the only point of intersection, the sole juncture, of those four lines of leadership responsibility and the constituencies they represent.

Yet, the demands and expectations pressing in upon the President propel him not alone toward enunciation, but delivery. Executive officials want decisions, congressmen want proposals, partisans want power, citizens want substance, friends abroad want steadiness and insight and assistance on their terms—all these as shorthand statements of complex material and psychological desires. These things are wanted *done*; given our Constitution and our politics, that means done by, or through, or with assistance from, or acquiescence of, the President. The very factors that contribute to his unique opportunities—and routinized responsibilities—as an initiator, make him essential also as protector, energizer, implementor, of initiatives once taken. His special place in government requires of him, indeed, thrusts upon him, a unique responsibility—and opportunity—to oversee and assure execution.

But while responsibility for the initiative has now been routinized and even institutionalized, authority to implement the courses set remains fragmented in our system. In most respects and for most purposes, the President lacks any solid base of assured, institutionalized support to carry through the measures he proposes. His four constituencies are capable of constant pressure, but not of reliable response to downward leads. The "executive" is not a unity with a firm command-and-subordination structure, nor is the Government, nor is the political party, in Congress or out, nor is the nation, nor the alliance system overseas. All these are feudalities in power terms; pluralistic structures every one of them. Our Constitution, our political system, our symbolism, and our history make certain that the President alone assumes, in form, the leadership of each; and guarantee, no less, that he will not have systematic, unified, assured support from any. Indeed, precisely the conditions vesting him alone with leadership responsibility for all prevent the rendering of any one of them into tight-welded followings. The constitutional separation of powers—really, of institutions sharing powers—the federal separations of sovereignty, hence politics, the geographic separations of electorates, these and their consequences at once have helped the Presidency to its special place and hindered the creation of a strong supporting base. And, at a time when the executive establishment has grown too vast for personal surveillance, when Congress is controlled in form by narrow, shifting partisan majorities, in fact by factional coalition, weighted against the President's electorate, the hindrances are bound to be enhanced. Ours is that sort of time.

This does not mean that Presidents are powerless; far from it. Their four-way leadership position gives them vantage points aplenty for exerting strength in Government, in party, in the country, and abroad; collectively, by all odds, an array of strong points quite unmatched by any other single power-holder in our system. It does mean, though, that presidential power must be exercised *ad hoc*, through the employment of whatever sources of support, whatever transient advantages can be found and put together, case by case. It means the President can never choose a policy with certainty that it will be approximated in reality or that he will not have it to unmake or make again. It means he cannot, as he pleases, moderate, adjust or set aside the rival, overlapping, often contradictory claims of his constituencies. *He has no option but to act, at once, as agent of them all, for their conjunction in his person is the keystone of his potency*; none is dispensable, hence the demands of none are automatically disposable at his convenience. Events, not his free choices, regulate their pressures and condition his response.

Dilemmas, consequently, are the Presidency's daily bread. The President must now initiate specific policies and programs for all fields of federal action; he has become the focus for all forward planning in our system; whatever leads the government and country and his party (and indeed, the opposition, also) are to have, will stem from him. Yet, not his preferences only, but events in an inordinately complex world, not his reasoning alone, but his constituencies' felt requirements, contradictory as they may be, mold his determinations, limit his choices, force his hand. What he initiates he must attempt to implement. He must try so to manage the executive establishment, and Congress, and his party oligarchs, and the other party's also, and "public opinion," and overseas support, that the essential things get done—so far at least as government can do them—to keep administration reasonably competent, the country reasonably prosperous, the cold war reasonably cold, and his party in the White House; objectives which will seem to him synonymous (no President in memory, Mr. Eisenhower naturally not excluded, has ever thought his policies could best be carried forward by the other party's men). Yet, none of these agencies of action, of execution, are subject to his management by fiat; not even those closest to home, his own administration, his own party, are constructed to provide him with assured support. Rarely can he order, mostly must he persuade. And even were his controls taut and sharp, there would remain, of course, those agencies beyond his power to command, events.

No doubt, in times of great emergency, sharp crisis seen and felt as such throughout the country, the Presidency's measure of assured support from public, party, and administration tends to increase dramatically, if temporarily, while "politics as usual" abates, at least until the sharpness wanes; witness the situation circa 1942. But it is characteristic of our circumstances at mid-century—in all the years since the Second World War—that while our government's responsibilities retain a trace of every prior crisis, no comparable sense of national emergency pervades our politics. If this is an "era of permanent crisis," it is one in which Presidents must manage without benefit of crisis consensus.

Given the underlying situation here described, the balance of this paper is, perforce, a study of dilemmas; dilemmas nurtured by disparities between the Presidency's obligation to initiate and its capacity to achieve, the one nailed down, the other relatively tenuous, both bound to be so by the nature of our institutional adjustment, up to now, to the complexities of governing this country at mid-century.

What, currently, is the American Presidency? A cat on a hot tin roof.

THE PRESIDENT IN THE PRESIDENCY

So far in this discussion, "President" and "Presidency" have been used almost interchangeably; the man and his office equated in an effort at capsule characterization. But since it is our purpose to appraise the man *in* office, the *President* at work, we must now differentiate between the individual and his official tasks, between the work done by the White House occupant and that performed by others in his name.

What does the President, himself, contribute to the conduct of the Presidency? What, in an office now so institutionalized that it encompasses six hundred "professional" aides, has he, himself, to do? What, in a government of vast and complicated undertakings, in a substantive environment demanding every sort of expertise, can there be *left* for him to do? To put the case in current terms, what is there that no "chief of staff" can do without him? . . .

[The] President's own specialties within the Presidency, the contributions none can make without him, consist of acts of choice and of persuasion; choices not in foreign policy alone, but in all spheres of action and of men as well as measures; persuasion not only of congressmen, but of administrative officers and politicians, of private interests and "the public" generally, of foreign governments and their publics; choice and persuasion exercised, in short, throughout the range of problems and of persons covered by his four constituencies.

These things are his to do because he is the sole, accountable human embodiment of an office which, in turn, is uniquely the center of responsibility and motive-power in our system. No President, of course, takes to himself more than a fraction of the choices, efforts at persuasion, made on his authority and in his name. But beyond a certain point—a point, of course, that varies case by case—choice-making and persuasion become personalized, of necessity, because his aides and auditors insist that it be so; because no one will accept others' choices, because no one will heed others' persuasions, because no others dare or care to run his risks on their discretion or their risks on his authority. Beyond another point—which may or may not coincide—persuasive acts and choices become ripe for his personal attention as a matter of desirability in his own interest, because his personal perceptions of that interest are ultimately untransferable; because save secondhand, by empathy, not even Harry Hopkins, Sherman Adams, can know fully what it feels like to sit where he sits (endowed with his intelligence, his temperament) at the solitary juncture of his four constituencies, "President of the United States"—hence, no one else can bring to bear precisely his own "feel" for risks to him, to the totality of his unique position, inherent in alternatives of doing and not doing.

If a look at the Presidency without a working President shows choices and persuasion as the man's own occupation, that impression cannot be strengthened by a glance at what takes up his time when on the job. Nowadays, the normal presidential working week revolves around a series of fixed sessions: one set meeting apiece with the National Security Council, and the Cabinet, and (when Congress is on hand) the legislative leaders, and the press, each preceded and followed by appropriate staff briefings, consultations;

one set appointment apiece with the Secretary of State, the Secretary of Defense, the Chairman of the Joint Chiefs of Staff, and (an Eisenhower innovation, now suspended) the Chairman of the Council of Economic Advisers. Truman had, besides, a daily morning conference with his principal staff aides to make *ad hoc* assignments and receive routine reports; such sessions Sherman Adams has conducted under Eisenhower.

When one includes the chores of getting ready, cleaning up, these regularly scheduled consultations pre-empt a substantial portion of the President's own working hours, week by week. In the case of a President like Eisenhower, who finds these mechanisms to his taste and uses them to the exclusion of much else, that share of hours occupied mounts high. And what is the object of this outlay of his time? Such sessions serve, in part, as occasions for others to put their concerns, their views before him; partly as occasions for him to impress his personality and attitudes *on* others. Which of these parts has major place will vary with each sort of session, influenced by subject matter, membership, and *his* proclivities. But whatever their variation, the components are the same: one part material for choice-making, the other part the stuff of personal persuasion.

As for the balance of the presidential working week, the bulk of it is turned to comparable account; the documents signed, the persons seen, the places filled, the arguments resolved, the messages sent, the speeches made, the ceremonies held, all these are characteristically acts of choice or efforts at persuasion, often both at once—even the formal ceremonials contributing a portion of his power to persuade, even their performance contingent on his choice.

The preoccupations of the presidential week will vary with the seasons of the presidential year, from budget and message seasons in the fall, through early, middle, and late stages of the legislative season, through the rush of adjournment and enrollments, to that precious period, the post-adjournment lull (if any), season for recovery and repairs, and so to fall again—a round, successively, of planning to decision, campaigning to compromise, recuperating to resumption; a peacetime rhythm set primarily to legislative tasks but liable constantly to interruptions on account of mishaps and emergencies in operating spheres. Inevitably, presidential choices, efforts at persuasion, reflect in their intensities, their objects, and their scope these swings of emphasis throughout the year. And even more may they reflect swings in the cycle of the presidential term, from early groping through a first consolidation and a forward push up to the test at midterm, then regrouping and a second forward effort dwindling toward hiatus in the final year. But whatever their application in a given context, choice-making and persuasion remain the components of the President's own work; comprising what he does himself, both on the insistence of others and at his own inner promptings.

These are, in short, his means; the means by which he, personally, exercises influence within his office and upon the course of government; the means by which he makes his own mark on the tasks of office sketched above. As such, these "means" are not for him mere instruments employed at will to carry out those tasks. Rather they are the concrete manifestations of the tasks themselves, applying to him personally; the work he has to do, no act of will required. In literary terms, one may say that he sets the tone, provides the lead in government by choosing and persuading. In operating terms, though, one must put it in reverse: that acts of choice and of persuasion cumulated over time produce an ultimate effect of tone and lead which may or may not correspond to any prior blueprint, purpose, or intention. Such is the consequence of disentangling the President from the Presidency.

That ultimate resultant labeled "leadership" will be compounded of two types of actions by the President: those he may reach for in his own discretion and those thrust on him of necessity; the one type, opportunities, the other, compulsions. And, as the compound will be viewed by his constituents and history, more than these enter in; the multifarious things done or left undone by others in his name, or the government's, and happenings beyond the government's discretion, plain events.

No President is free to concentrate upon his opportunities at the expense of his compulsions; he can but hope to find room for the things he may do amidst all things he must. Nor is he free to wave away those other actors on the scene; he can but hope to channel and deflect their impacts on his audience. To the extent he wants to make his own will dominate the conduct of his office, his regime, he has no recourse but to choices and persuasion exercised within these narrow limits. The purposeful President, his face set against drift (and any President, these days, will so regard himself), is thus confronted by an operating problem of immense complexity and large proportions, or more precisely by two problems tightly linked: Given those limits and in furtherance of his own purposes, how is he to maximize the efficiency of his choice-making? How maximize the efficacy of his power to persuade?

The proportions and complexities of these two connected problems it now becomes our object to explore.

THE FREEDOM TO CHOOSE

If Presidents were free to choose the matters they made choices on, their problems of choice-making would be relatively simplified; but Presidents are not. The flow of issues they must face cannot be turned off like a water tap; to know that, one has but to note its sources.

Why do men in government and politics (and in the country and the world) bring issues to a President, invoke his act of choice? To amplify the foregoing analysis, it may be said that they do so for one, or another, or all of three reasons. First, there are matters that by law or custom require some sort of personal performance on his part, his signature, his presence or his voice. Second, there are matters on which others, theoretically competent to act, want the loan of his potency or the cover of his prestige, his impetus behind their preferences, his brand on their performance. Third, there are the matters he himself wants made his own, that on his own initiative he has marked "count me in," matters on which he exercises the discretion we have already discussed. And in the circumstances of mid-century, no President will lack for quantities of matters of each sort.

In the first of these three categories, volume is adjustable, at least to a degree. . . .

As for the second category, the most a President seriously can hope to do is slow the rate of flow, shut out the marginal case. . . .

There remains the third category, where interventions come at *his* initiative. There, he has the option, theoretically, of moving not at all. But this is fatal; also quite impracticable. No doubt, some Presidents may relish, others shy away from forcing matters into their own hands. No doubt, each will evolve some special preferences according to his particular competences, interests. But every President will find some issues that he wants to seize and ride— Truman on Point Four, Eisenhower on Atoms for Peace—and each will find a plenitude he feels *impelled* to take upon himself. . . .

Since acts of choice are often negative, there are, of course, more instances of such "enforced" discretion than will appear in current press reports: Eisenhower choosing time and again, as Donovan records, *not* to blast McCarthy; Truman choosing—as he sometimes did—not to leap, guns blazing, into loyalty cases that aroused his ire; so forth, *ad infinitum*. The "I don't know about that" in press conference is deceptive as a guide to presidential doings. In most such cases, this would remain the expedient response, assuming he did know. Yet every President, one may suppose, will now go out of office wishing that in some respects he had pushed further still, discretion *un*enforced, toward taking over at times and in places where contemporary happenings did not push him.

One wonders whether Truman never wished that he had intervened more actively in the affairs of his Attorneys General. One wonders whether Eisenhower may not come to wish that he had done the same regarding some of *his* department heads. No President finds pleasure in waiting upon "messes" for his cue to intervene. But none can be sure, either, that initiatives of others will suffice to flash a warning to him in good time. There is an obverse of the second category named above: those issues men bring to the President out of their fears, uncertainties, are matched by those kept from him out of confidence, or cussedness, or independent power (even ignorance). . . . Far from reducing his discretionary range, a President is bound to end by wishing he could widen it.

But time stands in his way. He cannot afford to do nothing at his own discretion; but neither can he manage to do everything. Priority of place on his choice-making production line belongs of sheer necessity to matters with *deadlines* attached. And in most days of his working week, most seasons of his year, a President has quite enough of these to drain his energy, crowd his attention regardless of all else. It is not "policy" but pressure that determines what comes first.

What makes a "deadline"? For one thing, constitutional or statutory obligations: the President must send his annual messages to Congress, must sign or veto its enactments. Or, for another, items on political agendas all across the country: the nomination and election contests over offices, both partisan and public, the distribution of the patronage, the management of national conventions and campaigns. Or, for a third, turns of events in diplomacy or war: the approach to the "summit" spurring a disarmament departure, "open skies"; the outbreak in Korea forcing a new Formosan policy. Or, for a fourth, "outside" events at home: a sharpened economic trend (whether up or down), a dragged-out strike, a natural disaster, a race riot; not necessarily the great things only but the small-with-bite, as when a Texas waitress would not serve the Indian Ambassador. Or, finally, for a fifth, such operational disorders in administration, day by day, as dot the preceding pages—plus, of course, their congressional counterparts. Dates-certain make for deadlines, so does heat; dates generated by our laws, our politics, and our diplomacy; heat generated by events impacting on the needs and expectations of presidential constituents. Singly or together—though most readily

inflammable combined—dates and heat start the fires burning under-
neath the White House.

The President, of course, has influence on deadline-making and
unmaking, but only to a limited degree. He sets or evades dates
when he voluntarily decides upon a message or a meeting or a
speech. He turns heat on when he permits himself to arouse expectations, as Eisenhower did in his press conferences before Geneva.
He turns heat aside, if not off, when he finds plausible grounds,
proper-looking means for "further study," as was done so notably
in 1953. But these are marginal endeavors relative to the totality of
dates and heat potentially imposed upon him from outside. And
even these are usually reactions or responses to pressures not intrinsically his own. For the most part, even deadlines self-imposed
are only nominally self-engendered. Save in rare instances, a mid-
century President, however talented, simply has not time to man
both ends of the choice-generating process.

The result is to put him in a paradoxical position anent the whole
discretionary range of his choice-making. To reach out and take
over *before* the dates are nigh or the heat on—publicly at least—
can be crucially useful in his interest; yet, he always has to deal first
with deadlines already at his desk. As has been said above, he cannot count on the initiatives of others to spur him into interventions
timely in *his* terms; yet he is poorly placed to be his own self-starter.
He needs to be an actor, yet he is pre-eminently a reactor, forced
to be so by the nature of his work and its priorities. Since Eisenhower made Atoms for Peace his response to the heat expressed by
cries for "candor" and to the dates required for a UN presentation
in 1953, one may suppose he has not been entirely happy with its
slowness to get off the ground. One may suppose, besides, that had
he arrogated to himself all implementing choices and given them
first call upon his time, the matter might have moved a little faster.
Similarly, in the case of Truman and Point Four: had he, not State
and Budget, implemented his inaugural's fourth point and made
of this his first priority (as it never was for them), the sixteen
months after his 1949 inauguration might have produced more results than one meager piece of legislation newly on the books. But
whatever these Presidents might have done differently or "better"
than they actually did, one thing they could *not* do: accord that
hypothetical priority in terms of their own time.

Washington correspondents frequently complain that Eisenhower
talks a better line than his administration takes; that he proposes
better than his own regime disposes. Complaints of the same sort
were made in Truman's time, oftener than not by the same corre-

spondents. And these complaints—along with the realities behind them—symptomize the underlying problem here described. For in a time of routinized responsibility to take the policy lead, a President himself will have few deadlines more compelling than those clustering around the choice of measures to *propose*, of policies to *state*. Except, perhaps, in general war or comparable emergency, these gain and take his time more surely and more regularly than the general run of operating choices bound to follow in their wake. The weight which Robert Donovan's book gives to the *proposing* side of Eisenhower's "story," presumably reflects that skewing of the latter's workaday preoccupations. And if there is an implication that the White House sometimes came to look on messages and speeches as ends in themselves, delivery equated with accomplishment, such is a natural by-product, one not unknown in Truman's time, a point of view, indeed, by no means wholly unrealistic.

Ideally, a President concerned for the efficiency of his own choice-making in furtherance of his own purposes as *he* conceives them, should have free rein in choosing what to choose—and when—within the range of matters subject to his choice at his discretion. In practice, though, that is precisely what he *cannot* have. His discretionary range, while not a sham, is nowhere near as open as the term implies. Only his compulsions are potentially unbounded; his opportunities are always limited. Ideals apart, he is in no position to do more than seek some finite widening of those confines; he has no chance to break them down. But paradoxically, the only practical direction which his search can take—given the conditions here described—is toward some means of putting pressure on himself, *of imposing new deadlines on himself*, to come to grips with those things he would want to make his own if only he had time to contemplate the world about him, interfering at his leisure. And it is ironic that the very measures that a President may take to spare himself for "bigger things" by staffing out the "small," tend to work in the opposite direction. Of this, more later.

The limitations upon "what" and "when" which so restrict freedom of choice are reinforced by certain other limits of a different sort: limits on the substance of alternatives in choices actually made. The President's discretion is restricted by these limits also; they, too, are features of his landscape subject to some rearrangement but beyond his power to remove. What are these limitations on alternatives? Mainly three: limits of presentation, of substantive complexity, and of effectuation, each term loosely descriptive of a whole array of complications worth a chapter to themselves, though necessarily denied it here.

By "presentation" is meant time, form, and manner in which

issues reach a President for his determination. If his desk is where
the buck stops, as Truman liked to say, by the same token, it is the
last stop on the line. Most matters reach him at a late stage of
their evolution into issues calling for his choice; and many when
they reach him warrant action fast. Wherever they occur, lateness
and urgency—singly or combined—are bound to narrow options and
to curtail chances for fresh looks or second thoughts. As for the
form which issues take, the *context* of their presentation to a President, his settling of a budget sum, or phrasing of a speech, or
soothing of a legislator, each in its own terms may mean disposal
of an issue multi-faceted in terms of but one facet, thereby fore-
closing options anent others. There is no counting the occasions on
which Presidents have backed themselves—or been backed—into
corners by this route. Moreover, those who brief a President, who
can appeal to him, who can argue before him, have interests of their
own which grow remote from his with every increment of organizational distance, institutional independence. Rarely will they see an
issue wholly in his terms; oftener in some hybrid of his and theirs,
sometimes in theirs alone. And Presidents are no less vulnerable
than others (rather more so, in the circumstances) to the lure of
wrong answers rightly put.

A tracing out of many of the illustrations posed above would
show the workings of these presentation limits; signs of their presence are, of course, no novelty to readers of *The New York Times*.
Nothing is intrinsically new about them nowadays, nor anything
particularly obscure, though they are none the easier for being old
and obvious. But when it comes to limits raised by substantive complexity, the case is rather different. Though not by any means a mid-
century invention unknown to earlier times, the magnitude (and
durability) of complications in the substance of issues with which
Presidents must deal, these days, is greater in degree, to some extent
in kind, than we have known before.

Take the question of the military budget which has haunted
Eisenhower as it haunted Truman. That budget represents more than
half the dollars of federal outlay year by year, four-fifths of the persons on all federal payrolls, half the government's civilian personnel.
It represents a mainstay of deterrence and recourse in the cold
war, a bed-rock stabilizer in the national economy. Its annual determination raises issues of strategy, of economics, politics, administration, and (emphatically) technology; none of which is really
manageable in annual or financial terms (the limit of form, again);
none of which is really soluble by reference to anybody's certain
knowledge, for nothing is certain save uncertainty in these spheres.
To estimate what the American economy can "stand" is not to

answer what Congress and interest groups will "take" (or what would be required to equate the two). To estimate what new weapons may do is not to answer what may be demanded of them, or opposed to them, years hence. To estimate the Russians' *capabilities* is not to answer what are their *intentions*.

Yet, on some sorts of "answers" to these questions must military budgets now be built. And limited in terms of what is knowable, a President has no recourse but to select among the "guesstimates" of others—or to compound a compromise among them—by way of searching for his answer-substitutes. In such a search, the signs most readily discerned are bound to be those rendered most concrete by visibility, or pressure, or personal proclivities, or "common sense." No doubt a President needs better signposts in times of cold war, technological revolution; but given the uncertainties these generate, whence are such signs to come?

Parenthetically, it may be said that whatever the answer to that question, the "experts" are unlikely candidates. For if the real technicians see far more than a President can see, the record up to now suggests that they, least of all, show a capacity to ask themselves, out of their expertise, the questions pertinent to him; to translate their vision (and language) into his terms. Shifting the illustration, one thinks in this connection of an aspect of the thermonuclear "crash-program" controversy during 1949, as rendered by the transcript in the Oppenheimer case: that for weeks AEC's consulting scientists debated what the President should do in terms rendered obsolete, for him, by the mere fact of their debate.

Finally, there is the problem of effectuation, the third of the stated factors limiting alternatives in choice. How is a President to make "no" stick; to translate "yes" into performance, actuality? He is not bound to make each choice dependent on his response to these questions, but in the normal course he cannot fail to ask them and to give the answers weight. When Truman chose intervention in Korea, it happened that the necessary military means lay near at hand across the Sea of Japan; a factor, surely, in his choice. The obverse holds, of course, for our passivity in the last days of Dienbienphu; the means that *were* at hand were scarcely suited to the circumstance. But to cite instances of capability in military terms is to belittle the complexity of the how-to-do-it factor; in other terms, there are few choices blessed by aspects so nearly absolute or so readily calculable. Mostly the problem for the President is both more tenuous and more complex in character: how far can he hope to carry matters by persuading those whom he cannot command to do those things he lacks capacity to compel?

"I sit here all day," Truman used to remark, "trying to persuade people to do the things they ought to have sense enough to do without my persuading them." And on each posed alternative, in every act of choice, the question becomes whether to that workload he should add one thing more; with what prospect, at what risk. That question asked and answered may suffice to cancel options of all sorts; the President's choice-making ultimately interlocking with his power to persuade.

THE POWER TO PERSUADE

Concrete acts of choice engender concrete efforts at persuasion. Persuasion of whom? In general, of the President's constituencies, any or all as the case may be. In particular, of those who do the daily chores of governing this country: administrators, congressmen, and organization politicians. To these one might add certain foreign notables and private persons prominent at home, on whom the government depends for something in particular, a boost, a service or a sacrifice; but since such dependence is *ad hoc*, intermittent, their case can be ignored for present purposes.

In the main, day by day, it is the public officers and party politicians whom a President must reach to get his choices rendered into government performance. He may move toward them indirectly through public or interest-group opinion, sometimes his only routes, but they remain his objects because they, not the "public," do the close work; his preferences conditioned on their doing. To influence these men at work, he has at his disposal a quantity of instruments —refined and crude in varying degree—derived from his prerogatives of office as filtered through his personality.

Those instruments of influence, tools of persuasion, are common knowledge, no mystery about them and none pretended here: There is the aura of his office, coupled to the impact of his person and prestige, such as they may be. There are the varied forms of help, concrete and psychological, that congressmen want from the White House in dealing, as they must, with the executive establishment. There are, in turn, the various assistances desired by executive officialdom in dealing with the Congress. There are also the loyalties, varying in depth, of administrators to their chief, of party members to the boss, of congressmen (and citizens) to the head of State and Government. In party terms, there are, at once, supplies of federal patronage, such as it is, a presidential record which no party nowadays can shake, the prospect of a renewed candidacy (for first termers, anyway), and—save for Democrats, perhaps—a constantly replenished campaign chest, centrally controlled. These things, among others, are available to Presidents for use, reversibly, as carrots and as sticks in aid of their persuasion.

This listing has a formidable ring. In theory, it deserves it. For if a President could bring to bear that whole array effectively and all at once upon a given point, one may presume he would be irresistible. But practically speaking, such conjunctions are not easily arranged; far from it. Oftener than not, one or another of these tools will turn out ineffective of itself or in the hands of its prospective user, unsuited to use, by him, in any combination of resources he contrives. Why should this be so? What dulls their cutting edge and limits their employment? These questions become our immediate concern. Full answers would run far beyond the compass of this essay; no more can be attempted here than a suggestion of some factors that seem specially significant in the contemporary setting.

First among these factors—in order of discussion, not importance—is the uncertainty of a President's own hold upon his instruments of influence. They may attach to his office but can slip away from *him*. One doubts that at any time since 1935, or thereabouts, and not often before, have Presidents got half the mileage out of patronage the textbooks advertise. One doubts that Eisenhower can be sure from day to day of his control over the stockpile of administrative actions sought by congressmen. Most of these, certainly, are not under his sole lock and key. Others than he have the arts of persuasion to practice, and keys of their own. The story is told that a powerful House Democrat was traded off the same dam twice; once in Truman's time and once in Eisenhower's. If so, the Budget Bureau ought to be commended for its careful husbanding of presidential trading-stock. But such care is by no means universal in this Government (not even in the Budget). Moreover, a supply of trading-stock may prove insufficient just when the need is greatest. Appetites are insatiable and fears short-lived; a situation summed up in the phrase "What have you done for me lately," as amplified by "or *to* me."

In addition, sources of supplies to aid persuasion on one front may be endangered by the very effort at persuasion on another. A great share of a President's potential trading-stock with Congress is actually in the hands of the executive departments: jobs, expertise, publicity, administrative actions of all sorts. No less a share of his potential leverage with the departments is actually in the hands of his congressional supporters: protection or defense, consideration or support, in every sort of legislative situation. Too many sticks applied too often on the Hill may tend to uproot the supply of carrots growing there for use downtown, and vice versa.

A second factor is the tendency of certain presidential tools to cut in opposite directions, thereby impairing their simultaneous employment. It is not easy for a President to combine partisan approaches with attempts to crystallize support around the symbol of his office. He courts trouble when he tells his party's congressmen that his proposals will help them at the polls and simultaneously exhorts the other party's men to do their patriotic duty by their President. He courts trouble when he tries to draw upon the loyalties of subordinate officials and at the same time offers up their kind as human sacrifices on the altar, say, of adequate appropriations for their work. Such troubles come in infinite varieties; in every instance, they will tend to limit hypothetical effectiveness of each paired instrument. To say this is not to suggest, of course, that all these troubles are escapable. Carrying water on both shoulders—plus, perhaps, in both hands, also strapped around the waist—is frequently imperative for Presidents, a natural resultant of their four-way leadership position. But the complications are no less for often being unavoidable. So Truman found on many memorable occasions and even Eisenhower, now and then, especially in those first years of turmoil over "cleaning out the Communists" and Senator McCarthy.

A third factor complicating the persuasion process can be stated, most simply, as general dissatisfaction with the product to be "sold." It is difficult, in other words, to press a course of action intrinsically lacking much appeal to *any* of the persons whose support is being sought. Instruments of influence, however handled, are poor substitutes for genuine enthusiasm on the part of somebody among the movers and shakers in the case. And if the substitution must be made, as not infrequently occurs, the limits on the efficacy of persuasive tools will tend to be severe. The President's health-reinsurance scheme of 1954 is very much in point. So is the complex struggle over foreign aid in the 1956 session of Congress. There, Eisenhower pitted his own personal prestige, plus other sorts of pressure, against the disappointments, disenchantments, irritations, and forebodings which had penetrated every corner of both Houses. The result was a sharp check to the President—how serious in program terms one cannot know from the outside—a check administered, moreover, by traditional supporters of his course among the Democrats, together with a great proportion of *his* party's membership, election year or no. It is quite conceivable, in all the circumstances, that another President, in another year, might have done worse. But why did this President in this year not do better?

No doubt, his ileitis operation and its aftermath blunted Eisenhower's own persuasive influence at a crucial time. Perhaps there were things poorly done or left undone at other times as well. But however healthy and adroit he might have been last summer, there are no indications—not, anyway of public record—that by then his persuasion could have bettered the result in any *marked* degree. For the great lack, apparently, was not of influence in mechanistic terms, but of program in substantive respects. A sense of changing world relationships pervaded the debates, providing ammunition for old enemies of Mutual Security and worries for old friends. Yet, the administration's program appeared cast from the same mold as all its predecessors back to 1951, when the world wore a very different look. And Eisenhower's troubles in July seem, by hindsight, an inevitable outcome of his choices in December; the efficacy of persuasive instruments conditioned, in their turn, upon the exercise —and limits—of choice-making.

Alongside these three factors there is need to place a fourth, which looms at least as large under mid-century conditions: the factor of too many things at once, as represented, classically, by FDR's fight for reorganization powers amidst controversy over his "court-packing" plan. In that instance, Roosevelt was criticized for moving for his management reform at a time when his influence was mortgaged to another cause. Perhaps he had an option then— though that can be debated—but not so his successors. In 1956, in a relatively quiet time at home and abroad, the Eisenhower influence has been demanded in three closely spaced, competing, legislative fights of first importance to his regime—farm, education, foreign aid—to say nothing of those headed off, like tax reduction, or of the many other issues on which White House labels were affixed to controversial aspects: Hells Canyon, highway aid, social security amendments, the civil rights commission, and numbers more. In Truman's time, the list was often longer, the controversial aspects sharper, the presidential temperature higher, and, besides, in many of his years, such legislative struggles were accompanied by operational involvements—military, diplomatic, economic, or administrative—also calling his persuasion into play on a grand scale.

A President's tools of persuasion are put under great strains when used on many projects simultaneously. Look at the tools themselves, and that becomes quite obvious. Yet, such use is the normal practice, nowadays; often mandatory, always wanted. No more as persuaders than as choice-makers are contemporary Presidents at liberty, discretion unconfined, to choose the "what" and "when" of their endeavors to persuade.

Four factors have been named, so far, as limiting the efficacy of persuasive instruments. But there remains a fifth, a factor so important as to dominate the rest, continually affecting the dimensions of all four. This is the element of "setting" in persuasion, a matter not of instruments, as such, but of the *background* against which they are employed. As a rough rule, it may be said that for a fraction of the persons on whom Presidents depend, continuing exposure to the White House and its occupant provides a background favoring—though not, of course, determining—effective exercise of presidential influence upon them. The bigger the "staff system," the smaller the fraction; but even an open door could not enlarge it into a preponderance. For most officials, both public and partisan, a favorable background will be differently derived. Derived from what? To this we may now turn.

In the case of executive officials, all sorts of variables of time, place, situation, substance, tend to affect actual responses to a particular pressure from the President. But there would seem to be one variable always present, always influential: their own instinctive estimate of his prestige with Congress, his potency on Capitol Hill. This may not square with visions conjured up by the tag "Chief Executive"; it is, however, entirely natural. For Congress, day in and day out, means life or death to programs, institutions, personnel. Putting the matter in its crudest terms (and thus rather larger than life): if Presidents can make much difference in these respects, either way, their own officialdom will be well disposed toward their wishes; if not, so much the worse for them; many a bureaucrat, like many a congressman, was there before and will be after.

Of course, such bureaucratic estimates of presidential prowess will vary from time to time. George Kennan once remarked that diplomats must rethink foreign policy each morning; so bureaucrats must reappraise their attitudes toward a President, and so they do, day after day. Such estimates will vary, also, from place to place. The weaker an agency, in terms of institutional entrenchment, program support, the more its officials will tend to view the President as a resource, no matter what the state of his congressional relations; thus Labor is traditionally a "tame" department. And every agency, however "strong," will make its calculations with reference, mainly, to those elements in Congress and those issues before Congress that affect it the most; even as between Army and Air the President is not appraised alike.

This does not mean that there is any one-to-one relationship between a President's congressional prestige and agency compliance with his wishes—though sometimes, certainly, the correlation is that close—but rather that a favorable background for persuasive efforts at his end of Pennsylvania Avenue is markedly dependent, over time, upon his prestige at the other end, with Congress. And in precisely the same sense—no more, no less—a favorable background for persuasion of the Congress is provided by his prestige with the country. As in the bureaucratic case, Senators and congress-men differently situated, institutionally and electorally, will not see that matter all alike; place, time, party, and electorate make for dif-fering appraisals, though by no means along strict party lines: wit-ness Republican and Democratic attitudes in the Eighty-fourth Congress. No more than with the bureaucrats are estimates of this sort to be taken as controlling the congressional response in given instances of presidential pressure, but there can be no doubt that they contribute most significantly to the background against which such pressure is applied.

As for a President's own party's politicians outside Congress, they are quite comparably circumstanced, with the important qualification that at certain moments in the cycle of his term, their own enforced commitment to his record and his name may enhance their respon-siveness regardless of his momentary popular prestige; a qualification applicable, equally, to certain of their brethren on the Hill.

In short, the President's persuasive power with those who do the daily chores of governing, is influenced by a sort of *progression of prestige*, a sequence culminating in the regard of the "general pub-lic," the country-at-large. Woodrow Wilson once wrote, in an aca-demic vein, that a President "may be both the leader of his party and the leader of the nation or he may be one or the other." What-ever the case fifty years ago, no such option is open to him now. He must endeavor to lead "party" (for which read public officers as well), since "nation" does not run the government machine, cannot itself effectuate his choices. But if he is to manage those who make the wheels go 'round, he needs public opinion at his back, must seek consensus as his context for persuasion. And in that dual compulsion lies the *ultimate dilemma* of the presidential operation at mid-cen-tury.

How describe this dilemma? One may begin by pointing to the sources of that popular prestige which so affects the President's own power to persuade. His general public—in our terms, national and partisan constituencies combined—actually comprises a diversity of presidential publics, their expectations nurtured variously by claims on him as "government," by respect for his office, or by ties to his personality: "interest" publics, "capacity" publics, and "personal" publics, each subdivided many times, all linked by the crisscrossing lines of overlapping membership, collectively encompassing the country, or that part of it which cares about the President.

His national prestige, therefore—which congressmen and politi-cians watch and weigh—is simply the net balance of favorable re-sponse these many groups, in sum, accord their varied images of him (a matter always to be gauged, not scientifically determined, the result influenced, of course, by the affiliation of the gauger). Those images and the responses to them are not static; they can and do vary over time. And what are the determinants of variation? Happenings, mainly, or the appearance of happenings, ascribable—or anyway ascribed—to him: the reward or frustration of a bread-and-butter want, an ethical attitude, a psychological identification; to such as these his publics will react wherever and in whatever degree they see his office or his person as the cause. Inevitably, every concrete choice he makes, both positive and negative, and every effort at persuasion will set off some reactions of the sort, and not all of one kind; if somebody is pleased, then someone else is bound to be offended.

For the President to give offense is to risk blurring his own image in the eyes of those offended, hence to risk lowering their favorable response to him. But on a maximum of such response, as aggregated all across the country, must he depend for the effectuation of his choices. And on choice-making he depends for the impression of his person on the product of his office. But the conduct of office is liable to require policy initiatives in all directions, not as free will, but as constituency pressures and events decree. Hence, acts of choice and of persuasion become mandatory, inescapable. Yet, they are bound to give offense.

This, then, is the ultimate dilemma, the vicious circle Presidents must tread by virtue of their unique placement in our system, the personal equivalent for them, as individuals, of that disparity which haunts their office, routinely responsible for programming without assured support to carry through. No President, of course, is wholly helpless in this situation. He gains from office when he enters it a sizable initial fund of favorable response; if he is fortunate enough to be an Eisenhower, he brings still more to office. Once installed, his actions bring him gains as well as losses. Approbation, no less than offense, is bound to follow, from some quarter, everything he does or fails to do. And nobody in government is better placed than he to focus public interest and attention where he wants it, to foster certain images, obscuring others, to make desired happenings occur, to give events a nudge.

These are not insignificant resources. Particularly in a time of sharp emergency—which a preponderance of publics see or can be made to see as such—their use with skill, accompanied by luck, should help a President to break out of that circle altogether, in a fashion advantageous to his person and his cause; enabling him to gain from what he does far more by way of favorable response than negative reaction. For such a time, a crisis-time, tends to put premiums on affirmative action, to make the very act of doing almost its own reward, not doing almost its own penalty; so Hoover found to his discomfiture and Roosevelt to his taste a quarter-century ago. Of course, if circumstances are precisely opposite and times all peace and quiet, the outcome may be no less advantageous for a President; so Coolidge made a virtue of *not* doing and was well rewarded for it

But our situation at mid-century fits neither of these models; the years since the Second World War have neither been perceived, widely, as crisis-times, nor have they been, in fact, peace-times in any familiar sense. And nowadays, the things that Presidents must do and those they may be called upon to do expose them regularly to the penalties of *both* such times with no assurance that they can gain the rewards of either. These days, both doing and not doing give offense in indeterminate proportion to offsetting approbation; almost all actions now *tend* to produce a negative reaction more concrete than favorable response. Both forms of action are abrasive; from neither can our Presidents now *count* upon a bonus of response. Yet, they are constantly impelled to actions of both sorts and so it has to be, these days, their preferences notwithstanding.

Consider what a President must do in times we now call "peace": keep taxes relatively high, armed forces relatively large, the budget "swollen," the bureaucracy "outsize"; inject himself into labor disputes just when tempers grow highest, into defense of overseas constituents just when they seem, at home, most irritating or unwise. And so the list goes on. Consider, also, what a President now may be called upon to do: intervene with arms in Korea, Indo-China; intervene with counsel in ·Southern school segregation; back the Benson plan for aid to farmers; endorse the Hobby plan for aid to schools; accept the Rockefeller plan for aid abroad; impose the New York Bar committee plan for personnel security; keep Nixon or take Herter; choose silence on McCarthy or attack; these among others. Such "musts" and "mays," as manifested in his acts of doing or not doing, are bound to outrage some among his publics (and anger may last long), to be accepted grudgingly by many as unpleasant facts of life, to warm the hearts of an uncertain number whose warmth may be short-lived. Whichever way he acts, his penalties may outrun his rewards in prestige terms. And rarely can he calculate with certainty, in advance, the net balance either way. Yet act he must.

By virtue of his unique place in government, a President gains unequaled opportunities to mold the images his publics have of him. But, for these opportunities, he pays a heavy price. Even for Eisenhower, immune, so far, to many of the payments levied on his predecessors, there is now the real price his illnesses exact: the issue of his health in the 1956 campaign; an issue taking its dimensions from the nature of his office at mid-century. . . .

PROSPECTS AND PROPOSALS

"Mid-century" will not endure forever. If the cold war holds its present course and if our national economy continues, generally, to climb, we may face six, eight, even ten years, perhaps more, that will bear an affinity, in presidential terms, to the decade just past. Beyond another decade, though, our population, science and resources, our industrial development, urbanization, regional realignments, will have brought us to such a point that even if affairs abroad held constant—which they cannot do—what has been described here may be wholly out of date. Even a decade may turn out too long a period to bracket as a portion of "our times." But there is likelihood, at least, that the next two, perhaps three, presidential terms will have much in common with the three since the Second World War.

How then might the next few Presidents be helped to ease the likely operating problems of the office? The answer, plainly, is that nothing fundamental can be done to help them. Nothing short of really revolutionary party centralization bids fair to eliminate that basic and dilemma-nurturing disparity between the Presidency's obligation to initiate and its capacity to achieve. Of course, were our parties fully nationalized and centralized, the party oligarchs might well command the capacity and would tend to assume the obligation, relieving the Presidency, as such, both of burdens and of unique place. But it has been six years now since a committee of the American Political Science Association summoned the revolution to commence, and I am prepared to predict that our parties will endure, for one more decade anyway, substantially unnationalized as in the last.

Barring fundamentals, one can try to nibble at the fringes of the Presidency's problems via piecemeal structural reforms. But those a President might find most fun cannot be had, as a practical matter: witness the item veto. And those most certain to affect him for the worse are only too likely to be thrust upon him: as now we have the two-term amendment and still might find ourselves some day with Bricker's or with Mundt's. As for the many proposed statutory changes which fit neither of these two extremes, opinions differ; their proponents, though, would be well advised to reflect upon Rossiter's admonition: "Leave Your Presidency Alone." In my own view, that caution makes great sense and applies equally to all proposals of a structural and statutory sort. For all of them—all, anyway, of which I am aware—incur a common risk: that they will produce *wayward side-effects,* however unintended by their sponsors, which may make matters worse, or at least put new problems in the place of old. Even the twentieth amendment, widely heralded as an essential modernization, made matters difficult for Eisenhower his first year, and scarcely would have aided FDR, and easily might have been ruinous in Lincoln's time, the classic case of grave emergency it is intended to relieve. This is not to suggest we should repeal the "Lame Duck" amendment, or even alter its required starting-dates for the congressional and presidential terms; the point, rather, is that if so logical and seemingly so slight a change produces wayward side-effects, it might be well to avoid others more complex or more obscure.

Some risks, of course, accompany all change; this is no argument for never changing anything. But when one can foresee a wayward consequence, however unintended by proponents, then is the time, it seems to me, to move on their proposals very cautiously indeed. So, in the legislative cabinet scheme, as recently revived by Professors Corwin and Koenig, one is confronted with the prospect, all other things aside, that formal cabinet rank for leading Senators would transfer from an Eisenhower to Knowland, say, and Bridges, some part of his privacy, prestige, and nominal authority, without in any way diminishing their independent power base, or guaranteeing him improvement in the quality of counsel and advice they have provided up to now. If there should be a President who wished to try this one-way transfer, he could find means without a statute. The privilege remains his; why then impose a mandate? Of course, if one's concern is less with easing operational dilemmas than with checking arbitrary power, the matter wears a wholly different look. But if the Presidency now is dangerously powerful, this essay's premises and argument are all awry.

In terms of easing burdens, hence of strengthening the President, by means externally imposed, there is but one proposal that in all good conscience I could urge without equivocation, a proposal once made (but not patented) by a former Roosevelt aide: to guarantee new Presidents a solid partisan majority in both Houses of Congress, composed of men dependent on the President's own electorate. But in the circumstances of mid-century, this, above all, is never to be guaranteed; indeed it is not even to be hoped for.

Where does this leave us then? It leaves us with the Presidents themselves, with what they might do for themselves in their own self-defense, within the confines and environs of their office.

To make suggestions to them, without knowing them or their specific situations, imposes certain limitations on would-be suggestors, one limit above all: that each suggestion be adaptable for use by an incumbent, whatever his work-habits and his style; that each be usable by men so various in those respects as Eisenhower, Truman, FDR. Truman's White House rather resembled a senatorial establishment, writ large: the staff informal, almost family-like, assignments shifting casually among jacks-of-all-trades, organization plastic, hierarchy slight, and anything liable to be mulled over with the President. Eisenhower, one supposes, could not have abided it. But no more could Truman have abided—much less politically afforded —the military sort of staff system as adapted and on display in Eisenhower's White House. Yet this is the way Eisenhower works and that was the way Truman worked and the next President may want to work like one, or the other, or like neither. There is no point in urging upon any of them a suggestion he could not adopt without foregoing his accustomed way of work.

To illustrate the sort of thing thereby put out of bounds, a number of observers assert that the current regime is a "regency" and urge that Eisenhower should dispense with Sherman Adams. But if this were a regency, then Eisenhower and not Adams must be presumed First Regent. The military have their rules for chiefs of staff, and those who cannot keep them do not long retain the place. There is no evidence that Eisenhower lacks acquaintance with these rules or that his principal assistant has not learned to work within them. If Adams were to vanish overnight, no doubt there would soon appear in his place another such abrasive, intense concentrator. That is the Eisenhower way, and so it was long before 1953. In terms of personal performance, we might as well accept the moral and forbear to debate here whether Eisenhower's system, in the abstract, is a good thing or a bad. Some Presidents will find they cannot stand it, others that they cannot get away with it politically, while others, still, may try to proceed much as he has done.

I have stressed Eisenhower's case because among those of all recent Presidents his most restricts the range of the suggestible. Our need is for things Presidents might do to help themselves, on their initiative, at their discretion. Suggestions that seem reasonably practicable for a man of military background, entrenched behind the paraphernalia of elaborate staff, are likely to be usable, as well, by those schooled in more fluid, personalized, working-ways of civil government and politics, whence one supposes the next Presidents will come. But having so delimited the field of search, what remains to be found? In such a narrow ground, what is there to discover that may help a President resolve—or live with—his dilemmas? Tentatively, I would hazard the following response.

First, the fewer a President's illusions about the limitations on his power stakes and status in our system, the better his performance on the job. The more nearly he sees his power problem as I have endeavored to describe it here, the greater his chance to master his circumstances or at least hinder them from overwhelming him. Of course, a man wants the illusions that sustain him at his work, and if he needs to look upon the world in terms other than jungle, then so he must. It might help, though, if Presidents who felt impelled to find identification with a forerunner, would look to Lincoln, not as myth or symbol, but as man-in-office. For in their wartime crises, FDR and Wilson seem more removed from our mid-century state than Lincoln does, despite the fact of war. In its operational dilemmas, his was a very modern Presidency, contrasts notwithstanding. And should they seek such parallels, I suggest that the image of his operating burdens and his power problem, rather than, say, Washington's (or Jackson's or a Roosevelt's), be graven on the minds of our next Presidents.

Second, of all the self-perceptions that can help a President, nothing helps so much as an awareness of his absolutely unique place—of his aloneness at the only juncture of his four constituencies —and an alertness, consequently, to the fact that he can count on no one else in Government to sense his interests in precisely his own terms. To stress the "team" and teamwork is a fine thing for morale and useful, too, in binding others to one's cause. But any President who regards the blithe spirit all-for-one-and-one-for-all as a reality which may assume full right-and-title to his interests is assured disenchantment and distortion of his aims.

It follows that he needs to widen, so far as he can, the confines of his own freedom to choose what he himself would think he were well advised to make choices on and undertake persuasion on and when. As we have seen, he cannot hope to widen these confines more than a little; how might even that little be accomplished? On the one hand, I would suggest, by rendering the regular assistance he receives more representative of the totality of his constituencies; on the other hand, by building into government and his own staff the sorts of competitions which will create "deadlines" for him at times and on issues useful in his terms.

Perhaps we do not recognize sufficiently the deep distortions, in constituency terms, of staff assistance now officially available to a President. Without exception, his department heads and institutional staff aides are tightly linked to, actually are part of, his "government" constituency. The same thing can be said for his legislative leaders and for such White House aides as he may draw from agency or congressional sources to help with liaison in both directions. Many of these people also represent, in varying degree, some portions of his "partisan" constituency; so, of course, does the National Committee Chairman, whose office is more or less part of presidential staff facilities. And all of them can claim to be in some sense representative of "national" constituency as well. But taking them together as a collectivity, their representative character is decidedly different than his own; greatly overweighing the governmental element, especially its executive side, while relatively slighting partisan, underweighing national, and virtually ignoring overseas components. Even in the White House staff, none but the Press Secretary is free of institutionalized routines which pull particularly in the government direction (perhaps explaining why that post becomes so powerful when manned by a superb technician).

To compensate for these distortions, Presidents must break out of their official families and so they do, with ceremonials and visitors, with trips, and tête-à-têtes, with consultations and with confidants, each in his fashion. But I submit that these are frail reliances which need the utmost buttressing by Presidents themselves in conscious, purposeful awareness of official insufficiencies. And not the means but that awareness becomes crucial in this case; if that be strong enough, the man makes his own means. His aides, of course, can help and so they will, provided his insistence is incessant, but their reach is no *substitute* for his, nor their awareness either.

As for the matter of "created" deadlines, this was a specialty with FDR which, suitably adapted, I commend to his successors. Roosevelt is commonly supposed a "poor" administrator; lines of authority confused, the same assignments in the hands of numerous subordinates, doors opening and closing unpredictably, nobody knowing everything of anybody's business and everybody horning in on everything. Yet with all this and *by* it, he kept in his own hands more power of judgment and decision than most Presidents before or since. In the administration of the Presidency, what could be more important? This is not to suggest that future Presidents should try to play by ear, *ad hoc*, in Roosevelt's special way. They cannot if they would—nor could he either, at the end—for government has grown too big, its scope too broad, their own responsibilities too routinized, their office far too institutionalized. What is suggested, rather, is a search for substitutes compatible with their more complex circumstances. The building-in of competition seems to me the key.

Without attempting an exhaustive exploration, let me mention two means by which competitive relations might be fostered: namely appointments and reorganizations. The President who wishes to enhance his prospects for free choices in an area of policy will do well to arrange that opposed attitudes in country or in Congress, or in his own mind are represented among appointees charged institutionally with its consideration *and* administration. By "represented" is meant not in form alone, but in a balance that suffices to force underlying issues on the table, up the line, and in good time, without exhausting institutional support for a decision *either* way. Thus,

Eisenhower seems to run tremendous risks of foreclosed freedom in the sphere of foreign aid, when all the posts of massive institutional power are held by men reportedly conservative in view, with "balance" furnished mainly by a brace of White House aides.

One sympathizes with the wish of both of Roosevelt's successors to avoid such unseemly public struggles as were carried on from inside his regime. But foreclosed freedom can be harder on a President than struggling subordinates. Indeed, unless they are sufficiently well-matched to carry controversies to the press, he loses one among the early warning signals built-in-competitions can provide. If he is lucky and adroit and granted a respectful opposition, perhaps he can hold down the public outcries though he keep his fighters matched, and can devise internal signals as a substitute. But if, to keep the public peace, he rigs fights overmuch, he pays an exorbitant price, or so it seems to me. Indeed, under the circumstances of mid-century, an outward look of total harmony in a regime might well be taken as itself a warning sign.

As for reorganization, it is obviously useful, often essential, as a supplement to the appointive power in building or in equalizing institutionalized competitions. There is one disability, however: my colleague, Wallace Sayre, has propounded the sound "law" that any benefits of a reorganization are immediate, while disadvantages are cumulative over time. To this I would append the simple corollary that as for a President's own freedom, gains are short-range, risks long-run. And this applies with greater force the closer one approaches his own person. The moral appears plain. It cannot be enough to reorganize, one must keep on with it. In their relations to each other and the President, his official associates need stirring up; not with such frequency that they shrink into immobility, but just enough so that they are never absolutely confident in unchecked judgment of their chief's own judgment, or of their colleagues' either.

With that I would conclude. These several imprecise suggestions of what Presidents might do in their own self-defense are neither very bold nor very new; assuredly, they are neither my own last testament nor anybody's. In that regard, one final word: if we, as citizens, cannot rescue our Presidents from their dilemmas but must leave them to help themselves as best they can, there is one thing that we, as students and observers, might do to render their self-help a little easier. We might take more care in the future than sometimes in the past, lest we foster stereotypes and expectations not within their capacities or even their own interests to fulfill.

In the two decades since the report of the President's Committee on Administrative Management, great numbers of experts, in universities and out, have been hard at work seeking solutions for the managerial dilemmas of the federal government. And whether the focus be on budgeting, on organization, or on personnel—in order of prevailing fashion, then to now—the outcome tends to be the same: "The President, himself, must take command."

Faster than perhaps we realize, the frame of reference underlying such investigations, such solutions, becomes popularized (and over-simplified), eventuating in those plain truths nobody learns but everybody knows: "The President, of course! As in business, so in government; the title is the same and so should be the function." Perhaps it would not be amiss to remind the managerial enthusiasts of Woodrow Wilson's wise prognosis half a century ago: ". . . as the business of government becomes more and more complex and extended . . . the President is becoming more and more a political and less an executive officer . . . incumbents will come more and more [to be] directors of affairs and leaders of the nation—men of counsel and of the sort of action that makes for enlightenment."

For so it has turned out; these and not management are the great objects of their work and sources of their troubles at mid-century.

☆

JAMES DAVID BARBER: *The Presidential Character*

When a citizen votes for a Presidential candidate he makes, in effect, a prediction. He chooses from among the contenders the one he thinks (or feels, or guesses) would be the best President. He operates in a situation of immense uncertainty. If he has a long voting history, he can recall time and time again when he guessed wrong. He listens to the commentators, the politicians, and his friends, then adds it all up in some rough way to produce his prediction and his vote. Earlier in the game, his anticipations have been taken into account, either directly in the polls and primaries or indirectly in the minds of politicians who want to nominate someone he will like. But he must choose in the midst of a cloud of confusion, a rain of phony advertising, a storm of sermons, a hail of complex issues, a fog of charisma and boredom, and a thunder of accusation and defense. In the face of this chaos, a great many citizens fall back on the past, vote their old allegiances, and let it go at that. Nevertheless, the citizen's vote says that on balance he expects Mr. X would outshine Mr. Y in the Presidency.

This book is meant to help citizens and those who advise them cut through the confusion and get at some clear criteria for choosing Presidents. To understand what actual Presidents do and what potential Presidents might do, the first need is to see the man whole — not as some abstract embodiment of civic virtue, some scorecard of issue stands, or some reflection of a faction, but as a human being like the rest of us, a person trying to cope with a difficult environment. To that task he brings his own character, his own view of the world, his own political style. None of that is new for him. If we can see the pattern he has set for his political life we can, I contend, estimate much better his pattern as he confronts the stresses and chances of the Presidency.

James David Barber is James B. Duke Professor of Political Science at Duke University. The selection is from *The Presidential Character* (Englewood Cliffs, N.J.: Prentice-Hall, Inc., 1972; 2nd. ed. 1977), pp. 3-14, 445-454. Copyright © 1972, 1977 by James David Barber. Reprinted by permission of the author and the publisher.

The Presidency is a peculiar office. The Founding Fathers left it extraordinarily loose in definition, partly because they trusted George Washington to invent a tradition as he went along. It is an institution made a piece at a time by successive men in the White House. Jefferson reached out to Congress to put together the beginnings of political parties; Jackson's dramatic force extended electoral partisanship to its mass base; Lincoln vastly expanded the administrative reach of the office, Wilson and the Roosevelts showed its rhetorical possibilities — in fact every President's mind and demeanor has left its mark on a heritage still in lively development.

But the Presidency is much more than an institution. It is a focus of feelings. In general, popular feelings about politics are low-key, shallow, casual. For example, the vast majority of Americans knows virtually nothing of what Congress is doing and cares less. The Presidency is different. The Presidency is the focus for the most intense and persistent emotions in the American polity. The President is a symbolic leader, the one figure who draws together people's hopes and fears for the political future. On top of all his routine duties, he has to carry that off — or fail.

Our emotional attachment to Presidents shows up when one dies in office. People were not just disappointed or worried when President Kennedy was killed; people wept at the loss of a man most had never even met. Kennedy was young and charismatic — but history shows that whenever a President dies in office, heroic Lincoln or debased Harding, McKinley or Garfield, the same wave of deep emotion sweeps across the country. On the other hand, the death of an ex-President brings forth no such intense emotional reaction.

The President is the first political figure children are aware of (later they add Congress, the Court, and others, as "helpers" of the President). With some exceptions among children in deprived circumstances, the President is seen as a "benevolent leader," one who nurtures, sustains, and inspires the citizenry. Presidents regularly show up among "most admired" contemporaries and forebears, and the President is the "best known" (in the sense of sheer name recognition) person in the country. At inauguration time, even Presidents elected by close margins are supported by much larger majorities than the election returns show, for people rally round as he actually assumes office. There is a similar reaction when the people see their President threatened by crisis: if he takes action, there is a favorable spurt in the Gallup poll whether he succeeds or fails.

Obviously the President gets more attention in schoolbooks, press, and television than any other politician. He is one of very few who can make news by doing good things. *His* emotional state is a matter of continual public commentary, as is the manner in which his personal and official families conduct themselves. The media bring across the President not as some neutral administrator or corporate executive to be assessed by his production, but as a special being with mysterious dimensions.

We have no king. The sentiments English children—and adults —direct to the Queen have no place to go in our system but to the President. Whatever his talents—Coolidge-type or Roosevelt-type —the President is the only available object for such national-religious-monarchical sentiments as Americans possess.

The President helps people make sense of politics. Congress is a tangle of committees, the bureaucracy is a maze of agencies. The President is one man trying to do a job—a picture much more understandable to the mass of people who find themselves in the same boat. Furthermore, he is the top man. He ought to know what is going on and set it right. So when the economy goes sour, or war drags on, or domestic violence erupts, the President is available to take the blame. Then when things go right, it seems the President must have had a hand in it. Indeed, the flow of political life is marked off by Presidents: the "Eisenhower Era," the "Kennedy Years."

What all this means is that the President's *main* responsibilities reach far beyond administering the Executive Branch or command-ing the armed forces. The White House is first and foremost a place of public leadership. That inevitably brings to bear on the President intense moral, sentimental, and quasi-religious pressures which can, if he lets them, distort his own thinking and feeling. If there is such a thing as extraordinary sanity, it is needed nowhere so much as in the White House.

Who the President is at a given time can make a profound differ-ence in the whole thrust and direction of national politics. Since we have only one President at a time, we can never prove this by comparison, but even the most superficial speculation confirms the commonsense view that the man himself weighs heavily among other historical factors. A Wilson re-elected in 1920, a Hoover in 1932, a John F. Kennedy in 1964 would, it seems very likely, have guided the body politic along rather different paths from those their actual successors chose. Or try to imagine a Theodore Roosevelt ensconced behind today's "bully pulpit" of a Presidency, or Lyndon Johnson as President in the age of McKinley. Only someone mes-merized by the lures of historical inevitability can suppose that it would have made little or no difference to government policy had Alf Landon replaced FDR in 1936, had Dewey beaten Truman in 1948, or Adlai Stevenson reigned through the 1950s. Not only would these alternative Presidents have advocated different policies—they would have approached the office from very different psychological angles. It stretches credibility to think that Eugene McCarthy would have run the institution the way Lyndon Johnson did.

The burden of this book is that the crucial differences can be anticipated by an understanding of a potential President's character, his world view, and his style. This kind of prediction is not easy; well-informed observers often have guessed wrong as they watched a man step toward the White House. One thinks of Woodrow Wilson, the scholar who would bring reason to politics; of Herbert Hoover, the Great Engineer who would organize chaos into progress; of Franklin D. Roosevelt, that champion of the balanced budget; of Harry Truman, whom the office would surely overwhelm; of Dwight D. Eisenhower, militant crusader; of John F. Kennedy, who would lead beyond moralisms to achievements; of Lyndon B. Johnson, the Southern conservative; and of Richard M. Nixon, conciliator. Spotting the errors is easy. Predicting with even approximate accuracy is going to require some sharp tools and close attention in their use. But the experiment is worth it because the question is critical and because it lends itself to correction by evidence.

My argument comes in layers.

First, a President's personality is an important shaper of his Presidential behavior on nontrivial matters.

Second, Presidential personality is patterned. His character, world view, and style fit together in a dynamic package understandable in psychological terms.

Third, a President's personality interacts with the power situation he faces and the national "climate of expectations" dominant at the time he serves. The tuning, the resonance—or lack of it—between these external factors and his personality sets in motion the dynamic of his Presidency.

Fourth, the best way to predict a President's character, world view, and style is to see how they were put together in the first place. That happened in his early life, culminating in his first independent political success.

But the core of the argument (which organizes the structure of the book) is that Presidential character—the basic stance a man takes toward his Presidential experience—comes in four varieties. The most important thing to know about a President or candidate is where he fits among these types, defined according to (a) how active he is and (b) whether or not he gives the impression he enjoys his political life.

Let me spell out these concepts briefly before getting down to cases.

PERSONALITY SHAPES PERFORMANCE

I am not about to argue that once you know a President's personality you know everything. But as the cases will demonstrate, the degree and quality of a President's emotional involvement in an issue are powerful influences on how he defines the issue itself, how much attention he pays to it, which facts and persons he sees as relevant to its resolution, and, finally, what principles and purposes he associates with the issue. Every story of Presidential decision-making is really two stories: an outer one in which a rational man calculates and an inner one in which an emotional man feels. The two are forever connected. Any real President is one whole man and his deeds reflect his wholeness.

As for personality, it is a matter of tendencies. It is not that one President "has" some basic characteristic that another President does not "have." That old way of treating a trait as a possession, like a rock in a basket, ignores the universality of aggressiveness, compliancy, detachment, and other human drives. We all have all of them, but in different amounts and in different combinations.

THE PATTERN OF CHARACTER, WORLD VIEW, AND STYLE

The most visible part of the pattern is style. *Style is the President's habitual way of performing his three political roles: rhetoric, personal relations, and homework.* Not to be confused with "stylishness," charisma, or appearance, style is how the President goes about doing what the office requires him to do — to speak, directly or through media, to large audiences; to deal face to face with other politicians, individually and in small, relatively private groups; and to read, write, and calculate by himself in order to manage the endless flow of details that stream onto his desk. No President can escape doing at least some of each. But there are marked differences in stylistic emphasis from President to President. The *balance* among the three style elements varies; one President may put most of himself into rhetoric, another may stress close, informal dealing, while still another may devote his energies mainly to study and cogitation. Beyond the balance, we want to see each President's peculiar habits of style, his mode of coping with and adapting to these Presidential demands. For example, I think both Calvin Coolidge and John F. Kennedy were primarily rhetoricians, but they went about it in contrasting ways.

A President's *world view consists of his primary, politically relevant beliefs, particularly his conceptions of social causality, human nature, and the central moral conflicts of the time.* This is how he sees the world and his lasting opinions about what he sees. Style is his way of acting; world view is his way of seeing. Like the rest of us, a President develops over a lifetime certain conceptions of reality — how things work in politics, what people are like, what the main purposes are. These assumptions or conceptions help him make sense of his world, give some semblance of order to the chaos of existence. Perhaps most important: a man's world view affects what he pays attention to, and a great deal of politics is about paying attention. The name of the game for many politicians is not so much "Do this, do that" as it is "Look here!"

"Character" comes from the Greek word for engraving; in one sense it is what life has marked into a man's being. As used here, *character is the way the President orients himself toward life* — not for the moment, but enduringly. Character is the person's stance as he confronts experience. And at the core of character, a man confronts himself. The President's fundamental self-esteem is his prime personal resource; to defend and advance that, he will sacrifice much else he values. Down there in the privacy of his heart, does he find himself superb, or ordinary, or debased, or in some intermediate range? No President has been utterly paralyzed by self-doubt and none has been utterly free of midnight self-mockery. In between, the real Presidents move out on life from positions of relative strength or weakness. Equally important are the criteria by which they judge themselves. A President who rates himself by the standard of achievement, for instance, may be little affected by losses of affection.

Character, world view, and style are abstractions from the reality of the whole individual. In every case they form an integrated pattern: the man develops a combination which makes psychological sense for him, a dynamic arrangement of motives, beliefs, and habits in the service of his need for self-esteem.

THE POWER SITUATION AND "CLIMATE OF EXPECTATIONS"

Presidential character resonates with the political situation the President faces. It adapts him as he tries to adapt it. The support he has from the public and interest groups, the party balance in Congress, the thrust of Supreme Court opinion together set the basic power situation he must deal with. An activist President may run smack into a brick wall of resistance, then pull back and wait for a better moment. On the other hand, a President who sees himself as a quiet caretaker may not try to exploit even the most favorable power situation. So it is the relationship between President and the political configuration that makes the system tick.

Even before public opinion polls, the President's real or supposed popularity was a large factor in his performance. Besides the power mix in Washington, the President has to deal with a national climate of expectations, the predominant needs thrust up to him by the people. There are at least three recurrent themes around which these needs are focused.

People look to the President for *reassurance,* a feeling that things will be all right, that the President will take care of his people. The psychological request is for a surcease of anxiety. Obviously, modern life in America involves considerable doses of fear, tension, anxiety, worry; from time to time, the public mood calls for a rest, a time of peace, a breathing space, a "return to normalcy."

Another theme is the demand for a *sense of progress and action.* The President ought to do something to direct the nation's course — or at least be in there pitching for the people. The President is looked to as a take-charge man, a doer, a turner of the wheels, a producer of progress — even if that means some sacrifice of serenity.

A third type of climate of expectations is the public need for a sense of *legitimacy* from, and in, the Presidency. The President should be a master politician who is above politics. He should have a right to his place and a rightful way of acting in it. The respectability — even religiosity — of the office has to be protected by a man who presents himself as defender of the faith. There is more to this than dignity, more than propriety. The President is expected to personify our betterness in an inspiring way, to express in what he does and is (not just in what he says) a moral idealism which, in much of the public mind, is the very opposite of "politics."

Over time the climate of expectations shifts and changes. Wars, depressions, and other national events contribute to that change, but there also is a rough cycle, from an emphasis on action (which begins to look too "political") to an emphasis on legitimacy (the moral uplift of which creates its own strains) to an emphasis on reassurance and rest (which comes to seem like drift) and back to action again. One need not be astrological about it. The point is that the climate of expectations at any given time is the political air the President has to breathe. Relating to this climate is a large part of his task.

PREDICTING PRESIDENTS

The best way to predict a President's character, world view, and style is to see how he constructed them in the first place. Especially in the early stages, life is experimental; consciously or not, a person tries out various ways of defining and maintaining and raising self-esteem. He looks to his environment for clues as to who he is and how well he is doing. These lessons of life slowly sink in: certain self-images and evaluations, certain ways of looking at the world, certain styles of action get confirmed by his experience and he gradually adopts them as his own. If we can see that process of development, we can understand the product. The features to note are those bearing on Presidential performance.

Experimental development continues all the way to death; we will not blind ourselves to midlife changes, particularly in the full-scale prediction case, that of Richard Nixon. But it is often much easier to see the basic patterns in early life histories. Later on a whole host of distractions — especially the image-making all politicians learn to practice — clouds the picture.

In general, character has its *main* development in childhood, world view in adolescence, style in early adulthood. The stance toward life I call character grows out of the child's experiments in relating to parents, brothers and sisters, and peers at play and in school, as well as to his own body and the objects around it. Slowly the child defines an orientation toward experience; once established, that tends to last despite much subsequent contradiction. By adolescence, the child has been hearing and seeing how people make their worlds meaningful, and now he is moved to relate himself — his own meanings — to those around him. His focus of attention shifts toward the future; he senses that decisions about his fate are coming and he looks into the premises for those decisions. Thoughts about the way the world works and how one might work in it, about what people are like and how one might be like them or not, and about the values people share and how one might share in them too — these are typical concerns for the post-child, pre-adult mind of the adolescent.

These themes come together strongly in early adulthood, when the person moves from contemplation to responsible action and adopts a style. In most biographical accounts this period stands out in stark clarity — the time of emergence, the time the young man found himself. I call it his first independent political success. It was then he moved beyond the detailed guidance of his family; then his self-esteem was dramatically boosted; then he came forth as a person to be reckoned with by other people. The *way* he did that is profoundly important to him. Typically he grasps that style and hangs onto it. Much later, coming into the Presidency, something in him remembers this earlier victory and re-emphasizes the style that made it happen.

Character provides the main thrust and broad direction — but it does not *determine*, in any fixed sense, world view and style. The story of development does not end with the end of childhood. Thereafter, the culture one grows in and the ways that culture is translated by parents and peers shapes the meanings one makes of his character. The going world view gets learned and that learning helps channel character forces. Thus it will not necessarily be true that compulsive characters have reactionary beliefs, or that compliant characters believe in compromise. Similarly for style: historical accidents play a large part in furnishing special opportunities for action — and in blocking off alternatives. For example, however much anger a young man may feel, that anger will not be expressed in rhetoric unless and until his life situation provides a platform and an audience. Style thus has a stature and independence of its own. Those who would reduce all explanation to character neglect these highly significant later channelings. For beyond the root is the branch, above the foundation the superstructure, and starts do not prescribe finishes.

FOUR TYPES OF PRESIDENTIAL CHARACTER

The five concepts — character, world view, style, power situation, and climate of expectations — run through the accounts of Presidents in the chapters to follow, which cluster the Presidents since Theodore Roosevelt into four types. This is the fundamental scheme of the study. It offers a way to move past the complexities to the main contrasts and comparisons.

The first baseline in defining Presidential type is *activity-passivity.* How much energy does the man invest in his Presidency? Lyndon Johnson went at his day like a human cyclone, coming to rest long after the sun went down. Calvin Coolidge often slept eleven hours a night and still needed a nap in the middle of the day. In between the Presidents array themselves on the high or low side of the activity line.

The second baseline is *positive-negative affect* toward one's activity — that is, how he feels about what he does. Relatively speaking, does he seem to experience his political life as happy or sad, enjoyable or discouraging, positive or negative in its main effect. The feeling I am after here is not grim satisfaction in a job well done, not some philosophical conclusion. The idea is this: is he someone who, on the surfaces we can see, gives forth the feeling that he has *fun* in political life? Franklin Roosevelt's Secretary of War, Henry L. Stimson wrote that the Roosevelts "not only understood the *use* of power, they knew the *enjoyment* of power, too.... Whether a man is burdened by power or enjoys power; whether he is trapped by responsibility or made free by it; whether he is moved by other people and outer forces or moves them — that is the essence of leadership."

The positive-negative baseline, then, is a general symptom of the fit between the man and his experience, a kind of register of *felt* satisfaction.

Why might we expect these two simple dimensions to outline the main character types? Because they stand for two central features of anyone's orientation toward life. In nearly every study of personality, some form of the active-passive contrast is critical; the general tendency to act or be acted upon is evident in such concepts as dominance-submission, extraversion-introversion, aggression-timidity, attack-defense, fight-flight, engagement-withdrawal, approach-avoidance. In everyday life we sense quickly the general energy output of the people we deal with. Similarly we catch on fairly quickly to the affect dimension—whether the person seems to be optimistic or pessimistic, hopeful or skeptical, happy or sad. The two baselines are clear and they are also independent of one another: all of us know people who are very active but seem discouraged, others who are quite passive but seem happy, and so forth. The activity baseline refers to what one does, the affect baseline to how one feels about what he does.

Both are crude clues to character. They are leads into four basic character patterns long familiar in psychological research. In summary form, these are the main configurations:

Active-positive: There is a congruence, a consistency, between much activity and the enjoyment of it, indicating relatively high self-esteem and relative success in relating to the environment. The man shows an orientation toward productiveness as a value and an ability to use his styles flexibly, adaptively, suiting the dance to the music. He sees himself as developing over time toward relatively well defined personal goals—growing toward his image of himself as he might yet be. There is an emphasis on rational mastery, on using the brain to move the feet. This may get him into trouble; he may fail to take account of the irrational in politics. Not everyone he deals with sees things his way and he may find it hard to understand why.

Active-negative: The contradiction here is between relatively intense effort and relatively low emotional reward for that effort. The activity has a compulsive quality, as if the man were trying to make up for something or to escape from anxiety into hard work. He seems ambitious, striving upward, power-seeking. His stance toward the environment is aggressive and he has a persistent problem in managing his aggressive feelings. His self-image is vague and discontinuous. Life is a hard struggle to achieve and hold power, hampered by the condemnations of a perfectionistic conscience. Active-negative types pour energy into the political system, but it is an energy distorted from within.

Passive-positive: This is the receptive, compliant, other-directed character whose life is a search for affection as a reward for being agreeable and cooperative rather than personally assertive. The contradiction is between low self-esteem (on grounds of being unlovable, unattractive) and a superficial optimism. A hopeful attitude helps dispel doubt and elicits encouragement from others. Passive-positive types help soften the harsh edges of politics. But their dependence and the fragility of their hopes and enjoyments make disappointment in politics likely.

Passive-negative: The factors are consistent—but how are we to account for the man's *political* role-taking? Why is someone who does little in politics and enjoys it less there at all? The answer lies in the passive-negative's character-rooted orientation toward doing dutiful service; this compensates for low self-esteem based on a sense of uselessness. Passive-negative types are in politics because they think they ought to be. They may be well adapted to certain nonpolitical roles, but they lack the experience and flexibility to perform effectively as political leaders. Their tendency is to withdraw, to escape from the conflict and uncertainty of politics by emphasizing vague principles (especially prohibitions) and procedural arrangements. They become guardians of the right and proper way, above the sordid politicking of lesser men.

Active-positive Presidents want most to achieve results. Active-negatives aim to get and keep power. Passive-positives are after love. Passive-negatives emphasize their civic virtue. The relation of activity to enjoyment in a President thus tends to outline a cluster of characteristics, to set apart the adapted from the compulsive, compliant, and withdrawn types. . . .

The President is not some shapeless organism in a flood of novelties, but a man with a memory in a system with a history. Like all of us, he draws on his past to shape his future. The pathetic hope that the White House will turn a Caligula into a Marcus Aurelius is as naive as the fear that ultimate power inevitably corrupts. The problem is to understand—and to state understandably—what in the personal past foreshadows the Presidential future.

☆

Before a President is elected, debate centers on his stands on particular issues, his regional and group connections, his place in the left-right array of ideologies. *After* a President has left office and there has been time to see his rulership in perspective, the connection between his character and his Presidential actions emerges as paramount. Then it becomes clear that the kind of man he was stamped out the shape of his performance. Recognizing this, we ought to be able to find a way to a better prescience, a way to see in potential Presidents the factors which have turned out to be critical for actual Presidents. That is the idea of this book.

Its message is: look to character first. At least by the time the man emerges as an adult, he has displayed a stance toward his experience, a proto-political orientation. The first clues are simple: by and large, does he actively make his environment, or is he passively made by it? And how does he feel about his experience—is his effort in life a burden to be endured or an opportunity for personal enjoyment? From those two starting points, we can move to a richer, more dynamic understanding of the four types. The lives of Presidents past and of the one still with us show, I think, how a start from character makes possible a realistic estimate of what will endure into a man's White House years. Character is the force, the motive power, around which the person gathers his view of the world and from which his style receives its impetus. The issues will change, the character of the President will last.

In and beyond the eighth decade of the twentieth century, Presidential character will meet new versions of old themes. The swirl of emotions which will surround the next President — and the one after that and the one after that — cannot be wished away. For better or for worse, the Presidency remains the prime focus for our political sentiments and the prime source of guidance and inspiration for national politics. The next and future Presidents will each inherit a climate of expectations not of his making. If he is lucky and effective, he can call forth from that climate new energies, a new vision, a new way of working to suit a perennially new age. Or he can help us drift into lassitude or tragedy. Much of what he is remembered for will depend on the fit between the dominant forces in his character and the dominant feelings in his constituency.

Deep in the political culture with which the President must deal are four themes, old in the American spirit, new in contemporary content. A President to suit the age must find in these themes a resonance with his own political being. The dangers of discord in that resonance are severe.

POLITICS AND THE DRIVE FOR POWER

Americans vastly overrate the President's power — and they are likely to continue to do so. The logic of that feeling is clear enough: the President is at the top and therefore he must be able to dominate those below him. The psychology is more complicated. The whole popular ethic of struggle, the onward-and-upward, fight-today-to-win-tomorrow spirit gets played out vicariously as people watch their President. The President should be working, trying, striving forward — living out in his life what makes life meaningful for the citizen at work. Life is tough, life is earnest. A tough, earnest President symbolizes and represents that theme, shows by the thrust of his deeds that the fight is worth it after all. Will he stand up to his — and our — enemies, or will he collapse? Has he the guts to endure the heat in the kitchen? Will he (will he please) play out for us the drama that leads through suffering to salvation?

To a character attuned to power, this popular theme can convey a heady message. It comes through loudest to the active-negative type, whose inner struggle between aggression and control resonates with the popular plea for toughness. For Wilson, Hoover, Johnson, and

Nixon, and for active-negative Presidents in the future, the temptation to stand and fight receives wide support from the culture. The most dangerous confusion in that connection is the equating of political power—essentially the power to persuade—with force. Such a President, frustrated in efforts at persuasion, may turn to those aspects of his role least constrained by the chains of compromise— from domestic to foreign policy, from foreign policy to military policy, for instance, where the tradition of obedience holds. Then we may see a President, doubtful within but seemingly certain without, huffing and puffing with *machismo* as he bravely orders other men to die.

Short of that, the active-negative character may show his colors not in some aggressive crusade but in a defensive refusal—as Hoover did in his adamant stand toward direct relief. Although such a stand may undermine his immediate popularity, it too resonates with the culture's piety of effort. Paradoxically, the same public which may turn against a President's policy may respect him for resisting their demands. The President shares with them the awareness of an historical tradition of the lone hero bucking the tide of his times in favor of some eternal purpose. Particularly now that the President is restricted to two terms, in that second term the temptation to clean up one's integrity and long-term reputation with some unpopular heroism may be very strong indeed. This may not require an active-negative President to feel he must follow the martial model. What he may well feel impelled to do is to rigidly defend some position previously occupied, to translate some experiment into a commitment.

Nowadays, two developments work against this hard-line attitude. One is popular despair over the war in Indo-China, which has brought into discredit, perhaps for a majority of Americans, the style of thought which equates patriotism with slaughter. The revelation that the tough-minded earnestness of a secret elite around the President led not only to extraordinary cruelties but also to repeated defeat has called into question the military version of the ethic of struggle. The pose of toughness can still call forth a primal response, especially from people determined to deny their own doubts, but this first televised war has undercut a good deal of that. At a minimum, Presidential appeals for backing in new military ventures will be subject to hard questioning.

So in a different way will be appeals to the popular enthusiasm for hard work. For the active-negative President especially, hard work has brought him where he is—to the top. Whatever his background, he is and sees himself as a dramatic success, living proof that the way to the stars is through adversity. Clearly he shares that feeling with millions of Americans, themselves successful or not, who want to believe that work pays off in life-meaning as well as in dollars. Yet amid many cultural fads and temporary aberrations, the evidence of disillusionment in the meaningfulness of the work many Americans find themselves doing seems to be deepening in the eighth decade. From housewives to assembly-line workers to corporation executives and professionals, people are questioning the traditional assumption that hard work—and by implication the ethic of struggle itself—is meaningful *because* it is difficult; what is more, they are questioning it not in some abstract sense but in the all too concrete experience of their own working lives. The small minority of children of the middle class who have wandered away from gung-ho schools and tensed-up homes is a symptom of a larger erosion of the confident belief that the hard way is always the best way. Too much could be made of this change; we have been through such tides before. But for the middle-run at least, Presidents will find less and less response from projections of themselves as long-suffering laborers, bearing up under the immense burdens of an awful job.

The President as tragic hero, then, may have a hard time winning public belief in himself. He will have to wage his domestic and/or foreign "Wars on" this or that amidst a good deal of public skepticism. Yet for a long time, potential Presidents attuned to the ethic of struggle will continue to appear in the candidate lists. For the child is father to the man, and they received their basic cast of mind a long time ago—as did many of their constituents.

POLITICS AND THE SEARCH FOR AFFECTION

Betimes the people want a hero, betimes they want a friend. The people's desire for community in an age of fragmentation, their need to sense themselves as members sharing in the national doings, strikes a chord within the passive-positive President. From his youth he has personified the politician as giver and taker of affection. There he found reward for his air of hopefulness in the scads of friends he attracted and the smiles he helped bring to their faces. Raised in a highly indulgent setting, he came to expect that almost everyone would like him and that those who did not could be placated by considerateness and compromise. He needed that. For behind the surface of his smile he sensed how fragile the supply of love could be, how much in need of protection was the impression he had that he was lovable.

The affectionate side of politics (much neglected in research) appeals to a people broken apart less by conflict and rivalry than by isolation and anxiety. Most men and women lead lives of *quiet* desperation; the scattering of families, the anonymity of work life, the sudden shifts between generations and neighborhoods, the accidents a wavering economy delivers, all contribute to the lonesome vulnerability people feel and hide, supposing they are exceptions to the general rule of serenity. Politics offers some opportunities for expressing that directly, as when brokenhearted people line up to tell their Congressman whatever it is they have to tell. But for many who never tell anybody, politics offers a scene for reassurance, a medium for the vicarious experience of fellowship.

This can affect a President or Presidential candidate. He can come to symbolize in his manner the friendliness people miss. Whatever he is to himself, his look-on-the-bright-side optimism conveys a sense that things cannot be all that bad—and God knows he has more to worry about than I do. So there can develop between a President's cheerfulness and his people's need for reassurance a mutually reinforcing, symbiotic ding-dong.

Every President is somewhat passive-positive (and partly each of the other types); all have drawn a sustenance of sorts from the cheering crowds and flattering mail. At the extreme this sentiment can lapse over into sentimentality or hysteria, as with the "jumpers" for Kennedy screaming "I see him, I see him." Then the show business dimension of politics comes to the fore. The President as star brings his audience together in their admiration of him, lets their glamorization of him flow freely around the hall, where, for a moment at least, all experience simultaneously the common joy of his presence. The transformation of a middle-aged politician into a glamorous star is a mysterious process, one perhaps understood best by the managers of rock groups. A most unlikely case would be the political beatification of Eugene McCarthy. Somehow the man catches on, becomes an "in" thing; he ceases to be a curiosity and becomes a charismatic figure. What is important in that, besides the gratification it supplies the public, is what it can do to the star himself. For a Lyndon Johnson it meant a confirmation of power. But for a passive-positive type, a modern-day inheritor of the Taft-Harding character, such adulation touches deeper. The resonance is with his inner sense that such fleeting expressions of allegiance are the reality of affection.

These themes reinforce the obsession with technique that affects so much of contemporary political rhetoric. Political cosmetology becomes a fine art, despite the lack of evidence that it changes votes or polls. The money floods into the hands of those who know how to make a silk purse statesman out of a sow's ear politico. Politics is sexualized; the glance and the stance are carefully coached; the cruciality of just the right rhetorical flair is vastly exaggerated; the political club becomes a fan club. Ultimately the technique itself becomes an object of evaluation: people admire the man who does the most artful job of conning them. There are present-day equivalents aplenty of whom Harry Daugherty could say, as he said of Harding, "Gee, what a great-looking President he'd make!"

All of this can make an incompetent like Harding think he is not only qualified for high office but also personally attractive. That is the dividing line for the individual comparable to the transition to charismatic followership in the audience. The personal need for such pseudo-love is fundamentally insatiable—the applause pours into a bottomless pit. The larger political danger is that such a man will convince himself and others that he has untapped talents, only to discover later that he does not, and to reveal that to all who inquire.

Yet on the way, a man's very ordinariness can seem to him and them a sign of grace.

The Abraham Lincoln story spells out a persistent theme in American political mythology—not just rags to riches, but innocence to political stardom, like Jimmy Stewart in "Mr. Smith Goes to Washington." A man of common virtue is drafted by his neighbors to go off to deal with the sophisticates; there he is tempted—nearly seduced—by the slick and pompous wiseacres; but in the end his naïveté itself wins out: the sophisticates are beaten or won over by his simplicity. The story celebrates sincerity and along the way tells the citizen he is like the best of the bunch. It tells the candidate to emphasize not his superior talents but his ordinary feelings, those he shares with the better half of each constituent, to make a virtue of his ordinariness. What this means in terms of content will change as the culture changes. Jimmy Stewart's apple pie aw-shucksism will not do it for the age of Aquarius; perhaps the contemporary equivalent is Ralph Nader's emotional image (the Nader reality being another matter).

The affection problem of a realistic politics in the eighth decade is to help us love one another without lapsing into sentimentality or hero-worship. The passive-positive character feels the problem, but is too easily diverted by the sham and sentimentality of politics as show business.

POLITICS AND THE QUEST FOR LEGITIMACY

The Presidency exists solely in the minds of men. The White House is not the Presidency any more than the flag is the nation. This "institution" is nothing more than images, habits, and intentions shared by the humans who make it up and by those who react to them. There is not even, as in a church, a clearly sanctified place for it; the Oval Office is no altar—it is an office. The reverence people pay the President, the awe his visitors experience in his presence— all that is in their heads—and his. A fragile base for Presidential stability? Only to those who see in the tangible appurtenances of life a foundation more secure than man's sense of life's continuities.

In our culture the religious-monarchical focus of the Presidency —the tendency to see the office as a sort of divine-right kingship—

gets emphasized less in chiliastic, evangelical, or even ecumenical ways than in a quest for legitimacy. Seldom in history was the popular need for legitimacy more evident than at the start of the eighth decade. It was then that the President of the United States, chief among the governors, said that most people were fed up with government. The sentiment takes different forms — the credibility gap, the crisis of confidence, the Nixon administration's own plea to "Watch what we do, not what we say," as if to confess to verbal distortion even before the fact. The essential legitimating quality is trust, and a great deal of trusting seemed to have leaked out of the system. The problem is not in the succession — the transfer of power from one rightful ruler to the next; even after assassinations Americans do not hesitate to accord authority to the new President. Rather, it resides in a fear that the men entrusted to rule are proving all too human, are politicking away the high dignity and ancient honor of the Republic for hidden reasons of their own.

The dangers people seem to fear are two, pride and perfidy. Mechanically these come down to too little and too much compromise, but it is not a mechanical matter. Pride is feared when a President seems to be pushing harder and faster than the issues call for — and doing that more and more on his own, without proper consultation. FDR's attack on the Supreme Court is an example. The primal version is the fear of tyranny growing out of hubris. The response is to wish for a return to the Constitutional restraints, a reassertion of the basic system Americans have elevated to an article of political faith. Similarly Kennedy's conflict with U. S. Steel seemed to many businessmen an illegitimate forcing of power.

Perfidy stands for characterological betrayal, subtler than the constitutional form. Legitimacy is threatened not so much by one who would break the rules as by one who seems to break trust in the image of the President as dignified, episcopal, plain, and clean in character. Part of the public mind always realizes that the President is only a man, with all man's vulnerability to moral error; part wants to deny that, to foist on the President a priestliness setting him above the congregation. There is a real ambivalence here, one that makes it all the more necessary to reassert legitimacy in the Presidency when the pendulum swings too far. Presidents realize this. They try to be careful not to "demean the office." But especially after a time when the feeling has been growing that the Presidency is getting too "political" and that evil persons (Communists, grafters) are crawling too close to the throne, the call for a man of unquestionable honor will go out.

The appeal for a moral cleansing of the Presidency resonates with the passive-negative character in its emphasis on *not doing* certain things. It also reinforces the character attuned to moral appeals to duty. A man who cares little for the roils of politics or the purposes of policy may respond much more strongly to the appeal: save the nation, keep the faith, bring back the oldtime way of our forefathers. Such a man is eminently draftable. In the end he has no answer to the question, if not you, who? So he serves. In serving, the moral themes push his mind upward, stimulate whatever pontifical propensities he has. Especially if he is basically an apolitical man, unused to the issues and the informal processes of negotiation, he will find ways to rise above all that. For Coolidge the tendency was toward a proverbial, increasingly abstract rhetoric, for Eisenhower the drift was toward a Mosaic role—final arbiter of otherwise unresolvable conflicts.

Moral rhetoric in the eighth decade may well take a different tack. Neither the calls for energetic sacrifice (New Freedom, New Deal, New Frontier, New American Revolution) nor the reiteration of the Constitution's holiness may quite ring true to a generation sore with the wounds of disillusionment. The President may be seen less as Jeremiah or Job or Moses, more as John the Baptist, a man whose vision reaches beyond the currents of the present day, and who reflects in his own life the character of that vision. Certainly the present-day fluctuations of popular interest between the past (the cult of nostalgia) and the future-after-next (Consciousness III) seem to represent an uncertain wavering in time, a thrashing about in search of models and exemplars different from those at hand. The alternation in Nixon's politics between surprise and delay further fractures the sense of reliable continuity in the government, a flow of development linking a valued past with an imaginable future. The public expectation that things will be better for them and for their nation in the future—traditional American optimism—has had hard enough knocks in recent years that many doubt things will turn out that way. Science fiction paints pictures of a dismal antisepsis, a brittle, mechanical, soul-crushing world in the future, or of chaotic utopias.

CREATIVE POLITICS

But in the culture also is an awareness of these ills and dangers. The sham of the typical Presidential campaign has not gone unnoticed. The militant tough guys, the technocrats who counsel so coolly about kill-ratios and free-fire zones, and puffed-up claims for low-budget programs, the violations of Constitutional rights rationalized as protections of Constitutional order, the substitution of abstract moralisms for substance—I am not the first to point out these pathologies. Amidst much confusion, the public, especially in an election year when attention is paid, sees with a slow but stubborn vision the very distortions its own needs have helped to create. The press and television help with that; a President or candidate who knows how to say simply what many feel deeply can make an even greater contribution to cutting away the underbrush of lies and bluster.

Nor does the people's disillusionment easily sour into despair. Kennedy's call for vigor stopped short with his murder; Johnson's initial politico-religiosity fell apart; Nixon pleaded for national reconciliation and then polarized opinion. Yet aside from a few pathetic Weathermen and their Birchite counterparts, most Americans want to make the system work and are capable of doing so. The generation which went through the Wilson-Harding-Hoover disillusionments did recover. The cultural memory of that recovery has not disappeared, even in this age of the momentary. Beyond the candid confession of failure, the task of Presidential leadership these days is to remind the people that their past was not without achievement and that their future is not yet spoiled.

That is in the active-positive spirit. Those themes resonate with a character confident enough to see its weaknesses and the potentialities it might yet grow into. The active-positive Presidents did not invent the sentiments they called forth. They gave expression in a believable way to convictions momentarily buried in fear and mistrust. From their perception of a basically capable public they drew strength for their own sense of capability. For like everyone else, active-positive Presidents feed on reinforcements from the environment. What is different about them is their ability to see the strengths hidden in public confusion and to connect with those strengths.

A goodly part of the contemporary disillusionment is the gap between what people see governments doing and what they hear politicians telling them. In Washington, interest in policy falls off rapidly once a bill is passed or an executive order issued. Legislative "victories" are declared when the money is appropriated. By the time a program goes into operation, Washington is onto some new drama. The whole process lurches forward on the basis of the more or less plausible hope that some good will be done by the minions out in the "field" far away. Lacking knowledge of what their programs are doing to people, the policy-makers fall back on theories drawn nearly at random from current academic ologies, the columnists and editorial writers, and/or wise-seeming comments at committee hearings. There are exceptions. The exceptions are rare. The rule is policy-making by-guess-and-by-God, always in a hurry. The odds of success — that is, actual, significant improvements in the lives of citizens — are reduced by the general lack of attention to the real results of policy. When people see the contrast between headline Washington "victories" and how it is to get to work in the morning, they wonder.

The active-positive Presidents help get past that gap by focusing on results beyond Washington. FDR's insistent curiosity about how life was going for people, Truman's hunger for "the facts," Kennedy's probing questions in the Cuban missile crisis illustrate how a character in concord with itself can reach for reality. Active-positive Presidents are more open to evidence because they have less need to deny and distort their perceptions for protective purposes. Their approach is experimental rather than deductive, which allows them to try something else when an experiment fails to pan out, rather than escalate the rhetoric or pursue the villains responsible. Flexibility in style and a world view containing a variety of probabilities are congruent with a character ready for trial and error and furnish the imagination with a wide range of alternatives. A people doubtful about government programs as the final answer to anything might well respond to a candid admission of uncertainty, a determination to try anyway, and a demonstration of attention to results.

For the rest, there is laughter. Americans do a lot of that—at themselves, at politicians, at all the pomposities and cynicisms that stand in the way of genuine experience. We have yet to be immobilized by irony. A Presidential character who can see beyond tomorrow—and smile—might yet lead us out of the wilderness.

THE LIMITS OF PRESIDENTIAL POWER

From Vietnam/Watergate to the Present

☆

ARTHUR M. SCHLESINGER, JR.: *The Imperial Presidency*

. . . Of the many consequences of Watergate, one of the worst will be the panaceas it puts into circulation. Generals fight the last war, reformers the last scandal. Reformers therefore run the risk of deforming the constitutional system forever in order to put to rights a contingency of the fleeting moment. In his great opinion in the steel-seizure case, Justice Jackson warned against the infirmity "of confounding the permanent executive office with its temporary occupant. The tendency is strong to emphasize transient results . . . and lose sight of enduring consequences upon the balanced power structure of our Republic." There is no fail-safe mechanism guaranteed to contain presidential power; and the effort to devise such a mechanism may lead to forms of constitutional or statutory overkill damaging to other national interests, such as efficiency or even liberty.

Let us instead return to where we began: the Founding Fathers. They had two things in mind: creating a strong and effective national government and holding that government within a strong and effective system of accountability. The system of accountability, alas, had one grave weakness—foreign affairs. The decay of accountability under the pressure of international crisis created the imperial Presidency, which may be briefly defined as the condition resulting when the balance between presidential power and presidential accountability is destroyed. The problem after Vietnam and Watergate is how to restore the balance.

Arthur M. Schlesinger, Jr. is Albert Schweitzer Professor of the Humanities at the City University of New York. The first selection is from *The Imperial Presidency* (New York: Popular Library by arrangement with Houghton Mifflin Co., 1974), pp. 464-466. Copyright © 1974 by Arthur M. Schlesinger, Jr. Reprinted by permission of the author and the publisher. The second selection is a television interview published in Philip Dolce and George Skau, eds., *Power and the Presidency* (New York: Charles Scribner's Sons, 1976). Copyright © 1976 by P. C. Dolce and G. H. Skau. Reprinted with permission of the publisher, the editors, and the interviewee.

There are two ways to restore the balance. One is to cut down presidential power. The other is to build up presidential accountability. One approach envisages a Presidency diminished and circumscribed by congressional statute, judicial decision and institutional change. The other wishes to preserve the Presidency as the robust office that has served the republic nobly, despite a bad apple or two toward the end, but to prevent the abuse of power by reinvigorating and enforcing the system of accountability. The essence of the first approach is structure, of the second, politics.

Structure means proceeding by constitutional amendments, laws and formal changes in institutions and their relationships, rules and rigidity; it is what political scientists like. Politics assumes a broadly workable constitution and means proceeding by debate, education, persuasion, opinion, civility, comity. It is congenial to historians. Of course, when constitutions are not broadly workable, there is no escape from structural change. But one doubts whether Vietnam and Watergate finally prove the unworkability of the American Constitution. These disasters surely resulted less from provisions than from transgressions of the Constitution, which suggests that the better course may be not to alter the Constitution but to apply it.

Constitutions are not self-executing. Their application requires Presidents, Congresses and voters who are sensitive to constitutional issues. Perhaps the aim after Watergate should be to launch a campaign of national education, or rather, to borrow an invaluable term from the Women's Liberation movement, a campaign of national consciousness-raising. The object must be to raise the consciousness of future Presidents so that they will hereafter remember and respect the system of accountability; to raise the consciousness of future Congresses, so that they will hereafter accept and discharge their own constitutional responsibilities; and to raise the consciousness of citizens so that they will hereafter, as they enter the voting booth, think about a candidate's openness, integrity and constitutional sensitivity as well as about his rhetoric on issues.

Citizens have a particular responsibility. They should reject the latter-day myth of the President as a man above the rest, a myth bulwarked by the ghastly theory of the New Conservatives that institutions of authority must have respect, whether or not they have done anything to earn it. Nothing is more mischievous than the singular idea of recent years that the President has a sacred right to be protected from secular exposure and confrontation—the idea summed up in Nixon's idiot phrase about "respect for the Presidency." An American President is entitled to full courtesy, like every other citizen in the land; but let his fellow citizens never forget that he is simply a politician luckier than the rest—the one who has made it, in Disraeli's phrase, to the top of the greasy pole. Shinnying up the pole does not transform him into a demigod and carry him out of our sight and jurisdiction; and he can expect to stay on top only so long as he remains in touch with those below and operates within the disciplines of consent. The transubstantiation of the President has gone far enough. It is a modern development; it is not inherent in the process. If the electorate will secularize the Presidency and get it back into proportion, future Presidents should be quite as much tethered to the reality principle as the great Presidents of the past have been. . . .

☆

PHILIP C. DOLCE: Professor Schlesinger, for many years you have been a chronicler of famous Presidential administrations. One thinks of _The Age of Jackson, The Age of Roosevelt_, and A _Thousand Days: John F. Kennedy in the White House._ In these books you were a firm advocate of Presidential power. You saw Presidential power as necessary to overcome government inertia and to enable the nation to meet crises. Now you are plainly worried about the growth of Presidential power. In fact you use the term "imperial Presidency" to describe it. Do you still retain your faith in the strong Presidency?

ARTHUR M. SCHLESINGER, JR.: I still believe in a strong Presidency. I really do not see how a system based on the separation of powers can move and act without leadership from one of the branches, and historically the President has provided that leadership. But I think that some of us, I among them, were a little uncritical in the past in the way we have defended the strong Presidency. We should have said, "A strong Presidency _within the Constitution._" The men who made the Constitution wanted a strong and energetic national government. They expected the President to be a leader. But they expected him to operate within an equally strong and effective system of accountability. What has happened in recent years is that a state of imbalance has developed between the President's power and his accountability. Presidential power has grown, and Presidential accountability has weakened. This produces the situation I have described as the "imperial Presidency."

PHILIP C. DOLCE: You stated that the "imperial Presidency" is essentially the creation of foreign policy after World War II. Could you explain why you think that is where the "imperial Presidency" grew from?

ARTHUR M. SCHLESINGER, JR.: I mentioned the system of accountability. That system has historically embraced certain formal modes of accountability—the written restraints on Presidential power in the Constitution, the President's accountability to law, to Congress, to the courts. Then there evolved in the early republic various informal modes of accountability: accountability to one's colleagues in the

Cabinet and the executive branch, to one's political party, to the media of opinion, to public opinion in general. But the historic system of accountability has had one grave weakness, and this is in the field of foreign affairs. In foreign policy Presidents often had to take, or thought they had to take, actions on their own initiative and without Congressional authorization, actions they thought necessary to preserve the safety of the republic. Confronted by such Presidential initiatives, Congress, the courts, and public opinion had much less confidence in their own information and judgment, felt much less sure of their ground, and therefore were much less inclined to challenge and check and balance as they were accustomed to doing in domestic policy. Thus, international crisis increased Presidential power and weakened the system of accountability. Since 1939 or thereabouts we have been in a state of protracted international crisis. Moreover, this age of crisis was preceded by a period between the two world wars of active Congressional intervention in foreign affairs — intervention which even members of Congress themselves later agreed to have been unfortunate and mistaken. With that background our contemporary international crisis has carried power faster than ever to the Presidency. For Congress has readily abdicated its responsibilities in the international field because of its own inferiority complex. This has laid the basis for the "imperial Presidency." More particularly, the "imperial Presidency" is the compulsion to use against American citizens the powers that have flowed to the Presidency to meet international emergency. That happened very freely in the Nixon administration, where, under the all-purpose incantation of national security, powers that had been bestowed on the Presidency to meet foreign crises began to be turned against Americans at home.

PHILIP C. DOLCE: How has the "imperial Presidency" permeated the domestic scene?

ARTHUR M. SCHLESINGER, JR.: There have, of course, been occasions when Presidents have received unusual powers to cope with domestic crises. For example, Congress gave Franklin D. Roosevelt unprecedented powers to deal with the depression in the 1930s. But powers bestowed on Presidents to meet domestic crises do not have a spillover effect into foreign affairs. Roosevelt used the powers he had been granted in the domestic field with great skill. He was an exceptionally popular President. Nonetheless, Congress tied him hand and foot in foreign affairs through the neutrality acts. Roosevelt was still struggling to get out of those knots weeks before Pearl Harbor. On the other hand, power given to the Presidency for foreign affairs does spill over into domestic policy. President Truman could hardly have been lower in the polls than he was in 1952. Yet he seized the steel industry on the ground that it was necessary to prevent a steel strike which might stop the flow of ammunition to our troops in Korea. This was a case in which the Supreme Court declared Truman's actions unconstitutional, and he immediately complied with the action. In the Nixon case, you had a President threatening the liberties of the people far more directly in the belief that he could do almost anything in the name of national security—that he could, for example, privately declare a state of national emergency which, he felt, empowered him to create a secret posse in the White House and to release it to break the laws and the Constitution. This is a very clear case, it seems to me, of the way power flowing to the Presidency for foreign reasons is turned against the republic itself.

PHILIP C. DOLCE: Less than a decade ago, there was no cry against the growth of the strong Presidency by Congress, by public opinion, or even by the media. Most intellectuals sang the praises of the strong Presidency and sought to increase its power. Was this uncritical national attitude in part responsible for the growth of the "imperial Presidency"?

ARTHUR M. SCHLESINGER, JR.: I am sure you are right. The growth of the "imperial Presidency" is not so much the result of the rapacity of Presidents for power as it is of Congressional abdication and popular acquiescence or even popular demand. This is, after all, a turbulent and baffling world. It is much easier to have the weight of responsibility taken off one's shoulders and let the President make the decisions. For a time, we elected Presidents who, on the whole, made fairly good decisions and, on the whole, did not abuse their power, Presidents who operated within the system of accountability. That is why there was no great criticism of Presidential power. But, when Presidents began to abuse their power and reject their accountability, then we suddenly realized where the uncritical cult of Presidential power had led us.

PHILIP C. DOLCE: The federal government has been taking powers away from the states and cities for years. Is the "imperial Presidency" part of a great centralization of power that this nation has undergone in the twentieth century?

ARTHUR M. SCHLESINGER, JR.: I would agree that Franklin D. Roosevelt, for example, was a very strong President and that the centralization of authority which took place under the New Deal was certainly part of that larger wave of institutional centralization you mention. But on the whole Roosevelt was a President who respected the system of accountability. He held Cabinet meetings twice a week. He held press conferences twice a week—more during his first three months than Nixon held in his first four years. He was very accessible to members of Congress. He liked to see them and talk to them individually; he did not just receive them en masse as has become the recent Presidential fashion. In other words he did not run a "closed Presidency." I think the peculiar characteristic of the "imperial Presidency" is that it is a "closed Presidency." It rejects the system of accountability. I think we must have strong Presidents. We must have a measure of centralization. But strong Presidents must be open, they must want to be legal and they must respect the system of accountability.

PHILIP C. DOLCE: You mention the word "accountability" and I wonder what that means. While it is true that FDR did speak informally to members of Congress, does that mean he was truly accountable — the way the Constitution would have had it? What I am really making a distinction between is informal consultation and formal accountability.

ARTHUR M. SCHLESINGER, JR.: Well I would think in FDR's case he was probably good at both of them — except during the time of national emergency he proclaimed in 1941. The essence of the thing was well put by Theodore Roosevelt when he said that the President ought to be a very strong man and he ought to use all the powers the office yields but because of that he should be sharply watched and held to the strictest accountability. I think Nixon's view was rather different. Obviously he did not like to be sharply watched or held to strict accountability. His view was essentially that a President is accountable only once every four years — that an election confers a mandate and the mandate empowers the President to do what he thinks best for the safety and welfare of the country: to spend money appropriated by Congress or to impound it, to give out information requested by Congress or withhold it, to make war or to make peace; and that between elections the mandate ought to protect the President from harassment from Congress or by the press or by political opposition and so on. It is essentially a plebiscitary theory, well summed up in that wretched phrase one used to hear during the Nixon Presidency: "Let's all get off his back and let him do his job." That idea, of course, is quite contrary to the conception of the Constitution, which is that the country should always be in a sense on the President's back, and that accountability is a continuous matter, not a quadrennial matter.

PHILIP C. DOLCE: For years conservatives have been crying out against the extension of governmental power and now they see some of their cries of anguish recognized by others. At least one of them has said that the "imperial Presidency" is really a creature of the "welfare state," that we have entrusted too much power to government to solve social and economic problems and in doing so have created the "imperial Presidency." Do you think that is true?

ARTHUR M. SCHLESINGER, JR.: I do not see that because it seems to me that the Presidency on the whole does not have a great deal of power in domestic affairs, particularly in economic affairs. American Presidents probably have much less power over economic policy than the head of any other democratic country in the world. Take the question of taxes. I can well remember in 1962 when President Kennedy had gone to Congress with a tax-reduction bill which he considered necessary to reduce unemployment and stimulate growth. About the same time Harold Macmillan went to the British Parliament with a tax-reduction bill of his own. In the English case the bill was voted on in a few weeks, but in the American case it was introduced in the spring of 1963 and passed about a year later. In that respect I think American Presidents do not have a great deal of power. As for the relationship between the "imperial Presidency" and the "welfare state," I see none at all—that seems mythological. If there are American institutions on which the "imperial Presidency" has drawn heavily, I would say that they are institutions like the FBI—and the CIA—and these are hardly institutions of the "welfare state." One of the oddities is that the conservatives, who are to some degree justifiably smug for having warned against Presidential power, have never been notable for their criticism of the FBI.

PHILIP C. DOLCE: You have drawn an interesting distinction between the domestic Presidency and the foreign-policy Presidency. In your book *The Imperial Presidency* you mention that in foreign policy the American President has more power over war and peace than any other leader in the world with the possible exception of Mao Tse-tung. In domestic policy you say the President has much less power. Since World War II, however, are not most issues so intertwined that you cannot separate them into these categories?

ARTHUR M. SCHLESINGER, JR.: In many cases they are. It is an artificial distinction and there are many issues which involve both foreign and domestic policy. Nonetheless, when one makes an analysis of Presidential recommendations to Congress, those that fell clearly in the field of foreign policy in the period say from 1946 to 1966 had a much better chance of acceptance than those that fell in the field of domestic policy. It seems to me that since World War II the President has enjoyed much more scope and discretion in the field of foreign policy than he has in the field of domestic policy.

PHILIP C. DOLCE: Many people have claimed that the growth of Presidential power was in response to emergency or crisis. Should the President be able to go beyond constitutional limits in the times of crisis?

ARTHUR M. SCHLESINGER, JR.: Obviously one cannot say that there are no conceivable circumstances in which a President might have to move beyond or even against the Constitution. John Locke, in his famous chapter "Of Prerogative" in his *Second Treatise of Government*, argued that this might be necessary. When the life of the nation is involved, Presidents have acted on their own. But responsible Presidents must declare publicly what the reasons are for the emergency and for the unconstitutional acts they may have taken, and in general they try to get retrospective Congressional sanction for what they have done. Moreover, the times and occasions when the life of a nation is really at stake are damned few. There have been only two, in my judgment, in American history. One was the Civil War, and the other was World War II. These were both periods of clear and present danger to the United States. Lincoln and FDR both did things they were not authorized to do by the Constitution. But they proclaimed national emergencies, they explained why they thought the life of the country was in danger, and on the whole Congress and the people supported them in those acts. Such situations occurred in the past and may occur in the future, and I would not for a moment argue for any conception of Presidential power that would deny Presidents the power to act in an emergency.

On the other hand it is plainly essential to have criteria for what constitutes a genuine emergency. You cannot allow the President to make such a judgment on his own personal say-so and expect everyone to surrender automatically to that judgment. One criterion certainly is to proclaim the emergency as Lincoln did and as FDR did. Nixon went into a private panic in 1970 because of the Weathermen or something and in 1971 because of the Pentagon Papers. But he proclaimed no national emergency. He did not go to the country and say, "I think the life of the republic is in danger." He just sat in the White House and communed with himself and set up the Plumbers and let them commit robberies and forge cables and so on. So one criterion is that the President is under an obligation to state plainly and publicly what the emergency is. Second, he can act himself only if Congress is unable or unwilling to prescribe a course of action. Then he must go to Congress and get retroactive sanction for what he has done. There are other criteria. He must never, for example, commit acts against the political process itself, as Nixon did. Presidents who ignore these criteria get into trouble.

Take the case of Jefferson. Jefferson acted, as he said, "beyond the Constitution" in the case of the Louisiana Purchase, but the Congress and the nation agreed that this was an emergency and that he was justified in his action. When he took things into his own hands in the case of the Burr conspiracy, the courts resisted. Congress and the people did not think it was an emergency, and Jefferson's course was rejected. I have mentioned Truman and the steel-seizure case. Both Jefferson and Truman at least sent messages to the Congress explaining why they thought the Burr conspiracy and the steel strike were going to threaten the life of the nation. What Nixon did was to reject all the criteria by which the emergency power has been exercised in the past—and still claim the right to exercise that power.

PHILIP C. DOLCE: You make an interesting distinction between the usurpation and abuse of Presidential power. In times of emergency the President might have to usurp power, but this should never be institutionalized. Is that correct?

ARTHUR M. SCHLESINGER, JR.: Yes, because if usurpation is recognized as usurpation it does not create a precedent and therefore does not legalize that kind of use of power for future Presidents.

PHILIP C. DOLCE: Does the increase of Presidential power and Presidential responsibility show that the office is just too much for any one man to handle, either psychologically or physically?

ARTHUR M. SCHLESINGER, JR.: I do not think so. I think the problem of the Presidential work load has been much exaggerated. Presidents never have to worry about the things that take up time for people like you and me. They have every convenience of life. They are surrounded by people who want to do things for them. No ordinary citizen spent as much time in his vacation places as Nixon did. All Presidents appear to have a great deal of leisure time. Their psychological burden is much more wearing than the physical work load. But I think one man can handle the Presidency better than two. In addition, if you have more than one man, the problem of accountability becomes much more difficult, which is why people like Alexander Hamilton opposed the idea of the plural executive when it was first brought up in the Constitutional Convention.

PHILIP C. DOLCE: One of your principal concerns is that the revolution against the "imperial Presidency" might lead to institutional limits on the office. After all the abuse we have seen, should there not be institutional limits on the Presidency?

ARTHUR M. SCHLESINGER, JR.: On the whole, my view is that the office has served the republic well. I think the problem is not so much that of reducing the power of the Presidency as of rehabilitating and enforcing the system of accountability. The great virtue of strengthening the system of accountability is that it will preserve Presidential power and at the same time will discourage future Presidents from abusing that power. The great virtue of impeachment, for example, is that it punishes the offender without punishing the office.

PHILIP C. DOLCE: What are some of your suggestions for reforming the office itself?

ARTHUR M. SCHLESINGER, JR.: The important approach, it seems to me, lies in the realm of consciousness-raising rather than of structural reform. We must raise the consciousness of future Congresses so they will begin to acknowledge and meet their responsibilities. This is far more important than structural reforms. There are some structural reforms of consequence. Cleaning up campaign financing would be very useful. Congress might well increase its own research and analysis capacity by setting up a Congressional counterpart of the Bureau of the Budget. Congress should establish effective oversight committees for the FBI and CIA. But all this is essentially marginal.

Congress has only to exercise the powers given it in the Constitution to restore the balance of the system. The real question, it seems to me, is not one of structure but of will. It is the question whether Congress really wants to contain the "imperial Presidency" and it is the question whether the American people really want to contain the "imperial Presidency." If they do, the way to do it is within the Constitution by invoking the remedy prescribed by the Founding Fathers.

AARON WILDAVSKY: *The Past and Future Presidency*

In the third volume of *The American Commonwealth*, Lord Bryce wrote, "Perhaps no form of Government needs great leaders so much as democracy." Why, then, is it so difficult to find them? The faults of leadership are the everyday staple of conversation. All of us have become aware of what Bryce had in mind in his chapter on "True Faults of American Democracy," when he alluded to "a certain commonness of mind and tone, a want of dignity and elevation in and about the conduct of public affairs, an insensibility to the nobler aspects and finer responsibilities of national life." If leaders have let us down, they have been helped, as Bryce foresaw, by the cynical "apathy among the luxurious classes and fastidious minds, who find themselves of no more account than the ordinary voter, and are disgusted by the superficial vulgarities of public life." But Bryce did not confuse condemnation with criticism. He thought that "the problem of conducting a stable executive in a democratic country is indeed so immensely difficult that anything short of failure deserves to be called a success. . . ." Explaining "Why Great Men Are Not Chosen," in the first volume of his classic, Bryce located the defect not only in party politics but in popular passions: "The ordinary American voter does not object to mediocrity."

Aaron Wildavsky is Professor of Political Science at the Survey Research Center, University of California at Berkeley. This article appeared in *The Public Interest* No. 41 (Fall, 1975), pp. 56-76. © 1975 by National Affairs, Inc. Reprinted with the permission of the author and the publisher.

Ultimately, Bryce was convinced, "republics Live by Virtue"—
with a capital "V," meaning "the maintenance of a high level of
public spirit and justice among the citizens." Note: "among the
citizens," not merely among public officials. For how could leaders
rise so far above the led; or, stemming from the people, be so superior
to them; or, held accountable, stray so far from popular will? Surely it
would be surprising if the vices of politicians stemmed from the
virtues of the people. What the people do to their leaders must be at
least as important as what the leaders do to them. There are, after all,
so many of us and so few of them. Separating the Presidency from the
people—as if a President owed everything to them and they nothing
to him—makes as much sense as removing the people from the
government it has instituted.

If the reciprocal relations between political leadership and social
expectations could be resolved by exhortation, the problem would
long ago have ceased to be serious. If expectations are not being met,
it is leaders who are not meeting them, and either lower expectations
or higher caliber leadership is required. But both may be out of kilter.
Should one or two leaders fail, that may well be their fault. When all
fail (Kennedy, Johnson, Nixon, and now Ford), when, moreover, all
known replacements are expected to fail, the difficulty is not individual but systemic: It is not the action of one side or the reaction of
another but their mutual relationships that are flawed. That the
people may reject their Presidents is obvious; that Presidents might
flee from their people is less so. Once Presidents discover the embrace
of the people is deadly, they may well seek to escape from it. Presidents who tried to exercise powers they did not have might then be
replaced by Presidents unwilling to exercise the powers they do have.
The future of the Presidency will be determined not by the Presidency alone but by how Presidents behave in response to the environment "We-the-People" create for them. Presidents, we shall
learn, can retreat as well as advance.

PRESIDENTIAL POPULARITY

In the future, Presidents will be more important but less popular than
they are today. The Presidency will be more powerful vis-à-vis institutional competitors but less able to satisfy citizen preferences than it is
now. Unwilling to play a losing hand, future Presidents will try to
change the rules of the game. If they cannot get support from the
people, they can increase the distance between themselves and their
predators.

The importance of Presidents is a function of the scope of government; the more it does, the more important they become. No one
believes that the federal government of the United States is about to

do less — to abandon activities in which it is now engaged, to refuse involvement in new ones, to go below instead of above the per cent of the Gross National Product it now consumes. Hence Presidents must, on the average, be more important than they used to be. Even if one assumes the worst — a weak President opposed by strong Congressional majorities — the President's support will make it easier for proposals to receive favorable consideration and his opposition will make it less likely that legislation will be considered at all or be passed over his veto. Limiting Presidential importance would require the one thing no one expects — limiting what government does.

Presidents remain preeminent in foreign and defense policy. Formal authority is theirs; informal authority, the expectations as to who will do what, is almost entirely in their domain. There does not have to be a discernible foreign policy but, if there is, Presidents are the people who are expected to make it. The exceptions — the Jackson Amendment on Soviet Jews, restrictions on aid to Cambodia, Vietnam, and Turkey — prove the rule. They show that Presidents are not all-powerful in foreign policy; they do not get all they want when they want it. But these incidents are just what they seem — minor. The Turks would not be behaving differently in Cyprus if they continued to receive American aid, and détente, if there ever was such a thing, has evidently not been disturbed by Russian repudiation of their undertaking on the emigration of Soviet Jews. Reluctance to provide funds for Cambodia and Vietnam was, at most, a matter of deciding when — under the present Republican or a future Democratic President — rather than whether these governments would fall. Congress may anger foreign governments and dismay Secretaries of State; it may point to itself as evidence of national disagreement; but it will not succeed in making foreign policy. The main recommendation of the Congressional delegation to Cambodia, after all, was to send the Secretary of State there post haste!

I risk belaboring the obvious because, in the backlash of Watergate, it has become all too easy to imagine a weakening of the Presidency. Not so. Does anyone imagine fewer groups will be interested in influencing a President's position in their own behalf or that his actions will matter less to people in the future? The question answers itself. The weakening of the Presidency is about as likely as the withering away of the state.

To be important, however, is not necessarily to be popular. Let us conceive of Presidential popularity as a vector of two forces: long-term dispositions to support or oppose the institution and short-run tendencies to approve or disapprove what the occupant of the office is doing. Either way, I believe, the secular trend in popularity will be down.

By far the most significant determination of Presidential popularity is the party identification of the population. Since the proportion of people identifying with the major parties has shown a precipitous decline, future Presidents are bound to start out with a smaller base comprised of less committed supporters. This tendency will be reinforced by a relative decline of the groups—the less educated and the religious fundamentalist—who have been most disposed to give unwavering support regardless of what a President does or fails to do. Education may not make people wise, but it does make them critical. As the number of critical people in the country increases, criticism of Presidents will naturally increase. Thus future Presidents will have to work harder than have past Presidents to keep the same popularity status, so to speak. To offset long-run decline they will count on good news in the short run. But the news is bound to be bad.

PUBLIC POLICY AND POLITICAL RESPONSIBILITY

There is no consensus on foreign policy; the lessons learned from the past have not proved helpful. The 1930's apparently taught the United States to intervene everywhere, and the 1960's to intervene nowhere. Neither lesson is supportable. Under the spell of Vietnam, the instinctive reaction to foreign policy questions is "no." Foreign policy requires faith: Evils must be avoided before their bloody consequences manifest themselves to the doubtful. But there is no faith. As in the parable of the Doubting Thomas, Congressmen would not believe the President concerning the situation in Cambodia until they actually went there, plunged their hands into the wounds of the people, and saw they were red. For Presidents the adaptive response will be inaction until it is too late, after which there is no point in doing anything.

Reaction to the oil embargo and the manyfold increase in oil prices is a portent of things to come. When it came in the midst of an Egyptian and Syrian invasion of Israel, the United States did not react at all. Why were the American people not told of the inevitable consequences of the oil price increase, from mass starvation in poor countries and financial havoc among allies to inflation at home? Because then the President would have had to do something about it.

Future Presidents will allow foreign events to speak for themselves after the fact so they don't have to speak to them beforehand. They may reluctantly give in to popular demands for strong action but they will not act in anticipation. Followership, not leadership, probably will best describe future Presidential foreign policy.

There is not today, nor is there likely to be in the near future, a stable constituency in support of social reform. The 1930's through the 1950's were easy to understand. The "haves" did not like to pay, and the "have nots" preferred the benefits they received to the alternative. By the late 1960's, however, the poorer beneficiaries had learned from their leaders that they did not benefit, which led the richer providers to add ingratitude to their list of complaints. Then the extreme passion for equality, against which Tocqueville warned, asserted itself to label anything the government was able to accomplish unworthy of achievement. Too little, too late; or too much, too soon, the result was always the same: a feeling of failure. For as long as directly contradictory demands are made on public policy, governments (and hence Presidents) will be unable to get credit for what they do.

Public housing is a good example of how to make an evident failure out of an apparent success. The nation started with a low-cost shelter program for the stable working poor. Public policy concentrated the available resources into housing projects, so some people could be helped; and resident managers used their discretion to screen out "undesirables," so tenants could live in peace. It was not necessarily the best of worlds for all, but it was better for some. But all that changed in the 1960's. Screening was condemned as racism and worse: Didn't justice require that the worst-off be given preference? Not long after, public housing was attacked as a failure for all the crime it attracted. The dynamiting of buildings in St. Louis' Pruitt-Igoe Project symbolized, unfairly but persuasively, the blowup of hopes for public housing.

More medical care for the poor and aged is incompatible with easier access and lower costs for the whole population. By now the poor see doctors about as often as anybody else. This might be considered an accomplishment of Medicare and Medicaid — except that no one wants to accept responsibility for the consequences. Because access increases faster than facilities, the medical system gets crowded; because doctor and patient are motivated to resolve their uncertainties about treatment by using the insurance and subsidies at their disposal, the system gets expensive; because medical care is only moderately related to health, morbidity does not decline and mortality does not decrease in proportion to expenditure. Hence we hear that the system is in crisis because it is overcrowded, too expensive, and doesn't do much to improving aggregate health rates.

Examples of incompatibilities could come from almost any area of public policy — training the hard-core unemployed at low cost or decreasing dependency by increasing payments to people on welfare — but I will content myself with one less obvious example: party reform. The evils besetting our major political parties are supposed to be excessive influence of money and insufficient power of participation. But participation requires more meetings, conferences, primaries; in a word, more money. Told that money is the root of all evil, on the one hand, and required to dig deeper for it to promote participation, on the other, the position of our parties must be as perilous as that of Presidents, who are urged simultaneously to limit their powers and to lead the people.

Where will support for Presidential power come from? The only time a constituency appears is when there is a threat of curbing or eliminating existing programs. Then one discovers there are really recipients of medical care, aid to dependent children, food stamps, and the whole panoply of subsidies, transfer payments, and tax expenditures. But when they are safe, one could never guess from the torrent of abuse (money matters more than men, forms triumph over functions) that they had something worthwhile to lose. But they do and they will.

The mega-increase in the cost of energy means a decline in our standard of living. We pay more and get less. There will be fewer resources available to support social programs. Race relations may worsen as the poor (and black) do worse. Conservationists and producers will disagree more over strip-mining, oil shale, atomic power plants, and the like. Contradictory demands on government— produce more energy with less damage to the environment at lower cost—will increase.

It will be difficult to reduce defense expenditures because allies and dependents will be poorer and weaker than they were. It will be hard to avoid the threat of force because international events will become more threatening, and it will be difficult to use force because the nation will be torn between recent memories of Vietnam ("No more foreign adventures!") and older recollections of the Second World War ("Intervene before it is too late!"). As foreign news becomes less favorable, government will seek to apply more pressure at home. Is a tariff on imported oil a foreign or a domestic policy? Obviously, it is both. Yet there is no reason to believe that people will become less attached to their lifestyles or less interested in benefits from expensive spending programs. Demands on government will increase as the willingness of citizens to pay for them decreases. Reduction and redirection of consumption will become inevitable. The lot of a President will not be a happy one.

In view of these circumstances, the barest extrapolation from current events, it hardly seems likely that the nation will have to worry about a too powerful Presidency, a legislative dictatorship (as President Ford claimed in over-zealous campaign rhetoric), judicial tyranny, or any of the other scare slogans of the day. There will be enough blame for everyone. The complaint will be that our political institutions are too weak in comparison to their responsibilities, not that one is too strong in relation to another.

PRESIDENTIAL POWER

If it is a question of who gets the blame, a President will still be first in war, in peace, and in the hearts of his countrymen, for he will remain the single most visible and most accountable political actor. If it is a question of whose views will prevail on the largest number of important issues over the longest period of time, Presidents will still beat out their competitors.

In order to be a consistent competitor Congress would have to speak with a single voice. The days are gone when House Speaker "Uncle" Joe Cannon held so much internal power that Presidents Theodore Roosevelt and William Howard Taft had to deal with him as if he were a foreign potentate. I refer not merely to independent Congressional election through a decentralized party system in which no person owes election to another (though it is worth reminding ourselves of this fact of life) but also to the continuing dispersal of power. The tendency of every procedural reform (save one) is to disperse substantive power. The more Congressmen are forced to work out in the open, the less they are able to concert with one another in private. The more difficult it is to compromise their differences, the less they are able to oppose the Chief Executive. The decline of seniority may permit talent to be substituted for age; it also guarantees that Congress will provide less attractive careers for people with whom Presidents have had to deal, not once but indefinitely. Participatory democracy may have many virtues but institutional cohesion is not likely to be one of them. Enhancing the ability of individual legislators to express themselves is not equivalent to uniting them in behalf of a common program.

The exception is the budget reform. If successful, it would, by relating revenue to expenditure, enable Congress to maintain its power of the purse. But the prognosis is problematic. The impetus for change came from the excessive and extreme use of impoundment by President Nixon. Whether this was only a temporary abuse, or represents adaptation to a situation in which Congressmen like to get credit for spending but blame Presidents for taxation, remains to be seen.

If the new House and Senate budget committees attempt to act like cabinets on the British model, which enforce their preferences on the legislature, they will fail. Cabinets are committees that tolerate no rivals and Congress is composed of rivals. If the budget committees permit too many deviations, or are overruled too often, it will become clear that expenditures are out of control. Power will pass to the Executive. Impoundment *de facto* will be replaced by impoundment *de jure*, for everyone will know that without fiscal responsibility there can be no financial power. Since future increases are built into present budgets — increases in social security benefits may well take

up all the slack for over a decade unless there are to be huge deficits —
Congressional restraint in the face of desire for social programs may
collapse.

Parties would not be anyone's current "man-on-a-horse" to control
Presidents. The Republican National Committee avoided implication in Watergate because President Nixon was able to brush it aside
in order to run his own campaign. Nevertheless, the party must
accept a large share of the blame. If party leaders may be excused for
not stopping Watergate before it got started, they must surely be
faulted for not halting the cover-up once it became visible. The
remarkable thing was the President's perseverance in the pattern of
secret . . . forced revelation . . . new secret . . . new forced revelation
. . . ad nauseam. Had there been party leaders (Congressmen, national committee members, governors, state chairmen, city "bosses")
with power in their own jurisdictions, they could have descended on
the President en masse and said they would denounce him if he did
not do the right thing. They, at least, had to be told the truth so they
could judge the truth to tell. But this scenario did not occur. Why
not?

The nation lacks party leaders because its parties are weak. The
same weakness that allows a Barry Goldwater or a George
McGovern, candidates without substantial popular support, to take
the nomination for President also makes party leaders ineffective in
bringing pressure to bear on their President. At a time when the
nation most needs the restraint on office holders exercised by organizations with an interest in the long-term repute of their party, it can
no longer call on them. The price of making parties too weak to do
harm turns out to be rendering party leaders too useless to do good.

What is in it for anyone to be a hardworking member of a political
party? Except for the few who go on to public office, all the party
activist can expect is abuse. What used to be candidate selection is
now determined in primaries; what used to be patronage is now called
civil service; what used to be status has turned into sneer. The
politician has replaced the rich man as he who will as soon enter
heaven as a camel passeth through the eye of a needle.

Reform, which one might think would strengthen parties, is in fact
designed to weaken them. Once a candidate gets financial support
from the government, he has less use not only for "fat cat" financiers
but for "lean kitten" party politicians. The latest version of "The
Incumbent Protection Act" will not make legislators more amenable
to party considerations. New rules for party conferences and conventions stress expression at the expense of election. It is as if the
Democratic Party did not know itself but had to discover who it was at
the last minute by descending into the streets. Instead of being a place
where the party meets to choose candidates who can win elections,

conventions become a site for expressing the delegates' awareness of who they are. The politics of existentialism replaces the existence of politics.

The demise of parties is paralleled by the rise of citizen lobbies like Common Cause whose main thrust is to weaken other intermediary organizations—parties, labor unions, trade associations—that stand between citizen and government. Largely middle-class and upper-middle-class in composition, these "public interest" lobbies seek to reduce the influence of "private interests" by limiting the money they can contribute or the activities they can carry on to mold politicians or shape legislation. The sun that these laws are supposed to bring to politics, however, does not shine equally on all classes. Without strong unions and parties, workers will find that "open" hearings will, in effect, be "closed" to them. Corporations will continue to use lobbyists but they can pack no meetings. Only citizen lobbies combine the cash and the flexible hours of middle-class professionals needed to produce "mass" mobilization aimed at specific targets. Eventually as intermediary groups decline, the idea will grow that lively citizen lobbies should replace moribund political parties. But as the lobbies weaken the capacity of social interests to bargain, they will discover that they cannot perform the integrative function of parties.

POLITICS IN THE LIBERAL SOCIETY

If party and legislature cannot constrain Presidents, can the press do the job? It can do its jobs—to expose and to ventilate—but it cannot do the President's job: to provide leadership in critical areas of public policy. So long as people are concerned with abuse of power, the press will be powerful. Its essentially negative role is then viewed in a positive light. But when the pervasive problem in government is lack of power, the critical virtues of the media of information will become their carping vices.

Today we have become accustomed to certain constants: Presidents are rarely satisfied with their portrayal in the media of information, and reporters and commentators constantly complain about attempts to mislead or control them. They never seem to find a President who loves public criticism; he never seems to find a press and television that love him. It is in the President's interest to put the best gloss he can on things, and it is the reporter's vocation to find out what is "really" happening. Presidents are judged on the news and they can't help wishing it were good. But the news cannot be good when conditions are bad. No President in the near future will get good grades and every President will want to flunk the press.

The media, after all, are part of society. They reflect the dissatisfactions with government that grew in the 1960's. Scoops used to go to reporters who played along; today Pulitzer prizes go to reporters who get things they are not supposed to have. The leak of the Pentagon Papers, which did so much to galvanize the Nixon Administration in precisely the wrong way, would not have been possible without a public opinion to which challenging government had become infinitely more respectable than it was a decade before. Any reporter in Britain, whatever his party and policy preferences, is more a part of the permanent government (the elites that rule this time or expect to next time) than is any reporter in America, even if his favorite occupies the White House. Newsmen are not merely observers; they are also, in David S. Broder's apt title, "Political Reporters in Presidential Politics."

The perennial quarrel between the press and the President inadvertently points up an aspect of their relationship that is more important than whether one institution gets along with the other: Like everyone else in America, the press is fascinated by the Presidency. If its exaltation of the incumbent has declined, its fixation on him has not. Whom the press talks about is as important as what it says (if not more so). The media reinforce the identification of the Presidency with the political system.

People generally ask why their Presidents are doing so little rather than so much. Since America is a liberal society, it is not surprising that its people developed a liberal theory of the Presidency. All power to the Presidency? We never quite went that far. What is good for the Presidency is good for the country—we came near to that. The people wanted a New Deal, and a President gave it to them. They wanted egalitarian social legislation and, on the whole, Presidents were disposed to give it to them. The people wanted more, and Presidents could promise more. They wanted novelty, and Presidents provided it—new frontiers, great societies, fair deals, crusades. . . .

By comparison, Congress appeared confused, courts seemed mired in precedent, and bureaucracies were tangled in red tape. Checks turned into obstructions and balances became dead weights. The separation of powers looked like an 18th-century anachronism in a 20th-century world. In short, we were concerned with results, and unconcerned with institutions. The idea that the Presidency was implicated in a system of checks and balances, that the safety of the nation lay not in individual virtue but in institutional arrangements, was, though given lip service, in fact given short shrift. Once again, soon enough, the people will want a strong, action-oriented President to override obstructive courts and dilatory and divided Congresses.

BUREAUCRATIC FRUSTRATIONS

The real rival to the Presidency will be the bureaucracy, if not by intent, then through inadvertence. It is not so much that bureaucrats might resist a Presidential lead, though they might, but that such leads will be increasingly hard to give. The sheer size of government means that the Executive Office inevitably knows less about what is going on and what to do about it than it has in the past. Nor can any one person, including the President, know more than a small proportion of what his staff knows, which in turn is only part of the picture. The more frequently that government tries to intervene more deeply in society, the less anyone is able to control events and further removed the Presidency is bound to be from what is actually going on. When government is over-burdened, bureaucracy becomes unbearable; the march of complexity is mainly responsible for the mounting frustration of Presidents with "their" bureaucrats.

When Richard Fenno first published his classic study *The President's Cabinet* in 1959, it appeared that this cadre was at its lowest ebb. Its lack of a collective interest in decisions made by others and its dependence on the President rather than on Cabinet colleagues explained why it had never really been strong in the history of American politics. Under Presidents Kennedy, Johnson, and Nixon, however, the Cabinet appeared not merely weak but virtually non-existent. Its former low ebb seems, in retrospect, almost to have been its high tide.

What happened? In the old days, Presidents mistrusted the Cabinet because they were not entirely free in choosing its members. They had, in effect, to "give away" appointments to important party factions outside the government and to powerful Congressmen inside. The decline of party in American political life, however, has meant that recent Presidents have not been beholden to it. The increasing diffusion of power within Congress has also meant that there were correspondingly fewer powerful leaders whom Presidents have had to cater to in making appointments. Yet their increased freedom in selecting Cabinet members apparently has not led Presidents to confer greater trust on their appointees. Why not?

Secretaries of the great departments must serve more than one master. They are necessarily beholden to Congress for appropriations and for substantive legislation. They are expected to speak for the major interests entrusted to their care, as well as for the President. They need cooperation from the bureaucracy that surrounds them, and they may have to make accommodations to get that support. A Secretary of Agriculture who is vastly unpopular with farmers, a Secretary of Interior who is hated by conservationists, and all Secretaries whose employees undermine their efforts, cannot be of much use to the Chief Executive. Nevertheless, Presidents (and especially their personal staffs) appear to behave as if there were something wrong when Cabinet members do what comes naturally to people in their positions.

To the White House staff the separation of powers is anathema. They have wonderful ideas, apparently, only to see them sabotaged in the bureaucratic labyrinth. How dare those bureaucrats get in the way! The notion that the departments might owe something to Congress or that there is more to policy than what the President and his men want flickers only occasionally across their minds. It is as if the Presidency were THE government. The President's men tend to see themselves not as part of a larger system, but as the system itself.

Alternatively, going to the other extreme, consider the image of a beleaguered outpost in the White House with all the insignia of office but without the ability to command troops in the provinces. As Arthur Schlesinger, Jr. put it when reflecting on his experiences as an adviser to President Kennedy in A *Thousand Days*, "Wherever we have gone wrong . . . [it] has been because we have not had sufficient confidence in the New Frontier approach to impose it on the government. Every important mistake has been the consequence of excessive deference to the permanent government. . . ." Small wonder, then, that Presidents in later times have interpreted discontent with their policies or their behavior not as evidence of the intractability of the policy problems themselves but as another effort by the "big bad bureaucracy" (readily expanded to include the "establishment press") to frustrate the people.

COURTS AND THE CURBING OF POWER

The protection afforded by the courts in the Watergate case really shows how limited their role must be. If we are to depend on future criminal actions to control Presidents, if they can do anything they please that isn't plainly illegal, then they can do "most anything." It is no derogation of the courts to say that they are (with a few notable exceptions) reactive. They may tell others what to do after (usually a long time after) the fact, but they cannot compete with executives and legislatures for control of future choices. Indeed, efforts to alter future behavior by writing into law (or interpreting) prohibitions against specific past events are bound to fail.

The legal profession has the right aphorism: Hard cases make bad law. Congress has, after the fact, passed the War Powers Act to restrict Presidents in the future. In my opinion, the gesture was futile and possibly dangerous. Basically, the act provides that within 60 days of the commencement of hostilities the President must receive positive Congressional approval, or the military action grinds to a halt. Would this law have stopped Vietnam? That is doubtful because of the spirit prevailing at the time of the Gulf of Tonkin Resolution. Will it enable a President to respond when necessary and restrain him when essential? Such judgments, I fear, are more readily made in retrospect than in prospect. My concern is that the War Powers Act can be converted too easily into a permanent Gulf of Tonkin Resolution bestowing a legislative benediction in advance on Presidential actions, by which time Congress has little choice left. Now Presidents can point to a statute saying that they can do what they want (the Mayaguez affair should dispose of the requirement for consultation) for up to 60 days. The lesser defect lies in trying to anticipate the specific configuration of events by general statutory principles. The greater defect lies in trying to frame general principles on the basis of the most recent horrible event. And the greatest defect resides in treating a systemic problem, whose resolution depends on the interaction of numerous parts in a dynamic environment, as if it were a defect in a single component operating in a static situation.

History shows, to be sure, that constitutions are often written against the last usurper—the United States Constitution against the Articles of Confederation, the Fifth French Republic against the Fourth and the Third, Bonn against Weimar, the United Nations contra the League of Nations. So, too, do generals frequently end up preparing for the last war. But this is not quite so bad as aiming living constitutional provisions at dead targets. The nation has not been well served by the anti-third-term (read anti-Franklin Roosevelt) amendment, which guarantees that if the people ever find a President they deem worth keeping in office, they will have prohibited themselves from doing so. In the guise of denying power to Presidents, it has, in fact, been denied to the people. Were it not for the two-term limitation, moreover, we would be spared the current nonsense of proposing a single six-year term. Why some people think popular control over Presidents would be increased by taking them out of the electoral arena after they assume office must remain a mystery.

The difficulties judges face in trying to capture a probabilistic process of institutional interaction in a deterministic principle is nowhere better illustrated than in the recent pronouncement of the Supreme Court on executive privilege. In the old days an assertion of executive privilege had no legal status. No one knew what it meant, which was just the way things should be. Presidents needed confidentiality; Congress needed information; these self-evident truths were left to contend with each other according to the circumstances of the time and the pulling and hauling of the participants. Eventually an accommodation was reached that lasted until the question was raised again under altered conditions. Richard Nixon changed all that by bending the principle so far that it broke in his hands. Although the

Supreme Court could not quite put executive privilege back together
again, it went one step beyond by giving legal sanction to a doctrine
that never had one. .n order to achieve a unanimous opinion that
President Nixon had to give up the tapes, the Supreme Court apparently felt it necessary to distinguish this case from all others by
declaring that executive privilege might exist in other cases but
manifestly not in this one. For the first time, future Presidents will be
able to cite an opinion to the effect that there is a legal basis for
executive privilege.

Suppose all the other institutions—Congress, courts, bureaucracies, parties—ganged up on the Presidency: Couldn't they curb
Presidential power? No doubt they could. But the likelihood of their
all getting together is small, unless they face a common threat. Now
what President would be so foolish as to attack each and every other
institution all at the same time? Nixon, of course—the House on
expenditures, the Senate on foreign policy, the media on misinfor-
mation, the courts on credibility, and on and on. Are we then to think
of Watergate as the modal condition of the Presidency? No, it is more
like a limiting condition: Many things have to go wrong at once
before the Presidency enters into a knockabout against all comers. If
future Presidents have to do all that Nixon did before their wings are
clipped, they will win every race against their institutional competitors.

There are, to be sure, contrary trends that might lead to the
emergence of demogogic Presidents who would hold sway over the
multitudes. The decline in party identification leaves latitude for
personality differences among the candidates to show up in the form
of landslide majorities. And the growing influence of issue enthusiasts in national nominating conventions means that the major
parties are more likely to nominate candidates preferred by their
extremes but rejected by the population at large. This is what happened to the Goldwater Republicans in 1964 and the McGovern
Democrats in 1972. But the popularity of the winners, Johnson and
Nixon, did not last long.

It is also possible that the very absence of consensus on foreign
policy and the very presence of contradictions at the heart of domestic
policy would lead to a call for a leader to overcome (or more accurately, suppress) these disturbing conditions. Under these circumstances, threats to liberty are likely to arise less from a desire for
personal Presidential aggrandizement, and more from mass insistence that power be exercised to eliminate ambiguity. The Presidential problem will not be power but performance.

THE FLIGHT OF THE PRESIDENCY

Perhaps the most interesting events of our time are those that have not occurred—the failure of demagogues, parties, or mass movements to take advantage of the national disarray. Maybe the country is in better shape than we think, or they (whoever "they" are) are waiting for things to get still worse. In any event, it now appears that the United States will have to get out of its predicaments with the same ordinary, everyday, homespun political institutions with which it got into them. How will its future leaders (preeminently its Presidents) appraise the political context in which they find themselves? For leadership is not a unilateral imposition but a mutual relationship, in which it is as important to know whether and wither people are willing to be led as why and where their leaders propose to take them.

When you bite the hand that feeds you, it moves out of range. That is the significance of the near-geometric increase in the size of the Executive Office from Truman's to Nixon's time. Originally a response to the growth of government, it became a means of insulating Presidents from the shocks of a society with which they could no longer cope.

As government tried to intervene both more extensively and more intensively in the lives of citizens, the executive office, in order to monitor these events, became a parallel bureaucracy. The larger it grew and the more programs it tried to cover, however, the more the Executive Office inadvertently but inevitably became further removed from the lives of the people who were being affected by these new operations. Then the inevitable became desirable and the inadvertent became functional; for as Presidents discovered that domestic programs paid no dividends—see Nixon's comment in the Watergate tapes about the futility of building more outhouses in Peoria—insulation from the people didn't seem such a bad idea.

After Watergate, it became necessary to reduce the size of the Executive Office and to increase the number of people reporting directly to the President, so as to show he was as different as possible from his predecessor. Disassociation from Watergate, however, is not the same as organization for action. Faced with a lack of consensus in foreign policy and an absence of support for domestic policy, future Presidents may well retreat in the face of overwhelming odds.

In the first months of Richard Nixon's second term, when his Administration was at full strength and he was attempting to chart a new course, he tried both to reorganize radically the federal bureaucracy and to alter drastically his own relations to it. In part, the idea was old—rationalize the bureaucracy by creating a smaller number of bigger departments, thus cutting down on the large number of people previously entitled to report directly to the President. Part of it was new—creating a small group of supersecretaries who would have jurisdiction over several departments, thus forming, in effect, an inner Cabinet. Part of it was peculiarly Nixonian—drastically reducing demands on his time and attention. Part of it, I believe, is likely to be permanent—adapting to the increasing scope and complexity of government by focusing Presidential energy on a few broadly defined areas of policy. Presidents have to deal with war and peace and with domestic prosperity or lack of it. There will continue to be a person the President relies on principally for advice in foreign and defense policy, and another on whom he relies for economic management. The demands on Presidents for response to other domestic needs vary with the times—so that there will undoubtedly be one or two other superadvisers, called by whatever names or holding whatever titles, to deal with race relations or energy or the environment or whatever else seems most urgent. The rest will be a residual category—domestic policy supervised by a domestic council—reserved for a Vice President or a Cabinet Coordinator.

The response to ever-increasing complexity will continue to be ever-greater simplicity. This is the rationale behind wholesaling instead of retailing domestic policies; behind revenue sharing instead of endless numbers of categorical grants; behind proposals for family assistance and negative income taxes instead of a multiplicity of welfare policies; behind a transfer to state and local governments of as much responsibility (though not necessarily as much money) as they can absorb. "Here is a lot of trouble and a little money," these Presidential policies seem to say, "so remember the trauma is all yours and none of mine."

THE "OFFENSIVE RETREAT"

Future Presidents will be preoccupied with operating strategic levers, not with making tactical moves. They will see their power stakes, to use Neustadt's term, in giving away their powers; like everyone else they will have to choose between what they have to keep and what they must give up. Not so much running the country (that was Nixon's error) but seeing that it is running will be their forte. The Cabinet, or at least the inner "Super-Secretary" Cabinet, will undergo a visible revival because Presidents will trade a little power for a lot of protection. The more prominent a President's Cabinet, the less of a target he becomes. When Presidents wanted to keep the credit, they kept their Cabinets quiet; but they will welcome Cabinet notoriety now that they want to spread the blame.

The "offensive retreat" of the Presidency will not be the work of a single President or a particular moment in time. Nor will this movement be unidirectional. Like most things, it will be a product of trial and error in which backsliding will be as prominent as forward movement. But as Presidents discover there is sickness in health and ignorance in education, they will worry more about their own welfare.

Presidents, and the governments for which they stand, are either doing too much or too little. They need either to do a great deal more for the people or a great deal less to them. They must be closer to what is happening or much further away. At present, they are close enough to get the blame but too far away to control the result; for government to be half involved is to be wholly abused. Which way will it move?

One way is nationalization. The federal government would take over all areas of serious interest; there would be a National Health Service, a National Welfare System, and the like. Industry would go to the top but so would the power. Presidents would literally be running the country. The danger of overload at the center would be mitigated by mastery of the periphery. Uncle Sam would be everybody's tough Uncle and it would not be wise to push him around. Before it comes to this, however, Presidents will try to move in other directions.

Presidents will seek the fewest levers but those with the most consequential effects. They will be money men, manipulating the supply to citizens through income floors and the supply to business through banks. Taxes will vary with expenditures; if government spends more, taxes will go up, and if it spends less, they will go down, with the upper limit set by constitutional limitation. Income will determine outgo. Regulatory activities and agencies will be severed from all Presidential connection; why should Presidents get into trouble for fixing the price of milk or determining routes for airlines or setting railroad rates? States and localities will undertake whatever supplementary programs they are willing and able to support.

Presidents will handle systemic crises, not ordinary events. They will be responsible for war and peace abroad, and life and death at home, but not much in between. The people will not call on their President when they are in trouble. The President will call on his people when he is in trouble, for Presidents will represent the general interest in maintaining essential services and institutions, not the private and personal interests of every individual in his and her own fate.

PRESIDENTIAL PROSPECTS

The framers of our Constitution intended that its overarching structure should restrain each institution through the mutual interaction of its parts. Citizens should now see that their safety lies in that restraint. So long as the Presidency is seen as part of the system, subject to its checks and balances, citizens retain hope and show calm. The institutional lesson to be learned, therefore, is not that the Presidency should be diminished but that other institutions should grow in stature. The first order of priority should go to rebuilding our political parties, because they are most in need of help and could do most to bring Presidents in line with strong sentiments in the country. Had there been Republican "elders" of sufficient size and weight, the President representing their party could not have so readily strayed in his perception of the popular will. Whatever its other defects, a party provides essential connective tissue between people and government. So do the media. So does Congress; strengthening its appropriations process through internal reform would bring it more power than any external threat could take away. The people need the vigor of all their institutions.

Strengthening the political system as a whole will not necessarily weaken the Presidency. On the other hand, making the Presidency into the government would not only threaten liberty but leave it without support in times of adversity. No one wants to be president of a bankrupt company; Chairman of the board of a going concern is more like it. The national objective should be to increase total systemic capacity in relation to emerging problems. One way to do this is to lower people's expectations of what government and its leaders can do for them. Maybe that is what Watergate has tried to tell us. Another way is to depend on leadership. Maybe that is what President Ford's pardon of his predecessor should teach us not to do.

For 30 halcyon days the people of the United States had a President they could trust. This hope and trust was a precious national resource. Its dissipation was a national calamity. For it did not belong to Ford alone but was bestowed upon him by virtue of the circumstance under which he entered office. His task was to husband and preserve it for the dark days ahead. This was not only his but also the nation's most precious stock of political capital and he squandered it with a sudden wastefulness. If it were a question of the former President suffering more and the people less, Ford clearly mistook his priorities.

The voice of Ezekiel—"Son of man, trust not in man"—has a contemporary echo. If only Nixon went, the hope was, a leader would arise among us. Apparently not. The resignation and pardon warn against passive dependence on leaders. The wisdom of a democracy must lie in its "separated institutions sharing power." The virtues of a democracy must ultimately be tested, not in the leadership of its fallible men, but in the enduring power of its great institutions.

But institutions are not everything. They function in a climate of opinion that both limits and shapes what they can do. Those who operate them respond to the rewards and punishments of the environment in which they are situated. A people who punish truthfulness will get lies; a people who reward symbolic actions will get rhetoric instead of realism. So long as the people appear to make contradictory demands for domestic policies, they will be supplied by contrary politicians. Until the country is prepared to support a foreign policy that is responsive to new events, it will continue to nourish old misunderstandings.

Long before the current disenchantment, Henry Fairlie, in his book *The Kennedy Promise*, had questioned whether Americans did not have too exalted an opinion of what politics (and hence Presidents) could do. To some, Kennedy's Camelot recedes in the shimmering distance as nobility thwarted, its light tragically extinguished before its time. Fairlie discerned in the Kennedys an excessive conception of what government could do, a sense of politics over society that would come to no good. As he puts it, "The people are encouraged to expect too much of their political institutions and of their political leaders. They cease to inquire what politics may accomplish for them, and what they must do for themselves. Instead, they expect politics to take the place religion once held in their lives. . . ." When leaders were gods, it is worth recalling, they punished their people.

Public officials need to know they cannot lead by following a people that does not know where it wants to go, or how to get there. They must persuade themselves—and, in so doing, the people they wish to lead—that no one can have it all or at the same time. As officials seek to improve their public performance, they must simultaneously strive to shape popular expectations, for unless the two meet there can be no hope for (and perhaps no distinction between) the leaders and the led. If they fail, leaders will move not with but from their people. If they succeed, then the short-term predictions of this essay—the flight of the Presidency from its people—need not become the longer-run prognostication for the larger political system.

☆

THOMAS E. CRONIN: *The Presidency and Its Paradoxes*

Why is the Presidency such a bewildering office? Why do presidents so often look like losers? Why is the general public so disapproving of recent presidential performances, and so predictably less supportive the longer a President stays in office?

The search for explanations leads in several directions. Vietnam and the Watergate scandals must be considered. Then, too, the personalities of Lyndon B. Johnson and Richard M. Nixon doubtless were factors that soured many people on the office. Observers also claim that the institution is structurally defective — that it encourages isolation, palace guards, "groupthink" and arrogance.

Yet something else seems at work. Our expectations of, and demands on, the office are frequently so paradoxical as to invite two-faced behavior by our presidents. We seem to want so much so fast that a President, whose powers are often simply not as great as many of us believe, gets condemned as ineffectual. Or a President often will overreach or resort to unfair play while trying to live up to our demands. Either way, presidents seem to become locked into a rather high number of no-win situations.

Thomas E. Cronin is Professor of Political Science at the University of Delaware and Visiting Research Professor at Colorado College. This article is from Thomas E. Cronin and Rexford G. Tugwell, eds., *The Presidency Reappraised* 2nd ed. (New York: Praeger Publishers, 1977). Copyright © 1977 by Praeger Publishers. Reprinted by permission of the publisher and the author.

The Constitution is of little help in explaining any of this. The Founding Fathers purposely were vague and left the Presidency imprecisely defined. They knew well that the Presidency would have to provide the capability for swift and competent executive action; yet they went to considerable lengths to avoid enumerating specific powers and duties, so as to calm the then pervasive popular fear of monarchy.

In any event, the informal and symbolic powers of the Presidency today account for as much as the formal ones. Further, presidential powers expand and contract in response to varying situational and technological changes. Thus, the powers of the Presidency are interpreted in ways so markedly different as to seem to describe different offices. In some ways the modern Presidency has virtually unlimited authority for nearly anything its occupant chooses to do with it. In other ways, however, our beliefs and hopes about the Presidency very much shape the character and quality of the presidential performances we get.

The modern (post-Roosevelt II) Presidency is bounded and constrained by various expectations that are decidedly paradoxical. Presidents and presidential candidates must constantly balance themselves between conflicting demands. It has been suggested by more than one observer that it is a characteristic of the American mind to hold contradictory ideas simultaneously without bothering to resolve the potential conflicts between them. Perhaps some paradoxes are best left unresolved. But we should, at least, better appreciate what it is we expect of our presidents and would-be presidents. For it could well be that our paradoxical expectations and the imperatives of the job make for schizophrenic presidential performances.

We may not be able to resolve the inherent contradictions and dilemmas these paradoxes point up. Still, a more rigorous understanding of these conflicts and no-win or near no-win situations should make possible a more refined sensitivity to the limits of what a President can achieve. Exaggerated or hopelessly contradictory public expectations tend to encourage presidents to attempt more than they can accomplish and to overpromise and overextend themselves.

Perhaps, too, an assessment of the paradoxed Presidency may impel us anew to revise some of our unrealistic expectations concerning presidential performance and the institution of the Presidency and encourage, in turn, the nurturing of alternative sources or centers for national leadership.

A more realistic appreciation of presidential paradoxes might help presidents concentrate on the practicable among their priorities. A more sophisticated and tolerant consideration of the modern Presidency and its paradoxes might relieve the load so that a President can better lead and administer in those critical realms in which the nation

has little choice but to turn to him. Whether we like it or not, the
vitality of our democracy still depends in large measure on that
sensitive interaction of presidential leadership with an understanding
public willing to listen and willing to provide support when a President can persuade. Carefully planned innovation is nearly impossible without the kind of leadership a competent and fair-minded
President can provide.

Each of the ten paradoxes following is based on apparent logical
contradictions. Each has important implications for presidential
performance and public evaluation of presidential behavior. A better
understanding may lead to the removal, reconciliation, or more
enlightened toleration of the contradictions to which they give rise.

1. THE GENTLE AND DECENT BUT FORCEFUL AND DECISIVE PRESIDENT PARADOX

Opinion polls time and again indicate that people want a just,
decent, humane "man of good faith" in the White House. Honesty
and trustworthiness repeatedly top the list of qualities the public
values most highly in a President these days. However, the public just
as strongly demands the qualities of toughness, decisiveness, even a
touch of ruthlessness.

Adlai Stevenson, George McGovern, and Gerald Ford were all
criticized for being "too nice," "too decent." (Ford's decisive action in
the *Mayaguez* affair was an exception, and perhaps predictably, his
most significant gain in the Gallup Poll—eleven points—came
during and immediately after the episode.) Being a "Mr. Nice Guy"
is too easily equated with being too soft. The public dislikes the idea
of a weak, spineless, or sentimental person in the White House.

Morris Udall, who was widely viewed as a decidedly decent candidate in the 1976 race for the Democratic nomination, had to advertise himself as a man of strength. He used a quotation from House
Majority Leader Thomas P. O'Neill in full-page newspaper ads that
read, "We need a Democratic president who's tough enough to take
on big business. Mo Udall is tough." The image sought was unquestionably that of toughness of character.

Perhaps, too, this paradox may explain the extraordinary public
fondness for President Dwight D. Eisenhower. For at one and the
same time he was blessed with a benign smile and reserved, calming
disposition and yet also was the disciplined, strong, no-nonsense
five-star general with all the medals and victories to go along with it.
His ultimate resource as President was this reconciliation of decency
and decisiveness, likability alongside demonstrated valor.

During the 1976 presidential campaign, Jimmy Carter appeared to
appreciate one of the significant by-products of this paradox. He
pointed out that the American male is handicapped in his expressions

of religious faith by those requisite "macho" qualities of overt strength, toughness, and firmness. Carter's personal reconciliation of this paradox is noteworthy: "But a truer demonstration of strength would be concern, compassion, love, devotion, sensitivity, humility — exactly the things Christ talked about — and I believe that if we can demonstrate this kind of personal awareness of our own faith we can provide that core of strength and commitment and underlying character that our nation searches for."

Thus this paradox highlights one of the distinctive frustrations for presidents and would-be presidents. Plainly, we demand a double-edged personality. We, in effect, demand the *sinister* as well as the *sincere*, President *Mean* and President *Nice* — tough and hard enough to stand up to a Khrushchev or to press the nuclear button; compassionate enough to care for the ill-fed, ill-clad, ill-housed. The public in this case "seems to want a softhearted son of a bitch," as a friend of mine, Alan Otten, aptly put it. It's a hard role to cast, a harder role to perform for eight years.

2. THE PROGRAMMATIC BUT PRAGMATIC LEADER PARADOX

We want both a *programmatic* (committed on the issues and with a detailed program) and a *pragmatic* (flexible and open, even change-able) person in the White House. We want a *moral* leader; yet the job forces the President to become a *constant compromiser.*

On the one hand, Franklin D. Roosevelt proclaimed that the Presidency is pre-eminently a place for moral leadership. On the other hand, Governor Jerry Brown aptly notes that "a little vagueness goes a long way in this business."

A President who becomes too committed risks being called rigid; a President who becomes too pragmatic risks being called wishy-washy. The secret, of course, is to stay the course by stressing character, competence, rectitude, and experience, and by avoiding strong stands that offend important segments of the population.

Jimmy Carter was especially criticized by the press and others for avoiding commitments and stressing his "flexibility" on the issues. This prompted a major discussion of what came to be called the "fuzziness issue." Jokes spread the complaint. One went as follows: "When you eat peanut butter all your life, your tongue sticks to the roof of your mouth, and you have to talk out of both sides." Still, his "maybe I will and maybe I won't" strategy proved very effective in overcoming critics and opponents who early on claimed he didn't have a chance. Carter talked quietly about the issues and carried a big smile. In fact, of course, he took stands on almost all the issues, but being those of a centrist or a pragmatic moderate, his stands were either not liked or dismissed as nonstands by most liberals and conservatives — especially purists.

What strikes one person as fuzziness or even duplicity appeals to another person as remarkable political skill, the very capacity for compromise and negotiation that is required if a President is to maneuver through the political minefields that come with the job.

Most candidates view a campaign as a fight to win office, not an opportunity for adult education. Barry Goldwater in 1964 may have run with the slogan "We offer a *choice* not an echo," referring to his unusually thematic strategy, but Republican Party regulars who, more pragmatically, aspired to win the election preferred "a *chance* not a *choice*." Once in office, presidents often operate the same way; the electoral connection looms large as an issue-avoiding, controversy-ducking political incentive. Most presidents also strive to *maximize their options*, and hence leave matters up in the air or delay choices. JFK mastered this strategy, whereas on Vietnam LBJ permitted himself to be trapped into his tragically irreparable corner because his options had so swiftly dissolved. Indeed, this yearning to maximize their options may well be the core element of the pragmatism we so often see when we prefer moral leadership.

3. THE INNOVATIVE AND INVENTIVE YET MAJORITARIAN AND RESPONSIVE PRESIDENCY PARADOX

One of the most compelling paradoxes at the very heart of our democratic system arises from the fact that we expect our presidents to provide bold, innovative leadership and yet respond faithfully to public-opinion majorities.

Walter Lippmann warned against letting public opinion become the chief guide for leadership in America, but he just as forcefully warned democratic leaders: Don't be right too soon, for public opinion will lacerate you! Hence, most presidents fear being in advance of their times. They must *lead us*, but also *listen to us*.

Put simply, we want our presidents to offer leadership, to be architects of the future and providers of visions, plans, and goals, and at the same time we want them to stay in close touch with the sentiments of the people. To *talk* about high ideals, New Deals, Big Deals, and the like is one thing. But the public resists being *led* too far in any one direction.

Most of our presidents have been conservatives or at best "pragmatic liberals." They have seldom ventured much beyond the crowd. John F. Kennedy, the author of the much acclaimed *Profiles in Courage*, was often criticized for presenting more profile than courage; if political risks could be avoided, he shrewdly avoided them. Kennedy was fond of pointing out that he had barely won the election in 1960 and that great innovations should not be forced upon a leader with such a slender mandate. Ironically, Kennedy is credited with encouraging widespread public participation in politics. But he repeatedly reminded Americans that caution was needed, that the important issues are complicated, technical, and best left to the administrative and political experts. As Bruce Miroff writes in *Pragmatic Illusions*, Kennedy seldom attempted to change the political context in which he operated:

> More significantly, he resisted the new form of politics emerging with the civil rights movement: mass action, argument on social fundamentals, appeals to considerations of justice and morality. Moving the American political system in such a direction would necessarily have been long range, requiring arduous educational work and promising substantial political risk. The pragmatic Kennedy wanted no part of such an unpragmatic undertaking.

Presidents can get caught whether they are coming or going. The public wants them to be both *leaders* of the country and *representatives* of the people. We want them to be decisive and rely mainly on their own judgment; yet we want them to be very responsive to public opinion, especially to the "common sense" of our own opinions. It was perhaps with this in mind that an English essayist once defined the ideal democratic leader as an "uncommon man of common opinions."

4. THE INSPIRATIONAL BUT "DON'T PROMISE MORE THAN YOU CAN DELIVER" LEADER PARADOX

We ask our presidents to raise hopes, to educate, to inspire. But too much inspiration will invariably lead to dashed hopes, disillusionment, and cynicism. The best of leaders often suffer from one of their chief virtues — an instinctive tendency to raise aspirations, to summon us to transcend personal needs and subordinate ourselves to dreaming dreams of a bolder, more majestic America.

We enjoy the upbeat rhetoric and promises of a brighter tomorrow. We genuinely want to hear about New Nationalism, New Deals, New Frontiers, Great Societies, and New American Revolutions; we want our fears to be assuaged during a "fireside chat" or a "conversation with the President"; we want to be told that "the torch has been passed to a new generation of Americans . . . and the glow from that fire can truly light the world."

We want our fearless leaders to tell us that "peace is at hand," that the "only fear we have to fear is fear itself," that "we are Number One," that a recession has "bottomed out," and that "we are a great people." So much do we want the "drive of a lifting dream," to use Nixon's awkward phrase, that the American people are easily duped by presidential promises.

Do presidents overpromise because they are congenital optimists or because they are pushed into it by the demanding public? Surely the answer is an admixture of both. But whatever the source, few presidents in recent times have been able to keep their promises and fulfill their intentions. Poverty was not ended; a Great Society was not realized. Vietnam dragged on and on. Watergate outraged a public that had been promised an open Presidency. Energy independence remains an illusion just as crime in the streets continues to rise.

A President who does not raise hopes is criticized for letting events shape his Presidency rather than making things happen. A President who eschewed inspiration of any kind would be rejected as un-American. For as a poet once wrote, "America is promises." For people everywhere, cherishing the dream of individual liberty and self-fulfillment, America has been the land of promises, of pos-sibilities, of dreams. No President can stand in the way of this truth, no matter how much the current dissatisfaction about the size of big government in Washington and its incapacity to deliver the services it promises.

William Allen White, the conservative columnist, went to the heart of this paradox when he wrote of Herbert Hoover. President Hoover, he noted, is a great executive, a splendid desk man. "But he cannot dramatize his leadership. A democracy cannot follow a leader unless he is dramatized."

5. THE OPEN AND SHARING BUT COURAGEOUS AND INDEPENDENT PRESIDENCY PARADOX

We unquestionably cherish our three-branched system with its checks and balances and its theories of dispersed and separated powers. We want our presidents not only to be sincere but to share their powers with their cabinets, Congress, and other "responsible" national leaders. In theory, we oppose the concentration of power, we dislike secrecy, and we resent depending on any one person to provide all of our leadership. In recent years (the 1970s in particular), there have been repeated calls for a more open, accountable, and de-royalized Presidency.

On the other hand, we reject a too secularized Presidency. We reject, as well, the idea that complete openness is a solution; indeed, it has been suggested, instead, that the great presidents have been the strong presidents, who stretched their legal authority, who occasion-ally relied on the convenience of secrecy, and who dominated the other branches of government. This point of view argues that the country, in fact, often yearns for a hero in the White House, that the human heart ceaselessly reinvents royalty, and that Roosevelts and Camelots, participatory democracy notwithstanding, are vital to the success of America.

If some people feel we are getting to the point where all of us would like to see a demythologized Presidency, others claim we need myth, we need symbol. As a friend of mine put it, "I don't think we could live without the myth of a glorified Presidency, even if we wanted to. We just aren't that rational. Happily, we're too human for that. We will either live by the myth that has served us fairly well for almost two hundred years or we will probably find a much worse one."

The clamor for a truly open or collegial Presidency was opposed on other grounds by the late Harold Laski when he concluded that Americans, in practice, want to rally round a President who can demonstrate his independence and vigor:

> A President who is believed not to make up his own mind rapidly loses the power to maintain the hold. The need to dramatize his position by insistence upon his undoubted supremacy is inherent in the office as history has shaped it. A masterful man in the White House will, under all circumstances, be more to the liking of the multitude than one who is thought to be swayed by his colleagues.

Thus we want our President not only to be both a lion and a fox, but more than a lion, more than a fox. We want simultaneously a secular leader and a civil religious mentor; we praise our three-branched system, but we place capacious hopes upon and thus elevate the presidential branch. Only the President can give us heroic leadership, or so most people feel. Only a President can dramatize and symbolize our highest expectations of ourselves as almost a chosen people with a unique mission. Note too that only the President is regularly honored with a musical anthem of his own: "Hail to the Chief." If it seems a little hypocritical for a semisovereign people deferentially to delegate so much hierarchical stature and semiautocratic power to their President, this is nonetheless precisely what we continually do.

We want an open Presidency, and we oppose the concentration of vast power in any one position. Still, we want forceful, courageous displays of leadership from our presidents. Anything less than that is condemned as aimlessness or loss of nerve. Further, we praise those who leave the Presidency stronger than it was when they entered.

6. THE TAKING THE PRESIDENCY OUT OF POLITICS PARADOX

The public yearns for a statesman in the White House, for a George Washington or a second "era of good feelings" — anything that might prevent partisanship or politics-as-usual in the White House. In fact, however, the job of a President demands that he be a gifted political broker, ever attentive to changing political moods and coalitions.

Franklin Roosevelt illustrates this paradox well. Appearing so remarkably nonpartisan while addressing the nation, he was in practice one of the craftiest political coalition-builders to occupy the White House. He mastered the art of politics — the art of making the difficult and desirable possible.

A President is expected to be above politics in some respects and highly political in others. A President is never supposed to act with his eye on the next election; he's not supposed to favor any particular group or party. Nor is he supposed to wheel and deal or to twist too many arms. That's politics and that's bad! No, a President, or so most people are inclined to believe, is supposed to be "President of all the people." On the other hand, he is asked to be the head of his party, to help friendly members of Congress get elected or re-elected, to deal firmly with party barons and congressional political brokers. Too, he must build political coalitions around what he feels needs to be done.

To take the President out of politics is to assume, incorrectly, that a President will be so generally right and the general public so generally wrong that a President must be protected from the push and shove of political pressures. But what President has always been right? Over the years, public opinion has been usually as sober a guide as anyone else on the political waterfront. Anyway, having a President constrained and informed by public opinion is what a democracy is all about.

In his re-election campaign of 1972, Richard Nixon in vain sought to display himself as too busy to be a politician: He wanted the American people to believe he was too preoccupied with the Vietnam War to have any personal concern about his election. In one sense, Nixon may have destroyed this paradox for at least a while. Have not the American people learned that we *cannot* have a President *above* politics?

If past is prologue, presidents in the future will go to considerable lengths to portray themselves as unconcerned with their own political future. They will do so in large part because the public applauds the divorce between the Presidency and politics. People naively think that we can somehow turn the job of President into that of a managerial or strictly executive post. (The six-year, single-term proposal, reflects this paradox.) Not so. The Presidency is a highly political office, and it cannot be otherwise. Moreover, its political character is for the most part desirable. A President separated from, or somehow above, politics might easily become a President who doesn't listen to the people, doesn't respond to majority sentiment or pay attention to views that may be diverse, intense, and at variance with his own. A President immunized to politics would be a President who would too easily become isolated from the processes of government and removed from the thoughts and aspirations of his people.

In all probability, this paradox will endure. The standard diagnosis of what's gone wrong in an administration will be that the Presidency has become too politicized. But it will be futile to try to take the President out of politics. A more helpful approach is to realize that certain presidents try too hard to hold themselves above politics — or at least to give that appearance — rather than engage in it deeply, openly, and creatively enough. A President in a democracy has to act politically in regard to controversial issues if we are to have any semblance of government by the consent of the governed.

7. THE COMMON MAN WHO GIVES AN UNCOMMON PERFORMANCE PARADOX

We like to think that America is the land where the common sense of the common man reigns. We prize the common touch, the "man of the people." Yet few of us settle for anything but an uncommon performance from our presidents.

This paradox is splendidly summed up by some findings of a survey conducted by the Field Research Corporation, a California public-opinion organization. Field asked a cross-section of Californians in 1975 to describe in their own words the qualities a presidental candidate should have. Honesty and trustworthiness topped the list. But one of the organization's more intriguing findings was that "while most (72%) prefer someone with plain and simple tastes, there is also a strong preference (66%) for someone who can give exciting speeches and inspire the public."

It has been said that the American people crave to be governed by men who are both Everyman and yet better than Everyman. The Lincoln and Kennedy presidencies are illustrative. We cherish the myth that anyone can grow up to be President — that there are no barriers, no elite qualifications — but we don't want a person who is too ordinary. Would-be presidents have to prove their special qualifications — their excellence, their stamina, their capacity for uncommon leadership.

The Harry Truman reputation, at least as it flourished in the mid-1970s, demonstrates the apparent reconciliation of this paradox. Fellow commoner Truman rose to the demands of the job and became an apparent gifted decision-maker, or so his admirers would have us believe.

Candidate Carter in 1976 nicely fitted this paradox as well. Local, down-home farm boy next door makes good! The image of the peanut farmer turned gifted governor and talented campaigner contributed greatly to Carter's success as a national candidate, and he used it with consummate skill. Early on in his presidential bid, Carter enjoyed introducing himself as a peanut farmer *and* a nuclear physicist — yet another way of suggesting he was down-to-earth but cerebral as well.

A President or would-be President must be bright, but not too bright; warm and accessible, but not too folksy; down-to-earth, but not pedestrian. Adlai Stevenson was witty and clever, but these are talents that seldom pay in politics. Voters prefer plainness and solemn platitudes, but these too can be overdone. For instance, Ford's talks, no matter what the occasion, dulled our senses with the banal. Both suffered because of this paradox. The "catch 22" here, of course, is that the very fact of an uncommon performance puts distance between a President and the truly common man. We persist, however, in wanting both at the same time.

8. THE NATIONAL UNIFIER-NATIONAL DIVIDER PARADOX

One of the paradoxes most difficult to alleviate arises from our longing for a President who will pull us together again and yet be a forceful priority-setter, budget-manager, and executive leader. The two tasks are near opposites.

Ours remains one of the few nations in the world that call upon their chief executives to serve also as their symbolic, ceremonial heads of state. Elsewhere, these tasks are spread around. In some nations there is a Monarch *and* a Prime Minister; in other nations there are three visible national leaders—the head of state, a Premier, and a powerful party head.

In the absence of an alternative, we demand that our presidents and our Presidency act as a unifying force in our lives. Perhaps it all began with George Washington, who so artfully performed this function. At least for a while, he truly was above politics and a near unique symbol of our new nation. He was a healer, a unifier, and an extraordinary man for all seasons. Today we ask no less of our presidents than that they should do as Washington did.

However, we have designed a presidential job description that impels our contemporary presidents to act as national dividers. They necessarily divide when they act as the leaders of their political parties, when they set priorities that advantage certain goals and groups at the expense of others, when they forge and lead political coalitions, when they move out ahead of public opinion and assume the role of national educators, and when they choose one set of advisers over another. A President, as a creative executive leader, cannot help but offend certain interests. When Franklin Roosevelt was running for a second term, some garment workers unfolded a great sign that said, "We love him for the enemies he has made." Such is the fate of a President on an everyday basis; if he chooses to use power he usually will lose the goodwill of those who preferred inaction over action. The opposite is, of course, true if he chooses not to act.

Look at it from another angle. The nation is torn between the view that a President should primarily preside over the nation and merely serve as a referee among the various powerful interests that actually control who gets what, when, and how and a second position, which holds that a President should gain control of government processes and powers so as to use them for the purpose of furthering public, as opposed to private, interests. Obviously the position that one takes on this question is relevant to how you value the Presidency and the kind of person you'd like to see in the job.

Harry S Truman said it very simply. He noted that 14 million or 15 million Americans had the resources to have representatives in Washington to protect their interests, and that the interests of the great mass of other people, the 160 million or so others, were the responsibility of the President of the United States.

The President is sometimes seen as the great defender of the people, the ombudsman or advocate-general of "public interests." Yet he is sometimes (and sometimes at the same time) viewed as hostile to the people, isolated from them, wary of them, antagonistic to them, inherently their enemy.

This debate notwithstanding, Americans prize the Presidency as a grand American invention. As a nation we do not want to change it. Proposals to weaken it are dismissed. Proposals to reform or restructure it are paid little respect. If we sour on a President, the conventional solution has been to find and elect someone we hope will be better.

9. THE "THE LONGER HE IS THERE, THE LESS WE LIKE HIM" PARADOX

Every four years we pick a President, and for the next four years we pick on him and at him, and sometimes pick him entirely apart. There is no adequate prepresidential job experience, so much of the first term is an on-the-job learning experience. But we resent this. It is too important a job for on-the-job learning, or at least that's how most of us feel.

Too, we expect presidents to grow in office and to become better acclimated to their powers and responsibilities. But the longer they are in office, the more they find themselves involved in crises with less and less public support. There is an apocryphal presidential lament that goes as follows: "Every time I seem to grow into the job, it gets bigger."

Simply stated, the more we know of a President, or the more we observe his Presidency, the less we approve of him. Familiarity breeds discontent. Research on public support of presidents indicates that approval peaks soon after a President takes office and then slides downward at a declining rate over time until it reaches a point in the latter half of the four-year term when it bottoms out. Thereafter it rises a bit but never attains its original levels. Why this pattern of declining support afflicts presidents is a subject of debate among social scientists. Unrealistic early expectations are, of course, a major factor. These unrealistic expectations ensure a period of disenchantment.

Peace and prosperity can help stem the unpleasant tide of ingratitude, and Eisenhower's popularity remained reasonably high in large part because of his (or the nation's) achievements in these respects. For other presidents, however, their eventual downsliding popularity was due nearly as much to the public's inflated expectations as to the presidents' actions. It was often as if the downslide in popularity would occur no matter what the President did. If this seems unfair, even cruel, it is, nonetheless, what happens to those skilled and lucky enough to win election to the "highest office in the land."

And all this occurs despite our conventional wisdom that the *office makes the man* — "that the presidency with its built-in educational processes, its spacious view of the world, its command of talent, and above all its self-conscious historic role, does work its way on the man in the Oval Office," as James MacGregor Burns puts it. If we concede that the office in part does make the man, we must admit also that time in office often unmakes the man.

10. THE "WHAT IT TAKES TO BECOME PRESIDENT MAY NOT BE WHAT IS NEEDED TO GOVERN THE NATION" PARADOX

To win a presidential election takes ambition, ambiguity, luck, and masterful public-relations strategies. To govern the nation plainly requires all of these, but far more as well. It may well be that too much ambition, too much ambiguity, and too heavy a reliance on phony public-relations tricks actually undermine the integrity and legitimacy of the Presidency.

Columnist David Broder offered an apt example: "People who win primaries may become good Presidents — but 'it ain't necessarily so.' Organizing well is important in governing just as it is in winning primaries. But the Nixon years should teach us that good advance men do not necessarily make trustworthy White House aides. Establishing a government is a little more complicated than having the motorcade run on time."

Likewise, ambition (in very heavy doses) is essential for a presidential candidate, but too much hunger for the office or for "success-at-any-price" is a danger to be avoided. He must have boldness and energy, but carried too far these can make him cold and frenetic. To win the Presidency obviously requires a single-mindedness, and yet we want our presidents to be well rounded, to have a sense of humor, to be able to take a joke, to have hobbies and interests outside the realm of politics—in short, to have a sense of proportion.

Another aspect of this paradox can be seen in the way candidates take ambiguous positions on issues in order to increase their appeal to the large bulk of centrist and independent voters. Not only does such equivocation discourage rational choices by the voters, but it also may alienate people who learn later, after the candidate has won, that his views and policies are otherwise. LBJ's "We will not send American boys to fight the war that Asian boys should be fighting" and Richard Nixon's "open Presidency" pledges come readily to mind. Their pre-presidential stands were later violated or ignored.

Political scientist Samuel Huntington calls attention to yet another way this paradox works. To be a winning candidate, he notes, the would-be President must put together an *electoral coalition* involving a majority of voters advantageously distributed across the country. To do this, he must appeal to all regions and interest groups and cultivate the appearance of honesty, sincerity, and experience. But once elected, the electoral coalition has served its purpose and a *governing coalition* is the order of the day. This all may sound rather elitist, but Harvard Professor Huntington insists that this is what has to be:

> The day after his election the size of his majority is almost—if not entirely—irrelevent to his ability to govern the country. What counts then is his ability to mobilize support from the leaders of the key institutions in society and government. He has to constitute a broad governing coalition of strategically located supporters who can furnish him with the information, talent, expertise, manpower, publicity, arguments, and political support which he needs to develop a program, to embody it in legislation, and to see it effectively implemented. This coalition must include key people in Congress, the executive branch, and the private-sector "Establishment." The governing coalition need have little relation to the electoral coalition. The fact that the President as a candidate put together a successful electoral coalition does not insure that he will have a viable governing coalition.

Presidential candidate Adlai Stevenson had another way of saying it in 1956. He said he had "learned that the hardest thing about any political campaign is how to win without proving that you are unworthy of winning." The process of becoming President is an extraordinarily taxing one that defies description. It involves, among other things, an unflagging salesmanship job on television.

Candidates plainly depend upon television to transform candidacy into incumbency. Research findings point out that candidates spend well over half their funds on radio and television broadcasting. Moreover, this is how the people "learn" about the candidates. Approximately two-thirds of the American public report that television is the best way for them to follow candidates, and about half of the public acknowledge that they got their best understanding of the candidates and issues from television coverage.

Thus, television is obviously the key. But the candidate has to travel to every state and hundreds of cities for at least a four-year period to capture the exposure and the local headlines before earning the visibility and stature of a "serious candidate." For the most part, it becomes a grueling ordeal, as well as a major learning experience. In quest of the Democratic nomination for President, Walter F. Mondale of Minnesota spent most of 1974 traveling some 200,000 miles, delivering hundreds of speeches, appearing on countless radio and television talk shows, and sleeping in Holiday Inn after Holiday Inn all across the country. He admits that he enjoyed much of it, but says, too, that he seldom had time to read or to reflect, not to mention having time for a sane family life. Eventually he withdrew on the grounds that he simply had neither the overwhelming desire nor the time, as an activist United States senator, to do what was necessary in order to win the nomination.

Mondale would later—in 1976—show that he is an extremely effective national campaigner, but his frustrations about his 1974 presidential bid are worth remembering:

> I love to ponder ideas, to reflect on them and discuss them with experts and friends over a period of time, but this was no longer possible. It struck me as being unfortunate and even tragic that the process of seeking the Presidency too often prevents one from focusing on the issues and insights and one's ability to express them, which are crucially important. I believe this fact explains many of the second-rate statements and much of the irrational posturing that are frequently associated with Presidential campaigns. In any case, after eighteen months I decided this wasn't for me. It wasn't my style and I wasn't going to pretend that it was. Instead of controlling events in my life, I was more and more controlled by them. Others have had an easier time adapting to this process than I did, and I admire them for it. But one former candidate told me, three years after his campaign had ended, that he *still* hadn't fully recovered emotionally or physically from the ordeal.

What it takes to *become* President may differ from what it takes to *be* President. It takes a near megalomaniac who is also glib, dynamic, charming on television, and hazy on the issues. Yet we want our presidents to be well rounded, careful in their reasoning, clear and specific in their communications, and not excessively ambitious. It may well be that our existing primary-and-convention system adds up to an effective obstacle course for testing would-be presidents. Certainly they have to travel to all sections of the country, meet the people, deal with interest-group elites, and learn about the challenging issues of the day. But with the Johnson and Nixon experiences in our not too distant past, we have reason for asking whether our system of producing presidents is adequately reconciled with what is required to produce a President who is competent, fair-minded, and emotionally healthy.

CONCLUSIONS

Perhaps the ultimate paradox of the modern Presidency is that it is always too powerful and yet it is always inadequate. Always too powerful because it is contrary to our ideals of a government by the people and always too powerful, as well, because it must now possess the capacity to wage nuclear war (a capacity that unfortunately doesn't permit much in the way of checks and balances and deliberative, participatory government). Yet always inadequate because it seldom achieves our highest hopes for it, not to mention its own stated intentions.

The Presidency is always too strong when we dislike the incumbent. On the other hand, its limitations are bemoaned when we believe the incumbent is striving valiantly to serve the public interest as we define it. For many people, the Johnson presidency captured this paradox vividly: Many who felt that he was too strong in Vietnam also felt that he was too weakly equipped to wage his War on Poverty (and vice versa).

The dilemma for the attentive public is that curbing the powers of a President who abuses the public trust will usually undermine the capacity of a fair-minded President to serve the public interest. In the nearly two centuries since Washington took office, we have multiplied the requirements for presidential leadership and made it increasingly difficult to lead. Certainly this is no time for mindless retribution against the already fragile institution of the Presidency. Neither presidents nor the public should be relieved of their respective responsibilities of trying to fashion a more effective and fair-minded leadership system simply because these paradoxes are pointed out and even widely agreed upon. It is also not enough to throw up our hands and say, "Well, no one makes a person run for that crazy job in the first place."

The situation analyzed in this essay doubtless also characterizes the positions of governors, city managers, university presidents, and even many corporate executives. Is it a new phenomenon, or are we just becoming increasingly aware of it? Is it a permanent or a transitory condition? My own view is that it is neither new nor transitory, but more comparative and longitudinal analysis is needed before we can generalize more systematically. Meanwhile, we shall have to select as our presidents people who understand these paradoxes and have a gift for the improvisation necessitated by their contrary demands. It is important for us to ask our chief public servants to be willing occasionally to forgo enhancing their own short-term political fortunes for a greater good of simplifying, rather than exacerbating, the paradoxes of the Presidency.

While the Presidency will surely remain one of our nation's best vehicles for creative policy change, it will also continue to be a hard-pressed office, laden with the cumulative weight of these paradoxes. We urgently need to probe the origins and to assess the consequences of these paradoxes and to learn how presidents and the public can better coexist with them, for it is apparent that these paradoxes serve to isolate a President from the public. Whether we like it or not, the growing importance of the Presidency and our growing dependence on presidents seem to ensure that presidents will be less popular, and more often handy scapegoats when anything goes wrong.

Let us ask our presidents to give us their best, but let us not ask them to deliver more than the Presidency—or any single institution—has to give.

☆

RICHARD M. PIOUS: *The Presidency in the 1980s*

Presidential scholars make poor forecasters. Creators of the office were convinced by the end of the eighteenth century that incumbents would either subvert the Constitution or prove too weak to preserve it. Prior to the Civil War, constitutional lawyers, reacting to the presidencies of Jefferson and Jackson, argued that the office was the chief defect of the governmental system and should be checked by Congress or by a council of state. Few realized that the real danger to the Union would lie in a succession of weak incumbents incapable of uniting the sections to a common purpose. Near the turn of the nineteenth century the public-law scholars in the graduate schools of political science thought that the presidency was evolving into a ceremonial office, and would be displaced by an emerging parliamentary system. Most recently we had political scientists, using case-study and behavioral methods claiming that incumbents governed in the national interest primarily through their powers of persuasion rather than by command—just at a time when several presidents used veto and impoundment prerogatives for domestic affairs and war-making powers for their foreign policies.

It is clear that the only certain forecast about the presidency is that no forecast is certain. With this caution in mind I should like to conclude with some words about present trends and possible developments in the next decade.

Richard M. Pious is Associate Professor of Political Science at Barnard College. This selection is from his book *The American Presidency* (New York: Basic Books, 1979), pp. 416-422. Copyright © 1979 by Basic Books. Reprinted by permission of the author and the publisher.

THE ACCOUNTABILITY OF POWER

Presidents are not likely to become popular or party leaders. The mean turnouts of eligible voters will remain low and may decrease in the next several elections. Media techniques used during campaigns raise public expectations, whereas subsequent performances of incumbents in office result in a disillusioned and cynical electorate. The increase in the number of primaries and the changes in party rules leave incumbents vulnerable to intraparty challenges, and midterm policy conventions may embarrass the administration and provide ammunition for partisan opponents. Legislators will remain disassociated from the presidential electoral system, and the White House will be unable to purge dissidents or use the caucuses to impose party discipline.

Presidents will be tempted to appeal to the people. They will emphasize their expertise, their unique "vantage point," and equate their proposals with the national interest. But incumbents are not experts; worse, they are not perceived by legislators as effective politicians, nor by the public as competent managers. Interest groups all challenge the president when he attempts to define a national agenda. The media delight in putting incumbents on the defensive, and relish serving up the evidence of double-talk or double-dealing in the executive branch. The legacy of Watergate is wolfpack journalism, which will confirm the worst fears of the public. The White House will remain in a state of siege, as the normal transactions of the political system are unearthed, magnified, and then distorted by the media. Presidential attempts to control the national agenda seem destined to fail on most issues.

THE LOCUS OF POWER

Presidents will continue the decentralization of domestic policymaking and program management. Bureau chiefs and program managers will maintain their ties with congressional committees and subcommittees, and with interest and clientele groups. Presidents are not likely to take more than a passing interest in struggles between departments and bureaus, or between state and federal officials, for in most cases their stakes are limited. Executive Office agencies, particularly the Office of Management and Budget and the domestic staff in the White House Office, will continue to participate in departmental business, thus maintaining the appearance, if not the reality, of intense presidential participation in domestic program planning. But the major stakes for the White House will be political and economic rather than programmatic or managerial: to retain some influence in the distributive process to build support in Congress and with state parties; to influence the magnitude and timing of national commitments so that aggregate spending levels do not exceed White House targets.

Presidential domestic priorities will involve management of fiscal and natural resource policymaking. In both areas Congress has traditionally played a major role, and it has created mechanisms in the budget, impoundment, and fiscal processes that require the administration to collaborate with it. There are substantial differences between the two parties in these areas, and a president who could capitalize on these differences might succeed as a legislative leader. But the problem for a Democratic president is that he might be tempted to rely on national agenda politics and so split his party on ideological or sectional lines. For a Republican president the danger is that party differences will be expressed institutionally through the checks and balances system, with an antiadministration majority in Congress dominating policymaking through the new fiscal and budget mechanisms. Split government might produce deadlock, followed by presidential subversion of the spirit or letter of the new mechanisms. It is likely that instead of party government, decentralized policymaking in the executive branch will be matched by autonomous legislative leaders working closely with interest groups to develop policies, which will then pass Congress through transactional methods. That is why prospects that the White House can develop, for example, serious energy and natural resource policies for long-term development without relying on emergency powers are not good.

THE LIMITS OF POWER

Presidents will not be able to manage foreign relations well. The various foreign policy communities remain at odds with one another and with the White House: Defense wants more funds for advanced weapons systems and opposes concessions in arms limitation negotiations; the CIA remains demoralized as a result of cutbacks in personnel and increased White House supervision; State does not receive the authority it requests to manage foreign policy, and friction between it and the National Security Council staff seems to have become an institutionalized feature of the foreign policy machinery. The situation will not improve because foreign affairs in the next decade will center on economic negotiations, and both State and the NSC staff remain poorly equipped to deal with these matters. In the resulting vacuum the Treasury, special White House aides, the ambassador to the United Nations, and even the vice-president, all stake out their "turf," or meddle in the business of State and the NSC. There are too many rhetorical flourishes, too many "policies" enunciated in too many speeches—and too little policy, direction, or coherence. Camp David successes remain sweet, and rare.

Presidents will continue to rely on their prerogative powers. Nixon, Ford, and Carter all argued that their powers as commander in chief could not be diminished by the War Powers Resolution. Each used constitutional authority to expand the functions of the intelligence community, strengthen secrecy systems, and make commitments to foreign nations. Presidents argue that they cannot be held legally liable by the judiciary for violations of constitutional rights of citizens in national security matters.

But presidents must contend with the "backlash" effects produced by Vietnam and Watergate. Congress has passed laws designed to provide it with more information about executive branch activities. These may require the president to specify the constitutional or legal authority for his actions, or provide Congress or its committees with information. Even when such information is classified or closely held, some committees have arranged to be briefed on a regular basis by administration officials. Each year Congress passes more laws that require briefings or formal reports. It is not clear, however, that presidents will provide timely or complete information to Congress. Nor is it certain that legislators have the time, the interest, or the ability to digest and act upon massive amounts of information that they now require be transmitted to them by the executive branch.

Congress has also legislated action-forcing mechanisms that limit or affect statutory presidential authority. These include requirements for the concurrence of committees of one or both chambers before action may be taken, concurrence if action is to be continued past a specified deadline, "vetoes" of actions already taken, and termination of an existing situation or repeal of presidential authority by concurrent resolution. These systems have not always worked well. Congress sometimes acts perfunctorily and acquiesces in important matters without thorough review of executive action. In other circumstances it uses these mechanisms to dominate the distributive process rather than to make policy. Occasionally the legislature uses these mechanisms as part of the checks and balances system, to require constructive modifications of administration proposals, as in the cases of arms sales to Iran and Saudi Arabia. The constitutionality of some of these mechanisms has been challenged by the White House, especially in circumstances where they seem to infringe on the constitutional prerogatives of the president. It is possible that some committee vetoes and concurrences will be struck down by the courts. Congress might then respond by tying its systems of administrative oversight directly to the appropriations process. What seems certain is that Congress intends to legislate more veto and concurrence systems, especially in national security affairs.

Presidents have at times evaded the letter or spirit of some of the action-forcing systems. Ford worked grudgingly within the impoundment system but tried to overload Congress with trivia. He avoided full compliance with the reporting provisions of the War Powers Resolution. Carter tied various arms sales to nations in the Middle East in a single package, pressuring Congress to approve all components by threatening to withdraw all sales if a single element were disapproved. He canceled the B-1 bomber in a way that evaded the mechanisms of the impoundment process. He did not concede the constitutionality of some of the provisions of the War Powers Resolution. He also questioned the constitutionality of several committee and chamber veto systems.

In the future presidents will continue to oppose such provisions, especially in national security matters. They argue that the government can speak no longer with one voice, since the executive may make promises or commitments that Congress will delay, modify, or refuse to honor. Foreign leaders will charge presidents with bad faith, or will conclude that the White House can neither make nor carry out a foreign policy. These leaders may be tempted to deal directly with members of Congress rather than confine their official representations and negotiations to the Department of State and the president. They will attempt to influence Congress not only by force of argument, but if past history is any guide, by national agenda politics and through transactions or corruption.

Presidents will be tempted to pass the buck and blame Congress for all setbacks in foreign policy. The stage seems set for a replay of the period just prior to World War II, when attempts by Congress to restrict presidential freedom of maneuver—which succeeded all too well—ultimately led the generation that assumed power in the postwar period to conclude that Congress was incapable of sharing power in foreign policymaking. However poorly some presidents have performed in recent years as world leaders, there is little evidence to suggest that Congress, as it presently operates, is in a position to formulate better policies. There is some evidence to suggest that without executive leadership, Congress is likely to blunder terribly in alliance politics. The challenge for Congress is to demonstrate that it can collaborate effectively with the executive in making foreign policy and in managing foreign relations, for if it fails to do so, its use of the new action-forcing mechanisms simply to check the president will leave it discredited, and a backlash will set in against the mechanisms it has created. In major crises the White House is likely to institute some form of prerogative government and disregard provisions of the mechanisms Congress has legislated; such seem to be the lessons of the *Mayaguez* incident and the evacuations in Indochina.

THE USES OF POWER

Like generals who plan for the next war around the lessons of the last one, presidential scholars have focused attention on the "dirty tricks" of the recent past. Preventing another Watergate by decreasing the size of the White House staff, preventing political police from functioning in the Executive Office, extending public financing of elections, providing for fuller disclosure of lobbying activities, and establishing mechanisms for a special prosecutor to investigate charges of malfeasance involving the White House — these are commendable reforms, and some will probably be instituted. But they do not address the central problem of presidential power: how to make collaborative government work.

Congress must demonstrate that the action-forcing collaborative mechanisms it has created can work in crises, and that they are a viable alternative to prerogative government. Collaboration means more than sharing superintendence of the departments with the executive branch in order to control the distributive process for the benefit of constituents, interest groups, and voting blocs. It involves more than dominating bureaus that administer routine programs. Rather, it involves interactions between the branches that result in important national policies; and it calls for effective use of mechanisms that require the president to inform, consult, and propose, and require Congress to concur, perfect, and if necessary veto presidential initiatives within a limited period of time. Perhaps the most important use of collaborative mechanisms is to keep presidents in a consultative and persuasive frame of mind, which involves a purpose as much psychological as institutional.

Presidents do their part when they invite full and timely consultation within the executive branch, permitting careerists to work closely with political executives in formulating options. They act in the spirit of the system when they give advance notice of their intentions to legislative leaders, provide them with adequate and relevant information, and allow congressional thinking to influence their own deliberations.

Congress does its part when it uses its pooled resources and staffs to obtain its own information and develop its own options. It then can evaluate presidential proposals against alternatives, prior to concurring, perfecting, or vetoing his initiatives. But as yet Congress has not demonstrated that it is prepared to assume a major role in a collaborative system. Incentives for legislators to take the initiative in making policy are lacking. Congress is still not committed to using advanced techniques in the budgetary process. It does not interact early enough with the departments to make a significant impact on overall expenditure levels or on program options. It continues to react, and therefore continues to acquiesce, while making "paper" policies or legislating irresponsible amendments in its budget resolutions. In some policy areas, such as taxation and energy, the committees go their own way; the net result is that the executive controls the resolution of some issues by default, while on other issues the chaotic, decentralized, patterns of committee government are maintained.

Americans want presidents to solve problems. But the party system, the legislature, and the subgovernments each deny the White House the political power or legal authority necessary to manage public affairs. Because we emphasize the limits to power rather than the uses of power, incumbents must substitute rhetoric for achievement. In real or manufactured crises they institute forms of prerogative government, and such crises will continue to occur precisely because presidents remain too weak to manage most problems until they get out of hand. Prerogatives are still seen by the White House as the antidote to paralysis.

There are no easy answers to the problems of a presidential office that remains the major destabilizing factor in the political system by oscillating between too little and too much power. Decentralizing responsibility for most domestic programs to subgovernments and the federal system, strengthening collaborative mechanisms for management of the economy and foreign affairs, and setting new and stricter standards for the exercise of prerogative powers in genuine national emergencies — these might be steps toward placing presidential power and accountability in better constitutional balance.

☆

LOUIS W. KOENIG: *The Swings and Roundabouts of Presidential Power*

Compared to the chief executives of other political systems, the power and influence of the American President in foreign policy-making are fluctuating and uncertain. In the American system, more than in other systems, the chief executive is unable to stabilize his political influence. His competitor, Congress, is more powerful in foreign policy-making than any other legislative body in the world. In American society and culture, potent forces and traditions are in play that also cause swings and discontinuities in the President's role. An overview of American foreign policy experience discloses rises and falls, ebb and flow in the President's impact and performance. If this description has merit, it provides an alternative perception to the contention that there is an "imperial Presidency."

Partly these characteristics spring from the circumstance that power is shared between the Executive and Congress, but the precise patterns of sharing are tentative and unclear, and, even after nearly two centuries of constitutional practice they remain largely unpredictable. Also contributing to the erratic swings of power are the shifts in public moods which proceed to a degree unmatched in any other major nation. The American mood swings widely between high ideals and willingness to sustain heavy burdens in foreign policy, to absorption in domestic affairs and even to moods of disillusionment and resignation, induced when foreign policy fails to satisfy activist expectations, whereupon the country resorts to withdrawal and isolation. The swings between involvement and withdrawal, their breadth and recurrence, are distinctly an American phenomenon, and they are indulged in by all categories of public opinion, the general public, the attentive public, and elites.

Louis W. Koenig is Professor of Politics at New York University. The selection is from *The Tethered Presidency* edited by Thomas M. Franck. Copyright © 1981 by New York University. Reprinted with permission of the author and the publisher.

To be sure, the earlier Presidents, from Washington to Monroe, faced imposing foreign policy problems and were engaged in diplomacy of the most involving kind. There was no other alternative; most of the problems could not be avoided. But from Jackson to the Civil War, the country was preoccupied with domestic problems, and its foreign policies seldom reached beyond relations with our immediate neighbors. In the Civil War, foreign policy was important although ancillary, and no President between Lincoln and Cleveland emerges as more than a modest presence in foreign affairs. The Spanish-American War, which first brought the United States to stage-center in world affairs in modern times, was a Congressional war, promoted by legislators and supported by public opinion inflamed by the yellow press, and reluctantly acquiesced in by a peace-minded President, William McKinley.

America was kept at stage-center by the bellicosity and other hyperactivity of Theodore Roosevelt, the dollar diplomacy of Taft, and Wilson's messianic mission to make the world safe for democracy and peace. A mood of isolationism and the modest talents of Coolidge and Harding prompted the Presidential presence to recede. World War II, followed close-on by the Cold War, caused a soaring Presidential activism for two and a half decades. Then as the nation tired of the long-dragging Indochina war and the Watergate scandals set in, a tainted Presidency passed into a diminished role, accompanied by a mood, heavily tinged with neo-isolationism, which makes the public and its officials wary of foreign commitments potentially involving the engagement of American combat forces.

Clearly each political branch, Congress and the Executive, has enjoyed ascendancy at different intervals and in different fields of foreign policy. The performances of both branches are mixtures of successes and failures. Neither branch has a monopoly of error or virtue. Presidents have successfully waged wars, proclaimed creative and utilitarian long-range policies like the Monroe Doctrine, instituted imaginative programs like Eisenhower's Atoms-for-Peace and Kennedy's Peace Corps, and Nixon opened up relations with Communist China. But the Presidential boxscore declines when Wilson fails to win the Senate's approval of American membership in the League of Nations, when the Bay of Pigs invasion goes awry, when a succession of Presidents becomes entrapped in the protracted war in Vietnam, including a secret war in Cambodia.

But Congress' performance is also mixed. The country's most senseless and least defensible conflicts, the wars of 1812 and 1898, were Congressional wars. And it was the Senate or Congress that blocked our entry into the League of Nations, withheld full support for the World Court, that continuously reduces foreign aid, and passes resolutions mixing in the affairs of other countries for political

rather than diplomatic reasons. Congress served as a most sympathetic audience for General Douglas MacArthur and his call for "total
victory," and when Kennedy struggled to establish a prudent policy in
the 1962 Cuban missile crisis, Congressional leaders urged an
immediate air attack on the island.

But Congress also has a sturdy credit side. It established, for
example, the exchange of persons program and the use of agricultural
surpluses in foreign aid. Ideas for a Peace Corps and to create an Arms
Control and Disarmament Agency, and employing foreign policy to
enhance human rights abroad began in Congress.

It is further evidence of the volatility of both the Presidency and
Congress and their functioning in the political and policy-making
systems, that each in recent times has been looked to admiringly by
both liberal and conservative opinion. In the 1930's and '40's, the
Presidency was favored by liberals and dreaded by conservatives who
were driven to sponsor the Bricker amendment by which they confidently proposed to make a good Congress the watchdog of a bad
Presidency. In the 1960's and '70's, liberals, distressed by the Presidency's war involvements, looked to Congress to rein in the office.

This notion of fluctuation and uncertainty is affirmed if we consider foreign policy-making to be most frequently a continuum, that
is, from an idea and plan, it passes through many stages of formation,
adoption, implementation, and the degree of the President's personal
or institutional control is normally quite different at each stage. It is
one thing for Nixon, acting autonomously and with dramatic effect,
to journey to China. Far less is his and his Presidential successors'
control over the countless detailed decisions to give actuality and
substance to his important symbolic act. It is easy to be over-
impressed with the importance of Presidential policy-making, to
undervalue the progression of concrete steps to implement his
choices. The farther down the road that policies go toward implementation, the remoter they become to his control, the more
dependent he becomes on the discretion and support of others. He
can decide to escalate the war in Vietnam, but he depends on others
to finance and wage it; he can encourage inventions to improve
American technology and productivity and our international trade
balances, but the brains of others must incubate the ideas and write
the laws. . . .

PATTERNS OF FOREIGN POLICY-MAKING

An historical review of American foreign policy-making discloses at
least four common patterns of Presidential role performance. In each
the President as policy-maker does not function as a solitary, self-
willed official, but interacts with other members of the political

system, and the relationships have important impacts in different stages of his foreign policy activity. The President shares power with others, especially Congress, is counseled by department heads and staffs, faces criticism by political opponents, and review by public opinion. Let us examine these contentions in the context of the following common policy-making patterns.

Conflict. Foreign policy-making often proceeds in a milieu of conflict and doubtless provides the readiest support for our thesis that Presidential power is largely shared power. The treaty-process, requiring a super-majority, the two-thirds vote, is an invitation for minority opinion in the legislature to be asserted. The opposition party, the President's rivals in an upcoming election — Senators who would rather be President — provide the seeds of conflict.

The Jay Treaty (1794) was a conflict-type episode of foreign policy-making, illustrative of the variety of external forces that impinge upon the President, question his judgment, challenge his decisions. As President Washington's special emissary, John Jay was assigned to clear up issues remaining under the Treaty of Paris of 1783 which ended the revolution, and new issues stemming from the Franco-British War, such as British depredations on U.S. shipping, and cutting off our trade with the West Indies.

Within the administration, the principal department secretaries, Jefferson (State) and Hamilton (Treasury), battled over the negotiations, and their embroilment caught up Washington and required his deliberation and decision. In Congress, the treaty was clearly a party issue, with Madison organizing the Republican opposition, and directing parliamentary maneuvers. In the Senate, to foil the Federalist majority and the required two-thirds treaty vote, Republicans strove to split off the Southern Federalists by moving to seek compensation for impressed Negroes. The effort failed by three votes.

Ultimately, the Senate approved the treaty, by 20 votes to 10, whereupon the Republicans carried the fight to public opinion. Bonfire rallies were held in the cities, and letters, petitions, and newspaper editorials opposing the treaty poured into Washington, driving the President to exclaim, "The affairs of the country cannot go amiss. There are so many watchful guardians of them, and such infallible guides, that one is at no loss for a direction at every turn." Madison also extended the conflict to the state legislatures, seeking resolutions opposing the treaty, and the Virginia legislature, at his prodding, proposed an amendment to the federal constitution to make treaties subject to a majority vote of the U.S. House of Representatives, center of Republican strength.

Finally, the Jay Treaty required not only Senate approval, but implementing legislation, which enabled Madison and the Republicans again to flay the treaty. The legislation squeaked through the

House by 51 to 48. Washington attributed his success in that close result to popular petitions the Federalists had accumulated to counter the Republican attack.

Consensus. Occasionally consensus overtakes public affairs, and one of the stellar practitioners of that brand of politics was James Monroe, whose tenure coincided with "the era of good feeling." The Federalist Party had now disappeared and the Democratic-Republicans flourished as the country's only party. Monroe's most memorable foreign policy is, of course, the Monroe Doctrine, ideally suited for consensus politics. According to Dexter Perkins, the leading scholar of the Doctrine, its original power stemmed from the fact that it "expressed what many men, great and humble, had thought, were thinking then, and were to think in the future. The ideas which it set forth were in the air."

But notwithstanding the unanimity at every side, the consensus politics of the Monroe Doctrine subjected Presidential policy-making to the discipline of challenge, deliberation and discussion. Monroe faced questions about facts and their assessment in the international environment and how to proceed with the Doctrine's immediate implementation. In the cabinet, opinion divided over how serious the danger was of European intervention in the newly independent countries emerging from Spain's former Latin-American possessions.

According to Secretary of State John Quincy Adams, Monroe was "alarmed" and Secretary of War John Calhoun "moonstruck" by the danger that the Holy Alliance would intervene in South America. Adams cooly discounted this possibility. Attorney General William Wirt opposed the proclamation of the Doctrine unless the country were willing to go to war to protect South American independence, but, he contended, public opinion would not tolerate that step. Adams and Calhoun argued against and prevailed over Wirt's position and the development of the Doctrine proceeded.

Despite the high unanimity it engendered, the Doctrine encountered hard questions and serious opposition in Congress. Senator John Branch of North Carolina feared that the Doctrine would "excite the angry passions and embroil us with foreign nations." James Buchanan led a maneuver of introducing amendments to eviscerate the Doctrine. Again the Doctrine prevailed. Ironically, neither Monroe, his friends, nor his opponents, really grasped the large importance the Doctrine was to have, its enduring vitality, its influence on future foreign policy.

Autonomy. Not only are alternate paths of politics open to the President's choice. He also can sometimes choose between several methods of policy-making—whether to act autonomously or in collaboration with other members of the political system such as

Congress. Franklin Roosevelt largely followed the autonomous path at a crucial interval of foreign policy-making in the months before Pearl Harbor and after the Axis conquest of France (June 1940-December 1941). During this interval, Britain stood alone, threatened with invasion. Faced with Congressional and public opinion closely divided between isolationism and intervention, Roosevelt chose to act on his own initiative and discretion, including, when necessary, the committing of warlike acts.

Among other things, Roosevelt handed over to beleagured Britain fifty over-age but still serviceable destroyers in return for grants of bases for American forces on British territories in the Western Hemisphere. After Germany overran Denmark, Roosevelt dispatched forces to occupy Iceland and Greenland, an overt act of participation in the European war. To assure the delivery of American arms to Britain, Roosevelt provided naval convoys, and ultimately ordered the shooting of Axis naval craft at sight, and several violent encounters took place.

In this extraordinarily difficult and critical wartime situation, Roosevelt clearly took into his own hands matters which in earlier and easier times either belonged to Congress or were handled by the branches jointly. In expiation of Roosevelt's seemingly imperious conduct, elements of the larger context in which he operated, as well as several other of his methods, are noteworthy. His autonomous actions cannot be judged in isolation.

First, Roosevelt was sensitive to public opinion, alert to assessing its reaction to his policies, and in undertaking the educative function of the Presidency respecting which he was extremely diligent. Time and again in speeches, he pointed out to the public the deadly peril afoot in the world, the necessity for wider awareness of the danger, and the inevitability of citizen sacrifices. Even with his best efforts prior to Pearl Harbor, public opinion remained mixed, even incoherent, although it provided a sufficient base for the President's initiatives.

Roosevelt regularly ran the gauntlet of Congress, where isolationist sentiment was strong. The foundation of large-scale aid to Britain and subsequently to other allies was the Lend Lease Act, appropriately called the "blank check" bill. An opponent, Senator Robert Taft, attacked the contrivance of "lend-lease," observing that "Lending war equipment is a good deal like lending chewing gum. You don't want it back." In effect, the Act was a legislated abandonment of neutrality, an unofficial declaration of war on the Axis, and largely a ratification of Roosevelt's previous autonomous course. Roosevelt also had to renew the Selective Service Act, which squeaked through the House by one vote. And he had to traverse the Presidential election process in 1940, on a Democratic platform mirroring the ambivalence of public opinion by pledging abstention from "foreign wars" while promising aid to countries resisting aggression.

Collaboration. Both the Constitution and the practicalities it imposes on foreign policy-making require active cooperation between the legislative and executive branches, and the large volume of their combined actions and routine cooperation goes unnoticed. Some eras, such as the years immediately following World War II, are marked by exceptional outputs of collaborative policy-making: approval of the U.N. Charter, aid to Greece and Turkey, Point 4, the regional security treaties—Rio, NATO, SEATO—and the Marshall Plan.

Sometimes these collaborations are criticized as excessive, as speeding the ascendance of the Presidency and lowering the impact of Congress. But a closer look at these policy ventures, for example, the Marshall Plan, discloses that the distribution of influence between the branches was not really so one-sided.

The Marshall Plan was enacted in 1948, a rare interval when the Republican Party controlled Congress. Through Truman, the Democrats controlled the White House. The dominant Republican motif was the necessity of cutting taxes and the worst of sins was government's penchant for pouring money down a "rathole." Since the Marshall Plan, at least in some eyes, threatened these imperatives, President Truman looked for help to the Republican chairman of the Senate Foreign Relations Committee, Arthur Vandenberg, a former isolationist recently converted to internationalism.

The evolution of the Marshall Plan from a kernel of an idea in speeches of the State Department's leaders, George Marshall and Dean Acheson, to enacted legislation and a brilliantly implemented foreign policy is a saga of collaboration between the European powers, eager to recover from the ravages of World War II, and the United States, between government and the private sector, between the White House and the bureaucracy, between the Executive Branch and Congress. The last was by no means Presidentially dominated.

Vandenberg, an imperious personality, with great capacity for instant indignation, wrested important concessions from the Truman administration. For example: Vandenberg insisted that a business executive run the program and his handpicked candidate, Paul Hoffman of Studebaker, was appointed. The Senator rebuffed the Administration's plan to have the State Department run the program, and substituted a new separate agency of cabinet-level rank, the Economic Cooperation Administration. Other Vandenberg additions included pulling the Administration away from a proposed but politically impractical four or five year authorization and substituting a generalized authorization and yearly cash appropriations. Vandenberg inserted a watchdog committee into the legislation and provisions stipulating the obligations of the recipient countries. That the balance of Vandenberg's stewardship favored internationalism, is suggested by the protests of isolationist legislative friends that he had sold them out, and Truman's gratitude for his indispensable help.

THE PRESIDENCY TODAY

Since Watergate and Vietnam, the Presidency has been sustaining a downward turn in its efficacy and impact. Partly this is the harvest of those events, of the flawed talents of recent incumbents, of changes in institutions of the political system which interact with the Presidency, changes which, on the whole, are deleterious to the office and its policy-making effectiveness in both domestic and foreign affairs. Clinton Rossiter's observation that the Presidency's responsibilities exceed its powers has special force today. The question is not whether there is an imperial Presidency, but whether there still is a Presidency as that office has traditionally been known.

Recent changes in the political system, changes which are still transpiring, are debilitating to the Presidency. Certain of these changes are the following:

—A vital two-party system is an historic foundation stone of the strong responsible Presidency. But our major parties are declining, the body of independent voters continues to expand, the historic Presidential selection system is superseded by a Presidential primary system run amuck. Unfortunately, the latter can produce Presidents and Presidential entourages whose talents apply more to electoral campaigning than to governing.

—Congress, too long a little changing institution, is now changing markedly and in ways detrimental to an effective Presidency. Theodore Roosevelt once said that a strong Presidency required a strong Congress. Unfortunately, current trends are leading to increasing dispersal of power in Congress. Committee chairmen have lost power, which has flowed to a multitude of subcommittees, largely secluded and dealing with public policy idiosyncratically. The power of the Speaker and other party leaders has faded; "Tip" O'Neill, however gifted, is not in the same power-league as Sam Rayburn. The historic function of Congressional party leaders to assemble votes to support the President's major foreign and domestic policy projects, after ample legislative review, is gravely impaired.

Increasingly, Congress is limiting the President's foreign policy options. By one recent count, Congress has used its appropriations power to impose more than 70 "constraints" on the President, such as insisting that no American foreign aid be spent on abortions, barring military assistance to Thailand unless authorized by Congress, and direct financing of any assistance to Angola. Subsequently, President

Carter complained that because of Congressional restraints the United States was unable to provide assistance to indigenous forces in Angola fighting the Cubans.

Congress is also increasingly inserting its own veto provisions into legislation. The legislative veto allows Congress to negate a given Presidential action without going through the process of enacting legislation requiring the President's signature. The legislative veto enables Congress to neutralize Presidential power by circumventing the normal procedures of legislation. The veto can be cast by both chambers acting concurrently, by a single chamber, or by a legislative committee. In the past four years, provisions for 48 such vetoes have been inserted into laws. President Ford protested that the inclusion of the legislative veto in a pending foreign aid and arms sales bill "would forge impermissible shackles on the President's ability to carry out the law and conduct the foreign relations of the United States." Carter said that his administration would not be bound by what it considers abuses of the legislative veto.

The Senate is increasingly immersing itself in the negotiation, actually the renegotiation, of treaties made by the Executive Branch. Sometimes this heightened Senatorial activity comes at the consent stage rather than the advice stage. The farther reaches of these possibilities became evident when Senate Majority Leader Robert C. Byrd and Minority Leader Howard H. Baker negotiated treaty changes in Panama City with Panama's chief of government.

—The presence of domestic interest groups in foreign policy-making is expanding. Important domestic groups are aroused over foreign policy issues, for example, Greek-Americans over the Cyprus dispute, American Jews over Israel, and black civil rights groups over African and Middle East issues. Political Action Committees (PACs), predominantly business organizations, well financed, politically sophisticated, and often hard-driving on one or several issues, will become increasingly assertive in foreign economic policy-making as that sector of foreign policy continues to expand.

—Of all the historic forms of communications technology and organization, television, far more than the press and radio, is the most ambivalent in its impacts on the Presidency. In some respects, television has clearly weakened the office.

Television has indeed enhanced the Presidency's position as the supreme symbol of the political system. But the trouble is when events take a downturn—when Middle East oil prices soar, when inflation and unemployment worsen, when the Soviet-Cuban axis makes a new sortie—the President is the readiest symbol on which to affix blame, a national scapegoat, even though his powers for dealing with those eventualities are extremely limited. It is the President who is blamed for soaring oil prices, not the American motorist who insists on driving in his car alone, at high speed.

Since Watergate and Vietnam, television has sprouted with reporters who not only follow the historic journalistic priority for bad news over good news, but have a fillip of frequent moralizing over the policies and performance of Presidents and their administrations. Since public policies seldom constitute clear-cut moral choices and their implementation is easily hobbled by unexpected, untoward events and the frailties of the many human beings on whom their implementation depends, the President and his administration are easy prey for televised moralizing which reinforces the scapegoat function.

—America's position in world affairs has changed from its ready predominance after World War II and through much of the 1960's to a position in the 1970's where its power is more easily challenged and rebuffed. During that interval, the Soviet Union rose from a state of clear military inferiority to a state of essential nuclear equivalence, attained in the 1970's, thanks to an extraordinary arms build-up, unequalled in history. The military superiority that strengthened Kennedy's hand in the 1962 Cuban missile crisis has disappeared. Events, it is clear, have their own fluctuations which effect swings in the President's powers.

As Presidents struggled to extricate the United States from the futile Indochina war in the 1970's and to persuade the nation that not every foreign involvement could "lead to another Vietnam," Soviet-Cuban adventurism progresssed on several fronts in Africa, and the American petroleum pipeline to the Middle East was jeopardized by war in Somalia, by the overthrow of the Shah in Iran and his replacement by the hostile regime of the Ayatollah Khomeini, and by the Soviet takeover of Afghanistan. Like North Vietnam and Cuba, Khomeini's Iran demonstrated the capacity even of relatively weak countries to defy the United States. In the 1970's, the Presidency was constrained by the increasing inefficacy of its formidable military power to command results, and by the impact of new kinds of power, derived from the possession of oil and other energy resources by militarily less powerful countries, to whose manipulations the United States proved extremely vulnerable.

THE FUTURE

A major factor in the Presidency's historic success in surviving the major swings and roundabouts in its usable powers is its remarkable capacity to adapt to the changing circumstances of the environment in which it functions.

The outline of its necessary adaptations in the 1980's is beginning to emerge. Most likely, the Presidency will need to develop more of its foreign policy in collaboration with Congress, with the latter a genuine and active partner. Congress' foreign policy-making role will continue to expand, fostered by its practice of remaining almost continuously in session in contrast to the lengthy adjournments of the past, by its enlarged professional staffs, and by the likelihood that future foreign policy will be more substantially economic in character, embracing topics such as inflation, unemployment and energy. In the economic realm, Congress enjoys broad Constitutional powers which will give it ample leverage in future foreign policy-making. The successful President of the 1980's will need to be skilled in the politics of inter-branch collaboration.

The greater sharing of power as a modus operandi must also be pursued by the Presidency in its future relations with America's allies. The economic foreign policies of the 1980's will require the synchronized efforts of many national economies, and the role of the President will no longer be that of enforcing the will of a vastly dominant power, but of building consensus among allies enjoying full status as partners.

If the Presidency appears to be in a downswing both for the present and possibly in the immediate future, history counsels continued reliance on the Framers' balancing mechanisms which ought soon to move the Presidency into an upswing. History also counsels caution toward even well-motivated fundamental reforms of the system's messy architecture: whether in the form of constitutional amendments or institutional changes. They seldom work out the way we hope and anticipate. A better course is to rely upon the Presidency's amply proven capacity to adjust to new circumstances and to regain and restore powers that have been diminished or weakened, and to find new uses for its powers for new problems.

☆

FRED I. GREENSTEIN: *Change and Continuity in the Modern Presidency*

Although my main concern here is change in the American presidency since 1960, it is necessary to begin with an extended prefatory account of the evolution of the presidency from Franklin D. Roosevelt's inauguration through the end of the Eisenhower administration. This is because the most striking changes in the institution occurred during the first three modern presidencies, and many of those that have occurred since Kennedy took office appear to have been oscillations in patterns that began under Kennedy's three predecessors.

I am using the phrase "modern presidency" to distinguish the Roosevelt through Carter presidencies from the previous "traditional presidencies." Up to the Hoover administration, there were variations from President to President in how the chief executive conducted his duties. Periodically there were stable shifts in the functioning of the institution itself—for example, the shift to popular election with Jackson and the increased tendency of Presidents to interest themselves in legislation beginning around the turn of the century. With Franklin Roosevelt's administration, however, as part of the general increase in the size and impact of American government, the presidency began to undergo not a shift but rather a metamorphosis. The eight post-Hoover presidencies, those I have called modern, have been different from their thirty traditional predecessors in the following aspects:

Fred I. Greenstein is Henry Luce Professor of politics, law, and society at Princeton University. This article appeared in *The New American Political System*, edited by Anthony King (Washington: American Enterprise Institute for Public Policy Research, 1978). Copyright © 1978 by AEI. Reprinted by permission of the author and the publisher.

451

(1) From a state of affairs in which there was at best a somewhat grudging acceptance that the President would be "interested" in the doings of Congress, it has come to be taken for granted that he *should* regularly initiate and seek to win support for legislative action as part of his continuing responsibilities. The President also has come to be far more active in evaluating legislative enactments with a view to deciding whether to exercise the veto than traditionally was the case.

(2) From a presidency that normally exercised few unilateral powers, there has been a shift to one that is provided — via statutes, court decisions, and informal precedents — with many more occasions for direct policy making through executive orders and other actions not formally ratified by Congress.

(3) From a presidency with extremely modest staff support, there has evolved one in which the President has at his disposal in the Executive Office and "on loan" from elsewhere in the executive branch an extensive bureaucracy to implement his initiatives. It is only because of the rise of a presidential bureaucracy that it has been possible for Presidents to follow through on (1) and (2).

(4) Finally, there appear to have been major changes in the quantity of public attention to incumbent Presidents. For many Americans the complex, uncertain political world of our times seems to be dealt with by personification, in the form of perceptions of the quality of performance and personal virtue of the incumbent President. Presidents are expected to be symbols of reassurance, possessing extraordinary "nonpolitical" personal qualities that traditionally were associated only with long deceased "hero presidents" of the past, such as George Washington. At the same time they are expected to be politically effective, bringing about favorable national and international social conditions. They have become potential beneficiaries of anything positive that can be attributed to the government, but also scapegoats for social and political discontent.

THE FORMATIVE PERIOD OF THE MODERN PRESIDENCY

The emergence of the physical and symbolic defining characteristics of the modern presidency is evident in the several city blocks surrounding 1600 Pennsylvania Avenue. William Hopkins, who began working as White House stenographer under Hoover in 1931, went on to become executive clerk, and held his White House position until his retirement in the Nixon years, remembers that he had shaken hands with President Hoover the year before going to work in the White House. Hoover still found it possible to carry on the leisurely nineteenth-century New Year's Day tradition of personally greeting any person who cared to join the reception line leading into the White House.

In Hoover's time, the presidency had not become so central a symbol for public emotions and perceptions about the state of the nation that elaborate procedures for protecting the White House from potentially dangerous intruders were deemed necessary. The White House of our time is surrounded by a high, electronically sensitized fence; its gates are locked and carefully guarded; and the fence extends across West Executive Avenue to the ornate Old Executive Office Building, creating a two-block "presidential compound." In Hoover's time, the lower, unelectrified fence surrounded only the White House grounds and had open gates. Anyone walking east of the White House from what then was not a presidential office building, but rather the site of the State, Navy, and War Departments, customarily did so by strolling across the White House grounds.

Moreover, when Hoover was President, the West Wing of the White House had sufficient space to accommodate the modest presidential staff. The bureaucracy of the modern presidency now occupies not only the building across the street from the West Wing, but also the red-brick, high-rise New Executive Office Building on 17th Street. Extensions of the presidency are to be found in many other nearby buildings, including the Georgian-façade edifices facing Lafayette Square. There is even a house on the square to accommodate and provide office space for ex-Presidents.

ROOSEVELT: THE BREAKTHROUGH TO THE MODERN PRESIDENCY

The first stage in the transformation that accounted for these physical changes was an almost overnight rise in expectations about the appropriate duties of the chief executive. This resulted from the convergence of a deep national (and later international) crisis with the accession and long incumbency of perhaps the most gifted entrepreneurial President in American history, Franklin D. Roosevelt. Nothing was "inevitable" about the appearance in 1933 of entrepreneurial, innovative presidential leadership. FDR's nomination in 1932 had not been a sure thing. As President-elect he barely escaped assassination. It is impossible to believe that the impact of the leader next in succession, Vice President-elect John Nance Garner, would have been very different from Hoover's. One can argue that, whether under Hoover, Garner, or the various other "available" presidential contenders of the time, "social conditions" would have fostered demands for strong leadership. But the outcome, if any, of these demands might well have been some form of indigenous dictatorship, such as that described in Sinclair Lewis's novel *It Can't Happen Here*. Crisis was a necessary but far from sufficient condition for the modern presidency that began to evolve under Roosevelt.

The premodern historical record—especially the record of the nineteenth century—contains countless examples of congressional antipathy to mere suggestions by the President that particular legislation be enacted. There were even congressmen who held that presidential vetoes could not legitimately be used as an expression of policy preference by the chief executive, but rather must be reserved for occasions when he deemed legislation to be unconstitutional. FDR promptly established the practice of advocating, backing, and engaging in the politics of winning support for legislation. By the end of Roosevelt's long tenure in office, presidential legislative activism had come to be taken for granted, if not universally approved.

This activism began within four days of Roosevelt's taking office. The relentless succession of "Hundred Days" legislative enactments passed by the special session of Congress that met from noon, March 9, to 1:00 a.m., June 15, 1933—including such major policy departures as the banking act, the securities act, the Civilian Conservation Corps, and the National Industrial Recovery Administration—was appropriately viewed as the result of Roosevelt's leadership. In some cases his leadership involved bringing about the enactment of programs that had long been on the public political agenda, such as the Tennessee Valley Authority, but which needed the impetus of the Hundred Days legislative campaign to achieve approval. In one case—the Federal Deposit Insurance Corporation—Roosevelt received praise for passage of a program that he personally opposed but acceded to after realizing it had too much congressional support to be defeated.

That FDR was given credit for the initiatives of others points to the fact that during his administration people tended more and more to think of the President as a symbol for government. The public dealt with the increasing complexity of government by personifying it. Even before Congress could convene, as the nationally broadcast inaugural ceremony proceeded, the chief executive was almost instantly transformed from a remote, seemingly inert entity to a vivid focal point of national attention. FDR's confident comportment; the high oratory of the inaugural speech, with its grave warning that he would request war powers over the economy if Congress failed to act; his ebullience; the decisiveness of the following day's "bank holiday" executive order—all of this elicited an overwhelmingly favorable public response to the new President. William Hopkins, who was then in the White House correspondence section, remembers that "President Roosevelt was getting about as much mail a day as President Hoover received in a week. The mail started coming in by the truckload. They couldn't even get the envelopes open."

Significantly, the volume of presidential mail has never tapered off. Recent estimates are that over a million letters come to the

President annually. Roosevelt evidently was able to wed his own great powers of personal communication to the general sense of national urgency, channeling what hitherto had been a static patriotic sentiment—American veneration of the great Presidents of the past— into a dynamic component of the incumbent President's role. In initiating this characteristic of the modern presidency, he undoubtedly enhanced his ability and that of his successors to muster public support in times of perceived national crisis. But he also undoubtedly established unrealistic and even contradictory standards by which citizens tend to judge both the personal virtue of Presidents and their ability to solve the typically controversial social and political problems that arise during their administrations.

FDR also innovated in accustoming the nation to expect that the President would be aided by a battery of policy advisers and implementers. At first these aides were officially on the payrolls of diverse non-White House agencies but were unofficially "the President's men." Best remembered now is the sequence of academic braintrusters who advised FDR as governor of New York and early in his first term; the lawyers who drafted and politicked for the next stage of New Deal legislation; and Harry Hopkins, who served as war-time presidential surrogate in international diplomacy.

Politically attentive Americans tend to regard unoffical presidential advising—for example, Jackson's use of his Kitchen Cabinet and Wilson's of Colonel Edward House—with suspicious fascination. The fascination draws on the titillation of identifying the "real" powers behind the throne. The suspicion arises from the fear of illegitimate, legally irresponsible power—an especially strong concern in a polity in which so many of the political actors are lawyers inclined to invoke constitutional principles, even in debates over matter-of-fact interest-group conflicts.

In any case, in the fishbowl context of American mass communications, grey eminences do not remain grey for long. The two leading young lawyers who were Roosevelt's principal agents during the so-called Second New Deal, Thomas Corcoran and Benjamin Cohen, were pictured on the cover of *Time* magazine. This visibility of the unofficial aides who were essential to maintaining FDR's momentum as policy initiator threatened the legitimacy of his leadership. To the degree that such aides upstaged him, they also detracted from his centrality as a symbol of national leadership. These costs of using visible unofficial advisers must have contributed to Roosevelt's interest in procedures that would provide the presidency with aides who *were* official and who were *not* conspicuous.

Just such a corps of aides was proposed in the 1937 recommendations of the Brownlow Committee, the Committee on Administration of the Federal Government that Roosevelt appointed. Arguing that because of the mushrooming responsibilities of the executive branch, "the President needs help," the Brownlow Committee proposed that an Executive Office of the President be established, including a White House Office staffed by skilled, energetic aides who were to have "a passion for anonymity." After extensive political bargaining, the Reorganization Act of 1939 was passed and implemented by executive order.

The shift from exclusive use by Roosevlt of behind-the-scenes advisors to use of a staff authorized by statute is recorded in the *United States Government Manual* released in October 1939. Listed immediately following the page identifying the President of the United States is what continues to be the umbrella heading under which presidential agencies are grouped — the Executive Office of the President (EOP). The White House Office (WHO) is listed next. (In October 1939 only three WHO aides had been selected. In the 1970-1971 *Manual,* about the peak year for size of WHO staff, over fifty were listed.)

Each *Manual* since 1939 has listed next in sequence, following the WHO, the Bureau of the Budget (after 1970, the Office of Management and Budget). BOB/OMB has consistently been by far the most influential Executive Office appendage, except for the White House Office itself. The BOB originally had been established in 1921, after a decade of efficiency-minded lobbying by "good government" reformers who sought to substitute a consolidated and centrally screened Executive Budget as the communication submitted for congressional action, rather than the disaggregated requests from individual agencies that had been submitted until then. Until the passage of the 1939 Reorganization Act, however, the bureau was not a policy-framing agency, but rather a kind of bookkeeping department which sought to achieve mechanical economies in budgetary requests based, in some cases, on exercises of parsimony as picayune as saving paperclips and pencil stubs. Although officially an agency of the President, the old "green eyeshade" BOB was lodged in the Treasury Department and did not attend to presidential policy goals, apart from the general 1920's policy of holding down budgetary requests and expenditures.

The post-Reorganization Act bureau received a new director, Harold D. Smith, who was both passionately anonymous and assiduously devoted to building an organization of highly able public administrators who would have a continuing responsibility to the presidency, no matter who the incumbent was, as well as serving the man who was in office at the time. Smith's unpublished diaries and the memoirs of the Washington insiders of that period make it clear that he privately assumed an active, if invariably diffident, advisory relationship with President Roosevelt. FDR and Smith conferred regularly. The bureau itself was moved in 1939 from the Treasury Department building to office space in the frequently renamed building directly across the street from the West Wing of the White House. Smith continued to have similar regular conferences with the new President during the first year of the Truman presidency. Instructively from the standpoint of anonymity, the bureau was rarely discussed in the press, and during his tenure as director, Smith's name appeared only twice — both times in neutral contexts — in the *New York Times Index.*

Because the great changes between 1933 and 1945 in expectations about the magnitude, impact, and nature of the presidency were the outcome not only of the political climate during Roosevelt's time in office, but also of FDR's highly personal style, it was not inevitable that what I now confidently describe as "the modern presidency" *had* to continue into subsequent administrations. Roosevelt's personality-centered presidency might simply have been one of many transitory highs in the recurring cycle of presidential passivity and activism, such as the intense but rather brief legislative activism of the early Wilson administration. Roosevelt's monopoly of political attention and his capacity to arouse public feeling were reminiscent of the visibility and appeal of his cousin, Theodore Roosevelt. His use of emergency powers in response to crisis had strong precedents in the Lincoln administration. Therefore, when Roosevelt died, World War II ended, and a virtually unknown "little man" succeeded him, there was reason to expect, fear, or hope that, much as in the Wilson-to-Harding transition, the presidency would again move from center stage in national government to a position closer to the wings.

TRUMAN: INSTITUTIONALIZATION OF THE MODERN PRESIDENCY

Truman's impact on substantive public policies was at best uneven; his impact on the modern presidency as an institution was profound. Under Truman, the presidency did in fact continue to be central in national politics. There was, however, a shift from the ad hoc, personally stimulated policy initiatives of Roosevelt to the methodical development of policy by Truman in consort with WHO and BOB staff members, as well as other public officials. This shift is aptly described by Max Weber's phrase "the routinization of charisma."

As tattered and imprecise as the term "charisma" has come to be, it could not be stretched to described Truman's leadership, especially the flat, uninspiring impression he communicated during his first eighteen months in office. Truman's initial extremely high Gallup poll rating (87 percent) expressed national mourning for FDR and sympathy for Truman in what obviously was going to be the monu-

mental task of attempting to succeed Roosevelt. After that first Gallup
poll, Truman's performance as President frequently garnered more
disapproving than approving poll responses. This was an effect of the
unsettled political times over which Truman presided. (Roosevelt,
like Lincoln, died in time not to face postwar problems virtually
guaranteed to erode presidential popularity.) Truman's seeming substantive and rhetorical shortcomings as a national leader also contributed to his endemically low popularity. But he had the added
burden that would have been faced by any successor of Roosevelt
(and perhaps Roosevelt himself had he survived his fourth term)—
that of living up to the standard FDR had set in the depression and
during the war as an inspirer of public confidence.

Whatever his inspirational inadequacies, Truman was no back-
to-normalcy Harding. This was evident as early as September 1945,
when in a twenty-one-point reconversion message he anticipated the
major themes of what soon evolved into the Fair Deal program.
Truman also was not the inexperienced "failed haberdasher" his
critics alleged him to be. In leading a major wartime investigating
committee that scrutinized the performance of "home front" activities and in his earlier service on the Senate Appropriations Committee he had over a decade become closely familiar with the operations and policies of the federal government. Moreover, before his
entry into the Senate, his extensive experience as a county administrator and his omnivorous reading had left him well furnished with
political skills and ideals.

We can see harbingers of the future President in the handful of
documents that the Truman Library has been able to salvage from
Truman's years in local government. Some of them, in which he
methodically accounts for county revenues and expenditures and
proposes reforms, anticipate Truman's exceptionally close work with
his Budget Bureau staff in examining the many policy issues that
quickly fell into the bailiwick of that institution. Other early Truman
documents include speeches to patriotic and other civic groups
which presage many aspects of his presidential leadership—speeches
extolling the centrality of the President in the constitutional system;
praising good (that is, decisive, manly, and moral) leaders, including
great Presidents; and conceiving of social process as the outcome of
the triumph of good over bad leaders.

Much of Truman's impact on the presidency is illustrated by
comparing his and Roosevelt's ways of dealing with the Bureau of the
Budget. In Harold Smith's diaries, a repeated theme during the
Roosevelt years is Smith's concern that he would fail to build a
continuing staff agency that could serve successive presidencies. So
incorrigibly informal was Roosevelt's way of operating that he often
treated Smith simply as if he were another of Roosevelt's many

unofficial advisers, rather than the head of a statutory presidential staff agency. Smith expressed in his diaries a concern that the agency he was in the process of carefully filling with the most promising administrators he could find would be compromised institutionally by FDR's continuing impulse to make use of the director as a mediator among feuding departments and wartime agencies. He was distressed, as he put it, at being Roosevelt's "Mr. Fixit."

Under Truman, the bureau itself as well as its director became an integral part of the presidency. During Smith's holdover period and the tenure of his exceptionally able successor, James Webb, the bureau rapidly assumed the role of central coordinating institution for framing and formalizing annual presentations of what came to be called "the program of the President." Truman was a direct party to the soon taken-for-granted expanded role of the Bureau of the Budget, the enlargement of the White House Office staff, and the conversion of that staff into a team meeting daily with "the boss," dividing a workload beyond the capacity of the traditional presidency. By 1947 the efforts of the White House staff and of the Bureau of the Budget had become closely coordinated as a result of Truman's, Smith's, and Webb's efforts.

From time to time BOB aides, especially if they developed strong Fair Deal political convictions, "crossed the street" and became White House aides. Meanwhile, the bureau itself continued to develop its joint roles of helping the President to frame his policy program and examining policy proposals in terms of their consistency with the overall outlines of that program as well as their technical feasibility. It was during Truman's first two years in office that the bureau began, as a standard operating procedure, to examine all departmental appropriations requests in terms of their consistency with the President's program. Even more important (and less probable, given the title of the agency), the bureau became centrally involved in the legislative process. It became a regular BOB duty to clear and coordinate all legislative requests originating within federal departments, to help draft legislation emanating from the White House, to clear and draft executive orders, and to do all of this in terms of program of the President. These actions were in addition to the continuation of a bureau function acquired in the late 1930s — review and clearance with other relevant agencies of all congressional enactments with a view to recommending whether they be signed or vetoed.

The annual BOB compilation of proposed legislation and the final budget document provide the basis for what has become the set-piece initiation of each political year—a state of the union message, backed up by draft legislation. Delivered by the President with dignified republican ceremony to a joint session of Congress and other assembled dignitaries, the contemporary state of the union message enunciates the general outlines of the President's program, as well as containing traditional rhetoric about present national conditions and future prospects.

The state of the union message is one of three major presidential communications that go to Congress in January. The second is the budget document itself, accompanied by the budget message and the *Budget in Brief*, complete with graphic illustrations. The third is the Report of the President's Council of Economic Advisers (CEA). The CEA, which was provided for in the Employment Act of 1946, is one of two continuing accretions to the Executive Office added during the Truman years. Truman's first council had a chairman who wanted the annual report to be an independent assessment of the economy not coordinated with the political emphasis of the overall presidential program. This view of the role of the CEA did not prevail, however. The council became part of the President's team, and its report and the other two January messages quickly became complementary assertions of the same program. A second statutory body, the National Security Council (NSC), grew out of the legislation that brought about the unification of the armed forces. Initially the NSC was conceived of by many congressmen who had supported unification as a potential check on Presidents' autonomy in their commander-in-chief role. Truman, however, "domesticated" the NSC as well as the CEA. Ever since the Truman years both of these, plus numerous more transient EOP agencies, have been further institutional underpinnings of the modern presidency.

Just as the professional staff of the BOB acquired some of the qualities of those British civil servants who perennially aid the executive, whatever party is in power, so the President's January communications have become roughly akin to the messages to new British parliamentary sessions, ghostwritten by the Government in power for delivery by the monarch. But American Presidents face one of the most vigorously autonomous legislatures in any parliamentary democracy. Hence their messages only help set the *terms* of the next legislative session's political debate, whereas the proposals voiced by the British monarch almost invariably are enacted into law. The many legislative defeats Truman received from the 79th through 82nd Congresses illustrate how a presidential program may be consistently blocked by an opposition coalition. In Truman's case the amount of Fair Deal domestic legislation that he succeeded in passing was minuscule, although there were major triumphs in assembling a sufficiently large bipartisan foreign policy coalition to authorize the Truman Doctrine, the Marshall Plan, and other postwar reconstruction and cold war initiatives.

Truman was also responsible not merely for initiating but also for carrying through policy making in areas included in the expanded domain of independent presidential action. Among the most consequential exercises of executive initiative by this believer in a presidency with substantial autonomous powers were the decision to use atomic weapons at the end of World War II, the decision to commit American troops to Korea, and the executive order integrating the military. Many of Truman's autonomous decisions were politically costly, including a number that reflected his commitment to maintaining the independent powers of the presidency — for example, the steel seizure and the relief of General MacArthur.

Despite domestic policy stasis, his low general popularity, and the political costliness of some of his decisions, Truman's practice of executive assertiveness entrenched the tendency of all but the most conservative policy makers to look at the President as the main framer of the agenda for public debate — even when much of the debate consisted of castigation of his proposals. Truman, like Roosevelt, was not alone responsible for the changes in the presidency that occurred during his years in office. Key advisers like Smith and Webb were also influential. Moreover, Truman was operating in an environment of big government, the welfare state, and American international involvement that inevitably tended to place major responsibilities on the executive branch. Nevertheless, like Roosevelt, Truman himself does emphatically seem to have been a major independent influence on the shape of the modern presidency. Not everyone in the postwar period was convinced that the welfare state should continue or that the United States should maintain its international commitments. Conservatives of both parties felt that the New Deal welfare innovations should be repealed or cut back. Conservative isolationists and left-leaning supporters of Henry Wallace's 1948 Progressive party, out of wholly different motivations, opposed American involvement in the international arena. And during the post-World War II years not all democracies acquired assertive, stable executive leadership, the French Fourth Republic being an obvious example of a nation in which the top political executives (although not the permanent bureaucrats) were highly limited in influence and unstable in tenure in office. What then was to be expected of the evolving "center stage" presidency when another President replaced Truman — one who had frequently echoed his newly adopted party's claim that the "balance" of political leadership should be redirected toward Congress?

EISENHOWER: RATIFICATION OF THE MODERN PRESIDENCY

When the Republicans returned to power in 1953 and the institutional changes and role expectations of the modern presidency were not fundamentally altered, the Great Divide had been crossed. As is well known, drawing on his long military exposure to staff work, Eisenhower arranged for the establishment of a White House office that was more formally organized and, incidentally, larger than Truman's WHO. At least in the official scheme of things, the Eisenhower White House was an organizational hierarchy. Directly under the presidential apex was a chief of staff—for the first six years, the zealous Sherman Adams. As The Assistant to the President, Adams was listed first in the *Organization Manual*; other White House aides were enumerated in an indented list that visually conveyed their subordination to Adams. Adams's counterpart in foreign affairs—again for the first six years—was Secretary of State John Foster Dulles.

We know from a variety of sources, including the newly opened private and confidential files of the President's personal secretary, that Eisenhower was far from being a mere puppet of Adams and Dulles. He was intimately involved in national security policy making and had multiple sources of information about domestic as well as foreign affairs. As a domestic political conservative without a strong desire to innovate, except in modest incremental ways, Eisenhower does, however, seem to have left to Adams and his associates a variety of substantive decisions that would have been made by the President himself in the previous administration, as well as making use of Adams as a framer of alternatives under circumstances where Truman would have canvassed alternatives on his own.

Other steps toward formalization in the Eisenhower White House were the regular and systematic practice of holding cabinet meetings (although, as in other presidencies, the cabinet was not a decision-making body); the establishment of a Cabinet Secretariat; and the creation of an elaborate National Security Council structure, in which special attention was paid not only to formal presentations in weekly meetings of the NSC, but also to the use of a coordinating mechanism (later scrapped by Kennedy) to attend to the implementation of policy.

Many of Eisenhower's formal mechanics of White House organization were supplemented by informal, unpublicized proceedings. The NSC meetings, for example, which by the end of the 1950s had come to be thought of as mechanical rituals, were in fact coordinating and teamwork-generating occasions. Preceding the official meetings, however, there were off-the-record meetings by the President with a subgroup of the NSC, and these appear to have been occasions for a genuine process of hammering out policy in which the President arrived at decisions after hearing contending points of view. And members of the cabinet had individual access to the President to discuss matters that cabinet members invariably find impolitic to discuss openly in the Cabinet Room. Moreover, for the first time the

White House Office staff acquired an official legislative liaison office (staffed by a skilled lobbying team that Eisenhower "appropriated" from the Pentagon). As Eisenhower came to be more and more aware that even a conservative who wished to put curbs on policy innovation needed effective representation of his views to Congress, this staff became increasingly systematic in its efforts to advance the President's program.

Above all, under Eisenhower there continued to *be* a President's program. Having talked of "restoring the balance," Eisenhower quickly found himself to be a presidentialist—that is, a defender of the accrued responsibilities of the modern presidency. This ratification of the overall properties of the modern presidency during Eisenhower's two terms is manifested at both the formal and the symbolic levels. On the formal level, his position favoring presidential prerogative is instructive. Eisenhower immediately became intensely active, for example, in the campaign that successfully defeated the Bricker Amendment, which would have made presidential executive agreements with other nations subject to Senate ratification. In terms of maintaining the symbolic function of the office, Eisenhower was able to draw on his longstanding public credit as the most popular figure to emerge from World War II in order to maintain a remarkably consistent high level of prestige and popularity with the electorate, even at times when Washington insiders derided him for his seeming lack of political skill and knowledge. In this sense he was able—with what seems to have been minimum effort—to live up to the high expectations established under FDR that Presidents be endowed with virtuous personal qualities but nevertheless be sufficiently politically competent to carry out their tasks in a way that leaves citizens broadly satisfied with the state of the nation.

A third, and from the standpoint of this essay especially consequential, aspect of the Eisenhower presidency was his continued use of the institutional resource that made it possible for there to be a "program of the President"—the Bureau of the Budget. Eisenhower's first bureau director, Joseph Dodge, became attuned to the bureau's procedures before assuming office, taking advantage of Truman's offer of interelection "internships" for Eisenhower appointees. Dodge quickly recognized the high quality of the bureau's senior personnel and their readiness to shift from shaping a Truman program to shaping an Eisenhower program. Although there was no first-year Eisenhower legislative program, there was one to accompany his January 1954 state of the union message. The requests for proposed legislation from federal agencies were routinely sent out by the bureau's professional staff in 1953. Before the year was over it became evident that an Eisenhower program would be submitted to Congress.

464EXPERT VIEWS

In August 1956 Eisenhower's secretary, Ann Whitman, replied to an inquiry from Milton Eisenhower as to how the President's workload might be reduced. Her letter, from which I quote selectively, suggests how a basically conservative President, working in a tightly staffed White House, allocated his energies. During much of the previous year the President had been recovering from two major health setbacks, so her remarks apply primarily to Eisenhower's practices up to his September 1955 heart attack. We see his very great attention to national security policy and his greater willingness to delegate policy initiation in domestic than in international affairs.

Regular Weekly Meetings:
1. The National Security Council seems to be the most time-consuming, from the standpoint of number of hours *in* the actual meeting, the briefing before the meeting that has seemed to become a routine, and the time that the President must give, occasionally, to be sure that the meetings reflect exactly the decisions reached. . . . [Mrs. Whitman thought that frequently the President was already well informed on the substance of the prior briefings and of the meetings themselves. She noted "he himself complains that he knows every word of the presentations as they are to be made. However, he feels that to maintain the interest and attention of every member of the NSC, he must sit through each meeting. . . ."]
2. The Cabinet meetings are not usually so long as NSC, but the President feels in some instances that to fill out an agenda, items are included that are not necessarily of the caliber that should come before the Cabinet. . . .
3. The Press Conferences. These meetings are preceded by a half to three-quarter hour briefing by staff members. [Mrs. Whitman felt that in most cases Eisenhower was already sufficiently informed to meet the press without briefings, but added "the meetings do serve the purpose of letting him know how various members of the staff are thinking. . . ."]
4. Legislative Leaders Meetings. When the Congress is in session, these are held weekly but do not last, on the average, more than an hour and a half and only about five minutes' preparation is required.
5. The President has a weekly meeting with the Secretary of Defense.
6. The President usually has a half-hour meeting with [Economic Advisers] Dr. [Gabriel] Hauge and Dr. [Arthur] Burns. I think he finds these meetings valuable and do not believe the sessions are unduly prolonged.

Mrs. Whitman also noted that the President had a half-hour daily intelligence briefing from Colonel Andrew Goodpaster, and she listed roughly a dozen categories of "other items that occupy his time," some of them taking up very little time (for example, independent agencies), some of them involving him in time-consuming ceremonial duties (receiving ambassadors, meeting dignitaries and civic groups, state dinners, and signatures), and others involving policy and intermittently consuming much time. The latter included the State Department ("meetings with the Secretary are irregular, based upon the urgency of the particular crisis of the moment"); additional defense matters ("here is a great time-consuming area. . . . I can't always see why some of the inter-Service problems cannot be resolved before they come to the President"); "other Cabinet matters" ("The President is available at all times to any Cabinet member for consultation"); "personnel, appointments, domestic matters" ("My general impression is that all such items have been pretty well digested [by Sherman Adams] before they reach the President and that only his final judgment is required"); and speeches ("The President spends a great deal of time personally on his speeches, but I don't think that routine can ever be changed. I think only by the process of editing and reworking does the speech become truly his own — and I think the hours — and I guess he spends twenty to thirty on each major speech — are inevitable.")

THE PRESIDENCY SINCE 1960:
STRUCTURAL CHANGES, OSCILLATIONS, AND CONTINUITY

In any institution it is difficult in the short run to distinguish between permanent changes and changes that will turn out to have been only ephemeral. Many changes in the post-Eisenhower presidency were thought to have been permanent at the time but from the perspective of the late 1970s appear to have been rather drastic zigs and zags in patterns that had been established during the formative first three modern presidencies. Taking as a combined basis of classification the actual functioning of the presidency and the way in which the more widely read commentators on American politics have evaluated its functioning, the Kennedy-to-Carter years can be divided into three phases.

Phase one is the period beginning with Kennedy's efforts — "vigorous" efforts — to initiate a wide range of policies, some of them long-term inheritances from the Democratic party's New Deal-Fair Deal agenda, others projects with a distinctive Kennedy stamp. This period continued through the enactment of the extraordinary volume of Johnson Great Society legislation by the heavily Democratic 89th Congress. The bulk of commentators on the presidency viewed this as a period during which a previously "stalemated" presidency was steadily increasing both in its impact on public policy and also in the merit of its contribution to the political system. Merit, of course, is in the eye of the beholder. The beholders I have in mind are the politically liberal academics and publicists who provide most of the "serious" commentary on public affairs. During the formative presidencies . . . most such political commentators had become convinced of the institutional desirability of a "strong" presidency. Experiencing the Kennedy qualities of personal leadership, the posthumous idealization of Kennedy, and the passage of Johnson's sweeping domestic policy program during the period from Kennedy's death to roughly the end of the 89th Congress, these commentators typically felt that the presidency was beginning, in practice, to perform precisely the functions in the political system they had long felt that it ought in principle to be performing.

The period of Great Society legislative enactment overlaps with the second phase, from the advent of serious protest at Vietnam escalation through Watergate and President Nixon's resignation. Even before the end of the 89th Congress, increasing American military involvement in Vietnam began to induce commentary on the presidency, which, as in the first post-1960 phase, stressed the growing capacity of Presidents to shape public policy, but which now emphasized "excessive" presidential power. By late in the Watergate sequence, the view that the presidency was a dangerously unchecked institution was no longer monopolized by liberal political commentators. For convenience, I adopt for this period the label that came to be virtually automatic for many writers: "imperial presidency."

The first two phases, that of celebration of presidential strength and that of lamentation about the "imperial" practices of Presidents Johnson and Nixon, have been followed by a phase that, using the most recent catchword, I shall call "postimperial." During the time since President Nixon left office, one President, Gerald Ford, has joined the select ranks of William Howard Taft and Herbert Hoover as the only twentieth-century incumbents to run unsuccessfully for reelection. Ford's successor, Jimmy Carter, limped through an initial year in office, during which he encountered what could charitably be called limited response to his ambitious legislative and foreign policy goals and a substantial erosion in his Gallup poll ratings.

Presidential politics in phase three, at the advent of the final quarter of the century, seems remarkably like the pattern of politics of the formative pre-Kennedy modern presidencies as described in Richard Neustadt's influential essay, "The Presidency at Mid-Century." As a former Truman aide who had worked on the unsuccessful Fair Deal domestic program and who was also aware of the inability of FDR to win support for similar policies after 1938 and of

Eisenhower's difficulty in achieving even limited policy goals, Neustadt saw the presidency as a highly restrained institution. Granting that modern Presidents had acquired far enhanced formal powers and role expectations, Neustadt argued that Presidents nevertheless were exceptionally limited in their capacities to turn formal power into effective policy making. Further, the tension between the demands on them and the limitations on their ability to make policy and hence to live up to expectations put them in a position Neustadt likened to that of "a cat on a hot tin roof."

The rather drastic and rapid alternations since 1960 in the way in which the presidency has functioned and, possibly as important, in the way in which it has been perceived to function are to a considerable extent a consequence of one continuing property of the presidency. Among all American national political institutions, none is so profoundly affected by the personal characteristics and performance in office of the incumbent and of the other personalities he chooses or permits to act as his chief associates. One reason why the Roosevelt, Truman, and Eisenhower presidencies *could* be formative was that their long duration accustomed political actors, including Presidents themselves and the public at large, as well as other members of the policy-making community, to broadly consistent practices in the conduct of the presidency. Between 1933 and 1961 the *three* formative modern Presidents held office for the equivalent of *seven* four-year terms. Since then *five* presidents have been in office for the equivalent of just over *four* four-year terms.

Just as it was by no means predetermined that the three formative Presidents would have the cumulative impact that they did have in shaping the basic qualities of the modern presidency, there was nothing inexorable about the way the institution has developed since. On the contrary, it has been plausibly maintained that each of the post-Eisenhower Presidents had a major personal impact on the phases through which the presidency has moved since 1960. Would the three phases described above have occurred if the individual named Richard Nixon had defeated Kennedy in 1960? What would have happened if Kennedy had served two full terms? Or if Nixon had never become President?

Although there is no definitive way to answer such questions, it is possible to apply systematic evidence and inference to them. "What if?" questions are the grist of historical explanation. It is only possible to say that *x* caused *y* in a historical sequence by inferring that some plausible non-*x* would have led to a result different from *y*. Putting this concretely, and in terms of the effects of presidential psychology on the evolution of the presidency, we may note that, quite appropriately, there continue to be debates about whether Kennedy would have escalated the Vietnam conflict in the fashion that Johnson did, whether FDR would have presided over the same Truman-led sequence of cold war events that occurred after his death, and so forth. The entire enterprise of psychological interpretation of Presidents and their behavior is dependent on such speculation.

By the late 1970s the rapid turnover in Presidents had become an important quality of the presidency itself, as well as helping to explain the sequence of cyclical rather than secular changes in certain overall properties of the office. Modern Presidents, at least since the Twenty-second Amendment, have generally been recognized by political observers as short-run participants in Washington policy making, who therefore tend to have a hurried approach to the making of policy. The more enduring fixtures of the Washington political community—senior members of Congress, justices, lobbyists, and Washington attorneys, for example—can better afford to play a waiting game. If the impact a President seeks is policy innovation rather than the maintenance of the status quo, the President's relatively brief tenure of office encourages him to engage in activities that are politically risky: simply to win office he needs to raise aspirations about what he will be able to contribute to the nation; once in office, the difficulty of meeting those aspirations opens up temptations to cut corners—for example, to rush legislation through Congress and leave considerations of practical implementation for later on, or to circumvent slow-moving or otherwise recalcitrant departments and bureaus by moving policy making into the White House, say, by augmenting the role of the assistant for national security affairs over that of the secretary of state or by establishing a White House "plumbers" group. The temptation to cut corners therefore seems bound to increase. . . .

THE INTRACTABLE POLITICAL ENVIRONMENT
OF THE POSTIMPERIAL PRESIDENCY

At what Neustadt called "mid-century," Presidents were severely restrained in their ability to affect policy, especially in spheres other than those that permitted unilateral action. They were surrounded by an intractable political environment. As the last quarter of the century begins, after a period during which Presidents seemed to be riding high, intractability is back. Many of the restraints on Presidents that seemed unnecessarily oppressive to liberals in the 1950's and early 1960's are precisely those that so often restrained Ford and that make Carter's efforts at policy achievement so difficult. The *way* in which these restraints manifest themselves does seem to have changed, largely as the result of factors that make it even harder in the late 1970's than it was during the three formative modern presidencies for Presidents to live up to the continuing belief of many citizens that the President is singly responsible for the state of the entire nation.

The most conspicuous obstacle to presidential policy influence is Congress. From the rise of the congressional conservative coalition following the 1938 presidential election through Johnson's landslide election in 1964, the major source of congressional resistance to presidential initiatives was — especially in the Roosevelt, Truman, and Kennedy years — the resistance by conservative Republicans and southern Democrats to liberal presidential policy proposals. Eisenhower's domestic policy conservatism was sufficiently disguised by his advocacy of "modern Republicanism" to make this seem to be the case even during the single Republican presidency of that period.

The 95th Congress, which in Carter's first year in office passed none of his major substantive legislative proposals, had approximately the same one-sided Democratic majority as the 89th Congress, which in a comparable period of time enacted a sizeable proportion of Johnson's Great Society program. One major difference between them was that Carter's was operating in an "end of liberalism" climate — a time when the failures of many Great Society programs had produced widespread skepticism about the efficacy of legislative attacks on major social problems. In fact, the phrase, "the end of ideology" seems more applicable to the political discourse of the 1970s than it was to the period in which it was coined, the 1950s. In the 1950s there were still many political activists and practitioners who took it for granted that *broadly* liberal or *broadly* conservative political programs, if only enacted, would rectify what they felt to be the nation's social and political shortcomings. In the present era of economic "stagflation" and of such cross-cutting conflicts as those between liberal policy reformers favoring environmental protection and liberal labor union activists favoring economic growth, clear-cut lines of cleavage and hence the bases for organizing coalitions are harder to identify than they were even in the ostensibly unideological 1950s.

Closely related to the decline of predictable ideological groupings in Congress (as elsewhere in society) is a decline since the 1950s in the ability of congressional leaders to serve as effective intermediaries between their colleagues and the President, knowing that on achieving agreement with the President they can deliver significant blocs of votes and bring about the passage of the desired legislation. Consider the negotiations that shaped the final outcome of the Civil Rights Act of 1957. The point at issue was a provision of the legislation that enabled federal judges to exact fines and prison sentences in cases when state officials deprived citizens of their voting rights. If such cases were not decided by judges, but rather by the lily-white southern juries of the time, there would have been no effective sanction against southern officials who ignored the act's provisions. Through the efforts of the two Texas power brokers who led the majority

Democratic party, Speaker Sam Rayburn and Senate Majority Leader Lyndon Johnson, a group of swing congressmen had been won
over to the provision, which finally became law: fines as great as $300
and jail sentences up to forty-five days would be acceptable without
the requirement of a trial. Johnson, who considered this a more
favorable compromise than he had hoped for, telephoned President
Eisenhower and

> . . . asked the President to see quietly if his boys would agree to
> that. The President asked for ten minutes. He called [the Republi-
> can leaders, William Knowland and Joseph Martin] off the floor;
> both agreed. . . . [Eisenhower] called Lyndon Johnson back and
> said everything was okay. He asked for a little time so the proceed-
> ings would be in order, which Lyndon agreed to. . . . The Presi-
> dent called [his chief of legislative liaison] who was delighted at the
> compromise.

Even if Carter had managed to establish such solidly grounded
bargaining relations with the congressional party leaders of the 95th
Congress, there was little likelihood that the leaders themselves
would have been able to deliver the goods. Some of the reasons for
this change [as detailed by Thomas Patterson, are that]: no subsequent congressional party leaders have been as skilled at molding
coalitions as Johnson and Rayburn were; there has been an increasing
tendency for incumbent congressmen automatically to be returned to
office if they run for reelection, and this undoubtedly increases
congressmen's independence in dealing with both their party leaders
and the President; and a massive growth in congressional staffs has
further decentralized congressional power by giving congressmen
their own decision-making resources. Above and beyond these
changes, there appears to be a general post-Watergate congressional
resistance to cooperation with the White House.

In the 1950s it was widely taken for granted that Congress was a
major check on executive autonomy and that the "weakness" of
congressional parties limited the chances that partisanship would
serve to "bridge the separation of powers" even when the same party
was in control of both branches of government. Who would have
thought that a quarter-century later one explanation of a President's
difficulties in influencing his party would be a still greater decline in
the capacity of congressional leaders to mediate between members of
Congress and the President? This decline does seem to have occurred, however, and it parallels still another institutional decline —
that of the power of party leaders in the states and localities to mediate
between their constituencies and the President, especially in presidential-selection politics.

During the formative period of the modern presidency, the "decentralized" national party system was widely viewed as a restraint on the mobilization around the President of national policy-making coalitions. By the 1970s state and local party organizations were so fragmented that, by contrast, the 1930s through the 1950s seem to have been high points of party government. At least in the earlier period there *were* party organizations and leaders with whom Presidents could bargain and who viewed a successful President as a political asset. Accompanying the general decline in the strength of state and local party organizations throughout the 1960s there was a striking decline in candidacies and campaigns using traditional grass-roots party channels. The older decentralized party fiefdoms were at least entities with which Presidents could bargain—for example, when the time came for renomination or for influencing the choice of one's successor. Today there is much less to bargain with "out there." Moreover, the change in presidential-selection rules toward multiple primaries, caucus states that are penetrable by disciplined candidate organizations, the disappearance of unit-rule voting at national conventions, and other "democratizing" party reforms further invalidate the textbook description of the President as chief of his party. In 1968, if Johnson had not withdrawn his candidacy, it was by no means certain that he would have been nominated. Ford fought an extremely demanding battle for the 1976 nomination. And while Nixon's renomination was superficially in the traditional pattern of partisan renomination of incumbent Presidents, his main resource was the Committee to Re-elect the President, not the Republican party.

Clearly much of what is intractable about the political environment of the late 1970s results from the inability of Presidents to work effectively with institutions that also restrained the early modern Presidents. The difference is in the nature of this inability. In the past, the resistance came from institutions that possessed sufficient structure and leadership so that bargaining and negotiation were possible. In the present, institutions are more amorphous, less responsive to their own leadership or any other, and are therefore less well suited for presidential coalition-building.

This amorphousness also appears increasingly to apply to cabinet departments, as Heclo suggests in his ... study of the executive branch. The President's appointees—the cabinet secretaries and assistant secretaries—seem less and less likely to be professional politicians or public figures who have independent bases of political influence. Rather, they are professional participants in the policy domains that concern their departments. In this respect they tend to have views that converge with those of the career officials in the departments—the latter having increasingly become advocates of the substantive policy directions of the programs that they administer. Cabinet secretaries have always "gone native" and civil servants have always had views about their programs, but if Heclo is correct, there is now less difference between the political appointees and the career bureaucrats than there once was. Above all, the departments are decreasingly available to the President as firm entities with which he can work out alliances in the course of policy making and implementation.

Under the heading of intractability (if not amorphousness) it also is appropriate to mention the mass media, which nowadays expose the President to a kind of scrutiny that probably accounts both for the evanescent high popularity of many Presidents during their early months in office and for their subsequent sharp declines in support. Roosevelt was rarely photographed from the waist down; many Americans do not appear to have been aware of the extent of his physical disability. George Wallace's physical disability was publicized in minute clinical detail; his physical limitations and his emotional state were described in ways that could scarcely have encouraged support for his presidential aspirations. In part, microscopic focus on real or attributed presidential acts and traits (Carter's folksiness, Ford's physical ineptness, Nixon's outbursts of temper during the late stages of Watergate) is a result of the shift from print journalism to television newscasting as the principal source relied upon by most Americans for political news. Without accepting the indictment by Nixon loyalists of the "liberal establishment" mass media, I think that Nixon speech-writer Raymond Price is undoubtedly right in his comment that

Television has vastly changed the nature of the news business. . . . People turn to the news, whether print or broadcast, for both information and entertainment. Whereas print journalism has tended more toward the presentation of information that entertains, the structure of television news is such that it is designed to be an entertainment that informs.

Media coverage of the President-elect and the first few months of an administration tends to emphasize the endearing personal touches — Ford's preparation of his own English muffins, Carter's fireside chat in informal garb. No wonder both of these Presidents enjoyed high poll ratings during their initial months in office. But the trend can only go downward. Even if the media coverage simply shifts to rather straightforward reporting of initial administration efforts to get organized and develop a program, the impact is bound to be unfavorable in contrast to the idyllic initial presentations of the President. Further, after idealizing Presidents, the media quickly search out their warts. More and more it is the shortcomings in presidential performance that are newsworthy. Moreover, tough investigative journalism now is a prime means of making a professional mark. Such journalism may have been an invaluable counterweight to Johnson credibility gaps and Nixon stonewalling. For present purposes, however, what needs to be noted is that aspiring Woodwards and Bernsteins constitute still one more environmental obstacle to presidential leadership.

THE PRESIDENTS' REACTIONS TO THEIR POLITICAL ENVIRONMENT

During the years when Presidents were widely viewed by liberal political commentators as having an edge over other members of the policy community in their ability to identify and to promote successfully the public interest, some of these commentators were sensitive to the "Caesarist" potential of a politics in which sustained efforts were made to enhance a single leader's influence over other policy makers without providing him with legitimate instruments of leadership. The now barely remembered "responsible party" proposals that were endorsed by many political scientists in the 1950s were designed to domesticate strong presidential leadership by harnessing it to party organizations that would be ideologically cohesive and that would also have a base in widespread participation by idealistic local party members. Needless to say, there has been no move toward strong, responsible political parties along the lines that the party reformers advocated, or along any other lines.

The reformers' concern with Caesarism does, however, seem to have been prophetic. It anticipated the perceived increases in the arbitrary use of presidential command powers during the Johnson, Nixon, and, some would claim, Kennedy years. Some of the excesses of imperial presidential leadership seem to have been attempts to flail out at the very aspects of the political environment that make the presidency a potentially stalemated institution: if bureaucrats seem disloyal, wiretap them; if the media and Congress will surely object to a desired military action, carry it out in secret. Obviously individual Presidents differ in the degree to which they perceive their political environment in adversary terms and are prepared to act ruthlessly. Nevertheless, as the authors of an article reporting the sharp policy differences between Nixon supporters and supergrade civil servants comment, "even paranoids have enemies."

GROWTH AND EVOLUTION OF THE PRESIDENTIAL BUREAUCRACY

From early in the 1960s through the end of the Ford administration, the number of people working in the White House Office increased substantially. There have been various published itemizations of the changes, but since practices such as borrowing personnel from other agencies in the executive branch have periodically changed and are difficult to monitor, I simply refer the reader to the several complementary attempts at year-by-year tabulation. There has also been growth in the remainder of the Executive Office of the President, but here the statistics are even less susceptible to summary discussion because the EOP has frequently been used to house agencies that are not engaged in staffing the presidency but have line responsibilities. The most obvious example has been the Office of Economic Opportunity, which for many years was located in the EOP out of a fear that its program would be "absorbed" and that it would lose its innovative aspects and public visibility if it disappeared into the sprawling Department of Health, Education, and Welfare.

Something more than Parkinson's Law has been at work in the growth of the White House staff. In 1961, an administration took office committed to introducing new programs and energizing continuing programs. The Johnson administration was even more activist than Kennedy's, especially if "activism" is used to describe both the monumental outpouring of Great Society programs and also the expansion of hostilities in Vietnam. In these two administrations, the desire to innovate, combined with an impulse to circumvent resistance of the sort discussed in connection with the intractable political environment, led to an increasing tendency "to run the government from the White House." The need to coordinate interdepartmental programs had also expanded greatly. With Nixon, the desire to curb many of the innovations of the previous two administrations in the context of what seemed to Nixon and his associates to be a uniquely hostile environment (a Democratic Congress, administrators committed to carrying out New Frontier-Great Society programs, and mass media that in their view were not disposed to portray the President favorably) led to an even further expansion of the White House Office staff. Nixon's intense concern with foreign affairs and his close cooperation with Henry Kissinger and the much enlarged National Security Council staff, which served as Kissinger's EOP replica of the State Department, further contributed to the size of the bureaucracy attached to the presidency, as did Nixon's concern with domestic political enemies, which came to a head with the Watergate break-in and its aftermath.

Other important changes in the Executive Office of the President, especially changes in the Bureau of the Budget, which eventually led to a renamed agency with a somewhat changed mission, were underway throughout the post-Eisenhower period. We have seen that much of the Truman domestic program was drafted by Bureau of the Budget staff, working closely with Truman's (by present standards) small White House Office team, especially the aides of the successive special counsels, Clark Clifford and Charles S. Murphy. The bureau proved to be remarkably capable of shifting gears and of responding to Eisenhower's deep commitment to budgetary restraint. After the eight Eisenhower years, however, the bureau did not seem to Kennedy and Johnson to be an administrative entity well suited for framing a large volume of new policy, some of it without much precedent. Even before taking office, Kennedy appointed task forces to help shape his legislative agenda. Johnson made regular use of task forces, linking them to a much expanded White House domestic policy staff. Task forces typically were composed of people from the private sector, presidential aides, and federal officials. Use was made of individual Budget Bureau officials, but frequently they acted not in their institutional status as bureau officials, but rather as individuals who were chosen because they were viewed as personally knowledgeable and imaginative.

The Bureau of the Budget and its successor agency, the Office of Management and Budget (OMB), continued to clear legislation and executive orders, but more and more, routine rather than innovative policies bore the agency's imprint. Perhaps the most stable aspect of the bureau's role since 1960 has been its review of congressional enactments with a view to examining their consistency with the president's program and their practical efficacy. There has been no systematic change in presidential responses to OMB's recommendations about whether or not to exercise the veto.

The 1970 reorganization in which the BOB became the OMB was a direct response to the Nixon administration's desire to have a political impact through the assertive use of the executive branch in policy making—for example, by the impoundment of funds appropriated to maintain Great Society programs. Yet the change was anticipated in Kennedy's and Johnson's view of BOB as too slow-moving and cautious to keep up with their policy-making efforts. Under Kennedy and Johnson and under Nixon, the bureau seemed ill-equipped to meet presidential desires, whether desires to initiate policy or to retrench.

The most distinctive feature of the OMB (which in many ways did continue to carry out the BOB's basic functions) was the introduction of a "layer" of presidential appointees directly under the OMB director. These officials were, in effect, line officers. Their counterparts were the White House Office domestic policy aides. The new layer of politically appointed assistant directors and the bolstered White House staff were intended to make the bureau more systematically responsive to White House directives. During this period, OMB directors also tended to become detached from the professional staffs of their agency. More and more, they were used as personal staff advisers to the President, sometimes physically located in the West Wing and at any rate rarely in touch with the detailed work of the agency in such matters as the legislative clearance of less visible components of the presidential program and the examination of agency budget requests.

At the time of the 1970 transition, a number of long-time senior members of the agency, including some who had held positions of responsibility from as far back as the Smith era, found other employment or went into retirement. At least some of the exodus reflected unhappiness with the agency's changed mission. As Berman's research and other studies show, the OMB is populated with aides who have spent far less time in the agency than was traditionally the case with the BOB and who tend to be reconciled to the notion that their responsibility is directly to the incumbent President. Undoubtedly there is much idealization in the BOB veterans' view that they served both President and presidency and in their feeling of commitment to "neutral competence." Nevertheless, there is reason to believe that the shift from BOB to OMB weakened a valuable restraint on grandiose presidential aspirations. One reason why many of the implementation failures of Great Society programs were not anticipated or more promptly detected was that the BOB staff (which has *not* increased in proportion to the growth of the White House staff) did not have the time and resources to evaluate the cascade of new programs and policy proposals.

Under present circumstances, however, it is far from certain that, even with sufficient resources, the OMB will be as disposed to warn Presidents that proposed policies have hidden costs and impracticalities as the BOB traditionally would have been. Further, an agency with few officials who have long records of service and with a rather high rate of personnel turnover is bound to lack what is commonly called "institutional memory"—the ability to evaluate current proposals in terms of its experience with previous endeavors to accomplish the same ends.

Both the change from BOB to OMB and the great expansion of White House staffs in the 1960s and early 1970s clearly rose out of presidential efforts to respond to a sense that, in spite of the center-stage status of the modern President, he is surrounded by a cast of actors more committed to stealing the show from him than to allowing him to live up to the nation's expectations that his performance be the extraordinary one. There is, however, no evidence that a larger White House staff and a more deferential BOB/OMB have in fact made recent Presidents more successful. On the matter of White House size, Nixon's experience provides the strongest evidence of a contrary effect, as the innumerable memoirs and other Watergate-induced revelations so extensively document. A White House Office that envelops the entire Old Executive Office building and harbors an armed member of a political espionage unit and a special counsel whose safe contains unaccounted-for cash campaign contributions — in short, an office that leaves room for "White House horrors" — symbolizes the broader problem of a presidential bureaucracy that has expanded to the point where the President is victimized rather than helped by members of a staff whom he himself cannot begin to supervise.

Under Ford, the size of the White House staff did not decline markedly, though one of Nixon's innovations for imposing the presidential will on public policy, John Ehrlichman's Domestic Council, fell into disuse. Carter has sharply cut the size of the White House staff and substituted a domestic policy staff for a council, but the consequences of Carter's reorganization cannot yet be assessed. Much of the reduction is cosmetic — for example, certain personal services are no longer tabulated under the heading White House Office and much White House business will now be conducted by personnel detailed from other agencies. The political layer of OMB has in fact been expanded rather than reduced.

PRESIDENCY-CURBING LEGISLATION

In the days when the Bricker Amendment was narrowly defeated by a coalition led by a Republican President, the notion that an already politically restrained presidency needed added legal restraints was abhorrent to liberal commentators on American politics. They saw the presidency as the political institution most likely to have a benign impact on public policy. Opponents of the Bricker Amendment in most cases felt that there had already been a recent and unfortunate presidency-weakening constitutional change — the 22nd Amendment, restraining the President from running for a third term. Many of these same commentators sympathized with such exercises of presidential prerogative as Truman's deliberate refusal to seek a congressional resolution authorizing American military intervention in Korea — a refusal Truman made with some awareness that he was increasing his potential political vulnerability, but on the principled ground that he wanted to avoid setting a precedent that, he felt, would weaken future Presidents. Yet, as Averell Harriman, who at the time recommended that Truman seek such a resolution, has since noted congressional authorization would have "tied the hands" of many later opponents of "Truman's War."

In connection with the general alterations in views about the presidency that occurred during the Vietnam conflict and Watergate, presidency-curbing legislation came to receive increasing support — much of it from former defenders of a broad construction of the

President's power. Largely during the Watergate period, Congress enacted an unprecedented array of presidency-curbing legislation. Most of these laws have not been tested or, when they have been, have not had much effect on existing practices. All told, however, it is hard to believe that their total impact on Presidents will be nil. Certainly if the laws had been in force many past acts of presidential initiative would have had to be carried out with more systematic attention to congressional support than they were. Here are some of the major legislative changes, beginning with one that is a logical consequence of BOB's transformation into OMB, a more explicitly political agency:

• After fifty-three years during which BOB/OMB had existed as an agency wholly in the President's preserve, in 1973 the OMB director and deputy directors for the first time became subject to congressional confirmation. (P.L. 93-250, 88 Stat 11, 1974).

• In 1973 Congress allowed the lapse of a presidential power to propose executive branch reorganization plans, which would go into effect unless rejected by Congress within sixty days. In 1977 President Carter succeeded in winning restoration of this power (the Reorganization Act of 1977), but with restraints on the elimination of statutory programs and the provision that no more than three reorganization plans can be pending at any time.

• The Impoundment Control Act of 1974 (Title X of P.L. 93-344) requires that if a President does not want to expend appropriated funds he must report "recission" to Congress. If he wants to *defer* spending funds, he is able to do so unless one house of Congress votes disapproval. Recissions must be approved by both houses within forty-five days.

• The Case Act, passed in 1972 (P.L. 92-403), requires that all executive agreements with foreign powers be reported to the Congress. In fact, however, the Nixon administration failed to report a number of international agreements, notably several made with the government of South Vietnam.

• The War Powers Resolution of 1973 (P.L. 93-148) requires the President to consult with Congress "in every possible instance" before committing troops to combat and to submit a report on his action to Congress, and makes it necessary for the Congress, unless physically unable to meet, to authorize the military action. In the one case to which this has applied, President Ford's rescue of the ship *Mayaguez* and its crew, there was congressional briefing but not consultation, and the episode did not last the sixty days allowed until congressional action was required; most important were the political realities: numerous members of Congress promptly praised Ford's action.

In describing these changes I have used the term commonly applied to them — "President-curbing" legislation. Yet we have also noted the potentially high costs of presidential command actions, especially when these are based on broad interpretations of the extent to which the vague language of Article II entitles the President to engage in autonomous action. At least in the case of Truman and Korea, the War Powers Resolution probably would have yielded the equivalent of the congressional resolution that Harriman urged Truman to seek. And this in turn could have provided Truman with protection from some of the criticism he received as the war lingered on. (Indeed one objection to the resolution by those who felt it did not sufficiently curb presidential war powers was that just such a possibility might occur.) In the legalistic context of American politics it is possible that more explicitly bounded Presidents will be more, rather than less, able to maintain sustained support for their political goals.

SUMMARY AND CONCLUSIONS

Thomas Patterson in his analysis of the contemporary Congress . . . notes that if Henry Clay had been resurrected and placed in the 95th Congress he would begin to see that, in spite of many detailed changes in the structure of the institution, it continues to function in ways reminiscent of the period before the Civil War. By contrast, we have seen that even a 1920s President would have difficulty making sense of the modern presidency. The changes that have transformed the traditional presidency were evident by the end of the Eisenhower administration. The turbulent experience of the institution since 1960 has also left a few apparently enduring residues — for example, the legislation just summarized and the changes in the White House Office and Executive Office of the President more generally. During the Kennedy, Johnson, and Nixon administrations, more fundamental changes in the presidency seemed to be underway; but to an extraordinary degree the politics of the post-Nixon presidency have been reminiscent of the severely restrained "mid-century" presidencies.

In commenting on the changes in evaluations of the merits of the presidency as an institution that occurred during the post-Eisenhower years, I have not sought to summarize the views of the institution that have been prevalent in the years since Nixon resigned. There are many views of how Ford and (to date) Carter have comported themselves in office, but the "data base" for evaluating the postimperial presidency as an institution is too thin. Even more important, the intellectual resources for such an evaluation are not yet available. The old presidency-celebrating imagery of "lonely grandeur" and "awesome power," and of the need for more power, cannot be resurrected. A common prescription during the Johnson and Nixon years — that the presidency be "demystified" — may slowly be coming to pass, particularly if the nation continues to undergo a series of one-term presidencies. Yet Presidents still do seem to be expected to perform wonders.

My own discussion of the President-curbing legislation stressed the possible contributions that a firmer statutory basis of power might make to effective presidential leadership. I cannot imagine, however, that legislative changes will fundamentally alter dilemmas that arise from high expectations of presidential performance and the low capacity of Presidents to live up to those expectations.

Today's presidency is an institution in search of new role definitions. This is evident in the actions of the President himself, as we see Carter floundering through episodes of self-conscious image-building, self-imposed demands for policy enactments which do not come to pass, a state of the union message stressing the need for lowered expectations from government, and attempts at tough old-fashioned political arm-twisting in connection with Panama Canal Treaty roll calls. Perhaps a President who had not come up as a political outsider, belaboring standard Washington political practices, would have been off to a more effective start. But even as Washington-wise a President as Johnson, whose administration started with widely acclaimed successes, came to grief.

Taking it for granted that FDR's political skills and the wide-spread sense of crisis that enabled him to put them to work were sui generis, it may be instructive to consider the view of the presidency held by the last two-term incumbent — Eisenhower. As I noted, archives now available at the Eisenhower Library emphatically refute the image that President-watchers of the time had of Ike as a "captive hero," cherubically soothing the American people with his infectious grin and golfing while others ran — or failed to run — the government. We discover a "modern Republican" whose modernity consisted of being an internationalist and of favoring moderate departures from conservative political principles in the interest of providing the Republican party — or at least its President — with sufficient electoral strength to win the support of an electorate unprepared to see basic New Deal programs, like Social Security, repealed. More interestingly, we see a man for whom leadership had been a life-long preoccupation and who in extensive correspondence with his associates enunciated in detail how he conceived of leadership in general and of the presidency in particular.

In my own reflections on what a contemporary presidential role definition might be, I have found instructive such assertions of Eisenhower's as the following comment in a letter to Henry Luce, written in August 1960, ruminating on his tenure in office:

The government of the United States has become too big, too complex, and too pervasive in its influence on all our lives for one individual to pretend to direct the details of its important and critical programming. Competent assistants are mandatory; without them the Executive Branch would bog down. To command the loyalties and dedication and best efforts of capable and outstanding individuals requires patience, understanding, a readiness to delegate, and an acceptance of responsibility for any honest errors — real or apparent — those subordinates might make.

Eisenhower, with his popularity and his limited domestic policy aspirations, could make such a statement with more assurance than a normal survivor of domestic political wars, especially one committed to substantial political changes. And one doubts whether Sherman Adams would fully have endorsed the last sentence in Eisenhower's statement. Nevertheless, the gist of his message — that the President is not the political system — might usefully inform political thought today. It may be easier to convince Presidents of this than the general public. Presidents have an interest in their own "demystification" if they are to keep from falling into the perennial trap of seeking overachievement and accomplishing dismal underachievement.

Elsewhere in his letter to Luce, Eisenhower commented that, having had for two years a slim Republican majority and for six years a Democratic majority in Congress, "the hope of doing something constructive for the nation . . . has required methods calculated to attract cooperation, although the natural impulse would have been to lash out." This may be no more than a self-serving way of saying that one has practiced the art of the possible. Again, however, I think Eisenhower's comments suggest a point that may contribute to a redefining of the role of the modern President in more workable terms. The most appropriate redefinition would seem to be one that educates both citizens and political leaders (and, in particular, the President himself) to view the office in terms of a realistic assessment of what Presidents can in fact accomplish in American politics.

This role definition would make it perfectly clear that the buck — a term that presumably refers to all major policy making — neither stops nor starts only in the Oval Office. It circulates among many political actors. Depending upon the President's skill, his interest, the nature of the issues being considered, and the state of the national and international political environment, the President can have a major impact on how the buck circulates and with what results. But he neither is, nor can be, nor should be an unmoved mover.

PRESIDENTS OF THE UNITED STATES

PRESIDENT	PARTY	TERM
1. George Washington	Federalist	1789–1797
2. John Adams	Federalist	1797–1801
3. Thomas Jefferson	Democratic-Republican	1801–1809
4. James Madison	Democratic-Republican	1809–1817
5. James Monroe	Democratic-Republican	1817–1825
6. John Quincy Adams	Democratic-Republican	1825–1829
7. Andrew Jackson	Democratic	1829–1837
8. Martin Van Buren	Democratic	1837–1841
9. William Harrison	Whig	1841*
10. John Tyler	Whig	1841–1845
11. James Polk	Democratic	1845–1849
12. Zachary Taylor	Whig	1849–1850*
13. Millard Fillmore	Whig	1850–1853
14. Franklin Pierce	Democratic	1853–1857
15. James Buchanan	Democratic	1857–1861
16. Abraham Lincoln	Republican	1861–1865†
17. Andrew Johnson	Union	1865–1869
18. Ulysses Grant	Republican	1869–1877
19. Rutherford Hayes	Republican	1877–1881
20. James Garfield	Republican	1881†
21. Chester Arthur	Republican	1881–1885
22. Grover Cleveland	Democratic	1885–1889
23. Benjamin Harrison	Republican	1889–1893
24. Grover Cleveland	Democratic	1893–1897
25. William McKinley	Republican	1897–1901†
26. Theodore Roosevelt	Republican	1901–1909
27. William Taft	Republican	1909–1913
28. Woodrow Wilson	Democratic	1913–1921
29. Warren Harding	Republican	1921–1923*
30. Calvin Coolidge	Republican	1923–1929
31. Herbert Hoover	Republican	1929–1933
32. Franklin Roosevelt	Democratic	1933–1945*
33. Harry Truman	Democratic	1945–1953
34. Dwight Eisenhower	Republican	1953–1961
35. John Kennedy	Democratic	1961–1963†
36. Lyndon Johnson	Democratic	1963–1969
37. Richard Nixon	Republican	1969–1974‡
38. Gerald Ford	Republican	1974–1977
39. Jimmy Carter	Democratic	1977–1981
40. Ronald Reagan	Republican	1981–

* Died in office
† Assassinated
‡ Resigned

BIBLIOGRAPHY

Abel, Eli, *The Missile Crisis* (New York: Bantam Books, 1968).
Abraham, Henry, *Justices and Presidents: A Political History of Appointments to the Supreme Court* (New York: Oxford University Press, 1974).
Acheson, Dean, *Present at the Creation* (New York: W. W. Norton, 1969).
Adams, Sherman, *First-Hand Report: The Story of the Eisenhower Administration* (New York: Harper, 1961).
Albertson, Dean, ed., *Eisenhower as President* (New York: Hill and Wang, 1963).
Alexander, Herbert E., *Financing Politics* (Washington: Congressional Quarterly, 1976).
Allen, Roger S. and William V. Shannon, *The Truman Merry-Go-Round* (New York: Vanguard, 1950).
————, "The American Presidency in the Last Half Century," *Current History*, Vol. XXXIX (October 1960).
Allison, Graham T., *Essence of Decision: Explaining the Cuban Missile Crisis* (Boston: Little, Brown, 1971).
————, and Peter Szanton, *Remaking Foreign Policy: The Organization Connection* (New York: Basic Books, 1976).
Anderson, Donald F., *William Howard Taft: A Conservative's Conception of the Presidency* (Ithaca, N.Y.: Cornell University Press, 1973).
Anderson, Patrick, *The President's Men* (Garden City, N.Y.: Doubleday, 1968).
Asher, Herbert. *Presidential Elections and American Politics* (Homewood, Ill.: Dorsey, 1976).
Austin, Anthony, *The President's War: The Story of the Tonkin Gulf Resolution and How The Nation Was Trapped In Vietnam* (Philadelphia: Lippincott, 1971).
Bach, Stanley and George T. Sulzner, eds., *Perspective on the Presidency* (Lexington, Mass.: D.C. Heath, 1974).
Bailey, Thomas A., *Presidential Greatness: The Image and the Man from George Washington to the Present* (New York: Appleton-Century-Crofts, 1972).
————, *Woodrow Wilson and the Great Betrayal* (New York: Macmillan, 1945).
————, *Woodrow Wilson and the Lost Peace* (New York: Macmillan, 1944).
Bayh, Birch, *One Heartbeat Away: Presidential Disability* (New York: Bobbs-Merrill, 1968).
Barber, James David, ed., *Choosing the President* (Englewood Cliffs, N.J.: Prentice-Hall, 1974).
————, *The Presidential Character: Predicting Performance in the White House* (Englewood Cliffs, N.J.: Prentice-Hall, 1972).
————, *The Pulse of Politics* (New York: W. W. Norton, 1980).
————, *Race for the Presidency: The Media and the Nominating Process* (Englewood Cliffs, N.J.: Prentice-Hall, 1978).

Barnett, Richard, *The Roots of War* (New York: Atheneum, 1972).

Bell, Jack, *Presidency: Office of Power* (Rockleigh, N.J.: Allyn and Bacon, 1967).

Benedict, Michael, *The Impeachment and Trial of Andrew Johnson* (New York: W. W. Norton, 1973).

Berdahl, Clarence, *The War Powers of the Executive in the United States* (Urbana: University of Illinois Press, 1921).

Berger, Raoul, *Executive Privilege: A Constitutional Myth* (Cambridge, Mass.: Harvard University Press, 1974).

―――, *Impeachment: The Constitutional Problems* (Cambridge, Mass.: Harvard University Press, 1973).

Berman, Larry, *The Office of Management and Budget and the Presidency, 1921-1979*. (Princeton, N.J.: Princeton University Press, 1979).

Bernstein, Barton J., ed., *Politics and Policies of the Truman Administration* (Chicago: Quadrangle, 1970).

Binkley, Wilfred E., *The Man in the White House: His Powers and Duties* (Baltimore: Johns Hopkins, 1970).

―――, *The Powers of the President* (Garden City: N.Y.: Doubleday, Doran, 1937).

―――, *The President and Congress* (New York: Alfred A. Knopf, 1947).

Bishop, George F., et al., *The Presidential Debates: Media, Electoral and Policy Perspectives* (New York: Harper & Row, 1978).

Black, Charles L., Jr., *Impeachment: A Handbook* (New Haven, Conn.: Yale University Press, 1974).

Blum, John Morton, *Woodrow Wilson and the Politics of Morality* (Boston: Little, Brown, 1956).

―――, *The Republican Roosevelt* (Cambridge, Mass.: Harvard University Press, 1961).

Borden, Morton, ed., *America's Ten Greatest Presidents* (Chicago: Rand McNally, 1961).

Brams, Steven, *The Presidential Election Game* (New Haven, Conn.: Yale University Press, 1978).

Brant, Irving, *Impeachment* (New York: Alfred A. Knopf, 1972).

―――, *James Madison*, 6 vols. (Indianapolis: Bobbs-Merrill, 1941-61).

Brauer, Carl M., *John F. Kennedy and the Second Reconstruction* (New York: Columbia University Press, 1978).

Broder, David S., *The Party's Over* (New York: Harper & Row, 1971).

Brogan, Denis, *Politics in America* (Garden City, N.Y.: Doubleday, 1960).

Brown, Stuart G., *The American Presidency: Leadership, Partisanship, and Popularity* (New York: Macmillan, 1966).

―――, *The Presidency On Trial: Robert Kennedy's 1968 Campaign And Afterwards* (Honolulu, Hawaii: University Press of Hawaii, 1971).

Brownlow, Louis, *The President and the Presidency* (Chicago: University of Chicago, 1949).

Bryce, James, *The American Commonwealth* (London: Macmillan & Co., 1888).

Buchanan, Bruce, *The Presidential Experience* (Englewood Cliffs, N.J.: Prentice-Hall, 1978).

Bundy, McGeorge, *The Strength of Government* (Cambridge, Mass.: Harvard University Press, 1968).

Burner, David, *Herbert Hoover: A Public Life* (New York: Alfred A. Knopf, 1978).

Burnham, Walter Dean, *Critical Elections and the Mainsprings of American Politics* (New York: W. W. Norton, 1970).

―――, and Martha Weinberg, eds., *American Politics and Public Policy* (Cambridge, Mass.: M.I.T. Press, 1978).

Burns, James MacGregor, *The Deadlock of Democracy* (Englewood Cliffs, N.J.: Prentice-Hall, 1963).

―――, *John Kennedy: A Political Profile* (New York: Harcourt, 1959).

―――, *Leadership* (New York: Harper & Row, 1978).

―――, *Presidential Government* (Boston: Houghton Mifflin, 1965).

―――, *Roosevelt: The Lion and the Fox* (New York: Harcourt, 1956).

―――, *Roosevelt: The Soldier of Freedom* (New York: Harcourt Brace Jovanovich, 1970).

Califano, Joseph, *Governing America* (New York: Simon & Schuster, 1981).

———, *A Presidential Nation* (New York: W. W. Norton, 1975).

Campbell, Angus, et al., *The American Voter* (New York: Wiley & Sons, 1960).

Campbell, Bruce, A., *The American Electorate* (New York: Holt, Rinehart and Winston, 1979).

Ceaser, James W., *Presidential Selection: Theory and Development* (Princeton, N.J.: Princeton University Press, 1979).

Commission on Organization of the Executive Branch of the Government (Hoover Commission). Reports. Washington, D.C.: Government Printing Office, 1949 and 1953).

Chamberlain, Lawrence H., *The President, Congress, and Legislation* (New York: Columbia University Press, 1946).

Chester, Lewis, et al., *American Melodrama: The Presidential Campaign of 1968* (New York: Viking, 1969).

Childs, Marquis, *Eisenhower: Captive Hero* (New York: Harcourt, 1958).

Chomsky, Noam, *American Power and the New Mandarins* (New York: Pantheon, 1969).

Christian, George, *The President Steps Down* (New York: Macmillan, 1970).

Clark, Keith and Laurence Legere, *The President and the Management of National Security* (New York: Praeger, 1969).

Cleveland, Grover, *Presidential Problems* (New York: Century Co., 1904).

Cochran, Bert, *Harry Truman and the Crisis Presidency* (New York: Funk and Wagnalls, 1973).

Commager, Henry Steele, *The Defeat of America: Presidential Power and the National Character* (New York: Simon & Schuster, 1975).

Committee on Government Operations, Senate Subcommittee on National Policy Machinery. Reports. (Washington, D.C.: Government Printing Office, 1959 and after).

Congressional Quarterly. Presidential Elections Since 1789. (Washington, D.C.: Congressional Quarterly Press, 1975).

Cornwell, Elmer E., Jr., *The American Presidency: Vital Center* (Chicago: Scott, Foreman, 1966).

———, *Presidential Leadership of Public Opinion* (Bloomington, Ind.: Indiana University Press, 1965).

Corwin, Edward S., *The President: Office and Powers*, 4th rev. ed. (New York: New York University Press, 1957).

———, *The President's Control of Foreign Relations* (Princeton: Princeton University Press, 1917).

———, *Total War and the Constitution* (New York: Alfred A. Knopf, 1947).

——— and Louis W. Koenig, *The Presidency Today* (New York: New York University Press, 1957).

Cotter, Cornelius P. and J. Malcolm Smith, *Powers of the President During National Crises* (Washington, D.C.: Public Affairs Press, 1959).

Cronin, Thomas E., *The State of the Presidency* (Boston: Little, Brown, 1980).

———, and Sanford D. Greenberg, eds., *The Presidential Advisory System* (New York: Harper & Row, 1969).

———, and Rexford G. Tugwell, eds. *The Presidency Reappraised*, 2nd ed. (New York: Praeger, 1977).

Crouse, Timothy, *The Boys on the Bus* (New York: Random House, 1973).

Coyle, David C., *Ordeal of the Presidency* (Washington: Public Affairs Press, 1960).

Cunliffe, Marcus, *The American Heritage History of the Presidency* (New York: American Heritage, 1968).

Daniels, Jonathan, *The Man of Independence* (Philadelphia: Lippincott, 1950).

David, Paul, et al., *Presidential Nominating Politics* (Washington, D.C.: Brookings Institution, 1954).

———, ed., *The Presidential Election and Transition 1960-1961* (Washington, D.C.: Brookings Institution, 1961).

Davie, Michael, *LBJ: A Foreign Observer's Viewpoint* (New York: Duell, Sloan & Pierce, 1966).

Davis, James, *Presidential Primaries* (New York: Thomas Y. Crowell, 1967).
————, *The National Executive Branch* (New York: Free Press, 1970).
Dean, John W., *Blind Ambition* (New York: Simon & Schuster, 1976).
Destler, I. M., *Presidents, Bureaucrats, and Foreign Policy: The Politics of Organization Reform* (Princeton, N.J.: Princeton University Press, 1972).
DeToledano, Ralph, *One Man Alone: Richard M. Nixon* (New York: Funk and Wagnalls, 1969).
DiClerico, Robert E., *The American President* (Englewood Cliffs, N.J.: Prentice-Hall, 1979).
Dolce, Philip and George Skau, eds., *Power and the Presidency* (New York: Charles Scribner's Sons, 1976).
Donald, Aida Di Pace, ed., *John F. Kennedy and the New Frontier* (New York: Hill and Wang, 1966).
Donald, David, *Lincoln Reconsidered* (New York: Alfred A. Knopf, 1956).
Donald, John C., *The Policy Makers* (Indianapolis: Pegasus, 1970).
Donovan, Robert J., *Conflict and Crisis: The Presidency of Harry S Truman, 1945-1948* (New York: W. W. Norton, 1977).
————, *Eisenhower: The Inside Story* (New York: Harper, 1956).
Dorman, Michael, *The Second Man: The Changing Role of the Vice President* (New York: Dell, 1970).
Downes, Randolph C., *The Rise of Warren Gamaliel Harding, 1865-1920* (Columbus, Ohio: Ohio State University Press, 1970).
Downs, Anthony, *Inside Bureaucracy* (Boston: Little, Brown, 1967).
Dunn, Delmer D., *Financing Presidential Campaigns* (Washington, D.C.: Brookings Institution, 1972).
Dunn, Charles, ed., *The Future of the American Presidency* (Morristown, N.J.: General Learning Press, 1975).
Edwards, George C., *Presidential Influence in Congress* (San Francisco: Freeman, 1980).
Eisenhower, Dwight D., *Mandate for Change* (Garden City, N.Y.: Doubleday, 1963).
————, *Waging Peace* (Garden City, N.Y.: Doubleday, 1965).
Ellsberg, Daniel, *Papers on the War* (New York: Simon & Schuster, 1972).
Evans, Rowland and Robert Novak, *Lyndon B. Johnson: The Exercise of Power* (New York: New American Library, 1968).
————, *Nixon in the White House: The Frustration of Power* (New York: Random House, 1972).
Fairlie, Henry, *The Kennedy Promise* (Garden City, N.Y.: Doubleday, 1973).
Feerick, John D., *From Failing Hands: The Story of Presidential Succession* (New York: Fordham University Press, 1965).
Fenno, Richard F., *The President's Cabinet* (Cambridge, Mass.: Harvard University Press, 1959).
Finer, Herman, *The Presidency: Crisis and Regeneration* (Chicago: University of Chicago Press, 1959).
Finn, Chester, *Education and The Presidency* (Lexington, Mass.: Lexington Books, 1977).
Fisher, Louis, *The Constitution Between Friends* (New York: St. Martin's Press, 1978).
————, *President and Congress* (Riverside, N.J.: Free Press, 1972).
————, *Presidential Spending Power* (Princeton, N.J.: Princeton University Press, 1975).
Fitzsimons, Louise, *The Kennedy Doctrine* (New York: Random House, 1972).
Flash, Edward S., *Economic Advice and Presidential Leadership* (New York: Columbia, 1965).
Flexner, James Thomas, *Washington: The Indispensable Man* (Boston: Little, Brown, 1974).
Ford, Gerald R., *A Time to Heal: The Autobiography of Gerald R. Ford* (New York: Harper & Row, 1979).
Freeman, Douglas Southhall, *George Washington,* 7 vols. (New York: Charles Scribner's, 1948-1957).

Freeman, J. Leiper, *The Political Process*, rev. ed. (New York: Random House, 1965).

Freidel, Frank, *Franklin D. Roosevelt* 4 vols. (Boston: Little, Brown, 1973).

Gatewood, Willard B., Jr., *Theodore Roosevelt and the Art of Controversy* (Baton Rouge, La.: University of Louisiana Press, 1970).

George, Alexander, *Presidential Decision-Making in Foreign Policy* (Boulder, Colo.: Westview Press, 1979).

————, and Juliette L. George, *Woodrow Wilson and Colonel House: A Personality Study* (New York: John Day, 1956).

————, et al., *The Limits of Coercive Diplomacy* (Boston: Little, Brown, 1971).

Gilbert, Robert E., *Television and Presidential Politics* (North Quincy, Mass.: Christopher Publishing House, 1972).

Glad, Betty, *Jimmy Carter: In Search of the Great White House* (New York: W. W. Norton, 1980).

Goebel, Dorothy B. and Julius Goebel, Jr., *Generals in the White House* (Garden City, N.Y.: Doubleday, Doran, 1945).

Goldman, Eric F., *The Tragedy of Lyndon Johnson* (New York: Alfred A. Knopf, 1969).

Goldsmith, William M., *The Growth of Presidential Power: A Documented History* (New York: Chelsea House, 1974).

Gosnell, Harold, *Harry Truman: A Political Biography* (Westport, Conn.: Greenwood Press, 1980).

Graber, Doris A., *Public Opinion, The President and Foreign Policy: Four Case Studies from the Formative Years* (New York: Holt, Rinehart and Winston, Inc., 1968).

Graff, Henry, *The Tuesday Cabinet* (Englewood Cliffs, N.J.: Prentice-Hall, 1970).

Greenstein, Fred, et al., *Evolution of the Modern Presidency: A Bibliographical Survey* (Washington, D.C.: American Enterprise Institute for Public Policy, 1977).

Griffith, Ernest S., *The American Presidency: The Dilemmas of Shared Power and Divided Government* (New York: New York University Press, 1976).

Grossman, Michael B. and Kumar, Martha J., *Portraying the President: White House Press Operations and the News Media* (Baltimore: Johns Hopkins, 1980).

Grundstein, Nathan D., *Presidential Delegation of Authority in Wartime* (Pittsburgh: University of Pittsburgh Press, 1961).

Hadley, Arthur, *The Empty Polling Booth* (Englewood Cliffs, N.J.: Prentice-Hall, 1978).

Haight, David E. and Larry D. Johnson, eds., *The President: Roles and Powers* (Chicago: Rand McNally, 1965).

Halberstam, David, *The Best and the Brightest* (New York: Random House, 1972).

Haldeman, H. R., *The Ends of Power* (New York: New York Times Books, 1978).

Halperin, Morton H., *Bureaucratic Politics and Foreign Policy* (Washington: Brookings Institution, 1974).

————, and Daniel Hoffman, eds., *Freedom vs National Security* (New York: Chelsea House, 1975).

Halpern, Paul, ed., *Why Watergate?* (Pacific Palisades, Calif.: Palisades Press, 1975).

Harbaugh, William Henry, *Power and Responsibility: The Life and Times of Theodore Roosevelt* (New York: Farrar, Straus, 1961).

Hardin, Charles M., *Presidential Power and Accountability* (Chicago: University of Chicago Press, 1974).

Hargrove, Erwin C., *The Power of the Modern Presidency* (New York: Alfred A. Knopf, 1974).

————, *Presidential Leadership: Personality and Political Style* (New York: Macmillan, 1966).

Hart, James, *The American Presidency in Action* (New York: Macmillan, 1948).

Hassler, W. W., Jr., *The President As Commander in Chief* (Reading, Mass.: Addison-Wesley Publishing Co., 1971).

Heath, James, F., *John F. Kennedy and the Business Community* (Chicago: University of Chicago Press, 1969).

Heller, Francis, *The Presidency* (New York: Random House, 1960).

Henderson, Charles P., *The Nixon Theology* (New York: Harper & Row, 1972).

Henkin, Louis, *Foreign Affairs and the Constitution* (Mineola: Foundation Press, 1972).

Henry, Laurin L., *Presidential Transitions* (Washington, D.C.: Brookings Institution, 1960).

Herbers, John, *No Thank You, Mr. President* (New York: W. W. Norton, 1976).

Herring, E. Pendleton, *Presidential Leadership* (New York: Farrar, Straus, 1940).

Hess, Stephen, *Organizing the Presidency* (Washington, D.C.: Brookings Institution, 1976).

————, *The Presidential Campaign: The Leadership Selection Process After Watergate* (Washington, D.C.: Brookings Institution, 1978).

Hickel, Walter J., *Who Owns America?* (Englewood Cliffs, N.J.: Prentice-Hall, 1971).

Hilsman, Roger, *To Move a Nation* (Garden City, N.Y.: Doubleday, 1967).

Hirschfield, Robert S., *The Constitution and the Court* (New York: Random House, 1962).

————, ed., *Selection/Election: A Forum on the American Presidency* (New York: Aldine Publishing Co., 1982).

Hobbs, Edward H., *Behind the President* (Washington, D.C.: Public Affairs, 1954).

Hofstadter, Richard, *The American Political Tradition* (New York: Alfred A. Knopf, 1948).

Holtzman, Abraham, *Legislative Liaison: Executive Leadership in Congress* (Chicago: Rand McNally, 1970).

Hoopes, Townsend, *The Limits of Intervention* (New York: McKay, 1969).

Hoover, Herbert, *The Memoirs of Herbert Hoover* (New York: Macmillan, 1951-1952).

House of Representatives, Impeachment of Richard M. Nixon, President of the United States, Final Report. (New York: Bantam Books, 1975).

Hoxie, R. Gordon, *Command Decision and the Presidency* (New York: Reader's Digest Press, 1977).

————, *The Presidency of the 1970's* (New York: Center for the Study of the Presidency, 1973).

————, ed., *The White House: Organization and Operation* (New York: Center for the Study of the Presidency, 1971).

Hughes, Emmet John, *The Living Presidency* (New York: Coward, McCann & Geoghegan, 1973).

————, *The Ordeal of Power* (New York: Atheneum, 1963).

Humbert, W. H., *The Pardoning Power of the President* (Washington, D.C.: Public Affairs Press, 1941).

Hyman, Sidney, *The American President* (New York: Harper, 1954).

Jackson, Henry M., ed., *The National Security Council* (New York: Praeger, 1965).

James, Dorothy B., *The Contemporary Presidency* (New York: Pegasus, 1969).

Javits, Jacob, *Who Makes War?* (New York: William Morrow, 1973).

Johnson, Donald B. and Jack L. Walker, eds., *The Dynamics of the American Presidency* (New York: Wiley, 1964).

Johnson, Lady Bird, *A White House Diary* (New York: Holt, Rinehart and Winston, 1970).

Johnson, Lyndon B., *The Vantage Point: Perspectives of the Presidency* (New York: Harper & Row, 1971).

Johnson, Richard, *Managing the White House* (New York: Harper & Row, 1974).

Johnson, Walter, *1600 Pennsylvania Avenue: Presidents and the People, 1929-1959* (Boston: Little, Brown, 1960).

Johnstone, Robert M., Jr., *Jefferson and the Presidency* (Ithaca, N.Y.: Cornell University Press, 1978).

Kallenbach, Joseph E., *The American Chief Executive* (New York: Harper & Row, 1966).

Katz, James E., *Presidential Politics and Science Policy* (New York: Harper & Row, 1978).

Kaufman, Herbert, *The Limits of Organizational Change* (University, Ala.: University of Alabama Press, 1971).

Kearns, Doris, *Lyndon Johnson and the American Dream* (New York: Harper & Row, 1976).

Keech, William and Donald Matthews, *The Party's Choice* (Washington, D.C.: Brookings Institution, 1976).

Kennedy, John F., *Profiles in Courage* (New York: Harper & Row, 1956).

Kennedy, Robert F., *Thirteen Days: A Memoir of the Cuban Missile Crisis* (New York: W. W. Norton, 1969).

Keogh, James, *President Nixon and the Press* (New York: Funk and Wagnalls, 1972).

Kessel, John, *The Domestic Presidency* (Scituate, Mass.: Duxbury Press, 1975).

————, *Presidential Campaign Strategies and Citizen Response* (Homewood, Ill.: Dorsey, 1980).

King, Anthony, ed., *The New American Political System* (Washington: American Enterprise Institute for Public Policy Research, 1978).

Kirkpatrick, Jeane, *The New Presidential Elite* (New York: Russell Sage Foundation, 1976).

Kistiakowsky, George B., *A Scientist at the White House* (Cambridge, Mass.: Harvard University Press, 1976).

Klein, Philip Shriver, *President James Buchanan* (University Park: Pennsylvania State University Press, 1962).

Koenig, Louis, *The Chief Executive*, 4th ed., (New York: Harcourt, Brace and World, 1981).

————, *The Invisible Presidency* (New York: Holt, 1960).

————, *The Presidency and the Crisis* (New York: King's Crown Press, 1944).

————, *The Truman Administration* (New York: New York University Press, 1956).

Kolko, Gabriel, *The Roots of American Foreign Policy* (Boston: Beacon Press, 1969).

Labovitz, John R., *Presidential Impeachment* (New Haven, Conn.: Yale University Press, 1978).

Lammers, William W., *Presidential Politics: Patterns and Prospects* (New York: Harper & Row, 1976).

Landecker, Manfred, *The President and Public Opinion: Leadership in Foreign Affairs* (Washington, D.C.: Public Affairs Press, 1968).

Larson, Arthur, *Eisenhower: The President Nobody Knew* (New York: Charles Scribner's Sons, 1968).

Laski, Harold J., *The American Presidency* (New York: Harper, 1940).

Lasky, Victor, *JFK: The Man and the Myth* (New York: Macmillan, 1963).

Latham, Earl, *J. F. Kennedy and Presidential Power* (Lexington, Mass.: D. C. Heath, 1972).

Lengle, James I. and Byron E. Shafer, eds., *Presidential Politics: Readings on Nominations and Elections* (New York: St. Martin's Press, 1980).

Leuchtenberg, William E., *Franklin D. Roosevelt and the New Deal, 1932-1940* (New York: Harper & Row, 1963).

Link, Arthur S., *Wilson*, 4 vols., (Princeton: Princeton University Press, 1956-1964).

Liston, Robert, *Presidential Power: How Much Is Too Much?* (New York: McGraw-Hill, 1971).

Longaker, Richard P., *The Presidency and Individual Liberties* (Ithaca, N.Y.: Cornell University Press, 1961).

Longley, Lawrence D. and Alan G. Braun, *The Politics of Electoral College Reform* (New Haven, Conn.: Yale University Press, 1972).

Loss, Richard, ed., *Presidential Power and the Constitution, Essays by Edward S. Corwin* (Ithaca, N.Y.: Cornell University Press, 1976).

Lowi, Theodore J., *The End of Liberalism* (New York: W. W. Norton, 1969).

Lyon, Peter, *Eisenhower: Portrait of a Hero* (Boston: Little, Brown, 1974).

MacMahon, Arthur W., *Administering Federalism in a Democracy* (New York: Oxford University Press, 1972).

Magruder, Jeb Stuart, *An American Life* (New York: Atheneum, 1974).

Mailer, Norman, *Presidential Papers* (New York: G. P. Putnam's Sons, 1963).

Malone, Dumas, *Jefferson and His Time*, 3 vols., (Boston: Little, Brown, 1948-1962).

Manchester, William, *Portrait of a President: John F. Kennedy in Profile* (Boston: Little, Brown, 1967).

Mansfield, Harvey C., Sr., ed., *Congress Against the President* (New York: Harper & Row, 1975).

Marcus, Maeva, *Truman and the Steel Seizure Case: The Limits of Presidential Power* (New York: Columbia University Press, 1979).

Matthews, Donald R., ed., *Perspectives on Presidential Selection* (Washington, D.C.: Brookings Institution, 1973).

May, Ernest R., *The Ultimate Decision* (New York: Braziller, 1960).

Mazlish, Bruce, *In Search of Nixon: A Psychohistorical Inquiry* (New York: Basic Books, 1973).

Mazo, Earl and Stephen Hess, *Nixon: A Political Portrait* (New York: Harper & Row, 1968).

McClure, Wallace M., *International Executive Agreements* (New York: Columbia University Press, 1941).

McConnell, Grant, *The Modern Presidency* (New York: St. Martin's Press, 1967).

————, *Steel and the Presidency, 1962* (New York: W. W. Norton, 1963).

McCoy, Donald R., *Calvin Coolidge: The Quiet President* (New York: Macmillan, 1967).

McGinness, Joe, *The Selling of the President 1968* (New York: Trident Press, 1969).

McPherson, Harry C., *A Political Education* (Boston: Atlantic-Little, Brown, 1972).

Michener, James, *Presidential Lottery* (New York: Random House, 1969).

Miller, Merle, *Lyndon: An Oral Biography* (New York: G. P. Putnam's Sons, 1980).

————, *Plain Speaking: An Oral Biography of Harry S Truman* (New York: Medallion, 1974).

Miller, William Lee, *Yankee From Georgia: The Emergence of Jimmy Carter* (New York: New York Times Books, 1978).

Milton, G. R., *The Use of Presidential Power, 1789-1943* (Boston: Little, Brown, 1944).

Minow, Newton, et al., *Presidential Television* (New York: Basic Books, 1973).

Miroff, Bruce, *Pragmatic Illusions: The Presidential Politics of John F. Kennedy* (New York: McKay, 1976).

Moe, Ronald, *Congress and the President: Allies and Adversaries* (Pacific Palisades, Calif.: Goodyear, 1971).

Moley, Raymond, *After Seven Years* (New York: Harper, 1939).

Mondale, Walter F., *The Accountability of Power: Toward a Responsible Presidency* (New York: McKay, 1975).

Moos, Malcolm, *Politics, Presidents, and Coattails* (Baltimore: Johns Hopkins Press, 1952).

Morey, William C., "The First State Constitutions," *The Annals of the American Academy of Political and Social Science*, Vol. 4, (Philadelphia: American Academy of Political and Social Science, 1894).

Morgan, Edward P., et al., *The Presidency and the Press Conference* (Washington, D.C.: American Enterprise Institute for Public Policy, 1971).

Morgan, Ruth, *The President and Civil Rights: Policy-Making by Executive Order* (New York: St. Martin's Press, 1971).

Morris, Richard B., *Great Presidential Decisions* (Philadelphia: Lippincott, 1960).

Mowery, George F., *The Era of Theodore Roosevelt, 1900-1912* (New York: Harper & Row, 1958).

Moynihan, Daniel P., *Maximum Feasible Misunderstanding* (New York: Free Press, 1969).

Mueller, John, *War, Presidents, and Public Opinion* (New York: Wiley, 1973).

Mullen, William F., *Presidential Power and Politics* (New York: St. Martin's Press, 1976).

Murray, Robert, *The Harding Era: Warren G. Harding and His Administration* (Minneapolis: University of Minnesota Press, 1969).

Nash, Bradley D., *Staffing the Presidency* (Washington: National Planning Association, 1952).

Nathan, Richard, *The Plot That Failed: Nixon's Administrative Presidency* (New York: Wiley, 1975).

Nessen, Ron, *It Sure Looks Different from the Inside* (New York: Playboy Press, 1978).

Neustadt, Richard E., *Alliance Politics* (New York: Columbia University Press, 1970).

————, *Presidential Power* (New York: Wiley, 1960, rev. ed. 1980).

Nevins, Allen, *Grover Cleveland: A Study in Courage* (New York: Dodd, Mead, 1932).

Nie, Norman, Sidney Verba, and John Petrocik, *The Changing American Voter* (Cambridge, Mass.: Harvard University Press, 1976).

Nixon, Richard M., *RN: The Memoirs of Richard Nixon* (New York: Grosset & Dunlap, 1978).

Novak, Michael, *Choosing Our King* (New York: Macmillan, 1974).

Novak, Robert and Rowland Evans, *Nixon in the White House: A Critical Portrait* (New York: Random House, 1971).

"The Office of the American Presidency," *Annals of the American Academy*, Vol. CCCVII (September 1956).

O'Brien, Lawrence, *No Final Victories: From John F. Kennedy to Watergate* (Garden City, N.Y.: Doubleday, 1974).

Orban, Edmond, *La Présidence Moderne Aux États-Unis* (Montreal: University of Quebec Press, 1974).

Osborne, John, *The Nixon Watch* (series) (New York: Liveright, 1970-1975).

Page, Benjamin I., *Choices and Echoes in Presidential Elections* (Chicago: University of Chicago Press, 1978).

Parmet, Herbert S., *Eisenhower and the American Crusades* (New York: Macmillan, 1972).

Parris, Judith H., *The Convention Problem* (Washington, D.C.: Brookings Institution, 1972).

Patterson, Caleb Perry, *Presidential Government in the United States* (Chapel Hill: University of North Carolina Press, 1947).

Peirce, Neal R., *The People's President: The Electoral College in American History and the Direct-Vote Alternative* (New York: Simon & Schuster, 1968).

Pfiffner, James P., *The President, the Budget and Congress: Impoundment and the 1974 Budget Act* (Boulder, Colo.: Westview Press, 1979).

Phillips, Cabell, *The Truman Presidency* (New York: Macmillan, 1966).

Pious, Richard M., *The American Presidency* (New York: Basic Books, 1979).

Pollard, James E., *The Presidents and the Press* (New York: Macmillan, 1947).

Polsby, Nelson W., *Congress and the Presidency* (Englewood Cliffs, N.J.: Prentice-Hall, 1964).

————, ed., *The Modern Presidency* (New York: Random House, 1973).

————, and Aaron B. Wildavsky, *Presidential Elections: Strategies of American Electoral Politics* (New York: Scribner, 1968).

Pomper, Gerald, *The Election of 1976: Reports and Interpretations* (New York: McKay, 1977).

————, *Elections in America* (New York: Dodd, Mead, 1970).

————, *Nominating the President: The Politics of Convention Choice* (New York: W. W. Norton, 1966).

————, ed., *Party Renewal: Theory and Practice* (New York: Praeger-Holt, 1980).

————, et al., *The Election of 1980: Reports and Interpretations* (Chatham, N.J.: Chatham House Publishers, 1981).

"The Presidency," *American Heritage*, Vol. XV (August 1964).

"The Presidency," *Current History*, Vol. XXV (September 1953).

"The Presidency in Transition," *Journal of Politics*, Vol. XI (February 1949).

"The Presidential Office," *Law and Contemporary Problems*, Vol. XXI (Autumn 1956).

President's Committee on Administrative Management (Brownlow Committee), *Report with Special Studies* (Washington, D.C.: Government Printing Office, 1937).

Pressman, Jeffrey and Aaron Wildavsky, *Implementation* (Berkeley: University of California Press, 1973).

Pringle, Henry F., *The Life and Times of William Howard Taft*, 2 vols. (New York: Farrar, Straus, 1939).

————, *Theodore Roosevelt* (New York: Harcourt, 1931).

Public Papers of the Presidents of the United States (Washington: Government Printing Office).

Pusey, Merlo J., *Eisenhower: The President* (New York: Macmillan, 1956).

————, *The Way We Go to War* (Boston: Houghton-Mifflin, 1969).

Randall, James G., *Constitutional Problems Under Lincoln*, rev. ed. (Urbana: University of Illinois Press, 1964).

————, *Lincoln the President*, 4 vols. (New York: Dodd, Mead, 1945-1955).

Rankin, Robert, *When Civil Law Fails: Martial Law and Its Legal Basis in the United States* (Durham, N.C.: Duke University Press, 1939).

———— and Winfried Dallmayr, *Freedom and Emergency Powers in the Cold War* (New York: Appleton-Century-Crofts, 1964).

Ranney, Austin, *Participation in American Presidential Nominations, 1976* (Washington, D.C.: American Enterprise Institute for Public Policy, 1976).

————, ed., *The Past and Future of Presidential Debates* (Washington, D.C.: American Enterprise Institute for Public Policy, 1979).

Reagan, Michael, *The New Federalism* (New York: Oxford University Press, 1972).

Reedy, George E., *The Presidency in Flux* (New York: Columbia University Press, 1973).

————, *The Twilight of the Presidency* (New York: World, 1970).

Richardson, James, comp., *Messages and Papers of the Presidents* (New York: Bureau of National Literature, 1897).

Rienow, Robert and Leona Train Rienow, *The Lonely Quest: The Evolution of Presidential Leadership* (Chicago: Follett, 1966).

Rivlin, Alice M., *Systematic Thinking for Social Action* (Washington, D.C.: Brookings Institution, 1971).

Roberts, Charles, ed., *Has the President Too Much Power?* (New York: Harper, 1974).

Roche, John and Leonard Levy, *The Presidency* (New York: Harcourt, 1964).

Rogers, James G., *World Policing and the Constitution* (Boston: World Peace Foundation, 1945).

Romasco, Albert U., *The Power of Abundance: Hoover, the Nation, the Depression* (New York: Oxford University Press, 1965).

Roosevelt, Theodore, *Theodore Roosevelt: An Autobiography* (New York: Charles Scribner's Sons, 1920).

Rose, Richard, *Managing Presidential Objectives* (New York: Free Press, 1976).

Rosebloom, Eugene H., *A History of Presidential Elections* (New York: Macmillan, 1959).

Rosenman, Samuel I., *Working with Roosevelt* (New York: Harper, 1952).

————, comp., *The Public Papers and Addresses of Franklin D. Roosevelt*, 13 vols. (New York: Random House, 1938-1950).

Rossiter, Clinton, *The American Presidency*, rev. ed. (New York: Harvest, 1960).

————, *Constitutional Dictatorship* (Princeton: Princeton University Press, 1948).

————, *The Supreme Court and the Commander-in-Chief* (Ithaca, N.Y.: Cornell University Press, 1951).

Rourke, Francis, E., *Bureaucracy, Politics, Public Policy* (Boston: Little, Brown, 1969).

Rudoni, Dorothy, *Harry S Truman: A Study in Presidential Perspective* (Ann Arbor, Mich.: University of Michigan, 1969).

Saffell, David C., ed., *Watergate: Its Effects on the American Political System* (Cambridge, Mass.: Winthrop, 1974).

Safire, William, *Before the Fall: An Inside View of the Pre-Watergate White House* (Garden City, N.Y.: Doubleday, 1974)

Sayre, Wallace S. and Judith H. Parris, *Voting for President: The Electoral College and the American Political System* (Washington, D.C.: Brookings Institution, 1970).

Scammon, Richard M. and Ben J. Wattenberg, *The Real Majority* (New York: Coward-McCann, 1970).

Schachner, Nathan, *Thomas Jefferson: A Biography*, 2 vols. (New York: Appleton-Century-Crofts, 1951).

Schlesinger, Arthur M., Jr., *The Age of Jackson* (Boston: Little, Brown, 1945).

————, *The Imperial Presidency* (Boston: Houghton Mifflin, 1973).

————, *A Thousand Days: John F. Kennedy in the White House* (Boston: Houghton Mifflin, 1965).

———— and Alfred de Grazia, *Congress and the Presidency: Their Role in Modern Times* (Washington: American Enterprise Institute for Public Policy, 1967).

———— and Fred Israel, eds., *History of American Presidential Elections 1789-1968* (New York: Chelsea House, 1971).

Schubert, Glendon, *The Presidency in the Courts* (Minneapolis: University of Minnesota Press, 1957).

Scigliano, Robert, *The Supreme Court and the Presidency* (New York: The Free Press, 1971).

Seidman, Harold, *Politics, Position and Power* (New York: Oxford University Press, 1970).

Sherrill, Robert, *Accidental President* (New York: Grossman Publishers, 1967).

Sherwood, Robert E., *Roosevelt and Hopkins* (New York: Harper, 1948).

Shull, Steven A., *Presidential Policy Making* (Brunswick, Ohio: King's Court Communications, 1979).

Sichel, Werner, ed., *Economic Advice and Executive Policy: Recommendations from Past Members of the Council of Economic Advisers* (New York: Harper & Row, 1978).

Sickels, Robert J., *The Presidency: An Introduction* (Englewood Cliffs, N.J.: Prentice-Hall, 1980).

————, *Presidential Transactions* (Englewood Cliffs, N.J.: Prentice-Hall, 1974).

Sidey, Hugh, *John F. Kennedy, President* (New York: Atheneum, 1963).

————, *A Very Personal Presidency: Lyndon Johnson in the White House* (New York: Atheneum, 1968).

Silva, Ruth C., *Presidential Succession* (Ann Arbor: University of Michigan Press, 1951).

Silverman, Corinne, *The President's Economic Advisers* (University, Ala.: University of Alabama Press, 1959).

Sindler, Allan P., *Unchosen Presidents: The Vice President and Other Frustrations of Presidential Succession* (Berkeley: University of California Press, 1976).

————, ed., *America in the Seventies: Problems, Policies and Politics* (Boston: Little, Brown, 1977).

Sirica, John J., *To Set the Record Straight: The Break-In, The Tapes, The Conspirators, The Pardon* (New York: W. W. Norton, 1979).

Small, Norman J., *Some Presidential Interpretations of the Presidency* (Baltimore: Johns Hopkins Press, 1932).

Smith, Harold, *The Management of Your Government* (New York: McGraw-Hill, 1945).

Smith, Malcolm J. and Cornelius Cotter, *Powers of the President During Crises* (Washington: Public Affairs Press, 1960).

Sorensen, Theodore C., *Decision-Making in the White House* (New York: Columbia University Press, 1963).

————, *Kennedy* (New York: Harper, 1965).

————, *Watchman in the Night: Presidential Accountability and Watergate* (Cambridge, Mass.: M.I.T. Press, 1975).

Spalding, Henry D., *The Nixon Nobody Knows* (Middle Village, N.Y.: Jonathan David, 1972).

Steiner, Gilbert Y., *The State of Welfare* (Washington, D.C.: Brookings Institution, 1971).

Stockwell, John, *In Search of Enemies: A CIA Story* (New York: W. W. Norton, 1978).

Strum, Philippa, *Presidential Power and American Democracy* (Pacific Palisades, Calif.: Goodyear, 1971).

Sullivan, Dennis, et al., *Explorations in Convention Decision Making* (San Francisco: Freeman, 1974).

Sulzner, George and Stanley Bach, eds., *Perspectives on the Presidency* (Lexington, Mass.: D. C. Heath, 1974).

Sundquist, James L., *Making Federalism Work* (Washington, D.C.: Brookings Institution, 1969).

————, *Politics and Policy: The Eisenhower, Kennedy, and Johnson Years* (Washington, D.C.: Brookings Institution, 1968).

Sutherland, Arthur, ed., *Government Under Law* (Cambridge, Mass.: Harvard University Press, 1956).

"Symposium: United States v. Nixon," *UCLA Law Review*, Vol. 22, No. 1 (October 1974).

Taft, William Howard, *Our Chief Magistrate and His Powers* (New York: Columbia University Press, 1916).

Thach, Charles, *The Creation of the Presidency* (Baltimore: John Hopkins Press, 1922).

Thomas, Benjamin P., *Abraham Lincoln* (New York: Alfred A. Knopf, 1952).

Thomas, Norman C., *Politics in National Education* (New York: David McKay, 1975).

———— ed., *The Presidency in Contemporary Context* (New York: Dodd, Mead, 1975).

———— and Hans W. Baade, eds., *The Institutionalized Presidency* (Dobbs Ferry, N.Y.: Oceana, 1972).

Thompson, Hunter, *Fear and Loathing: On the Campaign Trail '72* (San Francisco: Straight Arrow Books, 1973).

Tobin, James, *The New Economics One Decade Older* (Princeton, N.J.: Princeton University Press, 1974).

Tolchin, Martin and Susan Tolchin, *To the Victor: Political Patronage from the Clubhouse to the White House* (New York: Random House, 1971).

Tourtellot, Arthur B., ed., *The Presidents on the Presidency* (New York: Russell and Russell, 1970).

Truman, Harry S, *Memoirs*, 2 vols. (Garden City, N.Y.: Doubleday, 1958).

Tugwell, Rexford, *The Democratic Roosevelt* (Garden City, N.Y.: Doubleday, 1960).

————, *The Enlargement of the Presidency* (Garden City, N.Y.: Doubleday, 1960).

————, *How They Became President* (New York: Simon & Schuster, 1968).

U.S. National Archives, *Public Papers of the Presidents of the United States* (Washington, D.C.: Government Printing Office, 1957 and after).

Vandenberg, Arthur H., *The Great American: Alexander Hamilton* (New York: G. P. Putnam's Sons, 1921).

Van Der Linden, Frank, *Nixon's Quest for Peace* (Washington, D.C.: Luce, 1972).

Vinyard, Dale, *The Presidency* (New York: Charles Scribner's Sons, 1972).

Wann, A. J., *The President as Chief Administrator: A Study of Franklin D. Roosevelt* (Washington, D.C.: Public Affairs Press, 1968).

Warren, Harris G., *Herbert Hoover and the Great Depression* (New York: Oxford University Press, 1959).

Warren, Sidney, *The Battle for the Presidency* (Philadelphia: Lippincott, 1968).

————, *The President as World Leader* (New York: McGraw-Hill, 1967).

Watson, Richard, *The Presidential Contest* (New York: Wiley, 1979).

Wayne, Stephen J., *The Legislative Presidency* (New York: Harper & Row, 1978).

————, *The Road to the White House* (New York: St. Martin's, 1980).

Westin, Alan, *The Anatomy of a Constitutional Law Case* (New York: Macmillan, 1958).

White, Theodore H., *Breach of Faith: The Fall of Richard Nixon* (New York: Atheneum, 1975).

―――, *The Making of the President 1960* (New York: Atheneum, 1961).

―――, *The Making of the President 1964* (New York: Atheneum, 1968).

―――, *The Making of the President 1968* (New York: Atheneum, 1969).

―――, *The Making of the President 1972* (New York: Atheneum, 1973).

White, William S., *The Professional: Lyndon B. Johnson* (Boston: Houghton Mifflin, 1964).

Wicker, Tom, *JFK and LBJ: The Influence of Personality Upon Politics* (New York: William Morrow, 1968).

Wildavsky, Aaron, *The Politics of the Budgetary Process* (Boston: Little, Brown, 1964).

―――, ed., *The Presidency* (Boston: Little, Brown, 1969).

Williams, Irving G., *The Rise of the Vice-Presidency* (Washington: Public Affairs Press, 1956).

Wills, Gary, *Nixon Agonistes: The Crisis of the Self-Made Man* (Boston: Houghton Mifflin, 1970).

Wilmerding, Lucius, *The Electoral College* (New Brunswick, N.J.: Rutgers University Press, 1958).

Wilson, Woodrow, *Congressional Government* (Boston: Houghton Mifflin, 1885).

―――, *Constitutional Government in the United States* (New York: Columbia University Press, 1908).

Winner Take All, Report of the Twentieth Century Fund Task Force on Reform of the Presidential Election Process (New York: Holmes and Meier, 1978).

Wise, David, *The American Police State* (New York: Random House, 1976).

―――, *The Politics of Lying* (New York: Random House, 1973).

Wise, Sidney and Richard F. Schier, eds., *The Presidential Office* (New York: Thomas Y. Crowell, 1969).

Witcover, Jules, *Marathon: The Pursuit of the Presidency, 1972-1976* (New York: Viking, 1977).

With the Nation Watching, Report of the Twentieth Century Fund Task Force on Televised Presidential Debates (Lexington, Mass.: Lexington Books, 1979).

Wolanin, Thomas, *Presidential Advisory Commissions* (Madison, Wis.: University of Wisconsin Press, 1975).

Wolk, Allan, *The Presidency and Black Civil Rights: Eisenhower to Nixon* (Cranbury, N.J.: Fairleigh Dickinson, 1972).

Woodward, Augustus B., *The Presidency of the United States* (New York: R. Worthington, 1884).

Woodward, Bob and Carl Bernstein, *All the President's Men* (New York: Simon & Schuster, 1974).

―――, *The Final Days* (New York: Simon & Schuster, 1976).

Wormuth, Francis, *The Vietnam War: The President vs the Constitution* (Santa Barbara, Calif.: Fund for the Republic, Center Occasional Paper, 1968).

Young, Donald, *American Roulette: The History and Dilemma of the Vice Presidency* (New York: Holt, Rinehart and Winston, 1965).

Young, James S., *The Washington Community 1800-1820* (New York: Columbia University Press, 1966).

Zinn, Charles J., *The Veto Power of the President* (Washington: Government Printing Office, 1951).

INDEX